CONTENTS

HUMAN RESOURCE MANAGEMENT

An International and Comparative Perspective on the Employment Relationship

Graham Hollinshead and
Mike Leat

London · Hong Kong · Johannesburg · Melbourne · Singapore · Washington DC

Dedicated to Jacob, Alex, Catherine Beaven and Thérèse.

PITMAN PUBLISHING
128 Long Acre, London WC2E 9AN

A Division of Pearson Professional Limited

First published in Great Britain in 1995

© G Hollinshead and M Leat 1995

ISBN 0 273 60333 7

British Library Cataloguing in Publication Data
A CIP catalogue record for this book can be obtained from the British Library

10 9 8 7 6 5 4

Typeset by 🅣 Tek Art, Croydon, Surrey
Printed and bound in Great Britain by Clays Ltd, St Ives plc

The Publishers' policy is to use paper manufactured from sustainable forests.

FOREWORD

Various writers throughout the twentieth century, from Taylor (*Scientific Management* 1911) to Peters and Waterman (*In Search of Excellence* 1982), have sought to ascribe organisational economic success to a particular style and approach to the management of human resources. Similarly, at different times during the postwar period, the poor economic performance and apparent failures of human resource management practices in the UK have been compared and contrasted with the US, then Sweden and Germany and, more recently, Japan in order to try to learn and emulate their 'secret of success'. Ouchi and Jaeger (*Type Z Organisations* 1978) have gone so far as to combine what they perceive as the 'best' features of American and Japanese approaches into a single universal, almost panacean, model of 'human resource management'. However, it is too simplistic to assume that because, at any particular point in time, any organisation(s) or country exhibits better economic growth and performance than others, their approach to managing people must be the 'right' or 'best' one.

Human resource management should not be viewed simply as a management or organisational phenomenon. We cannot fully understand it by limiting our attention to practices within the organisation (whether of an operational or strategic nature). The importance and implications of 'human resource management' developments stretch far beyond the boundaries of the organisation. To appreciate their significance requires us to integrate an examination of changes in objectives, styles, policies, strategies and practices within the organisation with an understanding of their inter-relationship with macro-economic, social and political issues and changes outside the organisation – both cause and effect. For example, management strategies to increase organisational labour efficiency (introduction of new technology, organisational de-layering, peripheral workers, time flexibility etc.) cannot be isolated from the wider socio-economic issues of combating continued high general levels of unemployment and its associated deprivation or responding to the aspirations of women, ethnic minorities, the disabled etc. for an equal opportunity to participate fully in the labour market.

Human resource management is inextricably linked, throughout the world, to economic activity. The general world economic recession coupled with the rise of 'newly industralised' economies (in particular Japan, Korea and South East Asian countries), the 'capitalist reformation' of the economies of the former Eastern European block and China and the renewed emphasis on 'free trade' as the solution (the Single European Market, NAFTA, ASEAN/APEC, GATT/WTO etc.) has resulted not simply in more intense international competition for markets and trade between the traditional 'industralised' countries but, perhaps more significantly, in a transformation of the world economy with increasing homogeneity of economies around the world. At the same time, governments in the 'industralised' countries (UK, Europe, US, Australia etc.) have instituted policies in varying degrees aimed at deregulating their labour markets and reducing the cost of social security benefits. This internationalisation of markets and economies has been accompanied by an increased emphasis on 'human resource management' as organisations across the world have sought to cope with the same issues – reduce labour costs, improve product quality and introduce organisational flexibility. There is now clearly international competition, both between organisations and countries, based on the quality and cost of labour – particularly the latter.

The potential for the convergence of human resource management approaches across the world, derived from confronting and seeking to resolve similar problems and issues, is further augmented by the continuing growth of multinational corporations, the increasing use of collaboration agreements, joint ventures etc. between 'independent' organisations and the resultant emergence of international management and managers. This multinational management dimension involves a two-way process of both working in and adapting to different national cultures and at the same time importing into and influencing those cultures (like the overlapping ripples on a pond when pebbles are thrown in at the same time in different places – each circle of ripples eventually meeting and interacting with the others but only *partially* combining).

Divergence of culture, goals and institutional arrangements to regulate labour both within the organisation and the labour market exists and will remain – resulting in different solutions to similar problems. It is important, therefore, to recognise the differing nature and dynamics of the cultural, economic, social and institutional arrangements within which organisations and countries are, in an increasingly competitive 'free-market' world, seeking solutions to human resource management and labour market issues.

We can then better understand the deep concern felt in the traditional industralised countries about the threat to employment and existing terms and conditions of employment (particularly wages) posed by not only the freer *import of products* produced in countries with lower wages and less employment rights (South East Asia, Eastern Europe, China) but also the *export of jobs* as organisations shift their locus of operations to these areas. There is a real fear of a world movement towards the 'lowest common denominator' in employment standards and the weakening or even abandonment of any real 'social security' net provided by either collective bargaining or state regulation. Recent pressure by the European Union to insert 'social' clauses and labour standards into trade agreements with South East Asian countries could be seen as an attempt to establish some form of international agreement and regulation about what is a 'fair' and 'unfair' basis for labour competition. However, from a South East Asian perspective there is concern about not only the *effect* (a form of economic trade protectionism which threatens continued economic growth and development) but also the *process* (the 'imposition' of unacceptable changes in the culture and institutions of human resource management and labour market regulation).

Finally, the 'culture' debate (in organisational theory, industrial relations and human resource management) has focused attention on its role in supporting and underpinning strategic organisational change, the interaction between organisation culture and national cultures (ethnocentric, polycentric and geocentric approaches of multinational organisations) and, in the case of the European Union, the potential to establish a supra-national culture to regulate, harmonise and standardise differing national cultures. It is perhaps significant that whilst organisations, in their drive to become 'leaner and fitter', have generally become smaller, the 'economies' within which they operate have become larger, moving from single nation state economies to supra-national interdependent economies. The existence (and expanding membership) of the European Union, NAFTA and ASEAN may well provide the basis for three distinctly contrasting and competing human resource management cultures rather than there being a convergence towards a more uniform approach – to which may be added the potential for an Islamic economic grouping and style of human resource management. However, we should not ignore the counter pressure, in many different parts of the world and for different reasons, for sub-national or regional economic, social and political identities to be expressed and recognised. Fragmentation of economic, social and political units may lead to greater, rather than less, diversity in the approaches to and institutions of human resource management at both organisational and labour market levels.

In this book the authors seek to examine the general applicability of the 'human resource management' concept by exploring the issues confronting the management of human resource in organisations, how the approach has been applied to these issues and how different national labour market institutions and arrangements impinge on its application.

Mike Salamon
Department of Management Studies
Universiti Brunei Darussalam

PREFACE

Human resource management (HRM), viewed as a distinct and innovative approach towards managing the employment relationship, has moved ever closer to centre stage in recent years. An explanation for this is that it has held out the promise of corporate success, and even national economic advantage, through connecting the effective management of human resources with the achievement of corporate strategic goals.

Not surprisingly the concept of HRM, which owes much to Japanese ideas and practices as well as American ones, has inspired practitioners and academics alike. The language of HRM is becoming widely spoken, and experimentation with new human resource (HR) initiatives seems to be commonplace.

Yet HRM is a term shrouded by rhetoric, and there has been a general paucity of analysis to examine what the term actually means, whether it has real applicability at workplace level, and whether the assumptions underlying it bear up to close scrutiny. In particular, can the link between HRM and economic advantage be sustained? Advocates of HRM are prone to discuss it in universal and general terms. However, there has been little actual research or analysis to prove that its prescriptions will automatically be valid in national systems other than those in which the concept is widely used, notably the US and the UK. One important aim of this book, therefore, is to question the applicability of the HRM concept in varying cultures and structures, notably in Europe. In doing so, we shall see that some important, yet perhaps neglected, factors come into play, for example the role of government, the role of trade unions, and the processes of interaction between representatives of major interest groups in industry, referred to as the 'social partners'.

The second main aim of the book is to provide the reader with information and analysis concerning employment and management practices across a range of national systems to enable meaningful cross-comparisons to be made.

Our aim is to provide an integrated and holistic view of different systems, and in pursuit of this we will apply relevant and available conceptual frameworks to guide discussion. We are conscious of the need for conceptual cohesiveness within the book, as we are aware of a number of texts in the field of comparative HRM and Industrial Relations (IR) which provide an informative yet eclectic and fragmented set of readings. Frequently, these are edited volumes in which authorities from different countries write about important features of their systems. In order to gain the benefit of such first-hand insights, while attempting to retain coherence, we have asked authorities in particular countries to validate, authenticate and augment material.

A further dilemma confronting authors of comparative texts is whether to proceed on a country by country basis, analysing the components of each country's system, or to take an issue or theme and discuss it in the light of observations and evidence gained from a number of national structures and practice.

Pitfalls may exist with respect to each approach: the first runs the risk of neglecting real and detailed analysis of specific issues on a cross-national basis. Interesting contrasts in, for example, forms of payment systems may remain only implied. The second approach, on the other hand, can sometimes involve discussion of an eclectic and disintegrated set of issues, and may not satisfy those who wish to obtain a complete and integrated view of each national system.

In order to provide insights into areas of comparison between national systems in Section 1 we have opted for the thematic approach. This, however, will be complemented throughout by 'snapshots' which will consist of essential facts and international profiles.

Section 2 of the book provides a more complete view of selected national systems.

A number of points should be made in order to explain the rationale underlying this plan. First, the authors feel it is necessary, in Section 1, to reflect on the nature of the employment relationship. This is because underlying the HR concept, which is discussed subsequently, there is a set of assumptions about managerial power and control. Important factors in this respect would include the degree of countervailing power exerted by groups of employees on management, as well as the extent to which the relationship between trade unions and management is legitimated and institutionalised, and how far governments (through economic and legal policy) promote managerial freedoms.

Secondly, in keeping with the views of leading authorities in the field of HRM, we investigate those situational or environmental factors which are likely to influence HRM. We hold the view that there is no single best practice in HRM, but rather, in the words of Beer *et al.*, that 'HRM policies and practices must be designed and implemented to fit a variety of important situational factors'.[1]

Thirdly, a significant theme which emerges throughout the text, but is particularly apparent in the section on HR policies and practices, is that of flexibility. As we shall discover, flexibility may take a variety of forms and may relate to the form of reward packages, the variety of tasks which employees carry out, or the degree of individuals' security of attachment to enterprises. There does seem to be an important trend towards flexible employment practices in the countries we consider, although the degree of change is clearly variable across national boundaries. Following our investigation of national systems in Section 2, we return to the theme of flexibility in the conclusion, and pose the question of whether or not shifts towards flexibility are promoting a convergence in employment practices across nations.

We should point out too, at this stage, that we have by necessity been selective in the countries we have included for coverage in this text. Our rationale for selection has been guided by the need to encapsulate a sample of countries which manifests a range of structural, cultural and institutional features, thereby promoting scope for meaningful cross-comparison. The selection is deliberately quite narrow, comprising the US, Japan, Australia, the UK, France, Italy, the Netherlands, Sweden and Germany, in order to promote a consistency of approach throughout the text, whereby a multiplicity of phenomena and practices impinging on the employment relationship are explained with continuous reference to these national systems. The approach should also promote a more in-depth analysis of those systems. We shall go on to explain how each of them may manifest institutional arrangements and practices which can be related at a more profound level, to a set of underlying perspectives on, or typologies of, the employment relationship. We would tentatively suggest, therefore, that some of our analysis may be extended to other countries of a similar type.

Notwithstanding this, we will provide further reading for those who are interested in broadening their perspectives to encompass a wider range of countries. Our selection is based on the view that although we are writing from the UK, it is necessary to cast the net wider than Europe to gain the benefit of cross-comparisons with some highly influential systems beyond it. We have, reluctantly, been unable to include countries from the former Eastern bloc, South Africa, South America, the Middle East or the Far East. We should also point out that we have fought against the temptation to write from a British perspective, and have attempted to think in a more detached and global way; nevertheless we accept that many of our perceptions are likely to be culturally determined.

PEDAGOGIC FEATURES OF THE BOOK

The text includes the following mechanisms to assist the reader in assimilating information.

Chapter Outline
This will indicate the broad structure of the chapter in advance.

Learning Objectives
These will point the reader towards key reference points within the chapter.

Snapshots
These will supplement the text by summarising the main components of national practices or phenomena.

Diagrams and Tables
Statistical and other data will be presented in an easily digestible form.

Newspaper cuttings and other articles
Areas of contemporary relevance and debate are included to supplement the text. A key feature of the text is its substantial use of material drawn from the *Financial Times*.

Case Studies
These will complement and illustrate the text, by placing the focus on developments at a real organisational level. The use of cases should also serve to integrate materials from within the text.

Chapter Summary
Key concepts will be reiterated.

Discussion Questions
These may be used for individual reflection or class discussion.

Overview of National Systems
Section 2 of the book provides comprehensive information for those who wish to obtain specific or more general data in relation to a complete national system. (Please note that we have used 'European Union' as a general term for the group of countries in question although, arguably, 'European Community' would have been more appropriate in some contexts.)

Further Reading
This provides opportunities for taking areas of specific interest further, and for exploring other national systems.

Index
To assist the reader in gaining access to the material at any point, a comprehensive index is provided. We have written the book in the knowledge that many readers may not need to read it from cover to cover.

ACKNOWLEDGEMENTS

The authors would like to thank Heather Hills, Denise Pitt, Barbara Gibbons and Jane Prendergrast for their help in preparing the manuscript.

Thanks to Sarah Cox for proofreading and making useful suggestions for improvement, to Koen Van Dijk at the Hogeschool West-Brabant, Breda, and Dr. Bernard James at the Business School, University of Hertfordshire for commenting on earlier versions of the manuscript. Also to Ian Grayston for providing contacts in selected countries and for discussing matters of international importance.

Thanks also to Penelope Woolf and Lisa Howard at Pitman Publishing for their support and tolerance.

Heartfelt gratitude to Thérèse for practical and moral support throughout.

The book is written in the hope that increasing international awareness will provide the stimulus for real investment into educating, training and developing the human resource.

Every effort has been made to trace and acknowledge ownership of copyright. The publishers will be glad to hear from any copyright holders whom it has not been possible to contact.

REFERENCE

Beer M, Spector B, Lawrence PR, Quinn-Mills D and Walton RE (1984) *Managing Human Assets*, Free Press, New York, p.23

PLAN OF THE BOOK

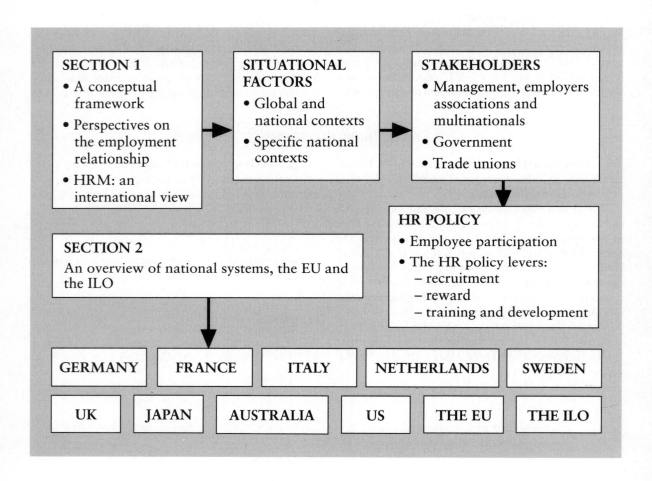

SECTION 1
- A conceptual framework
- Perspectives on the employment relationship
- HRM: an international view

SITUATIONAL FACTORS
- Global and national contexts
- Specific national contexts

STAKEHOLDERS
- Management, employers associations and multinationals
- Government
- Trade unions

HR POLICY
- Employee participation
- The HR policy levers:
  - recruitment
  - reward
  - training and development

SECTION 2
An overview of national systems, the EU and the ILO

| GERMANY | FRANCE | ITALY | NETHERLANDS | SWEDEN |
| UK | JAPAN | AUSTRALIA | US | THE EU | THE ILO |

Section 1

HRM THEMES AND ISSUES

1 · INTRODUCTORY THEMES AND PERSPECTIVES ON THE EMPLOYMENT RELATIONSHIP

OUTLINE

● **Why study international comparisons?**

● **Perspectives on the employment relationship: liberal individualist, liberal collectivist, corporatist and radical.**

● **The cultural context.**

LEARNING OBJECTIVES

You should be able to:

i understand why it is important to gain an insight into international comparisons in HRM;

ii understand some of the difficulties and hazards confronting those who are seeking to make international comparisons;

iii display an understanding of the main perspectives underlying the employment relationship;

iv investigate cultural perspectives on the employment relationship.

INTRODUCTION

A key motive for engaging in comparative analysis is to enable us to cast a critical eye over taken-for-granted aspects of domestic activity. Value judgements in many aspects of life, including the management of people, and corresponding prescriptions for change may be conditioned by underlying and rarely questioned ideological and cultural preconceptions which represent a bedrock for our thinking. The aim of this chapter is twofold. Firstly, to establish the importance of engaging in international comparisons, both for 'practitioners' and 'academics'. Secondly, in order to facilitate meaningful analysis, we aim to dig below the surface of international manifestations of HRM, by exposing some major cultural and ideological undercurrents which impinge upon the employment relationship.

Our view of ideology is that it represents a shared understanding of, and acquiesence towards, the distribution of power within a society by members of that society. This will have clear repercussions in the sphere of employment and, in particular, will affect the extent to which the sharing of power between the 'stakeholders' in the employment relationship is viewed as legitimate, or whether, alternatively, a high degree of managerial prerogative and control is tolerated or preferred.

The quite nebulous notion of culture may be taken to refer to shared values and beliefs within societies, and may be expressed in accepted patterns and modes of interaction between people, morality and ethics, views of human priorities and orientation to work. So, for example, a commitment to egalitarianism in the broader society will impinge upon pay determination and related processes.

In discussing major theoretical perspectives on an ideology and culture, we aim to provide a number of conceptual reference points against which we can map out, cross compare, and evaluate important features of the HRM terrain in our selected countries.

WHY STUDY INTERNATIONAL COMPARISONS?

Learning by comparison: the search for new ideas

Taking an international perspective and learning by comparison are nothing new. In the middle decades of the twentieth century the success of the Ford Motor Company in the US led to widespread emulation of 'Fordist' principles of work organisation, based on systems of mass production across industrialised countries.

The US has also provided much of the theory on employee motivation, through, for example, the work of Herzberg[1] in the 1960s, which is now accepted by many as conventional wisdom. His exhortation that work itself should be interesting, and that recognition of employee contribution is important, may be viewed as an important antecedent for the HRM movement.

More recently, the Japanese 'economic miracle' has encouraged academics and practitioners alike, in a search for the holy grail of productivity, growth and harmony, to be receptive to some of the pillars of Japanese organisational management. These include locating responsibility for quality at the point of production, encouraging employee influence through quality circles and other participatory mechanisms, breaking down demarcation between jobs to engender multiskilled and flexible working practices and entrenching well-developed internal labour markets.

A number of potential pitfalls associated with learning from Japan have been identified by Peter Nicholls[2], which may serve as a more general reminder for those interested in learning from abroad to proceed with caution.

- The temptation when conducting comparative research is to believe that the study is able to isolate key variables which can account for differences between the domestic and overseas system or process. Where authors have been cautious about any causal links, others, in their eagerness to find solutions, attribute qualities and outcomes which are unlikely to be realised.
- By the time explanations of particular overseas phenomena have been studied, popularised and given

currency in the domestic system, the original situation could well have changed significantly and this could jeopardise the claims made for the predicted outcomes when applied.
- In the case of Japanese management practices, little effort has been devoted to unravelling the variety that exists within Japan itself. Japanese practices are universally stereotyped, even though recent research clearly points to their variability in Japan and indicates that they are shaped by both the different sectors of the economy and the variety of forms of enterprise.
- Much of the recent research raises serious doubts about the original implicit connection between Japanese management and good business performance. Significant criticism is now applied to the validity of the 'excellence' literature and its claim to identify critical factors for business performance; it is difficult to envisage how research into the business system of Japan can make such a simple connection between management practice and business performance.

Consideration of the last point inevitably leads us to the work of the American management gurus, a number of whom have strong connections with the Harvard Business School. Peters and Waterman, Moss Kanter[3] and others have had a widespread influence on the language, and almost certainly the practice, of management on a worldwide basis over the last decade or so. Much of their work stresses the need for continuous organisational change in a changing and competitive market environment, and in the case of the best-selling *In Search of Excellence* by Peters and Waterman[4] a set of prescriptions is offered for corporate success, based on research into high-performing US companies at the time of publication. Despite being strongly criticised for methodological flaws and inconsistencies[5] the work has been taken on board with zeal by, in particular, Western managers searching for new ideas. The drive towards, for example, closeness to the customer represents a central plank of new management orthodoxy. A very important repercussion of this work has been to highlight the importance of effective management of human resources in the achievement of corporate success, which is, of course, integral to the human resource management movement.

The link between the prescriptions of American gurus and performance must, however, be questionable, not least in the light of a poor showing by the US itself. European economies which have been achieving higher levels of economic performance are not bathed in a similar limelight. This paradox is recognised by Tom

GM to sell European luxury car in US

By Kevin Done, Motor Industry Correspondent, in Detroit

General Motors is planning to produce a luxury car in Europe for sale in North America under the Cadillac brand name.

The project will mark the US carmaker's first substantial export of cars from Europe to North America since the early 1960s and will be the first European-produced GM car to be sold under a North American nameplate.

The programme is expected to be approved in the next few months, with the car going into production in early 1996 in Germany at the Rüsselsheim plant of Opel, GM's main European subsidiary.

The three-litre V6 engines for the car will be produced in the UK at Vauxhall's plant at Ellesmere Port, Cheshire, while automatic transmissions will be made at GM's plant at Strasbourg.

At the Detroit motor show yesterday,

GM unveiled a prototype version of the car, the Cadillac LSE (Luxury Sedan Euro-style).

It will allow the carmaker to compete for the first time with the Japanese luxury car brands Lexus and Infiniti, launched in the US at the end of the 1980s by Toyota and Nissan.

The European-built Cadillac is being developed as a derivative of GM Europe's new top-of-the-range Opel/Vauxhall Omega executive car, to be launched in Europe soon.

It is understood that GM is aiming to produce in Germany up to 40,000 units a year of the Cadillac.

The product marks an important step in the globalisation of GM's vehicle development and engineering, which is seen as a way to cut costs and make better use of the company's worldwide resources.

GM is also planning for the first time

to export to Europe a version of its next generation US-produced MPV (multi-purpose vehicle) for sale under the Opel/Vauxhall badges, to compete with vehicles such as the Renault Espace.

Mr Jack Smith, GM chief executive, yesterday said the programme for a European-produced Cadillac was "one of the most significant international projects GM had undertaken".

The new car represented a cost-effective way to integrate the group's global resources "with a fraction of the investment" that it would have taken under the more traditional approach of developing the car in North America.

"It makes little sense to build duplicate components or near-duplicate platforms [chassis] for different regional market segments, when one region can adapt or tailor what is being developed for another," he said.

Fig 1.1 Source: *Financial Times*, 5 January 1994

Peters, who admitted being dumbfounded when asked why Britain continued to seek inspiration from the US.[6]

THE PRACTITIONER'S VIEWPOINT

As we have stated, an important feature of the new management orthodoxy is an increased recognition of the contribution which HRM can make. HR practitioners must counsel their organisations against parochialism, and encourage the raising of international antennae. There are a number of related reasons for this.

Globalisation

According to Holden:[7]

Increasingly nations and multinational corporations cannot take a parochial view of the world. The transformation of Eastern Europe, the adjustments and challenges within the European Community (EC) and the advancement of rapidly industrialising countries on the Asia Pacific rim with their concomitant commercial potential are forces which cannot be ignored.

The world economic order is also being restructured by the growth of more prominent economies in Latin America, such as Brazil and Mexico.[8]

Not only are the forces of competition being felt from further afield, but the scope for economic integration and collaboration is being widened through advances in telecommunications and transport systems. An example of this is in the motor manufacturing industry, where a European luxury car is to be produced for sale in the US, with engines being made in Cheshire, UK, and automatic transmissions manufactured at GM's plant in Strasbourg, Germany (see Fig. 1.1).

For many organisations, therefore, competitive advantage can only be sustained by organising production facilities on an international basis, and by relating this closely to global marketing strategies.

Multinational enterprises (MNEs)

Bratton and Gold[9] state:

The global corporation is back in fashion as the embodiment of modernity; high technology, rich in capital, replete with skilled jobs. Moreover, some economic theorists suggest that economic activity will be controlled by fewer and fewer companies.

Practitioners may have to be receptive to approaches and techniques which are funnelled through the conduit of MNEs. Certainly Japanese concerns operating abroad have been instrumental in the spread of 'quality circles', their perceived success persuading non-Japanese concerns to emulate this and other practices.

Pucik[10], states that MNEs are increasingly developing international human resource strategies. A primary concern here is likely to be remuneration policies which are internally consistent, but also take account of local market rates. Holden also identifies the need for global management succession planning, the expatriation process, recruitment from the indigenous population, and awareness of labour and human resource practices in different countries and regions[11]. Many organisations are becoming more fully involved in language training as well as conducting elaborate experiments in cross-cultural training and development. HR practitioners will not only have a primary role in providing advice on such matters, but may also personally experience international redeployment, as the level of international executive mobility increases. Globalisation and the growth of multinationals also present challenges for trade unions which will need to consolidate international links in order to exert countervailing power effectively on multinational decision making. To date, only limited success has been achieved in this direction.

The Single European Market

The heightening of international economic activity received a further boost by the formal creation of the Single European Market on 1 January 1993, with the removal of national barriers to the mobility of capital, goods, services and labour. This may affect HR practitioners in a number of ways.

First, deregulation has prompted a wave of mergers and amalgamations across European concerns, particularly in steel, motor manufacture, banking, tool and transport industries.[12] The implications for HR practitioners include managing the implications of organisational restructuring and staff severance.

Secondly, freedom of movement of labour throws up a set of challenges in the areas of staff recruitment and development.

Thirdly, the moves towards economic deregulation are being counterbalanced by an important set of social and legal measures emanating from Brussels forming a 'Social Agenda' which defines a common set of standards on matters such as employee consultation, health and safety and equal opportunities.[13]

In summary, therefore, it would indeed be ostrich like if those interested in the management of human resources, a function which has claimed with more confidence over the past few years to make a key contribution to the achievement of corporate objectives, disregarded the potential impact of international developments in many areas of their domain.

THE 'ACADEMIC' VIEWPOINT

Analysing rather than describing

From a more theoretical viewpoint, it is worth considering how broadening perspectives to include the analysis of systems of work and employment in other countries can deepen and sharpen insights into the disciplinary area. It is worth pointing out that the field we are referring to embraces the sometimes discretely viewed areas of 'industrial relations' and 'personnel management'. An initial advantage which springs from engaging in international analysis is that the division between these and other related subjects becomes virtually meaningless. For example, approaches to recruitment in Germany cannot be understood without consideration of the role of works councils, which involve workers' representatives in decision making.

Bringing this broad area into the discussion, we move on to a cross-national perspective to help us adopt a more critical stance, and to throw domestic institutions, practices and processes into sharper relief.

A recent article in *The Guardian* included a quote from Beardwell and Holden's book *HRM – A Contemporary Perspective:*[14]

> An event seen from one point of view gives one impression. Seen from another point of view it gives quite a different impression. But it's only when you get the whole picture you fully understand what's going on.

Taking an international perspective helps us not only to obtain the fullest picture, but also to ascertain the value of what we perceive. It may inform debate on the following types of issues.

- Are high labour costs compatible or incompatible with high economic performance?
- Is performance-related pay likely to improve corporate performance?
- Is investment in training and development to be viewed as an overhead or is it fundamental to the

achievement of a high-quality and flexibly deployed workforce?

- Is a high-profile, strategically orientated personnel department fundamental to corporate success?
- Is a marginalised trade union movement a prerequisite to putting HRM-type initiatives into place, and does this promote economic success?
- What are the benefits or drawbacks of establishing works councils?
- Is there a connection between minimum social provision/wages and unemployment?

Moreover, one purpose of study is to look behind observed facts and phenomena and to seek to establish underlying principles. Establishing and incorporating theoretical perspectives is useful in a text of this nature and it helps to identify the fundamental causes underlying a multiplicity of apparently unrelated events, practices and phenomena.

IDEOLOGICAL AND CULTURAL PERSPECTIVES ON THE EMPLOYMENT RELATIONSHIP

A conceptual framework

It is our contention that HRM does not exist within a vacuum, but that surrounding it there exists a set of values and beliefs which both impinge on, and are exerted by, those with a stake in the employment relationship, including employers, managers, trade unions, employees, government and its representatives. Positions of respective power and modes of interaction between these parties will be set on a broader ideological platform.

What follows is an exposition of major ideological perspectives on the employment relationship. The perspectives possess great explanatory value in compar-

Ideology

According to Giner, an ideology is a conception of the social world explicitly and coercively maintained by a collectivity, which derives from it a general plan of action and an identification of the sources of legitimate authority, and attempts the control of its social environment in a way consistent with this conception.

ative and international analysis, as they encapsulate many of the implicit principles which guide the thoughts and actions of policy makers, practitioners and academics in varying national systems.

Liberal individualism

Liberal individualism, sometimes referred to as market individualism, has much in common with the views underpinning the original *laisser-faire* economic model: individuals are assumed to be rational, free and capable of pursuing their own self-interest through exchange in the marketplace. The market is believed to be the most efficient mechanism for allocating resources between different users, and resources are assumed to be mobile. Conflicts of interest, as for example between buyer and seller of labour, are best reconciled freely through the market and in the absence of combinations which are deemed as impediments to the efficient operation of the market. The emphasis is on contracts agreed between individuals, who it is assumed are of roughly equal power. Individuals are expected to take responsibility for their own actions. This kind of system emphasises private ownership and enterprise and decentralised decision making at the level of the individual.

This pure form of liberalist ideology has a number of implications for labour markets, the parties to the employment relationship, trade unions and the role of government, which are briefly as follows. Labour markets should remain unregulated, trade unions should be prevented or at least discouraged, and government should not seek to interfere, whether it be to regulate the relationship of the parties, protect one particular interest or resolve conflicts between them. The parties should be left to reach their own decisions with respect to the terms and conditions of the employment contract.

Liberal individualism is not and has never been a perspective or ideology common to governments of developed market or advanced capitalist economies. However, there has been evidence in recent years of a resurgence of this orthodoxy, particularly in the UK and arguably also in the US. International and other pressures that emphasise the need for labour flexibility and a diminished role for the public sector may encourage a wider return to governmental approaches of this traditional kind.

Liberal collectivism

A very much more common approach adopted by several governments since the second world war constitutes an adaptation of the original liberalist perspective, and is referred to as liberal collectivism or voluntarism. It is an approach which differs from traditional liberalism in that it recognises and to some extent takes account of one of the main criticisms of the original model, that employees as individuals are not equal in bargaining power to the buyers of labour who, in advanced capitalist economies, are quite likely to be large and relatively powerful organisations and not individuals. The liberalist notion that in free markets exchange will take place between equally powerful individuals is seen to be an illusion, such freedom and individualism giving employers the opportunity to be paternal or exploitative in their approach and dealings with labour.

The liberal collectivist approach seeks to take account of this weakness in the liberal individualist perspective by allowing for labour combinations or collectives. The majority of enterprise is still seen as being best dealt with via private ownership and the operation of market forces, but within certain constraints. These constraints comprise both interaction between employing organisations and collective labour unions to determine jointly the terms and conditions on which labour is to be employed, and a marginally more protectionist and interventionist role for government. The latter is consistent with the Keynesian and welfarist economic policy often exhibited by liberal collectivist governments, which are themselves in part a response to the inequalities of income and wealth distribution that often seem to be the product of unrestrained and unfettered market or liberal individualism.

The nature of the interaction between employers and labour collectives that is favoured by the liberal collectivist approach is collective bargaining, freely entered into. The nature of collective bargaining is discussed elsewhere in this book, but can be simply described as a process of negotiation and compromise resulting in agreement, joint determination and regulation. Inevitably, collective bargaining results in regulated labour markets. No longer are employees and employers able freely and individually to engage in an unregulated process of exchange; the collective bargaining outcomes constitute limits within which the process of market exchanges between employer and employee takes place. Government intervention to protect particular interests or achieve particular economic or social objectives is similarly likely to create limits within which the process of individual exchange is to occur. It is, however, part of the liberal collectivist approach that such intervention should be kept to the

minimum necessary to afford genuine protection, and it may well be that management or employer interests require this government protection as much as do employees' interests. Liberal collectivism is not consistent with wholesale government intervention to determine, whether by legislation or other means, terms and conditions of employment.

The rights of or freedom for individuals to join together or associate in labour collectives may require government legislative intervention, especially if a liberal collectivist system is developed from a liberal individualist one, in which such an association might well have been unlawful. It is usually crucial to effective trade union organisation that the legislative system supports or at least allows such an association.

In the liberal collectivist context, trade unions and voluntary collective bargaining are perceived as institutions and processes consistent with democracy and the national interest. Collective bargaining is perceived as a fair, efficient and flexible mechanism for institutionalising and resolving conflicts between the two interest groups of employer and employee. Critics of liberal collectivist systems perceive trade unions as monopolistic, overly powerful and anti-democratic and, in combination with free collective bargaining, sources of labour inflexibility, labour market rigidities and inflationary wages, all of which contribute to declining efficiency and competitiveness. Alternatively, more radical critics perceive collective bargaining as a mechanism limited in its participatory scope and useful for limiting the power and activities of trade unions, thereby preserving the essence of capital's exploitation of labour.

Corporatism

In liberal systems, even those which are liberal collectivist, the political and economic spheres of society remain largely disassociated, with economic decision making being relatively decentralised and the product of interaction between competing interests. As society becomes more complex and the demands on government to achieve and maintain economic and political stability grow more insistent, pressures may develop for a less competitive and less disruptive system of decision making and administration. Government may feel that leaving a considerable proportion of economic decision making to market- and/or power-based processes is increasingly unwise and inefficient, since outcomes remain unpredictable and the processes often result in inequalities and unfairness.

In such circumstances, government may seek to devise mechanisms which integrate the interests of capital, labour and government, usually through some process of exchange and political institutions which facilitate tripartite discussion and decision making with respect to economic, industrial and social policies, and perhaps in particular the pursuit of economic growth, full employment and price stability. Such perspectives and resulting systems are referred to as corporatist. The government plays an active role, mediating the interests of capital and labour and, in partnership with these competing interest groups, directing the activities of the still privately owned enterprises. The national interest has been used to justify such arrangements, the argument being that the various interest groups should recognise their interdependence and seek to work in partnership for the benefit of all. In some countries such as Germany, the Netherlands and Sweden, which have lengthy corporatist traditions, it has been quite common for the partnership to be emphasised by the use of the term 'social partners' when referring to the representatives of capital and labour; indeed, this is the term used within the European Union. Commonly representatives of capital and labour participate with government representatives in a tripartite administration of the mechanisms established to achieve the agreed policy objectives.

Gospel and Palmer[15] make the point that corporatist arrangements may extend from the voluntary and almost *ad hoc* tripartism involving elements of bargaining between the parties which has occasionally been tried in the UK, through the very much more elaborate systems of interest representation and concerted action which have been characteristic of the systems operating in countries such as Germany, the Netherlands and Sweden, to the highly coercive and regimented administrative structures and systems associated with fascism.

The voluntary, bargained version of corporatism often results in a temporary agreement whereby non-governmental interest groups agree, for example, to moderate their demands for wage or price increases in return for concessions from the other parties which might take the form of increased social security benefits, enhanced co-determination rights for employees or renewed commitments by both government and employers to full employment. For employers, the concessions might involve investment allowances, tax allowances or reductions in company taxation. A massive range of social, economic and industrial objectives can be pursued through such arrangements and,

as noted above, one of the most common is income restraint. The July 1993 Accord in Italy is perhaps a particularly good example of this form of quite complex exchange.

Crouch[16] notes that corporatism ostensibly provides the ideal solution to the central problem of modern capitalism – the maintenance of order where market relations are no longer supreme, where the division between economy and polity can no longer be sustained, and where both capital and the working class are organised.

Corporatist arrangements and institutions are not necessarily easy to establish or maintain. However, it is possible to identify institutional and structural factors that would seem likely to help, as opposed to hinder, such developments. These helpful factors would include:

- capital and labour market interest groups that are representative, coherent, organised in a manner facilitating centralised decision making, and able effectively to control their respective memberships;
- a government that has close ideological and personal links with the labour movement;
- a prevalence of centralised decision-making structures within employing organisations.

Conservative or right-wing governments are much less likely to be ideologically sympathetic to notions of corporatism. Interest groups that are not strong, coherent, representative, centralised and able to control their membership will not carry sufficient authority with the other parties. The Trade Union Confederations in Italy and employers in Australia have found it difficult to satisfy these 'conditions' even when the will was there. They may not be able to agree among themselves and come to decisions within the necessary timescales and, perhaps most crucially, they will not be able to deliver what they have agreed. Corporate decision-making structures that are not consistent with the centralism intrinsic to corporatism at a macro level will probably hinder the effective implementation of any agreements or positions reached.

Even where the above conditions exist, it is common for such arrangements to break up or fall into disrepair. As Keller[17] points out, the participants are likely to continue to take part only so long as they are satisfied with the outcomes.

In addition to encouraging and establishing corporatist systems at a macro or national level, government can also influence the existence and practice of micro-corporatism. Micro-corporatism refers to a system whereby employee interests within the firm are incorporated into the administrative structure, often in the form of a productivity coalition or alliance[18]. Japanese organisations with their enterprise unions are sometimes given as examples of micro-corporatist arrangements.[19]

Critics of macro-corporatism tend to emphasise the dangerous powers acquired by the different interest groups, the active interventionist role required of government and the difficulty it has in remaining neutral between the other interest groups. Instead critics favour a return to liberalism and argue the advantages of competition, free markets and decentralisation.

Radical perspectives

Radical perspectives on the employment relationship are based on the fundamental belief that industrial conflict is too deeply rooted and profound to be resolved by a process of compromise. The Marxist perspective, which has influenced trade union movements in a number of Southern European countries, views processes of control as being inescapably bound up with antagonistic class relations. According to this standpoint industry does not exist in isolation, but vastly unequal power relations in industry are buttressed by processes of government, education, access to housing, health care and so on.

It is argued that employers have a vested interest in retaining a 'reserve army' of unemployed people, which is likely to promote progressive intensification of work for those who fear redundancy. Moreover, employees are systematically denied the fruits of their labour in terms of profits or production; these are unfairly appropriated by employers for themselves and other vested interests responsible for perpetuation of the *status quo*. This denial of what employees have invested in work leads to feelings of 'alienation' from the products of their labour.

Trade unions which are influenced by radical perspectives are likely to have reservations about collective bargaining, as it may be viewed as a manipulative process on the part of employers to encourage worker representatives to enter into false truces. Instead, trade unions would be used as vehicles for revolutionary change to bring about worker control. In those countries where radical perspectives are influential, management can expect a higher degree of statutory regulation to compensate for the absence of orderly bargaining arrangements, and a high level of overt conflict, particularly at shopfloor level.

Culture

According to Poole and Kluckholm and Strodtbeck culture value orientations 'include views of human nature, the relationship of man to nature, time orientation, orientation towards activity and types of relations between people.' Cultural values may be expressed in moral codes (especially in employment relations), commitments to legalism or voluntarism, regionalism, religious values, and the extent to which social integration and accommodation are widely accepted social goals.

Sources: Poole M (1986) *Industrial Relations: Origins and Patterns of National Diversity*, Routledge and Kegan Paul.
Kluckholm F R and Strodtbeck F L (1961) *Variations in Value Orientations*, Row Peterson, New York.

To what extent can differences in approaches to management of the employment relationship be traced back to, and explained by, variations in national culture? This is a difficult and controversial area for discussion, not least because of the problems in defining 'culture'. Hofstede views culture as the 'collective programming of the mind of members of a group which is reflected in its particular assumptions, perceptions, thought patterns, norms and values.'[20]

Such a definition would appear to attach a level of tangibility and degree of deliberation in its creation to something which is highly amorphous and which just seems to happen. Moreover, in most societies many would resist the notion that they are party to a set of national characteristics which somehow set them apart from other societies. Clearly most advanced countries now comprise heterogeneous and diverse subcultures. Leeds, Kirkbride and Durcan[21] attempt to overcome this by asserting that 'whatever are described as mainstream cultural traits are best considered as a central tendency or average. Individuals will differ in the extent to which they share the values associated with any particular country.' Although the emphasis here would still seem to be ultimately on conformity rather than diversity, it would have to be viewed as a realistic starting point if cultural explanations are to have any value.

Hall and Hall[22] define a distinction between high and low context cultures. According to the authors, context refers to 'the information that surrounds an event; it is inextricably bound up with the meaning of that event.' See Tables 1.1 and 1.2.

In low context cultures emphasis is placed on clear, unambiguous and explicit messages between people, because shared, mutual and informal understanding

Table 1.1 High and low context cultures

Low Context Culture	High Context Culture
Clear, unambiguous and explicit messages – shared, mutual and informal understanding not assumed.	Assumed that most information already vested in the person. Reliance placed on informal, subtle, face-to-face communication.
Emphasis placed on time management, deadlines and punctuality. Activities carried out simultaneously. Division between work and domestic life less rigid.	

Table 1.2 Locating low and high context cultures

Country	High context	Low context
West Germany		XXXX
German Swiss		XXXX
Scandinavian		XXX
North America		XXX
Belgium, Holland, Denmark		X
France	X	
Great Britain	XX	
Southern European	XXX	
Middle East	XXX	
Asia, Africa, Latin America	XXX	
Japan	XXXX	

Source: Kirkbride P S *et al* (ed.) (1994) *Human Resource Management in Europe, Perspectives for the 1990s*, Routledge, London and New York, p13

cannot be assumed. A greater emphasis is placed on time management, deadlines and punctuality.

In high context cultures it is assumed that most information is already in the person and therefore greater reliance is placed on informal, word of mouth, face-to-face methods of communication.

A degree of correlation may be discernible between low context cultures and more highly regulated employment systems. In the latter, there is a preference for absence of ambiguity, and a reliance placed on mutually agreed and established procedure.

Hall and Hall's work clearly has significance for HRM, particularly in the area of communications. Where interaction is between individuals from different backgrounds, empathy will be required to avoid misunderstanding. Comprehension of high and low contexts would have relevance to the form of employee communication systems, indicating the level of ambiguity and symbolism which can be tolerated.

The work of Geert Hofstede[23] has clear significance for a number of important areas of HRM. In an influential study, Hofstede sent a questionnaire about values to 160 000 employees of IBM across more than 60 countries. He analysed the results to show that there were four fundamental dimensions which correlated with nationality.

1. Power distance
The power distance index (PDI) measures the extent to which members of a society, including those less as well as more powerful, accept that power is distributed unequally.

2. Uncertainty avoidance
The uncertainty avoidance index (UAI) measures the degree to which people feel threatened by ambiguous situations, and create beliefs and institutions that try to avoid uncertainty.

3. Individualism
The individualism index (IDV) measures the extent to which people believe that their primary concern in life is the well-being of themselves and their immediate families (as opposed to an orientation towards a wider grouping with more extended responsibilities and a more extended network of support and loyalty).

4. Masculinity
The masculinity index (MAS) measures the extent to which achievement through such values as visible success, money and possessions is given priority over the more caring values of nurturing and sharing.

The values of each of these indices are listed in Table 1.3.

Individualism
The US, UK and Australia are high on individualism compared with Japan, for example. This may go some way to explain the preference for liberal individualism in the UK and US, and the associated HR practices of performance appraisal, individual payment by results and individualised career paths. In Japan, none of these feature much in the employment scene, where conformity to group norms is paramount. Italy and France are both high on PDI compared to the Netherlands, Germany, Sweden and the UK. This could explain the protected position of senior management

Table 1.3 Values of the four indices

Country	PDI	UAI	IDV	MAS
Argentina	49	86	46	56
Australia	36	51	90	61
Austria	11	70	55	79
Belgium	65	94	75	54
Brazil	69	76	38	49
Canada	39	48	80	52
Chile	63	86	23	28
Columbia	67	80	13	64
Denmark	18	23	74	16
Finland	33	59	63	26
France	68	86	71	43
Germany (FR)	35	65	67	66
Great Britain	35	35	89	66
Greece	60	112	35	57
Hong Kong	68	29	25	57
India	77	40	48	56
Iran	58	59	41	43
Ireland	28	35	70	68
Israel	13	81	54	47
Italy	50	75	76	70
Japan	54	92	46	95
Mexico	81	82	30	69
Netherlands	38	53	80	14
New Zealand	22	49	79	58
Norway	31	50	69	8
Pakistan	55	70	14	50
Peru	64	87	16	42
Philippines	94	44	32	64
Portugal	63	104	27	31
Singapore	74	8	20	48
South Africa	49	49	65	63
Spain	57	86	51	42
Sweden	31	29	71	5
Switzerland	34	58	68	70
Taiwan	58	69	17	45
Thailand	64	64	20	34
Turkey	66	85	37	45
USA	40	46	91	62
Venezuela	81	76	12	73
Yugoslavia	76	88	27	21
Mean	52	64	50	50
Standard deviation	20	24	25	20

Source: Hofstede G (1980) *Culture's Consequences*, Sage, London, p.315
Reprinted by permission of Sage Publications Inc.

in these countries, particularly France, and relatively highly stratified organisations. We have seen that in the Netherlands, Germany and Sweden, there is an emphasis on consultative decision making and co-determination is well accepted.

Uncertainty avoidance

Germany, Italy, France and Japan are all high on UAI, compared to, for example, Great Britain, the US and Sweden. This may explain the preference for adhering to rules in these former countries and referring to tried and tested procedures as opposed to taking risks. It would seem that the interest in regularity and predictability promotes a planned approach, as opposed to one which is short-term and reactive, and this is more consistent with economic success.

Hofstede comments: 'Interestingly, these security seeking countries seem to have been doing better economically ... than the risk takers, but the management theories that tell us that risk taking is a good thing were made in the US or Great Britain, not in Japan or Germany.'[24]

Masculinity

Compared with Italy and Japan, Sweden and the Netherlands are very low in terms of masculinity. A concern with nurturing and sharing may be viewed as consistent with a well elaborated and generously funded welfare state. Employment security is also likely to have a high priority in these countries, as opposed to there being a 'hiring and firing' attitude.

In conclusion, it is clear that such a categorisation depends on considerable stereotyping and neglects the nuances of organisational form. The basic premise that national cultures will directly determine organisational structures has also been questioned, especially by those who place a high priority on organisational autonomy and on contingency factors within companies, such as size, technology sector and stage of development.[25]

The newspaper article in Figure 1.2 illustrates how national characteristics impinge on organisational factors. It would be useful to read it in conjunction with Hofstede's analysis.

Criticisms of Hofstede

Although there is a degree of plausibility in such a report, Hofstede's analysis may be criticised on the following grounds:

● It neglects cultural diversity. For example, in the case of Germany there is a high degree of federalism within the nation-state, each 'Land' having different values and norms. Furthermore, in the 1960s there was an influx of foreign workers, largely from the Mediterranean. Five million immigrants now live in the country, with very different backgrounds.[26]

● It neglects change. Hofstede's main analysis occurred in the 1970s. Since then, as we have seen, the trend towards individualism has become more pro-

Alas, Schmidt and Jeaunes

France and Germany are at peace, aren't they? Not in the boardroom where cultures clash, says **Ludwig Siegele**

A disaster. The meeting was over in less than an hour and there was nothing to show for it, except the bile in the managers' throats. "Just what we expected: orders from the German steamroller," think the French. "Typically French," grumble the Germans, "a complete lack of substance." And both sides tell themselves: "We'll never make a go of this with them. Much better to do it without them."

And what caused the upset? Just a classic mistranslation. The Germans had tabled a discussion of their *Konzept*. The French translation of the agenda substituted the word *Concept*. The words only look similar. The Germans came to the meeting with a detailed plan of the new product. The French were prepared for a relaxed brainstorming session.

Politicians on either side of the Rhine may well have drawn a little closer since the Franco-German treaty of cooperation was signed in January 1963, but managers remain as far apart as ever. "When it comes to cultural understanding we still have a very long way to go," says André Laurent, a professor at the Paris Business School, INSEAD.

There are no statistics to tell us how much has been lost as a consequence of such misunderstandings. But there are plenty of opportunities: well over 1,000 German companies are in French hands. And double that number of French companies have a German shareholder. So there are a huge number of companies with Franco-German management.

The origins of this culture shock are as old as they are resistant to cure: "On one side of the Rhine business life has been shaped by Protestantism, while on the other side it was shaped by very particular French variety of rationalism," is how it is summed up by Günther Ammon, professor for business administration at the University of Erlangen-Nuremberg and author of the book The French Style of Business. In other words, an encounter between Luther and Descartes.

To bring the German *Unternehmen* and French *entreprise* into line is about as easy as squaring a circle. "The Germans make decisions together sitting at a round table. We French prefer the pyramid, with the boss at the top," says Henri Monod, Paris representative of German's privatisation agency, the Treuhandanstalt, and chairman of the Hoechst subsidiary Roussel Uclaf.

The management experts of the Banque Nationale de Paris have now got involved. After detailed research they have identified the relevant negotiator at the Dresdner Bank and there will now be an exchange with his opposite number at the French bank. It is reaching right up to the top: René Thomas, the president of the BNP

sees himself equal to a dozen board members of the Dresdner Bank.

Thomas can choose as he pleases. The head of the Dresdner Bank, Wolfgang Röller, first has to consult his board. "The French often think: either he has no power or he will pull a fast one on me," says Jochen Peter Breuer, a member of the management consultancy JFB, based near Paris, who has given seminars for 10 years in an attempt to cushion the Franco-German culture shock.

"In Germany the head of the company will often bow to the views of the majority. In France that would be regarded as showing weakness. People expect you to behave like a *patron*," says Udo Hück, who represents Germany's equivalent of British Telecom. "If in the morning the president of France-Telecom sneezes, by lunchtime the whole operation has caught a cold."

The head of a German company who holds meetings with French employees is often looked at with amazement. In France such a meeting, réunion, would not make a decision. The almighty PDG (Président Directeur Général) often just holds such a meeting to get information. "He will then take all the decisions by himself," says Monod.

This hierarchical way of thinking leaves its mark on how colleagues behave. "When German employees have an idea they discuss it with their colleagues. French employees go straight to their boss," says Hück. "Here information is power and you hang on to it."

"When I got my first job in Paris I couldn't understand why a colleague wanted to work with the door open, although there was a photocopier near it," recalls Breuer. "Only later did I realise the strategic importance of corridors: who has been to see the boss, what it says on discarded drafts. Fishing for information is a national sport in France."

It is also a matter of survival. Because people don't know what it says on files that are circulated, many employers have to find out fundamental information for themselves. German companies pass it around. "As most decisions are taken collectively," explains Breuer, "everyone should be equally well-informed. And that is best done on paper."

But this traffic of documents is a wearisome process to the fast-thinking French. "German companies are no doubt wonderfully structured but they are also ponderous," says Alfred Hirtz, president of SEMT Pielstick, the Paris-based diesel engine manufacturer, which is a subsidiary of the German companies MAN and MTU.

This is a view that Kurt Hollederer, general-director of Siemens Nixdorf France, shares: "The system of passing around transcripts can bring everything to a halt. In many companies nobody will lift a finger until they have received them. In France everyone makes their own notes – and gets on with it. Consequently we get on to the market quicker here."

Not only the structure of companies but the

different career ladders lead to conflict. To work for the same firm and in the same department for 25 years means something in Germany. In France the suspicion would be that people had been buried there. What counts in France are the elite schools, fast promotion and good political connections.

According to research by the consultants Heidrick & Struggles International, 30 per cent of the heads of the top 200 companies in Germany come from the same background. On the other side of the Rhine it is only 6 per cent. And while only 8 per cent of the German managers once worked for the state, in France it is 45 per cent. And most of them will have been to one of the Grandes Ecoles.

The teaching aims of these elite schools, such as the Ecole Nationale d'Administration (ENA), are almost always the same: originality, the ability to improvise, ambition, quick-wittedness, a breadth of knowledge, almost the opposite of what the German manager will meet as he works his way through his company.

The difference is clear in job applications. "The German candidate sends a heavy folder with umpteen references," says Klaus Walter Herterich who has spent 20 years as a personnel manager in Paris. A French applicant sends "only a CV in table form and a handwritten application. What counts is the interview."

It is very difficult to bring these two worlds together.

Different styles of work also cause annoyance. "A Frenchman tends to attempt too many things at once and consequently loses the thread," laughs Daniel Buclet, president of Euromissile, a joint venture of Aérospatiale and Germany's Eurospace. "But a German will often follow the line laid down – often far too rigidly."

Understanding oneself is often the first step to improvement. But many Germans and French managers don't want to take the second step. "Each believes that his own culture is universally valid," says the INSEAD professor André Laurent. "To go beyond acknowledging the problem is to question oneself. That is uncomfortable.

But comfort comes at a high price. "Those involved build an internal opposition and waste time and energy with manoeuvring, instead of working constructively towards fixed goals," warns Breuer. But he believes the French and Germans would be unbeatable if they could avoid their mutual misunderstandings. "Better than the Japanese."

Stéphane Charniot of BMW has other advice. "As in marriage the strengths and weaknesses of the partner should be accepted," she recommends. "The Germans are much better at rationalising production. French companies come up with far more ideas."

Perhaps that is why the BMW replacement parts manufacturing centre in Strasbourg is the most efficient in the whole company.

Fig 1.2 Source: *Guardian Europe*, 16 March 1993. Reproduced with permission. © *Guardian* 1993.

nounced, even in those countries with low individualism indices. It has also been argued[27] that homogeneity cannot be assumed over time, and that, again in the German context, subcultures are now important which conflict with the dominant values and that such subcultures have more in common with similar ones in Britain, France or the US.
● It is methodologically flawed. Not only was Hofstede's sample rather narrow, but also, as he

himself subsequently recognised, the four dimensions are too heavily drawn from Western concepts.[28] He suggests that the 'Uncertainty Avoidance Dimension' may not be relevant in Eastern cultures. Other culture theorists have received equivalent criticism, much of it centring on the difficulty they have faced in lucidly and rigorously analysing the diffuse and complex concept of culture.

SUMMARY

A comprehensive awareness of international comparisons is becoming increasingly important for practitioners and those engaged in the study of HRM. In order to be able to attribute meaning to the multiplicity of practices, institutions and phenomena one will encounter in examining international approaches to HRM, it is important to identify, at the outset, broader ideological and cultural perspectives which underlie the employment relationship. We will refer back to these as we proceed with our study.

DISCUSSION QUESTIONS

1 Why should domestic personnel practitioners be interested in learning from abroad?
2 What constraints exist on 'importing' new HRM ideas from overseas? How may they be overcome?
3 From your current knowledge of political/employment systems in different countries, identify at least two countries which fit most closely the four major ideological perspectives identified in this chapter.
4 Select four countries with which you are familiar. Would you accept Hofstede's stereotyping in respect of these? Why/why not?

5 Assuming Hofstede's stereotyping as valid, select four countries from Germany, France, Italy, Netherlands, Sweden, UK, Japan, Australia, US and predict how the cultural characteristics of these countries are likely to influence:
(a) organisation design
(b) approaches to
  – recruitment
  – remuneration
  – training and development
Compare your answers with the features described in our overview of national systems in Section 2.

NOTES AND REFERENCES

1. Herzberg F (1966) *Work and the Nature of Man,* Staples Press, New York

2. Nicholls P (1994) *Learning by Comparison: The search for new ideas, work and employment,* Spring issue, Bristol Business School, UK

3. Moss Kanter R (1983) *The Change Masters,* Simon and Schuster, New York

4. Peters TJ and Waterman RH (1982) *In Search of Excellence,* Harper and Row, New York

5. Guest D (1992) 'Right enough to be dangerously wrong' in Salaman G (ed), *Human Resource Strategies,* Sage, London

6. Quoted in the *Independent on Sunday,* UK, 12 June 1994, *The New English Babble*

7. Holden L (1994) 'International human resource management' in Beardwell I and Holden L, *Human Resource Management: A contemporary perspective,* Pitman, London, p.613

8. Bratton J and Gold J (1994) *Human Resource Management: Theory and practice,* Macmillan, London, p.43

9. Ibid

10. Pucik V (1984) 'The international management of human resources' in Fombrun CJ, Tichy NM and Devanna MA (eds). *Strategic Human Resources Management,* Wiley, New York, p.404

11. Holden L (1994) 'International human resource management', in Beardwell I and Holden L, *Human Resource Management: A contemporary perspective,* Pitman, London, p.600

12. IPD Brief, July 1994, *Personnel Management and Europe*, p.33

13. The Social Chapter, Maastricht Treaty, Meeting of European Ministers in 1989

14. Collins A (1984) 'Human resource management in context' in Beardwell I and Holden L, *Human Resource Management: A contemporary perspective,* Pitman, London, p.29

15. Gospel H and Palmer G (1993) *British Industrial Relations,* 2nd edition, Routledge, p.20

16. Crouch C 'The changing role of the state in industrial relations in Western Europe' in Crouch C and Pizzarro A (eds), *The Resurgence of Class Conflict in Western Europe since 1968,* vol 2, Comparative Analysis, Holmes and Meier, New York, pp.197–220

17. Keller BK (1991) 'The role of the state as corporate actor in industrial relations systems' in Adams RJ (ed), *Comparative Industrial Relations,* Contemporary research and theory, Harper Collins, p.83

18. Windolf P (1989) 'Productivity Coalitions and the Future of Corporatism: a comparative view on Western European Industrial Relations', *Industrial Relations 28,* 1–20

19. Gospel H and Palmer G, op. cit.

20. Hofstede G, *Cultures and Organisations,* McGraw Hill, Maidenhead, p.8

21. Leeds C, Kirkbride PS and Durcan J (1994) 'The Cultural Context of Europe: A Tentative Mapping' in Kirkbride PS, *Human Resource Management in Europe: Perspectives of the 1990s,* Routledge, London

22. Hall ET and Hall MR (1990) *Understanding Cultural Differences,* Intercultural Press, Yarmouth, Mass, p.6

23. Hofstede G (1980) *Culture's Consequences: International Differences in Work Related Values,* Sage, Beverley Hills, California

24. Hofstede G (1983) 'The Cultural Relativity of Organisational Practices and Theories', *Journal of International Business Studies,* volume 14, no 1, p.80

25. See Woodward J (1958) *Management of Technology,* HMSO, London

26. Conrad P and Pieper R (1990) 'Human Resource Management in the Federal Republic of Germany', in Pieper R (ed) *Human Resource Management, an International Comparison,* de Gruyter, Berlin and New York, pp. 130–1

27. ibid.

28. Hofstede G and Band M (1988) 'The Confucius Connection: from Cultural Roots to Economic Growth', *Organisational Dynamics,* Spring

FURTHER READING

Adler NJ (1986) *International Dimensions of Organisational Behaviour,* Boston, Kent

Crouch C (1982) *The Politics of Industrial Relations,* 2nd edn, Fontana, London

Hofstede G (1980) *Culture's Consequences: International Differences in Work Related Values,* Sage, Beverly Hills, California

Mole J (1990) *Mind Your Manners: Managing Culture Clash in the Single European Market,* Industrial Society, London

Poole M (1986) *Industrial Relations: Origins and Patterns of National Diversity,* Routledge and Kegan Paul, London and Boston

2 · THE HRM CONCEPT: AN INTERNATIONAL VIEW

OUTLINE

- **What is HRM? The Harvard concept and critique.**
- **The international applicability of the Harvard concept.**
- **Our approach.**

LEARNING OBJECTIVES

You should be able to:

i demonstrate an understanding of the main features of the 'Harvard' HRM concept;

ii relate the concept of the foregoing perspectives on the employment relationship in order to gain an insight into the assumptions underlying the concept;

iii explain the limitations to the international transferability of the HRM concept;

iv understand the principles guiding the structure of material in this book.

INTRODUCTION

Having identified various perspectives upon the employment relationship, we shall now focus specifically upon the HRM concept itself. A range of definitions and perceptions of HRM exist. However, for the sake of clarity we shall concentrate, in some detail, on a formulation of HRM which is widely viewed as being an 'original', that proposed by Beer and his colleagues at the Harvard Business School in the early 1980s.

Central to our thesis is the view that an association exists between current notions of human resource management and 'liberal individualistic' principles, which reflect prevailing economic, political and social conditions.

We go on to argue, however, that in other important parts of the world, particularly in continental Europe, the principles of 'liberal individualism' have less potency than is the case in, for example, the US and the UK. Here, the 'social partnership' model, in which managements, trade union representatives, and possibly agents of government collaborate in formulating employment policy, render transferability of the HR concept, and the assumptions of managerial autonomy underlying it, problematic.

We shall, therefore, discuss possible modifications to the HRM concept in order to give it broader, international applicability. This, we argue, calls for an enhanced recognition of the importance of all the 'stakeholders' in the employment relationship, to include not only management, but also the agents of employee organisations and government.

Furthermore, we place priority on the influence of 'situational factors' on HR policy and practice, which would include market, technological, social and legal environments.

We recognise that such external influences are included in the Harvard 'Map of the H.R.M. territory', and therefore we opt for the Harvard concept as providing the most satisfactory available template for guiding the sequence of our material throughout this text. Yet, as we have indicated, our major reservation with respect to the Harvard concept is the relatively modest degree of influence it allows stakeholders, and situational fac-

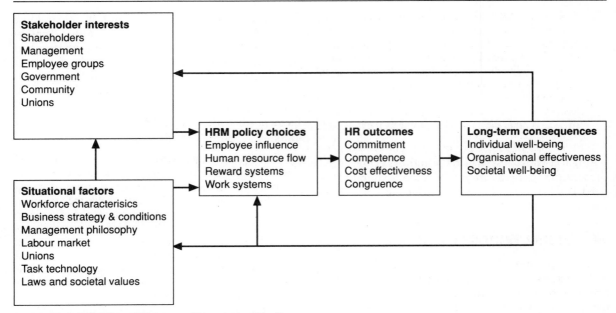

Fig 2.1 Map of the Human Resource Management Territory

Source: Reprinted with the permission of the Free Press, a division of Simon & Schuster Inc. from *Managing Human Assets* by Michael Beer, Bert Spector, Paul R Lawrence, D Quinn Mills and Richard E Walston. © 1984 by the Free Press.

tors, on managerial decision-making powers, and our subsequent analysis will aim to allow for this.

WHAT IS HRM?

Credit for the current conception of HRM can be taken by Beer and his colleagues at the Harvard Business School, who, in a highly influential text published in 1984, formulated the map of the HR territory shown in Figure 2.1.

The approach represented, in many respects, a departure from previous views of the nature and purpose of personnel management and, in essence, offered a set of prescriptions for managers to connect the effective management of HR with corporate success and broader positive consequences for society.

A number of important and innovative ideas are incorporated within the map, which have subsequently gained wide currency in managerial discourse. These are now distilled from the original text (page numbers refer to Beer *et al.*[1]).

CONSEQUENCES OF HRM POLICIES

HRM policies have immediate organisational outcomes and positive longer-term consequences for individuals and society. Factors such as physical fitness and lifestyle are given a high priority (pp.18–19). The

feedback loop signifies that the long-term consequences of HRM affect the context in which policies are formulated, so, for example, 'poor profitability over an extended period will affect shareholder interest and must inevitably result in changes of HRM policies regarding wages, training and perhaps employee influence' (p.17).

The authors state that the following questions are important ones when considering whether HR policy enhances the performance of the organisation, the well-being of employees, or the well-being of society...

1. *Commitment* To what extent do HRM policies enhance the commitment of people to their work and their organisation? Increased commitment can result not only in more loyalty and better performance for the organisation, but also in self-worth, dignity, psychological involvement, and identity for the individual.

2. *Competence* To what extent do HRM policies attract, keep, and/or develop people with skills and knowledge needed by the organisation and society, now and in the future? When needed skills and knowledge are available at the right time, the organisation benefits and its employees experience an increased sense of self-worth and economic well-being.

3. *Cost effectiveness* What is the cost effectiveness of a given policy in terms of wages, benefits, turnover, absenteeism, strikes, and so on? Such costs can be considered for organisations, individuals, and society as a whole.

4. *Congruence* What levels of congruence do HRM policies and practices generate or sustain between management and employees, different employee groups, the organisation and community, employees and their families, and within the individual? The lack of such congruence can be costly to management in terms of time, money, and energy, because of the resulting low levels of trust and common purpose, and in terms of stress and other psychological problems it can create.

A central facet of HRM philosophy relates to organisational effectiveness, which the authors define as the capacity of the organisation to be responsive and adaptive to its market and social environment.

SITUATIONAL FACTORS

A central premise of this work is that HRM policies and practices must be designed and implemented to fit the important situational factors specified in the map. Some key features of this are identified below.

Strategy and integration

Proposed HR policies should accord with situational factors and stakeholder interests. It is implied that there is no single approach to good HR practice, but that there is a significant element of contingency in effective HRM. A link is drawn between HR policy and practice and overall organisational strategy in its competitive environment, and with the immediate business conditions that it faces (p.25). So, for example, 'If quality is a key success factor, then HRM policies and practices must encourage concern and involvement of employees with the quality problem.'

Two reasons are given for the often poor match between HRM policies and business strategy. First, managers frequently develop business plans and make capital investments without adequate regard for the human resources necessary to support those plans. Secondly, the HR function itself commonly develops activities and programmes that are not relevant to line management's needs (p.26).

Integration should also exist between other HRM policies and systems (p.17). A proposed approach to designing work systems, for example, could require a change in the way employees are selected.

Management philosophy

Management philosophy is defined as the explicit or implicit beliefs of key managers about the nature of

the business, its role in society and how it should be run – particularly how it will treat and utilise employees (p.24). It is argued that where businesses have had powerful founders and leaders with a clearly articulated philosophy and set of values, then HRM policies are likely to be more internally consistent. In elaborating the importance of the link between management philosophy and HRM policies, the authors state:

> In fact the importance of that link has been acknowledged in recent efforts to create innovative work systems at the plant level aimed at developing high commitment among employees. These efforts typically involve the definition, in advance of plant start-up of a philosophy of management, that will guide the design of HR policies and practices. This process not only helps lead to a consensus among the management team about what the philosophy should be, thereby socialising them into a common view, but it also provides a guide-line for future action as new events and realities unfold. (p.28)

Labour market

Managers are advised to track long-term trends in labour markets, since these trends indicate how difficult it will be to acquire people with the skills their business may require in the future. It is argued that this information can help managers to assess the viability of their long-term strategic plans, and also to influence educational and training institutions to modify programmes or recruitment in order to ensure that the right skills will be available (p.30).

Managers are advised also to take account of the increased participation of women and minority groups in the labour force, as well as an ageing population as a result of the baby boom after the second world war, and the changing values of the workforce that make employees more resistant to arbitrary authority (p.31).

EVALUATING HRM

The authors propose that the success of HRM policies should be evaluated at individual, organisational and society level. At organisational level a number of possible methods are suggested.

- Performance evaluation by managers or third-party assessment of competence by personnel specialists, psychologists, other managers or assessment centres.
- Employee attitude surveys, through interviews or questionnaires administered by personnel specialists or outside consultants.

- Personnel records of voluntary turnover, absenteeism and grievances.
- Cost-effectiveness measures relating to wages and (with more difficulty) profit-sharing plans, pension plans, recruitment and employee development.
- Analysis of the cost of strikes/open conflict.

At the heart of the HRM map are the policy choices which have fundamental significance for the practice of HRM.

Employee influence

Employee influence is defined as encompassing collective bargaining between management and organised labour, legislated mechanisms for workers' participation (which would tend to occur on the European continent) and management's initiatives to allow more employee participation.

It is argued that general managers should consciously decide what their employee influence is and how much influence employees should be given. A general trend towards providing employees with more influence is noted, through pressures from unions and legislation, and also initiatives from management because of a belief that this is the best way to maintain a competitive and adaptive corporation (p.65).

Human resource flow

Human resource flow is defined as the flow of people in, through and out of the organisation and subsumes the traditional personnel areas of recruitment, internal staffing, performance appraisal and outplacement.

- *Inflow* encompasses recruitment, assessment and selection, orientation and socialisation.
- *Internal flow* refers to evaluation of performance and potential, internal placement, promotion and demotion, education and training.
- *Outflow* refers to termination, outplacement and retirement.

In carrying out these activities it is posited that managers should adopt more than an enterprise perspective, and that they should understand also:

- The perspective of the individual, with regard to what constitutes career development and satisfaction.
- The perspective of society, which involves an understanding of changing worker values, educational institutions that supply prospective recruits, legislation, government regulatory agencies and union policy.

A series of questions are specified to promote the development of effective flow policies.

- How can employees be recruited that will fit the corporation's needs and cultures?
- What is the optimum volume of personnel flow through the corporation consistent with good employee development and the strategic needs of the corporation?
- How is employee effectiveness defined and how shall it be evaluated?
- How can an organisational context be created that will encourage employee development?
- What mechanisms and processes can corporations install to meet employee expectations for fairness in connection with hiring, promotion and termination decisions?
- Should the company terminate, retire early, or otherwise encourage employees to leave when profits drop? What alternatives exist to this policy? (p.111)

Reward systems

A broad view is taken of reward systems which includes not only traditional concerns with pay, but also the symbolic significance of reward systems and their role in nurturing desirable attitudes and behaviour among employees. The main issues to be confronted by management are:

- The balance between intrinsic rewards such as feelings of competence, achievement, responsibility, significance, influence, personal growth and meaningful contribution, and extrinsic rewards such as promotions, salary, fringe benefits, bonuses, etc. (p.113).
- The application of systems which are most effective for maintaining employee perceptions of equity, both in terms of internal corporate relativities and external comparisons outside the organisation.
- Whether there are benefits in introducing performance-related pay (PRP) systems either at an individual or group/organisation level.

There is an emphasis on employee participation and communication in the design and administration of payment systems.

Work systems

The emphasis in this area is on establishing systems of work which foster high commitment on the part of employees. In order to achieve this a paradigm shift is suggested, from 'Model A' work systems which are characterised by factors such as:

- narrowly defined jobs;
- employee specialisation;
- pay for specific job content;
- close supervision;
- employees assigned to individual tasks;
- status differentials which enforce hierarchy;
- little employee influence

towards the more innovative 'Model B' systems, which may be applicable at shopfloor and office level as new information technology is introduced. These:

- define jobs broadly;
- rotate employees through many jobs;
- pay for skills mastered;
- emphasise self or peer supervision;
- assign whole tasks for teams;
- remove status differentials and emphasise egalitarianism;
- allow substantial employee influence and participation.

CONTRIBUTION OF THE HARVARD MODEL

We have defined the Harvard model at some length, and have made frequent reference to the original specification as, since its publication, different conceptions of HRM have proliferated. These have served to diffuse and obscure meaning as much as they have clarified what, if anything, is distinct about HRM. Many subsequent notions of HRM draw upon the fundamental tenets of the Harvard model, and by now the following ideas are quite commonplace:

- The need for HR policies to be integrated, to feed into corporate strategy, to promote organisational adaptability to rapid external change.
- The need to obtain employee commitment to change, through their empowerment.
- The importance of a strong 'culture' (referring to shared beliefs and norms across organisations).
- The need for longer-term planning to anticipate labour market changes.
- The need for the HR function to show a clear contribution to the achievement of corporate goals and, in particular, to meet line management's needs.
- The need for flexible working practices.
- The need to measure the success of change more rigorously through performance appraisal, attitude surveys, etc.

Despite its strengths, at the time of its inception the approach implicit in the Harvard model was not unchallenged. A competing text edited by Frombrun et al.[2] in 1984 took a harder view of HRM, placing less of an emphasis on viewing staff as a special and valued asset but leaning more towards equating them with all other organisational resources, so that principles of cost-effectiveness and optimisation would guide recruitment decisions, deployment and the dispensibility of staff.

Even though these contradictions within HRM have always existed, it does seem possible to identify some specific features of HRM which separate it from previous personnel practice. Mahoney and Deckop[3] specify the following differences:

in six specific areas:

(1) Employment planning: from a narrow technical focus to closer links with business strategy;
(2) communication with employees: from a collective, negotiating focus to a more general approach to more direct communication with employees;
(3) employee feelings: from job satisfaction to concern with the total organisational culture;
(4) employment terms: from selection, training, compensation policies focused on individuals to a concern with group working and group effectiveness;
(5) employment cost–benefits: from a concern with cost-reduction through such strategies as reducing turnover, controlling absenteeism to a focus on organisational effectiveness and the 'bottom line';
(6) employee development: from individual skills to longer-term employment capabilities.

Pervading all of these is the broader, visionary form of HRM which appeals to the emotions of managers and employees and which, through the language of transformation, aims to benefit not only organisations but societies.

HRM AS A PERSPECTIVE ON THE EMPLOYMENT RELATIONSHIP

The context and origin of HRM

In examining the principles and rationale underlying HRM it is instructive to locate its origins within a physical (northern US) and temporal (early to mid-1980s) context, and to consider the forces that stimulated a rethink of approaches towards the management of people which had been taken for granted. Beaumont[4] defines the following influences as typically highlighted in its inception:

- The increasingly competitive, integrated character-istics of the product market environment. These fac-tors are addressed more fully in Chapter 3.
- The positive lessons of the Japanese system and the good performance of individual US companies which accord HRM a relatively high priority.
- The declining levels of workplace unionisation in the US, particularly in the private sector.
- The relative growth of the service, white-collar sec-tor of employment.
- The relatively limited power and status of the per-sonnel management function in individual organi-sations owing to its inability to demonstrate a distinctive contribution to individual organisation-al performance.

Beaumont concludes therefore ,that HRM 'is viewed as a change or development driven by fundamental environmental changes' (particularly in product mar-ket conditions) which were not capable of being ade-quately responded to by the traditional concerns, orientations and power of personnel management func-tions'.

Although the concept of HRM originated in the US, according to Brewster and Bournois,[5] it has been 'taken up most enthusiastically in the related cultures of first Great Britain and then Australasia'.

A number of the influences noted by Beaumont as stimuli for the inception of HRM in the US have been reflected and elaborated in the UK context by Singh[6]. He notes:

- Increasing international competition, with old mod-els for the management of labour seeming not to be working effectively in a rapidly changing environ-ment.
- New technology, notably in manufacturing and office computerisation, facilitating moves towards flexible working arrangements and new reward sys-tems.
- The diminishing power of trade unions coupled with a strong trend towards individual achievement encouraged by government policy. A loss in the tra-ditional membership reservoir, as a result of decline in the coal, steel and manufacturing industries.
- Demographic changes, including an increasing pro-portion of women, part-timers and young people in the workforce. Singh contends that historically women have been more difficult to organise into trade unions than men, and more compliant with management ini-tiatives which would include moves towards HRM. He notes that companies which are associated with

HRM approaches employ a high proportion of women (e.g. Toshiba and Marks and Spencer).
- Japanese companies establishing plants in green-field sites providing the opportunity for the intro-duction of new initiatives in the management of labour. Features of such companies include a high-ly professional management, a carefully selected and trained labour force, and intrinsically rewarding work and security of employment. Singh argues that these companies actively pursue a careful and delib-erate policy of marginalising the influence of trade unions, or of avoiding the need for them altogeth-er. Management-led initiatives such as quality cir-cles, single status and staff consultative committees contribute to the achievement of this result.

Hendry and Pettigrew also point to certain similarities in the climate which HRM entered in the US and the UK, highlighting in the British context the restructuring effects of recession, loss of competitiveness and intro-duction of new technology. Alongside this, they argue, 'was the political climate of Thatcherism, a new legiti-macy for entrepreneurial, and anti-union legislation which encouraged firms to introduce new labour prac-tices and to re-order collective bargaining arrangements'.[7]

This brief look at the context in which HRM mate-rialised has suggested that the emergence of new approaches towards managing the employment rela-tionship can be explained by (a) the need for man-agements to bring about radical organisational change in order to survive and prosper in competitive and changing international markets; and (b) the ability of managements to see initiatives through based on new-found authority vested in a climate of entrepreneurial and free-market economics.

HRM and the role of stakeholders: contradictions within the concept

Returning to the HRM concept as defined by Beer et al., it is now possible to see that many of its prescrip-tions rest on quite strong free-market based assump-tions. This may be illustrated by referring to the following pivotal quotation, which supports the need for organisational adaptability.

In the long run, organisational effectiveness means that the firm has been flexible and responsive to its market and social environment. When the market demands lower costs, or product innovation, or improved service, the manage-ment of the corporation must sense the need for change and be able to mobilise the support of various shareholders, employee groups, unions, government, educational institutions, suppliers, and the community to make adjustments in their expectations and behaviour. (p.35)

From this quotation we would emphasise two premises:

1 The dominance of the market in determining organisational objectives and responses.
2 The supremacy of management in initiating action and mobilising support.

In subsequent sections of the book Beer et al. make it clear that management is in the driving seat in implementing HRM-type policies. Indeed, in citing firms which 'are effective in HR management' (p.24) a stress is placed on non-union firms: IBM, McCormack Spice, Hewlett-Packard, Donnelley Mirror and Lincoln Electric.

What then is the standing of the stakeholders?

Although the sections on employee influence suggest that Beer et al. are serious about encouraging employees to participate in management (p.25), the purpose of this, which is apparent from the above quotation, is hardly to share responsibilities or power with employees and their representatives, but rather to gain commitment to a course of action defined by management. Taken in conjunction with the propositions on management philosophy and the importance of strong culture (pp.27–9), one would question the extent to which managers adhering to the HRM approach would be prepared to take on board opinions, or ideas which deviated from 'explicit or implicit beliefs of key managers about the nature of the business; its role in society and how it should be run – particularly how it will treat and utilise employees'.

Perhaps for these reasons Strauss[8] argues that HRM literature ignored external economic variables, was potentially manipulative, was anti-union or ignored unions, and sought to have the organisation operate as a harmonious, co-operative system. Our reading of the literature would lead us to accept that the final three criticisms have greatest validity.

Turning to the importance given to market forces, and the need for HRM policies to be devised to ensure adaptability and responsiveness to competitive pressures, some authors have pointed to difficulties in reconciling the two requirements to keep costs down and invest in human resources.

Legge[9], in particular, cites circumstances in which matching HRM policy to business strategy calls for minimising labour costs, rather than treating employees as a resource whose value may be enhanced by increasing their commitment, functional flexibility and quality.

If a multi-business conglomerate's success is sought through acquisition, asset stripping and attention to its price/earnings ratio on the stock markets, its HRM 'policies' – if not entirely pragmatic – may logically call for actions (e.g. compulsory redundancy, reward based on short-term performance results) which, although consistent with business strategy, are unlikely to generate employee commitment.

Kochan[10] suggests that price-competitive markets are exerting increased pressure on both unionised and non-unionised concerns 'to lower labour costs, streamline staffing levels, adapt labour saving technologies and redeploy workers and assets'. This contradiction is exemplified by the case of IBM, a company singled out by Beer et al. as being effective in HRM, which in 1991 suffered massive financial losses and was forced to abandon its no redundancy policy.[11]

In order to reconcile the apparent contradiction between mission statements which visualise employees as 'valued assets' to be invested in and the economic necessity to keep labour costs down and sometimes to dispose of staff, it seems that managements are engaging in a form of denial and are turning to the use of rhetorical devices. Legge[12] finds that actions such as 'chopping out dead wood whose performance is not up to standard, or tying rewards closely to individual performance, or transferring employees to other jobs and parts of the organisation in the light of business requirements' may in fact be viewed as 'providing an opportunity for employees to develop their resourcefulness and competences'. She goes on to argue, 'If some employees prove unequal to the challenge and have to be dispensed with or if business circumstances dictate that some have to be sacrificed in the interests as a whole, this is really an example of tough love or care which does not shy away from tough decisions.'

Taking a broader view of current terminology and organisational characteristics associated with the HRM concept, Sisson casts a critical eye on how this may translate into reality (see Table 2.1).

HRM and trade unions

In Chapter 1, we say that a central tenet of liberal individualism is the notion that individuals are rational, free and capable of pursuing their own self-interest through exchange in the marketplace. In employment terms, this translates into the dominance of the individual relationship or contract between single employees and employers. The assumptions underlying this dynamic are of a rough equilibrium between the contractors, ease in entering into and terminating contracts, and an adherence to the provisions of the contract during its period of operation.

In contrast to the liberal collectivist perspective, trade unions would be discouraged as a form of cartel, artificially inflating the cost of labour, and as an unnecessary interference into the individual employment relationship.

Table 2.1 The HRM Organisation – Rhetoric or Reality?

Rhetoric	Reality
Customer first	Market forces supreme
Total quality management	Doing more with less
Lean production	Mean production
Flexibility	Management 'can do' what it wants
Core and periphery	Reducing the organisations' commitments
Devolution/delayering	Reducing the number of middle managers
Down-sizing/right-sizing	Redundancy
New working patterns	Part-time instead of full-time jobs
Empowerment	Making someone else take the risk and responsibility
Training and development	Manipulation
Employability	No employment security
Recognising contribution of the individual	Undermining the trade union and collective bargaining
Team-working	Reducing the individual's discretion

Source: Sisson K (1994) *Personnel Management, A Comprehensive Guide to Theory and Practice*, Oxford, Blackwell, p.15. Reprinted by permission of Blackwell.

To what extent is this view evident within the HRM concept? Beer *et al.* are quite circumspect on this matter, and resist overt statements to the effect that the implementation of HRM-type policies will be at the expense of a major stakeholder, the trade unions. However, in the final chapter of *Managing Human Assets* a move towards one-culture work systems is advocated, away from the traditional two-culture systems, on the grounds that the former are 'not only economically viable, but outstandingly successful and . . . are making life very difficult for their competitors'. (p.187)

In essence, the two-culture system refers to the division of labour between management and employees in larger organisations which is manifest in adversarial relations between these two groups and institutionalised through collective bargaining machinery.

Hewlett-Packard, a non-union concern, is used to exemplify the one-culture system with 'involved, enthusiastic and creative' employees testifying to the importance of founding a company on an explicit set of HRM beliefs (p.189). Beer *et al.* proceed (p.193) to argue the importance of management communicating values to all employees by means of company newspapers, speeches, and perhaps videotaped statements.

This proposition is a significant one, as direct communication from management to each employee, and vice versa, could well have the effect of sidelining trade unions and their representatives. Indeed, there is some evidence to suggest that there has been an important growth in systems of direct communication between management and employees which may bypass traditional trade union channels.[13]

It would also seem that a number of the proposals made by Beer *et al.* in respect of HR policy areas, particularly human resource flow, fit uneasily with the collective assumptions underlying trade unionism. So, for example, an emphasis is placed on individual career progression through enterprises for white and blue collar workers (pp.67–8). There is precious little evidence which casts light on whether HR-type initiatives have in fact been at the expense of trade unionism (an exception to this is Storey[14], whose findings are ambivalent on this matter).

Yet it is difficult to deny, in reading HRM literature and observing developments in practice, the proposition that the interventions of trade unions will not be welcome by management if they impede or transgress the transmission and application of fundamental managerial beliefs and values. It is therefore questionable whether pluralist or liberal collectivist principles, which legitimate a countervailing challenge to the authority of management under the auspices of trade unions, continue to be valued within the HRM model.

There are consequent implications for the power relationship between management and employees. As we have already said, original modifications in the liberal individualist perspective towards collectivism have occurred because of the realisation that employees as individuals are not equal in bargaining power to the buyers of labour who, in advanced capitalist economies, are quite likely to be large and relatively powerful organisations.

Palmer[15] reinforces this by stating, 'the nineteenth century assumptions and arguments of liberal individualism fit uneasily into a world where combinations both of employers and employees have gained unprecedented size and influence and where perfectly competitive markets are a rare feature of the world economy.'

If liberal individual principles are indeed evident within the HRM model, then it would seem that the position of individual employees is in fact quite precarious, with a high degree of dependency on the benevolence of employers.

DOES HRM HAVE INTERNATIONAL APPLICABILITY?

From the foregoing analysis it is clear that we associate the original conception of HRM closely with liberal individualist ideology, and with deregulated economies in which management has authority and discretion to put HRM-type initiatives in place. As we have already indicated, however, it would not be accurate to suggest that these ideological preconditions exist on a global basis. In much of continental Europe corporatist ideas carry considerable weight, and across the world liberal collectivist traditions are still well entrenched. The clash of ideologies is perhaps nowhere better demonstrated than in Europe, where the corporatist prescriptions contained in the Social Chapter of the Maastricht Treaty, which have aimed to provide a legally protected floor of individual and collective rights across Europe, have been resisted by the UK Government which advocates continued deregulation.

What seems to follow from this is one of the following:

● We should accept that the concept of HRM is a restricted one, and confine it to those countries where it is most applicable, notably the US and the UK. This position is implicitly taken by Pieper, a German who contends that 'In short, the industrialised nations of the Western world have developed characteristic approaches to HRM which do show some similarities, but are different, often contradictory, in many aspects. It seems that in practice a single universal HRM concept does not exist.'[16] Brewster and Hegewisch[17] find that critiques of any attempts to 'universalise' the American models have also come from France. Clearly this position would render difficult any meaningful study of international human resource management.

● We should accept that in principle the concept of HRM lends itself to international application but make necessary adaptations to allow this.

Michael Poole, in the editorial to the launch issue of the *International Journal of Human Resource Management* states,

At the outset, the original Harvard model will be used as a basis for definition and conceptualisation. As new European and other global regional models emerge, however, these will be incorporated, and it is certainly hoped that a variety of new paradigms will be developed that will be featured in this journal. We shall also accommodate the contributions of various related disciplines that help to develop the field of HRM internationally. At the moment though the Harvard model has certain advantages for the purpose of clarification,

(i) it is the most influential and most familiar approach so far as the international scholarly and business communities are concerned.

(ii) Its premises and scope are sufficiently broad for international purposes.

(iii) Its links with MBA programmes mean that large numbers of managers in the international business community will be familiar with its premises.

(iv) In the original Harvard studies, there are several references to international trends and patterns in human resource management in any case.

Poole, however, recognises that 'some of its [the Harvard model] features inevitably reflect its north American origin' and suggests three key modifications to accommodate:

● the global development of business;
● the power of different stakeholders;
● the more specific links between corporate and human resource strategies.[18]

Before examining further possible adaptations to the Harvard model to give it wider relevance, let us consider in more depth some of the preconditions on which it rests, which may not be universally present, particularly in the European context.

Much of the literature on HRM would seem to be based on the assumption that corporate management possesses sufficient autonomy to enable it to put HR policies into place. Management itself should have discretion not only to mould the culture of the organisation, but also to define HR policy in, for example, the areas of recruitment and remuneration.

In much of mainland Europe neither the creeds underpinning the HRM movement of managerial self-reliance nor governmental non-interference with the workings of the market have been as apparent as in the US and the UK. Germany, for example, has seen economic success built on the social market economy, underpinned by legal regulation, free collective bargaining and co-determination. Fundamental to this have been Keynesian approaches towards economic management, including tripartite consultation between government, employers and trade unions over economic policy and wage negotiation.

Decisions regarding pay, recruitment and training do not fall within the managerial sphere of influence in a number of European countries. This is because there are regulations from outside the enterprise, in the form of legislation or collective agreements between national associations of employers and labour, which constrain, or compel, actions by internal company management.

So, for example, collective agreements in Italy are negotiated at national level between employers' associations and trade unions and have a significant influence on pay and other terms and conditions. In France, companies with over 10 employees are obliged by law to contribute financially towards employees' training to the extent of a minimum of 1.2 per cent of gross salaries paid through the year.'

Managerial discretion can be constrained by requirements or preferences to consult. The system of co-determination in Germany means that some important decisions, relating to, for example, working hours, payment methods, hirings, social amenities or training programmes, require the approval of elected works councils. Indeed, works councils are becoming commonplace across Europe, a development spurred by the passing of the European Community statute.

Moreover, fundamental HRM assumptions about matters such as hiring and firing may not have universal applicability. It has been found, for example, that greater reliance is placed on developing internal labour markets in Germany than is the case in the UK or the US[19]. According to the Price Waterhouse/Cranfield study, 63 per cent of German organisations recruit less than 30 per cent of their managers externally, compared to 59 per cent of British organisations.[20]

Thus, HRM-type prescriptions about developing the sophistication of recruitment mechanisms and procedures may well carry less weight in Germany where the emphasis is on developing internal staff. This is the case too in Japan, where for many employees the assumptions are of a job for life and seniority-based payment systems.

The main planks which support the HRM construct cannot be taken for granted in every country. The international scene does not consist of green fields amenable to infinite replication, but rather the scene is of rugged and varied terrain. Europe, in particular, is 'in general, highly unionised'[21] and according to Towers,[22] 'The concept of social partnership between public and private sector employers and trade unions is deeply rooted in the EC, offering limited scope for the growth of

HRM policies acting directly on individual employees rather than collectively through other trade unions.'

AN ALTERNATIVE MODEL OF INTERNATIONAL HRM

In interpreting the results of the Price Waterhouse/Cranfield survey of strategic HRM in Europe, the Director of the Centre for Research in European HRM at Cranfield School of Management and his colleagues have called for a review of the HRM model so that it fits Europe more effectively. According to Brewster:[23]

> What is needed is a model of HRM that re-emphasises the influence of such factors as culture, ownership structures, the role of the state, and trade union organisation. Clearly the European evidence suggests that managements can see the unions, for example, as social partners with a positive role to play in human resource management; and the manifest success of many European firms which adopt that approach shows the explicit or implicit anti-unionism of many firms to be culture bound.

Drawing upon the work of Kochan *et al.*, who argue that governmental, market and labour management relations are interwoven, Brewster and Hegewisch arrive at the international model of HRM shown in Figure 2.2.

In justifying this model, the authors state that this different presentation of the HRM concept:

a) points towards a model which places HRM firmly within the national context, thus allowing for fuller understanding of situations which differ from that existing in the USA,

b) implies a less rigid approach on the part of consultants and commentators who have criticised employing organisations for not adopting the American model,

c) enables analysts to move beyond discussions of whether HRM should be accepted or rejected to a more positive debate about the forms and styles of HRM,

d) provides a closer fit between HRM and national success. By integrating personnel aspects into corporate strategy by culture, legislation and union involvement further explanation is provided as to why some countries that do not meet the traditional criteria of HRM are amongst the most successful in the world.[24]

OUR APPROACH

We would concur that, despite recognising the importance of situational factors and stakeholders, fundamental adaptations are required to the Harvard model so that it has broader applicability. In particular, we would suggest that, first, scope should exist to recog-

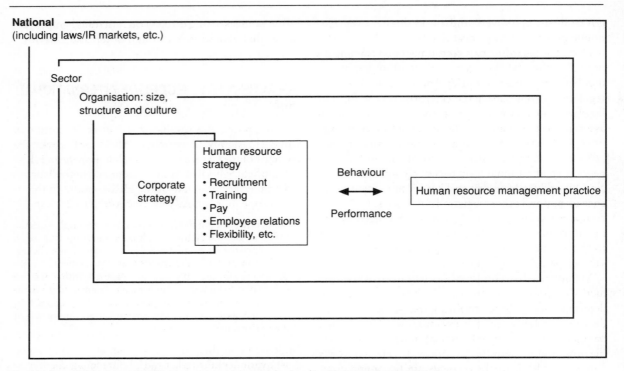

National ―――――
(including laws/IR markets, etc.)

Sector

Organisation: size, ―――――
structure and culture

Corporate
strategy

Human resource
strategy

• Recruitment
• Training
• Pay
• Employee relations
• Flexibility, etc.

Behaviour

Performance

Human resource management practice

Fig 2.2 A model for investigating human resource strategies: the European environment

Source: Brewster C and Hegewisch A (eds) (1994) *Policy and Practice in European Human Resource Management*, The Price Waterhouse/Cranfield Survey, Routledge, London and New York, p.6

nise that trade unions may be integral partners in the employment relationship involved within, and not marginal to, managerial decision making. Secondly, we hold the view that activities of government, through legislation, economic policy and other means, may significantly influence the employment relationship. Consequently, we believe that a more all-embracing definition of HRM inevitably draws in the major parties to the employment relationship, which are management, trade unions and government, and the processes of interaction between them.

Agreeing with Brewster,[25] we would argue that the industrial relations systems approach, devised by Dunlop in 1958, has renewed its usefulness in this respect. The approach emphasises:

• the nature of the actors of an industrial relations system, i.e. workers and their organisations, employers and their associations, and the government bodies that regulate and interact with workers, employers and their respective organisations;
• the context in which the actors operate as defined by the technological characteristics of industrial development, market structure, dominant factors,

and the power distribution within the society;
• the ideology common to all the actors, affecting their behaviour.[26]

Conventional notions of HRM are most likely to be appropriate in deregulated economies where governments abstain from overt economic intervention, and managements possess enough power and freedom to put such HRM-type initiatives in place. Where liberal collectivism is the dominant ideology, we would expect HR policies to be centred less on individual employees, and the emphasis placed on collectively determined terms and conditions of employment between managements and authoritative trade unions. In those countries where corporatism remains the prevailing ideology, we would expect HR policies to be determined through collaborative processes between powerful interest groups.

We would assert, therefore, that in the area of HRM there are no universally acceptable prescriptions for change, but rather that initiatives will be conditioned by the ideological and structural parameters of the country in question. So, for example, moving towards individual pay for performance may be viewed as a method of improving corporate and national performance where liberal individualist notions prevail. Moreover, this would explain why simple panaceas for economic success, based on the Harvard model, would not have universal application. Prescriptions which, for example, involve the marginalisation of trade unions may be appropriate in deregulated economies but, in contrast, where the emphasis is on corporatism, the road to economic success may be through developing even closer relationships with trade unions.

In conclusion, our view is that to date there is no conceptual model of HRM which is sufficiently rigorous and wide in scope to obtain a scientifically watertight approach to the making of international comparisons.

However, for the purposes of selecting material and ordering ideas we will adhere loosely to the principles of the Harvard model which, as Poole[27] has suggested, is the most influential and familiar approach so far as the international scholarly and business communities are concerned. However, in recognising more recent critiques of this model we will emphasise the position and strategies of stakeholders and the pervasive influence of situational factors.

SUMMARY

The Harvard concept of HRM has been influential well beyond the United States where it was initially formulated. In stressing the importance of situational factors, the concept has applicability in various national contexts and systems. In entering into comparative analysis, we will therefore be guided by the fundamental principles and interrelationships apparent within this concept. However, it is necessary also to recognise the potential limitations associated with the Harvard approach. These relate primarily to the emphasis it places on management possessing a high degree of autonomy to put HRM policies into place, an assumption which may not hold good in all national systems.

DISCUSSION QUESTIONS

1 Would you accept that the desired HRM consequences of 'commitment' and 'cost effectiveness' are reconcilable? Is there any conflict between them?

2 Would it be beneficial for 'stakeholders' in all countries to move towards 'HRM'? Why?/Why not?

3 Is there a place for trade unions within HRM? If so, what type of role would they play?

4 What areas of actual practice with regard to recruitment, reward, and training would you associate with HRM? Where possible, quote actual corporate practice.

5 What are the typical features of organisations which exemplify the HRM approach in terms of ownership, history, composition of the labour force, nature of business, and industrial relations traditions?

NOTES AND REFERENCES

1. Beer M, Spector B, Lawrence PR, Quinn-Mills D and Walton RG (1984) *Managing Human Assets,* Free Press, New York

2. Frombrun CJ, Tichy NM and Devanna MA (eds) (1984) *Strategic Human Resource Management,* John Wiley, New York

3. Mahoney TA and Deckop JR (1986) 'Evolution of concept and practice in personnel administration/human resource management', *Journal of Management* 12 (2):223–41, pp.229–34

4. Beaumont P (1982) 'The US human resource management literature – a review' in Salaman G (ed), *Human Resource Strategies,* Sage, London, p.22

5. Brewster C and Bournois F (1991) 'Human resource management: A European perspective', *Personnel Review* 20 (6), p.4

6. Singh R (1992) 'Human resource management : A sceptical look' in Towers B (ed), *A Handbook of Human Resource Management,* Blackwell, Oxford, pp.133–7

7. Hendry C and Pettigrew A (1990) 'Human resource management: An agenda for the 1990s', *International Journal of Human Resource Management* 1 (1), p.19

8. Strauss G (1986) 'Human relations – 1968 style', *Industrial Relations* 7, May, pp.262–76

9. Legge K (1989) 'Human resource management: A critical analysis' in Storey J, *New Perspectives in Human Resource Management,* Routledge, London

10. Kochan TA, Katz HC and McKersie RB (1986) *The Transformation of American Industrial Relations,* Basic Books, p.246

11. Towers B (ed) (1992) *The Handbook of Human Resource Management,* Blackwell, Oxford, p.xviii

12. Legge K (1989) 'Human resource management: A critical analysis' in Storey J, *New Perspectives in Human Resource Management,* Routledge, London, p.32

13. Storey J (1992) *Developments in the Management of Human Resources,* Blackwell, Oxford, p.106

14. Storey J (1992) 'Human resource management in action: the truth is out at last', *Personnel Management,* April, p.31

15. Palmer G (1983) *British Industrial Relations,* Allen and Unwin, London, p.21

16. Pieper R (ed) (1990) *Human Resource Management: An international comparison,* De Gruyter, Berlin, p.11

17. Brewster C and Hegewisch A (eds) (1994) 'Policy and practice in European human resource management', *Price Waterhouse/Cranfield Survey,* Routledge, London and New York, p.6

18. Poole M (1990) 'Editorial: Human resource management in an international perspective', *International Journal of Human Resource Management* 1 (1), pp.6–7

19. Brewster C and Bournois F (1991) 'Human resource management: A European perspective', *Personnel Review* 20, (6), pp.9–10

20. Brewster C and Hegewisch A (eds) (1994) 'Policy and practice in European human resource management', *Price Waterhouse/Cranfield Survey,* Routledge, London and New York, p.41

21. Brewster C and Bournois F (1991) 'Human resource management: A European perspective', *Personnel Review* 20, (6), p.8

22. Towers B (ed) (1992) *The Handbook of Human Resource Management,* Blackwell, Oxford, p.xx

23. Brewster C (1994) 'European human resource management versus the American concept' in Kirkbride PS (ed), *Human Resource Management in Europe,* Routledge, London and New York, p.81

24. Ibid pp.82–3

25. Ibid p.81

26. Dunlop J (1958) *Industrial Relations Systems,* Carbondale, Ill, Southern Illinois University Press

27. Poole M (1990) 'Editorial: human resource management in an international perspective', *International Journal of Human Resource Management* 1 (1), p.3

FURTHER READING

Beer M *et al.* (1984) *Managing Human Assets,* Free Press, New York

Begin JP (1992) 'Comparative Human Resource Management: A systems perspective' *International Journal of HRM* 3.3 Dec.

Dunlop J (1958) *Industrial Relations Systems,* Southern Illinois University Press, Carbondale, Ill

Kirkbride PS (ed) (1994) *Human Resource Management in Europe: Perspectives for the 1990s,* particularly Chapter 5, by Brewster C 'European HRM: Reflection of, or Challenge to, the American Concept?' Routledge, London, New York

Kochan TA *et al.* (1986) *The Transformation of American Industrial Relations,* Basic Books, New York

Pieper R (ed) (1990) *Human Resource Management: An International Comparison* particularly the Introduction, De Gruyter, Berlin, New York

Storey J (ed) (1990) *New Perspectives in HRM,* Routledge, London and New York

3 · THE GLOBAL AND NATIONAL CONTEXTS

LEARNING OBJECTIVES

You should be able to:

i identify a number of inportant factors occurring at a global level which are presenting challenges within the arena of HRM;

ii gain an insight into the specific features of significance within domestic contexts for HRM.

SITUATIONAL FACTORS AND STAKEHOLDERS

Underlying our approach is the view that there is an element of contingency in the way HR policies are formulated at organisational level. In other words, to an extent the form of such policies is conditional on critical influences exerted from outside the organisation.

HR policies are not only located within a set of economic, political, legal, social and technological conditions, which may occur at a national or international level, but they may also evolve through a process of interaction between those with a stake in the employment relationship, particularly the government and its representatives, and trade unions.

It is important to note that, to a varying degree across national systems, organisations have considerable autonomy in deciding which are the most appropriate and desirable HR policies to adopt in the circumstances which surround them. The notion of 'strategic choice' is therefore important. This implies considerable discretion over decision making[1] and rejects simple processes of 'environmental determinism' in which organisational decisions are viewed as merely reactive and dependent on environmental forces.

The framework we are adopting is in keeping with the Harvard model in suggesting that stakeholder interests and situational factors exert an important influence over HR policy choices. Yet the real picture is a complex one, as the various parties with an interest in the employment relationship have considerable scope for independent action and autonomous formulation of strategy. Moreover, HR policy choices, for example in respect of pay determination, may feed back into the environment and influence such matters as government or public policy in this area. Actual HR policies will thus be triggered by an interplay of forces, some of which may be viewed as entirely predictable and pragmatic responses to a national or international economic climate, others perhaps manifesting the strategic or even capricious judgements of an individual or management team.

Beyond the level of nation-states, global changes are occurring which are altering the shape of the context in which HRM occurs. It is the aim of the next section to highlight a number of these supranational, yet pervasive, developments, which represent international pressures on corporations across the world but which are prompting diversified responses.

THE INTERNATIONAL CONTEXT FOR HRM

Changes in the economic and political agenda: moving away from mass markets

The 1980s and 1990s have seen a change in governmental roles in national economic management. Ronald Reagan's era in the US in the 1980s, and Thatcherism in the UK, epitomised a move towards deregulation which involved governmental detachment from economic events, even if this meant the demise of weaker economic entities, as part of a belief in the transcendent potency of market forces. The function of the welfare state was reviewed and rationalised in this context, a development which is now occurring in more 'corporatist' structures such as Germany and Japan.

Shifts in the political fabric of national systems have been accompanied by changes in the nature of markets themselves. According to Sorge and Streeck,[2] a shift has occurred from 'standardised price-competitive production' to 'customised quality-competitive production'. Manufacturers can no longer assume that there is virtually unlimited demand for mass-produced items, and the necessity to attack niche markets and to anticipate or react quickly to rapidly changing tastes has in turn led to an overhaul of traditional principles and patterns of work. The singular success of Japanese manufacturers under these new market conditions in utilising new technology and innovative working practices to produce low-cost, quality items has sent an electric shock across the Western world.

Manzolini identifies:

● emerging jointly, with the gradual consolidation of an advanced 'factory sector' characterised by exclusive, personalised series, generally based on highly sophisticated technologies, a trend towards a new model of industrial development increasingly based on flexible response to market dynamics and less and less anchored to the logic of efficiency and production internal to companies;

● a departure from the logic of standardised mass production and rationalised production processes in order to establish forms of decentralisation and organisational flexibility that make it possible to identify and anticipate opportunities in markets which are now increasingly volatile and segmented;

● a growing level of interdependence between companies and between economic systems in various national contexts because of new integrated structures involving vertical and horizontal flows of inputs, information and finished products and services. The source of profit is no longer the individual operating unit, but rather the network between the different units, constituting a flexible structure ready to take advantage of change and of the opportunities offered by the international context in which it operates;

● at the level of job and task system planning, 'open roles' strongly oriented towards co-ordination and performance control.[3]

These changes imply fundamental transitions in the nature of capitalism which may be encapsulated by 'Fordist' and 'post-Fordist' ideal types of production systems (see Table 3.1). In essence, these paradigms relate dominant principles of organisation and production to the nature of surrounding product markets. 'Fordism' equates division of labour, standardisation of production, and collective labour relations with the existence of mass markets, whilst 'post-Fordism' connects the development of 'niche' and volatile markets with flexibility in the design of work. Ferner and Hyman locate Fordist and post-Fordist typologies in a broader political/economic and historical context by providing the following elaborations.

'FORDISM' (THOUGHT TO PREVAIL IN MIDDLE DECADES OF THE TWENTIETH CENTURY)

● based on mass production with largely semi-skilled labour;

● standardised products for price-competitive mass markets;

● macro-level state economic regulation, public welfare provision, standardisation of employment relations;

Table 3.1 Ideal types of Fordist and post-Fordist production systems

	Fordist	Post-Fordist
1 Technology	• fixed, dedicated machines	• micro-electronically controlled multi-purpose machines
	• vertically integrated operation	• sub-contracting
	• mass production	• batch production
2 Products	• for a mass consumer market	• diverse production
	• relatively cheap	• high quality
3 Labour process	• fragmented	
	• few tasks	• many tasks for versatile workers
	• little discretion	• some autonomy
	• hierarchical authority and technical control	• group control
4 Contracts	• collectively negotiated rate for the job	• payment by individual performance
	• relatively secure	• dual market: secure core, highly insecure periphery

Source: Warde A (1990) 'The Future of Work', in Anderson J and Ricci M (eds) *Society and Social Science*, Open University Press

• associated growth in public services, legitimisation of trade unionism and spread of collective bargaining.

'POST-FORDISM'
• quality-competitive products;
• shifting and differentiated markets;
• greater need for qualified labour;
• less state intervention in the labour market;
• greater personal or corporate responsibility for welfare provision;
• a more flexible and differentiated management of employment relations.[4]

The thesis of transition from Fordist to post-Fordist typologies has considerable intuitive appeal in relating moves towards flexible job design and changing product markets, and in making broader, macro-level corrections with changes in the welfare state and economic deregulation. The centrality of job design in HRM is argued by Bratton and Gold who relate it to key elements of the HRM cycle, as follows.

• **Selection:** a company producing small-batch, high-value-added products using skilled manual labour will have different recruitment and selection priorities to those of an organisation that specialises in large-batch production using dedicated machines operated by unskilled operators.
• **HR development:** changes in work problems will require some form of systematic training.
• **Rewards:** if an organisation fragments or combines tasks, alternative reward systems may be required.[5]

Nevertheless, at a national and organisational level it would seem appropriate to treat more exaggerated claims concerning the arrival of post-Fordism with a degree of scepticism. Mass production, albeit to a varying degree, still represents a common system of production in industrialised countries, while state intervention in economic matters and elaborate welfare provision remain pronounced in a number of mature political economies.

The accelerating pace of technological change

The driving force behind much of the change described above has been technological innovation, particularly information-based technology. Such technology has had a significant impact for the following reasons:

• It has provided the technological capacity to move away from systems of mass production towards more productive and modern, 'flexible' working methods. Smaller-scale, specialised batch production has been made possible by the introduction of such systems as computer-aided design (CAD) and computer-aided manufacture (CAM), which enable research and development functions to be integrated with production and marketing.[6] So opportunities exist to rethink the logic associated with mass production and the assembly line, and to move towards flexible forms of work organisation which are consistent with the need to respond rapidly to market change. Instead of items being 'pushed' through the production process via standardised assembly lines, they can be 'pulled' through flexible production systems designed to meet customer requirements head on.
• It has promoted organisational integration. Multinational corporations are increasingly domi-

Importance of manufacturing falls across western world ...

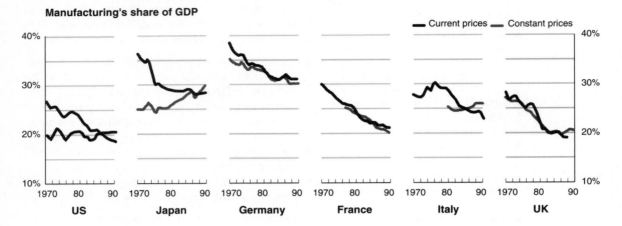

Manufacturing's share of GDP

— Current prices   — Constant prices

US   Japan   Germany   France   Italy   UK

... as Europe suffers largest job cuts ...

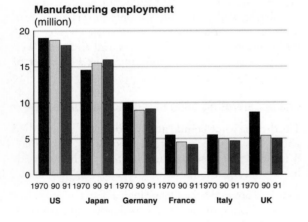

Manufacturing employment
(million)

1970 90 91 ... US Japan Germany France Italy UK

Shares of OECD trade in manufactures

Percentage	1970 total	1970 High tech	1970 Med tech	1970 Low tech	1990 total	1990 High tech	1990 Med tech	1990 Low tech
US	**20.3**	31.1	21.7	13.4	**17.4**	26.3	15.4	13.3
Japan	**11.0**	13.2	8.5	13.2	**15.0**	21.1	16.9	7.1
Germany	**18.9**	17.7	23.1	15.0	**20.6**	16.2	24.7	17.9
France	**9.3**	7.7	8.5	10.7	**10.3**	8.7	10.0	12.1
Italy	**7.3**	5.5	7.1	8.5	**8.6**	5.1	7.7	12.8
UK	**10.4**	10.5	11.9	8.9	**8.9**	10.2	6.5	8.5

Percentage of total manufactured exports of top 13 OECD countries

... and US reduces labour costs fastest

Changes in unit labour costs in manufacturing

1991 = 100

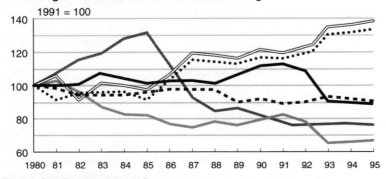

—— US
—⬜— Japan
·········· Germany
— — — — France
——— Italy
——— UK

Fig 3.1 Can Europe compete?

Source: *Financial Times*, 25 February 1994

Industrial countries' growth falls to pre-war levels...

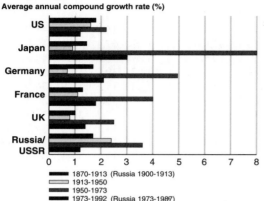

GDP per capita
Average annual compound growth rate (%)

US
Japan
Germany
France
UK
Russia/USSR

0 1 2 3 4 5 6 7 8

■ 1870-1913 (Russia 1900-1913)
□ 1913-1950
■ 1950-1973
■ 1973-1992 (Russia 1973-1987)

...as social security burdens rise and SE Asia closes wealth gap...

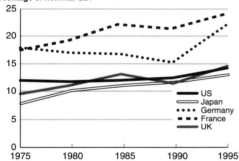

Social security transfers paid by general government
As a percentage of nominal GDP

US
Japan
Germany
France
UK

1975 1980 1985 1990 1995

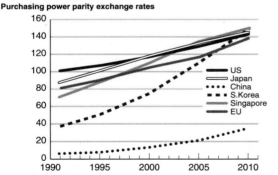

Income per capita (US 1991 = 100)
Purchasing power parity exchange rates

US
Japan
China
S.Korea
Singapore
EU

1990 1995 2000 2005 2010

...while US and Europe face shrinking share of world GDP

nating the world economic scene. Information technology can assist in establishing networks across these huge and diverse concerns.[7] More generally, the quality and effectiveness of information exchange between separate but increasingly interdependent enterprises is being revolutionised, thus minimising the need for physical transportation of people and papers.

● It has been instrumental in bringing about a more general economic shift from industry to services. Consumer and capital goods industries based on micro-electronics are themselves expanding rapidly, but the continued development of the service sector is also dependent on the continual need to raise the quality and sophistication of the service offered.[7] So, for example, in banks there is a continued trend towards the provision of personalised services based on highly sophisticated technology.[8]

Technological change has also transformed the shopfloor. One important manifestation of this has been the introduction of robotics into car manufacture. Although such change has been met with resistance, there is evidence that these robots can free the worker from the tedium associated with the assembly line.

Changes in economic structures

Throughout the western world there has been a continued transition from manufacturing to services.[9] According to Ferner and Hyman[10] in Western European economies traditional manufacturing sectors such as textiles, steel and heavy engineering have declined, while new sectors, such as micro-electronics-based consumer goods industries, have expanded.

In the wake of this structural change a long-term shift has occurred in the nature and composition of employment. The following related changes have been observed in the UK context, but they would have wider relevance.

● An increasing number of white-collar workers and women workers.
● The growing incidence of temporary/part-time and peripheral employment.
● The decline in the amount of workplaces employing large numbers of people.[11]

Such changes may impact on HR policy in a number of ways.

First, some commentators have noted that they present an adverse climate for trade unions to recruit and organise within. Consequently, different forms of interaction with employees, perhaps on a more individualised basis, may be required.

Table 3.2 Female labour force as percentage of total labour force 1960–89

Country	1960	1968	1974	1979	1980	1981	1982	1983	1984	1985	1986	1987	1988	1989
Austria	39.4	38.9	39.8	38.9	38.7	38.9	38.7	38.8	39.7	39.5	39.7	40.1	40.5	40.7
Belgium	30.2	32.0	33.7	36.7	37.2	37.7	38.2	38.7	39.1	39.7	40.2	40.7	41.2	41.3
Denmark	30.9	37.7	40.9	43.5	44.1	44.5	44.9	45.4	45.6	45.6	45.8	46.0	45.7	45.7
Finland	43.7	42.9	45.7	46.0	46.1	46.4	46.9	47.0	47.1	47.3	47.1	47.1	47.2	47.2
France	33.3	35.1	37.0	39.4	39.8	40.1	40.5	40.9	41.4	41.7	42.0	42.4	42.6	42.8
Germany	37.3	36.1	37.2	37.6	37.8	38.0	38.2	38.4	38.6	38.7	39.0	39.4	39.4	39.4
Greece	32.6	29.3	29.3	30.1	30.0	31.9	31.5	34.1	34.6	35.4	35.6	35.9	36.9	36.9
Ireland	25.6	25.6	26.8	27.8	28.7	29.1	29.5	29.8	29.5	29.6	30.0	30.9	30.5	30.7
Italy	30.7	28.5	29.7	32.8	33.3	33.5	33.7	34.2	34.6	34.9	35.5	36.1	36.3	36.6
Luxembourg	26.5	26.0	28.1	30.8	30.9	32.7	32.3	33.1	33.6	33.9	34.1	34.3	34.7	35.0
The Netherlands	21.5	23.0	25.7	29.2	30.4	31.4	32.0	33.8	34.2	34.5	34.8	37.6	38.3	38.4
Norway	28.2	29.4	36.1	40.3	40.9	41.4	41.6	42.2	42.6	43.2	44.1	44.3	44.6	44.4
Portugal	17.8	21.8	37.8	40.2	39.7	40.7	40.7	40.9	41.0	41.4	41.0	41.7	42.3	42.4
Spain	21.8	23.0	27.3	28.6	28.4	28.3	28.9	29.5	29.6	29.9	30.5	32.5	33.8	34.1
Sweden	33.6	38.1	41.8	44.7	45.2	46.0	46.2	46.6	46.9	47.1	47.6	48.0	48.0	47.9
Switzerland	34.1	33.4	34.5	35.8	36.2	36.7	36.8	36.9	37.1	37.0	37.0	37.3	37.6	37.8
United Kingdom	32.7	34.7	37.4	39.1	39.2	38.9	39.1	39.5	40.2	40.5	41.0	41.6	42.1	42.8

Source: OECD 1991. From Ferner A and Hyman R (1992) *Industrial Relations in the New Europe*, Blackwell, Oxford. Reproduced with permission of OECD.

Table 3.3 Employment in services as a percentage of civilian employment 1960–89

Country	1960	1968	1974	1979	1980	1981	1982	1983	1984	1985	1986	1987	1988	1989
Austria	37.1	43.1	46.3	48.8	49.3	49.8	50.0	51.3	52.4	52.9	53.6	53.7	54.6	55.1
Belgium	46.4	51.2	55.2	61.2	62.1	63.6	64.7	65.4	66.1	66.7	67.4	68.2	68.9	68.7
Denmark	44.8	49.9	58.0	60.3	62.4	63.3	64.2	64.2	66.5	65.2	65.9	66.1	67.1	66.9
Finland	32.2	41.1	47.6	51.6	51.8	51.9	53.0	54.2	55.2	56.5	57.0	58.4	59.6	60.2
France	39.9	45.8	49.9	54.8	55.4	56.4	57.3	58.3	59.3	60.4	61.3	62.2	63.0	63.5
Germany	39.1	43.0	43.2	50.0	51.0	51.8	52.8	53.6	54.1	54.5	54.9	55.5	56.1	56.5
Greece	25.5	32.6	36.2	39.2	39.5	40.4	42.0	41.5	42.8	43.7	43.4	45.0	46.2	47.1
Ireland	39.0	41.7	44.6	48.1	49.2	50.6	51.6	53.2	54.1	55.2	55.5	56.8	56.8	56.5
Italy	33.5	39.3	43.2	47.3	47.8	49.0	50.5	51.5	53.6	55.2	56.0	56.8	57.7	58.2
Luxembourg	38.4	43.1	47.9	55.7	56.5	57.7	58.7	59.9	60.6	61.9	62.3	63.2	64.4	65.4
The Netherlands	49.7	54.1	58.4	62.2	63.6	65.2	66.3	66.9	66.8	67.0	68.4	68.3	68.8	68.8
Norway	42.9	48.0	55.1	61.1	61.9	62.4	63.4	64.9	65.0	65.4	65.6	66.3	67.1	68.1
Portugal	24.8	34.0	31.3	34.4	36.1	37.0	37.3	41.5	42.2	42.2	43.9	42.9	44.2	45.7
Spain	31.0	36.5	39.6	43.4	44.6	45.9	47.3	47.8	48.8	49.9	51.9	52.5	53.1	54.0
Sweden	44.0	49.8	56.3	61.7	62.2	63.1	64.1	64.7	65.1	65.3	65.7	66.3	66.7	67.0
Switzerland	39.1	43.8	48.3	53.2	55.0	55.6	56.6	57.6	58.1	58.3	58.4	58.8	59.2	59.3
United Kingdom	47.6	51.3	55.1	58.6	59.7	61.5	62.7	63.9	65.1	65.8	66.7	67.4	68.0	68.4

Source: OECD 1991. From Ferner A and Hyman R (1992) *Industrial Relations in the New Europe*, Blackwell, Oxford. Reproduced with permission of OECD.

Secondly, the feminisation of employment and a move away from standard working patterns have implications for the design of jobs, the structuring of work, and the provision of childcare and related facilities.

Demographic changes

A number of significant demographic changes are occurring towards the end of the twentieth century,

but of greatest significance is likely to be the 'greying' of the population across much of the Western world. This 'greying' is an increase in the average age of the working population as births and deaths decrease. OECD projections indicate that in its 18 Western European member states, the number of people aged 65 and over will rise from 50 million in 1990 to more than 70 million by 2030. In the early 1990s, five people of working age were supporting each person over

65 and this will have reduced to three by 2030. Eurostat figures confirm these trends by forecasting a decline of 17 per cent per annum in the supply of labour in the age group 20–30 across Western Europe.[12]

Moreover, this trend will not be confined to Western Europe. Japan, the US and Pacific Rim countries will also experience a raising of national age profiles. In the US the Hudson Institute has predicted that by the end of the twentieth century, the average age of the workforce will be 36, six years older than at any time in the country's history.[13]

However, by comparison, the newly industrialised countries (including China and Brazil) will have much younger populations for the first half of the twenty-first century.

Within Europe, there will be variations in the extent of demographic change. Effects will be particularly pronounced in Germany, where the population will have declined by approximately 15 million over the 50 years to 2030, with 38 per cent of the population by then being over the age of 60.[14]

According to IRDAC:

> Even if the forecasts mentioned should be used with caution, they indicate that the starting base for the next decade is far from excellent. If no corrective action is taken there is a major risk that Europe will lose some of its competitive strength because of a lack of sufficiently qualified manpower.[15]

Demographic trends, in conjunction with the economic structural changes outlined above which are promot-

Recent unemployment levels
Average percentage of total workforce, 1980–92

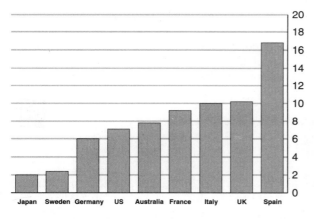

Total real GDP and employment growth, 1970–1992
Percentage

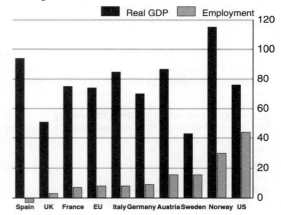

Changes in employment by broad sector
Average annual percentage change

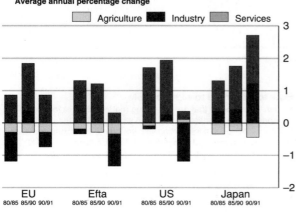

Expenditure on labour market measures
Percentage of GDP

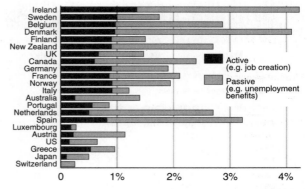

Fig 3.2 Unemployment: the dimensions of the crisis
Source: *Financial Times*, 14 March 1994

ing the need for more highly educated and technologically proficient workforces, are likely to promote skill shortages in a number of occupations. However, at least in the short term, labour shortages are likely to be mitigated by the international recession and persistently high levels of unemployment (see Fig. 3.2).

Nevertheless, the projected developments are likely to promote a review of HR policy in a number of respects:

● A review of approaches towards the recruitment and retention of older workers, particularly reconsideration of the desirability of early retirement.[16]
● Taking a broader view of potential labour pools to include a greater proportion of women and other groups who have been underused in the past. In the US, it is expected that the proportion of new entrants to the labour force who are young, white males will decline sharply. According to the Hudson Institute[17] women, minorities and immigrants will supply five-sixths of new additions to the workforce in the final two decades of the twentieth century. The growing requirement to bring relatively untapped groups into the labour force will have implications for the design of recruitment procedures and implementa-

tion of equal opportunities policy. These trends may represent a further pressure towards the redesign of traditional work organisation to ensure that time and place are amenable to female employees.
● The continuation of current arrangements for pensions and healthcare may become problematic. The level of social security contributions from those in employment to support those in retirement is likely to rise (see Fig. 3.3). At the time of writing it is estimated that social security contributions paid by German employers and employees have already risen to almost 40 per cent of the wage bill.[18] At a national level, public expenditure in those countries with high age profile populations may place those countries at an economic disadvantage compared to the new industrial economies. This problem is likely to be particularly pronounced in countries such as Sweden where welfare state provisions are highly elaborate.

In consequence, alternative approaches to pension provision and healthcare are likely to be demanded in future, with a greater emphasis being placed on private arrangements. In Japan the state pension is under review (see Fig. 3.4), while in the

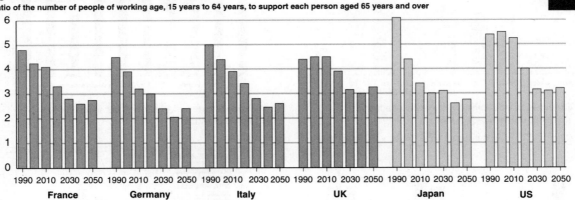

Age structure switches towards the elderly

Ratio of the number of people of working age, 15 years to 64 years, to support each person aged 65 years and over

Social expenditure

Burden per person aged 15–64 years

1980 = 100	2000	2010	2020	2030	2040
France	101	105	117	129	133
Germany	112	119	131	157	162
Italy	102	109	120	135	143
UK	98	101	106	118	117
Japan	112	133	138	136	150
US	97	100	118	133	132

How to advertise to older people
• Don't use models that are too young (not credible) or too old – people see themselves as 10–15 years younger than they are.
• Show older people interacting with younger generations in real situations, active and enjoying what they are doing.
• Information and facts are appreciated: cute puns and obscure abstractions are not.
• No hype, no loud music, no quick cuts – but don't cut out genuine emotions and feelings.
• Adopt an adult-to-adult tone of voice – people tend to acquire wisdom with age, not lose it.

Fig 3.3 Ageing in Europe

Source: *Financial Times*, 8 March 1994

Japanese face up to getting old

Emiko Terazono on planned changes to the pension system

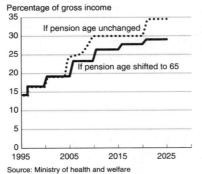

Pension contribution burden
Percentage of gross income

If pension age unchanged

If pension age shifted to 65

Source: Ministry of health and welfare

Workers supporting one pensioner
If pension age unchanged at 60

1992 6.4

2025 2.1

Mrs Setsuyo Uchida, a 71-year-old widow living on the outskirts of Tokyo, has been drawing a state pension for more than 15 years. "I really wouldn't know what to do without it," she says.

Mrs Uchida is one of 27m Japanese pensioners on the state system, which provides citizens over the age of 60 with pensions worth 70 per cent of average employees' salaries.

It is a tidy and generous system, but it is in for a change. Japan's is a rapidly ageing society, expected to have the highest percentage of people over 65 among industrialised nations by the turn of the century. Now the ministry of health and welfare wants to raise the pension eligibility age to 65 to decrease the contribution burden on workers supporting the system.

At the moment, by paying 14 per cent of their gross salaries, 6.5 workers support one pensioner. By 2020 some 2.2 workers will be supporting one pensioner with more than 30 per cent of gross salary. If however the retirement age is changed to 65 some 2.6 workers will pay 26 per cent of their salaries to support one pensioner.

The proposal has been met by fierce opposition from the influential trade union confederation Rengo. Mr Yoshio Tsuchida, director of Rengo's welfare policy planning department, points out that Japanese companies have just grown accustomed to the retirement age being raised to 60.

Although the goal of 60 as a standard retirement age is still not accepted by all companies, progress has been made over the past decade as the government has promoted a later retirement age through subsidies to companies that retain or re-hire older workers.

However, Japan's seniority-based employment system puts a large cost burden on companies retaining older employees, and although the government claims by re-hiring elderly work-ers companies can counter the expected labour shortage, job offers for workers over 55 remain at low levels.

"What are people supposed to do between the ages of 60 and 64 if the pension eligibility rate is raised to 65?" asks Mr Tsuchida.

The government, which reviews its state system and resets its premium rates every four years, needs to reach a decision by April next year, as it cannot afford to postpone the matter until the next review in 2007 when Japan's baby-boomers reach 60.

Although the pension council, an advisory group to the government made up of union leaders, bureaucrats, and representatives from the business community, failed to agree on a single reform blueprint, a recent report from the council suggests that a compromise deal is in sight.

On one hand, the ministry is easing its rigid stance on the shift in eligibility age by proposing a reduced benefit system for pensioners between the ages of 60 and 64 instead of no benefits until 65. The ministry admits it is aware that some sort of compensation needs to be made for that age group since at the moment two-thirds of pensioners start receiving their pensions between the ages of 60 and 64.

Meanwhile Rengo has agreed that workers' twice-yearly bonus payments should not be exempt from pension contributions. It has also accepted a change in the way pension increases are calculated. At the moment these are based on increases in average gross salaries.

However, by basing the increases in pension payments on the average growth of net income – gross income minus taxes and social security contributions – pensioners will also "share" the burden of increases of workers' welfare contributions and the government can avoid the possibility of workers taking home less net cash than pensioners.

Professor Noriyuki Takayama of Hitotsubashi University's Institute of Economic Research in Tokyo says basing pension growth on net salaries will ease the burden on the workers who support the system by 10 per cent and is more effective than altering the pension age. He says that the government has become enthusiastic over the plan after Germany implemented a similar scheme as a part of its pension system reform in 1992.

Over the next few months, Rengo and the government will need to work out what the levels of partial pension payments for pensioners aged 60 to 64 will be. Prof Takayama says the government should set up a special fund which companies would also be required to pay into. He suggests that an incentive system should be set up where the payments into the special fund would decline as the company takes on more elderly workers.

Fig 3.4 Source: *Financial Times*, 10 December 1993

US private pensions are big business, with HR managers taking the main responsibility for the design of pension plans as well as alternative healthcare packages.[19]

● The need to care for the elderly is likely to become an increasing concern for many employees, and therefore employers may have to consider the provision of career breaks and flexible working time for carers. Ford and Daimler Benz already offer such facilities.

The growth of women in employment (see Table 3.2) is, as we have indicated, an important trend. This, in itself, creates further issues to be taken into account in the management of employment, some of which are problematic. These are discussed in depth elsewhere. However, for our purposes we would note that nearly three-quarters of European women in employment are in the service sector, in a restricted number of low-paying, less prestigious occupations.[20]

Healy and Kraithman[21] find that in Europe, greater flexibility in working patterns for women normally takes the form of part-time and casual working. The growth of more precarious employment will have broader social significance where families are economically dependent on women's work. Furthermore if such employment is combined, as is the case in the UK, with a lengthening of male working hours, according to Healy and Kraithman, 'it is hard to envisage how a style of work which involves such a long commitment to paid employment could be emulated by anyone who had a major responsibility for children.'[22] Although legislation on atypical work is the main source of protection for workers in precarious jobs, there is little evidence that to date such legislation has achieved its objectives.[23]

It might seem that women are the main beneficiaries of the 'demographic time bomb', but optimism from proponents of equal opportunities has been dampened by the effects of recession. Furthermore, if more

Table 3.4 The top 25 multinationals (non-financial, ranked by foreign assets)

Rank		Industry	Country	Foreign assets ($bn)	Total assets ($bn)	Foreign sales ($bn)	% of total sales
1	Royal Dutch/Shell	Oil	Britain/Holland	na	106.3	56.0	49
2	Ford Motors	Cars and trucks	United States	55.2	173.7	47.3	48
3	General Motors	Cars and trucks	United States	52.6	180.2	37.3	31
4	Exxon	Oil	United States	51.6	87.7	90.5	86
5	IBM	Computers	United States	45.7	87.6	41.9	61
6	British Petroleum	Oil	Britain	39.7	59.3	46.6	79
7	Nestlé	Food	Switzerland	na	27.9	33.0	98
8	Unilever	Food	Britain/Holland	na	24.8	16.7	42
9	Asea Brown Boveri	Electrical	Switzerland/Sweden	na	30.2	22.7	85
10	Philips Electronics	Electronics	Holland	na	30.6	28.6	93
11	Alcatel Alsthom	Telecoms	France	na	38.2	17.7	67
12	Mobil	Oil	United States	22.3	41.7	44.3	77
13	Fiat	Cars and trucks	Italy	19.5	66.3	15.8	33
14	Siemens	Electrical	Germany	na	50.1	15.1	40
15	Hanson	Diversified	Britain	na	27.7	5.6	46
16	Volkswagen	Cars and trucks	Germany	na	41.9	27.5	65
17	Elf Aquitaine	Oil	France	17.0	42.6	12.2	38
18	Mitsubishi	Trading	Japan	16.7	73.8	41.2	32
19	General Electric	Diversified	United States	16.5	153.9	8.3	14
20	Mitsui	Trading	Japan	15.0	60.8	43.6	32
21	Matsushita Electric Industrial	Electronics	Japan	na	59.1	16.6	40
22	News Corp	Publishing	Australia	14.6	20.7	5.3	78
23	Ferruzzi Montedison	Diversified	Italy	13.5	30.8	9.1	59
24	Bayer	Chemicals	Germany	na	25.4	21.8	84
25	Roche Holding	Drugs	Switzerland	na	17.9	6.8	96

Source: *The Economist*, March 1993. Taken from Bratton J and Gold J (1994) *Human Resource Management: Theory and Practice*, Macmillan, p.44.

serious consideration of equal opportunities by employers is merely a pragmatic response to predicted skill shortages, a degree of scepticism is required to allow for the eventuality of demographic trends abating or even reversing in the future.

Multinational growth

According to Bratton and Gold, 'The global corporation is back in fashion as the embodiment of modernity, high technology, rich in capital, replete with skilled jobs.' MNEs possess a plethora of economic power. United Nations estimates suggest that, from a total of around 35 000 multinationals, the largest 100, excluding those in banking and finance, accounted for £3.1 trillion of global assets in 1990.[24] The top 25 multinationals are detailed in Table 3.4 above.

MNEs are also large employers of labour. A study by Sisson et al.[25] showed that there were over 8000 enterprises employing at least 1000 workers in EC member states in 1991, and over 900 multinational corporate groups having at least 1000 employees in two or more EC countries. The increasing dominance of multinationals raises issues concerning the integration of technological approaches and systems of work across national boundaries, and also 'social dumping', where the least attractive facilities are located in low-wage countries.

The growth of international competitive pressures outlined above, combined with the removal of trade barriers in the EU and other world economic blocs, has perpetuated the rationalisation of business on an international scale, with a growing incidence of mergers and joint ventures.

Managing staff reductions and the efforts of organisational restructuring have become central concerns of HR practitioners. Additionally, according to Ferner and Hyman, new organisational forms are emerging which 'devolve greater financial and operational responsibility to "strategic business units" in specific "product markets".'[26]

Green issues

There is an increasing recognition, particularly in larger organisations, of the importance of green issues and the steps industry can take to protect the physical environment. Many companies have appointed managers with direct responsibility for environmental issues, chiefly in high-risk sectors such as chemicals, pharmaceuticals and energy.

Some of the implications of environmental protection measures are outlined in Figure 3.5.

Germany

The context

Germany is the country with the largest population in Europe, nearly 79 million. Since 1990 Germany has been unified and now comprises both the previous Federal and German Democratic Republics, the old West and East respectively. In addition to an enlarged size and population, the unification of the two formerly separate states has posed many problems. At the outset it was envisaged that the old East, on unification, would become an extension of the old West as far as the political, legal, institutional and organisational framework regulating the management of human resources was concerned. Inevitably, given that before unification the two separate states had very different systems, this process of extension has not yet been completed and indeed has thrown up both challenges and opportunities for the participants. These are not limited to the East; in several areas the process of extension has raised questions about the efficacy of existing Western structures and systems, for example the structural suitability of trade unions and employers' associations and indeed the objectives of the parties. Unification and the subsequent process of extension have encouraged a reappraisal of some of the values and traditions that have dominated systems in the West since the 1940s.

If we look at unification in terms of it being a merger between two economies, we are immediately confronted by difficulty. The West was a technologically advanced, strong, successful social market economy in which gross domestic product had grown reasonably consistently[27] throughout the 1980s, inflation had been low,[28] unemployment had averaged about 6 per cent during the 1980s,[29] wages and living standards were high, and as an economy it was far less deindustrialised than its European competitors, with employment in industry in 1990 hovering slightly below 40 per cent, services employing 56.7 per cent and agriculture approximately 3.5 per cent of the civilian labour force.[30] Female participation rates were approximately 57 per cent.[31]

In contrast, the Eastern economy at unification was a socialist command economy characterised by technological backwardness, low productivity, stagnation, poor infrastructure, low wages and living standards, high female participation rates, relatively low official unemployment and high levels of industrial pollution.

The great clean-up ...

Origins of acid rain

(sulphur dioxide)
1985

Tonnes/Km2 per year

- ☐ Less than 0.999
- ▨ 1.000 to 3.999
- ▩ 4.000 to 9.999
- ■ 10.000 to over 40.000

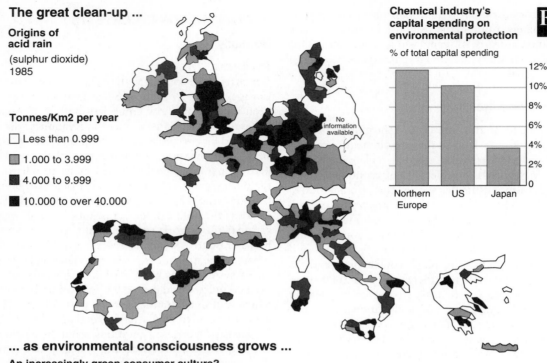

No information available

Chemical industry's capital spending on environmental protection

% of total capital spending

... as environmental consciousness grows ...

An increasingly green consumer culture?
Those who agreed that they...

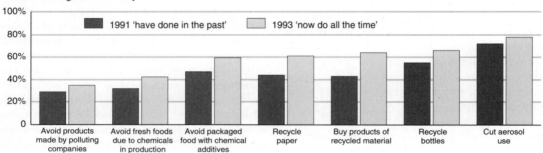

■ 1991 'have done in the past'   ☐ 1993 'now do all the time'

- Avoid products made by polluting companies
- Avoid fresh foods due to chemicals in production
- Avoid packaged food with chemical additives
- Recycle paper
- Buy products of recycled material
- Recycle bottles
- Cut aerosol use

... but regulation and costs rise

EU environmental directives and regulations passed each year

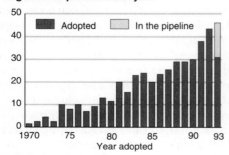

■ Adopted   ☐ In the pipeline

Year adopted

Pollution abatement and control expenditure
As % of GDP

	1985	1987	1988	1989	1990
Austria	1.0	1.0	1.0	—	—
Denmark	0.7	0.8	0.9	0.9	1.0
France	0.6	0.7	0.7	0.7	0.5
Germany	0.7	0.8	0.8	0.8	0.8
Italy	—	—	0.2	0.2	—
Netherlands	1.0	0.9	—	0.9	—
Portugal	—	—	0.5	0.4	—
Spain	—	0.5	0.5	0.6	0.6
Sweden	—	0.7	—	—	—
Switzerland	0.7	—	0.7	0.8	—
UK	0.7	—	—	—	0.4
Canada	0.7	0.7	0.7	0.8	0.9
Japan	0.9	1.0	1.0	1.0	1.0
US	0.6	0.6	0.5	0.6	0.6

Fig 3.5 The great clean-up

Source: *Financial Times*, 3 March 1994

By 1994, unification and the subsequent recession had had significant economic and labour market consequences. Unemployment in the East had risen substantially despite high levels of migration to the West and significant investment. Estimates of real levels of unemployment in the East vary enormously. Figure 3.6 gives a dramatic picture of the consequences of reunification on the labour market. Official figures in July 1994 put unemployment in the East at slightly less than earlier in the year, 14.8 per cent, with unemployment in the West also falling to an official figure of 8 per cent, a total of 3.59 million people.[32] The main causes of unemployment were failure to produce items and services that were competitive in terms of price and quality, hardly surprising given the technological antiquity of many of the production processes, the low levels of productivity and, it is argued by many, the foolish and unrealistic policy of raising wages in the East to match those in the West at too fast a rate. Employer reluctance to adhere to prior agreements to increase wage rates in the East in stages occasioned strike action in the steel and engineering industries in the East in the spring of 1993.

Germany, like many other developed economies, was in recession in 1993 and early 1994. GNP fell 1.2 per cent in 1993,[33] price inflation was being controlled by the Bundesbank's policy of high interest rates but was still 4.2 per cent in 1993 in the West,[34] a relatively high rate compared to average rates in the 1980s; by mid-1994 this had fallen back to below 3 per cent.[35] By early 1994 the German economy was in relatively dire straits, having lost nearly a million jobs in manufacturing in the preceding four years and confronting many more such losses as major manufacturing companies announced future reductions. Employers, employees and government were faced with the harsh realities of an economy that was no longer internationally competitive and high wage and associated social costs allied to a regulated labour market. The failures to open up new markets, the costs of reunification and a lack of product development were all seen to have contributed to the situation.

Presiding over unification and the process of integration was a coalition government comprising conservative Christian Democrats (CDU[36]/CSU, this latter the Bavarian sister party of the CDU) and the Liberals or Free Democrat Party (FDP).[37] The tradition in West Germany has been one of coalition government, with the CDU having been the dominant party since the 1940s. The Social Democrats (SPD)[38] have formed governments, but not since 1982; they are the second largest political party in terms of popular support, but

have been more likely to comprise the opposition. The Christian Democrats are market oriented and generally supported by employers, but they do have trade union support and indeed CDU trade unionists are guaranteed influence within the trade union movement as part of mechanisms for ensuring and maintaining unity. Governments of all persuasions have adhered to the principle of welfare improvement, whereby weaker groups are safeguarded. The majority of trade union political support would be for the SPD and there are close links between the party and the unions. The above are the three largest political parties but there are other smaller groups of Socialists, Greens and Republicans.

Germany is a Federation of Länder. Each Land has its own parliament and the prime ministers of each Land comprise the Bundesrat, which itself acts as a second chamber with power of veto over the Bundestag, the Federal Parliament. Considerable powers are delegated to the Länder.

Culturally, Hofstede[39] found that (West) German scores were relatively high on the masculinity, individualism and uncertainty avoidance indexes, and low on the power distance dimension. This would suggest a combination of values and attitudes consistent with male assertiveness, machismo and male domination of society, admiration of individual achievement and performance, considerable emphasis on money and possessions, and expertise, security, written rules and regulations, and nationalism all valued. Conflict and competition should be avoided, co-operation and consensus being preferable mechanisms. Aggression and emotions can be expressed but deviance is dangerous. The low power distance score indicates a belief in equality and interdependence, trust, harmony and co-operation, with power needing to be legitimised. Changes should be the result of redistribution not revolution. The high individualism score indicates a belief in looking after yourself and your family which influences motivation to work. It suggests that material gain and job security will therefore be primary concerns.

An introduction to the system of HRM

Germany is depicted as a social market economy underpinned by legal regulation, but one in which the principle of bargaining autonomy has been preserved by government and preferred by the participants. State intervention therefore is generally limited to the provision of a legislative framework. Part of the framework provides for mechanisms of co-determination within the company in addition to collective bargaining

The high price of national unity

FT

A steep fall in employment levels – 37 per cent of the eastern labour force is now idle

Rarely, if ever, has a labour force experienced such a radical and swift transformation as that which swept eastern Germany.

When the Berlin Wall was breached in November 1989, the 9.3m workers of eastern Germany were heavily concentrated in manufacturing and agriculture. More than 920,000 people worked on the land. That number has since dropped to 210,000, a 70 per cent reduction.

More significantly, the 3.17m employed in manufacturing are now down by 60 per cent to 1.29m. In mining and energy, production decreased by 39 per cent between 1989 and 1992.

Overall, the number of available jobs fell by at least 34 per cent from 9.3m in 1989 to 6.2m in 1993. Since that time, the total labour force has decreased to 8.2m, largely as a result of migration.

Several factors explain the steep fall in employment.

• Most of the products from east German manufacturing were aimed at markets in eastern Europe and the former Soviet Union.
• The competition caused by the merging of the GDR's Ost-Mark with the western D-Mark.
• The collapse of the Comecon socialist trading organisation, and the inability of the eastern European countries and the former USSR to pay for east German goods.
• The policies of the Treuhand privatisation agency, which sought to reduce overmanning, close or break up and restructure the large Kombinate, or state-owned enterprises, to prepare them for privatisation.
• The breakup of the LPGs, or collective farms.
• The wage levels, which imposed another brake on the demand side of the labour market. Since wages are set to equal west German levels by 1996, despite productivity often 60 per cent below west German levels, unit labour costs are around 170 per cent of west German levels.

"In reality, we would require a reduction by a further third of the work force if we were to match productivity levels of western Germany," commented one economist.

By March of this year, 16.8 per cent of the labour force, or 1.26m, were unemployed. That did not include those on short-time work (135,000), job retraining and job creation schemes (249,000, and 238,000 respectively) and those who had taken early retirement (205,000). All told, 37 per cent of the total eastern labour force is idle. Last year, the federal labour office paid out DM54.7bn in unemployment benefit.

The question is whether these very high unemployment levels have become permanent features of eastern Germany, and whether the federal government can continue to allocate nearly DM55bn each year as the price for maintaining social stability and for subsidising consumer spending in the east.

A recent report by the Berlin-based DIW Institute for Economic Research concluded that if the labour market in Germany did not radically change, there would be around 5m people without regular employment in the unified Germany by the end of the decade. It added that the economy would be burdened by higher taxes which would reduce enterprises' profits and could dampen the willingness to invest.

Against this background, few economists believe that - with the exclusion of women - the size of the labour market in eastern Germany will ever correspond to west German or western European levels.

Mr Wolfgang Scheremet, a labour expert at the DIW Institute, said that even when the recession ended in Germany, "there will simply be not enough new jobs in eastern Germany to absorb the high levels of unemployment."

The manufacturing base, overmanned before unification, and now in a state of collapse, could no longer be considered as a viable instrument for rebuilding mass employment.

Instead, Mr Scheremet believes that some positive and negative trends within the labour force are likely to emerge in the following sectors:

• Construction. This sector will continue to play an important role as the housing stock is modernised, the infrastructure is upgraded, and hotels and offices are erected. Mr Scheremet reckons that the construction industry already accounts for about 12 per cent of the labour market.
• Innovative technology. A lot of money is being spent on introducing innovative and high levels of technology which will quickly become competitive and find a niche in international market. For instance, Siemens is investing DM2.4bn in a new microchip plant in Dresden which will create more than 1,200 jobs. The success of such enterprises are underpinned by investment grants.
• Services and the Handwerk, (the small trades and craftsmen sector). These sectors are already capitalising on the construction boom. The DIW and other economic institutes see the Handwerk, embracing 700,000 people, as one of the engines of economic revival. "The number of people in the Handwerk are increasing as the manufacturing continues to decrease," says Mr Scheremet.

But these trends alone are not enough to absorb the high levels of unemployed. By 1993, western Germany was still supplying 90 per cent of the goods and services bought in eastern Germany. Meanwhile, the cheap labour in neighbouring eastern Europe could help to keep high unemployment figures in eastern Germany.

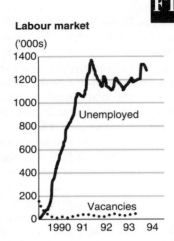

Labour market

('000s)

Source: Govt. and private estimates

The German economic institutes argue that if any small increase in the demand for labour emerges, especially for intensive labour, western German enterprises are more likely to shift production to the neighbouring countries of eastern Europe. The DIW study argues, that in the short term, this will deter investment both in west and east Germany.

In the medium and long term, it would benefit Germany as a whole because it would create a hinterland with very favourable cost conditions for suppliers. However, it concludes: "The positive effects of this will, however, not be felt until the beginning of the next decade at the earliest."

Women are the only sector of the labour market that appears to be matching western German levels. Eastern Germany's 8.1m women represent half the population. Before unification, more than 90 per cent of women, or 49 per cent of the total labour force in eastern Germany, were employed.

In contrast, of the 33.4m women in western Germany, more than 20m are classified as housewives while 13m are registered on the labour market.

Yet since unification, women, who are not more than two-thirds of eastern Germany's total unemployment, are being economically and socially forced back to the home as the labour market shrinks and radically different patterns of work take hold.

By late 1992, more than 4.2m east German women were registered as housewives, and 3.9m were registered on the labour market.

Yet even on the labour market, more than 905,000 are unemployed – not including those women on short-time work, job creation and job retraining schemes and early retirement. In western Germany, the number of unemployed women is 858,000.

Judy Dempsey

Fig 3.6 Source: *Financial Times*, 4 May 1994

outside the company between multi-employer associations and trade unions. The in-company institutions and processes are not open to the trade unions, although on the employee side they are usually dominated by union members and often rely on union facilities and support.

Additionally, many terms and conditions of employment are protected by the legislative establishment of employee rights, often taking the form of effective minima or maxima. If there is a dispute about the rights of the respective parties in the context of legislation or collective agreements, these can be resolved by referral to a local, regional or national/federal system of labour courts.

The multi-employer–trade union bargaining tradition at Land or federal level, allied to the fairly detailed legislative framework, has served to reinforce perceptions of the German system as centralised. However, the co-determination arrangements within the enterprise have to some extent countered this centralist tradition and there are increasing pressures for more issues to be determined within the workplace.

A criticism sometimes levelled at the system is that the dominant values emphasising cohesion, harmony and democracy have contributed significantly to a system which emphasises participation and consensus and its achievement at the expense of conflict resolution.

There is little doubt that consensus has been substantially achieved in recent decades, but since reunification, in 1992, 1993 and 1994, there have been signs of increasing discontent on the part of both employers and employees. There have been serious work stoppages in the steel and engineering industries and in the public sector, in both the West and the East. Economic recession and relative hardship and the social and financial costs and consequences of unification have undoubtedly contributed to feelings of discontent and a willingness to take action, with unions maintaining that jobs should be protected and that a fairer distribution of income and the profits from labour is justified. Employers and government thought that wage restraint was necessary and that pay rises must be affordable in the context of the increasingly competitive world economy. In fact, towards the end of 1993, as job losses mounted and more and more companies announced falling profits or losses, government ministers began publicly to question some of the traditions of the system. They alleged that German workers were overpaid and underperforming, that the system was overregulated, and that, if Germany was to compete successfully in the future in both European and international markets, costs would have to be reduced and

labour flexibility and productivity improved. In early 1994, the government agreed to further public spending cuts and an action programme to encourage job creation. This programme combined privatisation and deregulation. In May 1994 it was agreed to privatise the airline Lufthansa, but proposals to privatise the post and telecommunications businesses resulted in strike action in June on the part of employees anxious to secure guarantees of protection of benefits after privatisation. Such guarantees were eventually obtained through to 1996. In the case of deregulation, proposals were put forward to make it easier to hire people part time, and mechanisms were suggested to encourage employment of the long-term unemployed by facilitating an effective undercutting of minimum wages. Private employment agencies were also to be legalised. Such changes in Germany might have additional implications for the nature and direction of the social dimension of the European Union.

Time will tell whether existing structures and institutions are adequate for the task of conflict resolution, given the challenges thrown up by unification, recession and declining competitiveness, or whether they require adaptation or substantial revision.

France

The context
France is a country of 57 million people, of which some 25.3 million are economically active.[40] The female participation rate at the beginning of the 1990s had increased to 58 per cent from 54 per cent in 1979. The scale of the increase in the 1980s was not as great as in some other countries.[41]

The distribution of employment in France at the end of the 1980s was services 64 per cent, industry 29 per cent and agriculture 6.1 per cent.[42] France has experienced the same trends as most other European economies over the last two to three decades, i.e. shrinking industrial and agricultural sectors and an increasing service sector.

There has also been an increase in the number of part-time, temporary and fixed-term employment relationships. Part-time employment in 1990 was 12 per cent of total employment, a relatively low proportion by international standards.[43]

France still has a relatively large public sector employing 23 per cent of the active labour force in 1990 and comprising both civil service and public enterprises. In the mid 1980s the sector employed 2.4 million people and contributed in excess of 20 per cent of industrial output; this was subsequent to the nationalisation programme of the socialist government elected in 1981, during which banks and finance companies were taken into public ownership, as were the traditional utilities and major manufacturers such as Renault. The enlarging of the public sector looks set to be reversed by the right-wing government elected in March 1993 which has embarked on a major privatisation programme, including several banks and insurance companies, Elf oil, Rhône-Poulenc chemicals, Renault, Bull computers and Credit-Lyonnais. The position in July 1994 is shown in Figure 3.7. This reduction of the public sector is to some extent a continuation of the process begun by the cohabitation government of Chirac (1986–88) and not really reversed by the socialist government led by Rocard in the late 1980s.

France has experienced relatively high unemployment in recent years. In the 1980s it averaged 9 per cent[44] and it has increased since then, breaking through the 12 per cent mark at the end of September 1993 and rising to 12.7 per cent in May 1994.[45] (See also Figure 3.8.) Some of this unemployment is inevitably associated with the changing structure of industry and the decline of traditional extractive and manufacturing industries and agriculture, as well as cyclical factors.

In the early 1980s inflation[46] in France was relatively high, but the socialist governments elected in 1981 and 1988 managed to control inflation quite suc-

cessfully so that during 1992/93 it was around the 2 per cent mark and in April 1994 the rate was 1.7 per cent.[47] However, growth in GDP, after a surge in 1988/89, has decreased subsequently, growth in 1993 working out at about 1 per cent after negative growth for much of the 1992/93 period. The projection for 1994 stands at 1.4 per cent. Figure 3.9 illustrates these trends. Early in 1994, the prime minister of the right-wing government elected in 1993, Balladur, acknowledged that reversing the climbing unemployment rate was his highest priority and that unemployment among the under 25s was a particular concern, with approximately 25 per cent unemployment in this group in February 1994.[48]

Government has sought to encourage employment of the long-term unemployed (over three years) by giving employers two years' exemption from social security contributions in respect of such employees. In its anxiety to enhance employment among the under 25s the government proposed early in 1994 to reduce the minimum wage for such employees, but this had to be withdrawn in the face of considerable unrest and hostility from students' movements. Government reverted to a subsidy to the employer to achieve the same objective.

Politically, France is a republic with an elected president who has strong executive powers. There are five

	Company	Sector	Turnover*	Profit/loss	Percentage of capital held by state**
1.	Aérospatiale	Aerospace	FFr50.8bn	net loss FFr1.42bn	state holds 73.7 per cent
2.	Air France	Airline	FFr55.16bn	net loss FFr8.48bn	99.3 per cent
3.	Banque Hervet	Bank	n/a	net loss FFr1.2bn	73.5 per cent
4.	Banque Nationale de Paris	Bank	n/a	net profit FFr 1.02bn	Privatised Autumn 1993
5.	Caisse Centrale de Réassurance	Insurance	n/a		100 per cent
6.	Caisse Nationale de Prévoyance	Insurance	FFr64.3bn	net profit FFr1.26bn	42.5 per cent
7.	Groupe Bull	Computers	FFr28.25bn	net loss FFr5.07bn	72 per cent
8.	Cie Générale Maritime	Transport	n/a	n/a	100 per cent
9.	Crédit Lyonnais	Bank	n/a	net loss FFr6.9bn	52.51 per cent
10.	Pechiney	Aluminium and packaging	FFr63.03bn	net loss FFr980m	55.7 per cent
11.	Renault	Automobiles	FFr169.79bn	net profit FFr1.07bn	80 per cent
12.	Rhône Poulenc	Chemicals	FFr80.56bn	net profit FFr962m	Privatised Autumn 1993
13.	Assurances Générales de France	Insurance	n/a	net profit FFr977m	65.6 per cent
14.	GAN	Insurance	n/a	net profit FFr414m	79.4 per cent
15.	Union des Assurances de Paris	Insurance	n/a	net profit FFr1.42bn	Privatised 1994
16.	Seita	Tobacco and cigarettes	FFr14.14bn	net profit FFr585m	100 per cent
17.	Société Marseilleise de Crédit	Bank	n/a		100 per cent
18.	Snecma	Aerospace engines	FFr19.57bn	net loss FFr804m	97 per cent
19.	Elf Aquitaine	Oil	FFr210bn	net profit FFr1.1bn	Privatised 1994
20.	Thomson	Electronics	n/a	n/a	75.8 per cent
21.	Usinor Sacilor	Steel	FFr75.4bn	net loss FFr5.8bn	80 per cent

•1993 unless stated ••unless already privatised, at March 1993
Source: Ministry of the Economy and Finance , and the companies

Fig 3.7 The 21 companies on the privatisation list
Source: *Financial Times*, 12 July 1994

Real GDP

Change over previous year

Balance of payments

Current account balance (FFr billion ?)

Inflation

Consumer price index (annual percentage change)

Unemployment

Seasonally adjusted   Percentage of workforce

Source: Datastream

Fig 3.8 The French economy on the mend
Source: *Financial Times*, 12 July 1994

FT

main political parties spanning the spectrum of political perspective from extreme right wing to communist. There are also ecological movements.

1. Parti-Socialiste – PS.
2. Ressemblement pour la République – RPR – right wing with Gaullist traditions.
3. Union pour la Démocratie Française – UDF – a mixture of radicals, Christian democrats and republicans.
4. Parti-Communiste Français – PCF.
5. Front National – FN – right wing.

From 1981–86 and 1988–93 France had not only a socialist president but also a government predominantly socialist in orientation. However, as indicated above, in March 1993 a new right-wing coalition government was elected in what was a crushing defeat for the PS. However, it must be noted that there is still a Socialist President and this will be the situation until 1995 – another period of cohabitation. The new government under the leadership of Balladur was quick to begin public expenditure cuts and the process of privatisation.

Hofstede's research[49], which is commented on by Poirson,[50] concluded that French culture exhibited relatively high scores on three of the four cultural dimensions used – power distance, uncertainty avoidance and individualism – and a moderately low score on the femininity–masculinity index, indicating a tendency towards feminism. Such scores would indicate societal attitudes and values which encompass an acceptance of superiors and subordinates being different kinds of people with power holders entitled to privilege, a tolerance of elitism and fairly rigid hierarchical demarcations. However, there is a latent conflict between the powerful and the powerless, and society may only be transformed through the dethroning of those in power. Aggressive behaviour and showing emotions are acceptable. There is a concern for security and order; formality and rules and regulations are preferred. The expert is valued. In such a society employees' involvement with organisations is likely to be calculative as opposed to moral, and individual autonomy, achievement and initiative are valued, as is individual financial security. People work in order to live, and the quality of life and the environment are important, as is equality between the sexes. These cultural 'characteristics' don't indicate strong support for collective or consensual traditions or practices.

An introduction to the system of HRM

Employee relations in France have traditionally been conflictual and often antagonistic, unions being initially and primarily concerned with achieving political and social objectives and employers very much concerned with the maintenance of their prerogative. There is, therefore, no substantial tradition of shared decision making in the French system. Strikes have been viewed almost as an alternative to collective bargaining and very much a weapon to be used to achieve objectives of a political as well as an industrial nature. By and large, governments of the left have sought to enhance the position and power of trade unions and employees, and employers have found allies in Gaullist and other right-wing administrations. All actors in the system seem to accept the legitimacy of close relationships and alliances between unions, employers and political parties.

There is a tradition of collective bargaining at industrial level, but both the process and content of this bargaining has been prescribed and regulated by government, with legislation regarding many of the terms and conditions of employment being the norm. Governments have also involved the other actors at national level in a number of consultative bodies and in the administration of various dimensions of the welfare system.

Many critics have suggested that the socialist governments of the 1980s sought to transform industrial relations, in particular by seeking to extend collective bargaining and other forms of employee participation and employee rights in the workplace. They sought, in other words, to decentralise. In many respects the desire to decentralise industrial relations found more support among employers than trade unions since many employers were seeking to enhance flexibility and productivity and saw decentralisation and individualisation as necessary mechanisms for the achievement of these objectives.

The new 1993 government quickly announced its intention to help reduce labour costs and deregulate to a certain extent in order to promote employment. It has announced its desire to annualise hours of work regulations and change regulations preventing weekend working, thereby in both instances contributing to the potential for more flexible use of labour by employers. Particularly interesting is the proposal that annualisation should be negotiated at company level; given the relative absence of trade union organisation at this level, the proposal seems likely to enhance management's freedom and power. In early 1994, the government proposed to amend the laws concerning employee participation. Employees were to be encouraged to withdraw money from profit-sharing schemes for specific consumption, and there was also a suggestion that employees holding more than 5 per cent of their company's capital might be given the right to elect worker representatives to the Board.

Italy

The context

One of the main features of employment in Italy is the relatively low rates of active participation in the labour force. Both the overall and female rates, at 61.4 per cent and 46.5 per cent respectively[51], are higher only than those in Greece, Ireland and Spain within the European Union and lower than in any of the other countries covered in this text.

It is often suggested that one of the explanations for these relatively low participation rates is that they are a reflection of the unofficial, black or clandestine economy that is alleged to operate to a greater degree in Italy than elsewhere. By its nature it is difficult to estimate the size of the unofficial economy, but between 20 and 30 per cent of GNP and up to 30 per cent of the workforce are not uncommon assessments.[52]

Official unemployment throughout the 1980s averaged 9.5 per cent and the rate in 1990 was fractionally over 10 per cent.[53] Unemployment remained a problem into the early 1990s and in April 1994 was over 11 per cent and still rising.

Modigliani[54] stated in May 1993 that the Italian economy had for years suffered from four chronic diseases: high price inflation, high unemployment, high government expenditure and trade deficits. Only price inflation seemed to be under control at that time, being at a six-year record low of 4.2 per cent.[55] He attributed this in part to the agreement in July 1992 to abolish the automatic wage indexation system called the Scala Mobile, which was followed fairly rapidly in the autumn of 1992 by Italy's enforced departure from the European Community Exchange Rate Mechanism and the subsequent and significant devaluation of the lira.

Italy was relatively late to industrialise and still has a proportionally large agricultural sector, representing slightly under 9 per cent of total employment at the end of the 1980s, the largest of any of the countries in this text.[56] Italy is no longer industrially backward and throughout the 1980s exhibited rates of growth in GDP in excess of the norm for countries within the EU, averaging 2.5 per cent p.a. 1979–89.

The Italian state has traditionally intervened in the economy to take 'into ownership' a relatively large proportion of the manufacturing and service sectors of the economy, although significant rationalisations and job losses in these sectors occurred in the 1980s. Additionally, there is the public sector (excluding state-owned enterprise) which in 1990 accounted for approximately 16 per cent of total employment. Given the economic crises of the early 1990s, austerity packages including public spending cuts and public sector wage freezes were proposed in late 1992 and early 1993. This was followed by plans by the Ciampi government to privatise large sections of the public enterprise sector.

Another important feature that observers of employment relationships in Italy must bear in mind is the North–South divide. It seems likely at the time of writing that this will become increasingly important as an influence on government, given the political developments of the early 1990s which are described below.

While acknowledging the dangers of generalisation, it is possible to depict Italy as consisting of two major and different employment and social systems, one located in the north and centre, the other in the south.

The North is characterised as industrial and rich, particularly within the Milan–Turin–Genoa triangle, while the South is poor and industrially backward. The North is relatively closer to the attitudes and traditions of other Northern European members of the European Union, whereas the South is very much closer to those of Southern European Mediterranean members such as Greece, Spain and Portugal. In the South, figures for unemployment, agricultural employment, self-employment, unofficial and clandestine employment and unregulated employment relationships are all higher than in the North. Union membership is higher in the North and there are significant differences in political affiliations and traditions between the two areas.

Italian politics has a history of instability and coalition. Since the second world war ended and Italy returned to democracy, the Christian Democrats (DC), who as a party have a moderate and Catholic orientation, have been the largest single party in terms of share of the vote, averaging 30–35 per cent. They have, therefore, been continuously involved in government, since the second largest party was the Communists (PCI) and there was an effective conspiracy involving the other main party, the Socialists (PSI) who resemble Social Democrats, and no doubt external organisations determined to prevent Italy having a Communist government. Italy is sometimes described as exhibiting the characteristics of blocked democracy. The PSI has, on several occasions, held the balance of power and members of the party have participated influentially in government.

The 1990s, however, have seen a political instability and turmoil unprecedented in the post-war period. The demise of communism in Eastern Europe had profound effects; the Communist party (PCI) renamed itself the Democratic Party of the Left (PDS) and fragmented, with a smaller group of communist diehards forming a new group called the Communist Reconstruction (RC). The DC, on the other hand, have also been significantly affected since the *raison d'être* of the party was to resist communism and with this no longer necessary, the party has to some extent been rendered directionless. The DC–PSI links were strengthened in the early 1990s with the formation of an alliance, the CAF, named after the three main leaders, Craxi, Andreotti and Forlani. This alliance received particularly strong support in the South. In addition, new parties emerged catering for various sectional interests including neo-fascists, the relatively rich separatists of the North who formed the Lombard League also known as the Northern League. Other minority groupings of capitalist, elitist republicans and left-wing Catholics were also formed.

The instability caused by the demise of communism has been considerably worsened by the allegations of corruption, linking many influential members of both the DC and PSI to organised crime, particularly in the

South, and official patronage. By late 1992 the DC-dominated government with a Socialist prime minister, Amato, was confronted with economic and political crisis. The unions in the public sector were particularly incensed by proposals for a wage freeze in the public sector allied to cuts in public expenditure, and members of the Lombard League were proposing to stop paying taxes since they resented the government pouring the money away down the 'black hole' of the South. In spring 1993 the trade union confederations held a general strike against government's lack of direction in economic policy and violent conflicts occurred in the South between supporters of the socialist trade unions and neo-fascists. The summer of 1993 saw further scandal and allegations of corruption involving two former prime ministers, Craxi and Forlani; another new government under the premiership of Ciampi; and further political developments with the Lombard League and the PDS (the reformed Communists) sweeping the board in mayoral elections. The DC and PSI were annihilated as a result of the many revelations and allegations. By early 1994, conditions on the political stage were complicated further. Ciampi's government was still in power and faced a general election in which the PDS as the probable single largest party was being confronted by a new-right wing alliance encompassing Berlusconi's Forza Italiana (Forward Italy) 'party', the Lombard League and the neo-fascist Italian Social Movement (MSI). In January 1994, the DC transformed itself into the Popular party, with a relatively small splinter group going their own way and calling themselves the Centre Christian Democrats.

In the general election the new right-wing alliance was elected, and after some initial difficulties between the three alliance members, a coalition government was formed under the premiership of Berlusconi. The longevity of the government was problematic, but certainly in its early days it indicated its intention to pursue 'free market' policies with an emphasis on the control of inflation and public expenditure, reducing the size of the public sector, and privatisation. These intentions were accompanied by exhortations to the unions to be moderate in their wage demands and more ready to accept greater flexibility in the labour market. Initially both unions and employers' confederations reacted reasonably positively towards the new government, and certainly there is evidence that the intention is to continue with the reforms agreed in July and December 1993, which we examine later. Towards the end of 1994 the government and unions were in conflict over government proposals to reduce public expenditure and reform the state pension scheme and right at the very end of 1994 the Lombard League precipitated the break-up of the coalition.

The political dimension of the employment environment is perhaps particularly important in Italy since ideology and political allegiance thoroughly permeates Italian society in much the same way as in Holland and extends to trade unions, newspapers and other social and cultural activities and organisations. There are also traditions of highly regulated employment relationships and, as already noted, considerable state intervention in the ownership of enterprises.

Hofstede's research[57] indicates Italian scores on the power distance index to be moderate and high scores on the other three indices. This would indicate a culture emphasising the following values, attitudes and concerns: male assertiveness, machismo, clearly differentiated sex roles with women in a nurturing role, a male-dominated society in which big and fast are considered beautiful and successful achievers are admired, money and possessions are valued and economic growth is more important than concern for the environment. Emotions and aggressive behaviour are acceptable, nationalism is pervasive, experts and expertise are valued and respected, security is important and consensus is desirable, intolerance is likely and rules and regulations are necessary. Involvement with organisations and institutions is likely to be calculative and you are expected to show individual initiative and achievement and take care of yourself and your family.

An introduction to the system of HRM

As has been indicated in the preceding section, the state has played a significant role in Italy, regulating, intervening in ownership and setting an example. Terms and conditions of employment have tended to be determined through collective bargaining at an industry or multi-industry level between confederations of trade unions and employers. The outcomes of these negotiations are then given legislative effect and are often extended to bind employers and enterprises not signatory to the agreement but encompassed within the category of enterprise or activity covered by it.

Certainly until the 1990s, it was likely that 80–90 per cent of an employee's pay and benefits package would be determined this way.[58] The state has also granted legal rights and protection to employees in a number of important areas. There has been no attempt to regulate the process of bargaining nor, except in the public sector, the right to strike, but there is a corporatist tradition of tripartite arrangements, exchange and integration, even though Ferner and Hyman characterise it as informal and tacit.[59] A recent example is the tripartite accord in July 1993 that sought to deal with issues of inflation, pay, productivity, the structure of collective bargaining, additional labour market flexibility, vocational training and support for business restructuring, and which we deal with in more detail below.

One of the peculiar features of the system in Italy over the post-war period has been the nationally agreed wage indexation system – the Scala Mobile – which linked employees' pay to the rate of price inflation, and which has been blamed recently as a significant source of inflation[60] and criticised for contributing to a narrowing of differentials between white- and blue-collar workers, occupational and professional groups. For these two main reasons the system was abolished in July 1992 when the government obtained hard-won agreements with trade union and employers' confederations to do so.

The trade union movement and employers' associations have political affiliations, the trade union movement having been fragmented along ideological and political lines. Italy is renowned for having a poor strike record, the strike being a weapon of political as well as industrial protest, and this continued into 1994 with strikes in December 1993 and early 1994 in protest at job losses and the government's failure to propose acceptable solutions.

Workplace bargaining or participation mechanisms are relatively recent additions to the employee relations stage in Italy, and only over the last two decades have employers or employees taken initiatives at this level. Reform of the structure of workplace representation and bargaining arrangements was the subject of a central employers–trade union confederation agreement in December 1993. We examine this in more detail later.

Employers and unions have been involved by government in the determination and administration of various schemes of social protection. An example of this is the Cassa Integrazione Guadagni (CIG) – the earnings maintenance fund – which is administered by a tripartite body and pays laid-off employees up to 80 per cent of their earnings. The object of the fund is to assist restructuring and keep people in employment.

In February 1994, the government once again exhibited interventionist and neo-corporatist inclinations when it brought Fiat and its employees together in a deal which involved public provision for the costs of job losses, a public involvement with Fiat in funding the development of environmentally friendly cars, and the introduction of reduced hours of work and work sharing as an alternative to even more job losses. The state was again bankrolling labour peace.

The July 1993 accord

The tripartite accord has been presented as heralding significant change to the traditional systems of resolving conflicts and achieving consensus. The government appears to have played a very active part in achieving this agreement and some reports have suggested that the other parties were eventually and effectively bounced into an agreement by government ultimatums. The accord is comprehensive in its coverage and seeks to encompass an inflation-linked incomes policy, as well as reform of the structure of collective bargaining and workplace representation, various measures to enhance labour market flexibility and others representing additional support for business, including encouraging research and development, education and vocational training.

There are now to be only two levels of collective bargaining comprising:

- bargaining at sector level to determine national collective employment contracts (*contratto collectivo nationaledi lavoro*, CCNL), this to be undertaken at four-yearly intervals except on pay which can be renegotiated every two years. These pay negotiations are to take into account and indeed be consistent with planned inflation rates.
- bargaining at company or other appropriate level, such as the region, every four years. These agreements should not overlap with the CCNL above, and pay elements should be linked directly to company-level factors such as efficiencies or profitability.

The agreement also provides for a one-month cooling-off period after expiry of the contract before either party takes industrial action.

The union confederations' signature to the agreement can be seen to have traded wage moderation and restraint and some relaxation of labour market regulation in return for their continued 'dominance' of collective bargaining and employee representation, and in return also for some optimism with respect to job security and employment levels to be derived from additional expenditure on research and development and training. The February 1994 Fiat deal referred to above can be viewed as reflective of elements of this central tripartite accord.

The Netherlands

The context

One of the smaller countries in the European Union, the Netherlands has a population of approximately 15 million[61] and an overall labour force participation rate in the region of 70 per cent.[62] For many years the Netherlands exhibited relatively low labour force participation rates, but since 1986 there has been a substantial increase and this coincides with a particularly marked increase in female participation.[63] For many years female participation in the labour force after marriage was actively discouraged by Christian Democrat governments and the social partners. Membership of the European Community, and the various legislative initiatives and decisions of the 1970s and 1980s facilitating and requiring equality of access and treatment, undoubtedly had a beneficial impact on female participation rates, but so also did the trend towards employment in the service sector and employers increasing demands for part-time and more flexible working patterns. In 1992 62.9 per cent of women working were doing so on a part-time basis.[64] This was the highest proportion amongst OECD countries.

A relatively low proportion of employment is in the industrial sector. At the end of the 1980s industrial employment in the Netherlands at 26.3 per cent was the lowest in the European Community, with 69.1 per cent employment in services.[65]

In January 1994 official unemployment stood at 10 per cent, slightly below the European Union average at that time of 10.9 per cent. This level of unemployment was expected to fall in 1994 but was close to the average rate for the 1980s of 9.7 per cent.[66] This undoubtedly is somewhat lower than actual unemployment since many employees have been retired early and/or granted disability pensions as an alternative to unemployment. These mechanisms have been used extensively to ease industrial and employment restructuring, and are consistent with the pursuit of the socio-economic policies emphasising income maintenance, export growth and a stable currency rather than full employment that have been characteristic of the Netherlands in recent decades. Gross domestic product rose by only 0.2 per cent in 1993[67]; inflation in April 1994 was 2.8 per cent.[68]

The increasing tax and social charge burden of the highly developed welfare state has prompted government in the 1990s to propose reductions in the scale of, and length of entitlement to, various social security benefits, including sickness benefit and disability pensions, at the same time as they have been seeking to reduce the legislatively backed minimum wage in order to encourage further employment of unskilled labour. Government is keen to dismantle the comprehensive welfare state, in which benefits have tended to be universal and linked to previous earnings or the minimum wage, and replace it with a system that is geared towards the provision of benefits linked to a 'social minimum' to be topped up at the individual's choice via private insurance.

The total number in receipt of disability benefits exceeded 900 000 in the early 1990s. This represented some 13 per cent of the total labour force and disability benefit expenditure constituted approximately 6 per cent of GNP. Government proposals in 1991 to scale down entitlement and benefit levels led to considerable discontent and a series of mass demonstrations and strikes. The new rules were not enacted by parliament until January 1993 and the collective bargaining discussions between trade unions and employers in 1993 have frequently sought to 'make up' or repair the effects of these new rules.

Government has been dominated by Christian Democratic policies and ideologies since the second world war. There have been various centre-right and centre-left coalitions in power, but Christian democracy has been a constant influence even when the Labour party (PrdA) has been the dominant partner. Since 1989 the Labour party has been in coalition with the Christian Democratic Appeal (CDA).

The recession of the early 1980s had prompted government to begin to address the issues of rising unit labour costs, industrial regeneration and competitiveness, rising inflation and unemployment and, as already noted, the increasing burden of the welfare state on public expenditure. Various efforts were made through the 1980s to moderate wage increases and cease indexation of wages and social security benefits to price increases. Pay freezes were applied in the public sector and success was achieved in reducing inflation, labour's share of national income and unit labour costs. The long-term trend of income and wealth redistribution from capital to labour was reversed, wage differentials between skilled and unskilled began to widen, and profits increased, but the burden of welfare expenditure and relatively high unemployment has not been significantly eased. Government has not yet taken any significant initiatives to address the structural and supply side 'causes' of unemployment and the emphasis of government labour-market policy is still very much on income maintenance.

The influence of the social security system can also be seen in the failure to form a new government easily after the May 1994 general election. The Christian Democrats had started the year proposing to freeze the state-provided old age pension as a means of controlling the cost of the welfare state and facilitating job-creation programmes. They and the Labour party both lost seats in the election and were no longer able to form a majority coalition. By mid-July 1994 three parties were endeavouring to form a coalition, the Labour and Liberal parties and a smaller left-of-centre party called D66. These efforts were foundering on the issues of public expenditure and social security policy. The new parliament is compared with the old in Figure 3.9. A coalition between these three parties would produce the first government in modern times without the Christian Democrats.

On Hofstede's[69] original dimensions, the Netherlands' scores indicate relatively high individualism, quite low power distance and uncertainty avoidance scores and very low masculinity. As such, the Netherlands can be seen to share cultural characteristics with countries in both Ronen's[70] Nordic and Anglo clusters. Given this combination of scores, one would expect a society in which the dominant values include a concern for quality of life and the environment, a belief in egalitarianism, tolerance of different views, co-operation and autonomy for individuals. Organisations, to be consistent with these character-

istics, should exhibit rather flat hierarchies with minimal bureaucracy, delegated tasks and consultative management styles. Individuals are likely to have a relatively strong work ethic, be highly motivated and look after themselves and their families, and they are not likely to be too concerned by uncertainty.

An introduction to the system of HRM

In the decades after the second world war, corporatism and centralisation were dominant features of the system. Even before the war ended, employers and unions agreed that in order to assist with economic recovery, they would establish a joint negotiating body at national level. This bipartite forum was established within weeks of the war ending. Called the Foundation of Labour (SvdA), it was very soon accepted by government in an advisory role on socio-economic policy issues.

By 1950, government and other main actors had accepted the validity of tripartite discussion, compromise and consensus, and the Social and Economic Council (SER) was established. The Council is comprised of equal numbers of trade union and employers' representatives and government appointed experts. It is common for the groups of members to vote *en bloc* and often it is the government-appointed experts that have the deciding vote on specific issues. The maximum number of Council members is 45 and government is required to consult it on any and all proposals for legislation in the social and economic policy area. In addition to its advisory/consultative role, the Council also has roles stimulating new industrial developments, monitoring the application of relevant laws and indeed in some instances actively participating in the implementation of some decisions and laws. The Council does not normally address or advise on pay.

Initially the SvdA was primarily concerned with pay determination, but more recently the Foundation has sought to form common positions on other matters related to human resource management and employee relations , disability benefit schemes and provisions, recruitment and selection, absenteeism and unemployment. Positions adopted by the Foundation usually take the form of a non-binding accord but can, where appropriate and where agreed, take the place of legislative provision.

In addition to those two national-level 'advisory' bodies, there are a plethora of bi- and tripartite institutions and arrangements at lower levels, reinforcing and extending the practice of seeking consensus through the integration of the various interest groups in the decision-making and implementing processes

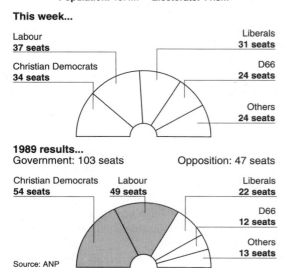

Parliament (lower house): 150 seats
Population: 15.4m   **Electorate:** 11.5m

This week...

Labour
37 seats

Liberals
31 seats

Christian Democrats
34 seats

D66
24 seats

Others
24 seats

1989 results...
Government: 103 seats   Opposition: 47 seats

Christian Democrats   Labour   Liberals
54 seats   **49 seats**   **22 seats**

D66
12 seats

Others
13 seats

Source: ANP

Fig 3.9 Netherlands elections

Source: *Financial Times*, 5 May 1994

that are characteristic of a voluntary but elaborate corporatist approach.

The need to industrialise and recover after the war encouraged the unions and employers to centralise collective bargaining to the level of the particular industry and policies via the government-appointed Board of Mediators. Wage control would facilitate competitiveness and export-led growth through lower unit labour costs, and the rewards of this centralised restraint were to be made available to all via the provision of a comprehensive welfare state. As the policy succeeded, pressures grew throughout the 1950s for greater freedom to allow the parties to negotiate rates more reflective of market forces. Entry into the EEC in 1958 added to the pressures for deregulation, as did tighter labour markets. The post-war policy of tight centralised control effectively ceased in the early 1960s, although on various occasions since then government has sought, and sometimes succeeded, to regain control of wage rises via various voluntary and compulsory income policies, cost-of-living indexation probably having been the most common. The Board of Mediators was abolished by the Wage Bill of 1968.

The significance of centralised consensus and negotiation has diminished over the last decade. The recession of the early 1980s, subsequent unemployment, a decline in government autonomy, pressures for greater democracy and participation in the workplace, the need to restructure industry and work organisation so as to respond more flexibly to international competition, and the requirement to introduce and utilise new technology have all contributed to a gradual decentralisation of decision making and bargaining over the terms of the employment relationship. The bargaining power of employers has been enhanced and labour weakened, and wage moderation has been achievable through the market without the need for centralised instruments of control. It is likely that pressures for decentralisation will also weaken the institutions and processes of centralised corporatism.

Another feature of Dutch society throughout most of the twentieth century has been fragmentation of institutions, activities and services on religious and ideological lines. This 'pillarisation'[71] permeated trade unions and employers' organisations as well as being an important element of politics. We have already noted that government has been dominated by Christian democrat ideologies and policies. Four main segments, strands or pillars can be readily identified: Catholic, Protestant, liberal and socialist. As Ramondt points out[72], pillarisation has often meant that dominant conflicts between worker and employer, union and manager, have been lessened by common religious ties. The significance of this characteristic has diminished over the last twenty years.

Sweden

The context

Sweden is one of the North European Nordic or Scandinavian countries and has a population of approximately 8.5 million, with 4.3 million civilian employees[73] and participation rates which have consistently been higher than in any of the other countries that we study in detail in this text.[74] Throughout the 1980s combined participation rates exceeded 80 per cent, reaching 86 per cent in 1990, and female participation rates increased gradually to be in excess of 80 per cent as Sweden entered the 1990s.[75]

Employment is now predominantly in the service sector, which provided 68 per cent of total civilian employment at the beginning of the 1990s, with industry accounting for nearly 30 per cent and agriculture slightly over 3 per cent.[76] As in many other countries in recent decades, Sweden has experienced a continuous increase in the size of its service sector, combined with a decline in agricultural and industrial employment as percentages of the total.

Unemployment in Sweden was maintained at an average of slightly over 2 per cent throughout the last three decades and this is a relatively low figure when compared with other countries.[77] However, unemployment has been at historically high rates in 1993 and 1994, with the June 1994 unemployment rate at 14.8 per cent including those on government training schemes.[78]

The average rates of inflation and economic growth in the 1980s were approximately 8 per cent and 2 per cent respectively[79], and both these figures reflect a worsening economic situation when compared with the earlier, post-war decades. Towards the end of the 1980s, government began to reappraise the long-term policy of pursuing full employment. Labour shortages and high levels of domestic demand were contributing to high rates of inflation and this was damaging Sweden's international competitiveness. Consequently, much greater emphasis has been given to controlling inflation and generating growth. This is reflected in the relatively high rates of unemployment in the 1990s[80] and the very much lower levels of inflation; at the end of 1992 inflation was running below 2 per cent.[81] Growth in GDP has been more difficult given the worldwide recession in the early 1990 but growth for 1994 is predicted at 2.7 per cent with a slight increase to about 3 per cent predicted for 1995.[82]

After a positive referendum in November 1994 Sweden became a full member of the European Union with effect from January 1995. Currency stability and international competitiveness are important issues confronting the Swedish economy which, in recent times, has seen many of its traditional export markets shrinking, largely due to rising costs and its non-membership of the EU.

Sweden is renowned as having generous welfare benefits, correspondingly high rates of taxation and a large public sector. The conservative coalition government of 1991–94 sought reductions in all three, an example being the decision in 1993 to revoke state sick pay for the first two weeks of absence. The public sector (excluding government-owned companies) accounted for 41 per cent of employed workers in 1990 and the majority of employees in the sector are female (over 70 per cent).[83] Public expenditure in mid-1994 accounted for 67 per cent of GDP despite government attempts over the preceding three years to reduce it.[84]

The Swedish industrial sector has been a mixture of a few large, internationally renowned engineering and manufacturing organisations and a large number of relatively small companies, the vast majority of which (approximately 85 per cent) employ less than 25 employees. Sweden's high cost base, combined with recession and non-membership of the European Union, has encouraged increased investment in foreign manufacturing capacity in recent years.

There has been remarkable political stability in Sweden. Government has been dominated by the Social Democrats (SAP) since 1932, with the exception of the periods 1976–82 and 1991 to September 1994, during which there were conservative-led coalitions. The 1991–94 government failed to control government expenditure and presided over historically high levels of unemployment. Throughout most of the period of social democrat government there was a rough equality of power between capital and labour. This can be detected as early as 1938 when employers and union federations concluded the first national 'basic agreement' which sought to establish certain basic rights and obligations and thereby to regulate future relationships (The Saltsjobaden Agreement).

One of the characteristics of Swedish society which sets it apart from many others is the emphasis on and apparent belief in egalitarianism. This is perhaps most apparent between the sexes. Swedish women partici-

pate in employment almost as frequently as men.[85] There is also a lack of class differentiation, and for many years the Swedish system produced a relatively undifferentiated wage structure. The trade unions in particular pursued what was referred to as a solidaristic wage policy, this policy having at its centre the narrowing of differentials between skill and status levels. This egalitarianism in income was also furthered by progressive and redistributive taxation and benefits schemes.

Hofstede's research[86] indicated Sweden (along with other Nordic countries) as a country in which scores on the masculinity, power, distance and uncertainty avoidance dimensions were all on the low side. This combination is consistent with a system in which the dominant values are co-operation, consultation and consensus, egalitarianism between the sexes and in society at large, concern for the quality of life and preservation of the environment, where both aggressive behaviour and the showing of emotion are frowned on, friendliness and personal relationships are considered more important than money, and there is a preference for small-scale enterprise and decentralisation of decision making within organisations and society.

An introduction to the system of HRM

The ground rules, basic rights and framework of the Swedish system were initially established by the Saltsjobaden Agreement in 1938. This agreement between the central trade union and employers' association confederations recognised the rights of both employers and workers to organise freely; acknowledged that agreements entered into by one of the central confederations would be binding on its members or subordinate organisations; stipulated that during the course of an agreement action by way of strike or lock-out should not be taken, although agreements could be cancelled; and asserted that the employer retained the right to determine production issues, including the organisation and distribution of work. The Social Democrat government elected in 1932 had encouraged the parties to regulate their relationships themselves. The belief in and reliance on self-regulation continued into the 1970s, when government began to intervene more directly via legislation and indirectly via the application of pressure on the parties to conclude agreements within particular limits.

The seeds of these more corporatist arrangements that arguably characterised the 1970s were in some senses sown in the early 1950s with the acceptance of the Rehn–Meidner proposals concerning economic and industrial policy.[87] The essence of these propos-als was that the union movement would help govern-ment in its pursuit of full employment, low inflation, steady economic growth and rapid structural change by pursuing a solidaristic wages policy incorporating wage restraint, equal pay for equal work, regardless of productivity, ability to pay or profitability, and the narrowing of differentials. Such a wage policy would also reduce inter-union competition. In return, gov-ernment should pursue restrictive and redistributive fiscal policies, thereby managing aggregate demand and controlling inflation, and make effective provi-sion via active and selective labour market policies to prevent structural unemployment by encouraging and facilitating both occupational and locational labour mobility. Subsequent to these proposals being adopt-ed, Swedish governments have spent far more on mobil-ity allowances, counselling services, training and job-creation initiatives than on unemployment bene-fits, and long-term unemployment was almost unknown for many years.

It was the implementation of the Rehn–Meidner plan that necessitated the development of effective cen-tralised bargaining arrangements between employer and employee organisations, and centralised wage bar-gaining remained a notable characteristic of the Swedish model or system of industrial relations until the early 1980s. Since then, the willingness of the par-ties to continue with the centralised bargaining tradi-tions has declined owing to tensions within the labour movement consequent on expansion of the service and public sectors and white-collar work; rank and file dis-satisfaction with narrow differentials; the consequences of economic policies aimed at economic growth, labour mobility and wage restraint; and increasing employer incentives to regain local control over wage determi-nation. The Social Democrat government after 1982 continued to argue for centralisation of wage bar-gaining and before the end of its period of office in 1990–91 instituted the Rehnberg Commission, a national tripartite mediation commission comprised of representatives from the major employers and trades union organisations and a national mediator. It was intended that the Commission would provide a frame-work for industry-level bargaining allied to a propos-al to prohibit local negotiations in 1991–92. The government desperately wanted to control wages and, in particular, locally determined wage drift.

This 'tripartite' corporatist experiment was, how-ever, short lived, given the election later in 1991 of a conservative-led coalition government with very different values, objectives and allegiances. With the support of employers' organisations, this new government began to take action legislatively to strengthen requirements for compulsory mediation in disputes, increase fines for wildcat strikes, require pre-strike ballots, reduce the influence of unions and employers in tripartite arrangements and reduce state funding for various trade union activities including education. Additionally, it was a government keen to reduce the size of the public sector and cut taxation and welfare benefits. There was a much greater degree of trust in the efficiency of the market and, as noted earlier, much less emphasis was given to the achievement and maintenance of full employment. Some of the consequences of the recession and different governmental approach are depicted in Figure 3.10.

The United Kingdom

The context

The United Kingdom, comprising England, Scotland, Wales and Northern Ireland, has a total population of close to 58 million and an employed labour force in excess of 25 million.[88] The 1980s and early 1990s have been a period of high unemployment compared with earlier post-war decades. The 1980–89 average unem-ployment rate was 10 per cent. The period since 1979 has been characterised by two major recessions, the first between 1979 and 1982, during which unem-ployment increased dramatically from 5 per cent to 11.3 per cent; and the second between 1990 and early 1993, during which unemployment again increased from slightly under 7 per cent to in excess of 10.5 per cent.[89] By mid-1994 official unemployment statistics indicated that 2.64 million were unemployed, a rate of 9.4 per cent.[90]

The recent trends in employment also exhibit sig-nificant decreases in male employment and employ-ment in manufacturing industry; the former declined by approximately 2.5 million between 1979 and September 1993[91], and the decline in the latter was even greater, from in excess of 6.7 million in 1979 to little more than 4.285 million in September 1993.[92] Indeed, in excess of 500 000 jobs in manufacturing industries were lost in 1990–92 along with almost 300 000 in services.[93] There was, however, evidence in mid-1994 that the almost continuous 25-year decline in manu-facturing employment might be coming to an end.

In the same period, since 1979, there has been a significant increase in female employment, from 9.4

Idle model city mourns a very Swedish past

Hugh Carnegy on a miracle cure that was no help at all for Uddevalla's ailing fortunes

There are few more forlorn sights in Sweden than the waterfront at Uddevalla, once a thriving shipbuilding city standing at the head of a deep inlet along the country's rugged west coast.

Wharfside cranes stand idle and rusting, their jibs dipped mournfully towards the water. The big dry dock lies half-flooded and deserted. Old brick-built workshops nearby are empty and silent.

It is a scene familiar from other former shipyard towns in northern Europe. But just across from the dry dock is a sight that makes the plight of Uddevalla especially poignant. There stands a huge factory built less than 10 years ago by Volvo, the car manufacturer. It was to have revitalised the city just as the old shipbuilding industry collapsed. But now it, too, is an empty shell.

Uddevalla, a city of 48,000 people, was supposed to be a shining example of what became known as the "Swedish model". In the 1980s, while the rest of western Europe began to struggle with high unemployment caused by the decline of traditional heavy industries, Sweden managed to keep jobless rates enviably low by a mixture of close co-operation between government, employers and trade unions and generous retraining schemes.

Faced with the closure of the state-owned shipyard in Uddevalla, the Social Democratic government used its clout – and some well-aimed incentives – to nudge Volvo into opening a car plant in the city. Volvo, at the time extremely profitable and keen to put into practice pioneering car making techniques which did away with tedious assembly line work, was happy to oblige.

It seemed like the perfect solution. Unemployment in Uddevalla actually fell after the shipyard laid off the last of its 4,500 workers in 1986 – to less than 2 per cent of the local workforce. Hotels sprang up and small companies moved in, encouraged by the Volvo investment.

But those heady days proved to be a false dawn. Crippled by falling car sales, Volvo closed its Uddevalla plant last year.

Unemployment in Uddevalla now stands at around 15 per cent – above the national average. The "Swedish model" has given way to a painful reality that is no different from the experience of other recession-struck European countries.

Officials at the Uddevalla Kommune (city council) admit they feel betrayed – and abandoned. "Now the government says the market must decide," says a bitter Mr Leif Molander, an elected member of the kommune board. But he and his colleagues are also realistic. "It seemed like a good solution at the time," shrugs Mr Lars Björneld, the planning director. "The problem was that Volvo couldn't sell enough cars."

In retrospect it is clear that the substitution of the Volvo plant for the shipyard was never as neat a solution as it appeared. Original plans to include a body and paint factory at the Volvo plant were dropped because of a row over emissions from the paint shop.

The assembly plant, which employed 930 people at its peak with an annual output capacity of 40,000 cars, did not start real production until August 1988, two years after the shipyard closed. By then most of the shipyard workers had found other work, leaving Volvo with a recruitment problem.

"In 1986 we had to say No to a number of very good people from the shipyard looking for work because we were not ready for them," said Mr Bengt Berntsson, a Volvo executive now seeking new tenants for the 100,000 sq metre factory. "Later, when we needed them, they weren't there any more."

This was especially ironic as much of the motivation behind Volvo's decision to build the Uddevalla plant, with its unique production system of small teams building whole cars, was to reduce the chronic problems of labour turnover and absenteeism it was experiencing at its headquarters in Gothenburg.

A keen debate persists within the motor industry over the viability of the team-based system. But the harsh reality was that a crash

in Volvo sales left the company with 30 per cent excess capacity and in November 1992 it decided to close two of its three Swedish assembly plants.

Uddevalla was abruptly exposed to Sweden's recession. Jobs disappeared at an alarming rate as former stalwarts such as the construction industry slumped. The government, too, had changed. In place of the interventionist Social Democrats was a right-centre coalition under Prime Minister Carl Bildt whose recipe for making Sweden competitive again was a radical dose of market policies.

After two years of reform and a big currency devaluation, growth is returning, but domestic investment is lagging and there has been a wave of overseas investment by Swedish companies. Volvo has production plants in Belgium and the Netherlands. SKF, the big ball bearing maker which grew up in Sweden's west, now produces only 10 per cent of its output in Sweden.

The biggest employers in Uddevalla are the kommune itself and the local health service. "Our problem is that we need a large industry that can employ a lot of people as an anchor around which we can build," says Mr Molander. Uddevalla is currently working with a private group on the possibility of re-opening the shipyard.

But it is a project that would require an investment of SKr3bn (£260m) and Mr Molander admits it is a long shot.

An example of the way forward for the city seems more likely to be found in a small corner of the Volvo factory where Mr Bengt Berntsson and two former colleagues from Volvo have set up a small components-sorting company employing 15 people.

"It is not realistic to go back to shipbuilding," says Mr Berntsson. He speaks not just for Uddevalla but for all of Sweden when he says: "The mentality has to change. There is no tradition of small industry. We still have a high cost base in Sweden. But we have good educated people who are flexible and do not need a lot of management. The future lies in smaller businesses, not big industries."

Fig 3.10 Source: *Financial Times*, 6 April 1994

million in 1978 to 10.5 million in 1993[94], and in employment in the service sector[95] and part-time employment[96], although there is evidence of declining service sector employment in 1994. The 1991 census confirmed that more than 80 per cent of working women were in service industries. Female participation rates increased from 58 per cent in 1979 to 65 per cent in 1991[97], and 1994 may have seen the number of women with jobs exceed for the first time the number of men in employment (see Fig. 3.11). Certainly

Plea for men as women take jobs lead

David Brindle
Social Services Correspondent

Ministers must help the millions of men with no prospect of holding a job, Frank Field, chairman of the Commons social security committee, said yesterday.

The number of women employees would this year for the first time exceed the number of men with jobs, Mr Field said. The consequences for society would be profound.

"The amount of pent-up violence I witness in some of my constituents who are in this position gives me a glimpse of what many wives have to endure," Mr Field, Labour MP for Birkenhead, told a conference on low pay, organised by Hyndburn council, in Accrington, Lancashire.

He called for measures including the reintroduction of technical schools for children being failed by the education system.

The gender gap among employees has narrowed sharply since 1978, when there were 13.4 million men and 9.4 million women. Latest Department of Employment figures show that last September there were fewer than 10.9 million male employees, compared with more than 10.5 million female. These seasonally adjusted figures exclude self-employed people, who are mostly men.

The trend was caused partly by women with full-time jobs holding on to them as men lost theirs. But it was mainly attributable to rapid growth in part-time posts – often by splitting full-time jobs – which had gone overwhelmingly to women.

Society was seeing the emergence of the "disenfranchised male", losing not only the prospect of work but also, with that, role of partner and father.

"The consequences of millions of males having no prospect of working is beginning to have the most profound effects on the society in which we live," Mr Field said.

He said ministers could take three steps. First, there needed to be measures to prevent men being sucked into permanent unemployment. These could include training and fall-back job guarantees, so that labour market flexibility could be achieved with a degree of security for workers in and out of employment.

Second, men unemployed for more than three years could for five years be guaranteed the same benefits if they took a low-paid job, with skills training guaranteed during the period.

Third, there could be greater emphasis on skills training in schools. This could be based on reintroduction of technical schools for over-11s.

Fig 3.11 Source: *Guardian*, 5 February 1994. Reprinted with permission. © *Guardian* 1994.

the rate of male unemployment in May 1994 exceeded that of females.[98]

During the 1980s gross domestic product (GDP) increased at an average rate of 2.3 per cent p.a. However, over the same period manufacturing output increased at approximately half this average rate, manufacturing output in 1990 equalling 112 per cent of the 1979 total.[99] As noted above, since 1990 the economy has experienced another recession, with GDP falling in 1991 and the early part of 1992, since when some recovery has taken place. 1993 saw a growth in GDP of 2 per cent over 1992[100], and 1994 second quarter figures indicate a rate of annual increase approaching 4 per cent p.a.[101] However, the May 1994 figures for manufacturing output were only 98.4 per cent of the 1990 base.[102]

On the consumer price front, the late 1970s and early 1980s saw very high rates of increase, 1980 being the year in which the rate peaked at 18 per cent.[103] In recent years the rate of increase has been considerably lower, and in June 1994 the annual rate of increase in the Retail Price Index was 2.6 per cent.[104]

The political system in the UK, which it must not be forgotten is still a monarchy, has resulted in single-party government. Only for the briefest of periods in the late 1970s has there been any hint of coalition government, and since 1945 the Conservative party has held office for approximately two-thirds of the total time and continuously since 1979. The election in 1979 of a Conservative government, headed by Margaret Thatcher, had a considerable influence on the human resource system within the UK; through the economic priorities chosen and policies pursued, through the impact of its ideology on perceptions of the public sector, and through its legislative interventions. Gospel and Palmer[105] appositely describe the period since 1979 as one characterised by 'Liberal individualism, monetary economics and restrictive legislation'. On each of these dimensions, the Thatcher government was significantly different from those that had preceded it, particularly perhaps the Labour government of 1974–79 which marked probably the only genuine attempt at bargained corporatism seen in the UK. The rejection of collectivism, Keynesianism and voluntarism that the Thatcher government represented was undoubtedly a watershed in the history of the employment relationship, employee relations and the management of human resources.

Hofstede's[106] work on cultural dimensions indicated that the UK exhibited relatively high individualism ratings, moderate masculinity and low(ish) power distance and uncertainty avoidance scores. This combination implies that success, money, etc. are relatively important and conflict quite common. Individual initiative is respected and should be rewarded. There is a willingness to take risks and not too much reliance placed on formality, rules and procedures. Also, people are not overly impressed by titles and power, accepting that others may quite legitimately have more power than they do. There is likely to be quite a strong adherence to the Protestant work ethic.

An introduction to the system of HRM

The system in the UK has a number of traditions:

- A coherent and relatively large trade union movement representing the interests of employees. This movement began among craft workers in the early nineteenth century and began to spread to unskilled and semi-skilled workers towards the end of that century.
- Employers' associations in many trades and industries again formed relatively early, in response to the activities of trade unions and subsequent legislation. These associations usually have trade as well as employee relations functions. There is also now a single peak association, the Confederation of British Industry (CBI).
- Multi-employer bargaining at the level of trade, industry or geographic area. Given impetus by the first world war, employers in manufacturing and extractive industries, public utilities and the public sector have for many years relied on multi-employer, centralised bargaining to set main terms and conditions, eliminate competition between them and prevent weaker ones being sacrificed.
- A reliance on collective bargaining as the main mechanism for resolving conflicts between the parties and for achieving employee participation in decision making, backed up by voluntary conciliation/arbitration. Relationships between employers and employees have been predominantly conflictual rather than consensual.
- A relatively strong procedural tradition, the parties to collective bargaining voluntarily determining and agreeing rules to govern their relationships. Impetus was given to this early on by the report of the Whitley Committee in 1916, which recommended the formation of Joint Industrial Councils (JIC) with formal written constitutions functioning at national, district and works levels, thereby also encouraging multi-employer bargaining. The committee's recommendations were widely accepted initially, although few in the private sector survived the inter-war period.

- A large public sector, significantly expanded after the second world war through the process of nationalisation, whereby many public sector utilities were taken into public ownership, and through the creation of the National Health Service and other institutions of the welfare state.
- Relative abstinence by government from participation via either legislation or economic regulation, although as a major employer for many years government participated in encouraging trade unionism and collective bargaining through which standards of terms and conditions were set which in many respects served as examples to the private sector.

Over the last 15 years, the system and the above traditions have been subject to considerable strains and changes have undoubtedly occurred. There are many factors that one could identify as influences for change and among the more significant must be the following:

- Increasing international competition for traditional markets and products, encouraging either significant initiatives on the part of employers to increase efficiency, productivity and reduce costs so as to remain competitive, or a retreat from the market altogether.
- The development of new technology at a seemingly ever-increasing rate, facilitating the development of new products and services but also rendering many traditional industries, skills and functions redundant.
- The work of the new management 'gurus' preaching excellence, quality and the importance of employee commitment and organisational culture, and increased exposure to Japanese management traditions and techniques.
- The election of a Conservative government in 1979, with liberal individualist, neo-classical ideological and theoretical convictions. These have formed the basis of its monetarist and supply-side economic management; its belief in the efficiency of the market as a mechanism for allocating resources and determining prices; its determination to reduce the size of the public sector and force that which remains to confront market forces; its legislative attack on the trade unions as a source of supply-side imper-

fections in labour markets; and its reassertion of the significance of financial reward as the main factor influencing individual motivation to work. It has sought to encourage the last factor through taxation policy, and exhortations to employers to stand firm against trade unions and reward individuals on the basis of performance and in accordance with local as opposed to national criteria.

By re-examining the traditions referred to above, it is possible to detect considerable erosion. Much of this forms the subject matter of the following sections, but briefly:

- The trade union movement has declined in size, trade union membership density having fallen substantially after 1979.[107] This decline in size is attributable in part to increased unemployment, structural change and legislative interventions. The movement is still coherent, certainly, and there is still only one peak association, the Trades Union Congress (TUC), but the size of the movement not affiliated to it has increased[108] and there have been some significant disagreements among TUC unions on subjects such as membership poaching and single-union agreements. Despite the decline in size there is no substantial evidence to suggest that union–non-union wage differentials have diminished.

- Again, employers and their organisations have retained one peak organisation, although other groups such as the Institute of Directors and the Industrial Society may have become more influential. Certainly as multi-employer bargaining, its relevance and efficacy have come under fire, the need for and role of employers' associations has been brought into question. The situation facing employers' organisations may not be as unfriendly as that facing the trade unions, but there are problems. The Workplace Industrial Relations Survey (WIRS) for 1990[109] found that private sector membership of an employers' organisation had declined from one in four to one in eight workplaces.

- Multi-employer bargaining had been under pressure in the 1960s from the development of the shop steward movement and workplace bargaining, often linked to piecework-based payment systems and frequently on an informal basis, and from the recommendations of the Donovan Commission in 1968 (Royal Commission on Trades Unions and Employers Associations), which identified lack of senior management responsibility for and involvement in employee relations at corporate level as a

weakness in the system and an abdication of their responsibility. Since that time, multi-employer bargaining has diminished in significance. There has been increased emphasis on individualism, ability to pay, local labour markets, organisational and individual performance, the need to introduce new technology in the workplace and health and safety issues. The decline of the trade union movement and its importance in traditional industries, and the relative absence of trade unions in many service sectors have all contributed to this diminished significance. The 1990 WIRS[110] confirms this decline in significance, finding that for manual workers only 25 per cent of establishments determined basic pay through multi-employer bargaining, compared with 40 per cent in 1984.

- Collective bargaining is still the main mechanism for jointly determining terms and conditions of employment and resolving conflict, but unilateral managerial determination has increased in significance. The 1990 WIRS[111] found that 54 per cent of employees had their terms and conditions of employment at least partially determined through collective bargaining, compared with 74 per cent in 1984. The extent to which the conflictual tradition has been affected is debatable. Employers and unions increasingly talk about the need to co-operate, seek consensus and enhance competitiveness, but one wonders about the extent to which traditions of confrontation between major interest groups have only partially and temporarily disappeared pending a new economic and political environment.

- As trade union membership and the significance of collective bargaining declines, to be replaced by individualism and unilateral managerial determination, one must expect the strong voluntary procedural tradition to decline also. To some extent, grievance and disciplinary procedures are required by legislation and judicial emphasis on due process and natural justice. It is also possible that the weakening of the procedural tradition will be limited to some extent by further legislative interventions consequent on the UK's membership of the European Union. The 1990 WIRS[112] found that grievance and disciplinary procedures existed in approximately 90 per cent of all establishments, but that there had been a slight decline in the incidence of procedures for resolving disputes of a collective nature over pay. In 1990, 65 per cent of establishments had such procedures compared with 68 per cent in 1984.

- The public sector had been substantially reduced in size by privatisation, compulsory competitive tendering and other mechanisms of exposing functions to market forces.
- Governments began to intervene more in the system as legislators and regulators from the early 1960s. In the 1960s and 1970s, there were several attempts made to regulate legally both prices and incomes. In the mid-1970s, the TUC's Social Contract with the Labour government (and employers as rather junior partners) was innovatory in the UK and reflected some of the attempts at macro-level bargained corporatism in other countries. Legislative intervention in other areas, establishing minimum employee rights and protections and regulating the activities of trade unions and employers, has expanded apace and is dealt with more fully in a later section.

The changes and developments referred to above may also have contributed to cultural change. If one looks again at the cultural dimensions which Hofstede[113] identified and concentrated on, one might postulate that long-term exposure to unemployment on a scale not known since the 1930s, allied to an increasing emphasis on individualism, individual performance and financial reward and materialism, may have contributed to rating shifts on the dimensions of uncertainty avoidance, individualism and masculinity.

Japan

The context

Japan is one of the industrial and economic success stories of the post-war decades, with GNP per capita rising at a faster rate than in other developed economies (the 1965–89 average annual rate was 4.25 per cent) and a GNP per capita that by the late 1980s exceeded that in any other similarly developed country including both the United States and Germany.[114] This economic success has included strong export growth, particularly in the automobile, motor cycle, electronic and office equipment sectors, and again the average rate of export growth over the 1965–89 period exceeded that in other developed countries, averaging almost 8 per cent per year. The need to export is prompted particularly by Japan's lack of basic, natural raw materials such as oil, iron ore, coal and bauxite, all of which it has to import and which it seeks to finance by the export of manufactured products.

The economic success of Japan has been based in part on the acquisition, development and use of advanced technology in manufacturing processes, for example the use and development of robotics, and on the development of production systems which are 'lean' in cost terms and emphasise quality. Nevertheless, Japan has been and is experiencing similar trends towards services and tertiarisation as are other developed economies[115] with decreasing proportions of the labour force employed in both manufacturing and secondary sectors and increasing proportionate employment in the service and tertiary sectors.

However, since 1991 Japan has also experienced recession with domestic demand, GDP and company profits declining.[116] Unemployment has been low, averaging below 3 per cent throughout the 1980s,[54] although there is undoubtedly some hidden unemployment and, perhaps most importantly, underemployment. 1993 saw negative economic growth and unemployment rising to a six-year high of 2.8 per cent at the year end[117], with unemployment among the under 25s at 7 per cent. In mid-1994, the rate of unemployment was still fractionally under 3 per cent.

Female participation in the labour force is approximately 60 per cent and women comprise less than 40 per cent of the total labour force.[118] Women are, by Western standards, treated as second-class citizens at work, they earn less than men, are much more likely to work in temporary and part-time capacities, and rarely have the rights and protections afforded to men. Equal opportunities legislation[119] was enacted in 1986 but its effect has been unexceptional, perhaps not surprising given dominant cultural values and a legal system which asks employers only to 'make efforts' to treat men and women equally. Women are commonly expected or required to resign on pregnancy or childbirth, and a woman is still expected to view looking after the home, children and husband as her primary role and responsibility (see Fig. 3.12).

Japan is densely populated and has approximately 125 million people crammed into relatively little space, since some 80 per cent of the land is mountainous and relatively uninhabitable. Many commentators identify overcrowding as one of Japan's most distinctive features. This has resulted in immensely expensive, relatively poor-quality housing, often some distance from places and centres of work, causing many employees to commute relatively long distances. It must be noted, however, that house prices have fallen substantially since 1990.

The Japanese are renowned as placing considerable emphasis on education, and the educational system is uniform, highly regulated and competitive. Educational attainment plays a considerable role in determining a

FAIRNESS AT WORK

TAKAO NAKAZAWA
Free-lance journalist

Differentiating between simple differences and discrimination in employment is difficult. In many respects, it seems that women are at a disadvantage compared with men in recruiting, education, transfers, promotions, etc. Few companies blatantly discriminate against women, but the great majority of women feel there is discrimination against them.

The average age of men whose education ended with elementary school or postwar, new-system middle school was high in 1991, at 48.6 years old, due to the fact that this generation is made up of workers who entered the labour market immediately after graduating (until the 1960s, when economic growth allowed more Japanese to get a higher education). The average age of male technical college and junior college graduates was low, because those systems are still relatively new.

The average compensation for middle school graduates was ¥276,000, but that for old- and new-system university graduates was ¥360,000, even

though their average age was 10 years younger. The number of Japanese who went on to prewar, old-system universities was only about 1 per cent of the population, so they were considered the elite. Most still alive are in top management positions, so it is only natural that their wages are high. In addition, because the number of Japanese who went on to college dramatically increased around 1970, the average age for this group is relatively low.

Furthermore, because the system in the typical Japanese company calls for promotions for university graduates to managerial positions after they have been employed for about 10 years, their salaries naturally increase more than those in lower positions. There is about a 30 per-cent difference in high school and university graduates' wages, even adjusting for length of employment.

The difference between men and women is greater than a simple difference in education would seem to indicate. The average pay for female university graduates is ¥239,000, a figure that is far lower than that for any male category. One of the key reasons is length of employment. Excluding middle school graduates, the length of employment for women is about one-half that for men. When the figures for old-system middle school and new-system high school graduates – which are roughly equivalent and which are the largest groups for both men and women (both exceeding 50 per-cent of the total) – are compared, however, there is an 80 per-cent difference in wages even though there is not much difference in average age and length of employment. It cannot be simply said that this is due to discrimination, but it is undeniable that there is a difference.

On wage management at companies, it is generally regarded as best if young women work for five to eight years and then quit, keeping their average wages low. The figures show that this is a feature of employment in Japan.

WAGES, ETC. BY SEX AND EDUCATION IN 1991

Education completed	M/F	Monthly wages (¥1,000)	Age	Years of employment	Percentage of total (by sex)
Elementary and new-system middle school	M	276.3	47.9	15.9	18.5
	F	160.3	48.9	11.1	17.1
Old-system middle school and new-system high school	M	288.2	38.5	12.6	50.9
	F	181.8	34.8	7.2	57.3
Technical and junior college	M	277.1	34.2	9.1	5.1
	F	196.6	29.0	5.1	19.8
Old- and new-system university	M	360.5	37.2	11.2	25.5
	F	239.7	30.7	5.3	5.8

NOTE: M = male, F = female

Fig 3.12 Source: *Japan Update*, May 1994

person's employment opportunities and long-term career (see Fig. 3.12).

As is discussed in subsequent sections, the human resource management system in Japan is distinctive. There are several dimensions of employment, the employment relationship, the nature of enterprises and the management decision-making process which, it is argued, are distinctive to Japan and which many claim set an example which the rest of the industrial world could, and perhaps should, follow. Many explanations have been forwarded to account for these characteristic features and among the more interesting of these is culture. Briggs[120], for example, in seeking to ascer-

tain whether Japanese workers really are more committed to their work than are workers in other countries, concludes that if they are, it is a different kind of commitment, and the most realistic roots and explanation for this are cultural.

The Confucian notion of *wa* has been significant in the cultural development of the Japanese. *Wa* signifies harmony, and harmony is most important. Harmony in society will only be achieved if individuals conduct their interpersonal relationships correctly, with compassion and acting in an appropriate manner. Each person should be continually aware of his or her position in society and act in strict accordance with what society expects from someone in such a position. Additionally, the most important Confucian social institution is the family, and the state is envisaged as an enlarged family. Children must obey and support their parents. It is very important to maintain social relationships as a way of facilitating harmony and social order. Society is a collection of groups not individuals, self is subordinate to the group, and the identity and self-concept of individuals is defined by their membership of groups. Individual status is a reflection of group status.

It is suggested that the Confucian base to the culture encourages social values such as duty, avoidance of shame, loyalty and a sense of group identity which distinguishes insiders from outsiders, thereby encouraging 'we Japanese' pride and isolation and the attachment of great value to networks. Zen, with its emphasis on discipline, practice and concentration on the path to enlightenment, complements this culture rooted in Confucian philosophy, valuing social harmony and order above all.

Hofstede's[121] research indicated Japan as a country exhibiting relatively strong uncertainty avoidance tendencies, low individualism, high power distance scores and a high masculinity rating (the Japanese rate money as an important motivator more than any other industrialised country). Some of the implications of these findings and the influence of Confucius and Zen are pursued in the following sections.

Politically, Japan has been dominated over recent decades by the Liberal Democrats (LDP) with the Japanese Socialist Party (JSP) as the main opposition. There are also Democratic Socialist and Communist parties and a number of other minority groupings, new parties and groups; by mid-1994 11 different parties had parliamentary representation.

Japan is a parliamentary democracy with the Emperor as the largely symbolic head of state. The parliament is called the Diet.

As indicated, the Liberal Democrats have dominated government over the last 40 years, but confronted by recession and many allegations of corruption and scandal, the electorate rejected the Liberal Democrats in the 1993 general election. However, by July 1994 there had been three coalition governments within 12 months and the LDP was back in government in coalition with the Social Democrats (SDP). The coalition of both left and right parties seems unlikely to be stable enough to alter existing economic and industrial policies to any great extent, at least in the short term, though in 1994 there has already been some evidence of economic and social policies that place greater emphasis on the quality of life and social infrastructure.

The 1993–4 period has been one of previously unknown political change and instability, and there is evidence of the old order, in which business, bureaucrats and politicians worked hand in hand, breaking down. Business has been seriously debilitated by recession and is increasingly critical of politicians and bureaucrats, particularly perhaps the latter who are seen as hampering the deregulation that business people feel is essential for economic recovery.

An introduction to the system of HRM

There are a number of features of the human resource system in Japan that collectively distinguish it from others, and it is popularly accepted that they are at least to some extent the product of the cultural dimensions and roots described in the last section. These features are variously referred to as 'pillars' and even 'sacred treasures'[122] of the system. They are:

- lifetime employment;
- seniority-based pay and promotion;
- consensus decision making;
- enterprise unionism.

The first point to make about these dimensions is that they apply only in the major industrial organisations, those that comprise the *keiretsu*[123], and by no means all employees of these organisations benefit or are entitled to participate. Briggs[124], for example, estimates that only 30 per cent of Japanese employees benefit from the lifetime employment guarantee. It is important to state that for the majority of employees employment conditions are not good, they have few rights and protections, are not represented by trade unions, are relatively poorly paid and are often used as a flexible and disposable resource. Certainly it can be argued that many employees work for below-average wages in unsafe conditions and in technologically driven environments which create fatigue and stress. Additionally, as indicated in the previous section, they are likely to live in relatively poor-quality and overcrowded housing.

Lifetime employment is a guarantee given to regular employees, often called 'salarymen', when they are recruited from university (see Fig. 3.13). Lifetime in this context means until compulsory retirement at between 55 and 60. The guarantee is not linked to any particular job, skill or functional area and even it is part of the salaryman tradition that they are mobile within an organisation and even between the main enterprise and one or more of its associates or sub-

FIRM OFFERS
The travails of job-seeking

TAKAO NAKAZAWA

The collapse of the "bubble economy" has had a widespread, deep impact on the labour market. Especially hardest hit are female students and graduates of four-year universities, for almost all the major companies listed on the Tokyo Stock Exchange have reduced recruitment of female students graduating next March.

These companies do so by subtle means, saying for instance that they only need graduates from technical schools. Their intention apparently is to recruit men only. Reality belies the Equal Employment Opportunities Law even eight years after its enactment.

Japan's labour market can be divided roughly into three components. One is a free market composed of medium-size and small businesses where jobs are offered and sought all year round.

The second is the market that comprises graduates from junior and senior high schools, junior colleges, special schools and universities.

The third is called an "intermediary market." It represents a shift of labor between allied companies in such forms as secondment and personnel exchange.

Why do young adults desperately try to enter the "new graduate market"? If new graduates fail to join a big company, they will have no more chance to get a job at a major company unless they possess special talents.

Japanese companies hire new graduates on the premise that they will work for a long time, and provide them with on-the-job training. Seldom do they recruit personnel not fresh out of school.

Japan's lifetime employment system is famous. Nearly 60 per cent of male graduates of universities with an enrolment of over 1,000 work permanently for one company. The rate of long-term employment, however, is much lower for women, senior high school graduates and employees of smaller businesses.

The chances for employment at well-known companies is very slim for women, except new graduates. Not a few companies hire "old graduate" women on the condition that they will retire by the age of 25. All these handicaps naturally make female graduates desperate in seeking jobs.

Young people have a lot of chances to find employment if they do not mind the type of company or job they get. The fact is, however, that a majority of new graduates are keen to work for a famous company.

Perhaps *company-hunting* rather than *job-hunting* most accurately describes the situation in Japan. What matters is not the job as such but the company for which one works. Of course, there are clear options to pursue, such as journalistic and technical jobs. But such posts are so scarce that most students try whatever companies they come across, like trading, non-life, transport and manufacturing companies, which have no direct relation to one another.

Some adults preach that graduates should seek jobs that suit their aptitudes, but it is almost inevitable for graduates to take every available chance. And young people often do not know what kinds of jobs suit them unless they try the jobs.

All that businesses want is to educate new recruits on technical knowhow. Even most older employees find their occupational niche only after having taken up various jobs. Perhaps if company employees can afford to keep looking for a job best suited to them, they are lucky.

In Japan, when one faces the question "What kind of work do you do?" it actually means "What company do you work for?" Japanese never introduce themselves by profession. Rather, they usually give the name of the company they work for.

This underscores the tendency among young job-seekers to be "brand-minded." So limited are the "brands" that first-rate companies pick virtually all their new employees as early as the June or July before the spring in which work will begin. Applicants not chosen in this period have to try their second-choice companies, and have to give up even those companies if they are not assured of employment during June or July. The danger is that they will come to say, "I don't care what company I join."

Some older adults tell young job-seekers of the meaninglessness of sticking to "brand" companies or advise them to change their values. But it is not the young people but the grumbling older generations who have created this trend.

Brand-orientation is a value held by the parents of those young people who send applications and resumes to 50 or 60 companies apiece and undergo interviews at 10 to 15. It stems from their past embarrassment of being asked what company they work for.

It is for this reason that telephones at university employment-counselling offices ring constantly every spring with calls from students' parents asking questions ranging from the scale of companies offering jobs and the university's percentage of successful applicants to assessment of individual businesses. Flooded with such questions, the exasperated men in charge may feel tempted to reply, "Why not try to make your children as eager as you are?"

Such parental questions are telephoned to companies as well. Most personnel officers at banks and manufacturing companies have responded to many such inquiries, especially from mothers. Their questions usually go like this: "My son (daughter) is a student of so-and-so university. Can you give him (her) a chance to take an entrance test?"

The answer, naturally, usually is "yes," because "no" is bound to spark a problem over discrimination against the applicant's university. The result is that the personnel desk of a company listed on the TSE is kept busy sending out 50,000 to 100,000 copies of its corporate brochure to students. During the June-July period, personnel officers are fully occupied with interviewing applicants.

Murmur personnel officers at most companies, "If only written tests decided successful applicants, like with public servants."

Companies, for their part, have criteria by which to select students. One example is that they may rely on a commonly accepted ranking of universities to evaluate the scholastic ability of students, because a school's deviation value shows the capability of students of "brand universities" to do the jobs they are given. It is proof of their past performance.

Past performance counts a lot when companies slash their job offers due to recession. First to be affected by such axing are female students and graduates of new universities.

In this sense, fortunate students graduate when business is booming. More often than not, some students stay on in school or go to the postgraduate level because they cannot find an attractive job. But in few cases does such a choice pay off.

Some observers, however, disagree that the present employment woes signify a serious job shortage. Students can find jobs if they are really determined, and can afford to be choosy about jobs because they still live in a blessed age.

Fig 3.13 Source: *Japan Update*, August 1994

sidiaries. Compulsory retirement used to be at the age of 55, but has been gradually moving towards 60 as Japanese government and industry began to grapple with the problems posed by an ageing population. However, recession in 1993–4 has occasioned a reappraisal of this policy and many companies have been using early retirement as a means of adjusting labour costs. Those regular employees who reach director level are not usually subject to any compulsory retirement age or requirement. Those who are compulsorily retired often leave their employment relatively unprovided for in terms of pension and future income and in the past many have had to take on alternative employment in retirement, often in a sector of the economy in which terms and conditions of employment are relatively poor. Regular employees are sometimes 'lent' or relocated to subsidiary organisations in their last years and sometimes found a job for the first couple of years of their retirement. It is argued by many, for example Komiya[125], that the guarantee of lifetime employment for regular employees is becoming increasingly difficult to fulfil in the face of pressures such as recession, rapid technological and structural change and increasing longevity. Indeed, in 1994 there are an increasing number of instances of large companies beginning to grapple with the problems of overmanning among white-collar workers, and some companies are introducing freezes on recruitment and cutting back on part-time workers.

A number of large manufacturing companies such as Toyota and Sony are discussing the need for greater labour force flexibility, and the introduction of fixed-term contract employees among the ranks of the traditional salarymen. Toyota has announced an experimental one-year contract system for designers, the insecurity of such contracts being compensated by higher salaries. Toyota is aiming at having 10 per cent of its salarymen on such contracts. In July 1994 Matsushita announced plans to reduce its administrative staff by 30 per cent (6 000 people) by 1996 at the same time as Sony was announcing its plan to close down a plant in Japan.

Regular employees are moved around the organisation; they are not considered as specialists, are trained within the company and as part of their reward for this loyalty and flexibility are paid and promoted very much according to their seniority or length of service. This mobility within the organisation is of considerable assistance to those regular employees because it facilitates the development of networks that are consistent with the Confucian philosophy and are also of immense use. Reasonably successful regular employees have, in the past, known that not only did they have job security from the lifetime guarantee, but also that their pay would continue to increase, often into their 50s, and that they would be likely to reach certain grades or ranks of management by certain ages. Whitehill[126] describes this process in some detail. The very lack of functional specialism is nowadays a further factor which is perhaps encouraging the gradual breakdown of the lifetime employment system, since technological advances are creating shortages of appropriately qualified engineers who are having to be recruited at reasonably senior levels from other organisations and other countries. As the complexity of production increases, the traditional salaryman may become less and less useful. The need, or at least perceived need, to incorporate individual merit or performance into the systems for determining reward and promotability are also factors that might advance the erosion of these traditional practices.

As with lifetime employment, we have seen in 1993 and early 1994 some large, household-name manufacturing companies introducing payment systems linking pay with performance or individual merit. Nissan is putting 3000 managers onto a performance-related pay scheme. Fujitsu and Honda are other examples.

Nevertheless, the practices of lifetime employment and seniority-based pay and promotion are very well-established in the major enterprises and groups, and are also consistent with the cultural traditions and values described previously. They may, therefore, prove very resilient (see Fig. 3.14).

Consensus decision making and enterprise unionism are pillars or dimensions of the system that we examine in later sections.

As has been indicated above, there is debate about the likelihood of these traditions continuing; additionally, there is considerable debate about the extent to which some of the popularly promoted conceptions of employees' values and behaviour are myth or reality. For example, certainly in Europe, Japanese employees are popularly viewed as loyal, industrious, committed and relatively content or satisfied, in many cases more so than the European or American equivalent. Increasingly research evidence is casting doubts on these assumptions.

Briggs[127] reviews some of these, indicating that the Japanese exhibit less job satisfaction than their British and American counterparts, they are more discontented with their jobs after technologically induced change, they feel their jobs to be less of an accomplishment, they show less pride in their firm than their American

Japanese companies squeeze their white collar workers

The tradition of jobs for life is forcing Japan's bosses to look at novel ways of getting more out of their office workers, writes **Emiko Terazono**

In Europe and the US companies simply cut staff. But Japan – where the tradition of lifetime employment remains deeply ingrained – the inexorable global trend towards flatter corporate hierarchies is posing an awkward challenge.

So far, the restructuring of Japan's business sector has focused mainly on cutting production lines and paring manufacturing costs. But during the past few months attention has switched, as it has elsewhere in the world, to the difficult issue of how to reduce the many layers of white collar workers.

The methods chosen by the Japanese have been necessarily different from those employed by western counterparts.

Some of Japan's blue chip companies have been forced to announce sackings and early retirement plans. But the public outcry has been so great that others are now trying to find new ways to increase the efficiency of their existing white collar staff without getting rid of them.

Some companies, for example, have tried to deal with the problem by shifting unwanted employees to subsidiaries or to smaller client companies. Others, such as the leading consumer electronics company Sony, are trying to introduce a more Japanese solution through comprehensive reorganisation schemes.

"For the first time in decades, Japanese businesses must rethink their functional priorities," says Shintaro Hori, director of Bain & Company Japan, the management consultancy.

Sony's plan, announced in March, is intended to tackle a bureaucracy which appears to have been seriously hampering the company's decision making.

The company has therefore reorganised its 27 departments and sales divisions into eight internal "companies" and cut the number of subdivisions and departments from 580 to 450. Sony believes this move will help to speed up internal communications and avoid duplication of projects in separate divisions.

Sony is typical of Japanese companies which concentrated on manufacturing efficiency while allowing executive grades to spiral out of control during the 1980s.

For instance, the consumer electronics company's manufacturing headcount increased by just 6 per cent during the eight years to 1992, but the ranks of its white collar personnel swelled by 139 per cent over the same period. Matsushita Electric Industrial, another large Japanese consumer electronics company, cut the size of its blue collar workforce by 24 per cent in this time, while its white collar staff rose by 47 per cent.

However, given the continued decline in corporate earnings and the lack of further room to cut production costs, companies are now finding that their bloated management bureaucracies are proving an unacceptable burden. The competitive disadvantage was illustrated by a Japan Productivity Centre survey in 1992, which found that Japanese manufacturing companies would have to eliminate 39 per cent of their head count to reach overall US productivity levels per employee.

Moreover, until recently, Japanese consumers indirectly subsidised low white collar productivity through higher prices for goods and services. However, the recent pressure on prices, arising from the slump in consumer confidence and new attitudes among shoppers towards discount retailing, have squeezed profit margins, thereby eliminating the "fat" which effectively subsidised inefficient performance.

Matsushita, which also implemented its corporate reorganisation last February, will move 300 administrative staff to its sales divisions, and reduce its 48 business divisions to 10. Susumu Ishihara, director of Matsushita, says the layers of administrative managers had caused the company to misread the market and to miss profit opportunities.

To measure its rise in productivity, the company has pledged to increase its ratio of pre-tax profits to sales from the current 1.4 per cent to 5 per cent over the next three years. Similarly, Sony is also pushing its managers for more efficient use

of capital. "Each company president will be responsible for not only the profits and losses, but also for the balance sheets of the organisation, including the return on equity," says Tamotsu Iba, Sony's executive deputy president who masterminded the company's reorganisation plan.

While some companies are trying to raise white collar productivity through structural changes, some are placing stricter quality requirements on their managers.

Honda, the automobile maker, recently announced that it would place a time limit on managerial posts. Starting from June, if a manager fails to be promoted within 12 years, he or she will be forced to a non-managerial post without subordinate staff.

The plan has provoked criticism among the Japanese media and business analysts, but Honda says that it is trying to provide more opportunities for its younger staff and to improve the productivity of its older managers. According to the company: "It's tough on the older workers but the younger employees are welcoming the move."

Spurred by this productivity drive, more and more Japanese companies and employees realise that the old definition of office work is no longer valid.

Tasks such as writing reports and filling forms have been traditionally regarded as office work, but the concept of white collar workers actually adding value to products or services has been absent.

Hori points out that Japan's business leaders have first to define what they mean by productivity of office work, set targets for improving it, and try to add value through strategic planning by companies and industries.

Ultimately, business leaders will need to set new ground rules for employees, as the traditional social contract breaks down. In the past companies guaranteed workers a path up the corporate hierarchy in return for loyalty and service. In situations where "bucho" or division managers find themselves losing their titles and becoming ordinary staff, companies need to map out a new direction for them.

In the meantime, more companies may have to face up to the inevitable – the reduction of overhead costs, western style. While many leading Japanese companies will continue to resist the concept of sacking staff, they may not achieve successful results without wielding the white collar axe.

"The magnitude of excess is too large," says Hori. "With too much organisational slack, bringing in new values is impossible to achieve in the short term."

A Sony manager's tale

Sony's reorganisation has been good news for Yoshihiko Yanagimoto, a 42-year-old general manager of one of the group's eight new in-house companies.

The reshuffle has streamlined his responsibilities, which previously included development and marketing of any sort of product linked to personal information hardware from personal computers to CD-Rom. "There was never a clear sense of direction because everyone was involved in everything," he says.

Now he is in charge of developing personal communication hardware around Magic Cap, a new communication software that integrates electronic mail, facsimile, telephones and paging systems. The other assignments he previously held have been shifted to the in-house Computer Systems Business Company.

Yanagimoto says this has allowed him to concentrate on the planning and developing of one theme. It has also meant that Sony itself is more focused on its plans in the next gen-

eration information and communications area. Meanwhile, the creation of internal "companies" has shifted power to the heads of groups from the central administrators.

"We are having to deal less with the corporate headquarters since most of the decision making is done within the [in-house] company," says Yanagimoto.

The removal of extra administrative layers has also meant that decisions made at headquarters rather than the individual internal companies are processed much more quickly than before. "I was always aware of the size of the company getting in the way of new business decisions," he says.

Sony's changes have not worked well for everyone. Unlike Yanagimoto, who has retained his old responsibilities in the same product area, and looks over the same number of subordinate staff, some managers have been given completely new assignments without staff directly under them." There are some people who are discouraged with their new mission," he says.

Fig 3.14 Source: *Financial Times*, 23 May 1994

counterparts and they show lower levels of organisational commitment. Additionally, we have the evidence referred to earlier, indicating that money is a great motivator.[128] Certainly Japanese employees do work longer hours and take fewer holidays than do employees in other developed economies, and many of them spend more time commuting to work. International comparisons show Japanese employees working between 200 and 500 hours a year more than those in other industrialised countries[129] and taking only 9 or 10 days' holiday per year (usually not all they are allowed), compared with averages of two and three times as much in Europe and America. It has been suggested in the past that this indicates that the Japanese are more industrious, loyal and committed, that they like work and have a strong sense of duty. However, the alternative view gaining credence as more research is undertaken is that the long hours and short holidays arise from a combination of it being expected and relevant to career progression, fear of leaving work before the boss, and a need for more money. The last reason is often related to people's desire to own their home and the relative expensiveness of property in Japan. Briggs[130] concludes that it is the overwhelming sense of duty, the feeling that the work must be done, which motivates the Japanese to subjugate their personal feelings and interests when and where necessary, but that this sense is culturally derived and is not akin to notions of commitment pertaining in Europe and America.

The government and its advisers have indicated their concern at the relatively low quality of life which the Japanese worker enjoys and on several occasions have announced plans to remedy the situation. In June 1992 the government announced proposals setting a goal of reducing annual hours of work by up to 500 to bring them down to around the 1800 hours per year worked in the West. This was to be achieved by 1996 and progress is obviously being made, since average working hours fell in 1992 to 1970 p.a. Government set an example to the private sector in 1992 by introducing regulations reducing working hours to 40 per week by 1994. The proposals put together by the Economic Council also called for cheaper housing nearer to places of work and better leisure facilities. These proposals were consistent with Prime Minister Miyazawa's recommendation that Japan's economic system should be transformed from one putting efficiency and economic growth first to one which gives greater consideration to fairness. Cynics might argue that these proposals had little to do with promoting fairness and a better quality of work life, and were really motivated by

Japan's need to expand domestic demand, particularly in the service and leisure sectors.

Taking the issue of fairness or egalitarianism further, it has often been claimed, that consistent with the dominant cultural values which emphasise the group rather than the individual and service rather than reward, there is a relative egalitarianism within Japanese companies when it comes to salaries and differentials, with presidents of companies receiving salaries only about seven or eight times those of new recruits. This compares favourably with the situation found in the West, where multiples of 50 or more are not unusual. What must also be borne in mind, however, is that massive perks and expense accounts are available for senior levels of enterprise management. Further detail of the components of typical pay and benefits packages is included in the later section on collective bargaining.

Australia

The context

Australia, a former British colony and currently a member of the British Commonwealth, is the smallest continent. It is one of the largest countries in the world, approximately 85 per cent of the size of the United States, but has a population of only approximately 17.5 million. There are therefore large expanses of thinly populated country.

Traditionally, Australia has had a relatively small industrial and manufacturing sector, importing many manufactured items and exporting largely unprocessed commodities including wheat, wool, iron ore and coal. The service sector is relatively large, exceeding 70 per cent, with agriculture employing 5.5 per cent and industry 25 per cent.[131] For many years, Australian manufacturing industry was protected to some extent by economic policies which erected tariff barriers against cheaper foreign imports. Unfortunately, the relative cosiness of this situation did not encourage employers to pay sufficient attention to production methods, costs and technology, and the international competitiveness of Australian manufacturers has been eroded. However, protectionism did facilitate the maintenance of relatively low levels of unemployment, and it also probably accounts in part for the relatively large degree of foreign ownership of Australian organisations. The balance of manufacturing trade moved into deficit in the 1980s, commodity prices fell and the economy slipped into recession. From the mid-1980s onwards, much attention has been given to the need to regenerate and reconstruct both industry and the economy, and these debates encouraged the parties to the human resource system to reconsider some of their traditional viewpoints, approaches and practices.

During the period after 1983, the Labour government sought to enter into partnership with both trade unions and employers so that economic and social objectives could be agreed and encouraged. However, while a number of 'accords' were agreed between government and trade unions, employers generally found such agreements more problematic. We return to this in later sections.

The 'accords' reached were problematic also since, in its desire to make industry more efficient and competitive, the government often sought union agreement to wage restraint at the same time as encouraging industrial policies and practices that inevitably threatened employment. The worldwide recession of the early 1990s also added to the difficulties of maintaining employment levels.

Nevertheless, some successes were achieved, and in the May 1994 budget statement the federal government estimated price inflation to be running at an acceptable rate of 2 per cent for 1993–4, and 2.25 per cent for 1994–5. Gross domestic product (GDP) grew 4 per cent in 1993[132] and the Australia Bureau of Statistics (ABS) figures for early 1994 showed GDP rising at an annual rate of 5 per cent. However, unemployment was another story – in April/May 1994 the rate was in excess of 10 per cent and government predictions were that, without intervention, it would remain above 7 per cent for the rest of the decade, even assuming a 3.5 per cent p.a. increase in GDP. Much of this unemployment was structural and long term.

Hofstede's research[133] found Australians to have high levels of individualism and relatively low ratings on the power distance dimension, indicating a strong belief in individual initiative with people doing things for themselves, and a belief in everyone being equal allied to a moderate belief in the Protestant work ethic, a willingness to disagree with authority and engage in co-operative and consultative arrangements. Ratings on the masculinity dimension were moderately high and on the uncertainty avoidance dimension slightly low, indicating a moderate degree of emphasis on money and material items as rewards for achievement, and a willingness to take risks allied to a tendency to take each day as it comes. Ronen and Shenkar[134] developed clusters of countries exhibiting similar cultures and located Australia into the Anglo cluster, including both the UK and the US.

There is a relatively large public sector incorporating government and public services operating at federal, state and local levels, as well as a number of business activities. Employment in the public sector comprises nearly a quarter of total civilian employment. Female participation rates have increased quite rapidly in the 1980s[135] with concentrations in the service sector and administrative and clerical occupational groups. There has been some equal opportunities legislation.[136]

As indicated above, government is undertaken at several levels and political power is relatively devolved. The role of federal government is circumscribed by the constitution which is interpreted by the High Court, and constitutional change is by referendum. At federal level, there are two houses of parliament, the House of Representatives which proposes legislative and economic policy, and the Senate which amends, approves or rejects this. Rarely have governments had a majority in both houses. There are considerable powers devolved to state level and this does result in legislative and policy differences between states. Government has tended to be either conservative (nationalistic and liberal) or socialist, the latter having close ties with the trade unions. As mentioned above, the Labour party has now (mid-1994) been continuously in power at federal level since 1983.

An introduction to the system of HRM

The most distinctive feature of the system in Australia is the extent to which it has used compulsory arbitration to determine main terms and conditions of employment. The Australian Industrial Relations Commission (AIRC) at federal level, which was created by the 1988 Industrial Relations Act and replaced the Conciliation and Arbitration Commission, is mirrored in each of the states and in some specific industries. The role of the various 'award'-making bodies has been legally prescribed and they have been able to intervene and make awards only if certain criteria are met, the judiciary being the final arbiters on disputes concerning eligibility and applicability. The main subject matter of awards has traditionally been substantive, but there are examples of 'procedural' awards; for example, the Termination, Change and Redundancy Decision 1984 established procedures to be followed with respect to informing and consulting with employees and unions and giving notice in circumstances of plant closure. In nearly all cases, these award-making bodies have a conciliation role in addition to arbitration, but it is the arbitration role which has been prominent.

Collective bargaining has always occurred between the parties, but access to legally binding arbitration has often proved attractive to one or more parties depending on their perceptions of relative bargaining power. It is often argued that the availability of the compulsory arbitration system hampered the development of effective alternative mechanisms for the parties involved freely and jointly to determine terms and conditions of employment, both at industry and workplace level. In the latter instance, this lack of development has made it more difficult to address issues of new and changing technology, production methods and work organisation, and their implications for productivity, efficiency and competitiveness, and to do so at the most appropriate level. Over the last decade, these issues have achieved much greater importance and prominence as the parties have tried to grapple with the need to become competitive in the face of declining protectionism and increasing international competition.

Other features of the system include a multiplicity of trade unions and employers' organisations. The trade union movement, with its craft origins, exhibits the influence of the trade union movement in Britain and structurally still reflects many characteristics of that movement, although efforts have been and are still being made to restructure. Employers and their organisations have had difficulty in achieving coherence and unity.

Over the last decade in particular, the Labour government at federal level has sought to adopt tripartite and corporatist approaches to many of the economic, social and industrial problems and challenges. Employers have often been unwilling or unable to participate in such arrangements at a macro level. Gospel and Palmer[137] argue that the system of compulsory arbitration, particularly as it applied at the level of the industry with the various interests being incorporated into administrative structures, is an example of mesa-corporatism.

Relationships between employer and employee have historically been conflictual, with management adopting a unitarist and individualistic approach while employees and their unions have tended to see things from a pluralist, collectivist perspective. There are examples in recent years of employers seeking to involve employees more in work-related decision making using essentially consultative and work-group- or team-based techniques. The trade unions have tended to treat such initiatives with scepticism, seeing them not so much as evidence of a widespread desire on the part of management to enhance the degree of participation or democracy within the firm, but as desperate attempts to achieve improvements in productivity, quality and efficiency. Government has also encouraged greater employee participation, usually in the form of consultation, as another means of improving productivity, quality and efficiency.

There is considerable concentration of employment and there are relatively few large employing organisations, which naturally tend to be located in the centres of population. The Australian Workplace Industrial Relations Survey (AWIRS)[138] found that the top 1 per cent of employing organisations employed 24 per cent of all employees. Therefore, large employing organisations often operate in monopolistic and oligopolistic markets and there is a relatively high incidence of foreign multinational ownership. These factors all influence the management of human resources – the policies, practices and style.

CONCILIATION AND ARBITRATION

The legislative base for this dominant process was set in 1904 in the Commonwealth Conciliation and Arbitration Act. The federal legislation provided for trade unions to register under the Act with the Industrial Registrar and once registered they became entitled to make claims on behalf of employees in the industry. They also became entitled to have access to conciliation and compulsory arbitration. The essence of the system remains today, although it is under attack from the 1993 Accord. Employers and their organisations and trade unions are required to register in order to obtain corporate status. The 1988 Industrial Relations Act and an amendment in 1990 varied the traditional federal legislative requirements for registration of trade unions by specifying that unions applying for registration must have 1000 or more members (increased to 10 000 in 1991) and be organised on an industrial basis. These moves were designed to encourage structural change and rationalisation within the union movement, but were the subject of a Confederation of Australian Industry (CAI) complaint to the International Labour Organisation that the new requirements breached the Convention on freedom of association. Once registered, a union or employer has right of access to the appropriate arbitration commission or tribunal. Traditionally, the commission or tribunal has sought to conciliate a voluntary settlement, but if this failed, they were empowered to make an award that was then legally binding on the parties.

Trade unions will not be able to register if there is already one to which employees could conveniently belong, and the arbitration tribunals and commission have only been able to intervene if the subject matter of the dispute fell into an appropriate, legislatively determined category. The law has been interpreted by the High Court. The role of the commissions has been to prevent and settle disputes, with the power to intervene on their own initiative in the public interest. The commissions are autonomous within the law and are not an arm of government, although governments have often sought to persuade and influence commissions and their awards. The law has required that when settling a dispute, they act according to equity and conscience and the substantial merits of the case. Normally, the arbitration process has resulted in minima being determined.

At federal level, the AIRC can strictly speaking only deal with cases involving more than one state. However and perhaps inevitably, it seems that most important cases have been made to fit this criteria when necessary.

Over the years, a system of commissions and tribunals has developed at levels below federal, their jurisdiction being limited by state, industry or some other specific and relevant dimension. It has been common for awards made at federal level to set a pattern for, but not to be binding on, commissions or tribunals elsewhere.

The AIRC has additional responsibilities for policing the implementation of awards, ruling on unfair dismissal claims and making recommendations for change in the law and conduct of industrial relations where it thinks fit.

In recent years the AIRC, under pressure from other parties, has been actively seeking to restructure the somewhat antiquated structure of awards, requiring parties to engage in productivity bargaining and encouraging a movement away from Taylorist forms of management and work organisation towards ones which enhance flexibility and efficiency. The Commission has also sought to encourage greater employee participation via the utilisation of co-operative and consultative mechanisms. The Termination, Change and Redundancy Decision of 1984 required employers to consult employees and their representatives before introducing significant changes to organisational structure or production methods, and a number of recent national wage case decisions (1987, 1988, 1989 and 1991) have also contained recommendations that employers should make greater use of consultation.

Many awards made at all levels have been ratifications or endorsements of agreements between the parties, sometimes as a product of conciliation, and thereby given the force of law. Commissions, however, have been able to not endorse such agreements and impose their own award.

Criticisms of the system include that it has tended to emphasise substantive issues, arguably at the expense of the development of coherent and adequate procedures for negotiation and disputes and grievance resolution. It has inclined the system and participating institutions and structures towards centralism and overly complex and bureaucratic processes. The trade unions have in many cases not developed adequate workplace representation for members; the system has not facilitated the linking of pay to productivity and efficiency and has not been sufficiently flexible.

Advantages of the system may have been that it has facilitated trade union recognition and growth. Employees have been given a mechanism which they could use to combat the potentially exploitative power of the employer, and social need has been incorporated into wage rate determination (the 1907 Commonwealth Court of Conciliation and Arbitration ruling setting the standard of basic wages at a level intended to be sufficient to meet the normal needs of a family of five). Employers have been provided with a mechanism inhibiting competition between them on wages in times of labour shortage.

The 1983 Labour government established a Committee of Review into industrial relations law and systems which reported in 1985 (the Hancock Committee of Review). In their report, the Committee recommended retention of the Conciliation and Arbitration Commission, although they suggested that greater emphasis should be given to conciliation and that the dual role of the existing Commission should be split between an Australian Industrial Relations Commission and a Labour Court. It also suggested further integration of state and federal systems, and that arbitration awards should incorporate dispute-settling procedures. Many of these recommendations were encompassed in the 1988 Industrial Relations Act. As noted above and as we elaborate later, the system does currently seem to be under threat from the government Australian Council of Trades Unions (ACTU) agreement known as the 1993 Accord.

US

The context

The United States of America (USA) is the largest of the developed economies, with a population of 252 million and a civilian labour force of 126 million in

1990[139], expected to reach 141 million by 2000.[140] There has been very rapid growth in both the size of the civilian labour force and civilian employment in recent decades, e.g. the civilian labour force grew by 35 per cent between 1972 and 1986[141] and total civilian employment came quite close to doubling between 1963 and 1990, from 68 million to 126 million. Between early 1992 and June 1994 5.3 million new jobs were created, an increase of nearly 5 per cent.[142]

One of the distinguishing features of the US population and labour force is the substantial diversity of ethnic and racial minority groupings, and it is these groups that are expected to provide the majority of labour force growth through the 1990s. At the end of the 1980s the black, Hispanic and Asian groups comprised approximately 12, 8 and 3 per cent respectively of the labour force.[143]

The population is ageing and the youth share of the labour force (16–24 years) is projected to drop to 16 per cent by 2000 from 20 per cent in 1986.[144] This implies that the age distribution of the labour force is likely to shift in favour of older workers (55+), although this will depend on the extent to which they can be persuaded to remain as active labour force participants.

The US economy is furthest along the road of deindustrialisation, with a service sector accounting for 71.8 per cent of total civilian employment by 1991 and projected to continue increasing its share of employment. Agricultural employment accounted for 3 per cent and manufacturing and other industrial activities for 25.3 per cent.[145] Manufacturing industry has been staffed predominantly and traditionally by white workers, whereas the service sector is much more the province of females and ethnic minorities.

Female labour force participation rates are relatively high in the US, the 1993 figure being 69 per cent[146], and it is projected that by the turn of the century women will constitute 47 per cent of the total labour force.[147] Equal opportunities in employment, equal pay for work of comparable worth, gender and other minority group discrimination have all become significant issues, with substantial legislative intervention in recent decades. These issues are likely to continue to be in the forefront of the concerns of employers, government and trade unions in forthcoming years.

During the 1980s unemployment tended to vary between 5 per cent and 7.5 per cent. Having risen in the early years of the 1990s, by the end of 1993 unemployment was beginning to fall[148] and by May 1994 it had fallen to 6 per cent.[149] The economy was growing rapidly by the end of 1993 (an annualised rate of 7 per cent in the last quarter) and, while there was some slowdown in 1994 (first quarter growth in GDP being 3.4 per cent)[150], concerns were being expressed about the dangers to inflation even though the June 1994 rate was still a satisfactory 2.5 per cent.[151]

There are two main political parties in the USA: the Democrats and the Republicans. While both parties have subscribed to the dominant cultural dimensions of individualism and relative masculinity[152], thereby reinforcing the base of capitalism and wealth creation, nevertheless there are differences between them, with the Republicans generally being further to the political right and the Democrats occupying the centre-left ground. Certainly Democrats generally have the support of the trade union movement and are more willing to intervene in order to achieve objectives related to social and economic justice. The original civil rights legislation was enacted by Democrats in the early 1960s. The Democrat administration elected in 1992 quickly enacted legislation requiring employers to make provision for employees to be able to take maternity leave and leave to look after sick children and/or dependent relatives – the Maternity and Family Leave Act 1993. However, and perhaps unexpectedly, in 1994 the Democrats also proposed changes to the welfare system which seem likely to have most effect on single and long-term unemployed parents. The intention is to break the cycle of dependency through additional spending on childcare, education and training allied to cessation of benefit after two years. After this period the unemployed parent would be expected to undertake publicly subsidised work at the minimum wage rate and forego benefit. Critics argue that the proposals will force single parents out of the home and do nothing to assist the young unemployed and unskilled who lose benefit after six months. It would be unwise to characterise the Democrats as the party either of the left or of the labour movement. The resurgence of Republicans in the late 1994 elections seems likely to significantly impede the Clinton administration in pursuit of any 'left-wing' social or employment objectives.

An introduction to the system of HRM

The US system is characterised by the early development of large-scale employment in factories, mass-production technology, and the principles of scientific management, work design and organisation. Employers committed to the retention of their right to manage and fiercely hostile to collective organisation and representation by their employees eagerly implemented these techniques. These and the disastrous economic depression of the early 1930s served to create an environment in which a government somewhat more friendly towards organised labour intervened in order to regulate the relationship between employer, employees and their representative organisations – the trade unions.

Ever since, the system in the US has been buttressed by a legally backed regulatory framework, which supports both employer prerogative and collective organisation. Collective bargaining has been the main means of resolving conflict and freely entering into legally binding contracts specifying the main substantive terms and conditions of employment. Underlying this system is the notion that employees have no legitimate interest in the management of the enterprise, but they may have an interest in the distribution of the benefits generated.

Employers have remained largely hostile towards trade unionism and for this among other reasons trade unionism has not achieved the membership levels and influence that might be expected given the early legislative support and protection. In recent decades trade union membership has been decreasing as the industrial sector of the economy has declined and as employers and managers have introduced new technology, new working methods and in many cases also new approaches towards human resource management, approaches which they argue are more co-operative in nature and which encourage and facilitate greater employee participation, involvement and commitment, often outside traditional trade union channels. Certainly the US has a tradition of conflictual relationships between employers and employees, and there are examples in recent years of managements pursuing specific union-avoidance policies.

Governments have generally sought not to regulate terms and conditions of employment, although there are examples of such substantive intervention, as there are also examples of governments and the judicial system intervening to create and protect employee rights, particularly in the areas of equality and discrimination, and the rights of trade union members.

As indicated in the preceding section, the US is a society in which individualism and masculinity are strong cultural dimensions. Such dimensions are consistent with capitalism and an emphasis on individual enterprise and wealth creation, and are probably not helpful to the collective cause of trade unionism or to any other form of collective representation or participation. These dimensions are also likely partly to explain why trade unions have traditionally pursued a distributive approach and concentrated on terms and conditions of employment.

It must be remembered that the majority of employees do not have their terms and conditions of employment determined through collective bargaining and are only relatively marginally protected by federal or state legislation. The employment-at-will doctrine has formed the basis of the employment relationship and this doctrine really affords no protection to employees who can, in accordance with it, have their employment terminated at any time and for any or no reason; they are employed at the will of the employer. In recent years we have witnessed the development of another doctrine, the job-as-property doctrine, which argues that employees develop property rights in their job. Once accepted the employment relationship becomes 'protected' by the 14th Amendment to the Constitution which specifies that 'Nor shall any state deprive any person of life, liberty, or property, without due process of law'. Increasingly employees have sought to use this latter doctrine to combat the former via wrongful discharge suits.

Kochan et al.[153] in their particularly influential work postulate a transformation of the system of human resource management in the 1980s. They characterise the traditional model as one in which management retained prerogative over business strategy and policy making, engaged in the collective negotiation of binding contracts on terms and conditions of employment, relied on quasi-judicial grievance procedures to resolve disputes during the contract term and afforded seniority rights a crucial role in determining work allocation, career paths and lay-offs. This traditional model they label the 'New Deal' model.

Kochan et al.[154] suggest and to some extent recommend a change from the 'New Deal' model to the 'New Industrial Relations' model, which they argue is more suitable given the new environment and its associated pressures for efficiency and flexibility. The new industrial relations model is characterised by a much greater degree of co-operation between management and union, with unions having a legitimate consultative role in the formulation of business strategy on issues such as investment and technological change. This new mood of co-operation and collaboration at strategic level is accompanied by the expanding use of enabling agreements rather than legally binding contracts and, at workplace level, a greater willingness by both parties to experiment with flexibility and co-operative approaches on operational issues.

SUMMARY

HRM decisions are not made in isolation, but a degree of contingency exists between the making of HRM policy choices and an interplay of important contextual factors at both a national and international level.

At an international level, economic and technological changes, and an intensification of competition, are promoting the need for adaptable and flexible organisational responses. Yet, within each nation, distinct structural, institutional and cultural patterns and forms continue to set the parameters for the detail of the interaction between HRM 'stakeholders'.

DISCUSSION QUESTIONS

1 What forms of organisational flexibility exist? Why are organisations having to become more flexible?
2 What effects do multinationals have on domestic systems of HRM? How do they affect the power of employees?

3 What action should employers take in response to the demographic 'time bomb'?
4 How can 'cultural' and 'ideological' perspectives explain the distinct features of national HRM contexts?

NOTES AND REFERENCES

1. Poole M (1986) *Industrial Relations: Origins and Patterns of National Diversity*, Routledge and Kegan Paul, London, Boston, Henley, p.13

2. Sorge A and Streeck W (1988) 'Industrial relations and technical change: the case for an extended perspective' in Hyman R and Streeck W (eds), *New Technology and Industrial Relations*, Blackwell, Oxford, pp.19–47

3. Manzolini L (1993) 'Environmental dynamics and the organisational innovation process: Implications for human resource management in Italy' in Tyson S, Lawrence P, Poirson P, Manzolini L, Soler Vicente C, *Human Resource Management in Europe, Strategic Issues and Cases*, Kogan Page, London, pp.133–5

4. Ferner A and Hyman R (1992) *Industrial Relations in the New Europe*, Blackwell, Oxford, pp.xviii and xix

5. Bratton J and Gold J (1994) *Human Resource Management: Theory and practice*, Macmillan, London, p.61

6. Manzolini L op. cit. p.135

7. Ibid, p.133

8. Ibid, p.132

9. Ferner A and Hyman R (1992) *Industrial Relations in the New Europe*, Blackwell, Oxford, p.xvii

10. Ibid

11. Edwards P, Hall M, Hyman R, Marginson P, Sisson K, Waddington J and Winchester D (1992) in Ferner A and Hyman R, *Industrial Relations in the New Europe*, Blackwell, Oxford, pp.1–3

12. Reported in *Financial Times*, 8 March 1994

13. Hudson Institute (1987) *Workforce 2000*, a report prepared for the United States Department of Labor, Indianapolis, p.79

14. Reported in *Financial Times*, 8 March 1994

15. *Skill Shortages in Europe* (1990) Industrial Research and Development Advisory Committee of the Commission of the European Communities, p.8

16. Springer B and Springer S (1990) 'Human Resource Management in the United States – Celebration of its Centenary' in Pieper R (ed), *Human Resource Management: An international comparison*, de Gruyter, Berlin, New York

17. Hudson Institute (1987) *Workforce 2000*, a report prepared for the United States Department of Labor, Indianapolis, p.xx

18. Reported in *Financial Times*, 8 March 1994

19. Springer B and Springer S (1990) 'Human Resource Management in the United States – Celebration of its Centenary' in Pieper R (ed), *Human Resource Management: An international comparison*, de Gruyter, Berlin, New York, p.55

20. Commission of the European Communities (1989) Employment in Europe, Luxembourg

21. Healy G and Kraithman D, 'Patterns of Labor Market Participation in the United Kingdom and European Context: Forces and Constraints in Relation to Gender', Research in Personnel and Human Resource Management, supplement 3, pp.239–56

22. Ibid, p.242

23. Ibid, p.243

24. Bratton J and Gold J (1994) *Human Resource Management: Theory and Practice*, MacMillan, London, p.43

25. Sisson K, Waddington J and Whitson C (1992) 'The Structure of Capital in the EC: the Size of Companies and the Implications for Industrial Relations', *Warwick Papers in Industrial Relations*, 38, Coventry, IRRU

26. Ferner A and Hyman R (1992) *Industrial Relations in the New Europe*, Blackwell, Oxford, pp.xviii

27. See appendix 3

28. See appendix 4

29. See appendix 7

30. See appendix 2

31. See appendix 6

32. *Financial Times* 7 July 1994. See also appendix 8.

33. *Financial Times* 22 April 1994. See also appendix 3.

34. *Financial Times* 5 May 1994. See also appendix 4.

35. *Financial Times* 28 June 1994

36. CDU – Christlich-Demokratische Union – Christian Democrat Union

37. FDP – Freie Demokratische Partei – Free Democratic Party

38. SPD – Sozialdemokratische Partei Deutschlands – Social Democratic Party

39. Hofstede G (1980) 'Motivation: Leadership and Organisation – Do American Theories Apply Abroad?' in Lane H W and DiStefano J J *International Management Behaviour* (1992). PSW Kent pp.98–122. See also Table 1.3.

40. See appendix 1

41. See appendix 6

42. See appendix 2

43. See appendix 10

44. See appendices 8 and 7

45. *Financial Times* 1 July 1994

46. See appendix 4

47. *Financial Times* 12 May 1994

48. *Financial Times* 15 March 1994

49. Hofstede G op. cit. See also Table 1.3

50. Adapted from Poirson P (1993) 'Human Resource Management in France' in S Tyson *et al.*, *Human Resource Management in Europe*, Kogan Page, p.74

51. See appendices 5 and 6

52. Caplan J 'It's the climate that counts – Personnel Management in Italy' *Personnel Management*, April 1992

53. See appendix 7

54. Modigliani F 'The year of the great opportunity', *Financial Times* 5 May 1993

55. See appendix 4

56. See appendix 2

57. Hofstede G, op. cit. See also Table 1.3.

58. Caplan J op. cit.

59. Ferner A and Hyman R 'Italy between political exchange and micro corporatism', in Ferner A and Hyman R (eds), *Industrial Relations in the New Europe*, Blackwell, p.525

60. Modigliani op. cit.

61. Visser J (1992) 'The Netherlands, the end of an era and the end of a system' in Ferner A and Hyman R (eds) *Industrial Relations in the New Europe*, Blackwell, p.324

62. See appendix 5

63. See appendix 6

64. See appendix 10

65. See appendix 2

66. See appendix 7

67. *Financial Times* 29 April 1994 quoting data produced by the Central Bureau for Statistics. See also appendix 3

68. *Financial Times* 14 May 1994

69. Hofstede G op. cit. See also Table 1.3.

70. Ronen S (1986) *Comparative and Multi-national Management,* Wiley

71. Visser J 'The Netherlands, The end of an era and the end of a system', Ferner A and Hyman R (eds) *Industrial Relations in the New Europe*, Blackwell, p.32

72. Ramondt J in Blum A A, *International Handbook of Industrial Relations* p.398

73. See appendix 1

74. See appendix 5

75. See appendix 6

76. See appendix 2

77. See appendix 7

78. *Financial Times* 6 July 1994

79. See appendices 3 and 4

80. See appendix 7

81. See appendix 4

82. OECD forecast quoted in *Financial Times* 1 July 1994

83. Kjellberg A (1992) 'Sweden: can the model survive?' in Ferner A and Hyman R, *Industrial Relations in the New Europe*, Blackwell, p.93

84. *Financial Times* 1 July 1994

85. See appendix 6

86. Hofstede G, op. cit. See also Table 1.3.

87. Named after Trade Union economists Rehn G and Meidner R

88. See appendix 1

89. See appendix 7

90. Quoted in *Financial Times* 14 July 1994

91. Department of Employment Statistics quoted in *Guardian* 5 February 1994. 1978 13.4 million male employees, September 1993 10.9 million male employees.

92. *Employment News* February 1994

93. D.E Gazette various issues

94. Op. cit. *Guardian* 5 February 1994

95. See appendix 2

96. See appendix 10

97. See appendix 6

98. *Financial Times* 16 June 1994. 12.8% for males and 5% for females. See also appendix 8

99. NIER's Statistical Appendix adapted and quoted in Kessler S and Bayliss F (1992) *Contemporary British Industrial Relations,* Macmillan, p.42

100. See appendix 3

101. Central Statistical Office quoted in the *Times* 23 August 1994

102. UK Economic Indicators quoted in *Financial Times* 14 July 1994

103. See appendix 4

104. Quoted in *Financial Times* 14 July 1994

105. Gospel H and Palmer G (1993) *British Industrial Relations*, Routledge, p.252

106. Hofstede G, op. cit. and see Table 1.3

107. See appendix 14

108. Towers B (1992) 'British Industrial Relations and Trades Unions' in Towers B (ed) *A Handbook of Industrial Relations Practice*, Kogan Page, p.32. Towers estimates that in 1991 TUC affiliated membership comprised 82.3% of the total compared to a figure of 91.6% for 1979

109. Milward N, Stevens M, Stuart D and Hawes WR, (1992) *The 1990 Workplace Industrial Relations Survey – First Findings*

110. Ibid.

111. Ibid.

112. Ibid.

113. Op. cit.

114. Swift R 'The rise of Japan in Prisoners of Prosperity', *New Internationalist*, May 1992

115. See appendix 2

116. See appendix 3

117. See appendix 7

118. See appendices 6 and 9

119. Equal Employment Opportunity Law, 1986

120. Briggs P (1991) 'Organisational commitment: The key to Japanese success?' in Brewster C and Tyson S, *International Comparisons in HRM*, Pitman, p.33–43

121. Hofstede G (1984) 'The cultural relativity of the quality of life concept', *Academy of Management Review*, July, p.389–98. See Table 1.3.

Hofstede G and Bond M (1988) 'The Confucius Connection: from Cultural Roots to Economic Growth', *Organisational Dynamics*, 16.4 p.4–21

'Culture's consequences. International Differences in Work Related Values', Sage Publications, 1980

122. Whitehill AM (1991) *Japanese Management – Tradition and Transition*, Routledge. p.88

123. Keiretsu – large conglomerate groups of affiliated companies comprising contractors, suppliers and customers, see Whitehill A M Ibid. p.85

124. Briggs P op. cit. p.36

125. Komiyo F 'The Law of Dismissal and Employment Practices in Japan', *IRJ* 22.1 Spring 1991

126. Whitehill A M op. cit. Chaps. 7 and 8

127. Briggs P op. cit. p.33–4

128. Hofstede G op. cit.

129. See appendix 12

130. Briggs P op. cit. pp.41–2

131. See appendix 2

132. See appendix 3

133. Hofstede G op. cit. See also Table 1.3.

134. Ronen S and Shenkar O (1985) 'Clustering Countries on Attitudinal Dimensions: A Review and Synthesis', *Academy of Management Journal*, September, pp.435–54

135. See appendix 6

136. Federal Affirmative Action (Equal Employment Opportunity for Women) Act 1986

137. Gospel H and Palmer G op. cit.

138. Callus R, Moorehead A, Cully M and Buchanan J (1991) 'Industrial Relations at Work, The Australian Workplace' *Industrial Relations Survey*, Australian Government Publishing Service

139. See appendix 1

140. Bureau of Labor Statistics: Occupational Outlook Handbook 1990–91, Edit., Bulletin 2350, April 1990

141. Ibid.

142. *Financial Times* 13 July 1994

143. Bureau of Labour Statistics op. cit.

144. Ibid.

145. See appendix 2

146. See appendix 6

147. See appendix 9. Also Bureau of Labour Statistics op. cit.

148. See appendix 7

149. Quoted in *Financial Times*, 16 June 1994

150. *Financial Times* 30 June 1994

151. *Financial Times* 13 July 1994

152. Hofstede G op. cit. See also Table 1.3.

153. Kochan T, Katz H C & McKersie, R B, The Transformation of American Industrial Relations, 1986, New York, Basic Books

154. Ibid.

FURTHER READING

Gladstone A (ed) *et al.* (1989) *Current Issues in Labour Relations: An International Perspective*, De Gruyter, Berlin, New York

Starkey K and McKinley A (1993) *Strategy and the Human Resource: Ford and the search for competitive advantage*, Blackwell, Oxford

For further reading on these 'national' contexts refer to the later chapters on individual countries.

4 · MANAGEMENT, MULTINATIONALS AND EMPLOYERS' ASSOCIATIONS

OUTLINE

● Management styles and strategies.

● The significance of multinationals and their approach to HRM.

● The role and organisation of employers' associations.

LEARNING OBJECTIVES

You should be able to:

i understand the main managerial perspectives in approaches to the employment relationship;

ii explain the main management strategies in employee relations;

iii understand the purposes of employers' associations and variations in their organisation and role in different countries;

iv appreciate the growing influence of multinational concerns in the world economy and within the domain of HRM;

v demonstrate an insight into some specific HRM approaches of multinationals, and the significance of 'Japanisation'.

INTRODUCTION

In this chapter we turn the spotlight onto a major 'stakeholder' in the employment relationship: the employer. Indeed, it may be argued that the influence of employers and management in moulding the characteristics of the employment relationship has grown in recent years, and that the growth of HRM itself is a product of an ascendant managerialism.

Multinational concerns are highly influential entities on the international HRM stage and may stimulate important cross-cultural currents in employment practices as they organise productive facilities on an international basis.

In broad terms, employers may exert influence on the employment relationship at the level of the undertaking, with individual employers acting in a quite autonomous way; or collectively, through employers' associations at an industrial or national level. As we shall see, levels of centralisation/decentralisation in the way employers organise vary from country to country.

In the first part we shall focus primarily on the level of the establishment, and consider management styles and strategies for the management of employment at that level. Variations in the importance and potency of collective employer action through employers' associations will then be considered. Consideration of the shape and nature of employer organisation reveals that underlying ideological and cultural factors within societies determine not only the dominant level for employer decision making, with, for example, corporatism and structure tending to enhance the position of industry or national-level institutions, but also the selection of appropriate management strategies.

A consideration of the role of multinationals highlights the growing significance of internationalisation in HRM decision making.

STYLES AND STRATEGIES

There is a burgeoning literature on the management of the employment relationship. For our purposes we will concentrate discussion on the range of styles and strategies which may be exhibited by management, and how underlying ideological and cultural features within different societies may necessitate different approaches to management.

A useful conceptual framework for such discussion has been provided by Fox,[1] who distinguished between 'unitary' and 'pluralistic' views of the enterprise. The unitary perspective is clearly associated with the broader ideological liberal individualistic perspective which may apply to national political level, while 'pluralism' is closely linked to the doctrine of 'liberal collectivism'. Representing these as 'ideal types', they possess the following key features:

Unitary
- Management is the only source of authority and focus of loyalty.
- There is an overriding vision of a 'team approach' with everyone pulling in the same direction.
- There is no scope for factions or opposition.
- Common goals and values unite the enterprise.
- Conflict is abnormal, arising because of organisational or personality dysfunctions, such as poor communications or the 'deviance of dissidents'.[2]
- Trade unionists are viewed as agitators, who import alien concepts into the enterprise.[3]

Pluralist
- Organisations are complex social structures formed of a plurality of potentially conflicting interest groups.[4]
- Two main interest groups, management and trade unions, prevail. These have different aims and objectives, some of which conflict and some of which coincide.
- Each interest group has an independent power base, and may 'hurt' others.
- Conflicts arising from the clash of interests are resolved, if possible, by bargaining and compromise.
- Management has to compete with other sources of leadership, and must manage competing claims and tensions.

Fox argued that the pluralistic perspective represented a more realistic view of work life, although this seems to neglect what may seem to be a natural leaning of many managers towards the unitary approach.

A more sophisticated analysis was provided by Fox in 1975[5] which distinguishes separate organisational approaches towards the management of employment.

Purcell and Sisson[6] adapt Fox's work to suggest five ideal typical styles of industrial relations management (see Table 4.1).

1. Traditional
Organisations in this category would 'forcefully oppose' trade unions[7] and their treatment of employees is often overtly exploitative.

2. Sophisticated Human Relations or Paternalists
Most of these organisations refuse to recognise trade unions. However, there is considerable investment in terms of time and money to ensure that employees do not see the need to undertake collective action. Sophisticated policies for recruitment, selection, training, counselling and high pay are used to ensure that aspirations are mostly satisfied. IBM, Hewlett-Packard and Kodak may be fitted into this category.

3. Sophisticated Moderns: Constitutional and Consultative
For these organisations, the union role is accepted by management and legitimised in specified areas of joint decision making, with the purpose of encouraging employee participation and consent. Two types of sophisticated moderns are distinguished. First, constitutionalists, which formally codify the limits of collective bargaining within binding collective agreements. This 'legalistic' approach, which clearly delineates areas of managerial prerogative, is common in North America, and Ford may fit into this category. Secondly consultors, which recognise trade unions and have well-developed collective bargaining, but this is not formally codified in collective agreements. Instead, the emphasis is on co-operative or 'integrative' bargaining supported by wide-ranging procedures for consultation and communication. ICI could fit into this category.

4. Standard Moderns: Opportunists
These organisations are essentially pragmatic and opportunistic in their approach. Such organisations mix unitary and pluralistic approaches according to changing circumstances, and a consistent set of values or assumptions is not apparent. A fire-fighting approach is taken to industrial relations management. GEC, GKN and Tube Investments may fit into this category.

Although this model clearly implies different practices and tactics in the management of human resources, it may be argued that the first two styles both reflect a unitary frame of reference, while the latter pair tend to be based on more pluralistic values.

Table 4.1 Five styles of industrial relations management

Title	Description	Most likely to occur in these circumstances	Expected role of central personnel management
Traditional	Labour is viewed as a factor of production, and employee subordination is assumed to be part of the 'natural order' of the employment relationship. Fear of outside union interference. Unionisation opposed or unions kept at arm's length.	Small owner-managed companies (or franchise operations). Product markets often highly competitive, with the firm having a low share leading to emphasis on cost-control and low profit margins.	For personnel specialists.
Sophisticated human relations or paternalists	Employees (excluding short-term contract or sub-contract labour) viewed as the company's most valuable resource. Above-average pay. Internal labour-market structures with promotion ladders are common with periodic attitude surveys used to harness employees' views. Emphasis is placed on flexible reward structures. Employee appraisal systems linked to merit awards, internal grievance, disciplinary and consultative procedures, and extensive networks and methods of communication. The aim is to inculcate employee loyalty, commitment and dependency. As a by-product, these companies seek to make it unnecessary or unattractive for staff to unionise.	American-owned, single-industry, large, financially successful firms with a high market share in growth industries (electronics/finance sector).	Strong central personnel departments developing policies to be adopted in all areas of the company.
(a) Sophisticated moderns: Consultative	Similar to the sophisticated human resource companies except that unions are recognised. The attempt is made to build 'constructive' relationships with the trade unions and incorporate them into the organisational fabric. Broad-ranging discussions are held with extensive information provided to the unions on a whole range of decisions and plans, including aspects of strategic management, but the 'right of last say' rests with management. Emphasis is also placed on techniques designed to enhance individual employee commitment to the firm and the need to change (share option schemes, profit sharing, briefing or cascade information systems, joint working parties, quality or productivity circles/councils).	British/Japanese-owned single-industry companies which are large and economically successful, often with a high market share. Companies with relatively low labour costs (process industries) often adopt this style.	Central personnel departments produce policy guidelines or precepts providing advice and central direction when required.
(b) Constitutional	Somewhat similar to the traditionalists in basic value structures but unions have been recognised for some time and accepted as inevitable. Employee relations policies centre on the need for stability, control, and the institutionalisation of conflict. Management prerogatives are defended through highly specific collective agreements, and careful attention is paid to the administration of agreements at the point of production. The importance of management control is emphasised, with the aim of minimising or neutralising union constraints on both operational (line) and strategic (corporate) management.	Single-industry companies with mass production or large-batch production requiring a large unit of operation. Labour costs form a significant proportion of total costs. Product-market conditions are often highly competitive.	Relatively strong emphasis on the central personnel auditing/control function.
Standard moderns: Opportunistic	The approach to employee relations is pragmatic. Trade unions are recognised in some or all parts of the business, often inherited with company acquisition. Employee relations are viewed as the responsibility of operational management at unit and/or division level. The importance attached to employee-relations policies changes in the light of circumstances. When union power is high and product and labour markets buoyant, or when legislative needs dictate, negotiation and consultation is emphasised. Fashionable employee-relations techniques are adopted over short periods as panaceas. When union power is low, or product markets become unfavourable, or major technical change threatens existing practices, unions are 'rolled back', and management seeks to regain its prerogatives. There can be marked differences of approach between establishments or divisions and between various levels in the hierarchy.	Most common in conglomerate multi-product companies which grew by acquisition and diversification, especially in the engineering and heavy manufacturing industries with long traditions of unionisation.	Relatively weak central personnel departments with personnel specialists at operating-unit level having a fire-fighting role, reacting to union claims and the impact of labour legislation. The personnel function tends to have a chequered history: sometimes strong, sometimes weak.

Source: J Purcell and A Gray (1986) 'Corporate personnel departments and the management of industrial relations: two case studies in ambiguity', *Journal of Management Studies*, March pp. 214–15. Reprinted by permission of Blackwell.

The much vaunted move towards HRM-type approaches has implied greater professionalism and sophistication in the formulation and application of HR policies, therefore it may be mooted that HRM can be allied with sophisticated paternalist or sophisticated modern styles, depending on the status of unions within employing organisations.

These typologies may be viewed as representing strategic choices which may be taken by organisations defining their approach towards managing the employment relationship. Poole, however,[8] makes the useful point that culture and ideology have a bearing on managerial strategies and styles. In the absence of authoritative cross-national research in this area, Poole adopts an illustrative approach, examining the three distinctive national cultures of Japan, the US and Nigeria.

Poole argues, in the case of Japan, that the modified Confucian world view which prevailed in the late nineteenth century is vital in explaining 'benevolent paternalism' in the Japanese system of industrial relations. Drawing on the work of Dore[9], Poole states:

> Assuming original virtue [rather] than original sin it [the modified Confucian world view] encouraged employers to evoke moral appeals to authority and to stress the efficiency of benevolence. And it also helped to shape personal objectives (the desire of private industrialists and managers to appear to be good moral citizens) and economic goals (such as public reputation as well as greater profits and efficiency and faster expansion). Indeed, the patterns of institutionalisation which emerged in industrial Japan reflected a creative synthesis of new elements which conformed to cultural predispositions, the direct borrowing from abroad in certain circumstances and, in other aspects again, the institutional continuation of pre-industrial practices.[10]

Turning to the US, Poole finds that 'individualism' in the wider culture and prevalent private enterprise commitments[11] explain, in part, a pronounced 'unitary' perspective, which is evident in union avoidance practices and the deployment of sophisticated human relations and human resourcing techniques, such as careful screening of potential applicants prior to selection, and advanced systems of communication and information sharing.

In the case of Nigeria, Poole points towards an 'authoritarian but people centred African arbitrary paternalistic style'. This is reflected in an 'informal and frequently perfunctory treatment of trade union demands' by management, and a tendency for trade unions 'to strike over situations which are merely mis-understandings'.[13] Poole also identified 'persistent high handedness in the treatment of the workforce'.[12]

Poole's analysis, which demonstrates the importance of culture, may be complemented by Gallie's comparative study of oil refineries in France and Britain in 1978. This found that industrial relations in these countries were 'firmly locked in the institutional patterns of their societies'[13] which reflected differing cultural orientations and historical development of social structures.

In the British refinery, management exerted control with little direct intervention and through allowing the workforce involvement in decision making. A strongly organised shopfloor movement meant that, according to Gallie, management could be faced 'with severe economic losses if it failed to take into account their views, or to win their consent on issues which were felt to be of major importance by the workforce'.[14]

By way of contrast, in France trade unions possessed little organisational strength at workplace level. In these circumstances management was able to exert a tighter system of control than in the UK which involved a higher ratio of supervisors to workers, and to apply tougher disciplinary sanctions. An emphasis was placed on paternalistic management styles to enhance employee motivation and performance. Thus, quite distinct managerial styles were apparent in each country even within highly automated and almost identical sectors of the refining industry.

So although a range of potential strategies are available to management in exerting control over the employment relationship, it would seem not only that courses of action are influenced by broader cultural, ideological or institutional factors within societies, but also that approaches taken need to fit the prevailing circumstances. In particular, managerial predispositions towards making unitary prescriptions may have to be curtailed where the prevailing ethos is pluralistic, and where it is necessary to compromise authority.

Poole adds a further dimension to this analysis by suggesting that, in the UK context, managerial styles may shift over time. In some interesting research[15] it is found that the progressive evolution from 'unitary' to 'pluralist' conceptions has been superseded by a 'pronounced preference for a unitary frame of reference'. Furthermore, managements will be more equipped to give effect to these preferences the more they are able to formulate strategic policy at corporate level.

Thus a shift towards the unitary paradigm may be expected in those deregulated systems (particularly the

US and UK) in which there are few institutional or structural pressures on management to engage in 'constitutionalist' rule making with the representatives of trade unions and government (as is the case in more corporatist structures).

Indeed, this managerial paradigm shift may be reinforced by the necessity for managers to raise productivity and control labour costs in the light of growing price competition. In this context, habitual notions of retaining labour peace through traditional collective channels may give way to more assertive and detailed forms of employment management.

According to Poole, 'In short, a highly competitive product market leads to directive managerial "styles", the abandonment of constitutionalism and the focus on individual employees at the expense of trade union representatives.'[16]

Assertions that transformation is occurring must, however, be tempered by the knowledge that pluralistic ideology remains common in many systems. In continental Europe, and Scandinavia in particular, well-established institutional arrangements based on the principle of recognition of collective interests may have been modified in recent years, but they have hardly been transformed.

MULTINATIONALS

A multinational enterprise (MNE) is a company that is physically active in more than one country; the definition does not just include the business giants such as Ford, IBM and BP, but also smaller companies. Service sector companies, as well as manufacturing concerns, can be located across national boundaries. Examples of this are finance or property investment. Indeed it would seem that the inexorable trend is in the direction of globalisation. According to Mitroff:[17] 'Those individual businesses, firms, industries, and whole societies that clearly understand the new rules of doing business in a world economy will prosper, those that do not will perish.'

The development of trade blocs means that mobile and flexible organisations can create interests in those areas providing the greatest economic benefits, while the attractiveness of economies of scale is likely to prompt mergers and amalgamations across national boundaries. Companies in certain countries, Sweden being one example, because of their restricted markets at home, are compelled to physically locate in other countries in order to develop further market opportunities. The power possessed by multinationals is awesome. The top 500 manufacturing companies do over $3 trillion worth of business, which is around 10 times the size of Britain's gross national product, the measure of all economic activity in the country.[18]

Countries such as Britain and Canada are relatively open to multinationals and offer incentives to encourage foreign investment. Other countries such as Japan and India have exerted more restrictive controls. The primary reason is to protect local businesses and markets. Nevertheless, the general trend towards physical location of Western-owned companies in developing countries continues.

A useful set of typologies for the analysis of multinationals has been provided by Perlmutter[19], originally in 1969.

- The *ethnocentric* concern bases its operations on the assumption that tried and tested approaches to management can be extended from the country of origin to operating sites in other countries. Underlying this is a preference to keep the reins of the power in the country of origin. This is reflected in the centralisation of managerial authority. Ethnocentric MNEs are also likely to retain research and development and other 'knowledge' activity in the country of origin.

- In contrast, a *polycentric* company bases its operations on the assumption that local managers and workers are best placed to formulate policies which most realistically reflect local needs. This approach therefore rests on a preference for decentralisation, and provision of autonomy for operating sites.

- The *geocentric* position is perhaps the most complex one as it combines both local and international strengths. At senior corporate levels in particular, managers will be able to take a global view of the organisation, being able not only to respond flexibly to local needs but also to transcend them in the pursuit of corporate goals and values. Although the geocentric position is likely to be the most difficult to achieve, it can also be the most successful.

While it may be possible to place individual companies in a particular category reflecting their strategic choices, Perlmutter sees the three typologies as representing three consecutive phases in multinational development. The range of products or services provided will probably increase as the concern moves through the three phases of development. Policies are likely to wax and wane in importance as each phase is encountered.

Multinational typologies and HR approaches

(Adapted from Adler NJ and Ghador F (1990) 'Strategic Human Resource Management: A Global Perspective' in Pieper R (ed) *Human Resource Management: an International Comparison*, de Gruyter, p.246)

Ethnocentric

RECRUITMENT AND SELECTION
- Staffing procedures controlled from the centre.
- Local labour may be recruited.

REMUNERATION
- Remuneration systems are set up from the centre.
- Local market rates taken into account.

TRAINING AND DEVELOPMENT
- Professional development retained within country of origin.
- Little/no requirement for language or cross-cultural training.
- Basic skills training provided at operating sites.

Polycentric

RECRUITMENT AND SELECTION
- An emphasis on recruiting local staff.
- Considerable expatriation of executives (possibly reluctantly). Tranference of technology.

REMUNERATION
- Local market rates highly significant.
- An emphasis on pay/salary determination at domestic level.

TRAINING AND DEVELOPMENT
- Training needs established and provided for at domestic level.
- Some requirement for language training for expatriates and knowledge of local culture.

Geocentric

RECRUITMENT AND SELECTION
- An integrated approach towards recruitment ignoring national demarcation, especially at managerial level.

REMUNERATION
- Possible conflicts in attempting to balance fair internal relativities on an international basis, with responsiveness to market rates at all levels.

TRAINING AND DEVELOPMENT
- Considerable demand for language training and cultural sensitivity.

A key issue then for many multinationals is to combine being highly differentiated, so that there is sufficient flexibility to be able to respond to local conditions and particularly market requirements, with a level of integration that will promote corporate cohesiveness and economies of scale. HR strategies, for example, which promote expatriation and staff mobility could well assist the MNE to strike the optimum balance between centralised control and responsiveness to local needs.

Multinationals and organisational culture

Certain authors argue[20] that multinational concerns are applying a 'common industrial logic' across the peculiarities of specific national cultures, while others assert that there is no single best way to manage across cultures and that successful organisations will have to adapt their approach to meet the requirements of the specific cultural contexts in which they operate (see Fig. 4.1). At the centre of the question is whether powerful multinationals are able to manipulate or supersede national cultures.

Adler and Ghadar[21] makes the valid point that the impact of culture on the organisation depends on the strategy of that company. In the ethnocentric organisation, there will in effect be no attempt to manipulate the national cultures in which it operates, as cultural differences are paramount. The issue will gain more significance in the case of the polycentric set-up, which is establishing autonomy in its countries of operation. In this case, the concern will be bound to adapt, perhaps on a country-by-country basis, to the nuances of the cultures in which it operates. In the case of the geocentric company the greatest ambiguity is likely to arise, as there will be a need to match corporate and national cultures. Methods used to accomplish this may involve frequent visits and travel, international career planning, using IT and networking, language development and international conferences, publications and communications.[22]

In examining the degree of cultural penetration exerted by multinationals, it is likely that a range of contingent factors will be significant. Readiness, for example, to accept Japanese-type working practices in the UK will rest on how disposed indigenous workers

Styles of execution

In light of the BMW-Rover deal, **Christopher Lorenz** looks at the contrasting attitudes between German and British managers

As BMW and Rover begin to get to know each other, and start deciding how to achieve the Bavarian company's goal of collaborating without destroying Rover's motivation and British character, new evidence has emerged of the deep gulf which separates managerial attitudes and behaviour in many German and British companies.

The gap is so fundamental, especially among middle managers, that it can pose severe problems for companies from the two countries which either merge or collaborate, according to a study by a team of German and British academics called "Managing in Britain and Germany", which will be published this autumn.

The phenomenon manifests itself in the contrasting attitudes of many Germans and Britons to managerial expertise and authority, according to the academics, from Mannheim University and Templeton College, Oxford. This schism results, in turn, from the very different levels of qualification, and sorts of career paths, which are typical in the two countries.

These contrasting patterns encourage many German and British managers to hold opposed views of the nature of management itself, according to a working paper by the German side of the team, under Alfred Kieser.

The academics' conclusions are based on a comparative study of three industries – brewing, construction and insurance – but are in line with the results of several broader studies over the past 20 years.

The project leader, Rosemary Stewart of Templeton College, says the gulf in attitudes and behaviour may be narrowing in high-technology industries such as electronics, but she doubts whether they are doing so to the same extent in the motor industry.

German managers – both top and middle – consider technical skill to be the most important aspect of their jobs, according to the working paper. It adds that German managers consider they earn their authority with colleagues and subordinates from this "expert knowledge", rather than from their position in the organisational hierarchy. Half the German managers in the study did not even mention their leadership responsibilities.

By stark contrast, British middle managers see themselves as executives first and technicians second, says the working paper. The term "management", it continues, "was on everyone's lips", but more than a third of them did not even mention technical responsibilities. In some cases this may be because they do not possess the requisite technical expertise to do their jobs in a way which their German counterparts would consider effective, the academics suggest.

As a result, German middle managers may find that the only people within their British partner companies who are capable of helping them solve routine problems are "operatives" who do not have management rank, conclude Kieser and co. Such an approach is bound to raise status problems in due course, but "there seems to be no way out given the current lack of knowledge of each other's system".

Other practical results of these differences in attitude include a greater tendency of British middle managers to regard the design of their departments as their own prerogative, and to reorganise them more frequently than happens in Germany, say the academics.

German middle managers can have "major problems in dealing with this", they point out, since British middle managers also change their jobs more often. As a result, UK organisations often undergo "more or less constant change".

Of the 30 British middle managers in the study, 13 had held their current job for less than two years (compared with only three in Germany), and another 12 (seven in Germany) for less than four.

One British insurance company manager had changed jobs nine times in eight years, and a construction company manager seven times in 11 years. Many of the Britons had also moved between unrelated departments or functional areas.

In contrast, all but one of the Germans had stayed in the same functional area. Twenty of them had occupied their current positions for five years or more (12 of them for more than 10), compared with only five of the Britons.

The Mannheim researchers almost certainly exaggerate the strengths of the German pattern; its very stability feeds the rigid attitudes which stop many German companies from adjusting to external change. But the academics are correct about the drawbacks of the unstable and technically-deficient British pattern. And they are right in concluding that the two countries do not merely have different career systems but also, in effect, different ways of doing business.

That does not necessarily mean that the findings of the Mannheim-Templeton study should be taken as a direct warning to BMW and Rover. The latter's ability to learn from its long relationship with Honda has made the attitudes of many of its managers more Japanese than British – especially as regards the technical content of their jobs, as well as the source of their own organisational status. On both counts, Japanese and German attitudes are not too far distant from each other.

In contrast with the long line of academic studies cited by Stewart and Kieser, other researchers have concluded that the variance of managerial attitudes between industries can in some cases be greater than it is between countries.

If this reading proves correct, Rover's managers could find that they have relatively few differences with their new BMW masters. But the truth is likely to lie somewhere in the middle, with the Stewart-Kieser study having more than a modicum of relevance for both the Bavarians and the Brits. It certainly does for companies in many other industries.

Fig 4.1   Source: *Financial Times*, 23 February 1994

are to accept such practices, and this is in turn influenced by local economic factors. Selection procedures adopted by such organisations may also be designed to hire those staff who are most disposed to accept the goals and values of the company.

Multinationals and HRM

The increasing internationalisation of business is placing new demands on companies, particularly in the area of HRM, and at least some major organisations are responding to such challenges. In the area of recruitment, a number of multinationals are stressing the need to attract young employees, who are seen as being adaptable and who do not have any restrictions placed on mobility through family commitments. Furthermore it is argued that specific competencies are required for successfully mobile international managers, and that these should be considered in the selection procedure. IDV, a subsidiary of Grand Metropolitan, assesses candidates by a series of scales: expectations, open-mindedness, respect for others' beliefs, trust in people, tolerance, personal control, flexibility, patience, adaptability, self confidence and initiative, sense of humour, interpersonal interest, interpersonal harmony, motivation and spouse/family communication. This 'international assignment inventory' is followed up by a behavioural event interview.[23]

In the areas of training and development, Adler highlights the pressing need for cross-cultural sensitivity and language training.[24] However, she recognises that many firms, in particular those in North America, generally have not recognised the importance of cross-cultural effectiveness. BP and Finance Europe have used multicultural teamworking activities to examine cultural differences, team roles and effective communication, while at the Hong Kong and Shanghai Bank international managers attend two-day cultural awareness and team-building workshops and participate in a ten-day outdoor development exercise, highlighting such areas as trust, conflict, and intercultural relationships (see Fig. 4.2).[25]

Finally in the area of reward, multinational concerns are faced with the challenge of ensuring both equity across their operations in different countries, this being of particular significance to the executive whose career path may span a number of subsidiaries, and responsiveness to local market rates. Issues of the comparability of fringe benefits, hours of work, and performance-related elements are also likely to gain in significance.

The impact of multinationals on domestic HR systems

A power which multinationals possess, over and above that of domestic enterprises, is the ability, at least in theory, to switch production from one country to another if this is found to be economically advantageous. Since the inception of the Single European Market in Europe in January 1993, the potential for this has been widened and there has been similar economic integration in other parts of the world. As freedom of capital and labour is being established across trade blocs a further set of challenges are presented to domestic HR actors. If the original rationale for moving to a specific country ceases to be valid, the organisation in question may move again. This rationale may apply in respect of markets, transport and communications, availability of labour or corporate taxation and grants.

Within the domain of HRM, relative labour costs, the level of industrial conflict and the ability of management to make decisions unimpeded by laws or other regulations can influence decisions about location or relocation. This has been illustrated by the case of the US-owned Hoover company, which in 1993 completed a transfer of production from Dijon, France to Glasgow, Scotland. This highly visible move involved the creation of 400 jobs on two-year contracts, but 650 jobs were lost in Dijon. The move was coupled with an erosion of agreed terms and conditions which was made possible by the less regulated system of employment in the UK, combined with relatively low labour costs. As a further example, Bosch has invested in low-cost plants in South Wales and Spain. It has decided to locate a new plant at Reutlingen, near Stuttgart, on the basis of an agreement for a seven-day working week.[26]

In practice, there are limitations on such switches of production. It may be feasible for more mobile business services or light manufacturing sectors, but for capital-intensive heavy industries it is unlikely to make economic sense. At an international level concern is being expressed, by labour organisations and by some governments, that not only is there a need to protect skilled labour, but also to ensure basic minimum employment standards. The Social Chapter of the Maastricht Treaty can be understood as an attempt to avoid a downward spiral of labour cost-cutting, and deregulation on an international scale. This issue is likely to gain more prominence as the former Eastern bloc countries offer alternative sources of cheap labour, and as global trade blocs become more all embracing.

Start slow, end fast

FT

Jean Louis Barsoux offers advice on working in multicultural teams

When 3M recently restructured its European operations employing 21,000 people, it limited relocation to fewer than 40 managers. Yet about 1,000 of its managers have been given permanent and/or project responsibilities across national borders.

Increasingly, companies are asking employees to participate in multiple work groups – project teams, task forces, steering committees, commissions and boards – which transcend national boundaries.

The idea, confirmed by research, is that cultural diversity promotes creativity, overcomes group-think and leads to better decision making. "Establishing a situation that is unfamiliar and slightly uncomfortable forces people to look at things differently", says Irene Rodgers of the Paris-based consultancy ICM.

The gains from diversity, however, are not automatic. In order to fulfil their creative potential, multicultural teams have to overcome barriers that uniform teams resolve quickly, often instinctively. They have to confront differences in attitudes, values, behaviour, experience, background, and expectations, as well as language. The team's biggest problem though is the lack of trust. Multicultural team members often find it difficult to overcome long-held prejudices and stereotypes about people who speak and behave strangely and have different ideas from themselves.

From the very inception of the team, members will have different views about how to build up the level of trust – and about how much time should be devoted to relationship building prior to "getting down to business".

North American managers, for instance, tend to have an instrumental view of relationships. Teams can be put together mechanistically and expected to function effectively, or fixed if they fail to do so. The directness of the team-building approach reflects the directness of American culture.

Members from more relationship-oriented cultures such as southern Europe, the Middle East or Latin America may feel rushed or distrustful of colleagues if the get-ting-to-know-each-other phase is curtailed.

What is more, artificial efforts to speed up that team-building process may backfire. Consider the example of a French medical equipment maker, taken over by General Electric in 1988. GE decided to boost the morale of its new French employees by organising a training seminar for French and other European managers.

In their hotel rooms, the company left colourful T-shirts emblazoned with the GE slogan "Go for One". A note urged the managers to wear the T-shirts "to show that you are members of the team". The French managers wore them, grudgingly, to the seminar, but as one of them recalled: "It was like Hitler was back, forcing us to wear uniforms. It was humiliating."

The build-up of trust may prove especially problematic if it is a project team which only meets periodically. Not only will opportunities to develop trust be restricted, the need for trust will be higher since individuals rely on one another to advance work outside the formal meetings.

Trust is universally important but it is built up and sustained in different ways. For instance, in Germany, trust is heavily biased towards a person's dependability. Delivering on promises, honesty and punctuality all increase trust. If a task is not going to be completed by a promised date, the deadline must be renegotiated in advance to let people make arrangements. In other cultures, where time is more elastic, and words and statements taken less literally, not meeting a deadline is not critical and will not necessarily lead to a loss of trust.

A further problem is that cultural misunderstandings often happen in situations where trust may already be low. Disagreement and suspicion may therefore be magnified out of proportion. The misunderstanding serves as additional proof of lack of trustworthiness. There is no benefit of the doubt.

As Rodgers saw it: "People get hung up on a word and it flies up into a huge event, and becomes a focus for all sorts of displaced anger and frustration – a bit like domestic quarrels caused by leaving the lid off the toothpaste."

In America and Europe, trust is usually enhanced by looking people in the eye. This is considered a sign of respect and sincerity. But in East Asia, for instance, eye contact indicates anger or aggression.

That makes it easy to misinterpret cultural problems for personality differences. A manager may consider a colleague to be awkward or sabotaging group efforts when that person is merely responding to cultural upbringing and beliefs.

Digging into cultural differences is a high-risk activity for the team since all sorts of value-laden differences and prejudices can come to the surface.

Multicultural teams, therefore, have to find ways of describing and surfacing differences in a depersonalised way. For instance, one multicultural team of MBA students was exposed to the idea that cultures may have a polychronic (flexible) versus a monochronic (rigid) view of time.

An Italian student who turned up late to a session was teased about being polychronic. This served to mark his "violation" of team norms without attacking him personally. His colleagues gave him the "benefit of the doubt" by ascribing his lateness to cultural programming rather than to the individual's own behaviour.

Humour can also provide a means of putting the cultural differences "on the table". The level of shared humour within a group, therefore, serves as a kind of barometer of team integration. "If a team has reached a high level of emotional security and members can laugh, joke, question and play devil's advocate with each other while completing the task, then it has done well," observes Sue Canney Davison of the London Business School.

Every culture has its own particular insights and blind spots. So it is a question of using these differences, not just living with them. In neglecting to work through these differences at the beginning, multicultural teams are storing up problems for later.

All this may sound rather time-consuming but, as Canney Davison comments: "You have to start slowly and end faster; by starting too fast, you run the risk of not ending at all."

Fig 4.2   Source: *Financial Times*, 8 July 1994

Developments in information and communication technology can facilitate moves towards cheaper sites, where routine services need not be located in high-cost areas. First Direct has its telephone-banking service in Sheffield, while Zurich Insurance has moved to Portsmouth. Nestlé Rowntree has closed most of its Scottish factory and has established new interests in France.[27]

A related development, which has gained momentum following the removal of European trade barriers, has been the increase in mergers and takeovers, the steel, car, banking, tool and transport industries being those chiefly affected[28] (see Fig. 4.3).

As well as having to deal with organisational restructuring, rationalisation and general turbulence, further challenges have been presented by the need to manage within new international entities. The Kingfisher group, in merging with the French group of chain stores

Darty, has needed to adopt French structures by, for example, incorporating and maintaining the effective operation of works councils.

Such organisational transformations are likely to demand increasing preparedness to accept the work in hitherto unfamiliar organisational structures and cultures. Yet multinational concerns exerting alien influences on countries in which they operate is not a new phenomenon.

JAPANISATION

Although US-owned multinationals are considerably more widespread on a global basis than are Japanese concerns, in recent years the latter would seem to have exerted the greater influence on HRM practices. Lean and efficient production systems and cellular group

Foothold in a low-cost manufacturing base

By David Marsh

High up in the company's cylindrical tower block on the outskirts of Munich a few months ago, a BMW board member gazed wistfully in the direction of the Czech border. "They work there for a whole day for the wages we pay a German worker for one hour," – adding that BMW's largest challenge was to reduce costs.

One important aspect of the Rover takeover is that it gives BMW a high-level industrial foothold in a country now generally recognised as one of western Europe's lowest-cost manufacturing bases.

The deal extends a long list of German investments in Britain in recent years – underlining Britain's accelerated economic integration with the rest of the Continent.

The sale of a prestigious manufacturing name will be labelled by some British industrialists as an unsatisfactory "sell-out" to foreign interests. Negative effects on employment would certainly result from any transfer abroad of headquarters' functions such as marketing and development activities. However, the deal

marks further public recognition by a large German company that the UK is an effective place to do business – a step that should be positive for jobs and investment.

The deal sends a message to German workers about the need to keep costs down as German motor and engineering groups signal their desire to shift some production abroad.

Coincidentally, the takeover was announced on a day of warning strikes by the IG Metall trade union to press home demands for a pay rise of up to 6 per cent. One German investment banker said yesterday the acquisition would provide BMW with a "useful yardstick" to help press for more streamlined and lower-cost production at home. He said BMW could now effectively put its workers into competition with Rover employees on productivity and quality standards.

According to the German-British Chamber of Commerce, the value of German investments in the UK rose to DM26.1bn at the end of 1992 compared with DM22.1bn at end-1990 and only DM8.7bn at end-1985. British investments in west Germany have risen far more slowly, to DM13.6bn at end-1992

against DM10.7bn at end-1985.

A survey by the Chamber at the beginning of the 1990s cited good labour relations and high productivity as main factors encouraging German companies to boost UK investments.

At current exchange rates, British manufacturing wages are 65 to 75 per cent of German levels, although the differential can be smaller in high technology sectors such as chemicals. More importantly, British non-wage charges – primarily social security levies – are only about 40 per cent of wage costs, compared with 85 to 100 per cent in Germany.

Heading the league table of German takeovers in the UK have been the acquisitions in 1989 by Deutsche Bank of Morgan Grenfell, which cost £950m, and by Siemens and GEC of Plessey, valued at £2bn.

Although German groups have largely been satisfied with their UK experiences, not all German takeovers have been success stories. In the late 1980s, Hochtief, the construction group, bought a 25 per cent stake in Rush & Tompkins, but the deal turned sour when the UK contractor went into receivership in 1990.

Fig 4.3 Source: *Financial Times*, 1 February 1994

working have been established by Japanese concerns, and companies have emulated them in cultures as different as Australia, South Wales and East Germany. In Europe, the UK has been the prime European target for Japanese investment, with Sony, Nissan, Toyota and Honda all establishing sites. Incentives for doing this include the relatively weak state of domestic competition for cars and electronics and the need for Japanese concerns to gain a foothold in Europe before trade barriers came down at the end of 1992.

Japan – a critique

Delbridge and Turnbull,[29] in investigating the practices of Japanese-owned concerns when operating overseas, highlighted a number of the more negative features of Japanese-style management practices from the employee's point of view. These included the following:

- Just-in-time methods of production promoting continual intensification of work, which became only accessible to the young and the fit. 'A tendency for workers to be "spat out" prematurely.'
- Extreme peer pressure on work-group members to perform, sometimes leading to ostracising and humiliation.
- Faults being traced back to individuals who are then exposed in quality circles.
- Quality circle members being compelled to give suggestions, these being rated on a scale from one to nine.
- Employees undertaking surveillance of other workers during and outside working hours, and reporting 'deviant' behaviour.
- Growing evidence of health and safety problems, as a product of flexible work systems which sometimes involve 57 seconds of motion every minute for up to nine or ten hours a day, to coincide with machine cycles.
- Exhaustive recruitment procedures which are aimed towards 'weeding out druggies, rowdies and unionists' rather than assessing technical skills and competencies.

Nevertheless, the Japanese model has gained international influence, not only through the direct effect of Japanese-owned companies locating on foreign soil, but also through the powerful demonstration effect of Japanese best practice.

Ford, for example, has attempted to introduce quality circles, employee involvement, culture change and multiskilling, although there has been workforce resistance to such initiatives. In the UK Jaguar and Lucas have introduced 'just-in-time' production, as has General Motors in eastern Germany.

EMPLOYERS AND THEIR ASSOCIATIONS

Purposes

Within national contexts, combinations of different employers have occurred to carry out a variety of functions, not always solely concerned with employment matters. Indeed, the link between trade associations, which have existed in order to regulate commercial and training affairs, and employers' associations has sometimes been inextricable. For example, in the building industry the main body in France, Sweden, Germany, Italy and the UK is both an employers' and a trade association, since wage negotiations are not easily separated from matters such as agreed arrangements for contract tendering. In the industrial relations arena employers' associations may involve themselves in collective bargaining over wages and other conditions of employment, as well as providing advice in areas such as labour market rates and labour legislation. Miscellaneous services, for example training, may also be provided. Associations have in addition possessed an important role as a pressure group for employers, providing a unified voice for employer interests. At national level, this responsibility will probably fall on the 'peak' associations.

International variations in organisation

There are considerable variations in the extent to which employers see any purpose or benefit in combining with others. A central motive in combination will be that it is seen as a way of preserving the ability to manage. It seems that at least the initial impetus to combine with other employers for industrial relations purposes has been essentially a negative, reactionary one in order to defend interests against growing union power or the perceived threat of state intervention. Labour laws which are perceived as unfavourable, or social policy reform, may be viewed by employers as potentially undermining their position.

A number of factors can be held to explain the varying significance and potency of employers' associations in different countries.

Threat of trade unionism

Growing trade unionism is perceived as a threat and different strategies are utilised to respond to it. The growth of trade unionism has promoted parallel developments among employers in order to present a unified front, and to prevent weaker enterprises being 'picked off' by trade unions.

Particularly in European countries, where mass-based socialist unions represented a challenge to capitalism, both government and employers seemed to favour a strategy of recognising unions for bargaining purposes. The idea seemed to be to provide unions with important industrial rights, but to temper their socialist objectives and protect managerial prerogative through formal regulation of bargaining rights and obligations.

In contrast, unions in the US have retained an economic orientation and have not been linked to mass socialist movements. American employers were not coerced by governments into recognising trade unions, and employers, frequently on an autonomous basis, felt free to resist them.

Profile of the State

Following the second world war, a number of governments in Western Europe (particularly Germany and Sweden) pursued interventionist strategies which involved the making of accords with organised labour and employers' associations. The preference of such governments for authoritative employers' associations served to strengthen their position.

Structure of industry

Where the structure of industry comprises large units, as opposed to a multiplicity of smaller enterprises, similarities in organisational type (for example, in terms of production methods) will facilitate the combination of employers and make agreements between them easier to secure. This can be highlighted by contrasting the position in Sweden, where there is a high degree of industrial concentration, with that in France, where there is a preponderance of small firms. It also seems to be the case that smaller and medium firms are disposed towards combining for bargaining purposes to ensure that none gains a competitive advantage in respect of pay and conditions.

Accordingly, multi-employer bargaining does occur in small and medium firms in trucking, construction and retailing in the US. Some large concerns in the US and UK (e.g. Esso Petroleum and ICI) have, however, refrained from joining employers' associations, as the norms and standards they recommend may be viewed as restricting the decision-making freedom of these powerful enterprises.

Employers' associations and collective bargaining

Once employers' associations have become established they have exerted a definite influence over bargaining structures, which in turn could well have affected the overall shape and distribution of power within trade unions. Benefits seemed to flow from locating the level of bargaining at a central level, particularly in terms of protecting vulnerable members from 'victimisation', neutralising powerful shopfloor movements, and possibly adopting a policy of divide and rule. Thus in the UK employers initially introduced centralised procedural agreements and industry-wide agreements on pay and hours. In Sweden and Germany employers' associations also preferred centralised bargaining. However in France, where employers' associations were slow to develop, collective bargaining itself was not significant in the determination of terms and conditions of employment, which were instead largely determined by law.

Features of employers' organisations

UK

- The main umbrella group is the CBI (Confederation of British Industry), established in 1965. It is essentially a lobbying group and does not participate in collective bargaining.
- Associations typically do not present a unified force and there are problems of fragmentation and conflicting interests within associations.
- Important initiatives taken by employers' associations include the establishment of disputes procedures and the provision of advisory and consultancy services.
- Different organisations operate within the public sector.

Sweden

- Employers are well organised with four main confederations, one for the private sector (SAF) and three for the public sector.
- SAF is responsible for negotiation with national trade union federations of economy-wide agreements on wages.

Japan

- Employers are organised into regional and industrial associations. Only in private railways, bus services and textiles do associations engage in collective bargaining, as this normally takes place at establishment level.

- Nikkeiran, the Japanese federation of employers' associations founded in 1948, is generally advisory in function.
- The role of associations is declining as individual company performance is of increasing significance in collective bargaining.

Australia
- The main umbrella groups are the Confederation of Australian Industry (CAI) and the Business Council of Australia (BCA) which comprises chief executive officers of each member company.
- Associations are varied in structure and serve a diverse membership. The leading bodies have a high profile and associations often have direct involvement in industrial relations.
- Associations have engaged in industry-wide collective bargaining and influence pay and hours. However, the trend is towards single-employer bargaining, with associations becoming more advisory.
- Some large firms have left associations.

US
- Associations are relatively unimportant with regard to industrial relations activity.

- In the non-union sector, employers have combined to prevent unionisation (e.g. the National Association of Manufacturers).

Italy
- Confindustria is the most important organisation for private employers. It has a direct role in national-level bargaining and represents firms with more than three million employees.
- Public sector manufacturing enterprises have separate associations, the most important being Intersind.

France
- At national level CNPF covers more than three-quarters of French enterprises. It engages in collective bargaining, although wages are regulated at industry level, where law plays an important part.

Germany
- At national level BDA represents about 80 per cent of enterprises. It does not directly engage in collective bargaining, but provides information.
- Industry-wide associations carry out the main bargaining activities.

SUMMARY

Employers and management are exerting a growing influence on the character of the employment relationship, and multinationals, as powerful economic entities, have set into flow cross-cultural ripples which encompass HRM across nations, and are presenting important challenges to governments, employers and trade unions alike. The trend towards decentralisation of bargaining and pay determination has generally been at the expense of employers' associations, yet in some countries they remain important actors in HRM.

The section on employers' associations has been reproduced by kind permission of UNISON Education and Training.

DISCUSSION QUESTIONS

1 What determines different management styles and strategies (a) in different countries and (b) over time?
2 Is 'Japanisation' to be welcomed or resisted?
3 Do multinationals necessarily exert an homogenising effect on HRM across national systems?
4 What are the requirements for an effective multinational team of managers?
5 What is meant by 'social dumping'? How may it be avoided?

NOTES AND REFERENCES

1. Fox A (1966) 'Industrial Sociology and Industrial Relations', Research Paper number 3, *Commission on Trade Unions and Employers' Associations*, HMSO, London

2. Palmer G (1983) *British Industrial Relations,* Allen and Unwin, London, p.7

3. Purcell J and Sisson K (1983) 'Strategies and Practice in the Management of Industrial Relations', in Bain GS (ed), *Industrial Relations in Britain,* Blackwell, Oxford, p.113

4. Palmer G op. cit.

5. Fox A (1974) *Beyond Contract, Power and Trust Relations,* Faber, London

6. Purcell J and Sisson K op. cit. pp.113–16

7. Bain G S (1971) 'Management and White-Collar Unionism, Conflict at Work' in Kessler S and Weekes B, BBC Publications, London, pp.17–18

8. Poole M (1986) *Industrial Relations, Origins and Patterns of National Diversity,* Routledge and Kegan Paul, London, Boston, pp. 45–51

9. Dore R P (1973) *British Factory – Japanese Factory*, Allen and Unwin, London, pp.401–2

10. Poole M, op. cit., p.47

11. Poole M, op. cit., p.50

Damachi U G (1978) *Theories of Management and the Executive in the Developing World*, Macmillan, London, pp.113–21, pp.192–94

12. Poole M, op. cit., p.50

13. Gallie D (1978) *In Search of the New Working Class,* Cambridge University Press, Cambridge, p.182

14. Gallie D, op. cit., p.314

15. Poole M J F (1981) 'Industrial Democracy in Comparative Perspective', in Mansfield R and Poole M (eds), *International Perspectives on Management and Organisation,* Gower, Aldershot, pp.23–38

16. Ibid. p.51

17. Mitroff I (1987) *Business Not as Usual*, Jossey-Bass Publishers, San Francisco, (IX)

18. Channel 4 Television, 1985, Multinationals Broadcasting Support Services

19. Perlmutter H V (1969) 'The tortuous evolution of the multinational corporation', *Columbia Journal of World Business,* 4

20. Kerr *et al.* (1952) *Industrialism and Industrial Man,* Harvard University Press, Cambridge, Mass.

21. Adler N J and Ghadar F (1990) *Industrialism and Industrial Man,* Harvard University Press, Cambridge, Mass, pp.242–3

22. Open Business School, B884, Human Resource Strategies, Block 3

23. Open Business School, op. cit.

24. Adler N J and Ghadar F, op. cit., pp.254–5

25. Open Business School, op. cit.

26. Incomes Data Services, Focus Quarterly 66, April 1993, pp.4–7

27. Ibid

28. 'Institute of Personnel and Development Brief', *Personnel Management in Europe*, July 1994, p.33

29. Delbridge R and Turnbull P (1992) 'Human Resource Maximisation: The Management of Labour under Just-in-Time Manufacturing Systems', in Blyton P and Turnbull P, *Reassessing Human Resource Management*, Sage, London, California, New Delhi

FURTHER READING

Bartlett H C and Ghoshal S (1989) *Managing Across Borders,* Hutchinson Business Books, London

Blyton P and Turnbull P, *Reassessing Human Resource Management*, Sage, London

Evans P, Jank E and Farquer A (1989) 'Managing human resources in the international firm: Lessons from practice', in Evans P *et al.* (eds) *Human Resource Management in International Firms: Change, globalisation, innovation,* Macmillan, London

Neale B and Mandel R (1992) 'Rigging up multicultural teamworking', *Personnel Management*, January

5 · THE ROLE OF TRADE UNIONS

LEARNING OBJECTIVES

You should be able to:

i identify trade union movements according to the nature of their objectives and orientation and understand the significant influences on them;

ii explain the main influences on trade union structure, the different structural patterns and the relevance of structure to issues of internal democracy;

iii explore and assess explanations of cross-national variations in membership levels;

iv understand that trade union movements can be seen to be confronted by a number of common challenges and examine some of the factors influencing their responses.

INTRODUCTION

As Braverman[1], among many others, has pointed out, the logic of capitalism is that the labour resource is subject to exploitation as surplus value is created through the labour process and accumulates to capital. In unregulated labour markets, individual employees or units of labour resource are relatively weak participants in the process of market exchange between buyer and seller. Relative scarcity is, as in other market situations, a factor influencing bargaining power and market outcomes, and yet even scarce resources can be relatively weak as individuals in comparison with the bargaining power that can be derived by the same individuals in combination and through concerted action to control supply to the market. It is this market weakness of individuals and the strength derived from association and collective action that is at the root of trade unionism. Having formed themselves into collectives, employees have not stopped at seeking to influence market price and, as we see in the next section, trade union objectives in most of the countries considered transcend this initial market dimension, seeking, for example, to exert a wider control over the work environment and the labour process and, in some instances, to transform the nature of society.

The inherent relative weakness of the individual seller of labour when contrasted with the relative strength of the corporate buyer may well be at the root of trade union organisation, but we must not assume that this is necessarily the prime motivation for people when they decide to join an existing trade union. It is important to bear in mind that for most trade union members, availability in the workplace is a crucial prerequisite to membership. In some systems where trade unions have particular political or religious objectives and affiliations, it may well be that these constitute a significant factor in individual 'joining' decisions. However, other motives or reasons may include:

- some element of compulsion, whether this be the product of some form of agreement or legislation stipulating union membership as a condition for obtaining or retaining a specific employment, or the product of peer pressure;

● a moral concern that those who benefit should in some sense pay the price by joining. It is usual for benefits or improvements obtained by trade unions to be extended to all in the appropriate bargaining unit, irrespective of trade union membership;

● a belief that individual benefit will be derived from membership, either because, unlike the previous point, beneficial terms and conditions of employment are limited to trade union members only, or because the individual believes that the union's capacity to obtain or win benefits will be enhanced by his or her membership;

● the image of unionism at the time, including both public opinion and individual perceptions of the role being played by trade unions and their leaders;

● for protection, security and/or representation. Undoubtedly, many individuals join trade unions for one or more of these reasons. For example, it may be that they are primarily concerned with the risk of unemployment or threats posed to their standard of living by rising prices and feel that they will gain some measure of individual protection as a product of union membership. Alternatively, they may be attracted by the belief that the union will represent them as individuals in any grievance, disciplinary or dismissal proceedings and if necessary before a court of law;

● so that they can benefit from facilities and services offered by the union, such as:

(a) retirement and sickness benefits and facilities;

(b) preferential or discounted rates for members in the purchase of particular products and services;

(c) membership of other associations or clubs;

(d) unemployment services and benefits. Some trade unions act as recruitment and selection consultants for employers providing them with names of unemployed members, or it may be that the union circulates job vacancy information to its members, or that the union participates in some way in the administration of state financial unemployment and/or social security benefits;

(e) education and training opportunities, facilities and schemes;

● for career reasons, either because they seek a career within the union as an official or because they consider that experience as a union official may open up other career avenues, such as in management. It is by no means unusual for trade union officials who have shown themselves to be competent to be offered management opportunities.

Trade unions are secondary organisations in structural terms, being to some extent reflective of the way in which the other corporate actors and environment have structured industry and the labour force. Employers have usually formed employees into groups of one kind or another before trade unions are in a position to structure themselves. This is not to say that the unions can exert no influence or choice in these structural matters, they can and do, but they rarely have a green field in which to decide. There are a number of factors that can be readily identified as providing the context within which employers and government make their decisions with respect to the structure of industry and the workforce, these being, perhaps primarily, the nature and availability of technology and production systems, and the nature and extent of international competition and consumer demand. In recent years, there is evidence of considerable and rapid global change in these contexts, and the consequential pressures on the structure of industry and the workforce also constitute pressures on the structure of the trade union movement. We pursue this issue of structure, the influences on it and the cross-national variations in the second main section of this chapter.

Researchers and theorists, along with governments and the media, have exhibited a long-running fascination with the issue of trade union membership and membership density. Over the years, many different explanations have been proffered for variations in membership over time, between sectors of industry and the labour force, and between countries. Some explanations have emphasised the variables of size and concentration; some economic influences and outcomes; others have given precedence to socio-political influences; others emphasise institutional and structural paradigms and their development; while yet others have sought to emphasise the importance of the policies and strategies pursued by the unions themselves, arguing that trade unions are not simply the passive recipients of members. Membership and density levels are often regarded as indicative of union power and influence. Perhaps inevitably, the fairly widespread decline in union membership shown throughout the 1980s has given impetus to further recent investigations into the relevance of the various phenomena referred to above, and also to issues such as whether there is evidence of either international convergence or divergence in membership behaviour given the increasingly global nature of some of these phenomena. We examine these various issues and explanations, with particular emphasis on some recent contributions and cross-national variations, in the third section of this chapter.

These common global developments, the increasing investment by and influence of multinational organisations, and developments within the European Union such as the proposals regarding labour and capital mobility, European-level works councils and an enhanced role for the social partners, have all tended to encourage interest in the extent to which unions have developed cross-national or international contacts, structures and organisation, and the extent to which those that do exist can be viewed as appropriate and effective. The two main international trade union organisations are the International Confederation of Free Trade Unions (ICFTU) and the European Trade Union Confederation (ETUC). In the fourth section of this chapter we examine each of these in the context of the changes and developments referred to above.

Few analysts would contest the assertion that trade unions have in recent years been confronted by changes and challenges on a scale rarely, if ever, encountered before. Ferner and Hyman[2] describe unions as facing severe problems of representation, finance, organisation and mission. Many of these changes and challenges are the contextual ones noted earlier influencing the structure and location of industry and the labour force, new technologies and production systems, new systems of work organisation, changes in consumer demand and product markets, and an increased competitiveness in world markets. However, in addition, trade unions have been confronted by levels of unemployment and economic crisis unseen for many years, new managerial strategies and initiatives, the cross-national influence of particular models associated with foreign and inwardly investing multinationals, the emergence of new political realities and ideologies, changes in societal values and attitudes, and the development and emergence of new interest groups with different requirements and motives with respect to trade union membership.

In the final section of this chapter we examine the challenges posed to trade unions by these developments and their response to them, again keeping an eye on the question of whether there is evidence of convergence or divergence in these responses, and whether, as has often been suggested in recent years,

the trade union movements in countries such as the US, where Blanchflower and Freeman[3] envisage only a form of ghetto unionism remaining in the future, and France can be seen to be in a state of near-terminal crisis as movements of power and influence.

OBJECTIVES AND ORIENTATION

Alternative objectives: 'business' and 'political/welfare'

It has become common to distinguish trade unions and national trade union movements according to whether they have pursued essentially 'business' or 'political/welfare' objectives. 'Business' movements tend to be apolitical, not too interested in the pursuit of particular 'class' interests, and very much concerned with and focused on the provision of improved benefits and services to their members at their place of work. These benefits and services may well include aspects of job control and these movements often have craft origins and traditions. Movements in this category have tended to emphasise collective bargaining at the level of the enterprise and the use of the strike as their preferred mechanism for resolving conflicts and achieving control. Conflictual and co-operative approaches and relationships are both consistent with these objectives, since 'business' unions often accept that the interests of their members are closely interwoven with the success of the enterprise.

'Political' or 'welfare' movements do tend to pursue particular class interests, do have political or religious affiliations, do seek to transform society for the benefit of their members, and in particular attempt to influence economic, legal and social policy so as to protect and further their members' interests. It is not uncommon for such movements to mobilise their membership in such a way that fundamental change is achieved, if necessary outside the framework of the existing political system. Industrial action to achieve political and social change is consistent with this approach. These 'political' movements are commonly affiliated to and/or sponsored by political or religious groups, for example the Communist party and the Catholic church. Given the nature of their dominant objectives, movements in this group have often not given priority to the development of effective bargaining or other influencing mechanisms at the level of the firm or in the workplace.

Somewhere between these two extremes are those movements, perhaps best exemplified by those in some of the Northern European and Scandinavian countries, which have become social partners in neo- and bargained corporatist arrangements. These movements have been concerned to protect and further the interests of their members, but not primarily through activity at the level of the enterprise or through class-based and militant action aimed at transforming society. They have pursued the interests of their members predominantly through discussion, negotiation and concerted action at national level with the other main corporate actors – the employers and the state. Normally these movements see their interests as being consistent with the achievement of national economic and social objectives such as full employment, price stability, income and wealth redistribution and economic growth. Inevitably, if these arrangements are to flourish, the other parties must be sympathetic and, perhaps most importantly, such arrangements must be consistent with the ideology of government.

As we shall see, US and Japanese unions have been considered to fit most closely the mould of 'business' unions, concentrating their efforts on the improvement of terms and conditions of employment within the enterprise, and accepting as inevitable the broader economic and political system. In France and Italy, however, the union movements have tended towards the 'political' type, seeking change centrally through political affiliation and pressure, on occasion mobilising the membership into industrial action aimed at achieving specific political objectives. In both countries, the union movements are fragmented on both political and religious lines, have tended to place low importance on workplace activity and, in France particularly, there has been a neglect of collective bargaining and a reliance on legislation as the mechanism through which employees' terms and conditions of employment are regulated.

Clearly, there is scope for variation within countries, as is evidenced by the fragmentation within France and Italy. Also changes can occur over time: thus in the US, unions have become increasingly involved in campaigning in the political sphere for favourable legislation, whereas there is some evidence that in continental Europe, the 'rank and file' are becoming more 'instrumental' in their approach and rejecting the 'political' orientation of their leaderships in favour of a greater business orientation. In the UK in the 1980s and in the context of an anti-union government, declining union membership and evolving employer strategies in employee relations, there was also evidence to suggest changes in the objectives and strategies of some

unions. The new realist movement has emerged, expressing views and behaviour more consistent with business unionism than has been traditional. The issue of whether unions are predominantly concerned with the pursuit of business objectives at the level of the firm, or with exerting political influence on a national basis, evidently also has a bearing on how they structure themselves internally and how power is distributed at different levels of union organisation.

Significant factors influencing objectives/orientation

Explanations of these variations in the orientation and objectives of union movements are inevitably complex and numerous. We explain below some of the factors and variables that seem to have been significant in contributing to the development of objectives.

- The nature of the society before and in the early years of industrialisation. Where societies had traditions of feudalism or where, as in Australia, there were other specific historical circumstances, it seems much more common for union movements to have emerged with a 'class' dimension and with social change and transformation as an objective.
- The attitudes of government and employers. Where governments were sympathetic to trade unionism and where there were political affiliations, union movements seem to have been encouraged to seek a central role and pursue the interests of their members politically and consensually. Where employers were anti-union and strongly resisted union recognition, unions tend to have been encouraged to concentrate their activity at the level of the firm and to concern themselves with 'bread and butter' issues.
- Social homogeneity certainly favours the development of broad class-based movements, as compared with heterogeneous societies in which there are numerous and diverse interests and value systems.
- Cultural characteristics may well be relevant. Certainly the enterprise-based, business-oriented union movement in Japan is consistent with the cultural dimensions identified by Hofstede[4], and the solidaristic policies and objectives pursued by the Dutch and Swedish movements over many years seem consistent with an emphasis on egalitarianism.
- The prosperity of the population has also been proposed as an explanation, the argument being that the more prosperous workers were, the more likely they were to be content with the social *status quo* and hence incline towards business unionism.

- The speed or pace of industrial and/or technological change and development. Again, the argument is that the faster the rate of change, the greater the likelihood that unions would be forced to concentrate on job-related issues at or near to the workplace.

Snapshot 1

UNITED KINGDOM

The union movement in the UK has consistently pursued class interests and political and social objectives as well as seeking to regulate, or at least influence, the job and terms and conditions of employment through collective bargaining. The Trades Union Congress (TUC) affiliated movement has close political affiliations with the Labour party and plays an arguably overly influential role in the determination of Labour party policy, although this role is in decline. For much of the twentieth century, the formal focus of collective bargaining and union activity was at industry level, with local variations and improvements being agreed at lower levels.

In the mid-1960s and 1970s there were corporatist experiments with Labour governments, the most famous being in the 1974–7 period during which an agreement was reached between government and unions known as the Social Contract. However, these experiments were neither successful nor long lasting.

There is evidence that in the 1980s and early 1990s union objectives and orientation changed, with some unions arguing for a greater emphasis on co-operative approaches, enterprise-level bargaining and a concentration on directly relevant benefits and services with considerably less emphasis attached to seeking to exert influence nationally on economic, social and legal policy. To some extent, these changes can be seen as a reflection of the attitudes, values and interests of the new union constituencies occasioned by those influences encouraging restructuring of industry and the workforce. No doubt they are also a response to the changed economic, political and legal environment and new managerial strategies. Certainly, we can say that the union movement in the UK has begun to confront its objectives and mission critically over the last decade, and this was further evidenced by the TUC's decision to 'relaunch' itself early in 1994.

GERMANY

The current union movement was created in the aftermath of the second world war. Employers, government and employees, confronted with the need to reconstruct the economy, entered at a relatively early stage into voluntary corporatist relationships.

The unions have reasonably broad objectives, including social and economic policy, and have operated primarily at industry and national level. They have not neglected workplace issues and machinery, but have only an informal role in the context of co-determination at workplace level. Many have placed considerable emphasis on obtaining favourable legislation.

Post-reunification, and confronted with its consequences, recession, continuing technological change and increasing international competition, it is possible that consensus, co-operation and neo-corporatism will be subject to increasing strain. Certainly, there is already evidence that former East German union members have a more instrumental orientation, which may itself pose a threat in the future to the traditional objectives and approach.

SWEDEN

Sweden is probably the most frequently cited example of a movement exhibiting corporatist social partnership characteristics. For many years after the second world war, the peak union and employers' associations, in collaboration with government, negotiated a framework agreement nationally and sought to achieve rising real wages in conjunction with profit growth, full employment, income and wealth redistribution, price stability and economic growth. However, the Swedish movement has also placed considerable emphasis on achieving favourable legislation and has been relatively successful in combining national bargaining with the development of effective representative machinery within the workplace.

The movement has had close links/affiliation to the Social Democratic Party which, until 1991, had formed the government in Sweden for all but 6 of the preceding 59 years. The new right-wing coalition government is more sympathetic to the interests and concerns of employers and pressures for decentralisation. The union movement is now much more subject to the influence of new interest groups, particularly in the service and white-collar sectors, and these new interests have been influential in changing the emphasis of the movement away from its solidaristic and welfare traditions.

UNITED STATES

The trade union movement in the US has been the prime example of a business movement. The absence of feudalism and a class base combined with social heterogeneity, fierce employer opposition, anti-union governments, a culture emphasising individual achievement and a relatively prosperous labour force, all contributed to the movement's business orientation. There are national unions but the enterprise or workplace remains the dominant level for trade union activity.

The unions have not formally affiliated to a political party, although they have generally supported the Democrats and worked for and welcomed the election of a Democrat government in 1992. In recent decades the movement has lobbied more actively for the passage of favourable legislation.

The traditionally conflictual nature of the unions' approach has been challenged by management efforts to introduce teamworking, quality of worklife and other involvement programmes arguably demanding a more co-operative approach from both union and workforce. Union responses to such management initiatives have varied.[5] Indeed, these initiatives have engendered considerable debate within individual unions and the union movement about how the unions should respond. Katz[6] has distinguished co-operatist and militant strategies, and Verma and Kochan[7] have pointed out that union approaches to such schemes do seem to be influenced by the presence or absence of foreign competitors in the industry. The co-operatists tend to see such initiatives as opportunities for more varied and skilled work and consistent with long-term objectives for more union participation in organisational decision making, whereas the militant perspective sees them as mechanisms to achieve greater workloads, higher productivity, greater management direction and higher levels of stress among employees.[8]

American unions have continued to rely on the strike weapon, although the effectiveness of the all-out strike at the end of a contract has diminished over the last 20 years. However, there were signs in 1993, particularly in the airline industry, that the unions might be more successful when using strategies such as legal slowdowns, sullying the corporate image, rolling strikes from one department or section to another, and strikes of limited duration. The presence of a Democrat government may have given the unions concerned the confidence to take action and to experiment.

AUSTRALIA

The particular historical connection with the UK as a colony had a significant impact on the objectives and approach of the union movement in Australia. There have long been political affiliations with the Australian Labour party. The early introduction of compulsory arbitration and recognition, however, signalled a significant departure from the British tradition. Trade union activity has until recently been dominant at state or federal level rather than at the workplace, and plant-level activity has tended to be relatively informal.

Conflictual or adversarial union–employer relations have been the norm and, prior to the mid-1980s, Australian unions had resorted to the strike weapon frequently and their concerns had been dominated by terms and conditions of employment. However, since 1983 and the election of a Labour government, the unions have willingly entered into corporatist-style arrangements at federal level. Indeed, in many respects the unions can be seen as the architects of these arrangements and ACTU has referred to its 'strategic unionism'[9] approach which involves acting jointly with employers and government to manage wealth creation, rather than continuing to confront the others over wealth distribution.

In addition, the movement has placed much more attention recently on enterprise-level activity, particularly in pursuit of employee participation/industrial democracy and efficiency.

ITALY

The trade union movement is political/religious in orientation and has affiliations with objectives considerably broader than bargaining over terms and conditions of employment. The major union confederation has been communist and socialist, but with the demise of communism in Eastern Europe the communist element has become less evident, mirroring developments among the political parties. Catholicism has also been a strong influence. The movement is fragmented along political and religious lines and the federations have tended to compete with one another for members and influence. In some respects the movement can be seen still to be wrestling with the dilemma of whether it should seek to remain class based or take on more of the role of a social partner.

The union confederations have concentrated on collective bargaining at industry and national level and on exerting their political influence to achieve (sometimes through direct negotiations with government) their objectives on terms and conditions and on wider social and social security issues. Some tripartite corporatist experiments have been tried but the politicisation of the union movement has tendered internal cohesion difficult for any length of time.

Before the 1970s relatively little formal attention had been paid to union organisation and activity at the workplace, although in recent years the main confederations have become much more concerned with workplace activity, representation and organisation. In part this has been prompted by rank-and-file disaffection with the political objectives and activities of the leaderships, as well as with the outcomes of some national and local agreements. Union members are arguably exhibiting increasingly instrumental concerns and certainly, as in some other countries, new union constituencies have arisen which have different, less egalitarian interests and objectives and which have created new and rival organisations to the traditional confederations.

FRANCE

As in Italy, the union movement in France is politically and religiously fragmented and competitive. Again, objectives have traditionally been broader than terms and conditions of employment, with communist, socialist and Catholic factions all favouring different objectives, orientations and approaches. The unions have traditionally been classified as either revolutionary or reformist. They have tended to ignore the workplace and have concentrated on securing improvements in terms and conditions through collective bargaining at industry level, and through exerting pressures on governments to enact favourable legislation creating minima/maxima which could be extended and improved on. The unions also participate with employers in the administration of many public bodies, particularly in the areas of training and social security.

The socialist government(s) in the 1980s tried to encourage trade unions and collective bargaining within enterprises, with some success, but without great support from union leaders who saw it as a threat to their personal position, influence and power, and as a development that would enhance employer discretion and prerogative.

JAPAN

Employers in Japan successfully curbed the traditional union movement after the second world war and, with the assistance of the Allied administration, succeeded in ensuring that replacement trade unions were enterprise based. These enterprise unions are often members of industry wide confederations who represent them in the spring wage round, but the enterprise has remained dominant as the focus of union activity.

The unions concern themselves primarily with terms and conditions of employment and are 'business' in orientation but, unlike unions in the US, are essentially co-operative in their orientation towards the company. This approach is congruent with the national culture and employment traditions and practices such as lifetime employment and seniority-based wage systems. Loyalty to the company is important both to the employees and unions.

The industrial confederations do seek to lobby and exert influence on government policies, but they are not politically affiliated. The 1993–4 recession is putting pressure on the traditional consensus and co-operative relationships, and the 1994/95 pay rounds may see more union militancy in support of pay demands and job protection than has been witnessed in the previous decade.

THE NETHERLANDS

Trade unionism began with syndicalist-inspired attempts at association and mobilisation among the unskilled labourers of the pre-industrialised 1890s. In the first decade of the twentieth century, trade unionism was subject to the same process of religious and ideological segmentation that permeated all social and cultural organisations. The organisation and mobilisation of trade unions began before large-scale industrialisation and outside the workplace, the activists being prompted by religion and ideology. Not surprisingly, given these beginnings, the unions have always tended to have objectives of the political/welfare kind and have sought to achieve them outside the workplace and via political and ideological debate, negotiation and influence, creating rights, rules and conditions protected and reinforced where necessary by the law. The heterogeneity of the religious and ideological segmentation of society rendered it unlikely that the trade union movement would become a simple class-based one.

After the second world war, the movement can be seen as having shifted into a 'social partner' role. All the main actors readily accepted the need for 'corporatist' solutions to the immediate and immense problems of reindustrialisation and recovery. They acquiesced in a long period of central control of main terms and conditions of employment, and did so in a manner consistent with the achievement of a narrowing of income and wealth differentials and the creation of a comprehensive welfare system. In more recent times pressures have grown within the movement, as well as from outside, for a relaxation of this co-operative approach and perhaps more importantly for a reversal of such solidaristic objectives. There is evidence in the late 1980s/early 1990s of increasing instrumentalism on the part of union members and a desire for a widening of differentials to reflect skill and productivity levels. There is also some evidence of a greater concern with workplace issues.

TRADE UNION STRUCTURES

Differing patterns and their significance

In many countries trade unions have been classified by virtue of their membership base. In some countries, such as Japan, the dominant basis for organisation is employment by a particular company. In others, such as Germany, the dominant basis is employment in a particular industry. In yet others, such as France and Italy, the membership base is essentially ideological or religious; whereas in others it may be the possession of a particular skill or qualification or because of employment in a specific occupation. In some systems, there are trade unions of a general nature which recruit across trades, occupations and industries. It is common, therefore, in the literature to find unions being described as:

- company or enterprise;
- craft;
- occupational;
- industrial; or
- general.

The process of industrial and labour force evolution in response to changing tastes, new technology and production systems and international competition has had significant consequences for the internal structures of some movements. The decline in demand for the products of particular skills, occupations and industries has rendered the traditional structures inappropriate and many craft and some occupational and industrial unions have ceased to be viable as separate entities. Sometimes they have simply ceased to operate, but in many cases such decline has been accommodated by mergers and amalgamations and, where this has happened, there has been a consequential reduction in the numbers of trade unions.

Membership base is only one dimension of structure. Trade unions and movements vary also on other dimensions of organisation. One such dimension is concerned with level: the level at which activity and decision making dominates or is focused. Often we seek to distinguish between those unions and movements in which the dominance, focus or emphasis is centralised as opposed to decentralised. The other structural dimension that we incorporate in this section is concerned with the extent to which movements are unified or fragmented. For example, in some countries, movements are fragmented in that there are large numbers of unions, but nevertheless the movement is unified by experience, or by ideology and purpose, and represented by one 'peak' confederation at national level. Other national movements may comprise a relatively small number of independent unions but the movement is nevertheless fragmented at national level on ideological or some other ground.

The significance of structure can be illustrated in many ways. For example, movements that are centralised and unified are likely to find it easier to enter into effective corporatist arrangements than are decentralised or centralised but fragmented movements; whereas movements that are decentralised may well find it easier to adapt to and embrace 'new' team-based work organisation and involvement programmes. Kjellberg[10] has suggested that structures influence membership levels, and suggests that membership levels are 'assisted' by the co-existence of effective and integrated centralised and decentralised mechanisms.

To some extent, we can also argue a relationship between trade union structures and union membership density by adapting the work of Bean and Holden[11], Calmfors and Driffill.[12] If we assume a relationship between the degree of wage bargaining centralisation and trade union structures, then this work would tend to imply that centralised, coherent and co-ordinated movements engaging in wage bargaining centrally encourage or are at least consistent with high(er) membership density. Influences on membership levels and explanations of cross-national variations are the subject of a later section in this chapter.

Before looking at the structure of the movements in each of our selected countries, we need to examine the determinants of and influences on structure and, perhaps most importantly, we need to bear in mind that trade unions are secondary organisations, their members having already been organised into distinctive groups by employers. Trade unions have always had to be willing to adapt their structure and methods in the light of changes to production methods and the structure of employment. Unions are reactive organisations in structural terms if in no other; already we are beginning to address some of the determinants of union structure.

What determines differing union structures?

So how can these differences be explained? The following are some of the main influences.

The attitude and role of the state

The liberal collectivist tradition in the UK meant that unions were allowed to grow, often on a craft basis, from the 'bottom up' without attempts being made to mould a 'rational' structure through statutory provision. In contrast, in both the Netherlands and West Germany in the post-war period, there was close collaboration between unions and government at all levels of industry, a greater reliance by unions on legal provision, and in Germany at least, agreement on a structure that was 'industry' based. Where governments are corporatist or consensual, as in the Netherlands and Germany, they are also more likely to encourage centrality in the structures of the union movement, since unions will need to devise representative mechanisms directed towards government. Where governments, such as those in Australia, France and the UK over the last 10–15 years, seek to encourage decentralisation of collective bargaining, there are implications for the structure of the unions if they are to operate effectively and guard their members' interests.

Objectives and strategies of unions

If the unions are relatively interested in pursuing 'political' objectives (as in the Netherlands, Italy and France) they will tend to centralise and organise on an industrial or national basis so that pressure can be exerted on government. If, however, their main concern is with 'bread and butter' issues, craft and occupational union patterns will be more discernible and it is more likely that the workplace or enterprise will be the focus of organisation, such as in the US and Japan. Those movements that are political may well experience difficulty in achieving unity or coherence – the movements in France and Italy have had long experience of fragmentation and competition on ideological grounds. Interestingly, the Dutch movement is fragmented in this manner but sufficient coherence was achieved in the post-war period to facilitate effective corporatist concertation (the seeking/achievement of agreement from, or using, a corporatist approach). It may well be that explanations of this unexpected combination should be sought in cultural differences.

Employers

As noted in the preceding section, employers have a significant influence on union structure since it is they who initially organise union members into jobs and industries. Additionally, employers and their associations influence union structure to the extent that they determine collective bargaining structures, to which and within which unions have to respond. If employers, who in capitalist systems usually organise in response to trade union activity, decide to organise and bargain at the level of the industry, or the district or region, to some extent unions will have to adapt their structures to fit with this pattern.

Individual employers can also influence union structures within the enterprise. In many countries over the last decade or so, employers have decided to take more responsibility for conducting their own relationships with unions, as multi-employer bargaining has become less relevant and appropriate for dealing with issues such as relating pay to organisational performance and the pursuit of flexibility through new production systems and methods of organising work. Decisions about the nature of the technology to be used and the ensuing production systems are rarely joint, employers having retained their prerogative over such decisions in most countries. Often, operational decision making has been decentralised, encouraging an appropriate decentralisation of employee participation and collective bargaining with its implications for existing structural patterns and levels of activity within the unions.

Where unions were already relatively decentralised and focused on the enterprise or workplace, e.g. in the US and Japan, these moves by employers are likely to have less effect on union structure than is the case where the unions have traditionally been organised and structured towards the centre, e.g. in France and Australia, with little attention having been paid to the workplace. The German, Swedish and Italian movements have traditionally been centralised in terms of the dominant levels of activity and orientation, but they have not ignored workplace organisation and this may well have enabled them to withstand the negative influences on membership in the last 10–15 years.

Production methods and technology

In the UK and the US early methods of production promoted the formation of pockets of skilled craftspeople, and consequently craft unionism has been of considerable significance. In Sweden, however, the dominance of mass-production techniques has not promoted powerful occupational groups but has, on the contrary, led to a preponderance of semi-skilled mass-production workers for whom general and industrial union structures are most appropriate. While we do not wish to be too deterministic about the impact of technology on human resource structures and systems, it is nevertheless clear that the transition from 'Fordist' mass-production systems to those of a post-Fordist nature, emphasising labour flexibility, multi-skilling and in many instances dual labour markets for core and peripheral workers, obviously poses challenges for trade unions and may encourage structural adjustments.

Changing consumer demand and increasing international competition

These both contribute in determining the appropriate structures of industry and the labour force in any particular country. As the traditional Western reliance on manufacturing and extractive industries has been confronted by declining demand and enhanced competition on a global scale, these industries have been forced to contract, and as they contract, so does the labour force employed. Unions of an industrial nature then have to confront many of the same issues and dilemmas that have confronted craft unions as the demand for their particular and traditional skills has declined. These changes pose problems for particular unions but also lead to adjustments in the composition and structure of the movement. In most of the countries that we are studying, these pressures can be detected and, as noted earlier, movements may not only be forced to devise new structures and alignments, they may also be confronted by new interests and values.

Structure and democracy

To some extent organisational and structural characteristics can either enhance or restrict the scope for unions to be internally democratic. Michels[13] provided early fuel for debates concerning trade union democracy with his views that large-scale organisation encouraged bureaucracy and that the necessary emphasis placed on administrative efficiency and its pursuit were likely to facilitate oligarchies, arguably the enemy of democracy. The implication was that as trade unions grew in size, democracy would become more tenuous and difficult to maintain.

There are also numerous dimensions to democracy. One might generally argue that it is concerned with the extent to which the members of an organisation can or do participate in the formulation of policy and the organisation's government. This can have implications for the mechanisms through which officers are elected; membership participation rates in elections and attendance at meetings; the opportunities that are allowed to opposing factions to express and communicate their views; the extent to which sectional interests are represented and provided for; the levels at which decisions are taken; as well as the existence of constitutional and structural checks on the activities of the union leadership. While internal union democracy has been an issue of some concern to government in the UK since 1979, it is not apparent that this concern has been mirrored elsewhere, although governments in other countries have on occasion sought to regulate internal financial dealings with a view to limiting corruption.

Wedderburn[14], Fosh[15], Blanc-Jouvain[16] and Crouch[17] have examined the related issues of trade union autonomy, internal democracy and government regulation of internal trade union processes. Extracting from the latest work a comparison of six of our countries (excluding Australia, Japan and Sweden) on a range of dimensions of autonomy/democracy clearly indicates the UK movement in recent years to be the most regulated. The dimensions compared are:

- method of selection of union leaders;
- method of selection of union workplace leaders;
- means by which a union ascertains support for a call for industrial action;
- union freedom to discipline strike breakers;
- union freedom to indemnify union members and officials from the consequences of acts committed on behalf of the union.

It is possible to make a number of comments and draw some conclusions about the likelihood of union movements being internally democratic given their structural characteristics and the recent interests and activities of the rank and file membership. We can compare these observations with some of the dimensions of democracy referred to above.

We might suggest that large, centralised and efficient organisations are less likely to achieve internal democracy easily, whereas organisations that are relatively small and local, or large but with effective decentralised decision-making mechanisms, particularly if these are closely linked to the level at which collective bargaining takes place, are likely to find it easier to achieve internal democracy.

Similarly, evidence of any widespread rank-and-file dissatisfaction with the objectives or policies being pursued by union leaders might be indicative of a lack of internal democracy. Low levels of membership participation at meetings and in elections of officers and representatives on policy-making bodies might also indicate that union democracy is largely absent.

Snapshot 2

UNITED KINGDOM

The dominant pattern has been one of fragmentation and multi-unionism but with one peak association and with the majority of unions being traditionally job centred. There has been a tradition of multi-union bargaining at industry level and this has often occasioned loose federations of unions representing employees in that industry. Mergers and amalgamations have been increasing in frequency, but since the unions are free to enter or not into these arrangements, only some of these have been outwardly rational liaisons. Electricians and engineers have merged, as have various public sector groups, but so also have white-collar workers in manufacturing, science and finance industries. The movement is becoming more and more concentrated, and the large general and super-union is becoming more and more dominant to the extent that it is anticipated that by the turn of the century the movement will be dominated by 20 or so such unions.

The unions looked towards the centre more and more after the second world war as governments pursued Keynesian demand-management policies and became ever more interventionist. The central orientation and inadequacy of formal workplace organisation and representation facilitated the emergence and development of informal workplace bargaining, until in the 1970s, unions and employers both sought to regain control and develop more formal structures at enterprise or corporate level. However, workplace union organisation and activity, while now more likely to be incorporated into formal structures, is nevertheless still relatively autonomous. As pressures grow for decentralised bargaining and a union response to recent employer strategies and initiatives, so arguably does the need for trade unions to integrate these workplace structures successfully into the national structure.

The one peak federation, the Trades Union Congress, has performed a co-ordinating and representational role centrally, in addition to seeking to regulate inter-union relationships and resolve disputes between affiliated members, a role that may become both more necessary and more difficult given legislative intervention in recent years giving employees the right to belong to a union of their choice no matter which may be currently recognised. To some extent, the movement has succeeded in appearing unified within the auspices of the TUC. However, in recent years the non-TUC-affiliated movement has grown as a proportion of the total and this is a partial reflection of the union-isation of new groups of workers with non-traditional interests and values; although the TUC does still represent marginally in excess of 80 per cent of total union membership.

The internal affairs and autonomy of the movement have been subject to significant legislative regulation since 1979.

US

Traditionally the union movement has been relatively fragmented, the primary day-to-day focus of organisation and activity being the 'local' operating within an enterprise or workplace. These locals are in membership of national or international federations and financial and collective power resides at the national level. The movement is also highly concentrated in a relatively small number of industries and in the older industrial north-eastern and mid-western states and California. However over the last decade in particular employers, with the tacit and sometimes open support of government, have sought to break the unions in some of the major industries, e.g. coal mining, distribution, trucking and construction. The movement's relative failure to unionise expanding sectors of industry and the labour force has rendered it open to the suggestion that it is becoming a 'ghetto' movement. Arguably the movement, in concentrating on workplace and 'bread and butter' issues and in failing to centralise and form close political affiliations, has made it easy in recent years for employers supported, by a neo-*laisser-faire* conservative government, to engage in union busting. The union movement has often provided financial support to political candidates and campaigned for legislative changes, and certainly the Democrat victory in 1992 raised the spectre of a somewhat more supportive government stance.

The single national confederation is the AFL–CIO (American Federation of Labour – Congress of Industrial Organisations) which includes approximately 85 per cent of union members with nearly all the major national unions in membership. Interestingly, the AFL–CIO split in the 1930s on structural grounds; the AFL was craft orientated while the CIO wanted to organise on industrial lines. It has no direct role in collective bargaining but does seek to present an impression of unity and does have responsibilities in jurisdictional disputes among members.

GERMANY

Prior to Hitler's crushing of the union movement in 1933, German unions were craft and industry based and divided by ideology and political allegiances. Now the movement in Germany is highly centralised and industry based. There are 16 unions, each of which seeks to represent all employees within a particular industry. Since the second world war, successive governments have pursued consensus and co-operation, and unions and employers have responded in the national interest and against a background of prosperity and rising living standards. The dominant union confederation, the DGB (Deutscher Gewerkschaftsbund), which represents approximately 80 per cent of union membership, has no overt political affiliation, but there are close links to the SDP.

The unions have been relatively coherent as a movement and, while the focus of their attention has been the centre, they have not ignored other levels. There are regional links between the unions and within the workplace legislatively backed mechanisms of co-determination have been created. These workplace co-determination mechanisms are not union based, although some would argue that they are in fact union dominated, but they and the union-based processes of collective bargaining at industry level and tripartite arrangements at national level are, to a large extent, integrated into one coherent structure of employee representation and participation. As in any country, the structure of industry and labour force has changed, and even before reunification there were tensions developing between unions as distinctions between industries were blurred by new technology and new products and services.

Reunification has posed additional problems with respect to assimilating the previously East German and communist unions and union representatives, and there has been some evidence of Western unions in conflict over membership and jurisdiction in the East. It also seems that, at the time of writing, the costs of reunification on top of recession and change are creating pressure among the rank and file in both the East and West for the improvement and maintenance of living standards and employment levels. Whether this is evidence of an increasing instrumentalism that will have consequences for the structure of unionism over the next few years, only time will tell; certainly there are also pressures for merger/amalgamation based on the traditional advantages of larger scale.

One of the main issues confronting the movement in 1994 is the trend towards increased decentralisation of decision making and collective bargaining, and this may well force the movement to review its traditional organisational emphasis, possibly encouraging a strengthening of local organisation and involvement in works councils.

SWEDEN

Trade unions in Sweden are generally organised on an industrial basis, although in the white-collar and professional sectors occupation and education are common bases for membership. There are three main confederations: LO (blue collar), TCO (white collar) and SACO/SR (professional). Traditionally the LO has dominated matters and it was the LO in conjunction with government and employers that was instrumental in the development after the second world war of the centralised, corporatist arrangements that have been a characteristic of the Swedish system over the years.

The LO has close ties with the Social Democratic Party and for many years it was LO policies that dominated the labour movement. The other two main confederations are not politically affiliated. However, as the structure of industry has changed, exhibiting many of the same characteristics as the other countries discussed (declining manufacturing and manual sectors and increasing service, white-collar and professional sectors), the other federations have become more influential, confident and less prepared to accept the dominance of the LO and its social welfarism.

The overall emphasis is still centralist within industries and indeed within the unions themselves, but there are pressures to decentralise. Fortunately, a feature of Swedish trade unionism has also been effective workplace organisation and the integration of workplace 'clubs' into the industrial and national union structures.

ITALY

Unions have been organised on an industrial basis since the beginning of the twentieth century. There is no tradition of craft or job-centred unionism. There is a strong socialist and revolutionary tradition within the labour movement in Italy and political affiliation is common. The Catholic church also played a role in organising labour, and since the early decades of the century socialist and Catholic movements have been in competition. This is reflected by the three main old-style confederations, CGIL (socialist–communist), CSIL (Catholic, although diminished) and the UIL (socialist centre). These confederations have tried to work together at various times, but without great success since the different political ideologies have intruded. In recent years, there has been considerable expansion of other occupationally based, autonomous unions, catering for white-collar and semi-professional employees, and these do pose a threat to the traditional confederations at a time when the old political 'certainties' are very much in doubt and the movement is confronted by an increasing emphasis on decentralised, company-level activity and issues.

The corporatist influence of the Fascist period encouraged the centralisation of decision making and focus, although there are both vertical and horizontal structures. The vertical organisations represent everyone within an industry, while horizontal structures combine workers across industrial boundaries at city or regional level. At industry level, federations are usually represented by one of the 20 or more affiliated national unions. The unions are both fragmented and competitive and it is common to find members of unions affiliated to each of the main confederations present in each workplace. It is at the level of the workplace and through the mechanism of the factory council that the unions have worked most closely with one another. This has only happened since the 1970s. The 1993 July Accord and subsequent December agreement confirm the increasing importance of company-level organisation and in particular the RSU format within the newly confirmed two-tier bargaining structure (RSU stands for *rapprasentanza sindicate unitatria*, which are unitary union-based representative bodies at workplace-level, the product of a preliminary agreement in 1991 – see Chapter 11 for further explanation). However, at the time of writing, it does seem that industry/sector-level activity continues to dominate.

FRANCE

The trade union movement is fragmented and competitive. The fragmentation is on largely political and ideological grounds, as is reflected in the five national confederations: CGT (communist), FO (anti-communist), CFTC (confessional), CFDT (non-Catholic) and CGC (professional). Except for the CGC, all of these union confederations effectively recruit across all industries and trades and across all categories of employee. They compete for members and employees join the union that politically/religiously suits them. There are some autonomous and company unions, e.g. Peugeot and Citroën.

Traditionally, the unions have been relatively centralised in organisation and outlook, the focus being the industry. In fact, it was not until 1968 that unions were legally allowed to form branches at workplace level. The legislative interventions in the 1980s sought to encourage trade union organisation and collective bargaining within the enterprise and have required some adjustments to traditional structures and relationships, but do not appear to have been as effective as the government had intended. Indeed, there was some evidence in the late 1980s and early 1990s of a reawakening of activity at a national level with a number of orientation and framework agreements between the federations and employers. At workplace level the role of the unions is in a sense limited to collective bargaining, but in reality union representatives also play a significant role in the works councils and many are also employee delegates.

There are the usual pressures for decentralisation and plant-level activity from employers seeking improvements in flexibility and efficiency. The right wing of the union movement is generally in favour of such developments, while the left is concerned with the dangers they represent to unity and the struggle of the working class.

JAPAN

The vast majority of unions are enterprise based, autonomous and represent all categories of employees. There are some craft, general and industrial unions, e.g. seamen, but the number is relatively low. Most enterprise unions in the same industry join industrial confederations which provide a co-ordinating role, particularly with respect to the spring wage offensive, and these industrial confederations often belong to the one main peak association, Rengo. The movement is fragmented and decentralised but generally not competitive. There are a very large number of individual unions. The union movement is not affiliated to a particular party, but has tended to support the SDP. The shift away from manufacturing and towards the service sector does have implications for the overall composition of the movement, and recession and increasing unemployment may well threaten the enterprise-based structure of trade unionism, as it also threatens traditions of lifetime employment.

AUSTRALIA

The movement in Australia shows many structural similarities with that in the UK. There is a strong craft- and job-centred tradition, considerable fragmentation and multi-unionism, and political links with the Labour Party. Australian unions are small by international standards. The unions have necessarily adopted a centralist orientation and organisation in response to, and so as to cope with, the system of compulsory arbitration at federal and state levels. Organisation at the workplace has been largely ignored until recently, and the impetus for reform and development at this decentralised level has come from the pressures for enhanced efficiency and productivity and the need to introduce new technology and work practices.

The decade since 1983 has been one of unprecedented union influence centrally through the one peak association, the ACTU, and in conjunction with the corporatist tendencies of Labour governments. Nevertheless, both parties have realised the need to develop union organisation, skills and activity within the workplace as managements have pursued new initiatives at this level – a kind of managed decentralisation but integrated into the existing centralised structure. The 1993 'Accord' gave this additional impetus.

The government and ACTU have also taken steps to reduce the number of trade unions, on the one hand by encouraging mergers and amalgamations, and on the other by amending in 1988 and 1990 the legal requirements with respect to trade union registration, increasing the minimum number of members required for registration to 1000 in 1988 and to 10 000 in 1990 and insisting that unions should be industry as opposed to craft based. The legislation was to apply to existing unions as well as new ones, although there were to be opportunities for special pleading.

THE NETHERLANDS

The original orientations and objectives of the unions resulted in a movement that was religiously and ideologically fragmented and centralised. Little attempt was made to provide effective structures for participation at workplace/company level, and indeed little provision was made for ensuring that members could participate in decision making or that their interests and needs were catered for. Internally, the unions have tended to be run in a paternalistic and disciplined manner.

The early basis of membership and organisation was primarily ideological/religious and loosely industrial. Occupational interests have come to the fore in more recent times.

The initial ideological and religious fragmentation and centralism has remained, although the degree of fragmentation has been diminished through certain mergers, particularly that between the Catholic and Socialist Federations in 1981 to create the Dutch Federation of Trade Unions (FNV). However, there is

still a separate Christian (largely Protestant) Union Federation (CNV). In recent years new federations have been formed to cater for the needs/interests of clerical and managerial staff (MHP) and in 1990 the ACV was formed as a federation of public-sector unions. We see therefore the emergence of new interests and groupings within the movement that the older federations have been unable to encompass and satisfy.

It is surprising that, given the fragmented nature of the movement and the competition that has existed between them, the various federations were able to co-operate so effectively in the strongly corporatist determination and administration of industrial and socio-economic policy in the decades after the second world war. Many of the tripartite institutions created in that period remain and still function.

In recent years, the unions have been confronted by pressures for decentralisation of decision making and greater employee participation, and while plant union committees have been formed in a minority of instances, the main unions have rarely accomplished the organisational and structural transformation necessary to respond effectively to these pressures. The non-union works councils have been the main vehicle for the satisfaction and absorption of these pressures.

MEMBERSHIP

Problems of measurement

It is not easy to make cross-national comparisons of trade union membership owing to a number of problems associated with measurement. First, there are some differences in definition as to what constitutes a trade union. In the US, for example, professional associations may not define themselves as trade unions, although they are involved in collective bargaining. However, in the UK it is possible for an organisation to engage in collective bargaining but not be included as a trade union because it has not applied for a certificate of independence. Secondly, the source of the figures varies from country to country, and in some cases may be suspect. In many instances, for example, the sources of data are the unions themselves and there is obvious potential for these to be under- or overstated. It is also the case that national statistics on trade union membership may not be very meaningful, given that in some countries, e.g. Germany, France and the Netherlands, many non-unionised employees are by law covered by the terms of collective agreements, and that in others membership may include retired members, as in the Netherlands and Italy. The most meaningful measurement is that of trade union membership density, the proportion of potential members who actually are members; but even here comparisons can be difficult because the definitions of 'potential' are not the same. In some statistical series, potential will simply be the total actually in employment, in others, it is the total plus those registered unemployed, while in others the self-employed are also included in the potential calculation.

Reasons for variations

Despite the difficulties of measurement and comparison referred to above, there has nevertheless been a long history of attempts at explaining variations: over time, between industrial and labour force sectors and between countries. This interest has partly been fuelled by assumptions that trade union membership levels positively correlate with their bargaining power in dealings with employers and also with their political influence with governments.

Early explanations such as that of Commons *et al.*[18] tended to assert relatively simple business cycle–membership relationships. Union membership would grow in the upswing of the business cycle because there would be greater pressure from employees for concessions from employers, who would be in a better position and more willing to make those concessions. The opposite trends would be discernible in periods of downswing.

Attempts to explain union membership density variations by reference to such cyclical variables seem currently to have established that such factors can account for a considerable proportion of year-on-year variations, but cannot explain to anything like so great an extent the variations between, for example, Sweden, where the density has varied above 80 per cent for the last 20 years, and France, where over the same period density has varied below 23 per cent.

Bain and ElSheikh[19] established that in Australia, Sweden, Britain and the US in the period 1893 to 1970, between 68 and 80 per cent of annual variations in membership levels could be explained by:

- *the rate of change in prices:* as price inflation increases, union membership is likely to increase as people join in the belief that they will be better able to protect their living standards/real wages;
- *the rate of change in employment:* as unemployment rises, union membership tends to decrease,

less people are in work and, in most countries, union membership, collection of subscriptions and local organisation are geared to employment and the interests of the employed, not the unemployed;

- *the rate of increase in money wages:* unions seem to be perceived as achieving higher money wages and, in periods of relatively high price inflation, this will be an incentive to membership, especially since it also seems to be the case that in periods when employers find it relatively easy to increase product prices, they are more disposed to yield to wage increases;
- *the existing level of union density:* obviously it is possible where density is high for the market to be effectively saturated (e.g. Sweden); where density is lower, but nevertheless buoyant enough to persuade employers to recognise and bargain, further membership gains may be encouraged by virtue of these successes.

When it comes to explaining longer-term variations and movements, and particularly when addressing the question of cross-national variations in union membership, it seems clear that the above cyclical variations have relatively little influence and that the emphasis is on socio-political, socio-economic, structural and institutional explanations.

It is important for us to keep in mind that long-term movements and cross-national variations are not the same and that explanations of the one may not explain the other. Visser[20] illustrates this difference by pointing out that while there has been a discernible and general decline in union membership density in almost all of our countries over the last 15 years, and there has at the same time been a divergence between top and bottom starting with the lowest density levels (France and the US) losing proportionately the most, the cross-national rank order of density levels has hardly changed over the decades since the end of the second world war. Measured by the collective organisation of their workforce, capitalist democracies are as wide apart from one another as during the 1930s. He therefore argues that many of the factors that may be used to explain long-term trends in union membership, such as changes in the structure of demand and greater international competition; changes in the structure of industry; the structure and composition of the labour force and structural unemployment; the shift from manufacturing and extractive industries into services; and the increasing employment of women and ethnic minorities in part-time and temporary jobs, do not explain cross-national variations. These factors may partially explain the general decline referred to above, but certainly do not seem to account for cross-national differences such as those between the Scandinavian countries and, say, France or the US. (See Appendix 14 – Comparative Trade Union Density.) In this context, Visser[21] suggests the following generalisations which require explanation: unionisation rates in Europe tend to be higher than elsewhere, they tend to be higher in smaller countries, and they appear to be lower in countries with adversarial traditions.

In seeking to explain these cross-national variations, Visser[22] emphasises the importance of the existence of workplace organisation and the availability of union organisation to the potential member, and argues that we should not be sidetracked by issues related to why people join or do not join a union. The important variation is that of workplace organisation – people can only join unions that exist and are available. It is also suggested that it may well be the lack of availability of union organisation that explains common lower-density levels among women and the young, rather than a lower propensity on their part to join a trade union.

One of Visser's[23] early working hypotheses was that cross-national variations in workplace organisation and coverage were the product of the recognition strategies and representation and retention strategies of employers and unions respectively, the level of workplace organisation being seen as an organisational or institutional outcome of strategic choices on the part of the main actors. Many explanations have followed the same route, for example Clegg[24] identifies such outcomes as the extent and depth of collective bargaining and the degree of support from employers and the system for union security, whereas Poole[25] suggests that cross-national variations may be best explained by public policies supporting collective bargaining which are partly a reflection of labour strategies and partly a reflection of managerial and state policies on trade union recognition. Bean and Holden[26] report the positive correlation between union membership density and the degree of centralisation of wage bargaining, the extent of bargaining coverage in terms of numbers of employees, the size of the public sector and the degree of left-wing party control of government.

Visser[27] seeks then to identify the contextual factors that may explain or can be seen to account for the cross-national differences in strategies adopted by the actors and the institutional and organisational outcomes that influence union organisation availability and thence union membership density. The tentative conclusions on this are that size of country, economic and industrial concentration and, to a lesser extent, social homogeneity are important in explaining industrial relations outcomes, including the level of trade union membership at any particular time. However, care is taken to explain that the influence of these 'country' features is indirect and is mediated through the institutional and organisational characteristics of the national industrial relations system as well as through political influences. Size and concentration tend to be related in that smaller countries tend towards more concentrated industries and more specialised economies, and these encourage the collective organisation of employers and a relatively high degree of centralisation. Social, religious, linguistic and ethnic homogeneity seems to be linked to the degree of class voting and the strength of the political left, as well as determining the degrees of ideological and political unity within the union movement, coherence and unity facilitating both organisation and membership.

Price[28] has also sought to explain cross-national variations in terms of institutional paradigms or frameworks. He acknowledges the importance of strategic choices and socio-economic and other structural variables in the determination of these frameworks. He suggests that we can distinguish between periods of national institutional development and subsequent consolidation. Periods of institutional development are periods of acute socio-political change, constituting a kind of paradigm break, and they establish the pattern of institutional arrangements surrounding the employment relationship which then imposes key constraints on the developments, including collective bargaining and union organisation, that occur during the ensuing period of consolidation. As an example, he queries whether the election of a Conservative government in the UK in 1979 constituted the beginning of a period of acute socio-political change that has resulted in a new institutional framework within which unions will find life more difficult, and which can be seen to have created a new lower 'norm' of trade union membership. The periods of institutional development can be seen as establishing a framework of union recognition, state and employer policies and union organisation which then conditions the impact of subsequent changes, whether economic or socio-political.

A recent and different approach has been taken by Hancke.[29] Having examined and compared union density rates in seven Western European countries between 1960 and 1990, he argues that local organisation seems to be a crucial factor explaining cross-national variations in membership trends. The essence of his conclusion is that where workplace union organisation is well developed, and where unions have managed to use the official institutions for employee participation (for example the works council) as extensions of their operations, union membership held up better against the various negative pressures referred to before and examined in more detail in a later section of this chapter. In other words, unions with strong local organisation (and hence visibility) lost fewer members in the 1980s than those without. There are apparent connections between this new emphasis and the emphasis Visser[30] places on workplace organisation and availability.

An additional conclusion of Hancke's[31] examination is that perhaps the traditional typologies of union organisation, structure and type need to be revised and significantly simplified, the suggestion being that distinguishing and classifying union movements according to the type of local organisation may be both more fruitful and relevant. He therefore groups together France and the Netherlands as movements with weak local organisation; Italy and the US as having strong local movements but with a lack of involvement in firm-level channels for worker participation; and a third group, Belgium, Sweden and Germany, with strong local organisations that have successfully achieved involvement in firm-level participatory mechanisms and decision making. It is in this latter group that union membership has stood up the best.

He also notes that the widespread evidence of a trend towards decentralised decision making (referred to many times in this text) may well enhance the importance of local organisation and, in this context, the future of trade unions as meaningful representative bodies may depend on the strength of local workplace organisation. This obviously poses a considerable number of issues for industrial, national and even international levels of union organisation, their role and structures.

In commenting on previous explanations, he argues that their 'weakness' derives from the assumption that trade unions are central and national actors whose health is inextricably tied to the performance of national economies and national politics. He argues that this conventional emphasis on central institutions may explain union strategies but not the problems of union density. Union membership recruitment is central to the issue of union density and is most influenced by local organisation. In most instances, members join in

the workplace and he argues (as others have in the past) that they evaluate their membership mostly in terms of local visibility, access, effectiveness, representation and services.

To summarise this section on trade union membership, there is wide acceptance that within countries cyclical variables account for a significant proportion of year-on-year fluctuations. Over a longer period, membership may vary as trade union organisation availability varies in response to changes in the structure of industry occasioned by structural changes in demand, international competition and technological innovation. The socio-political, legal and institutional framework in a country, which is partially the product of the strategic choices that are made by the main actors (employers, trade unions and government) within the framework, will also influence levels of union organisation and membership and changes in this framework may explain long-term variations.

However, when it comes to explaining cross-national variations in union membership, there are at least two quite different views. One argues that there is a need to encompass country characteristics such as size, industrial and economic concentration and societal homogeneity, and the indirect influence they exert through their effects on the national actors, their strategic choices, structures and institutions. The other view, a relatively recent contribution to the debate, argues that the crucial explanation of these cross-national variations is not national characteristics, institutions, strategic decisions, etc.; it is the strength and effectiveness of local union organisation and activity. The former view notes that local organisation and availability are important to membership levels, but sees this as a product of the more dominant and important national characteristics, institutions, choices etc.; whereas the latter view rejects these national explanations as mistaken and argues that local organisation is the dominant variable.

Snapshot 3

THE NETHERLANDS

Union membership density reached a high point of around 40 per cent in the early 1950s and in recent years has been in substantial decline, reaching a low point of 23.2 per cent in 1988 according to Visser,[32] since when there appears to have been stability if not a slight increase. The majority of the membership are in unions affiliated to the FNV – somewhere around 60 per cent – with approximately 20 per cent affiliated to CNV unions.

Membership in the private sector is lower than in the public sector, and membership density among male workers is substantially greater than among females.

The decline in union membership density in the 1980s is almost certainly a product of various predictable influences, including changes in the structure of industry and hence the labour force shifting from manufacturing and extractive to services, the increased use of part-time and temporary labour, and unemployment with its associated insecurities.

It is not possible to assess the extent to which the decline was associated with an increasing disenchantment with the objectives and policies pursued by the union leadership, but there is evidence of a halt to the decline at or around the same time in the late 1980s that many unions began to pursue policies inclined towards achieving wage increases rather than job sharing. Certainly new interest groups have emerged which apparently do not share the traditional egalitarian objectives, and it would not be surprising if the decline was also linked to an increasing desire on the part of employees (and management) for involvement and participation in the workplace allied to the failure of the unions in the main to devise appropriate company-level structures and democratic procedures.

US

Membership has been in a relatively constant decline over recent decades. Governments have not been well disposed to the trade unions and have not created a favourable legislative framework. Employers are anti-trade union and in recent years there has been evidence of union busting and relocation of manufacturing capacity to non-union locations and plants. The unions themselves have never really sought to centralise, do not have any particularly strong political affiliations or liaisons, and have tended to believe in and accept the capitalist *status quo*. They have also been confronted by the international and technologically driven changes to the structure of industry that tend to militate against union membership and growth. Membership growth in recent decades has been almost exclusively in the public sector.

GERMANY

For the two decades preceding reunification, West German membership had been relatively stable around the 35 per cent mark. Until the recession of 1993, employment levels in manufacturing industry had not been so violently influenced by the effects of technological change, international competition and world-wide recession as had been the case elsewhere. It is also important to remember that the unions have preserved a reputation and position as responsible social partners and the centralised and coherent nature of the movement, with its co-operative orientation and willingness to enter into corporatist-style arrangements, has probably helped preserve membership levels. Rates of inflation and wage rises have not been high, but neither historically has the rate of unemployment.

However, it is undoubtedly the case that the period after 1991 through to mid-1994 has witnessed a significant decline in union membership. The DGB arguably has 'lost' 1.5 million members or more during this period. Recession and declining traditional membership strongholds have contributed to this decline, but only time will tell if there are other important contributory factors.

SWEDEN

Swedish traditions are of very high membership density; over the last couple of decades Sweden has consistently occupied the number one position in the OECD's league table of union membership densities. The movement has been both centralised and coherent, and has generally adopted a responsible, social partner orientation and role. There has been some decrease in membership density in the late 1980s and early 1990s, which may reflect changing economic and technological contexts allied to the impact of political change and some popular disaffection with the institutional framework that has existed for the last three or four decades. New union constituencies and non-solidaristic values and trends towards decentralisation may threaten membership levels and habits, but the movement may be sheltered by its role in administering job search and training schemes and the integration of workplace clubs into national organisations. Unions are very firmly entrenched within organisations although there is some recent evidence of declining influence.

FRANCE

The gradual decline over the last two decades has continued. Membership levels have traditionally been low and the movement has been centralised and fragmented. French industry has not traditionally been characterised by large scale or concentration, and employers have been resistant to union organisation.

Since the early 1980s, with politically sympathetic governments enacting apparently supportive legislation, one might have expected membership to rise, but this has not happened, perhaps because of negative features in the economic context leading to unemployment and decline in the manufacturing sector, and perhaps also because of a disaffection at shopfloor level with the ideological schisms, consequent competition and distance of the leadership from the rank and file. It is also evident that the favourable legislation has not been particularly assiduously applied. In addition the late and limited development of workplace organisation, allied to the traditions of substantive regulation and extension of agreements, may not have acted as incentives to union membership. Trade union membership statistics in France are perhaps particularly unreliable.

ITALY

In the last two decades, membership density levels and trends among the employed have been similar to those in the UK with a fairly significant increase in the 1970s and then subsequent decline. The proportion of retired membership is increasing. The union movement has traditionally been ideologically and politically orientated and fragmented, and individuals have joined at least in part on this basis. In the 1980s the confederations have been confronted by, but have not totally resolved, the challenge of developing from a class-based movement to one approaching social partner status.

The trade unions have been subject to similar negative economic, technological and structural environments over the last decade to those which have confronted other movements, and these have no doubt influenced membership decline. The fairly widespread use of check-off arrangements has probably prevented membership among the employed falling even further. The only sector in which membership has even remained relatively stable throughout the 1980s has been in public service, and, as noted elsewhere, it is unions outside the traditional confederations that have tended to benefit most from this.

JAPAN

Only very recently has Japan begun to experience the negative economic environment, decline of manufacturing industry and rising unemployment that have affected the other countries above, and so far the effects have been limited.

Union membership density has been in a gradual decline over the last decade, possibly reflecting the slight changes in the structure of industry towards the service sector as much as anything else. More sub-stantial decline in manufacturing employment and further restructuring in favour of services might have more dramatic effects on union membership density. However, it is also important to remember that much manufacturing is undertaken by non-unionised employees.

Overall levels of density and membership are relatively low and this would appear to be owing to cultural factors as well as the fact that in a large part of the manufacturing and contracting sector unions are resisted by employers and employees are exploited without a protective or sympathetic legislative framework. Substantial reductions of administrative overheads in the larger companies where the administrative and managerial labour force is unionised might also have significant consequences for union membership density, as might cultural change encompassing individualism.

UK

The high point of union membership was in 1979, since when the movement has been experiencing an almost exclusively negative political, governmental, economic and legislative environment. Unemployment has risen sharply, the union movement has been removed from any significant central role, and the structural changes in industry have been unfavourable. Government and managerial strategies have tended to emphasise individualism, performance-related pay and enterprise, and the legislative framework has been significantly altered to make it more difficult for unions to take industrial action or gain recognition.

AUSTRALIA

The trade union movement in Australia has experienced membership decline in the 1980s in common with the movements in many of the developed economies. The extent of the decline is difficult to establish, since statistics for earlier years apparently included some members who were union members in a second job. It now seems that membership at the beginning of the 1990s (only in an individual's main job) at around 40 per cent density is of a similar order to that in the UK and Italy. There has been no tradition of effective workplace organisation, although this is developing in response to an increasing emphasis on enterprise-level bargaining/activity.

Developments in the structure of industry and the labour force over the last decade (shifts into service and part-time and casual work) have generally not been helpful, as has been the case in most other developed economies. The movement is voluntarily undergoing substantial structural reform in order to serve its membership more effectively and reinforce its relevance to both employees and employers.

The closer relationship with government since the 1980s might have been expected to enhance or at least protect membership. Of course, we cannot judge what may have happened to union membership density had the Labour government not been in power since 1983.

INTERNATIONAL TRADE UNION ORGANISATION

There are a number of international organisations of trade unions. Most of these are craft, trade or industry based, but there are others which are confederations across trades and industries. One of the main problems confronting international co-operation, co-ordination and coherence among the trade union movement has been differing political affiliations and ideologies. Employers tend not to have these problems.

Traditionally the ICFTU (International Confederation of Free Trades Unions), which is anti-communist, has been the most important of these international organisations and this dominant position has been enhanced by the recent demise of communism and the WFTU (World Federation of Trades Unions), which was the international federation catering for communist associations. The ICFTU is the confederation to which most of the unions in the countries discussed are affiliated. The confederation is influential within the International Labour Organisation and its main activity is encouraging and representing internationally trade union activity within less developed and developing economies. The ICFTU has made some attempts to confront multinationals on behalf of members in a number of countries, but has not achieved collective bargaining at this level.

However, in many respects the ETUC (European Trade Union Confederation) is becoming the most important international trade union confederation since it has been accorded a formal consultative role in the legislative processes of the European Union via the Social Dialogue and EcoSoc. The social protocol and annexed agreement to the Treaty agreed at Maastricht in December 1991 envisages an enhanced role for the ETUC, in agreement with the relevant employers' associations UNICE and CEEP, in initiating and possibly implementing legislation on social and employment issues. The main thrust of the ETUC with respect to multinationals has been to try to achieve the formation of international (corporate) works councils with individual companies and also through lobbying for European Union legislation to require pan-European companies to form such councils for information and consultation purposes.

As noted above, there are many international organisations servicing and representing unions and employees in particular trades, crafts or industrial sectors. These international secretariats co-ordinate research and the gathering of information, seek to maintain union solidarity against multinationals and, while autonomous, are mostly sympathetic to the ICFTU. The largest of these organisations represents metalworkers.

It is likely that the consultative role of unions across national boundaries will increase, the pace of such increase in Europe being largely dependent in the medium term on whether the EU enacts appropriate legislation.

CHALLENGES AND RESPONSES

Trade union movements have been subject to a perhaps unrivalled series of threats and challenges over the last 10–15 years. In some instances one can identify these developments as general in that they seem to confront most movements, while others have been country specific. The impact of these developments also varies considerably and even those 'general' developments and challenges, such as the decline in trade union membership, differ considerably in terms of the scale and nature of their impact and its seriousness.

It is not difficult to draw up a brief list of relatively common threats and challenges:

- The decline in membership.
- The need to recruit and represent new types of workers.
- Changes in the structure of demand and the structure of industry.
- Management strategies in pursuit of labour force flexibility and labour market segmentation.
- New team-based methods of working.
- New technology and production systems.
- Other involvement and quality of work life programmes.
- New managerial strategies emphasising individualism.
- Increasing pressures for co-operation.

- The recession and declining employment levels.
- New neo-*laisser-faire* political initiatives.

Many of these can be seen to be interrelated and many pose a threat to the traditions of trade unionism in particular countries. However, as noted above, these threats or challenges will impact differentially. A simple example serves to illustrate this: in systems with union organisation and co-operative traditions at all levels, such as Sweden and Germany, management initiatives seeking further employee participation in task-based decisions, for example via quality circles, may well have relatively few implications unless management seeks to use them to bypass the unions or existing mechanisms. However, in systems with conflictual traditions, such as the US and UK, and where the union organisation locally is not integrated with the centre, the implications of such proposals are likely to be both greater and disparate in nature requiring different kinds of adjustment and response.

In a chapter of this length, it is not possible to look in any kind of detail at all of the threats and initiatives referred to above and we have therefore had to be selective. We have grouped some together and chosen to look at the decline in membership, new methods and practices, commitment and the search for competitiveness.

The decline in membership

All of the countries we concentrate upon with the apparent exception of Sweden have experienced a decline in union membership density, over recent years, although the scale of decline and the period over which it has been happening has varied considerably (see appendix 14 on comparative trade union density), as have the precise consequences. However, as Ferner and Hyman[33] point out, numbers are not all important; recognition and collective bargaining commonly cover more employees than are union members. The Price Waterhouse/Cranfield project data[34] suggest that trade union recognition has held up better than union membership and also that union recognition tends to vary less across national boundaries than does union membership density. They found that in organisations employing more than 200 people, trade unions were recognised by more than 70 per cent of them in most of the countries examined. The researchers also pursued the more perceptual dimensions of influence and discovered that there was certainly no evidence to suggest or confirm a universal withering away of union influence across Europe.

Nevertheless, Plankert[35] shows that the union confederations in most of the countries covered by this survey identify declining membership as a significant, if not the most significant, problem that they face, and also that in most cases they identify among the main 'causes' the common changes in the structure of industry and composition of the labour force that we have noted before: declining manufacturing, expanding services, more women working, more qualified technicians and more atypical workers or contracts. The foregoing discussion on cross-national variations in union membership makes it evident that if union movements seek to maintain membership density, they need to devise means of organising in these sectors, and having organised they then need to recruit. This may require tailored campaigns and training for trade union recruiting officials, and it is likely to be very much more difficult in countries with no statutory mechanisms for obtaining recognition. As was noted earlier, people will not generally join unions that are not present in their workplace or employing organisation, are not seen to be active and effective, or which make no effort to cater for their needs. Failure to come to terms with these issues may well result in what Blanchflower and Freeman[36] have called 'ghetto' unionism; that is, unionism that is limited in its coverage to a few ageing industries and public and non-profit-making sectors.

However, it is also important to note that where employees in the new or expanding sectors of industry or labour force have objectives, interests or values not consistent with the movement's traditions, a 'culture change' may be required by some or all of the unions concerned if they are to retain an appeal. The structure and composition of the labour movement and relative power distribution may also have to be amended. It may be that existing confederations are inadequate or inappropriate. The more heterogeneous the membership, the greater the difficulty of maintaining unity. In several of the countries discussed, some of these repercussions can already be identified. Sweden is perhaps the most apparent since it has probably witnessed the greatest degree of success in recruiting in such areas, but this success has posed cultural and structural difficulties.

In some movements where union structure and organisation are craft or job based as opposed to industry based, one response to membership decline has been merger. Unions whose members' skill is no longer required have often been faced with the choice of ceasing to exist as numbers decline and viability becomes tenuous, or merging, either with other unions of a similar nature and in a similar position, or with other larger, healthier organisations of an industrial or general nature. In either event, there are likely to be difficulties of adjustment which may pose organisational, structural and cultural difficulties as the different interests and traditions meet.

Managerial initiatives for numerical flexibility often pose particularly difficult recruitment and retention scenarios for trade unions. Sometimes they will find their members made redundant and re-employed on a subcontracting or casual basis. In other circumstances, their members are made redundant and others employed as and when necessary. As the 'peripheral' share of the labour force increases, unions in a number of the countries discussed face a difficult adjustment.

The impact of recession and unemployment on trade union membership is also potentially significant. Where, as has been the case over the last decade, unemployment is in those sectors of the economy traditionally amenable to union organisation and membership, then membership losses are suffered, although where trade unions participate in the administration of unemployment benefit and social security benefit schemes, as in Sweden and Germany, these losses appear to be substantially mitigated. However, where the unemployment occurs in the service or peripheral sectors, the impact on union membership is likely to be less significant. In this new world of segmented labour markets, if unions manage to recruit and retain core workers it is possible that cyclical unemployment will have relatively minor effects in terms of membership loss, since it will be likely that their members are protected.

New methods and practices, commitment and the search for competitiveness

Managements have taken many new and strategic initiatives in the pursuit of competitiveness, some of the more common of which are as follows:

- They have sought to enhance task flexibility through mechanisms such as multi-skilling, team-based approaches to production and job enlargement programmes.
- They have sought to take advantage of workers' knowledge and skills in order to enhance quality, sometimes making employees responsible for their own quality and sometimes via quality circles encouraging employees to identify and resolve quality problems.
- In addition to the above, managements have sought through a variety of means, some participative and some educational, to secure greater employee commitment to the values and work ethic of the organisation on the assumption that such commitment, if achieved, will engender a normative or moral compliance relationship in which employees become more co-operative, efficient and productive.
- Managements have also sought to individualise and deregulate the employment relationship consistent with a neo-*laisser faire* or liberal individualist perspective, a re-emphasis of management's prerogative; although Brewster's evidence[37] would appear to indicate that it is unlikely in Europe that managements have often taken this to the extent of derecognition.

The incidence and impact of such initiatives is variable, being more common and significant in some countries and sectors than others. What interests us here are the implications for and response of trade unions. At the outset, it should be clear that each of these initiatives poses a potential threat to trade unions. It may be that the threat is to traditional demarcations between unions, restrictive practices and other mechanisms of job control, or it may be that the threat is to employee loyalty to the union and its values and objectives. A new ideology of individualism and co-operation or submissiveness may replace one of collectivism and strength.

Trade union responses to such initiatives will vary. Factors influencing this response include:

- The extent to which management seeks to bypass or involve the unions or other representative structures in these initiatives, and whether managements themselves adopt a confrontational or co-operative approach.
- The traditions and ideology of the unions and their perceptions of the strategies and initiatives. If the unions seek greater involvement in decision making (as many covered by Plankert's survey[38] say they do), they are likely to welcome many of these initiatives and co-operate. If the traditions are corporatist, then they might well be looking for micro-corporatist arrangements at workplace level in which they participate in driving forward many of the efficiency-gaining innovations.
- The union's perception of its strength and ability to resist, which will be influenced by the economic, legal and political environments. Examples of relevant environmental features might include recession and unemployment; whether the unions are legally protected and secure; and the ideology of the government and whether it is supportive of employer initiatives to individualise.

Institutional and ideological factors, perceptions and the strategic choices made by the various actors may all additionally influence responses.

Streeck[39] has suggested that trade unions will only maintain their strength where they pursue a 'productionist strategy' and thereby make a realistic and positive contribution in the face of such initiatives; where they assist employers in developing a co-operative and committed workforce and in the reorganisation of production. This way they will join in employers' ambitions for low-cost options and avoid marginalisation and decline. They should accept management's objectives in return for an increased influence over their achievement.

Parker and Slaughter[40] have presented an alternative viewpoint with particular reference to teamworking initiatives which they see as pitting employees against each other and as a mechanism through which managements retain and in some cases extend their prerogative or discretion.

Katz[41] depicted two union responses to such initiatives: distinguishing the co-operatist strategic choice from the 'militant' and pointing out the significance of assumptions and ideology in these choices.

Grahl and Teague[42] take these possibilities further in their suggestion that two quite different trajectories can emerge from the pursuit of enhanced labour flexibility, the role and response of trade unions differing considerably between them. The constructive flexibility model or trajectory envisages the development of micro-corporatism and labour co-operating in the process of capital accumulation, in return for which managements agree to pursue strategies that enhance skill-based employment allied to an avoidance of social inequalities. In the competitive flexibility trajectory, unions are viewed as the enemy of flexibility, and their power has to be reduced along with government regulation if flexibility is to be attained.

SUMMARY

It seems reasonable to identify at least three different types of trade union movement according to their objectives and orientation:

(a) Those interested primarily in 'bread and butter' issues at the workplace and which accept the *status quo* with respect to the nature of society and ownership of the means of production. These movements tend to be decentralised, relatively fragmented, not politically affiliated and relatively easy targets for employer and governmental anti-trade union initiatives.

(b) Those with a political/religious orientation, at least initially seeking to change the nature of society. Some of these movements, however, seem to have found internal unity of orientation difficult to achieve and they tend in such circumstances to be fragmented along ideological lines and are often competitive with each other. The nature of their orientation has tended to encourage centrality and a lack of attention to workplace organisation and activity. There is some evidence that there is an increasing distance between the interests of the leadership and those of the membership, and to the extent that this occurs, it is likely to contribute to enhanced disaffection on the part of the members.

(c) Those which may have started out as in (b) above but which have achieved the status of social part-

nership at national level with employers and government. To achieve this status, the movements need to be coherent and well disciplined and have often been successful in achieving favourable legislative, economic and social policy, and a measure of co-determination or participation within the workplace. Even here, however, there are currently some signs of membership disaffection with the essentially co-operative nature of the movement's relationship with employers and government, and negative economic circumstances are facilitating tensions of a largely unprecedented dimension between the social partners.

It must be remembered that objectives and orientation can change over time and there is certainly evidence currently of movements in a number of countries wrestling with the appropriateness of their position given new environments and governmental and marginal strategies.

All movements have been confronted with negative and often hostile environments and other influential circumstances over the last decade. Nearly all movements have experienced decline in membership and membership density, and it seems that it is in those countries with the protections afforded by legal rights to trade union recognition and employee participation and where the unions have social partnership status and influence that they have fared best. Perhaps it is not so easy for employers and government to attack ruthlessly trade unions with which they have a tradition of co-operation and corporate partnership. Others emphasise the local level of organisation as crucial to explaining the maintenance of membership levels.

When examining variations in membership density, it is necessary to distinguish between variations over time and variations across national borders. When examining trade union influence and strength, it is

important to bear in mind that membership levels are not the only or perhaps most meaningful criteria.

The movements in the countries that we study in this text are all confronted with threats and challenges, many of which seem common. It is, however, clear that many factors influence the responses of the movements to these challenges, and that among those influences are the perceptions, values and strategic choices of the various national actors.

DISCUSSION QUESTIONS

1 Examine the main points of difference between 'business' and 'welfare' trades union movements.
2 To what extent is the traditional business-welfare distinction adequate as a typology in the world of the 1990s?
3 How might developments in the external technological and economic/market contexts influence trade union (a) objectives and (b) structure?
4 Examine factors that might encourage trades unions to develop (a) centralised structures (b) decentralised structures?
5 How would you explain the decline in trade union membership experienced in many countries in the last 10–15 years?

6 Consider the prospects for cross or international trades union associations and structures.
7 Explain the implications of 'ideology' upon trades union objectives, structure and membership.
8 How would you explain the relatively minor variations in the international rank order of national trade union membership density figures over time?
9 Examine the suggestion that influences for convergence in the role and structure of trades unions movements in different countries can be significantly mitigated by the strategic choices of the unions themselves.

NOTES AND REFERENCES

1. Braverman H (1974) *Labour and Monopoly Capital*, New York

2. Ferner A and Hyman R (1992) *Industrial Relations in the New Europe*, Blackwell, p.xxiii

3. Blanchflower DG and Freeman RB, 'Going Different Ways: Unionism in the United States and other OECD Countries', *Industrial Relations* 31, 56–79

4. Hofstede G (1980) *Culture's Consequence: International Differences in Work Related Values*, Sage

5. Kochan T, Katz HC and Mower NR (1984) *Worker Participation and American Unions: Threat or Opportunity?*, The WE Upjohn Institute for Employment Research

6. Katz HC (1986) *The Debate over the Reorganisation of Work and Industrial Relations within the North American Labor Movements*, Cornell

7. Verma A and Kochan T (1990) *Two Paths to Innovations in Industrial Relations: The Case of Canada and the United States*, IRRA

8. Parker M and Slaughter J (1988) 'Managing by Stress: The Dark Side of the Team Concept', *ILR Report*, Fall 19–23

9. Plankert A (1993) 'Adjustment Problems of Trades Unions in Selected Industralised Market Economies: the Union's own View', *The International Journal of Comparative Labour Law and Industrial Relations*, Spring 3–14

10. Kjellberg A (1992) 'Sweden: Can the Model Survive?' in Ferner A and Hyman R, *Industrial Relations in the New Europe*, Blackwell, 88–142

11. Bean R and Holden K (1991) 'Cross National Differences in Trade Union Membership in OECD Countries', *Industrial Relations Journal* 23, 52–59

12. Calmfors L and Driffill J (1988) 'Bargaining Structure, Corporatism and Macroeconomic Performance', *Economic Policy* 6, 41–61

13. Michels R (1966) *Political Parties*, Free Press

14. Wedderburn Lord (1988) 'Trade Union Democracy and Industrial Relations: United Kingdom', *Bulletin of Comparative Labour Relations*, 17, 107–44

15. Fosh P, Morris H, Martin R, Smith P and Undy R (1993) 'Union autonomy, a terminal case in the UK?', *Employee Relations* Vol 15, No 3, 3–21

16. Blanc-Jouvain X (1988) 'Trade Union Democracy and Industrial Relations: France', *Bulletin of Comparative Labour Relations* 17, 7–26

17. Crouch C (1993) *Industrial Relations and European State Traditions*, Clarendon Oxford

18. Commons J *et al.* (1918) *History of Labor in the United States*, Vol 1, Macmillan, New York

19. Bain GS and ElSheikh F (1976) *Union Growth and the Business Cycle: An Econometric Analysis*, Blackwell

20. Visser J (1993) 'Union Organisation: Why Countries Differ', *The International Journal of Comparative Labour Law and Industrial Relations*, Autumn, 206–221

21. Ibid.

22. Ibid.

23. Ibid.

24. Clegg H (1976) *Trades Unions Under Collective Bargaining*, Blackwell

25. Poole M (1986) *Industrial Relations: Origins and Patterns of National Diversity*, Routledge

26. Bean R and Holden K, op. cit.

27. Visser J, op. cit.

28. Price R (1991) 'The Comparative Analysis of Union Growth' in Adams RJ (ed) *Comparative Industrial Relations, Contemporary Research and Theory*, Harper Collins, pp.37–55

29. Hancké B (1993) 'Trade Union Membership in Europe 1960–90, Rediscovering Local Unions', *British Journal of Industrial Relations* Vol. 31, No. 4, 593–611

30. Visser J, op. cit.

31. Hancké B, op. cit.

32. Visser J (1992) 'The Netherlands: The End of an Era and the End of a System' in Ferner A and Hyman R (eds) *Industrial Relations in the New Europe*, Blackwell, p.330

33. Ferner A and Hyman R, op. cit. p.xxiv

34. Gunnigle P, Brewster C and Morley M (1994) 'European Industrial Relations Change and Continuity' in Brewster C and Hegewisch A, *Policy and Practice in European Human Resource Management*, Routledge, 139–53.

35. Plankert A, op. cit.

36. Blanchflower DG and Hyman R, op. cit.

37. Brewster C (1994) 'European HRM, Reflections of, or Challenge to, the American Concept' in Kirkbride PS (ed), *Human Resource Management in Europe*, Routledge, 56–89.

38. Plankert A, op. cit.

39. Streeck W (1987) 'The Uncertainties of Management in the Management of Uncertainty: Employers, Labor Relations and Industrial Adjustment in the 1980s', *Work Employment and Society* 1.3, 281–308

40. Parker M and Slaughter J, op. cit.

41. Katz HC, op. cit.

42. Grahl J and Teague P (1991) 'Industrial Relations Trajectories and European Human Resource Management', in Brewster C and Tyson S (eds), *International Comparisons in Human Resource Management*, Pitman, 67–91

FURTHER READING

Adams R J (1992) 'Regulating unions and collective bargaining: A global historical analysis of determinants and consequences', *Comparative Labor Law Journal*, 14 (3), 272–301

Barnouin B (1986) *The European Labour Movement and European Integration*, Pinter

Bean R (1994) *Comparative Industrial Relations: An introduction to cross-national perspectives*, 2nd edition, Routledge

Bendiner B (1987) *International Labour Affairs: The world trade unions and multi-national companies*, Clarendon

Blanpain R (ed) (1990) *Comparative Labour Law and Industrial Relations in Industralised Market Economies*, 4th edition, Deventer

Bridgeford J and Stirling J (1994) *Employee Relations in Europe*, Blackwell

Cella G and Treu T (1990) 'National trade union movements' in Blanpain R (ed), *Comparative Labour Law and Industrial Relations in Industrialised Market Economies*, Kluwer

Chang C and Sorrentinto C (1991) 'Union membership statistics in 12 countries', *Monthly Labor Review*, 12, 46–53

Crouch C (1982) *Trade Unions: The logic of collective action*, Fontana/Collins

Deery S and De Cieri H (1991) 'Determinants of trade union membership in Australia', *British Journal of Industrial Relations*, 2, 59–73

Disney R (1990) 'Explanations of the decline in trade union density in Britain: An appraisal', *British Journal of Industrial Relations*, 28 (2), 165–78

Edwards R, Garonna P and Tödtling F (eds) (1986) *Unions in Crisis and Beyond: Perspectives from Six Countries*, Auburn House

Flanders A (1970) 'What are unions for?' in Flanders A (ed), *Management and Unions*, Faber

Hyman R (1991) 'European unions towards 2000', *Work, Employment and Society*, 5 (4):621–39

Kassalow, E M (1969) *Trade Unions and Industrial Relations: An international comparison*, Random House

Kendall W (1975) *The Labour Movement in Europe*, Allen Lane

Lipset S M (1986) *Unions in Transition*, ICS Press

Regini M (ed) (1992) *The Future of Labour Movements*, Sage

Von Beyme K (1980) *Challenge to Power: Trade unions and industrial relations in capitalist countries*, Sage

Wallerstein M (1989) 'Union organisation in advanced industrial democracies', *American Political Science Review*, (2) 481–501

Windmuller J P (1980) *The International Trade Union Movement*, Kluwer

Windmuller J P (1981) 'Concentration trends in union structure: an international comparison', *Industrial and Labor Relations Review*, 35, 43–57

Zachert U (1993) 'Trade unions in Europe: dusk or new dawn?', *International Journal of Comparative Labor Law and Industrial Relations*, 9, pp.15–26

6 · GOVERNMENT INFLUENCES ON HRM

OUTLINE

- Approaches.
- Government as employer.
- Government as legislator.
- Labour market policies.
- Government and convergence.

LEARNING OBJECTIVES

You should be able to:

i understand the various ways in which governments influence the contexts for human resource systems and human resource management;

ii appreciate the importance of political ideology and perspective as an influence on government actions and objectives;

iii explore and compare the human resource system outcomes of government labour market policies and their inputs as employer and legislator;

iv appreciate that technical and market forces that may be encouraging a convergence of government role across national boundaries may be mitigated by government ideology and priority.

INTRODUCTION

In developed market economies, governments influence human resource systems, labour markets and human resource management in a number of ways. They constitute one of the main corporate actors in the system and are in a position to influence significantly the economic, legal, social and political contexts within which the systems exist and function.

As Crouch[1] points out, government is the only actor in the situation able unilaterally to change the rules. The degree, nature, direction, objective and mix of government influence vary from one country to another and also within countries over time. Crucial to this are the values, beliefs and perspectives of those elected to govern, since these significantly influence the kinds of society that they consider desirable, their willingness to intervene, their willingness to enter into a political exchange with the other actors, and their economic, industrial and social policy preferences. As Kochan *et al.*[2] suggest, government values and choices, with respect to macro-economic and social policy, influence both the processes and outcomes of employee relations. Relatively rarely do governments pursue particular human resource management or labour market objectives and strategies for their own sake; their interventions into these areas are much more likely to be contingent on the ideology and pursuit of particular political, economic and social objectives.

It is common these days for these contexts to be categorised according to whether they are liberal or corporatist. The liberal context is one in which private ownership and freedom of choice is emphasised and reliance is placed on the market to reconcile the conflicts. The corporatist context is consistent with both private and public ownership, but emphasises the government-inspired mediation of competing interests through centralised institutions. Liberalism is further categorised according to whether individual or collective decision making is favoured, whereas corporatism is distinguished by the degree of coercion exercised on the competing interests to participate in centralised decision making and conflict resolution and the extent of an exchange.

As noted above governments, in their management of the economy and choice of objectives and strategies, almost inevitably have an impact on both process and outcome. Fairly obvious examples of this phenomenon would be the impact of a decision to give priority to controlling inflation on the level of economic activity and hence employment, this then impacting on the bargaining power of the other actors. Another might be the implications for levels of economic activity and employment, perhaps particularly in the public sector, of decisions related to the level or desirability of public expenditure or ownership. In this latter context, many of the governments in Europe have embarked on active programmes of privatisation, divesting themselves of the responsibilities of ownership and the role of employer. In some instances this is the product of ideological objections, in others more a matter of seeking to reduce public expenditure and increase revenues.

In this role of employer, government is directly able to exert considerable influence on the terms and conditions of employment and management of a significant proportion of a country's labour force. Public sector employees commonly comprise 20 per cent or more of the total labour force in developed market economies. Through its role as an employer, government also often seeks to influence events and developments within the private sector as a model employer or as an example of best practice. This influence may be limited to basic terms and conditions of employment such as rates of pay or hours of work, but may alternatively extend into many other aspects of the management of human resources. Examples of the latter may include the recruitment, selection and treatment of women, ethnic groups and/or the disabled, or the procedures to be used in disciplining employees.

Governments also exert considerable influence through their ability referred to above to change the rules, to legislate. Commonly the nature of this legislative intervention is the creation or confirmation of positive rights, although in some instances it will prohibit and in yet others governments are content to rely on common law.

The direction or objective of legislative intervention can be broadly separated into that which is regulatory and that which is protective. These distinctions invariably become blurred in practice, nevertheless they can be used as a convenient structural framework. Regulatory legislation is commonly aimed at the interaction of the parties, the process and their behaviour.

It is often argued that it constitutes/provides a framework. In providing this framework of acceptability, the law also invariably impacts on the autonomy of the parties. Indeed, protective legislation is also likely to have an effect on autonomy – in protecting the interests of an individual or particular group, or even the national interest, the autonomy of others is limited. An example of this is that in creating protective rights for employees, the autonomy or prerogative of management/employer is limited. Protective legislation can have either substantive or procedural subject matter. Both regulatory and protective legislation can constitute impediments to the operation of market forces.

The above two roles, as employer and legislator, are particularly significant in most of the countries studied in this text. However, governments also tend to provide various services to the other actors, such as advisory and research services, and they also commonly seek to mitigate the most potentially damaging consequences of industrial conflict by requiring or encouraging the parties to make use of conciliation, mediation or arbitration as an alternative to industrial action. In some countries, government provides these facilities as one of the services mentioned above.

As also noted above, government policies and interventions sometimes limit the 'freedom' of the parties to the labour market and the process of exchange indirectly, or as a byproduct of achieving other objectives. However, governments do also seek to influence directly the operation of labour markets and the level and nature of activity within them. They may, for example, seek to influence the quantity and quality of labour supply through education, training and retraining initiatives; the provision of unemployment services by way of vacancy information, relocation and/or mobility advice and assistance; and the management of financial compensation to those unemployed. Government may also influence demand for labour, for example, through its provision of subsidies, regional programmes and even the financing of lay-offs or early retirements.

Governments, along with the other parties, are influenced by external developments and concerns, such as the increasing competition in global and changing product markets. For example, as an employer government may find itself directly affected by changes in demand for the product of its public enterprises, whereas in its role as guardian of the national interest such influence may oblige government to pursue alternative economic and labour market policies and strategies, such as deregulation of labour markets in order to facilitate the pursuit of labour flexibility and the new methods of working deemed necessary for the maintenance of competitiveness. Membership of the European Union is another potential source of pressure on governments to pursue different objectives and strategies in the human resource field.

In the remainder of this chapter we pursue these approaches, contexts and roles further. In the next section we look at ideological approaches in each of our sample countries. This is followed by a more detailed appraisal of the various roles that governments perform as employer, legislator, and as an active influence on the labour market. Finally, we assess the extent to which global or international developments might encourage governments to influence human resource systems in directions that are convergent.

APPROACHES AND IDEOLOGIES

The values and beliefs that help to form political ideologies inevitably also influence views as to the kind of economic, social and political systems that are desirable. These systems then constitute some of the contexts for human resource management. As noted in the introduction, the industrial, economic and social policy preferences exhibited by government reflect their underlying beliefs and influence the relative power of the other parties, the processes used and also the outcomes. We will now examine how the ideological perspectives discussed in Chapter 1 are manifested in our sample of countries.

Snapshot 1

AUSTRALIA

The role of the federal government has been circumscribed by legislation and the activities of the various Arbitration Commissions. Right-wing governments have generally pursued liberal approaches to management of the economy and industrial relations. However, Labour administrations have generally been more sympathetic to the unions and also more prepared to intervene to regulate and seek to influence commission decisions. The Labour administration since 1983 has sought to involve the other corporate actors at federal level in the formulation of economic, social and industrial policy and to influence commission approaches and outcomes. The weakness of and lack of coherence among employers and their representative organisations has made it difficult for them to participate fully and effectively at federal level with government and trade unions, even if they had had the inclination to do so.

The series of Accords between government and unions since 1983 are arguably indicative of a desire on the part of government to involve more fully and integrate the other corporate actors in decision making. The integration of the various interests into the administrative structures associated with the system of compulsory arbitration is perhaps evidence of mesa-corporatism.

In recent years, the actors at federal level have been encouraging greater freedom for the parties at enterprise level and while the freedom proposed is limited, it may be indicative of a gradual shift in the direction of liberalism.

ITALY

Government in recent decades has typically been the product of coalition and seeking consensus through bargaining. This approach also seems to have typified the involvement and integration of the interests of capital and labour in macro-level decision making with respect to economic, social and industrial policy, as evidenced by the Scala Mobile and more recently by the tripartite Accord in July 1993 that sought to limit pay increases, restructure collective bargaining, and improve labour flexibility and productivity as part of a strategy aimed at enhancing and assisting industrial restructuring. The tripartite agreement in February 1994 involving Fiat, the government and the main union confederations, resulting in the public funding of job losses and the state bankrolling industrial peace, is another example, at a micro level, of this approach. Notwithstanding the longevity of the Scala Mobile, governments have typically sought to involve the other parties on an *ad hoc* basis, usually in response to crisis, and it is possible that the relative absence of institutionalised arrangements is a reaction to the coercive state corporatism practised by Mussolini. The election in 1994 of a new right-wing coalition government raises the possibility of a more liberal approach in the future.

On the administrative dimension, the parties have co-operated and participated more regularly, examples being the scheme for earnings maintenance in the event of lay-offs, the CIG, and various other social and unemployment benefit schemes and services.

Representative status is a base for union participation in a range of these mechanisms, and it is arguable whether a more united and coherent union movement might have facilitated more institutionalised and relatively permanent corporatist decision-making arrangements at national level.

Governments have participated in fairly detailed and comprehensive regulation of the labour market, traditionally giving legislative effect to terms and conditions voluntarily agreed at industry level.

FRANCE

For many years now, governments have intervened to encourage and regulate both the processes and outcomes of employee relations, and the representatives of capital and labour have been involved in consultative bodies such as the Economic and Social Committee and also in the administration of many dimensions of the welfare system and specific employment and training programmes. However, the orientation of governments before 1982 was probably predominantly liberal rather than corporatist, and certainly the pro-labour stance of government between 1982 and 1993 was a break with tradition. The new right-wing government has already given evidence of its intention to be less protective of labour, less keen to retain enterprises in public ownership, and also to be in favour of some deregulation of the labour market in pursuit of flexibility, restructuring and competitiveness.

Both employers and union confederations have been somewhat reluctant to enter voluntarily into collective bargaining, although since the late 1960s government has successfully encouraged the other parties to enter into the process, thereby enabling the government to take a less directive role. Much of the legal regulation of terms and conditions of employment is now the product of voluntary agreements subsequently given legal effect, rather than the product of unilateral determination by government.

The relative fragmentation and weakness of the union movement and the reluctance of employers have not facilitated corporatist tripartite decision making and integration at a national level, not even during the 1980s when there was a government that one might have expected to be more receptive to such arrangements. The government elected in 1993 is certainly very far from corporatist in its outlook.

JAPAN

Government has been dominated by relatively conservative business interests and there has undoubtedly been a tradition since the second world war of relatively close co-operation between government, the bureaucracy and the Federation of Economic Organisations (Keidanren). The role of trade unions at this level has been relatively small and their influence weak. However, there are tripartite consultative mechanisms in which the trade unions participate that discuss economic, industrial and social policy. Government has pursued policies conducive to economic growth and generally consistent with employers' interests. Western models are often inappropriate to Japan, although it is possible to view it as a corporatist state with weak trade unions.

There are some other tripartite arrangements, for example the Minimum Wages Councils which annually advise government as to appropriate rates. It is the government that actually establishes the rate legally. The Labour Relations Commissions are also tripartite in composition.

There is some evidence that government is beginning to show a greater concern with issues of fairness and social justice than has been the tradition, although these concerns cannot be said to have replaced those of efficiency and growth. There is no significant record of government intervening either directly to determine terms and conditions of employment or between the parties at industry or enterprise level.

US

The traditions are very much of governments not keen to intervene in the employment relationship. A legislative framework was provided in the 1930s that was motivated by a desire to aid economic recovery rather than by a desire to protect or further particular interests. Since that time, governments have been liberal in their orientation, concerned to eliminate barriers to competition rather than mediate between the other interests. There is a distrust of government intervention at federal level. The move to the right in the 1980s served to emphasise liberal and individualist traditions and preferences. The election of a Democrat government in 1992 provides some possibility of a reawakening of collectivism and labour protection, but it is unlikely that, in the short term, President Clinton will be able to achieve significant inroads into liberal individualism as the dominant business and political ideology. The Democrat government is more concerned about the social dimension of work and the problems of unemployment.

The relative weakness of the trade union movement, the anti-union stance of most employers and the drive for labour flexibility combine to render the promotion by government of collectivism rather than individualism problematic in the foreseeable future.

SWEDEN

In the 1970s and 1980s, the Swedish system was characterised by voluntary corporatist arrangements at a national level, with all three parties participating in decision making in the pursuit of certain economic social and industrial policies, more often than not consistent with the modified Keynesian proposals of Rehn and Meidner. Elaborate systems of interest representation and mediation emerged, social welfarism flourished and many of the programmes were subject to tripartite administration. Governments pursued active labour market policies in pursuit of full employment and encouraged the central determination of the main terms and conditions of employment. The unions pursued solidaristic wage policies and employers welcomed the stability in pursuit of export markets.

As the 1980s progressed, employers were confronted by less favourable international markets and, aware of their relative lack of control over labour costs and workplace mechanisms for attaining greater efficiency, began to draw back from these corporatist solutions and arrangements. The final throw of the corporatist dice was the Rehnberg Commission of 1990–91, a government-inspired tripartite attempt at centralised wage control and mediation, rejected by both employers and union members. The emergence of new employee interest groups made concerted and disciplined union compliance with these arrangements less and less practical as the 1980s wore on, and certainly by the end of that decade it was not realistic to talk of a coherent, united or disciplined movement.

In the 1990s, a new government has rejected such corporatist approaches in favour of a liberal and decentralised system emphasising deregulation, labour flexibility and competitiveness, a greater trust in the efficacy of the market and a change in the direction of economic policy, with inflation rather than employment as the main priority. Employer and trade union representatives have been removed from many tripartite arrangements. It is argued that this change of direction has been influenced by the desire of the government to gain entry into the European Union, which was ratified in a referendum in November 1994; membership will commence in 1995.

UK

Before the mid-1970s the dominant governmental approach was a liberal collectivist one, with bargaining autonomy for employers and employee organisations and a non-interventionist stance adopted by government. The legislative framework was based on freedoms as opposed to statutorily confirmed rights. In the mid-1960s a Labour government had pursued a more interventionist policy of seeking to control wage rises, initially via voluntary tripartite agreement, and, on the failure of this approach and the failure of the central employers' and union organisations to obtain compliance from their members, a statutorily backed policy was adopted. Similar voluntary tripartite arrangements were tried again in the early and mid-1970s by both Conservative and Labour governments, but eventually with similar results – compulsion and failure.

The last 25 years have seen a great deal of statutory intervention and regulation of the employment relationship and the framework for collective relationships, and over the last 15 years there has been a perceptible shift by government in favour of market individualism and deregulation. Much of the statutory intervention since 1979 has been motivated by a belief in the efficiency of the market and the 'need' to remove barriers to competition and efficiency.

Economic objectives and policy approaches have changed. Keynesian concerns with full employment and social welfarism have been replaced by a dominant concern with the control of inflation, individual contract and self-help, the argument being that the successful control of inflation and removal of barriers to competition will form the basis of an improvement in international competitiveness and long-term economic growth.

Tripartite consultative and administrative arrangements have been largely dismantled and the strength and influence of both employer and employee organisations severely diminished.

GERMANY

The former West Germany has traditions of coalition governments seeking consensus with and among the other corporate actors, often known as the social partners. Over the years relatively elaborate systems of interest representation and concerted action have emerged at all levels, even though governments have by no means always been particularly sympathetic to labour. In the 1960s and 1970s it was relatively common for the government to involve the other actors nationally in a form of bargained corporatism. The employment relationship and industrial relations system are extensively regulated, although the principle of bargaining autonomy has been preserved.

Considerable emphasis has been placed on the social dimension and Germany can be described as a social market economy also exhibiting considerable voluntary tripartism. Both employer and employee movements have remained coherent and reasonably united, and both have also adopted a relatively disciplined approach ensuring member compliance with agreements reached on their behalf.

These traditions are currently threatened by recession, unemployment and the requirements of regaining competitiveness which have compounded many of the problems associated with reunification. Government sources in 1994 are referring to the need to deregulate, increase the scope for labour flexibility and reduce certain social costs associated with employment. There is also evidence of an increased informality emerging within the elaborate structures of interest representation, in particular an increase in the amount of workplace bargaining between works councils and employers, some of which falls into the category of concession bargaining with employees conceding wage cuts in return for job security.

THE NETHERLANDS

The ideological and religious fragmentation of Dutch society ran through all social institutions, including trade unions and employers' associations, and was reflected also in political associations. Since the second world war, government has been by various centre-left and centre-right coalitions but dominated by Christian Democracy. These do not constitute the stereotypical background to the development of the strong corporatism, centralised tripartite decision making and socio-economic policy making, and disciplined search for consensus that are the Dutch post-war traditions. The Nazi occupation, wartime destruction of industry and cultural characteristics emphasising co-operation and egalitarianism no doubt all contributed to the development of post-war corporatism as the way to reindustrialise and achieve the socio-economic objectives of economic growth, international competitiveness and a stable exchange rate.

The pre-war traditions and organisation of trade unions and employers' associations were centralised and orientated towards achieving objectives outside the workplace and via political influence. The existence of pre-war legislation facilitating the extension of collective agreements to all employers in an industry, allied to the discipline exerted by the central associations over their members, eased the creation and effective operation of corporatist institutions such as the SER.

Strongly corporatist arrangements persisted into the 1960s and 1970s and, while the corporatist approach is very much weaker now, many of the institutions are still in existence and still work reasonably effectively.

Economic prosperity and income maintenance policies have mitigated the worst effects of unemployment. However, unemployment has in a sense given employers the confidence to place greater reliance on the market than on corporatist regulation. The unions are clinging on to corporatist institutions and processes, since they have not yet devised work-based organisations and structures that would enable them to voluntarily exist and achieve equivalent influence at company or workplace level.

Governments over the last 20 years have sought to combat the pressures for decentralisation and deregulation by engaging in bargained corporatist approaches, the agreement of 1982 being an example. However, recent indications are that government is moving towards a more liberal approach advocating deregulation and a greater reliance on market forces.

GOVERNMENT AS EMPLOYER

Government participation in the economy as an employer is inevitably influenced by its perspective, as outlined earlier. Governments with a *laisser-faire* or liberal individualist approach are more likely to rely on private enterprise for the provision of utilities, goods and services; whereas those with liberal collectivist or corporatist perspectives are more likely to willingly intervene as providers. Approach or perspective is therefore likely to be one of the factors influencing the size of the public sector as well as the extent and nature of employee participation in decision making, the style and practice of human resource management, and employee relations processes and outcomes in those organisations that comprise it.

It is important to appreciate, however, that government as employer is not the sole determinator of these issues. There are other parties involved and they will also have an input and influence.

In all of the countries that we study in this text, government occurs at local as well as national level and administrative agencies at these levels also act as employers, so that the public sector tends to be made up of government administrative agencies and staffs at various levels as well as organisations acting as providers of utilities, goods and services.

It is not practical or indeed appropriate in this work to examine all the various human resource management and employee relations policies and practices pursued within public sector organisations.

Nevertheless, there are a number of issues, developments and themes that are sufficiently common to merit and reward comparative examination.

Frequently governments have sought to act as model employers, employers of best practice setting an example to the private sector. What constitutes 'best practice' of course varies according to the perspective of government and the traditions and culture prevalent in the country concerned, and it is quite likely to extend into procedures and practices as well as substantive terms and conditions of employment. Public sector organisations, because of the dominant influence of central or local government in policy determination and decision making, often exhibit centralised decision-making processes and many of the other features of bureaucracies. Management at lower levels is commonly diminished by this. It is also common for management and staff in public sector organisations, particularly those employed in the public and welfare services, to exhibit relatively high degrees of commitment to the values, objectives and activities of the 'service'. This commitment, however, can be diminished or enhanced by the management styles as well as by the human resource policies and practices pursued. Some governments have used their control of funding in the public sector to encourage particular approaches and styles. The UK is perhaps the best example of this in recent years, where public sector managements have been encouraged to pursue efficiency and performance and to take responsibility for wage determination locally rather than relying as is traditional on national-level bargaining.

Public sector trade unionism is often higher than that in the private sector and one of the reasons for this is that, whether as a model employer or not, governments have often encouraged trade union membership and collective bargaining. Having said that, it is also common for trade union membership and/or collective bargaining to be discouraged, if not against the law, in certain selected public sector activities such as defence, the armed forces and the police service. Industrial action by employees in the public sector is more commonly unlawful. Governments often use the national interest and employer prerogative as the justification for such discouragement or illegality. In the light of this, it is not surprising that conciliation and/or arbitration are widely used as mechanisms for the resolution of disputes.

In the civil, welfare and public service areas, terms and conditions of employment are often determined, either unilaterally or jointly, using some form of mechanism that seeks to compare them with those applicable in 'similar' private sector organisations or employment categories. Through its control of funding, government can also apply various forms of incomes policy to its own employees, and often does so as an example to the private sector. It is therefore quite common for these public sector employees to be continually seeking to 'catch up' with terms and conditions prevailing elsewhere, although it is also the case in some systems that 'non-wage benefits', perhaps particularly security of employment and retirement provisions, are better than those available in the private sector and in this respect at least the employees are privileged.

Public sector employees are vulnerable to governmental change, particularly if the perspective of an incoming government is of a liberalist nature. Privatisation, exposure to market forces and public expenditure cuts obviously contain the potential for insecurity of employment, but they also frequently herald imperatives for cultural change within the organisations that remain. Most of the European countries covered in this text, e.g. France, the UK, Italy, Sweden and even Germany, are in various stages of a privatisation programme. The motivation for this is ideological on the one hand and linked to a perceived need to control public expenditure on the other.

Snapshot 2
UK

Despite the programme of privatisation and exposure to market forces pursued by governments since 1980, the public sector comprising central and local government and some remaining services and enterprises accounts for in excess of 20 per cent of those in employment.

By and large, employees in this sector have the same rights and freedoms as those in the private sector, although there have been instances of rights to belong to a trade union and bargain with employers being withdrawn in the last decade, and recently government has proposed limitations on the right to strike in certain essential services.

Government, via its control of the public purse and its use of cash limits, does significantly influence rates of pay in this sector. The traditional use of comparability as a base for settling main economic or substantive terms and conditions has been forsworn by government as inflationary, although again there are some groups that have managed to cling to independent pay-review machinery where comparability may still play a part.

Government has encouraged decentralisation of collective bargaining and, where possible, individual contract, and it has increasingly turned against independent arbitration as a mechanism for resolving failures to agree.

The pursuit of efficiency and flexibility in the public sector has been paraded as an example to the private sector, as have the government's willingness to stand firm and resist the demands of employee organisations and its determination to exercise control over wage costs. Before the 1980s the public sector comprised an example of best practice to private sector employers in the area of employee rights, protections and participatory mechanisms, but this is no longer the intention or the fact.

The government's belief in the inefficiency of public ownership and provision continues to underpin a programme of public expenditure cuts and privatisation of the diminished public enterprise sector. The increasing emphasis on efficiency, flexibility and individualism in the public sector has been accompanied by the encouragement of a less paternalistic approach to management and a shift of emphasis away from the traditions of personnel management and towards a more unitarist style of human resource management, emphasising employee commitment and managerial prerogative.

It must also be said that government objectives have not always been achieved, and local managements have sometimes clung on to national arrangements, pluralist and personnel traditions, at least in the short term.

GERMANY

By and large, public sector employees have the same rights and freedoms as employees in the private sector. The exception to this are the *Beamte*, the civil servants, who do not have the right to engage in collective bargaining or to take industrial action. Public sector workers used to be privileged in that they enjoyed greater job security than those in the private sector. However, as is the case in a number of developed countries struggling with issues of competitiveness and the scale of public expenditure, public sector employees in Germany are being increasingly exposed to measures oriented to the achievement of efficiency and flexibility improvements.

Government at federal level has also begun to use its power to influence pay in the public sector and to control pay as an example to other sectors, although they do not yet seem to possess quite the necessary resolve. Certainly their efforts in 1992 backfired in

that the 'pattern' established by public sector negotiations was considerably closer to the aims of the unions than government. In 1994 the government sought to establish a zero norm or pay freeze in the public sector which did result in moderate agreements. The government does not formally negotiate as employer, this is done via employers' organisations, but in practice it sets the constraints within which the employers' side negotiates.

The government is also proposing a widespread programme of privatisation as part of a policy aimed at reducing public expenditure in addition to the pursuit of efficiency and flexibility. The proposals to privatise the post and telecommunications business resulted in strike action by employees seeking guarantees of protection of jobs and various benefits on privatisation. The burden of financing public expenditure, not perceived as a significant problem in the 1970s and 1980s boom period, has increased substantially in importance given the massive costs of reunification and subsequent rejuvenation of the East and the additional costs of recession.

We may well also see a hardening of the traditional consensual management style in the public sector if the imperatives for the future are public expenditure cuts and improvements in efficiency and flexibility.

SWEDEN

Renowned as having proportionately one of the largest public sectors among the developed economies and a public expenditure proportion of GDP commensurate with it, Sweden is exhibiting distinct signs of a change in mood and the new, more right-wing, market-oriented government elected in 1991 is keen to reduce the scale of both public sector employment and expenditure. Consequently, a programme of privatisation has been embarked on along with further exposure to market forces. To some extent its desire to reduce public expenditure has been thwarted by increasing unemployment.

Pay in the public sector is negotiated between employers' association representatives and unions, but in practice the Minister for Wages is the member of the government ultimately responsible and able to determine employment policies in this large sector of the economy. Usually the private sector has set the pace on pay, while the public sector has provided the example in other areas of the employment relationship. However, towards the end of the 1980s the public sector was leading the way on rates of pay as well, and this provoked private sector employers into calls for public sector pay restraint and probably contributed to the election of a right-wing government campaigning on public expenditure restraint.

Employees and their organisations enjoy the same rights and freedoms as in the private sector. The emergence of new union interests and groupings has been a particular feature of the public sector among salaried occupations and professional groupings, and they have contributed to the fragmentation of the traditional solidarity of the union movement.

ITALY

The public sector is characterised by large-scale public ownership in both manufacturing and service sectors. Two holding companies control and co-ordinate the public enterprise sector, and the companies that make up the sector have formed themselves into employers' associations for the purpose of bargaining with trade unions. Employees in the public sector generally have the same rights and protections as those in the private sector. The government has sought to limit the right to strike in certain essential services. Strikes in the public sector are not uncommon and in both 1992 and 1993 government attempts to enforce pay freezes in pursuit of the perceived need to reduce public expenditure and set an example were responded to by strike action.

Trade union membership is higher in the public sector, particularly among employees in white-collar occupations and the professions, and these groups have been particularly active in their opposition to wage indexation and other mechanisms serving to narrow wage differentials. As in other countries, these employees/public servants who used to be privileged are finding this privilege and associated job security threatened by the direction of government economic policies geared towards a reduction in public expenditure, the return of nationalised enterprises to the private sector and the pursuit of efficiency.

Before the 1993 Accord and December agreement on the structure of collective bargaining and workplace representation, the framework for collective bargaining in the public sector had been agreed in 1983 and confirmed by legislation. The scope of the subject matter of joint determination and an associated management rights clause were intended to set an example to the private sector, as indeed was the IRI protocol of 1984 with its 'blueprint' procedures for dealing with disputes and consultation.

The recent relative weakness of government has rendered pursuit of right-wing orthodoxy problematic.

However, the return of a right-wing coalition government in 1994 undoubtedly gave impetus to a programme of privatisation, reductions in public expenditure and reliance on market forces, though the demise of the government at the end of 1994 presents further uncertainty.

FRANCE

The tendency since the latter half of the 1980s, given fresh impetus by the return of a right-wing government in 1993, has been towards controlling inflation and reducing public expenditure and the size of the public enterprise sector. A fresh programme of privatisation has begun.

Cash limits have been used by right-wing governments in recent years to control public sector pay and set an example to the private sector, while left-wing governments have encouraged the public enterprise sector to set an example in areas such as encouraging collective bargaining, the establishment of corporate-level works councils and the election of employee representatives onto the board of directors.

By and large, employees in the public sector enjoy the same protections and rights, many of which are guaranteed by the constitution, as do employees in the private sector, although public sector employees are required to give five days' notice before a strike. In the latter part of the 1980s the incidence of strike activity in the public sector was relatively high and proportionately higher than in the private sector. Much of this activity was aimed at improving terms and conditions which were typically poor in comparison with the private sector, and on a significant number of occasions these actions were organised by unofficial co-ordination committees of employees in the workplace. It must be remembered that trade union activity in the workplace has not been a feature of the system in France.

JAPAN

The public sector in Japan is split into four subsectors and each has a separate legislative framework covering the employment relationship and interaction between the parties. Employee rights and protection with respect to collective action vary; some groups do not have the right to join a trade union, some have the right to join a union but there is no right to engage in collective bargaining. Most public sector employees are only allowed to discuss or bargain on a limited range of subjects and many are not able lawfully to take industrial action. These rights and protection are generally worse than those provided by the legislative framework governing the private sector, but it is important to remember that the private sector legislation in practice applies largely to the major corporations and not to the small enterprise sector. The 1992 proposals to reduce public sector employees' hours of work, ahead of developments in the private sector, is a relatively rare example of government seeking to use its role as employer to set an example.

Notwithstanding the above, trade union membership density and the incidence of industrial action have often been greater in the public sector.

So far the public sector has not been substantially exposed to market forces or pressure for improvements in efficiency and/or flexibility. Nevertheless, a programme of privatisation is in hand and, as recession bites, we may expect such pressures to emerge and threaten the relative security of the public sector labour force.

Pay and the main terms and conditions of employment are frequently the product of unilateral determination by management acting on behalf of the government.

AUSTRALIA

Public sector employment occurs at several levels – federal, state and local. The federal sector has tended to set the pattern in terms of pay and substantive conditions. Depending on the political orientation of federal and state governments, it is possible that quite different approaches are adopted to the employment relationship and collective issues and interaction.

Generally, government has proved to be an employer more favourably disposed towards trade unionism and public sector union density is higher. Left-wing state and federal governments have encouraged and facilitated greater employee participation via consultation with the Public Service Boards that constitute the employer at both state and federal levels. Public sector employers at local level have often been combined into associations to deal with unions at the level of the state. The Arbitration Tribunals covering public sector employees are more likely to be tripartite in terms of interest representation.

Employees generally have similar rights and protections as in the private sector. In some senses these are likely to be better, particularly in terms of job security and grievance handling, but there are some restrictions on employees in certain essential services which prevent them taking industrial action.

Government at federal level is encouraging decentralisation and enterprise-level bargaining in the private sector in pursuit of improvements in efficiency and productivity, and it will be interesting to see whether these pressures are extended to the public sector by a left-wing government.

The federal government's ability to use its role as employer to influence pay increases has been limited by the role of the Arbitration Tribunals.

US

Government occurs at federal, state and local levels. There is relatively little incidence of public ownership of enterprise and the size of the public sector in proportionate terms is relatively small, as befits a country in which the market and enterprise have always been dominant and government intervention has been distrusted.

Union density is generally higher in the federal public sector, and what little expansion there has been in union membership in recent decades has almost all occurred within the public sector and among white-collar, occupational and quasi-professional employees.

Many government employees have restricted rights to engage in collective bargaining and take strike action and the right to join a trade union is relatively recent (1962) for federal employees. In many states, state and local government employees are without such rights and opportunities; they may have rights to meet and confer with management, but not to engage in collective bargaining. Even at federal level, it is still quite common for the range of subject matter appropriate to collective bargaining to be limited to non-economic issues, with management retaining the unilateral prerogative to decide. The use of compulsory and binding arbitration is relatively common in the event of failure to agree, and separate and specific bodies exist at federal level to deal with such situations and to adjudicate on allegations of unfair labour practice.

The election of a Democrat government in 1992 may have beneficial effects on employee rights and protections within the federal sector, and it may be that a less authoritarian management style will emerge over time. Already measures have been taken to reopen the possibility of federal employment for air traffic controllers sacked by the Reagan administration in 1981 and to promote trade unionism in federal construction projects and federal agencies. However, it would be unwise to anticipate drastic change in this sector since, by

European standards, the Democrats occupy the centre rather than the political left wing, and there was a substantial shift to the right in the elections late in 1994 with Republicans seizing control in both Houses.

THE NETHERLANDS

Trade union density in the public sector is considerably higher than in the private sector and one of the main union federations (ACV), formed in 1990, is an organisation representing mainly public sector employees. The other main federations do also have public sector membership and have sought to bargain with government and its representatives over pay and other terms and conditions of employment.

Traditionally government has sought to control public sector pay and terms and conditions, and for many years government refused to bargain with unions representing its employees; consultation was as much as it would allow. Public sector employees have also been subject to unilaterally imposed pay freezes and between 1962 and 1982 their rates of pay were directly linked to rises achieved in the private sector. Since 1982 there has been a gradual relaxation in the direction of genuine collective bargaining, although periods of national austerity and retrenchment tend to be accompanied by efforts to control public expenditure; public sector employees are vulnerable in such circumstances as they are elsewhere.

GOVERNMENT AS LEGISLATOR

As noted earlier, the extent, nature and objectives of legislative activity and intervention by government and the precise means chosen vary from country to country, and over time are inevitably influenced by governments' values and beliefs, and their industrial, economic and social policies. Additionally, Brewster[3] points out the significance of national culture on legislation in his comparison of European traditions with those of the US.

It is difficult in a book of this length to do this subject justice, since in the countries chosen for specific study the variety of legislative subject matter and method is immense. Nonetheless, it is possible to devise broad categories of intervention according to: (a) whether the object of the legislation is essentially collective or individual and (b) whether the intent of the legislation is protective of particular interests or to provide a framework for and/or regulate the interaction and activities of the parties. To some extent, these typologies overlap, in that much of the protective leg-

islation is protective of individuals rather than collectives, and much of the framework legislation is indeed aimed at collective relations, interaction, activity and institutions. The usefulness of such typologies is as frameworks facilitating analysis and comparison and we intend to use the latter, the one which seeks to distinguish protective legislation from regulatory and framework legislation.

It is impossible to examine legal systems in detail in this section. Suffice to say that in countries other than the UK, the traditions have been of statutory intervention of a positive rights nature, whereas in the UK the traditions have been of common law freedoms and obligations and the statutory creation of immunities; although over the last 30 years this has changed and there has been a much greater emphasis on statutory intervention of a positive rights nature.

Regulatory and framework legislation

In most countries, trade unions developed in part in response to some of the consequences of market individualism, a perspective which disapproves of combination and the collective pursuit of sectional interests in conflict with others. In many of these countries, combination and collective action were unlawful and consequently legislative intervention was necessary in order to render lawful the formation and membership of collectives, particularly trade unions. The potential for disruptive collective action was considerable and it quickly became apparent that governments often then sought to regulate the activities of the parties and, in particular, to impose statutory limitations on such action and encourage alternative forms of dispute resolution.

Nowadays, legislation often provides not only rights to organise and belong to trade unions, but also statutory mechanisms whereby unions can obtain recognition for collective bargaining purposes from employers. In some systems, unions can attain 'representative' status entitling them to recognition and bargaining rights wherever they have members. In others the quest for recognition has to be pursued piecemeal, but it can nevertheless be enforced if certain conditions are met.

In all of the countries under examination, collective bargaining is at least one of the main interactive processes and its level, scope and conduct are sometimes regulated. Some systems require the parties to bargaining to do so in 'good faith' and with a view to reaching agreement, and sometimes the minimum subject matter is also prescribed. Occasionally areas of managerial prerogative or management rights are also prescribed, which further delineates the issues that may be open to collective bargaining. The frequency of bargaining is generally not legislatively prescribed, although there are systems in which this happens, as in France. If collective agreements are legally enforceable, as they are in most of our countries and for a fixed period, it is also quite common for legislative prescription to cover when and in respect of what kinds of subject matter it is lawful to take industrial action.

In several of the countries, a legal distinction is drawn between disputes of right and disputes of interest, the former being disputes concerned with the application or interpretation of existing agreements, whereas the latter category refers to disputes concerning new or revised terms and conditions, the subject matter of a new or revised agreement or contract. Where such a legal distinction is drawn, it is common that disputes of right can be processed during the terms of the existing agreement whereas other disputes may not be. Sometimes the law stipulates that industrial action in support of disputes of right is lawful, whereas action in support of a matter of interest is lawful only when the contract term has expired and once legislatively stipulated conditions are met. These conditions might refer to specific amounts of notice to employers and/or procedures to be followed by the parties before taking action, for example unions might be required to ballot their members and obtain particular levels of support.

Where industrial action is deemed to be against the national interest, governments sometimes reserve the right to impose a delay or cooling-off period and in some instances such action is unlawful. We have noted in a preceding section that in some public sectors or systems, industrial action is unlawful in all circumstances.

Australia has been renowned for its system of compulsory arbitration, and both conciliation and arbitration are legislatively specified in some other systems as alternatives that must be tried either prior to, or in place of, industrial action; although of course they are not always successful and indeed parties do not always comply with the legislative prescription. Government may fund agencies providing these facilities. In some systems, such as those in the US and Japan, government has created the notion of an unfair labour practice which, when alleged, may prompt the involvement of government agencies or courts which are charged with deciding such disputes.

As noted above, in most of our countries individuals have the legal right to belong to a trade union and the unions themselves have a legal right to exist so long as they fulfil certain criteria, such as being independent of employers. Registration or certification schemes exist in some countries which specify the criteria that organisations must meet if they are to be granted the legal status of a trade union. This legal status is then usually linked to statutory rights and benefits, for example those relating to recognition and collective bargaining.

Individuals may or may not have the right to join any union they wish; the union that they may join may be circumscribed by some form of closed-shop agreement, although these or at least the pre-entry varieties are unlawful in many countries. Individuals can also be limited by the fact that there may only be one union to join, as for example in systems where the one union has sole bargaining rights in a particular industry or enterprise. In other systems where the union tradition is more fragmented, it may be that the individual does have a choice and that this choice is preserved legally. In France, the Netherlands and Italy individuals may well have a choice between a number of unions, the basis of their separation being ideology or religion.

We have already commented on the fact that trade unions may be confronted by a legislative requirement that certain procedures must be followed before the union can take industrial action. The activities and conduct of trade unions may well be limited by the law in other ways. In some systems, government has granted itself or some other agency the right to investigate the financial affairs of unions, and in many of our countries there are legal duties imposed on unions in the conduct and reporting of their financial affairs. Concerns about racketeering and corruption have prompted this kind of intervention in countries such as the US, whereas in others the motivation may be related to the use of union funds for political purposes or to issues of internal democracy.

In the majority of systems, unions are allowed to determine their own internal arrangements with respect to membership participation, the election of officers and other dimensions of internal administration and government. However, in the UK and US governments have intervened to a greater extent in these issues in the name of enhancing membership rights and democracy and, in the case of the US in particular, as part of the post-war purge of communism.

In most systems unions are entitled to information and certain other facilities relevant to their legitimate activities, and it is common for these facilities to include some agreement with the employers whereby any union subscriptions can be either deducted at source or collected at work. In those countries that are members of the European Union, trade unions must have rights to information and consultation in certain circumstances, such as collective redundancies and the transfer of undertakings, and on many matters associated with health and safety at work.

As discussed elsewhere in this text, collective bargaining is only one mechanism that may be utilised to facilitate employee participation in decision making. In some systems, governments have legislated to encourage the use of other participatory mechanisms such as consultation, works councils and employee representation on boards of directors, the legislation often specifying in detail the nature of the processes, rights of the participants and issues appropriate for discussion. In Germany, which is regarded as a model for such participatory arrangements, and the Netherlands the rights of the parties, processes and subject matter are specified in detail.

Crouch[4] has produced some very useful tables indicating the presence and nature of national legislative regulations on many of the above issues in a range of European countries and the US.

Protective legislation

Protective legislation is usually concerned with the interests of particular groups within society, such as ethnic minorities, or alternatively it is concerned with the health and safety of people at work or with protecting, maintaining or improving living standards. Protective legislation often seeks both to protect and to improve the object and, as noted in the introduction to this chapter, the protection of one specific interest often impinges on the autonomy of another.

In all the systems under examination, government intervened legislatively to protect and further the rights of women in terms of pay and access to and treatment at work. The European Union has also been active in this area. Fewer of the systems have witnessed legislative intervention to provide similar rights to ethnic minorities, the disabled or other minorities such as older workers. By and large, legislation of this nature has protection and equality as its objectives and would seem to be most effective when supported by some form of agency given the role of publicising the law, encouraging organisations and, where necessary, enforcing the law by pursuing those employers that do not comply. The effectiveness of such legislation is influenced by its success in encouraging changes of

attitude, usually notoriously difficult, as well as by the existence and activity of an enforcement agency. Countries such as Japan and Australia have been perhaps particularly tardy in seeking to protect and further the interests of these groups.

Legislation on health and safety and that concerned with the protection of particular interests sometimes coincide, so that in some systems regulations limiting the hours that groups such as women and young people are allowed to work and the kind of work they are allowed to do are justified on health and safety grounds, despite the fact that in some senses they introduce or at least seek to preserve inequalities of access and treatment. Recent European Union directives and proposed directives on matters such as maternity pay and leave, young people at work and even those relating to the rights of part-time and temporary employees are defended on grounds of health and safety.

Some protective legislation seeks to protect by stipulating that certain procedures be followed in particular circumstances. We have already noted European Union intervention in areas such as requiring informational and consultative procedures to be followed in the event of collective redundancies, transfers of undertakings and on many health and safety issues. There are other areas in which most systems have some form of legislative protection via procedural requirements. An example of this is the procedure to be followed when dismissing an employee. Even in the US in recent years, the courts have increasingly paid attention to procedural fairness in such cases, despite the traditional importance attached to the principle of employment at will. There is evidence of the pressures for labour force flexibility encouraging some European governments to relax certain of these protective procedural requirements.

Legislation geared towards the protection of the living standards and maintenance of income of those at work is common in many systems and tends to centre around legally supported minimum wage rates and indexation to some measure of price inflation. The Netherlands, Sweden and Italy have provided good examples of such systems in the past, and while minimum provision is still popular, indexation has tended to suffer in recent years under the weight of arguments that such schemes are inflationary and thereby damage competitiveness and economic growth which can be detrimental to the national interest. It is in this sense that one can arguably label the statutory regulation of pay and increases in pay as protective. Certainly these schemes, to the extent that they succeed in limiting the rate of price inflation, can be seen to protect the living standards of various unemployed groups in society. Such statutory incomes policies are not common to all systems, but they have been experimented with in several, usually as part of wider corporatist arrangements, and often as an alternative when voluntary corporatism fails. In recent years, one of the more durable attempts at such a policy has been in Australia since the election of the Labour government in 1983.

One of the continuing dilemmas facing governments that acknowledge a responsibility to low-paid groups is deciding the extent to which they should seek to achieve minimum income levels through wage legislation, as opposed to dealing with the issue via social security benefits and allowances, the latter having a less direct impact on labour markets. Once again, governmental perspective will be a significant influence on the decision; although there is evidence of much greater pressure on European governments, in particular from employers and other organisations such as the OECD, to shift the balance away from the employer and thereby limit the impact on labour costs and competitiveness.

Snapshot 3
GERMANY

The system in Germany is usually characterised as being highly regulated via a series of legislative interventions which provide and serve to regulate both the individual and collective relationships between employers and employees. Both sets of actors are given 'positive' rights and have obligations imposed on them, and there is a considerable amount of protective regulation of the terms and conditions of and treatment at work.

Employees have rights to join trade unions and to participate via various mechanisms (collective bargaining, worker representation on the board and works councils) in decisions concerning specified ranges of subject matter. In some instances the rights are to co-determination, in others there is a right of veto, while in yet others the rights are to consultation and/or information. Where employees are given rights to participate, this inevitably constitutes a limit on management's right to determine issues unilaterally. Where there are no such rights to participate, it can be argued that management's right to decide unilaterally is protected and, on some issues, this is specific. The parties are required to participate in these processes in a spirit of mutual trust and benefit.

Collective agreements are legally binding, and can be extended by government to cover all employers in the sector. The parties only have a right to take industrial action lawfully at the expiry of the agreement or contract term and on matters of interest, and trade unions are legally required to undertake a ballot of relevant members to gain approval for industrial action. A structure of Labour Courts exists at all levels to deal with or resolve disputes concerning matters of right, interpretation or application.

Labour market regulation is extensive via protections extended to labour; minimum rates of pay, hours of work, rights and mechanisms and procedures for hiring and dismissing are all regulated, as are types of permissible employment contract. Recession, unemployment and competition are resulting in pressures for relaxation of most of these 'protections', the argument being that they impose unacceptable constraints on the flexibility now required, and make employment too expensive.

Aspects of the working environment, health and safety, gender discrimination and protections for other minorities or specific groups are also covered by legislation.

UK

For many years governments resisted legislative intervention in the employment relationship; reliance was placed on contract and common law. The interaction of employers and employees as collectives was deemed to be a matter for the parties, supported if necessary by a system of freedoms, negative rights and legal immunities and the government provision of third-party assistance. Government intervention via legislation was to be avoided where possible and undertaken only where it was clear beyond doubt that particular interests could be protected in no other way, and even then such protection was not to be provided via the creation of a structure of positive rights.

Since the early 1960s the traditions of voluntarism and non-intervention have been mortally wounded, but those of negative rights, freedoms and immunities as opposed to positive rights remain significant, despite some greater willingness to create positive rights. A specialised system of industrial tribunals has been created to adjudicate claims that individual rights have been infringed.

Collective agreements are not legally enforceable except in that they become incorporated into individual contracts of employment. No legal distinction is drawn between disputes of right and interest; individuals do not have a positive right to take industrial action and can be lawfully dismissed for doing so. Individuals have only recently been given a right to join a trade union and trade unions have no right to recognition by an employer for bargaining purposes, and no means apart from persuasion of encouraging an employer to recognise them whether it be for bargaining or other purposes. There are no legislative requirements regarding other forms of employee participation, as for example, in works councils or board-level representation.

Trade unions are lawful institutions but have to comply with a series of legislative requirements regarding the election of officers, calling of industrial action, maintenance of political funds and collection of union dues. Union members have been given legal rights as members not to be discriminated against and not to be disciplined for not taking part in properly instituted industrial action. With respect to industrial action, trade unions retain an immunity from being sued for damages, so long as they comply with legislative requirements regarding the subject matter of the dispute (the range of acceptable subject matter has been narrowed in recent years), the balloting of members and the giving of notice to the employer. Closed shops are lawful but not legitimate subject matter for industrial action; lawful secondary/sympathy action is barely possible and picketing in support of industrial action is lawful but regulated.

There is relatively little legislative protection of individual security at work. There are circumscribed rights not to be unfairly dismissed or discriminated against on grounds of sex and race, but otherwise reliance is placed on contract. Living standards are not protected via minimum wage legislation and generally there are no legislative limitations on hours of work. Individuals do have rights to minimum periods of notice if dismissed and payments in the event of redundancy. Women also have specific protections regarding employment during pregnancy, a right to return to work and certain minimum payments during a period of maternity leave. There is fairly extensive legislative provision with respect to the health and safety of employees. Some of these protections are the result of European Union initiatives and directives, although the UK government has generally resisted initiatives which it considered would damage industrial competitiveness. The labour market in the UK is one of the least regulated among industrialised nations and much of the legislative intervention over the last 15 years has been specifically directed towards achieving this deregulated status.

SWEDEN

Before the 1970s, government had intervened relatively little via legislation to regulate the employment relationship or to provide the framework within which collective 'relations' occurred. The main actors, employers and trade unions, had voluntarily taken care of the collective relationship in their agreement at Saltsjobaden in 1938, and thereby they set the tone of centralised self-regulation that has been a crucial feature of the Swedish model. Rights to free organisation, binding agreements, limits on industrial action during the period of an agreement, the right to terminate agreements on notice and employer rights to determine production issues unilaterally were all covered by this agreement. A distinction is drawn between matters of right and interest. Industrial action in pursuit of a matter of right is not lawful, further negotiation or referral to the structure of labour courts being the solution to such disputes. Legislative intervention in 1977 gave the unions priority of interpretation in such disputes pending a subsequent outcome.

The considerably increased level of legislative intervention in the 1970s and 1980s was initially prompted by a desire to enhance employee participation and improve the working environment. The 1970s saw legislation on worker directors, trade union safety representatives' rights and duties, the formation of safety committees, the extension of the rights to information and consultation before dismissals and changes to working arrangements, and time-off facilities for shop stewards. The intentions with respect to the extension of collective bargaining subject matter were not really effectively achieved, since the parties were left to deal with detail and implementation via a development agreement; eventually this was largely on management's terms.

Recent legislative proposals have been very different in nature and tone, increasing fines for unlawful strikes, enforcing pre-strike ballots and imposing mediation on the parties in certain kinds of dispute. These are indicative of a shift in the direction of protecting employers rather than employees, and there is no doubt that the centre-right coalition government elected in 1991 did see a reduction of trade union power as one of its main priorities. Historically the protection of individuals and minority groups has been largely achieved through the unions agreeing to operate egalitarian and solidaristic wage policies, effectively creating adequate minima allied to government, fiscal, economic, social and active labour market policies consistent with objectives of full employment and social welfare.

ITALY

The 1948 Constitution and 1970 Workers Statute collectively gave employees the right to establish, join and take part in trade union activities. Government has not imposed rights or obligations with respect to taking part in collective bargaining, but for many years now (since 1959) collective bargaining at industry level has been supported by government via the mechanisms of giving legal effect to the outcomes, thereby effectively regulating many of the substantive and economic dimensions of the employment relationship.

Generally, governments have not sought legislatively to regulate the process of collective bargaining or to limit the right to strike, and no legal distinction is drawn between matters of right and interest. However, the 1970 statute did seek to encourage the formation of a unified, union-based employee representative structure and collective bargaining in the workplace, and gave employees some protections from discriminatory or disciplinary action against them because of their trade union activities.

The legal regulation of many substantive terms and conditions of employment has, as noted above, been the product in many cases of giving legislative effect to the outcomes of bargaining, but there have also been instances of specific legislative interventions to give employees protection. In all, a considerable range of dimensions of the employment relationship are regulated, including minimum rates of pay, maximum hours of work, types of contract, recruitment processes, disciplinary and dismissal processes, and management's unilateral right to introduce change.

In the 1980s and since, there has been considerable pressure to relax the regulations in many of these areas with a view to enhancing labour flexibility and job creation. The 1993 Accord introduces further possibilities of legislative relaxation, as well as a threat of legislative intervention as an incentive to the other parties to reach agreement on reforming workplace representation.

JAPAN

Governments in Japan have not been renowned for their interventionist approach. Once the legislative framework was established in the years immediately following the second world war, there have been relatively few employment relationship issues on which the government has felt obliged to legislate. In recent years, legislation has been introduced to encourage equal opportunities to facilitate the raising of mandatory retirement ages, although its requirements are not particularly demanding, and proposals have been made to encourage a reduction in working hours thereby beginning to address issues associated with the quality of working life. 1992 saw the legislative provision of a version of paternity leave.

The framework established in the late 1940s and periodically amended since then provides employees with rights to organise, bargain and take strike action, and the notion of an unfair labour practice. It also requires employers to have works rules which effectively constitute minimum terms and conditions of employment or standards on issues such as rates of pay, hours of work and holidays; but again, the law does not specify the standards, simply that employers must have them. The government in this period also created legislative machinery for conciliating, mediating, arbitrating and dealing with allegations of unfair labour practices. Only employers can commit an unfair labour practice such as failing to bargain (in good faith) on discriminating against employees because of their trade union activities.

More recently, mechanisms have been created to advise the government on appropriate minimum rates of pay which the government then sets. Collective agreements are legally enforceable, but there is no legislative distinction drawn between matters of right and interest, and also no legislative encouragement of employee participation other than through collective bargaining.

Substantive terms and conditions are generally not legislatively prescribed or protected, and the working environment including health and safety are only relatively recent concerns.

US

The legislative framework for the conduct of collective relationships between employers and employees was established initially in the 1930s, with subsequent amendments in the late 1940s and 1950s. Since then, legislative interventions have been relatively few and far between, and have been primarily aimed at extending private sector rights and responsibilities into the public sector and the protection and furtherance of particular minority interests and equality, the nature of this protection often being anti-discriminatory and concerned with civil rights. Just recently, new statutory rights have been provided to facilitate family care.

Governments since the 1930s have been generally anti-trade union and pro-employer, and the 1940s and 1950s amendments to the framework legislation were consistent with this general orientation. The initial legislative interventions, in contrast, were concerned to create rights for employees to organise and bargain with employers, with duties at the same time being imposed on employers to bargain in good faith, and not to exert undue pressure on employees with a view to encouraging them not to join or participate in unionism. Such latter actions constitute unfair labour practices. The early legislation also created the machinery for allegations of unfair practices.

Employees have a right to join a trade union or to refrain from joining. With sufficient support recognition for bargaining can be enforced, and the parties are required to bargain in good faith. The subject matter of bargaining is also regulated in terms of permissible, mandatory and prohibited topics. Collective agreements are legally enforceable contracts, and generally industrial action is lawful only on expiry of these agreements or in the event of an unfair labour practice. Employers are frequently able lawfully to dismiss employees on strike. Governments have problems with legislating to afford employee protection against dismissal, since it is not consistent with the doctrine of employment at will. However, judicial interpretation of constitutional rights with respect to property and just cause has helped in this respect.

The trade unions are also covered by legislation governing their internal government and financial affairs and individual members have certain legislative rights in respect of these matters.

Generally governments have not sought to regulate substantive terms and conditions, although there are mechanisms for determining and establishing minimum rates of pay, overtime premiums and maximum hours of work. The working environment is regulated via legislation on health and safety.

FRANCE

Employees have a constitutional right to a job, to join a trade union and defend their interests, to take action and to have representatives with rights to information and consultation. Depending on their ideological orientation, governments have generally legislated either to protect and preserve the unilateral rights of man-

agement/employers and minimise the rights and protections afforded to employees; or alternatively to encourage trade unionism, collective bargaining and other participatory mechanisms such as works councils and to regulate terms and conditions of employment in the interests of employees. Over the last decade, socialist governments sought to encourage collective bargaining on pay at company level on an annual basis. The new right-wing government is seeking to deregulate in areas such as hours and times of work and types of employment contract so as to give greater flexibility to employers in their pursuit of efficiency and competitiveness. Legislative proposals to enable undercutting of minimum wage legislation in respect of the under 26s in order to encourage employment occasioned mass public protests early in 1994 and the government withdrew them.

The traditions are of substantial legal regulation of terms and conditions of employment such as minimum rates of pay, redundancy rights and pay, maternity leave and pay, and hours of work, and government extension of collective agreements. Collective agreements are legally enforceable, although there is no legal obligation to bargain in good faith or to reach agreement and there is no legislative distinction between rights and interests. It seems as if individual signatory unions may be about to be given an effective veto over changes to collective agreements with which they disagree, even if other signatory unions have agreed to them.

Employees also have legislatively created rights of direct expression outside trade union arrangements. In support of the legislative encouragement of company-level bargaining, employees were granted rights to elect workplace delegates and committees for bargaining purposes.

Works councils (which are joint bodies) should be created in companies above a certain size and large, multi-plant companies are required to establish such councils at corporate level. The role of these councils is essentially informational and consultative, and the legislation specifies the appropriate subject matter. These councils do not have co-determination rights.

AUSTRALIA

Federal governments' opportunity to influence legislatively and/or regulate the employment relationship has been severely limited by the legislation creating and reinforcing the system of compulsory arbitration. In recent years, they have intervened in areas such as sex discrimination, equal opportunities and health and safety, and since 1988 legislation has been enacted changing the membership requirements for trade union registration. The object of this latter intervention is to assist in the restructuring of the trade union movement. Generally employers' prerogatives over business and production issues have not been contested by legislation.

Government has not commonly legally regulated substantive terms and conditions; this has usually been a consequence of an appropriate and legally enforceable arbitration award. The Arbitration Tribunals are independent of government.

Collective bargaining has not been a particularly common feature of the system, although it can result in a consent award by a tribunal which certifies and gives legal effect to the agreement. Enterprise level agreements certified by tribunals are encouraged by the 1993 Accord.

THE NETHERLANDS

Government has intervened relatively little via legislative provision of a framework or regulation of the relationships between the main parties. Collective agreements are legally binding as contracts, and can be extended to employers not in membership of a signatory association via the Collective Agreement Extension Act of 1937. However, there is relative freedom for the parties outside these legislative constraints, no legal compulsion to bargain, no legislative distinction between disputes of right and interest; although action during the period of an agreement can be unlawful since agreements are legally binding and there is no requirement to seek conciliation or arbitration as an alternative to industrial action. There is no statutory requirement to give notice of strike action but failure to give such notice can render such action unlawful on the grounds that it is 'premature and unconsidered'. Unofficial action is unlawful as may be certain other kinds, such as political strikes. Recognition of trade unions affiliated to one of the main federations is automatic, but given the relative absence of union activity at levels below the industry, recognition at company level has tended not to be an issue.

Government is itself constrained by the requirement to consult the SER before enacting legislation on social and economic issues.

One of the main items subjected to centralised control, often via statute, has been wages. For much of the post-war period, wages in the private as well as

the public sector have been subject to such controls. This control, whether statutory or voluntary, was perceived as essential to economic recovery after the war and periodically since as an essential instrument for achieving international competitiveness and export-led growth, as well as assisting in the desired redistribution of income/wealth.

The main statutory means used to constrain employer freedom to decide issues unilaterally has not been via a legal requirement to bargain or to decide in good faith, but rather via the legislative requirement that enterprises employing over 35 employees should create a works council, which once created has statutorily backed rights to information and consultation on some issues and to give its consent and approve others. Other legislation is derived from European Union membership which grants information and consultative rights to employees in certain specific circumstances. The law on works councils does also give effective primacy to collective agreements.

On the protective dimension, legislation has been used to protect living standards via a combination of a statutory minimum wage and various comprehensive welfare benefits covering disability, unemployment, sickness and retirement. There is also, as in other member states of the EU, fairly substantial legislative creation and protection of individual employment rights in areas such as health and safety, equal pay, access and treatment, maternity leave and pay, and acquired rights on the transfer of control of an undertaking and redundancy. The works council has been used as the vehicle for ensuring some of this protection.

Individual rights of association and collective rights of assembly are specified in the constitution in articles 8 and 9, and generally individuals are protected from dismissal for taking part in a strike. Hours of work, holidays and notice periods are also subject to statutory regulation.

LABOUR MARKET POLICIES

The significance of perspective is again apparent the moment one begins to examine the extent and nature of government intervention to influence either the supply of or demand for labour, or both.

Liberal individualist, laisser-faire, neo-classical governments tend not to espouse active intervention, given their belief in the efficacy of the free market as a resource allocator and individual decision making and responsibilities. However, consistent with their preference for supply-side measures for regulation of the economy, they also tend to favour supply-side measures if and when they do intervene actively or directly in labour markets. Such governments are likely to argue that the most effective way of increasing supply is through attacking and reducing barriers to mobility and flexibility, such as those enforced by trade unions, and reducing taxation and/or 'too high' unemployment and social security benefits, both of which, it is argued, will encourage people to want to work, on the one hand because they will keep more of what they earn, and on the other because unemployed life will no longer be so comfortable. Underlying such arguments is a belief in and a reliance on money or income as an effective incentive to work. Such measures might address quantity issues with respect to labour supply, but are much less likely to address issues associated with quality.

With respect to quality, measures would need to address matters such as education, training, skills and competencies. With the exception of pre-work education, governments of a *laisser-faire* persuasion are likely to emphasise the role and responsibility of the private sector in ensuring that the quality of their labour supply is adequate. The private sector would be expected to train and retrain both current and future employees. Government is likely to accept some responsibility for pre-work education, but even here it may well advocate a greater role for private sector employers, possibly in financing, but more probably in contributing towards the determination of the subject matter and direction of pre-work education.

In addition to reducing the real value of unemployment and/or other social security benefits, governments of this perspective may well acknowledge that they have a legitimate role to play in the organisation and provision of vacancy information to the unemployed. They may also provide services to the unemployed which might help them to obtain work, such as mobility or relocation assistance of a financial kind, and training in how to fill out application forms, devise curriculum vitae, and present and conduct themselves at interviews. They are likely to be more reluctant when it comes to the issue of providing job-related training opportunities for those unemployed, and are much more likely to see this as desirably and more effectively provided through some mix of individual initiative and private enterprise funding.

On the demand side, governments of this persuasion are likely to be even more reluctant to intervene directly at a macro level. They are unlikely to be willing to manage aggregate demand in order to achieve full employment, and they are unlikely to be prepared to increase public expenditure with a view to job creation, even on infrastructure projects. However, at a micro level, such governments may be prepared to help in job creation via various mechanisms such as tax reliefs and incentives or subsidies to employers for locating in areas of high unemployment, and specific assistance to small and medium-sized employers, arguably the main creators of new jobs. Those countries within the European Union have access to several Union-wide schemes of this nature.

Governments of a liberal collectivist and certainly of a corporatist perspective are much more likely to have accepted Keynesian explanations and prescriptions with respect to economic management. Consequently, they are likely to give a higher priority to the maintenance of full employment and accept that government has a legitimate and effective role to play in influencing the level of employment through the management of aggregate demand. It is always important to bear in mind that the demand for labour is derived from the demand for its products. Consequently, government policies which expand the level of aggregate demand for goods and services are likely to have a positive impact on the demand for labour and thereby the levels of employment/unemployment. Such governments are also more likely to use taxation and public expenditure for the purpose of job creation, thereby influencing more directly the demand for labour.

They are much more likely to invest in infrastructure schemes and to favour public ownership, and many will see this as a mechanism for protecting industries and saving jobs. Liberal collectivist governments are somewhat less likely to intervene directly via other mechanisms than are those of a full-blown corporatist perspective, but when they do they may well favour demand-side initiatives.

Corporatist governments, with their emphasis on interest mediation, will almost certainly involve representatives of capital and labour in the management of the economy, emphasising co-operation if not partnership. They are also much more likely to adopt a directly interventionist approach on both the demand and supply sides of the market, using public expenditure to create work and embarking on publicly funded and administered training initiatives for the young and the unemployed, perhaps even using public funds to assist employers with the training and retraining of their existing employees. Certainly, such governments are likely to provide financial and other assistance with labour mobility and relocation, and will willingly fund job-finding mechanisms, sometimes involving the 'social partners' in the administration of these arrangements and of unemployment benefit schemes. It is relatively difficult for corporatist governments to take direct measures to diminish whatever restrictions trade unions may impose on the supply of labour, but it is quite possible that they may seek to encourage liberalisation of working practices and demarcations where these are a hindrance to flexibility.

In periods of recession, liberal collectivist and corporatist governments are both more likely than liberal individualists to seek to protect and enhance employment levels through the promotion of schemes such as job sharing and reductions in working hours, as well as seeking to protect living standards through more generous redundancy, lay-off, unemployment and social security payments and provisions.

Brewster[5] illustrates the generally more interventionist approach of European governments as compared with the US by drawing attention to the percentages of GDP spent on active labour market programmes, including training, retraining, job-transition support, job-creation schemes and programmes to help both the younger and long-term unemployed.

Late 1993 and 1994 has been a period in which the different perspectives and approaches referred to in this section have been very publicly aired within the European Union, the OECD and between the G7 countries as part of the debates within all of these fora on unemployment, and perhaps particularly the European unemployment problem. While some measure of consensus has been achieved on both causes and solutions, there are clearly differences of emphasis at least between those favouring *laisser-faire*, market-force approaches and others who accept some necessity to deregulate but not at the expense of social justice. These issues are discussed in more detail in Chapter 19.

Snapshot 4
GERMANY
Governments in (West) Germany have pursued positive, active and preventative labour market policies over recent decades. The Work Promotion Act 1968 formed the base for much of this activity, promoting vocational training, job preservation and creation. However, these policies have been pursued within the context of substantial labour market regulation and

social protection, and an economic environment facilitating growth and employment. The Federal Institute for Labour has been the agency through which many of these schemes have been financed and administration has often been tripartite. Germany is renowned for its national system of vocational training/retraining and the relative success of manufacturing industry has derived in part from the skill levels and flexibility facilitated by this national scheme.

In 1994 government is confronted by a different context of rising unemployment and a declining manufacturing base, and in February it proposed a 30-point action plan of measures to deregulate and reduce unemployment. This programme incorporates the legalisation of private employment agencies, thereby ending the state monopoly; measures to encourage the unemployed to set themselves up in business; incentives to encourage the long-term unemployed to take seasonal work; deregulation of rules that make it difficult and unattractive for employers to hire part-time employees; and measures making it more difficult or less attractive to hire illegal immigrants. These are part of a package that also incorporates further privatisation and incentives and benefits for small businesses. It seems likely that these measures, if successful, will create employment that mirrors much of the employment created in the 1980s in the UK and the US, i.e. part time and in the service sector. With much labour-intensive and low-technology work already being exported to Eastern Europe, there is an obvious danger that Germany will in the future have very much higher and more intractable levels of long-term, structural, male unemployment. It is quite likely that government will come under considerable pressure to deregulate further and to reduce the non-wage costs of employment.

SWEDEN
The tradition before the election of a right-wing coalition government in 1991 was of consensus and tripartism with government pursuing active labour market policies aimed at easing mobility and re-employment. For many years, less was spent on unemployment benefit than on the combined programmes of mobility allowance, training and retraining, counselling and job creation. Many of these initiatives and programmes were operated by the Labour Market Board.

Since 1991 government policy has changed significantly. There has been a widespread and ongoing programme of privatisation and reliance on market forces. The greater reliance on market forces has been extended into labour markets. No longer are companies and jobs protected as they once were, and no longer is there the government will to intervene so actively in the creation and location of work and in the retraining, relocation and re-employment of displaced labour. Unemployment in Sweden has risen to historically record levels in the 1990s.

Many of the major Swedish manufacturing companies have invested abroad, sometimes to take advantage of the benefits of being located within the Single Market and, as in many other economies, employment growth seems most likely in the service and small enterprise sectors.

JAPAN

Traditionally, government in Japan has not been an active participant in labour market terms. Government has recently sought to encourage shorter working hours, but primarily for quality of work life reasons, and has relaxed the rules with respect to the employment of professional and skilled foreign labour at the same time as reinforcing controls on the immigration of unskilled people seeking work in Japan.

The coalition government of Hosokawa, which resigned in April 1991, sought to use income tax cuts and public expenditure increases to stimulate the economy in response to the recession and increasing unemployment, but political difficulties seem to have prevented effective action. Similar difficulties also confronted government proposals at the end of 1993 to create a fund to subsidise companies hiring workers over the age of 45 who have been shed by other firms, the previous age limit for such subsidy having been 55.

Governments have relied on creating conditions in which organisations could thrive and the economy expand without substantial regulation of the market. Training has largely been provided by employing organisations and, with demand for labour buoyant, unemployment has been low. The tradition of organisations emphasising internal mobility and promotion allied to lifetime employment assisted government in its passive labour market role. However, recession and enhanced international competition have combined in the 1990s to create a situation in which government may be confronted by pressures to become more active and interventionist.

FRANCE

There is a substantial tradition of governments intervening to influence the scale and nature of labour market activity. Many terms and conditions of employment are legally regulated, and there have been efforts in recent years to enhance flexibility in labour markets by varying rules with respect to the authorisation of redundancies, working hours, weekend and overtime working, and atypical arrangements such as part-time, temporary and fixed-term contracts. At the end of the 1980s, government encouraged the social partners to conclude framework agreements at national level that would ease the introduction of new technology and new working practices and facilitate retraining and reclassification of jobs. The parties were also encouraged similarly to address issues of equal pay for work of equal value.

Various attempts have been made to influence levels of unemployment (particularly among the young) and assist industrial restructuring via vocational training initiatives, and governments have also used macro-economic and fiscal policy instruments to encourage job creation and subsidies, nationalisation and other forms of state aid to protect jobs.

Two examples early in 1994 illustrate some of these approaches. First, government tried to counter the very high levels of unemployment among the under 26s by proposing to change the law so that young people on training contracts could be paid between 30 and 80 per cent of the appropriate minimum wage (SMIC). This caused student protest and mass demonstrations, which in turn encouraged government to revise the proposals to give subsidies to employers to encourage them to create jobs or training places for young unemployed people. The second example concerns restructuring, longer working hours and job losses at Air France. Employees eventually agreed to a package of measures, central to which was substantial additional state financial assistance amounting to the injection of 20 billion francs over three years. At the time of writing, these proposals have just been approved by the European Commission despite opposition by other European airlines which allege that it infringes fair competition rules.

UK

The thrust of recent government activity with respect to labour markets has been supply side and deregulatory, removing 'barriers' to mobility and flexibility and encouraging private sector provision of training and in many instances recipient purchase or partial payment. The latter principle has been extended into the state educational sector at higher levels and also into post-school vocational training. Government expenditure on training, enterprise and labour market services has been falling in real terms in the late 1980s and early 1990s.

Some initiatives have been taken to encourage the creation of self-employment and small businesses, but government has refrained from policies of active job creation via demand management, public expenditure or infrastructure schemes.

The emphasis of government policy has consistently been non-interventionist and deregulatory, reflecting its belief in the efficiency of the market, and unemployment has often been viewed as an inevitable consequence of the necessity to restructure, reduce unit labour costs and regain competitiveness. Individuals are assumed to be capable of looking after their own interests, and certainly government has emphasised individual responsibility as opposed to state provision and protection. In this context it has emphasised that the market mechanism should be allowed to determine wage and employment levels.

The May 1994 white paper on competitiveness does not indicate any significant departure from these traditions, nor have the government's contributions to debates within the European Union concerning unemployment and social policies.

ITALY

Government has intervened via regulation of terms and conditions of employment including wages, hours of work and restrictions on part-time and temporary contracts. There is also restrictive regulation of hiring and firing. However in many ways, the more significant activity has been in job creation and protection via infrastructure projects, public ownership and subsidies to employers in the private sector. Government has also funded substantial early retirement and temporary lay-off schemes. Many of these interventions have in the past been in the South and the often unproductive transfer of funds from North to South has provided a rallying point for the Lombard League and arguments in favour of separatism and federalism.

Governments in the early 1990s have taken some initiatives towards enhancing labour market flexibility, and certainly the newly elected right-wing alliance headed by Berlusconi's Forza Italia campaigned on the grounds of easing the restrictive rules on hiring and firing, further privatisation and fiscal incentives to employers to create jobs.

March 1994 has provided some examples of government intervening in a traditional way, funding early retirement and temporary lay-offs as part of both private and public sector packages encompassing job losses and 'solidarity contracts'.

Solidarity contracts in this context refer to agreements providing for work sharing and reductions in working time and pay. One of these state-funded packages was in the state-controlled steel group Ilva and was to fund 10 500 early retirements with a further 1200 jobs being saved through solidarity contracts. The other was at Fiat and additionally provided for state-subsidised retraining and job seeking, linked to government providing substantial research and development finance for work on a new 'environmentally clean' car. The Fiat funding was for 6500 early retirements and 3500 solidarity contracts. These agreements are very much consistent with the terms of the July 1993 Accord, which also included measures aimed at addressing regional imbalances and infrastructure projects.

US

The Clinton administration is keen to change the emphasis of government labour market policies from traditionally very passive, whereby government has relied on growth and a largely deregulated and therefore flexible labour market, to one which is much more active. In particular, the government accepts a need to ease the transition from school to work and from unemployment to employment. To this end it unveiled in March 1994 a set of proposals including an extension of unemployment benefits for people undertaking training, from a maximum of 26 weeks at present to a maximum of two years. Further proposals in June, aimed at ending the dependency cycle among the unemployed born since 1971, also seek to encourage employment after two years of unemployment with additional expenditure on education, training and job placement, counselling and childcare provision and services. Federal government is also seeking to produce a much more coherent unemployment counselling and retraining service from the fairly disparate activities and services currently offered at state level.

These new policy emphases are a recognition of the failure of the relatively unregulated labour market to produce both highly skilled and highly paid jobs or a highly skilled labour force. Average weekly real earnings in the private sector in the US actually fell slightly between 1960 and 1992, and at the same time there was an increase in the inequality of income distribution and an increase between 1979 and 1992 of those in full-time employment earning poverty-level wages.

Despite the change in emphasis, there are no signs that the Democrat government envisages further regulation of the labour market, and this has been made even less likely by the resurgence of Republican support in the 1994 elections.

AUSTRALIA

Federal government has been relatively passive as a labour market influence and government expenditure on active labour market measures has been relatively low, as a percentage of GNP only marginally above that in the US and Japan.

Nevertheless, over the last decade the government has sought to provide the private sector with financial incentives to encourage flexibility and training. Australia, like other developed economies, has begun to experience structural unemployment with its corresponding demands for labour mobility, flexibility and retraining. In 1994 the federal government proposed a set of measures encouraging employment, job creation and training which indicate the adoption of a more active approach.

The sorts of policies that might be pursued at federal level by a more conservative government have perhaps been indicated by the state government in Victoria, with its emphasis on deregulation and individualism.

THE NETHERLANDS

Governments have not tended to place much emphasis on active labour market policies to deal with unemployment or specific skills shortages. Most of government's attention has been paid to income maintenance and the provision of a comprehensive welfare state. Full employment has not been a specified objective, although undoubtedly it was assumed to be a national consequence of successful reindustrialisation and economic growth, and indeed for many years it was. In more recent times, however, unemployment has risen consistently and governments have been subject to substantial criticism for failing to address the issue constructively and, for example, for failing to engage in infrastructure expenditure as a means of job creation. Comparisons are often drawn with Sweden, where the emphasis of government expenditure and attention has been on 'getting people back to work' and not on income maintenance. Even when initiatives have been taken to promote employment, for example reductions in working hours and enhanced flexibility in the use of part-time and temporary labour, the motives have often been linked to the achievement of other objectives, such as wage restraint or facilitating a reduction in unit labour costs.

Government now faces great difficulty in seeking to reduce the scale of income maintenance, whether it be disability benefits, social security benefits or the minimum wage, because the proposals are seen as primarily motivated by the need to reduce public expenditure rather than as part of an active labour market programme geared towards resolving some of the causes and consequences of unemployment. Proposals by the CDA in January 1994 to freeze state old-age pensions so as to facilitate job creation programmes seem to have been met by the electorate with a similar scepticism.

GOVERNMENTS AND CONVERGENCE

As noted elsewhere, those countries that are members of the European Union are subject to pressures encouraging convergence on at least some dimensions of national human resource systems, employee relations and human resource management. Individual member state governments are obviously in a position to influence the extent to which convergence is both aimed for and achieved. They participate in the decision-making processes within the Council of Ministers and to some extent they also have the freedom to decide:

● whether to comply with Union directives and requirements; and
● if they choose to comply, which precise method to use, e.g. whether to legislate or rely on the social partners to agree and implement.

Pressure for convergence has increased considerably since the establishment of a Single Market and the attendant concerns over the dangers of 'social dumping'.

However, debate continues as to the extent of and real prospects for such convergence and indeed its nature. Certainly, the UK government's opposition to many of the proposals for European Union intervention and legislation that emanated out of the social charter and formed the social action programme, allied to its negotiation of an opt-out from the Social Chapter in the proposed Union Treaty signed at Maastricht, have made more problematic the achievement of even a gradual convergence on minimum terms and conditions of employment and issues such as employee participation. The current position adopted by the eleven, which does not insist on specific models of participation in appropriate multinationals, is perhaps indicative of a diminution in these pressures and prospects. This has not been assisted by the impact of the recession on other member states who in some instances are beginning to echo sentiments formerly the sole preserve of the UK government. The latter's success in achieving a relative decline in unit labour costs and deregulation of the labour market over recent years appears to have played a significant part in the considerable success that the UK has had in attracting inward investment from non-EU member states, particularly from companies originating in Japan and the US.

Other convergence debates tend to centre on the impact of global/international developments in terms of technology, competition, product markets and production systems and new methods of organising work. To some extent, the debate about convergence in this global context is a debate between technical determinists and others who emphasise the significance of strategic choice on the part of system actors and the relevance of national traditions, institutions, legislation and cultures. If governmental perspective or ideology plays a role in whether systems converge, it is likely that technical determinists will seek to minimise the significance of this variable, whereas those favouring strategic choice, institutional and cultural explanations will tend to emphasise its impact.

This debate is certainly not new and was given considerable impetus by Kerr et al.[6] who predicted that there was a global tendency for the technical and market forces associated with industrialisation to push national industrial relations systems towards uniformity or convergence. They have also suggested a logic of industrialisation that would encourage a larger role for governments in providing the necessary infrastructure and corporatist approaches and contexts.

We tend to the non-deterministic viewpoint and would emphasise the relevance and role of ideological, institutional and cultural factors in mediating the impact of common global and international developments. However, we acknowledge that to the extent that global technological and production system developments encourage or necessitate decentralisation of decision making and relevant institutions and structures, and deregulation of labour markets, there may be the implication of a diminished role for governments. Certainly the trend in Europe seems to be away from corporatism and interventionism towards deregulation, decentralisation and perhaps less protective legislation.

Grahl and Teague[7] identify two different flexibility system models emerging in Europe in response to these various global developments: competitive flexibility and constructive flexibility. Each model implies a different role for government, but it is also clear that whichever system emerges in a particular country, it

will be influenced by the traditions and values of the actors in it, including government. For example, the neo-liberal ideology of Conservative governments in the UK in recent years has supported the development of the competitive flexibility trajectory, whereas the social welfarism and corporatism of governments in Sweden and Germany have supported the constructive flexibility model. Grahl and Teague[8] further comment that the greater the influence of policies determined by governments at European Union level, the greater the likelihood that the Union will experience the installation of the constructive flexibility model. As noted above and elsewhere (Chapter 19)[9] there is evidence of an inclination within the European Commission to consolidate over the next few years rather than embark on a whole new programme of legislative intervention. Nevertheless, the role of the European judiciary should not be underestimated as a source of convergence.

Ferner and Hyman[9] claim that the common context of structural transformation and economic crisis has had a number of cross-national impacts on the role of government in a number of countries in Europe. First, they argue that the twin pressures of employers seeking greater labour flexibility and the necessity to tackle massive unemployment have encouraged governments to deregulate labour markets, in some cases by attacking sources of imperfection. Secondly, they perceive a general dynamic within and across Europe to curtail public expenditure and make the operation of the state more effective. In many countries this has resulted in pressures on government as an employer to curtail wage costs and jobs, particularly in the public enterprise sector. The third cross-national impact that Ferner and Hyman[10] identify is the weakening of corporatist and tripartite arrangements and solutions. However, they also emphasise the variability and independence of institutional arrangements and the influence these have in mediating these broad tendencies.

Keller[11] also acknowledges that the global developments comprising the new technologies and trends towards flexibility have implications for the role of the government which, he suggests, may well be generally a diminished role. However, he also attaches significant importance to the 'colour', ideology and priorities of governments in mediating the pace, extent and nature of the responses to those developments within individual countries. He suggests two likely scenarios depending on whether government is conservative or social democratic, and these scenarios seem not too far removed from the competitive and constructive flexibility models of Grahl and Teague.[12]

SUMMARY

The ideology of government is a significant influence upon the system. It influences, for example:

- its approach to the traditional government role of employer, legislator, conciliator;
- the policy choices made, including those concerning the operation of the labour market, labour supply and demand, and interest mediation;
- the roles available to and played by the other main participants;
- the process and practice of human resource management and employee relations;
- employment and employment relationship outcomes.

However, governments are themselves influenced, and there is some evidence to suggest that developments within the international marketplace, competitive pressures and technological innovation, and their contribution to changing work organisation and practice, are all continuing to encourage a convergence of government roles across national boundaries. Opinions differ as to the extent to which ideology, among other national features such as culture and history as well as the strategic choices made by other actors, may serve to mitigate any convergent tendencies.

DISCUSSION QUESTIONS

1 Examine why the values, beliefs and perspectives of those elected to govern are important influences upon HRM.
2 Distinguish briefly between the liberal and corporatist contexts.
3 Examine and illustrate the various roles that governments play and ways in which they can influence HRM.
4 Consider the arguments for and against government allowing and disallowing public sector trades unionism.
5 Examine the suggestion that government should seek to act as a model employer, setting an example which private sector employers should follow.
6 Explain and illustrate what is meant by governments intervening in order to create positive rights, and what might the alternatives be?
7 Explain how governments may seek to influence both the supply of and demand for labour.
8 Explain by comparing two countries the significance of ideology upon government pursuit of active labour market policies.
9 In what ways might governments impact upon the likelihood of human resource systems converging across national boundaries?

NOTES AND REFERENCES

1. Crouch C (1982) *The Politics of Industrial Relations*, 2nd ed., Fontana, p.146
2. Kochan T A, Katz H C and McKersie R B (1986) *The Transformation of American Industrial Relations*, New York Basic Books
3. Brewster C (1994) 'European HRM, Reflection of, or challenge to the American concept?' in Kirkbride P S (ed), *Human Resource Management in Europe – Perspectives for the 1990s*, Routledge pp.56–89.
4. Crouch C (1993) *Industrial Relations and European State Traditions*, Clarendon
5. Brewster C, op. cit.
6. Kerr C et al. (1973) *Industrialism and Industrial Man: The problems of Labour and Management in Economic Growth*, Penguin
7. Grahl J and Teague P (1991) 'Industrial Relations Trajectories and European Human Resource Management', in Brewster C and Tyson S (eds) *International Comparisons in Human Resource Management*, Pitman, pp.67–91
8. Ibid.
9. Ferner A and Hyman R (1992) *Industrial Relations in the New Europe*, Blackwell, Introduction, p.xxvii
10. Ibid.
11. Keller B K (1991) 'The Role of the State as Corporate Actor in Industrial Relations Systems', in Adams R J (ed) *Comparative Industrial Relations, Contemporary Research and Theory*, Harper Collins, pp. 88–9.
12. Grahl J and Teague P, op. cit.

FURTHER READING

Bean R (1994) *Comparative Industrial Relations: An introduction to cross-national perspectives*, 2nd edition, Routledge

Brewster C (1994) 'Trends in European HRM: Signs of convergence?' in Kirkbride PS (ed), *Human Resource Management in Europe,* Routledge

Giles A (1989) 'Industrial relations theory, the state and politics', in Barbash J and Barbash K (eds), *Theories and Concepts in Comparative Industrial Relations*, University of South Carolina Press, 123–54

Goldthorpe JH (ed) (1984) *Order and Conflict in Contemporary Capitalism*, Clarendon

Lehmbruch G (1984) 'Concertation and the structure of corporatist networks' in Goldthorpe J H (ed), *Order and Conflict in Contemporary Capitalism*, Clarendon

Lehmbruch G and Schmitter PC (1982) *Patterns of Corporatist Policy Making*, Sage, 60–88

Maier CS (1984) 'Preconditions for corporatism', in Goldthorpe J H (ed), *Order and Conflict in Contemporary Capitalism*, Clarendon, 39–59

Marks G (1986) 'Neo-corporatism and incomes policies in Western Europe and North America', *Comparative Politics*, 18 (3), 253–77

Teague P (1993) 'Between convergence and divergence: possibilities for a European Community System of Labour Market Regulation', *International Labour Review*, 123 (3), 391–406

Treu T (ed) (1987) *Public Service Labour Relations. Recent trends and future prospects: A comparative survey of seven industrialised market economy countries*, ILO

Wedderburn Lord (1989) 'Freedom of association and philosophies of labour', *Industrial Law Journal,* 18 (1), 11–38

7 · EMPLOYEE PARTICIPATION

OUTLINE

- **The meaning of participation.**

- **Collective bargaining.**

- **Joint consultation and works councils.**

- **Other mechanisms – employee/worker directors, quality circles, groups and teams.**

LEARNING OBJECTIVES

You should be able to:

i identify different interpretations of the meaning of participation and understand the multi-dimensional nature of the concept and associated arrangements;

ii explain the nature of collective bargaining and examine international variations and trends in bargaining structures;

iii understand the nature of joint consultation and how consultative arrangements can vary on the dimensions of participation and across national boundaries;

iv appreciate the varying popularity and effectiveness of worker directors, quality circles and certain other group and team arrangements as participatory mechanisms.

INTRODUCTION

The processes through which employees participate in decision making within organisations and human resource systems are many and varied and can be analysed and compared on a number of different dimensions.

Employees may participate directly as individuals or as members of a group, or indirectly via some form of representative arrangement. The participation may be unilateral, that is, employees may be making the decisions on their own; bilateral, where decision making is shared with one other party; or trilateral or tripartite, when employees participate in decision making with both the other main actors (employers and government).

The subject matter of the participation also varies considerably and may encompass one or more of:

- details of task and work organisation and issues of technology, efficiency and quality;
- working conditions, the work environment and matters relating to health and safety;
- terms and conditions of employment, rates of pay, hours of work, rest periods;
- 'personnel' issues such as discipline, terminations, transfers, promotions, training and development, appraisal;
- the policies and strategies of the organisation including significant business decisions relating to the what, where, when and how of the organisation's activities;
- the formulation and implementation of national, economic, industrial and social policy.

The above is not intended to constitute an exhaustive list of the potential subject matter of participation, but from it one can deduce that level is another important dimension of participation, and that level and subject matter may or may not be congruent. As an illustration of the latter point, participation might be appropriate for issues such as the detailed distribution and organisation of tasks to be determined at the level of the workgroup, but it would be inappropriate or inefficient for issues of organisation-wide policy to be determined at this workgroup level. The level at which employee participation takes place, therefore, can be expected to vary from the individual employee right up to national level, and commonly can be seen to occur at workgroup, site, establishment or plant, division or corporate, region, sector or industry, and national levels.

Another dimension on which employee participation can be examined is the extent to which it is voluntarily entered into by all the parties involved, compared with a situation in which it is supported, encouraged or required by law. The perspective or beliefs of the main actors are perhaps particularly relevant to this dimension. For example, the extent to which the parties 'believe' in the moral right of employees to share in decision making on issues affecting them will influence the extent of voluntary participation, as indeed will the converse view or belief that management or employer should have a right to decide unilaterally on issues.

Where actors have differing perspectives on these issues, it is perhaps more likely that the nature of any participation will be adversarial or conflictual rather than co-operative, and this is another dimension on which employee participation can be examined and compared. The purpose of participation may be to resolve conflicts between the parties or it may be to regulate or govern jointly or to solve and administer jointly, in which case it may approximate to the kind of micro-corporatism described by Gospel and Palmer[1]. It may be that the parties recognise their mutual dependence and need to address distributive issues, or it may be that the parties realise that through co-operation and integration each can benefit. There are many instances in recent years of employers initiating forms of employee participation (often the term 'employee involvement' is used to describe such schemes) with a view to enhancing efficiency, quality, productivity, competitiveness and profit and participation in such instances for functional rather than normative or structural purposes. On the other hand, participation may have democracy as its objective, and in such cases is much more likely to have been instituted as the product of employee or governmental pressures rather than being driven by employers.

One of the features of this area of subject matter are differences of approach and definition. Many commentators and analysts have sought to define and distinguish employee participation, employee involvement and industrial democracy, not always consistently. It is perhaps useful to illustrate some of the differences of approach and definition. Salamon[2] points straight away to this difficulty and acknowledges that employee participation is a term capable of at least three different meanings.

In one sense, it can be seen as a socio-political concept or philosophy of industrial organisation, and in this sense it is more appropriately termed 'workers control' or 'industrial democracy', since employee self-management or control is the objective.

A second use or meaning is as a generic term encompassing all processes and institutions of employee influence within an organisation. The widest interpretation of this includes the whole spectrum of management–employee relationships from simple information giving by management through to workers control. Gospel and Palmer[3] adopt a similarly wide approach and suggest that there is a continuum of the extent to which employees have a say in decision making and the creation and administration of rules affecting their working lives. The continuum ranges from unilateral management determination with employees exerting no influence and having no say at one end, through individual bargaining, joint consultation and collective bargaining, to unilateral employee decision making at the other end. This latter category encompasses informal mechanisms such as custom and practice and workgroup controls over the pace and hours of work, as well as the more formal institutions of self-managing teams or groups and worker co-operatives. Farnham[4] also adopts this generic approach and suggests that worker participation is any employee relations process enabling employees to share in the making of enterprise or corporate decisions, but he also distinguishes managerial and trade union definitions of the term; the former are employer centred and essentially task and work based and aimed at individual employees, while trade union definitions and interpretations of the term have much more in common with industrial democracy.

The third interpretation of the term employee participation which Salamon[5] identifies is one which seeks to distinguish it from the traditional process of collective bargaining and the subject matter of that bargaining. It is defined as a philosophy or style of management recognising both the need and right of employees to be involved with management in processes which extend employee influence into 'new' areas of organisational decision making and which are less 'distributive' in their concerns and orientation, and more concerned with the joint determination and resolution of problems. This third interpretation is a much closer fit with the kind of schemes initiated by management to enhance employee involvement and referred to above, and which may or may not be participative in the sense of facilitating employee participation in decision making.

Salamon[6] suggests that involvement schemes can be distinguished from participation on the dimension of purpose, involvement having employee commitment to the objectives and values of the organisation as its purpose, while participation schemes seek to provide employees with opportunities to influence and take part in organisational decision making. Ramsay[7] also seeks to distinguish participation schemes which are managerial approaches seeking employee involvement from those which are labour-oriented initiatives and controls and have more to do with industrial democracy.

Marchington et al.[8] also address the issue of definition and note that there are at least three identifiable sets of definitions. The first simply refer to employees taking part or having a say or share in decision making, with no attempt to quantify their impact on the process. The second set is more specific and refers to participation in terms of the extent to which employees may influence managerial actions. The third set links participation and control over decision making.

They decide to use 'participation' as an umbrella term defining the subject as a whole and to include collective bargaining. Industrial democracy is used to describe those practices with the objective of increasing employee rights to participate in decision making, excluding collective bargaining but including mechanisms such as employee representation on management committees and at board level. Employee involvement is used to describe those practices initiated principally by management and designed to increase employee information about and commitment to the organisation, but which do not necessarily involve or imply any sharing of managerial authority or power with employees.

Marchington et al.[9] also usefully identify and summarise four different perspectives or models of participation:

1 One which emanates from a belief that participation enhances job satisfaction.
2 A second which believes that participation, or perhaps more specifically involvement programmes, will enhance commitment and that commitment leads to enhanced performance.

3 A third approach links participation with enhanced co-operation and reduced levels of conflict.
4 The fourth approach links 'real' participation to those situations in which there is some actual transfer of control from management to labour, and tends to dismiss much 'participation' as no more than cosmetic or a sham.

While the above exemplifies some of the differences of approach and definition, there do seem to be some common features and characteristics. Many commentators do use employee or worker participation as a generic term encompassing both employee involvement schemes and those which are described as exercises in industrial democracy. Among the common characteristics of involvement schemes include managerial initiatives geared towards securing greater employee commitment to the activities, objectives and values of the organisation as perceived by management. They are likely to offer employees, as work groups or individuals but not as union members, the opportunity to influence decisions concerning their jobs and immediate work environment. They may have specific objectives such as improving quality or efficiency, but arguably do not imply any dilution of managerial prerogative and do not generally offer employees participation in the formulation of organisational policy or strategy.

Schemes described by the term industrial democracy seem to be rooted in collective organisation and representation, and may well be the product of labour movement or governmental initiatives. They commonly provide for some degree of participation in policy and strategy formulation, and do imply some dilution of managerial prerogatives and sharing of power with representatives of the labour force. Sometimes the term is used strictly to apply only to situations in which all workers share in the management of an organisation which is owned by them or the state and, in this sense, refers only to systems of employee self-management or worker control.

One often-forgotten dimension of participation is motivation and there is plenty of evidence to suggest, and indeed it coincides with 'common sense', that to be effective participation schemes, whether collective or individual, do depend in large measure on willing participants.

In contrast to the above approaches seeking to distinguish between participation and involvement, Storey and Sisson[10] take the somewhat refreshing view that since most practitioners use the terms employee participation and involvement interchangeably, and given that it is possible to make conceptual distinctions between involvement and participation with the latter being reserved for instances where employees share some decision making with managers, the utility of forcing the distinction seems limited.

They usefully adapt Lammers[11] model for classifying forms of involvement, distinguishing processes and institutions on dimensions of both level and scope. In this context, scope refers to whether the subject matter encompasses goals and means or means only. However, we feel that in the context of earlier attempts at definition and distinction, it would be more useful if Storey and Sisson[12] had chosen to use participation as the generic term rather than involvement. There are attractions to the suggestion that the pursuit of conceptual distinctions between participation and involvement may be of little value. However, we do see a difference and prefer to use the term participation as more expressive of the subject matter of this chapter.

OUR APPROACH

In this chapter we intend to use the term employee participation broadly and our approach shares a great deal with the generic approaches referred to above. We see no particular value in limiting the scope of the term to processes and institutions internal to the organisation. It seems to us that employees, via representatives, can participate through mechanisms external to the organisation and still be effectively influencing decision making within that organisation. We also feel that the distinction between real and pseudo-participation is worth pursuing. For employees or their representatives to be participating in decision making, they must have both the power and opportunity to exert influence before decisions are made, or alternatively have an effective right to veto decisions made by others before their implementation. The passive receipt of information does not seem to us to constitute participation in decision making, and indeed there are undoubtedly instances of 'two-way' communication which also fall into the category of pseudo-participation. They give a semblance of participation and the impression that employees can influence decisions, when the reality is that the decision is made unilaterally by management with no genuine notice being taken of the views expressed by employees, and with the employees having no power to veto. It is often difficult and impossible on some occasions to ascertain the extent to which a particular process or institution offers employees genuine or real opportunities for participation. We do, however, try in this chapter to concentrate on those mechanisms which have a clear potential for real or genuine participation and it is a dimension of participation which we comment on where appropriate. We also do not see any particular value in this comparative analysis in seeking to define participation to exclude collective bargaining and any other traditional mechanisms of joint regulation.

The remainder of this chapter is structured around the main mechanisms, processes and institutions of participation: collective bargaining, employee councils and consultative committees, and others such as worker representatives on boards of directors, quality circles and problem-solving groups, and self-managing groups or teams. We do not examine macro-corporatist approaches and arrangements in this chapter since these are dealt with elsewhere.

As we examine arrangements in each of the countries that constitute the base of this text, we compare them as appropriate on a number of different dimensions, including those discussed earlier in this introduction and listed again here:

- individual or collective;
- direct or indirect;
- unilateral or bilateral;
- the scope of subject matter;
- the level at which arrangements exist;
- whether voluntary or legally supported or required;
- the influence of perspective or ideology;
- whether distributive, adversarial, conflictual, co-operative or integrative in nature;
- the purpose of arrangements;
- their 'realness' or genuineness.

COLLECTIVE BARGAINING

Collective bargaining is one of the most frequently used and common mechanisms or processes through which employees and their representatives influence and participate in decision making within human resource systems. There are many dimensions on which the nature and structures of collective bargaining may vary and many of these are illustrated in the following pages. Nevertheless, despite its many variations, collective bargaining is arguably the dominant employee participation process in all of the countries that form the basis of this text.

Our first task is to define the process. The International Labour Office Convention 154[13] defines it as encompassing: all negotiations between employers (or employers' organisations) and workers organisations for the purposes of determining terms and conditions of employment and/or regulating relations between them.

Gospel and Palmer[14] describe it as 'a process by which trade unions and similar associations representing groups of employees, negotiate with employers or their representatives with the object of reaching collective agreements'.

Salamon[15], on the other hand, defines it as a 'method of determining terms and conditions of employment which utilises the process of negotiation and agreement between representatives of management and employees'.

These descriptions and definitions of the process of collective bargaining have common elements, since each identifies it as a process involving negotiations which are conducted between representatives of employees and employers. However, here the similarities cease. The ILO limits the subject matter to terms and conditions of employment and the regulation of relations between the parties. Salamon limits it to terms and conditions. On the other hand, the Gospel and Palmer description does not seek to limit the subject matter of the process. Another significant difference between these three descriptions is that while both Salamon and Gospel and Palmer specify the objective as one of agreement between the parties, the ILO makes no mention of this.

From our perspective, the Gospel and Palmer description seems the most useful since it emphasises the crucial components of the process, rather than worrying about or limiting the subject matter. They further illustrate the process by explaining that each party has something the other wants, is able to exert pressure on the other and this results in a process of give and take leading to a compromise agreement. We, therefore, intend to use this definition as it emphasises that the process is collective, representative, involves negotiation and has agreement as its objective. Readers will note that none of the definitions falls into the trap of limiting the process to one necessarily involving trade unions, as not all employee organisations are trade unions.

In some countries, parties enter into this process of bilateral decision making freely and voluntarily; in other systems, there is some degree of legal compulsion on or support for one or more of the parties if various conditions or circumstances are satisfied.

Once agreements are made, it is common for them to have some legal force (there are exceptions to this, of which the UK is an example). The nature of this legal obligation varies as to the penalties or remedies available in the event of non-compliance or performance. If the agreements made are for a fixed period, it is quite common for the parties not to have the legal right to renegotiate or to take action to exert pressure on the other party for the duration of the agreement. Sometimes the limitation applies to only certain kinds of issues, such as so-called matters of interest as opposed to rights. This distinction is relatively common and usually means that parties cannot take action in support of claims for new or amended terms and conditions or other substantive matters, whereas they might be able legally to take action in support of a dispute over the interpretation or implementation of an existing agreement (a matter of right as opposed to interest).

Over the years, many attempts have been made to describe and classify the nature, functions and conceptions of collective bargaining as a process. Most conceptions of collective bargaining see it at least in part as power based and a process that is used to resolve conflicts between the parties, the dominant conflicts being perceived as conflict over the price of labour and conflict over the control of the labour process. This partially explains why some observers[16] have depicted the process as being essentially economic in character, concerned primarily with the exchange between buyers and sellers of labour, while others see it as not a process of exchange so much as one which determines the terms on which exchange may take place. This latter view accords closely with Chamberlain and Kuhn's[17] marketing concept of the process which sees it resulting in a contractual relationship, an agreement on the terms on which labour may be bought and sold.

Others, perhaps most notably Flanders[18], have insisted that collective bargaining is a process resulting in joint job regulation, the joint creation of rules, both substantive and procedural, which on the one hand specify terms and conditions and on the other stipulate the procedures that the parties will use in dealing with each other and particular areas of subject matter. This notion is similar to Chamberlain and Kuhn's[19] governmental concept of collective bargaining which views the process as primarily one of joint law making implying a sharing of power and sovereignty, since the 'laws' also include mechanisms covering their application and adjudication. Management prerogative is thereby limited – management retains executive authority but only within the context of the 'laws' or 'constitution' agreed by the parties. It is a process that is also concerned with the implementation and administration of agreements reached. Chamberlain and Kuhn[20] also suggest that in certain relatively exceptional circumstances, collective bargaining may even develop into a process akin to joint management.

Dubin[21] suggested that collective bargaining provided a means of institutionalising industrial conflict and its resolution in much the same way as the electoral process and majority rule have institutionalised political conflict in a democracy.

More radical conceptions view collective bargaining as a process that may contribute to the politicisation of the working class thereby furthering the class struggle. Others may view it as a process which, through its institutionalisation of conflict and its resolution and its introduction of stabilising influences and procedures, will actually serve to preserve the capitalist *status quo* and as such should be avoided.

As noted above most if not all analysts acknowledge that the collective bargaining process is both power based and concerned with resolving conflicts. However, an additional dimension needs to be noted in order to explain why parties freely and voluntarily enter into this kind of process and relationship – mutual dependence. If the parties did not need each other, then they would not bother to go through the process but would simply walk away or make unilateral decisions which the other party could take or leave. Where there is a plentiful supply of appropriate and unorganised labour, managements are much more likely to take the view that they do not need unionised labour and do not need to enter into collective bargaining. They will simply and unilaterally determine substantive terms and conditions.

Walton and McKersie[22], in examining collective bargaining, identified two different types of relationship. The first of these is a distributive relationship in which the parties acknowledge their mutual dependence and seek to coerce each other into an agreement on the distribution of a limited resource, a fixed-sum game, in which one party's gain is the other's loss. The other kind of relationship they see as more integrative, more concerned with resolving problems facing them both and which may facilitate gain for both, a win–win outcome being possible, a variable-sum game. The latter type of bargaining relationship also acknowledges mutual dependence but is less conflictual and more co-operative in nature, emphasising notions such as partnership and consensus. These distributive and integrative models equate with Chamberlain and Kuhn's conjunctive and co-operative models.[23]

Readers should note that they will rarely find 'pure' examples of the above notions, concepts, types and models of collective bargaining. It is much more likely that examination of systems and instances will discover hybrids and examples of differing emphasis. Nevertheless we do, for example, refer to some systems as having distributive and conflictual traditions and others as more co-operative and consensual, and so it is necessary to understand what is meant by these terms.

In the preceding discussion, some of the benefits of collective bargaining have already been identified. For example, it frequently resolves conflict and produces an agreed statement of the terms and conditions on which labour may be bought and sold, thereby enhancing fairness and certainty. Additionally, it may produce rules and agreements on procedures that effectively regulate the relationship between the parties and provide mechanisms for disputes and grievances, whether about new issues or existing rights or interpretations, to be resolved fairly and efficiently. It can also be seen as enhancing democracy within industry. In short, it is a process through which unfairness, disorder, conflict, unilateralism and uncertainty can be converted into order, stability, democracy, fairness and productivity.

To some extent one's assessment of the value or desirability of collective bargaining as a process will be dependent on one's perspective. Most analysts of a pluralist, liberal collectivist, corporatist and in some cases radical or Marxist perspective will see it as a process with advantages of the kind referred to above and without any significant disadvantages. However, unitarist and liberal individualist perspectives are much less likely to view it favourably, since it is a process which inevitably dilutes managerial prerogative, enhances employee participation in decision making and contributes to inflation by facilitating greater employee bargaining power resulting in higher wage rates. Other disadvantages from this viewpoint include the view that collective bargaining introduces or worsens disorder (orderliness being achieved through unilateral regulation) and brings conflict into the relationship between an individual employee and his or her employer. These latter perspectives are likely to view favourably individual bargaining and individual employment contracts, emphasising the benefits of rewards linked to individual performance and the importance of individual freedom of choice.

More objectively, collective bargaining does often seem to be accompanied by higher wage rates and smaller differentials; lower levels of productivity and profit; higher levels of industrial action; lower levels of absenteeism and labour turnover; less wage competition; and higher levels of job satisfaction. However, causal relationships between the presence of collective bargaining and these other variables are much more difficult to establish.

We have already noted that the subject matter of collective bargaining can vary. One only has to re-examine Chamberlain and Kuhn's[24] three concepts or stages in the development of collective bargaining to be aware that bargaining may at one end of the spectrum be limited to the price of labour, while at the other end it may be that the process has been extended to include any decision affecting labour. Indeed, it is difficult to identify subject matter that could not be included in the bargaining process, since within organisations and industries most management decisions have some impact on labour. Additionally, we need to bear in mind that in some national systems, a form of collective bargaining may take place at national level and be tripartite in nature, involving government as well as employer and employee representation. In this case, it is probable that the term 'bargained corporatism' will be used to describe the nature of the arrangements and the subject matter of the process is quite likely to include issues of national economic, industrial and social policy, frequently incorporating some form of incomes policy or wage restraint. There is therefore room for massive variation in the subject matter or scope of collective bargaining both between and within national systems.

Analysts usually identify four dimensions or components of the structure of collective bargaining. One of these is the scope of the bargaining in terms of subject matter. The others are level, unit and form. In this chapter we are not particularly concerned with bargaining units, other than to note that they can vary enormously in both shape and size and that there is commonly a direct relationship between level and size of unit – the higher the level, the larger the unit is likely to be. The form of collective bargaining or agreements simply refers to whether they are written, or not. In most systems they are written, if for no other reason than that they are legally binding, and that the participating and other adjudicating parties require detailed documentation in order to establish the 'rights and wrongs' of any dispute over implementation or interpretation.

This brings us to the important subject of bargaining level. This can vary from the smallest of work groups, plants, sites or establishments up to the largest of industries, and in some circumstances bargaining may occur at a multi-industry or even more rarely at an international level. This dimension is one of the factors on which national systems have traditionally and significantly differed. In some systems the dominant bargaining level has been multi-employer at the level of the industry, sector or even region, and these have been compared to other systems in which the dominant level has been at the level of the company or enterprise, or at levels within companies such as a site, division or establishment. We have referred here to dominant levels since it is common for bargaining to occur at other levels in addition to the dominant one. The reasons for the development of these particular traditions and mechanisms vary considerably and include strategic choices made by the parties as well as a whole host of cultural, ideological, environmental and other factors, such as the time at which the system developed and the nature of society at that time. We also need to bear in mind that collective bargaining structures do not remain static and may well change over time in response to particular developments and stimuli, and will return to this later.

The Price Waterhouse/Cranfield Project[25] has produced a wealth of evidence concerning levels of pay determination and bargaining over basic pay. The study is limited to Europe but does illustrate clearly a number of the above points. Certainly for manual workers bargaining does occur at a number of levels in all national systems, and the dominant level of pay bargaining across Europe and in most countries remains multi-employer at industrial or national level. However, there are countries within Europe (particularly France and the UK) where company/establishment-level bargaining over pay dominates, and in both of these countries there have been deliberate efforts by government and employers in the 1980s to achieve decentralisation from the industrial sector level. The studies have also confirmed that in most countries pay bargaining in the public sector tends to be more centralised than in the private sector.

Having noted that there are numerous influences contributing to the development of and dominance of certain bargaining levels, we need to identify those which seem to be particularly influential. We can do this by imagining a scenario that would tend to encourage multi-employer bargaining, most commonly at the level of the industry. This would consist of:

(a) Many relatively small employers/producers in
(b) a relatively undifferentiated and competitive product market using
(c) common technology and

(d) confronted by a strong centralised national union that will seek to pick off individual employers so that

(e) management is prepared to relinquish some degree of control over terms and conditions of employment and possibly over grievance and dispute handling in return for the security and economy (in terms of specialist resources) offered by multi-employer bargaining. In some circumstances, managements may want to separate industrial relations decision making from operational structures, and multi-employer bargaining can facilitate this.

(f) If the union has political or social objectives, then it is also likely to favour centralised, multi-employer arrangements, and

(g) if the labour market is a national one, then this again may encourage multi-employer bargaining since local terms and conditions are likely to be relatively unimportant, and lastly

(h) the attitude or ideology of government is also relevant. Governments seeking corporatist arrangements are likely to need centralised employers, trade union and bargaining structures.

A scenario encouraging bargaining at the level of the individual employer might be:

(a) An industry comprised of relatively few, quite large employers who operate in a

(b) differentiated product market and are

(c) confronted by a number of locally based unions with no particular objectives other than to obtain good terms and conditions of employment for their members, and no desires to combine or co-operate with others.

(d) If a standard technology is used and

(e) management wants to retain control locally and have the skilled resources available and

(f) operate primarily in a local labour market and

(g) in an economy governed by those believing in the importance of the individual and the efficiency of the market mechanism, particularly at local level.

These two scenarios are only intended to be indicative of the sorts of factors that may influence bargaining levels at any one time. One is perhaps rarely likely to encounter scenarios that quite so clearly indicate the suitability of one bargaining level over another, and so we also need to bear in mind that parties sometimes opt for, or continue to operate at, bargaining levels that are not necessarily the ones that the overall set of circumstances might indicate as the most appropriate.

It is relatively common that bargaining at the more centralised level, whether this be 'national' or within organisations, establishes procedures and criteria which are then utilised for, or govern negotiations at, lower levels. Sometimes terms such as 'framework' or 'umbrella' are used to describe these types of 'centralised' agreements, indicating that they are in some sense paving the way or facilitating lower-level bargaining.

Centralised bargaining is sometimes the outcome of the tactic of 'pattern bargaining', a term often used to describe a situation common in many systems whereby a trade union makes an agreement with one employer in a particular industry, usually the one it thinks most able to pay, and then seeks to extend the pattern created by this agreement to other employers within the sector.

In recent years many commentators, including Ferner and Hyman[26], Clarke[27] and Thompson[28], have identified an international trend towards decentralisation of bargaining levels and structures. This decentralisation has been occurring within companies, as well as from multi-employer arrangements to single employer bargaining. These commentators also identify a number of explanations for this apparently 'general' trend. In the main, these explanations tend to reinforce Kochan et al.'s[29] view of the importance of strategic choices being made by actors in the context of changing environmental circumstances, although strategic choices are not always well informed or rational.

It seems as if these decentralisation tendencies have been largely at the behest of management, in some instances encouraged by government as in France and the UK, with the unions in some systems unable to resist owing to their weakened position. Increasingly, analysts have concluded that bargaining structures may be more significantly influenced by management than has traditionally been thought. By and large, the recent pressures on management are the product of increasing globalisation of product markets and increased international competition allied to the rapid development of new technology, particularly information technology and robotics, all of which are resulting in rapidly changing product markets requiring flexible responses and new forms of work organisation with a premium on flexibility and multi-skilling. As Ferner and Hyman[30] characterise it, this represents a shift from a system of standardised price-competitive production to one of customised quality-competitive production. This has similarities with notions of flexible specialisation and post-Fordism.

These changes and developments in the international environment are encouraging the decentralisation of existing decision-making systems, both operational and employee relations, since flexible response and flexible specialisation seemingly put a premium on decision making close to production and close to the customer, and on linking pay to performance. At the same time, new information technology renders easier central monitoring and control of decentralised cost and profit centres and decision-making mechanisms. This was suggested by the research conducted by Marginson et al.[31] In some instances, this decentralisation has been agreed and managed by the parties jointly, often with framework agreements being agreed at the traditionally dominant levels facilitating the changes.

Ferner and Hyman[32] also point out that the impact of these developments on national systems has varied, and they suggest that institutional persistence is a significant factor influencing the nature of the impact. Those systems with strong and inflexible institutions are the ones in which such transformations are most difficult to achieve.

Accompanying the downward trend in bargaining structures, in some systems at least, there has been a decline in the incidence and significance of collective bargaining as a rule-making, conflict-resolving, participatory mechanism. This has been partly and variably attributed to and explained by increasing unemployment, declining union influence and strategic choices by governments and management emphasising individualism, and perhaps particularly individually related pay. Also many managements have introduced employee-involvement programmes as preferable complements or alternatives to collective bargaining.

Negative economic circumstances have also contributed to a wider incidence of the phenomenon known as concession bargaining. This term is used to describe a situation in which the parties are not bargaining over 'gains' to be shared between them but over concessions to be made by both; typically a trade union may find itself agreeing to concessions on wages or hours of work in return for employers' making concessions on manning levels, thereby protecting jobs.

The overall international trends identified above would not, on the face of it, seem to be encouraging to those who seek development of collective bargaining at an international level, whether within multinational corporations or at some multi-employer, multi-sectoral or multi-state level, such as within the European Union. It has been anticipated that the agreement by European Union members (excluding the UK) that management and labour should play a greater role in the formulation of Union policy on an agreed basis, whether this be given legal effect via a Council decision or voluntarily implemented by the parties, would give a significant boost to international collective bargaining at both sectoral and multi-sectoral levels. At the time of writing, this expectation has not been fulfilled. The social partners' first attempt at reaching agreement on a stalled social action programme directive failed, and in its failure illustrated the difficulties of achieving agreement when there are so many vested interests.

Carley[33] examines the potential for collective bargaining at the three international levels referred to above, multi-sectoral, sectoral and within multinational corporations, and identifies many of the difficulties, including whether the central associations are sufficiently representative, have a mandate and can control or exert discipline over their affiliates in order to ensure compliance. The significant international variations in social and economic conditions and traditions also make such bargaining problematic, although they might have a less negative impact on bargaining that seeks to agree a procedural framework rather than substantive matters.

Within multinational corporations some of these factors may be less inhibiting, although for the most part the employers have not encouraged such developments. There have been some instances of agreements being reached at this level, a recent example being BSN's agreement with the International Union of Food concerning employee rights to belong to a trade union and take part in its activities. The recent agreement by 11 member states within the European Union (not the UK) to adopt a directive that will give employees within multinational corporations a right to request negotiations with management, to agree mechanisms and procedures for informing and consulting employees, should encourage collective bargaining at this multinational corporation level (see Chapter 19). However if employers are opposed to such developments, this agreement may have relatively little impact.

Snapshot 1

US

Since the mid 1930s, trade unions and employers have had available to them a legislatively supported mechanism whereby, with sufficient levels of support as exhibited in a properly conducted ballot, they have been able to force employers into recognition, collective bargaining and a requirement to bargain in good faith.

The bargaining that has resulted has been concentrated at the level of the firm or establishment and, certainly until relatively recently, has been distributive in nature, with relationships being traditionally conflictual between employees and employers.

Managements have tended to insist on management rights clauses which have served to confirm the distributive nature of the bargaining and limit the scope of the subject matter covered to a relatively common range of issues: wages, hours, holidays, pensions, health and life insurance, and the handling of grievances.

There has been an underlying accord that employees have no legitimate interest in the management of the enterprise, only in the distribution of benefits. The emphasis has been on economic and substantive issues, although there has been some procedural development in grievance handling, discipline and discharge rules, and also in terms of the operation of internal labour markets, in particular covering the operation of seniority rights. The legal distinctions drawn between mandatory, permissible and prohibited topics has served to limit scope. There is some evidence of a broadening of the scope of bargaining in recent years into areas concerned with job design, work practice and work organisation, but this is not extensive as yet.

Pattern bargaining within particular industries has been relatively common. Multi-employer bargaining does occur in some industries, usually those characterised by large numbers of relatively small employers offering a comparatively standard product or service and geographically concentrated.

Concession bargaining has been one response to increasing international competitive pressures and the recession. Effectively this is a process whereby management might agree to continue to co-operate, recognise and bargain and not cut jobs in return for concessions on the part of labour in areas such as pay, working practices and productivity. Experience in the airline industry in 1993 exhibits some interesting and novel forms of concession bargaining, with employees conceding on various substantive issues in return for an equity stake in the company.

The emphasis on enterprise-level bargaining has been a product of the wishes of both sets of actors and government has not sought to influence this, nor indeed has it sought significantly to influence or regulate the outcomes of the bargaining process.

Agreements are generally for a fixed period and are legally binding, with a legal distinction drawn between disputes of interest and rights with regard to the taking of lawful industrial action. Action can only lawfully be taken during the lifetime of an agreement in respect of an unfair labour practice by the other actor, and often this is risky since the action taken precedes a decision on the fairness of the practice. Actions in respect of disputes of interest must take place at the end of a contract; disputes of right are usually dealt with via appropriate state, federally funded or privately arranged conciliation and arbitration machinery.

In recent years, there has been considerable debate about whether the system was in the process of transformation, with bargaining relationships moving towards the co-operative and integrative, and indeed a movement towards consultation at corporate level and in connection with matters of policy and strategy.[34] Certainly, management has tended to have the upper hand and has been able to pursue a firmer stance, as is evidenced by the emergence of concession bargaining. Whether these trends will continue now that unions have had some successes in late 1993, and given the support of a Democrat government, remains to be seen.

Many state and federal employees do not enjoy the same bargaining rights as employees in the private sector. Rarely do they have bargaining rights in respect of pay or other economic benefits. Additionally, there are usually provisions requiring public sector disputes to be resolved via conciliation or arbitration through machinery especially created to deal with impasses or failures to agree in the state and federal sectors of employment.

AUSTRALIA

The dominant role of arbitration in the determination of terms and conditions of employment has significantly hampered the development of voluntary collective bargaining. As late as 1991, the Federal Commission rejected a greater reliance on and encouragement of voluntary enterprise bargaining because, in its view, the parties were not sufficiently mature.

However, collective bargaining has occurred on a voluntary basis between unions and employers and has, on occasion, achieved prominence. This has usually resulted, as in 1973–4, in relatively large wage increases leading to both government and Commission efforts to control wages. Not that collective bargaining has not resulted in many 'acceptable' agreements

– many Commission awards are confirmations of voluntary agreements. These awards are often referred to as consent awards.

Bargaining has in the past been typically conflictual and distributive in nature. Only recently have the parties begun to adopt more co-operative and integrative approaches as they have been faced with the need to modernise, restructure, introduce new technology, improve efficiency, enhance flexibility and introduce and adapt to new methods of work organisation. It is these new challenges which have shown up the inadequacies of existing, or non-existing, bargaining arrangements, particularly within the enterprise and workplace. The government has been seeking to stimulate the expansion of collective bargaining at this level as well as encouraging a wider range of bargaining subject matter. To this end, the Federal Industrial Relations Act was amended in 1992 reducing the power of the Federal Commissions to vet enterprise agreements. Any expansion of collective bargaining activity at enterprise level represents decentralisation in comparison with previous arrangements.

The traditions of both bargaining and arbitration awards have been essentially substantive rather than procedural, although there have been some efforts made by Commissions in more recent times to establish procedural requirements and encourage consultation between employers and employees, for example in circumstances of impending closure and redundancy, or in the event of significant changes to production methods or company structure as in the Termination, Change and Redundancy decision of 1984.

The incidence and significance of collective bargaining, particularly at enterprise level, should increase as a consequence of developments and agreements embodied within the 1993 Accord between federal government and the ACTU.

GERMANY

In Germany, collective bargaining between unions and employers or their associations occurs mostly at sector and regional or 'Land' level in accordance with the Collective Agreement Act 1949 (amended 1969), which effectively guarantees the rights of the parties to bargain freely and without state intervention. Generally the parties have been left to resolve matters between themselves. Government does not provide mediation or conciliation facilities, but the parties usually make some provision themselves for recourse to assistance of this kind in the event of difficulties of interpretation or achieving agreement. The legislative framework guarantees rights to bargain, renders agreements binding, seeks to impose 'peace' on the parties for the duration of the agreement, and provides a mechanism for the extension of agreements to other employers within the sector via a declaration of general applicability by the appropriate regional or federal government department. A clear legislative distinction is drawn between disputes of right and interest. Disputes of right must not constitute the subject matter of industrial action, but must be resolved either by mediation/conciliation or by the labour courts. Disputes of interest can result in lawful industrial action but only once the contract period has expired and before a new one is agreed. There is also some legal regulation of terms and conditions of employment and the rights and obligations of the parties, e.g. maternity benefits, minimum holiday entitlements and maximum hours of work.

It is possible to distinguish between three main types of collective agreement: pay agreements; framework agreements which tend to specify principles and systems, e.g. payment schemes or the introduction of new technology; and umbrella agreements which include and regulate other conditions of employment, such as working times and holidays. Over the years, the scope of collective bargaining has expanded to include a wide range of issues affecting pay, working times and conditions, and there are continuing pressures from employees and their unions for further expansion to include production issues, such as the design of jobs, work organisation and quality. At sector level, it has been quite common for pattern bargaining to emerge with one bargain being used as a yardstick for others.

In addition to multi-employer bargaining at sector or regional levels, there are examples of bargaining at enterprise and workplace level. Enterprise bargaining is more likely to occur in organisations that are not members of employers' associations; the majority of these are relatively small, but there are some large household names such as Volkswagen who engage in bargaining at this level and, as noted elsewhere, more and more employers are leaving the associations.

Workplace bargaining does occur between the works council and local management, and it is primarily concerned with the implementation and application of agreements made at higher levels. Workplace agreements ought not to break or contradict the agreements made at industry level, but it is quite common for them to improve on the terms of the higher-level agreement.

In recent years, one of the main bargaining trends has been to reduce working hours in return for greater flexibility as to when the work is conducted. Recently, confronted with recession and rising unemployment, employers have traded a reduction in working hours and even pay cuts for employment levels. The Volkswagen agreement in November 1993 was a pioneering example of such a bargain.

The nature of bargaining relationships has been relatively co-operative over recent decades. Time will tell whether these co-operative traditions can be maintained when the parties are faced with recession, unemployment and increasing pressures for labour flexibility.

The necessity to introduce new technology and working practices as employers search for enhanced efficiency, flexibility, productivity and quality have all contributed to increasing decentralisation, as has the desire of the parties within the workplace for more discretion and control. Many employers seem to feel that sector-level bargaining was resulting in agreements that were too generous and too expensive, and against the context of recession and significant unemployment, it seems in mid-1994 that many are actively seeking to extend bargaining within the enterprise.

JAPAN

The 1945 Trade Union Laws gave employees the rights to organise, bargain and take industrial action.

Bargaining in Japan occurs at both industry and enterprise levels, but the dominant level is that of the enterprise. The origins of bargaining at this level were in the wartime production committees, and refusal of an employer to bargain in good faith can constitute an unfair labour practice. The subject matter of collective bargaining at this level tends to be fairly narrow and essentially substantive in nature, the emphasis being on economic issues and the working conditions of permanently employed staff. The agreements themselves are often somewhat vague.

At industry level a form of pattern bargaining is sometimes utilised, with wage claims and responses being co-ordinated by union and employer confederations. The rate of increase determined via the first agreement is then used as a standard or pattern for subsequent rounds of enterprise bargaining. There are some union-inspired pressures for an expansion of bargaining at industry level and for the adoption of a system whereby agreements in unionised enterprises may be extended to others in the same industry or sector where union presence may not be so strong.

There is a system of minimum wage determination, the rates for an industry and/or region being deter-mined annually by tripartite wages councils and approved by government. These rates may typically constitute about 50 per cent of the rates applicable in the larger and unionised enterprises, but a great proportion of the labour force is not in this fortunate position.

Where bargaining occurs, the nature of the relationship is predominantly co-operative. However, failures to agree occur and there is machinery for conciliation, mediation and arbitration through the appropriate Labour Commissions. These disputes are often concerned with the application or interpretation of existing agreements, which are legally enforceable.

In the public sector, government employees typically do not have bargaining rights. Employees in the public corporations and enterprises have limited bargaining rights, with parliamentary approval required if the expenditure implications exceed budget. A distinction is often drawn between working conditions and matters of management and administration; the latter are excluded by law from collective bargaining and are open to interpretation by management.

Bargaining in Japan is already relatively decentralised, the enterprise being the dominant level. Discussions involving government, unions, employers and other interest groups do occur at national level when appropriate. However, these discussions are not appropriately described as collective bargaining.

ITALY

Collective bargaining remains the dominant participatory mechanism in Italy. The dominant level is still the sector or industry, although there has been some seesawing between national and industry levels over the years, and despite the new impetus given to company-level bargaining by the July 1993 Accord and subsequent tripartite agreement in December.

National-level bargaining, involving government as well as union confederations and employers' associations, has declined in importance with the abolition in 1992 of the national wage indexation system called the *Scala Mobile*, although the July 1993 Accord was a prime example of such arrangements. Over the years, national-level bargaining has been characterised by conflict between union confederations almost as much as by conflict between unions and employers.

Industry-level bargaining still determines between 80 and 90 per cent of employees' total terms and conditions and benefits packages, although employers are increasingly keen to expand their discretion locally.

In recent years, much greater emphasis has been placed in collective bargaining at industry level on the negotiation and agreement of procedures and arrangements to govern activity at lower levels. Some framework agreements have been achieved, as have agreements concerning matters such as the processing of individual and collective grievances and disputes within companies. An example of this procedural development is the IRI protocol in 1984 in the public enterprise sector which has to some extent set an example for the private sector.

Traditionally, there have been four main contracts at industry level – those in metals, textiles, chemicals and construction – and the metals agreement has often set the pattern for other industries. In all, there are about 25 major industries and about 100 industry-level agreements. These industry-level agreements have tended to be renegotiated every three years. The reorganisation envisaged in the 1993 agreements above specifies that industry bargaining on pay should occur every two years, and on other issues every four years.

In-company, workplace or plant-level bargaining has not been dominant in the past, although local tailoring of industry agreements has always been possible. In recent decades, the frequency and importance of collective bargaining at this level have increased. Employers have been seeking more local discretion and flexibility, and employees within organisations have been seeking greater influence. The difficulties of creating and maintaining unitary employee representative arrangements within the workplace made co-ordinated and effective bargaining at this level problematic.

However, the factory council developments over the last 25 years have eased matters, and it is hoped that the December 1993 agreement at national level on the formation, constitution and role of RSUs will greatly facilitate expansion of bargaining at company-level. Usually bargaining at plant level is conducted between representatives of both parties from provincial or industry-level institutions, even though the claim has probably been formulated by the factory council.

There is evidence of more co-operative relations in recent years, but it is unlikely that the tradition of conflictual relationships between employer and employee will quickly be overturned. It is certainly too early to suggest that the traditional distributive nature of bargaining is being replaced by a more integrative approach.

The process of collective bargaining in Italy is not legally regulated, but outcomes have frequently been given legal effect and extended to cover all employees within an industry, irrespective of whether their employer was party to the agreement. There is no legal requirement for either party to engage in bargaining, although there can be advantages if either party wants to weaken legislative standards.

Agreements are intended to be binding and are usually for a specific period of time, but there are no legal barriers to industrial action being taken during the period of an agreement, and no legal distinction between matters of interest and right. By and large, different areas of subject matter have been negotiated at each of the bargaining levels, and the guiding principle is that issues covered by higher-level agreements are not renegotiated at the lower level. However, where agreements at national or industry-level set minima or establish systems or frameworks, then supplementary negotiation is likely to occur lower down the structure. As an example, industry-level agreements tend to establish industry-wide job classification systems; individual jobs are allocated to the appropriate classification at company or plant level.

It is far too soon to assess the impact of the 1993 attempts and agreements to reorganise the system.

FRANCE

Despite the impetus given to company bargaining by the 1982 legislation (Collective Bargaining and Employee Participation Acts), the dominant level of bargaining still seems to be at the level of the industry, at least in terms of the numbers of people covered. It was the 1936 Collective Bargaining Act which confirmed industry-level bargaining as the essential level, and it was this Act which also created the legislative rights and mechanisms for agreements reached at industry or regional level to be extended by the appropriate member of government to cover other employers (and employees) within the sector, irrespective of whether they were members of the appropriate employers' association. Industry-level agreements need only be agreed by one of the representative unions before this process of extension becomes available.

Industry-level agreements were also encouraged by the 1982 legislation which required the parties at this level, and already bound by such a sectoral agreement, to meet annually to negotiate pay and hours and every five years to discuss job classifications.

These agreements provide a framework within which company-level negotiations can take place. The legislative requirements do reflect the somewhat limited scope and nature of collective bargaining in France. The nature of the relationship is traditionally conflictual, with an emphasis on distributive rather than integrative bargaining. Industry-level bargaining has been preferred by the parties. Employers could continue to avoid recognising unions in the workplace and wage competition was mitigated, and the main union confederations preferred bargaining at this level because it meant that large numbers of workers could be covered without massive expenditure of time and other resources in the organising of workplace representation. It also fitted with their social and political orientations.

There is also a history of national, multi-industry or multi-sectoral bargaining in France. In the early 1970s, there had been innovative multi-sectoral agreements on issues such as job security, vocational training, redundancy payments and working conditions. Some of these agreements were envisaged as providing a framework for and enabling lower-level bargaining, but others were precise, detailed and more substantive in nature.

The late 1980s saw something of a resurgence of multi-sector framework agreements with a series of 'orientation' agreements designed to facilitate the modernisation and enhanced competitiveness of French enterprise through the encouragement of both sectoral and plant-level bargaining. This resurgence was prompted in part by agreement on the European Union Single Market, and the subject matter of these orientation agreements included technological change, the more flexible organisation of working time, sexual equality, working conditions, fixed-term and temporary employment rules, and further information and consultation rights for works councils.

The impetus given to plant/company-level bargaining by the 1982 legislation has been successful but only to some extent. The legislation imposed a duty to open negotiations annually on the issues of pay and working time in organisations with union branches. There is no legal obligation to bargain in good faith or reach agreement, and little likelihood of organisations being effectively forced to comply with the legislation if they do not wish to. Nevertheless, company bargaining has been significantly extended since the legislation, with a near fivefold increase in the number of agreements reached in 1991 compared with 1982. Substantial proportions of the agreements reached have been geared towards enhanced flexibility of working time and individualisation of at least part of employees' pay. Many organisations are not covered by the legislation and not much

more than 20 per cent of wage earners seem to be subject to company or plant-level agreements, although the Price Waterhouse/Cranfield Project[35] indicates 46 per cent of the organisations surveyed bargaining over basic pay. There has also been substantial bargaining activity in the larger organisations in compliance with the 1982 Employee Participation Act requirement that unions and employers negotiate arrangements for employee participation within enterprises.

It is apparent from the above that collective bargaining in France has been significantly influenced by legislative intervention, and both content and process are substantially regulated. Agreements are usually for a fixed period and are often given legal effect and legislatively extended. The recently elected and more right-wing government seems set to reduce the extent of this legislative regulation. There is not a strong tradition of voluntary bargaining and many employees are still, despite the efforts and intentions of government in the 1980s, not covered by any system of joint regulation, either because they work in smaller organisations and are therefore not covered by the legislation, or because their employer has not complied with the legislation, or because the legislation does not stipulate that agreement should be reached.

SWEDEN

Rights to organise and bargain freely and the basis of co-operative, consensual and centralised relations and institutions were confirmed by the Saltsjobaden agreements in 1938. Subsequent to the Rehn–Meidner proposals regarding management of the economy and the role of organised labour, a form of centralised corporatist bargaining developed which certainly was the dominant process from the mid-1950s through to the early 1980s. This centralised bargaining has covered wages, differentials, equal pay, working hours, the working environment, joint consultation and equal opportunities for women. Many of these central agreements provided for variation and tailoring at lower levels, but it is only over the last 15 years that any significant pressures have built up encouraging an expansion of local plant and, in some instances, industry-level bargaining. To some extent there has been a seesawing between centralised and local bargaining during the latter period, but the emphasis certainly now appears to be in favour of decentralisation, with employers and the new government particularly favourably disposed towards processes and freedoms which facilitate management regaining control, the linking of pay to efficiency or performance, and which assist in the pursuit of flexibility, efficiency, productivity and competitiveness.

The nature of bargaining relationships have perhaps become more conflictual and distributive in recent years, as new interest groups have emerged that do not necessarily share the traditional belief in the value and equity of consensual/co-operative bargaining and its outcomes. Managements were always keen to protect their prerogative over production issues such as the design, organisation and distribution of work, and this was effectively accepted by the unions as part of the Saltsjobaden agreement. This area of unilateral decision making was not encroached on to any significant extent before the Co-determination of Work Act (MBL) in 1977. This legislation did seem to establish a framework for the extension of collective bargaining into these 'production' issues and areas. However, the intentions of the legislators were considerably frustrated by circumstances and time, the eventual framework agreements in the private sector in 1982 being largely on management's terms, acknowledging as they did the need for enhanced flexibility, decentralisation and common endeavour to improve efficiency, competitiveness and profit.

In recent years, there does appear to have been an expansion of the scope and complexity of bargaining as well as bargaining becoming more frequent at local level, but it seems to have been on management's terms and concerned with the outcomes and implications of change rather than, as was envisaged by MBL, genuine employee participation through bargaining before change decisions are taken – a genuinely joint decision.

The Swedish system has left the parties to regulate themselves, although there has been greater legislative intervention since the mid-1970s. Collective agreements are usually for a fixed period. There is a legal distinction between disputes of interest and right, with resolution of the latter eventually a matter for the national system of labour courts. MBL gave trade unions priority of interpretation in disputes of right. Industrial action is unlawful for the duration of an agreement, but agreements can be cancelled or terminated and notice of industrial action can be given.

UK

Collective bargaining has been the dominant participatory mechanism in the UK although, as the WIRS[36] shows, there has been a substantial decline in its incidence and significance since 1980.

Bargaining, both formal and informal, has occurred both simultaneously and separately at a number of levels, industry and trade, corporate and workplace. The relative popularity of these levels has varied over time. Before the 1960s, industry level was the most common, involving employers' associations and trade unions (confederations), but during that decade workplace bargaining, often on an informal or unofficial basis, became very popular. The latter development was facilitated by piecework payment systems and an emphasis on productivity bargaining. In the 1970s multi-employer and corporate-level bargaining became relatively popular again, and the 1980s and 1990s have seen considerable pressures to decentralise. This again is confirmed in the WIRS evidence which shows a decline in multi-employer bargaining towards the end of the 1980s.

Bargaining in the UK has traditionally been conflictual and distributive in nature and it still is, although there is some evidence of a more co-operative and integrative approach being adopted in recent years.

The subject matter of bargaining has been relatively broad, extending beyond the joint determination of a range of substantive issues to encompass negotiating, grievance, disciplinary, redundancy and a range of procedural dimensions, but not extending into the areas of business policy or strategy.

The traditions are of voluntary bargaining rather than legislative regulation and, while there has been a substantial amount of legislative intervention in the last 25 years, this has not generally been geared towards the regulation of substantive terms and conditions of employment, or regulation of the bargaining process. There are no legislative mechanisms that can be used to force unwilling employers to recognise and bargain with trade unions.

Collective agreements are not legally binding and no legal distinction exists between rights and interests as far as disputes and industrial action are concerned. Agreements may or may not be written, although procedural agreements usually are and they are also normally open-ended in terms of duration. Substantive agreements are more likely to have a time period linked to them, but since they are not legally enforceable this does not have the same significance as in other countries.

The parties often provide for conciliation or arbitration to be considered in the event of dispute or failure to agree, but there is no compulsion. The government does fund the availability of these facilities through the Advisory, Conciliation and Arbitration Service (ACAS).

In the public sector, national-level bargaining has been the norm. However, since 1979 the government has encouraged decentralisation, although arguably with only relatively little success so far.

THE NETHERLANDS

Collective bargaining has traditionally taken place at a multi-industry national level, often within the aegis of the Foundation of Labour created immediately at the end of the second world war, or at a multi-employer sectoral level. In the years immediately following the war, the imperative to reindustrialise and achieve economic recovery encouraged the corporate actors to co-operate and the nature of the relationship between them was essentially consensual. However, as economic and industrial objectives were achieved, national-level co-operative multi-sectoral bargaining tended to give way to more conflictual relationships and multi-employer sectoral bargaining.

The Collective Agreement Extension Act of 1937 was used much more frequently after the war to reinforce national/sectoral-level bargaining and the implementation of its outcomes. The bargaining coverage of employees has been and is much wider than might be indicated by levels of trade union membership and even employer membership of employers' associations.

Larger companies have for many years tended to negotiate their own agreements with the unions quite separately. However, over the last decade there has been an increase in company-level bargaining within the constraints of sectoral agreements. It is estimated that approximately one-third of employees are now covered by company agreements. Sectoral agreements are being made increasingly flexible, establishing minima as opposed to actuals and providing frameworks within which bargaining can tailor terms and conditions to the specific requirements and circumstances of the company.

The period since the war can then be seen to some extent to be one of gradual decentralisation and enhancement of flexibility from the centralised rigid control imposed in the immediate post-war years. This has not been a constant process of decentralisation. There have been numerous instances during the last 20 years when sectoral bargaining was the norm for government seeking to reawaken national-level co-operation between the parties in periods of economic crisis.

As noted elsewhere, the trade unions have been hampered from participating effectively in company-level negotiations by their lack of in-company organisation, and in this context works councils have undertaken a bargaining role in some organisations that was not envisaged by the works council legislation. However, there seems to be no great pressure or desire from or on the part of employers to widen the scope of works council activity into pay bargaining. Works councils are only legally allowed to engage in such bargaining if unions and employers have explicitly agreed to it.

Over the years there was also a tendency gradually to widen the scope of collective bargaining subject matter. However, the expansion of the role of the works council and the more recent desire on the part of many employers to reassert their own autonomy and extend individualism have combined to limit, and in some instances reverse, this trend.

The 1993 bargaining round was substantially concerned with 'repairing' the impact of reductions in disability and welfare benefits and entitlements.

JOINT CONSULTATION AND WORKS COUNCILS

Consultation is a common participatory mechanism or process, although like collective bargaining it varies considerably in extent, scope, level and nature. Essentially the term refers to a process whereby employers/management exchange views and information with employees. This may be done on an individual basis or through representative and collective arrangements. Like collective bargaining, consultation between employers and their representatives and employees may be legally supported or 'mandatory' and this is often linked to specific subject matter so that, for example, you will find in some countries that employers are legally required to consult their employees on matters such as health and safety issues. In some instances, consultative mechanisms are established as an outcome of collective bargaining. Joint consultation is sometimes supported by management as an alternative to collective bargaining and in some instances also as a means of discouraging trade unionism. It is common to find joint consultative arrangements that are based around trade union membership and representatives, but it is also common to find systems in which the employee representatives are not trade union members or representatives.

One of the difficulties with joint consultation is assessing the extent to which the employee participation is real or illusory, not so much because the employee representatives do not take it seriously, although there are undoubtedly instances in which they do simply go through the motions of formulating and expressing views, but because management do not take any notice or account of the views expressed by employees.

This brings us back to the issue of the nature of the consultative process. In its pure form, it is a process whereby management outlines proposals or problems to employee representatives who in turn comment on, consider and suggest amendments or alternatives. It is therefore an exercise in two-way communication and may up to this point be almost indistinguishable from collective bargaining, apart from perhaps the participants and the subject matter. However, the crucial difference between this process and collective bargaining or joint regulation is that joint consultation is not predicated on any commitment by management to seek agreement. They give up none of their prerogative or discretion. In a sense it is this feature of the process which both ultimately distinguishes it from collective bargaining and gives management the opportunity to disregard completely the views, proposals or criticisms expressed to them. For consultation to be meaningful, it should occur before decisions are taken or actions embarked on. Certainly, if it is to provide a mechanism for employees to participate in decision making, this must be the case.

The trouble that academic observers take to distinguish conceptually consultation from bargaining is by no means always echoed in practice, and it is not difficult in some systems to find the two processes co-existing in the same forum, with the parties switching between them as it suits them or as they agree. In systems where one or both of these processes are legally regulated, it is less common for them to co-exist at the same levels, let alone in the same forum. A relatively common example is legally supported bargaining at a multi-employer level underpinned in the workplace by legally supported consultative arrangements, as for example in Germany. However, even here informal practices may develop which effectively dilute the conceptual distinction and result in consultative fora actually engaging in bargaining and joint regulation.

Given the nature of the processes and its implications for the preservation of managerial prerogative, it is common that employers initiate consultation and that they prefer consultation to bargaining. Conversely trade unions may well be suspicious of consultation and prefer bargaining. However, there are instances in which this is not the case. Trade unions and other employees may prefer not to be jointly involved in the making of certain kinds of decision and consultation may suit their interests better, e.g. on issues such as discipline, dismissals and collective redundancies. Another example might be where employee representatives are content to be consulted on issues such as the organisation of production and the technology to be used, but insist on joint determination through collective bargaining when it comes to the implementation of new technology and the distribution of the rewards or benefits.

Arguably there is greater scope for the parties to adopt a co-operative or integrative approach to each other and to particular issues or problems in a consultative framework and, conversely, employee organisations are sometimes wary of consultation precisely because they fear that an integrative relationship will make it more difficult for them to stand up for members' interests when it comes to bargaining. The significance of the concern may be less in systems where both the processes and participants are clearly separated. To some extent, therefore, conflictual or consensual traditions will influence the acceptability and usefulness of consultative arrangements.

The subject matter of consultation varies and is influenced by a number of factors: the subject matter of collective bargaining and any other participative processes; legal regulation; the wishes and disposition of the parties where consultation is freely entered into; and the level at which the consultation occurs. As is also the case with collective bargaining, the structure of decision making within organisations is a factor to be borne in mind when designing consultative mechanisms and determining the level at which they should operate. The European Commission's desire to give employee representatives certain consultative rights at corporate level in qualifying multinational companies is a reflection of the realisation that certain issues and areas of subject matter of relevance to labour are dealt with at that level and that, if consultation with employees on those issues is to occur and be meaningful, it must occur at a congruent level. As indicated earlier, employers sometimes have a preference for consultation over bargaining because it impinges less on their prerogative, and this explains why employers are often prepared to consult on issues that they would not be willing to make the subject of a joint regulatory process. Inevitably employers may be reluctant if the system facilitates a drift from consultation into joint regulation and, from an employer perspective, agreeing to consult with employee representatives on issues of policy and strategy at corporate level may be easier if there is no such possibility, and perhaps also if the employee representatives are internal to the company.

The machinery of consultation can also take a number of different forms. As already indicated, sometimes there is only one forum combining employer representatives, employee representatives, joint regulation and consultation. However, in many of the national systems forming the base of this text, that is not the case. Bargaining and consultation are separated as processes, occur at different levels, involve different participants and deal with different issues.

Works councils is a term used to identify some of these consultative mechanisms and it is used in a number of European countries, however not with the uniformity and consistency that one might wish. Sometimes they are joint management–employee bodies, but more commonly they are councils of employee representatives only. Sometimes the representatives have to be elected from among the workforce, sometimes external trade union officials can comprise part or all of the membership of the council. Works councils occur at a number of levels, the most common being the site or establishment level, although they do also exist at divisional and corporate levels depending on the size and structure of the employing organisation.

In some systems the make-up, role, subject matter, etc. are legally regulated and supported, and in some they form part of an integrated and coherent structure of institutions and processes for achieving employee participation.

Multidivisional and multinational organisations have so far shown some reluctance to form works councils at corporate level, although there are instances of companies doing so even when confronted with a mix of different cultures and different legislative requirements. Eurotunnel, for example, intends to establish a works council at corporate level encompassing both the English and French sides of the Channel.

There are a small number of other reasonably well documented instances of multinational corporations establishing, usually in agreement with employee representatives, mechanisms at corporate level for information and consultation, the emphasis normally being on informing rather than consulting. As noted earlier, there are far fewer instances of bargaining arrangements being established at this level. Many of the well-known examples of this practice are French and this is undoubtedly related to the influence of the Socialist government in France in the early 1980s.

In 1985 Thomson–Grand Public and the European Metalworkers Federation (EMF) established the 'first' European works council. In fact, two fora were established covering operations in five European countries. One forum was called a liaison committee, comprising the company chairman and senior directors on the one hand and the EMF general secretary and full-time union officials from the various countries on the other. The second body was called the European branch committee, which differed from the liaison committee primarily on the employee side, as it was comprised of members of the works councils throughout the company. The liaison committee should meet every six months, the branch committee annually. Neither committee has bargaining rights and the company is not committed to taking their views into account.

In 1986, BSN–Gervais Danone agreed with the International Union of Food Workers (IUF) to establish a permanent, corporate-level consultative mechanism covering workers and plants in seven European countries. In this instance, the employee side is made up of equal numbers of works council members and trade union representatives.

Other multinational companies that have established arrangements of a similar nature include Bull, with an information committee comprising trade union representatives from 12 European countries, Volkswagen with a European-level works council covering its Audi and SEAT operations, as well as Elf-Aquitaine with a European information and consultation committee.[37]

Within the European Union there has been pressure from the Commission and a majority of member states for corporate-level works councils to be established as a matter of right for employees in large companies employing substantial numbers in at least two different member states. The intention is that these councils would be for the purpose of information and consultation. Agreement has recently been reached by the 'eleven' utilising the procedures adopted by them at the Heads of State meeting of the Council at Maastricht in December 1991. This agreement is examined in more detail in Chapter 19.

Snapshot 2
UK
There is no legislation in the UK which requires the establishment of works councils. However, there are legislatively imposed obligations on employers to enter into consultation with union representatives and/or

employees in certain circumstances and on specific areas of subject matter.

Where two trade union representatives request it, employers can be legally obliged to form a consultative committee on health and safety issues. There are also informational and consultative requirements on employers in circumstances of impending collective redundancies and transfers of undertakings, and also in respect of the administration of pension schemes where employees contract out of the state scheme in favour of membership of a company scheme.

Joint consultation as a formal process can be traced back to the Whitley Committee proposals in 1916 and it has gone through several phases of differing levels of popularity. In recent years it seems that joint consultation has once again declined in its incidence and overall significance, and this may be attributable to a greater propensity for management to act unilaterally or because managements have increasingly sought to individualise the employment relationship and employee relations. In some circumstances, alternative participatory mechanisms have replaced joint consultation.

In some organisations joint consultative arrangements have been established as an alternative to trade unionism and collective bargaining, and it is reasonably common to find joint consultative arrangements in non-unionised companies. However, formal consultative arrangements can also be found co-existing with collective bargaining, with the representatives being union based in both cases. In these circumstances, it is likely that the two processes will be separated on the grounds of appropriate subject matter as well as by the nature of the processes.

Trade unions have generally preferred collective bargaining to consultation, and consultative arrangements are usually initiated by management rather than by trade unions.

Consultation can occur at a number of different levels from national or sector level down to the level of the workgroup and individual. The majority of consultation occurs within organisations, and commonly at a number of levels within large, divisionalised or multi-plant companies. In the latter cases, the consultative arrangements at various levels can constitute an organisation-wide and coherent structure.

The range of subject matter covered by joint consultation is often wider than is the case for collective bargaining, particularly in circumstances where joint consultative arrangements co-exist with collective bargaining. The fact that management retains the right to decide often makes it easier for them to inform and consult on a wider range of issues.

FRANCE

Organisations employing 50 or more employees have been required since 1945 to establish works councils for the purpose of consultation. The councils are comprised of employee representatives elected via a two-tier or two-stage process, whereby the first round of the ballot is made up of trade union nominees, and only if insufficient votes are cast in the first round is the second round proceeded with. In the second round any employee, whether a union nominee or not, can stand for election. The union nominees' share of the vote has decreased in recent times.

Compliance with this law is not universal. Usually the works council, while made up of employee representatives, is joint in that the chair is usually taken by the employer or a nominated deputy.

In large organisations councils can occur at various levels, and certainly in some of the large state sector organisations, e.g. Thomson and Rhône-Poulenc, works councils have been established at corporate level and on a multinational basis. The 1982 Employee Participation Act requires multi-plant firms legislatively based in France to form group or combine committees that meet at least once a year to be given group-wide information on finances and employment levels.

The rights of works councils are regulated and in almost all areas of subject matter these rights are to information and consultation only. In limited areas such as changes in individual working hours and profit-sharing arrangements, the council's agreement to management proposals is required before they can proceed.

The range of subject matter on which the councils have legislatively supported rights to information and consultation is quite wide and was extended by a few specific legislative interventions in the 1980s. The range of subject matter covered includes:

- any large projects involving the introduction of new technology if they are likely to have consequences for employment, qualifications, pay, training or working conditions;
- the financial state of the business, the state of the order book and production figures;
- employment levels and the nature of employment contracts and details of subcontracting;
- changes to the economic and legal organisation of the business, sales acquisitions or mergers;
- health, safety and improvements in working conditions.

Depending on the subject matter, this information and, where appropriate, consultation have to be provided at specified and regular intervals. Similarly, the works councils may establish subcommittees to deal with specified areas of subject matter, such as health and safety. The councils also have rights in certain circumstances, depending on their size and subject matter, to appoint expert advisers to facilitate their understanding of the subject matter and contribute further to the discussion.

The fairly widespread legislative support for consultation within enterprises is to some extent a reflection of the long-term absence of trade union organisation and collective bargaining at that level, although as noted elsewhere, this was an issue also addressed by legislative intervention in the 1980s.

SWEDEN

The long-term co-operative relationship, emphasis on centralised joint regulation and strength and influence of the trade union movement did not encourage the development of joint consultative mechanisms within organisations until the Co-Determination at Work Act of 1977. As a result of this legislative intervention, local unions now have additional legislatively supported rights to information and consultation on issues such as significant changes, reorganisations or the introduction of new technology. Additional to the right of information, management is also required to allow union representatives the time to investigate and consult with their own experts and national organisation before the proposed changes are implemented. Enterprises of medium size and above are also likely regularly to engage in joint consultation on issues relating to the working environment including health and safety, and also to provide the unions with information regarding the performance of the enterprise. Commonly subject-specific committees are established to cater for consultation.

Consultative machinery and bargaining machinery are usually separated, so that where information and consultation lead to an issue about which the parties then need to negotiate, they will change the forum or the machinery.

ITALY

In Italy there is no strong tradition of joint consultation at any level. The IRI protocol in 1984 in the public enterprise sector provided for the establishment of joint consultative mechanisms at workplace, enterprise, sector and group levels. The protocol specified information and consultation rights for employees on a range of subject matter including elements of company strategy, industrial relations policies, and new technology and its introduction. It was intended to set an example or pattern to the private sector and in some instances it has done so. A number of relatively *ad hoc* responses and systems have been developed in a range of large companies, such as Pirelli and Zanussi, which accord employee representatives, nearly always via the unions, greater participation through information and consultation. The subject matter of these arrangements is often concerned with the introduction of new technology and working practices.

Factory councils exist in many organisations. The 1970 Workers' Statute facilitated the formation of trade union-based unitary representative councils, and this was further eased by the unification of the three main trade union confederations in 1973. The confederations accepted the factory council (CdF), which may be made up of both union and non-union elected delegates, as the basis for union organisation within the workplace. Since 1984 when the unitary confederation broke up, the main confederations have expended much time and effort in seeking to agree on and establish unitary mechanisms within the workplace which were 'equitable' in guaranteeing all of them some representation as well as responding to the wishes of employees. Before 1993 the most recent attempt had been in 1991 and was called the RSU (Unitary Union Representatives) and it is this concept on which the 1993 agreements seek to build.

Given the relative absence of legal regulation of processes, there is a considerable variety of extent, level, subject matter, role, nature and permanency of the consultative mechanisms that have developed over the last decade. There is also similar ambiguity about the nature and consistency of the relationship between consultation and bargaining. In some instances the distinction is clear and certain, while in other circumstances the two processes are often confused.

The last decade has also seen the development of more co-operative relationships in many sectors and organisations. This has often taken the form of enhanced consultation between the factory councils and management, the factory council in many respects representing a haven of constancy for management to deal with. Given the conflicts and difficulties between the unions and facing them at sectoral and national level, the extension of consultative arrangements has formed a significant part of the proceduralisation and institutionalisation of workplace relations that has been a feature of the Italian system over the last 10–15 years.

JAPAN

In Japanese companies the traditions of consensus decision making and employee–management co-operation have tended to take a bottom-up problem-solving direction rather than a joint consultative one. Unionism and collective bargaining both tend to be based in the enterprise and again this tends to leave relatively little scope for separate and formal joint consultative machinery. Managements have been generally reluctant to relinquish control over goal setting, and what sharing of decision making there is tends to be concerned with means and problem solving.

Some of the larger organisations have established joint consultative machinery at corporate level, but there are suspicions that the motives are more to confuse existing bargaining arrangements, dilute trade union influence and persuade employees of the 'rightness' of management's position, rather than a desire to enhance employee influence and participation in decision making at the corporate level. Indeed, Thompson[38] poses the question of whether consultation, currently a supplement to collective bargaining, could supplant formal negotiations.

There is no tradition of legislative support for consultation rights and arrangements, although in the public sector, where bargaining rights are limited, there is a greater use of consultative mechanisms.

GERMANY

The works council is the established and legislatively supported mechanism for achieving employee participation in the workplace. The Works Constitution Acts of 1952 and 1972 constitute the main supporting legislation, although works councils have a history going back to the first world war. This legislation, in addition to requiring the establishment of works councils, also regulates the subject matter and nature of their role. The works councils are not trade union bodies, the members of the council being elected from among employees with no requirement that they are trade union members. There is, however, a great deal of co-operation between the unions and the councils and their members, with trade union expertise and resources being available to many works councils. The unions tend to have a greater density among works council members than among the labour force as a whole, and

it is sometimes suggested that the visibility of the activities of the union members on the council can be a powerful membership recruitment aid.

The role of the councils varies according to the nature of the subject matter. Three distinct roles are identifiable, i.e. the right to give consent, the right to consultation, and the right to information.

The right to consent covers a range of economic and personnel issues including discipline, overtime and holiday allocations and schedules, payment systems, piecework rates, safety, welfare, employee performance, the pace of work, working environment, staff selection and training. Rights to information and consultation relate to a range of production and business matters, although when it comes to business performance and prospects, the rights are limited to those of information only.

The councils are not intended to take part in collective bargaining but they do, since they are often the only institution for employee representation within the workplace. Industry and enterprise-level agreements, where appropriate, need to be tailored within the workplace, often raising issues of interpretation and application which need to be resolved at this lower level. Some higher-level agreements provide for local-level management–works council bargaining via 'opening clauses'.

Overall, the role of the works council is to look after and protect the interests and safety of employees, and in this latter respect in particular they have a monitoring purpose in respect of company compliance with appropriate legislation as well as compliance with higher-level collective agreements.

The nature of the relationship between the main actors is traditionally a consensual one and this is supported by the legislative requirement that they work together in a spirit of mutual trust and for their mutual benefit. The rights and involvement of the works council are sometimes blamed for increasing labour costs, but it is also commended as a mechanism that has encouraged employees' commitment and co-operation, particularly with respect to the introduction and utilisation of new technology.

In the larger organisations it is relatively common to find councils at different levels, with different subject matter being dealt with at each, and there are already instances of agreements in some multinational German companies to create European Works Councils at corporate level. However, the main emphasis and direction of this form of employee participation has been decentralised.

As noted elsewhere, there appears to be an enhanced incidence of works councils engaging in collective bargaining against the background of recession, unemployment and more employers resigning from employers' associations keen to determine matters locally.

AUSTRALIA

Since 1983 the government has been encouraging participation within the workplace, and several Federal Commission wage case decisions (1987, 1988, 1989 and 1991) have sought to encourage consultation between employers and employees as a means of more effectively pursuing improvements in efficiency and restructuring. In some cases, experiments in joint consultation have led to a form of productivity bargaining.

The transition from the traditional conflictual relationship to the more co-operative approach consistent with joint consultation is difficult for both parties. There has been conflict over both the scope and timing of consultation, with managements often content to consult about implications and outcomes whereas the unions are much more likely to seek a consultative role prior to, and in the making of, strategic decisions. Health and safety issues are probably those most commonly subject to some form of joint consultation, and the 1990 AWIRS[39] confirms that health and safety committees are the only formal consultative committees present in more than 20 per cent of the workplaces surveyed. Other formal joint consultative arrangements were relatively rare in the private sector.

There are no legal requirements as yet requiring the formation of works councils. Federal government has required certain consultative arrangements to be established in the public sector at Public Service Board and departmental levels. These were extended by the Public Sector Reform Act 1984, and again the AWIRS data confirms a higher incidence of both formal and informal consultative arrangements in the public sector.

US

In the US there is no significant tradition of collective and joint consultative arrangements within the system. Certainly, some companies have emphasised an 'open' communications and management approach, but have generally stopped short of formal consultative arrangements. There is no tradition of legal support for or regulation of such arrangements and the law has generally supported the notion of managerial prerogative.

Works councils do not normally exist. Employees have sought to participate in decision making through collective bargaining on economic issues, but otherwise have tended to accept management's right (often supported by the law) to decide unilaterally and employ at will. The unions have shown no great interest in consultation, either as an adjunct or alternative to bargaining, and managements generally seem to have resisted employee participation via consultative mechanisms because they were keen to preserve their prerogative and, in some cases, because they were sceptical of employees' ability to contribute to decision making in a meaningful and co-operative fashion.

Kochan *et al.*[40] have suggested that the situation both has and is changing, and their model of the transformed system encompasses employee participation via consultation at business strategy and policy-planning levels, as well as a very much more co-operative approach by both parties within the workplace, the subject matter of the co-operation within the workplace being primarily about operational issues.

THE NETHERLANDS

Works councils went through a number of stages before they reached their current form. Initially they were created as joint bodies with a consultative role, and it was not until the legislation of 1979 that they were confirmed as employee-only bodies with a representational as well as consultative role.

Works councils are mandatory in organisations above a certain size (35 employees) and have powers and rights that are specified in some detail in the legislation, varying according to the size of the company. The legislation specifies the minimum frequency of meetings with management, the information about company performance and prospects that must be given to the council, distinguishes between subject matter on which councils have a right to be informed and consulted, and specifies that such consultation must take place at a time which allows the council's view to have a significant impact. The councils also have rights to consent on certain personnel issues, and in any event if the employer does not take the advice of the council, behaves unreasonably or proceeds without agreement, the council has recourse to legal remedy, implementation can be legally delayed and decisions can be declared null and void by the appropriate court. This possibility of delay and legal remedy often provides scope for bargaining between employer and council. Legally councils cannot bargain over pay unless specifically agreed by the unions, and should not contravene terms of existing collective agreements. Councils in enterprises with between 35 and 100 employees have fewer rights.

The councils are non-union bodies, although the unions can put forward candidates for election and the majority of council members are also union members. To some extent, works councils initially filled a vacuum within the workplace left by the trade unions' relative disinterest in affairs and interests at that level. In more recent times, the councils can be seen as a significant impediment to the development of effective union organisation within companies.

Legislation covers representation of the labour force and employee qualification to stand for election and to vote in them. Members of the councils also have legislative protection from discrimination and dismissal and rights to time off and various relevant facilities.

Councils exist in 80–90 per cent of enterprises with more than 100 employees and in a majority of the smaller ones covered by the legislation.

OTHER PARTICIPATORY MECHANISMS

In this section we examine the extent to which employee representatives on corporate-level boards, quality circles and other problem-solving groups and self-managing teams feature in the various national systems with which we are concerned.

Employee/worker directors

As indicated in the introduction to this chapter, employee/worker director schemes are often cited as examples of employee participation tending towards democracy. Where they occur, they are inevitably representative in nature, are often power centred, are usually initiated by the labour movement and/or government and are in many cases supported by legislatively created rights. While the intention often is that these employee representatives on the board should represent employee interests at that level and in the formulation of corporate strategy and policy, it is not unusual for the intention to be frustrated. Occasionally they attend in a purely 'observer' capacity.

To some extent the effectiveness of these mechanisms depends on the precise detail of the arrangements:

- the proportion of the total board membership that is constituted by employee representatives;

- whether employee representatives are full and voting members of the management committee or simply have a status similar to that of an observer;
- whether employee representatives have some right of veto on all or certain kinds of decision or subject matter;
- what happens if there is a deadlock even in a parity of membership system – whether there is a casting vote and who has it;
- what kind of access to information is made available, whether the employee representatives are able to call on their own specialist advisers and who pays for them.

These and other details will make a significant difference to the success of such schemes from the viewpoint of an employee and in terms of the participation experience.

Even where the scheme seems satisfactory against the above criteria, there are other issues that are likely to impinge on the effectiveness of the participation. These include:

- the motivation of employees, whether this form of participation is wanted by employees, and whether there are sufficient numbers of competent people actually willing to take the role on;
- the attitudes of the other board members and the precise nature of any legally imposed obligations and/or sanctions on them to participate genuinely;
- the knowledge and experience of, and training received, by the employee representative;
- whether the employee representatives are subject to periodic re-election or appointment, and whether they can therefore be replaced by a dissatisfied constituency;
- the extent to which proximity to senior management and concern with the interests of the organisation dilute the ability or inclination of the employee representatives to represent their constituents' interests.

As is evident from the above, there are many potential obstacles to the effectiveness of such mechanisms even where the parties are themselves positively orientated towards them, and it should be noted that often arrangements of this kind have been against a background of employer reluctance and reservation.

Quality circles and problem-solving groups

These schemes are usually management initiated with a number of motives and objectives that do not necessarily include enhancing employee participation or influence in decision making. In other words, the fact that such enhancement occurs is commonly an unintentional byproduct of their introduction. Managements' motives for introducing such mechanisms are much more likely to be based in a desire to increase efficiency, productivity and quality, allied to a belief that employees, through their knowledge and experience, may well have a contribution to make to the design and organisation of the task and work organisation systems which facilitates the achievement of these objectives. Allied to this, as noted earlier, may well be a belief that employee-involvement schemes of this nature enhance employee commitment to the organisation and, through enhanced commitment, facilitate improved performance.

Quality circles are probably the most famous of these schemes and are inextricably linked with notions of and experiments in Japanisation. However, the Price Waterhouse/Cranfield Project[41] data indicate that they were being used by less than a fifth of the Scandinavian employers and between a fifth and a third across the rest of the surveyed countries and organisations. They seem most popular in the private sector, in multinationals and in large rather than small employers. In essence, they are comprised of quite small groups of employees (6–10) meeting voluntarily on a regular basis to identify, examine and resolve quality or other operational problems. It is usually anticipated that in addition to improving quality, these groups may devise ways of reducing costs and improving the way in which the tasks are completed and work organised.

As Ramsay[42] points out, for the objectives of quality circles to be achieved it is unlikely that simply calling a group of employees together will be sufficient. The group will have to be led, it will probably have some resourcing and support, participants and leaders will probably require training and the system must be monitored and managed. At least as important to the success or failure of such schemes are the attitudes and support of both middle and senior management, and it should borne in mind that middle and lower levels of management may well feel threatened by such an initiative, perhaps particularly in organisations that do not have a participatory tradition or culture. Trade unions may also resist these developments, viewing them as management-inspired mechanisms for diluting employee support and loyalty to unions.

Other dangers that management should guard against are a loss of momentum once initial enthusiasm palls as longstanding issues and problems are resolved and improved, and the dangers of inaction or non-application of the group's recommendations. It is rela-

tively rare for a problem-solving group of employees to have the authority to implement their own recommendations.

The search for improvements in productivity, efficiency, flexibility and quality, prompted by international developments in technology and competition in product markets, has encouraged some organisations to delve deeper into the notion of teamworking. As Storey and Sisson[43] point out, the main features of teamworking as it develops in response to these pressures are:

- groups of multi-capable and multi-skilled workers;
- flexibility of task, team organisation and allocation of work;
- team responsibility for performance levels and quality, and possibly even team responsibility for such tasks as recruitment and selection of new members.

This development of teamworking in the direction of enhanced team autonomy and responsibility has employee participation consequences as well as implications for managerial roles and organisational design. It would be inaccurate to suggest that developments in this direction are common as yet, but they do perhaps have particular significance and potential for employee participation, since they appear to transcend problem solving and arguably require a degree of delegation of decision making that represents a significant dilution of managerial prerogative.

Snapshot 3
US

In the US there are no legislative requirements with respect to companies establishing mechanisms for employee participation at board of directors level. However, there have been some instances of voluntary agreements to this effect.

Kochan et al.[44] emphasise the strategic choice which many managements have made to alter the nature of their relationship with trade unions and employees, moving in the direction of co-operation. As evidence of this process there are examples of companies experimenting with mechanisms such as quality circles, problem-solving groups and self-managing teams.

Lewin,[45] among many others, questions the significance of strategic choice in these developments, arguing that many of them may be examples of management reacting again to environmental pressures rather than the product of strategic choice.

The motivation for these developments is generally enhancing employee commitment, productivity and quality of output, rather than a desire to facilitate employee participation in decision making about production and task issues. Nevertheless, Ford, General Motors, Chrysler, General Electric, General Foods, GTE Telecommunications, Honeywell and Eastman Kodak are all examples of internationally renowned companies which, to varying degrees and in various formats, have introduced elements of teamworking or quality problem-solving groups into production locations, often with trade union agreement and involvement.

FRANCE

Employee participation legislation in 1982 gave employees the right to express directly their views on the content and organisation of their work and working conditions. As a result of this legislation, it is common for employees in 'expression' and 'participation' groups of 15–20 to meet management every quarter or half-year for this purpose. Usually managements are required to respond to employee complaints or enquiries within specified periods, and it seems as if this mechanism has contributed to an improvement in working conditions and the organisation of work.

Traditional concerns with maintaining managerial prerogative and the pattern of low-trust relationships have tended to mitigate against voluntary experiments in and extension of employee participation within the enterprise and workplace. There have been many experiments with quality circles, but middle management concerns about the impact on their position and prestige and their control over information constitute barriers not easily overcome. Employers have also experimented with new methods of work and task organisation, but not generally involving the creation of teams or groups with enhanced participatory roles or relative autonomy. These experiments have often been the subject of collective agreements.

Board-level representation and participation were also enhanced by legislation in 1983. This legislation is relevant to the public sector and requires up to one-third of the seats on the boards of public enterprises to be reserved for employee representatives. In the private sector there is no statutory right to employee representation on the board of directors, although companies may provide for a number of employee representatives to attend and observe board meetings.

SWEDEN

Unions were given the right by the MBL in 1976 to appoint two representatives to company boards of directors in companies with more than 25 employees. While the nature of their role is essentially informational, Kjellberg[46] suggests that this is the main mechanism through which unions exert influence on strategic decision making at corporate or group level. These employee representatives ostensibly have the same rights and obligations as other directors, but inevitably their minority position limits their ability to influence decision making; although again the participative tradition in Sweden probably allows them a greater role and influence in many organisations than would be indicated by their numerical minority position.

The participative tradition has also facilitated some of the team-based, small-batch, semi-autonomous workgroup experiments in work reorganisation in the 1980s for which the Swedish car manufacturers Volvo and Saab-Scania are renowned. The experiments, particularly those at some of the Volvo plants, included concepts such as workgroups electing their own supervisors and scheduling, assigning and inspecting their own work, working at their own pace to meet targets and, at Uddevalla, in teams of about 20 assembling a complete car. Usually the significant decisions made by the teams had to be approved by a joint management–union committee.

There were other factors that played an important part in encouraging management to move in these directions. The need to be internationally competitive, allied to tight labour markets and union strength, placed a greater emphasis on production systems consistent with the creation and maintenance of a motivated, competent and satisfied workforce. Increasing unemployment and recession in the 1990s renders it likely that experiments of this nature will remain isolated examples.

AUSTRALIA

In Australia, the emphasis in the past has not been on enterprise or workplace-based participatory activities. There is no legislation requiring employers to establish works council arrangements, nor indeed any form of employee director.

Nevertheless, the pressures on employers to compete internationally and enhance efficiency and flexibility have in a few instances led companies to experiment with problem-solving groups, quality circles and team-based working arrangements, sometimes as parts of a new approach to human resource management emphasising involvement. Lansbury and Davis[47] have documented experience in some of the larger organisations. The trade unions have been sceptical of these developments, although they and the government since 1983 have been keen to encourage employee participation. The AWIRS[48] found that managers in about one-third of the workplaces claimed to have a philosophy of teamwork and/or consultation. In the larger workplaces and public sector proportions were higher, yet the actual incidence of formal arrangements was markedly lower.

ITALY

There is no legal requirement for companies to establish schemes for employee participation at board level. The vast majority of employee participation in decision making within organisations is accomplished via union-based mechanisms, and the 1993 reorganisations seem unlikely to alter this significantly, since the main confederations are guaranteed representation in the new arrangements. Some companies have introduced quality-circle approaches to work reorganisation and restructuring, but these have generally been introduced in the face of trade union opposition and are far from common.

JAPAN

In many respects Japan is the home of the quality circle. They are in relatively common usage and are consistent with notions of consensus decision making which are bottom-up and envisage changes in routine and procedures being originated by those involved. The recommendations of the circles are subject to approval at a higher level. Participation in these problem-solving groups is ostensibly voluntary, although there is clearly considerable pressure within the system encouraging employees to participate.

More recently, in the pursuit of quality and competitive advantage, team-based work organisation has become more widespread in manufacturing industry, and these schemes often provide considerable internal flexibility and team ownership of production planning and quality.

There is no legal regulation of these direct and task-related participatory mechanisms. There is also no legal requirement for companies to have employee directors representing their interests at board level, although it can be argued that, since executive directors are likely to have spent the whole of their careers in the company and progressed within it, employees' interests are inevitably taken into account.

GERMANY

The outstanding 'other' participatory mechanism used in Germany is the worker director. Increasingly, German companies are experimenting with problem-solving teams, quality circles and joint problem-solving groups looking for ways of enhancing flexibility and productivity. This has been particularly noticeable in the car and chemicals industries, where perhaps the impact of 'Japanisation' has been greatest. Opel, Mercedes-Benz and Volkswagen are all restructuring works organisation towards teams, usually by agreement with the works council. There has also been considerable joint activity in the development of humanisation of work programmes. However, these recent participatory developments are insignificant as yet in comparison with the international renown of the German worker director provisions.

Companies in Germany are required to have a two-tier board structure, the senior board being known as the supervisory board and the other the management board. The supervisory board has a non-executive role, has to approve significant business changes and, more importantly, appoints the management board. The management board is made up of full-time senior executives and it is this board of directors that has the executive role within the organisation.

It is on the supervisory board that employees and their trade unions have legislatively supported rights to participate. Depending on the industry and size of company, the employee directors may constitute up to one-third or half of the supervisory board; the other board members represent shareholders, major finance institutions and others with an interest. In companies outside the coal and steel industry (for which there is a specific scheme) and employing in excess of 2000 people, worker directors, who need not be employees of the company concerned, can make up half of the supervisory board, have the same rights to information and voting rights as other directors but, in the event of deadlock, can be effectively outvoted by the chairperson's casting vote. The chairperson is not an employee representative. The apparent parity of influence between employee representatives and others is further diluted by the requirement that at least one of the worker directors should be nominated by and represent the interests of senior executives employed by the company. In companies employing 500–2000 employees, senior executives may be represented by up to one-third of the directors on the supervisory board. Worker or employee directors are usually nominated via the appropriate works councils.

The system does not always work as it was intended to. Employee interests can be frustrated relatively easily at board level. In addition to the chair's casting vote, shareholder and other representatives can easily control the information flow to employee directors and they can also meet privately and agree tactics and approaches. Another way in which employee participation through worker directors can be frustrated is by management restructuring so that the legislation does not apply. Employee directors have no power of veto over supervisory board decisions on any issue.

Nevertheless, it does seem that the systems of worker directors has influenced each side's goals, attitudes and understanding. Employee involvement in strategic decision making, even if the involvement is somewhat peripheral, may well have contributed to a greater identification on the part of employees with the objectives of the organisation and a greater willingness to accept change in the interests of the organisation's future, its competitiveness and in a sense the employees' own security.

UK

There are no legislative requirements on employers to allow employee representation on boards of directors. There were some experiments in the 1970s in public sector enterprises such as the Post Office and the British Steel Corporation, but these did not last.

Some British employers have responded to the pressures for flexibility, productivity, quality and competitiveness by embracing notions of employee involvement and commitment and seeking them in part with new systems of labour and work organisation. Quality circles, special projects and special-purpose groups are in evidence, as are team-based production methods. The 1990 WIRS[49] confirms that there was substantial growth in the use of these new work-related participatory mechanisms in the late 1980s. The experiments in companies such as Rover, Digital and Bird's Eye have been documented and Marchington et al.[50] have examined developments in 25 organisations.

THE NETHERLANDS

Dutch employers have been subject to much the same pressures and influences as others in Europe and many have responded in similar ways, experimenting with involvement and quality-improvement programmes that enhance employee participation in task-related issues and for functional reasons. Companies with 100 or more employees may be required to establish supervisory boards and employees have variable rights of membership.

SUMMARY

The literature is awash with different definitions and interpretations of the concept of employee participation and the similarities and distinctions between it and others such as employee involvement and industrial democracy. In the introduction to the chapter we examined some of these and also identified some of the many dimensions of participation against which particular schemes and mechanisms can be assessed and compared.

We used the term generically to include a range of different mechanisms by which employees can be seen to influence decision making within organisations, thereby limiting managerial prerogative, however we have excluded mechanisms which seem not to allow a real or genuine influence.

Collective bargaining remains the dominant mechanism in the majority of the countries studied, although it can be argued that the traditional dominance is diminishing as a whole host of national and international pressures seems to have both encouraged and facilitated a renewed interest in and emphasis on consultation and the decentralisation of decisions about work organisation and the task to those actually involved. In many instances these developments have been accompanied by exhortations to the labour force to become more co-operative and more committed in the interests of efficiency, competitiveness and their position as stakeholders. However, there is also much evidence to suggest that these pressures and trends are mitigated by the strength and flexibility of the existing mechanisms and institutions, themselves a product of many national, environmental, cultural and ideological interactions and choices.

DISCUSSION QUESTIONS

1 Explain the relevance of 'purpose' to distinctions between employee participation, involvement and industrial democracy.
2 Consider whether employee participation necessarily implies that managerial prerogative is limited by the process.
3 Can Flanders' perception of collective bargaining be integrated into Chamberlain and Kuhn's model of its nature and functions?
4 Explain why some of the radical perceptions see collective bargaining as a process which employees should avoid.

5 Examine the various influences upon bargaining level and highlight those that might encourage bargaining at a multi-employer level.
6 Consider the prospects for collective bargaining at a cross-national level.
7 Assess the proposition that joint consultation requires an integrative or co-operative approach from the participants.
8 What have been the influences encouraging the formation of quality circles and development of various teamworking schemes?

NOTES AND REFERENCES

1. Gospel H and Palmer G (1993) *British Industrial Relations*, Routledge, p.20
2. Salaman M (1992) *Industrial Relations: Theory and Practice*, Prentice Hall, pp.340–42
3. Gospel and Palmer, op. cit., ch. 8
4. Farnham D (1993) *Employee Relations*, IPM, p.393
5. Salaman, op. cit.
6. Salaman, op. cit.
7. Ramsay H (1992) 'Commitment and Involvement' in Towers B (ed), *The Handbook of Human Resource Management*, Blackwell, p.208–13
8. Marchington M *et al.* (1992) 'New Developments in Employee Involvement', *Employment Department Research Series No 2*, p.6
9. Ibid. pp.9–10
10. Storey J and Sisson K (1993) *Managing Human Resources and Industrial Relations*, Open University, p.98
11. Lammers CJ, 'Power and Participation in Decision-making' in Formal Organisations', *American Journal of Sociology* 73(2), pp.200–204
12. Storey J and Sisson K op. cit.
13. International Labour Office 1986, Convention No 154
14. Gospel and Palmer op. cit., p.15
15. Salaman op. cit. p.309
16. Webb S and B (1902) *Industrial Democracy*, Longman
17. Chamberlain NW and Kuhn JW (1965) *Collective Bargaining*, McGraw Hill
18. Flanders A (1968) 'Collective Bargaining: A Theoretical Analysis', *British Journal of Industrial Relations*, Vol VI, pp.1–26
19. Chamberlain and Kuhn op. cit.
20. Chamberlain and Kuhn op. cit.
21. Dubin R (1954) 'Constructive Aspects of Industrial

Conflict' in Kornhauser A, Dubin R and Ross AM (eds) *Industrial Conflict*, McGraw Hill
22. Walton RE and McKersie RB (1965) *A Behavioural Theory of Labor Negotiations*, McGraw Hill, Chapter 3
23. Chamberlain and Kuhn op. cit.
24. Chamberlain and Kuhn op. cit.
25. Brewster C, Hegewisch A and Mayne L (1994) 'Trends in European HRM – Signs of Convergence' in Kirkbride PS (ed), *Human Resource Management in Europe, Perspectives for the 1990s*, Routledge, pp.114–32.

Hegewisch A (1993) 'The Decentralisation of Pay Bargaining: European Comparisons' in Hegewisch A and Brewster C (eds) *European Developments in Human Resource Management*, Kogan Page, pp.86–100.

Fillella J and Hegewisch A (1994) 'European Experiments with Pay and Benefits Policies' in Brewster C and Hegewisch A (eds) *Policy and Practice in European Human Resource Management*, Routledge, pp.89–106

26. Ferner A and Hyman R (1992) *Industrial Relations in the New Europe*, Blackwell, Introduction pp.xvi–xxxvi
27. Clarke O (1993) 'Conclusions in Bamber CJ and Lansbury R *International and Comparative Industrial Relations*, Routledge, pp.255–7
28. Thompson M (1991) 'Union-Management Relations – recent research and theory' in Adams RJ (ed) *Comparative Industrial Relations*, Harper Collins, p.101
29. Kochan TA, Katz HC and McKersie RB (1986) *The Transformation of American Industrial Relations*, Basic
30. Ferner and Hyman, op. cit.
31. Marginson P *et al.* (1988) *Beyond the Workplace: Managing Industrial Relations in The Multi Establishment Enterprise*, Blackwell
32. Ferner and Hyman, op. cit.
33. Carley M (1993) 'Social Dialogue' in Gold M (ed) *The*

Social Dimension – Employment Policy in The European Community, Macmillan, pp.105–34

34. Kochan, Katz and McKersie, op. cit.

35. As reference 25 above

36. Milward N *et al.* (1992) *1990 Workplace Industrial Relations Survey, Workplace Industrial Relations in Transition, Dartmouth*

37. *ILO World Labour Report* (1992), Geneva p.57

38. Thompson op. cit.

39. Callus R, Moorehead A, Cully M and Buchanan J (1991) 'Industrial Relations at Work', *The Australian Workplace Industrial Relations Survey*, Australian Government Publishing Service

40. Kochan *et al.*, op. cit.

41. Brewster *et al.*, op. cit.

42. Ramsay, op. cit., pp.216–18

43. Storey and Sisson, op. cit., p.92

44. Kochan *et al.*, op. cit.

45. Lewin D, 'Industrial Relations as a Strategic Variable', in Kleiner MM et al (eds) *Human Resources and the Performance of the Firm*, IRRA, p.1–42

46. Kjellberg A (1992) 'Sweden: Can the Model Survive?' in Ferner A and Hyman R, op. cit., p.130

47. Lansbury PD and Davis EM (1992) 'Employee Participation: some Australian Cases', *International Labour Review* Vol 131, No 2 231–48

48. Callus *et al.*, op. cit.

49. Milward *et al.*, op. cit.

50. Marchington *et al.*, op. cit.

FURTHER READING

Baglioni G and Crouch C (eds) (1990) *European Industrial Relations: The challenges of flexibility*, Sage

Bean R (1994) *Comparative Industrial Relations: An introduction to cross-national perspectives*, 2nd edition, Routledge

Blanpain R (1992) *Labour Laws and Industrial Relations of the European Union*, Deventer

Bridgeford J and Sterling S (1994) *Employee Relations in Europe*, Blackwell

Bulletin of Comparative Labour Relations (1992) Special Participation Issue, No. 23

Crouch C (1993) *Industrial Relations and European State Traditions*, Clarendon

Gold M and Hall M (1992) *Report on European Level Information and Consultation in Multi-National Companies: An evaluation of practice*, European Foundation for the Improvement of Living and Working Conditions

IDE (1993) *Industrial Democracy in Europe Revisited*, Oxford University Press

Windmuller JP (1987) *Collective Bargaining in Industrialised Market Economies: A reappraisal*, ILO

Lammers C and Szell G (eds) (1989) *International Handbook of Participation in Organisations*, Oxford

Poole M (1986) *Industrial Relations: Origins and patterns of national diversity*, Routledge and Kegan Paul

Ramsay H (1990) 'Reinventing the wheel? A review of the development and performance of employee involvement', *Human Resource Management Journal*, 1 (4), pp. 1–22.

Sisson K (1987) *The Management of Collective Bargaining: An international comparison*, Oxford

8 · HR POLICY AND PRACTICE

LEARNING OBJECTIVES

You should be able to:

i appreciate cultural and institutional 'constraints' on HR decision makers;

ii understand the main features of recruitment, training and remuneration policy in different countries and consider some 'typologies';

iii gain a thematic and conceptual overview of international HRM, as a basis for investigation of practices in selected countries in Section 2.

THE HRM CONCEPT REVISITED

In all organisations the fundamentals of human resource management must be carried out. There is always a need to recruit staff, to reward them, and to equip them with the skills to enable them to carry out their work.

In this chapter we shall focus on the main features of HRM activity, with particular reference to our selected countries. Although we would acknowledge that, in practice, a broader range of concerns is encompassed within HRM, for the sake of clarity and ease of comparison we shall concentrate on the HR 'policy levers' of recruitment and selection, reward and remuneration.

As we have already noted, underlying cultural, ideological and structural factors influence HR practice in different national systems. So, for example, 'hiring and firing' approaches more acceptable in the US will be restricted by law in Western Europe. In Germany, for example, decisions over recruitment and selection, transfer, regrading or dismissal require the agreement of the works council, and in German-speaking countries the high priority placed on vocational training is supported by joint state and enterprise co-operation. In France, where bureaucratic traditions are strong, most HRM matters are regulated by law.

Nevertheless, despite such differences, certain overall trends can be identified in the field of HRM. According to Pieper[1] there are two strong tendencies that have to be confronted by HRM in all countries. In introducing a set of international and comparative writings on HRM, he identifies a strong common tendency towards flexibility in work organisation, workplace and benefits systems. He argues that this is primarily the result of the potential flexibility of a number of new production and office technologies. A related development is 'the continuing individualisation of most western societies' which leads to divergent labour needs, and also necessitates, for example, individual benefit systems, and provides increased flexibility in work organisation and hours.

The importance of flexibility in the European context has been emphasised in reports derived from the

Price Waterhouse/ Cranfield Survey,[2] which found a significant growth in areas of non-permanent employment such as temporary and fixed-term contracts and subcontracting. The researchers found also that levels of communication and consultation between management and employees were on the increase. This has frequently been a strategy to bring about employee commitment to change. A central objective of most organisations is to lower costs at a time of economic unpredictability, and the key to this is often the speed of response to changes in markets or technology. Perhaps somewhat paradoxically, this has led to wide-ranging initiatives in worker participation. The rationale underlying such schemes is that imposing change on a resistant workforce is likely to be hazardous and lengthy, and therefore the most desirable approach is to have ideas 'pushed up' from below.

In the US there have been some notable experiments in industrial democracy. In particular, at United Airlines there is a worker-shareholder deal enabling the workforce to acquire majority control in the company in exchange for $4.5 billion worth of cost savings. In Japan, a system of reciprocity is still widely practised; flexibility is rewarded by a job for life. In a number of European countries workers' councils are consulted on a range of important issues before decisions are taken.

Placed in this context, in which flexibility of response to rapidly changing conditions outside organisations is paramount, human resource policy areas gain a new significance and the potential for HR 'policy levers' to be manipulated in order to contribute to the achievement of the broader goals of flexibility and commitment is integral to major formulations of the HRM concept.

Guest,[3] drawing on the Harvard model and making reference to the systems 'in and around the conventional territory of personnel management' notes:

> They are concerned with more than good selection, training and communication. Rather they are intended to achieve HRM 'policy goals'. [Therefore] selection should ensure both high quality and the potential for attitudinal commitment. Training should contribute to flexibility, communication should be goal directed rather than primarily concerned with process.

Figure 8.1 presents an 'ideal type' which connects HR policy choices in the areas of recruitment, training and development to contextual changes towards flexibility.

A factor of great importance in connecting HR practice with corporate success is the role of personnel function itself, and the extent to which it is strategi-

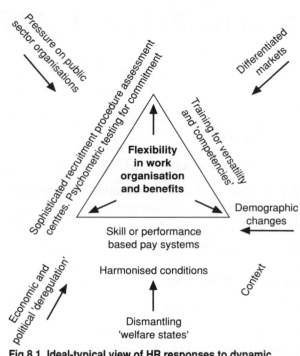

Fig 8.1 Ideal-typical view of HR responses to dynamic contexts

cally integrated into corporate management. In offering the HRM concept, Beer *et al.*[4] argue for a 'fit' between business strategy and HRM policies. The authors state that reasons for poor integration lie in the HRM function itself:

> That function often develops activities and programmes that are not relevant to line management's needs. This problem arises in part from the differences in perspectives between short-term profit oriented line managers and long-term people oriented human resource managers. But the problem also stems from the fact that many HR activities are not developed in close co-ordination with business planning.[5]

Guest also sees 'strategic integration' as an HRM policy goal. This concerns (1) the full integration of HRM into strategic planning; (2) coherence of HRM policies across policy areas and across hierarchies; (3) the acceptance of HRM practice by line managers.

Although advocates of HRM envisage operational personnel decisions being taken by line management, a more strategic and higher profile role is set aside for HR specialists, with representation at board level.

In Europe, however, the evidence suggests that this is too simple a connection to make, and that it disregards the important statutory, cultural and other influences being brought to bear from outside the enterprise which may intervene in the relationship between HR and senior line management.

In an interesting set of findings, the Price Waterhouse/Cranfield Survey[6] found considerable variation in the integration of HRM and corporate strategy across Europe. In Spain and France board representation of HR specialists is high, while in Italy and Germany the proportion is relatively low. However, perhaps not surprisingly, in most countries personnel specialists claim to be involved 'from the outset' in strategy formulation in around 50 per cent of organisations.

Consideration of the personnel role in Germany, which has been described as 'relatively reactive and legalistic'[7] is illuminating, as an apparently peripheral role for the function is combined with advanced features of personnel policy and a recent history of dynamic economic performance. This seemingly contradicts a central facet of 'strategic integration' within the HRM constraint.

ISSUES AND THEMES IN HR POLICY AND PRACTICE

Although the 'stakeholders' are experiencing many common international challenges, for example difficulties in recruiting and retaining sufficient skilled employees, or the need to respond flexibly to changing market conditions, an examination of practice in the area of human resource management reveals that prevailing cultural, ideological or structural features within domestic systems exert a potent conditioning effect on the selection of appropriate HR policies. Indeed, cross-cultural comparison in this area is hampered by difficulties in comparing like with like.

Dany and Torchy[8], for example, point to difficulties in comparing different forms of CV or interviews; while Filella and Hegewisch[9] suggest that performance-related pay translates most closely in Sweden and Denmark as 'individually negotiated pay'.

In considering the notion of management development in Japan, Holden[10] finds that no significant term exists for this, as 'they believe all workers should be developed and this should be an ongoing part of systematic employee development'.

Shared values and priorities and acceptance of the 'way things are done' will not only influence the formulation of personnel policies, but also the nature of the linkage between them.

In Japan, where economic regeneration and competitiveness have primarily expanded an effective utilisation of the country's greatest 'natural asset', its people, an emphasis has been placed on the continuous development of staff throughout their careers, connected with the principle of lifetime employment which continues to exist for 'core' employees in large companies.[11]

According to Holden:[12]

Lifetime employment allows for the long-term development of employees and enables the creation of a structured succession programme mutually beneficial to both the organisation and the individual employee. Decision making is shared at all levels and there is a strong sense of collective responsibility for the success of the organisation, and cooperative rather than individual effort is emphasised, although achievement is encouraged. Training and development is part and parcel of company policy in

Table 8.1 Head of personnel or human resources function on the main Board of directors or equivalent (%)

Country	Ch[a]	D(W)	DK	E	F	FIN	I[a]	IRL	N	NL	P	S	T	UK
	58	30	49	73	84	61	18	44	71	42	46	84	37	49

Note: [a] 1991 data

Table 8.2 HR involvement in development of corporate strategy (%)

Country	Ch[a]	D(W)	DK	E	F	FIN	I[a]	IRL	N	NL	P	S	T	UK
From the outset	48	55	47	54	54	48	32	50	65	50	42	56	45	53
Consultative	20	25	31	25	27	23	23	31	24	36	30	31	9	32
Implementation	6	10	15	18	16	10	17	10	9	10	18	8	33	9
Not consulted	14	10	7	4	3	7	3	9	3	3	10	6	13	7

Note: [a] 1991 data

Source (for Tables 8.1 and 8.2): Brewster C and Hegewisch A (eds) *Policy and Practice in European Human Resource Management*, The Price Waterhouse/Cranfield Survey, Routledge, p.28

helping to reinforce these working practices, as well as being used to improve skills in technology and other related working practices. Training and development is thus 'embedded' in Japanese companies, rather than extraneous, as in British organisation.

Japanese approaches to recruitment may also be understood with reference to the system of lifetime employment, which occurs predominantly, for the core labour force, and larger employers have developed links with universities and colleges and tap personal contacts for recruitment purposes. For 'special workers', who typically comprise women, mid-career recruits, temporary workers and foreigners, and who represent a more dispersed layer of staff surrounding the core, open approaches to recruitment are common, including direct application.

Approaches to reward also fit with the distinctive Japanese approach, with seniority-based pay systems remaining the norm for 'core' employees, with greater variability in pay being experienced by 'special workers'.

In Germany, the reserve of skills possessed by employees has been recognised as the main factor in German economic regeneration after the second world war, and the subsequent experience of the 'economic miracle'.

Here the tripartite approach to economic management exerts a profound influence on the determination of personnel policies. The vocational and educational training system (VET), which represents a dual system of vocational training, is defined in law and compels employers to fund training, and is administered by employers, unions and the state. Under this system, school leavers enter apprenticeships which combine attendance at vocational college with instruction from a skilled craftsperson who is also qualified in instruction techniques.[13]

The approach has engendered high rates of participation among young people in education and training, which has provided Germany with a skill base second to none. Consequently, vacant clerical and professional jobs can be filled through the apprenticeship system, rather than turning to external recruitment.[14]

Recruitment decisions themselves fall within the ambit of the system of co-determination, which involves consultation with workers' representatives; while reward systems, at least in the former West Germany, reflect the high level of skills possessed by workforces.

Taking a more specific view of the HR policy area, its clear that the degree to which management action is *directed* through statutory intervention, or perhaps through collective agreements or other consultative mechanisms, is an important determinant in the nature and form of HR policies.

With regard to recruitment, in the US and the UK, where liberal individualist principles are apparent, the state takes a minimal role in the recruitment process. Here organisations will be able to tap into relatively open labour markets, with mobility from organisation to organisation being relatively commonplace. Employees may decide on a range of selection mechanisms, although typically it is the interview that will be used, particularly in the UK.[15] In the US, there is some evidence of an elaboration of selection methods, to include psychometric testing and structured interviews.[16] Also, in these countries private recruitment agencies may be engaged by employers, particularly in respect of managerial professional positions.

An important exception to the 'non-directive' or voluntarist approach to recruitment in these countries is in the area of equal opportunities, where activities are circumscribed by law. In the UK, however, evidence would suggest that sex and race discrimination laws have only had limited success in achieving their objectives.[17] In the US, however, a large number of organisations have drawn up affirmative action plans and implemented quota systems to ensure legal compliance.

By way of contrast, in some European countries state agencies maintain an active role in the recruitment process. This is associated with broader corporatist tendencies. In Germany, for example, the state employment service has a monopoly in the placement of all labour, while in Belgium placement in the public sector is controlled by the state service.[19] In addition, in Germany employees are prohibited from using private recruitment agencies.

Despite variations in broad approach, Dany and Torchy[18] find remarkable similarity in the use of recruitment 'tools' in a number of European countries. It seems that the use of application forms, interviews and professional references is still widespread, although there is a preference for word-of-mouth methods in Southern European countries as well as in Southern Ireland.

Membership of the European Union has significance for those taking recruitment decisions in constituent countries. EU member states are obliged to respond to EU directives aimed at eliminating discrimination in gaining access to employment. Regulations passed in member states to comply with equal opportunities directives have taken various forms, and have applied to a wide range of discriminatory practices. Nevertheless, there is evidence to suggest that 'Enforcement, and the degree to which equal opportunities on grounds of race or sex are advocated positively, vary considerably between member states.'[19]

Also, the principle of free movement of labour enshrined within the Single European Act of 1987 formally removed barriers to mobility across Europe, which has implications for mutual recognition of qualifications, advertising and selection procedure, and pan-European approaches to human resource and individual career planning. Despite the opportunities presented, in practice there has been little mobility to date, and it seems that only those with scarce technical or entrepreneurial skills will find international career paths.

The Price Waterhouse/Cranfield Survey[20] has provided a wide-ranging exposition of recruitment practice in Europe, providing information not only on practice but also on policy, which examines where responsibility for recruitment is located in organisations.

In interpreting these findings, Dany and Torchy[21] arrive at a typology which groups countries together according to prevalent tendencies, and which is expounded as a provisional conclusion which is to be 'tested, explained and completed by further research':

Group 1 (former West Germany)

The leading features which are to be found are as follows:

Practices

1 Germany makes recourse largely to apprenticeship to fill vacant clerical and professional jobs. This can be easily associated with the dual training system which prevails in Germany. It brings to the fore the hypothesis that societal factors are of prime importance in the determination of management practices such as recruitment and selection.
2 In order to facilitate the recruitment of scarce resources in their national labour market, German companies develop flexi-time and part-time practices and neglect training and reskilling. This can be interpreted, within the German context, as a will to develop what has not yet been developed by the well-known German training system.
3 The categories in which most organisations find difficult to recruit are engineers and qualified manual workers.

Policies

1 Recruitment and selection policies are, more than anywhere else, determined at the subsidiary level, and less than anywhere else, determined at the

'site/establishment' level. This particular trend may reflect the way co-determination is organised in German companies.
2 There are some countries in which line management responsibilities have decreased over the last three years in comparatively more organisations, even if the general trend is – as seen above – the increase of line management responsibilities regarding recruitment and selection issues. Germany is among the countries in which these responsibilities have decreased most.

Group 2 (Denmark, Finland, Norway, Sweden)

The leading features which are to be found are as follows:

Practices

1 In these countries there are less recruitment problems than anywhere else, except for health professionals; they constitute the personnel category hardest to recruit in Scandinavian countries.
2 Line managers are very much involved in the management of recruitment and selection. Line managers' responsibilities have increased over the last three years. Line management and the HR department are responsible for recruitment and selection issues, the HR department being supportive of line managers.
3 The Group 2 countries are characterised by a wide use of internal and external advertising to fill vacant clerical, manual and managerial jobs.
4 Flexible working hours are widely used to aid recruitment. Relaxed qualifications, relaxed age requirements, increased pay and benefits are less used than in any of the other groups.
5 The staffing requirements are planned, more often than the other groups, for two years ahead. This feature particularly prevails in Finland (under the influence of the former USSR model).

Policies

The determination of recruitment and selection policies is carried out most of the time at the site/establishment level and not at the national level.

Group 3 (France, Ireland, United Kingdom, the Netherlands)

The leading features which are to be found are as follows:

Practices

1 Recruitment agencies are used in the process of filling vacant positions of all sorts (clerical, professional/technical, managerial).
2 The Group 3 countries are characterised by the large number of methods they use in order to fill vacant professional/technical and clerical positions.
3 France, Ireland, UK and the Netherlands are among the countries that have introduced the recruitment of foreigners more widely in order to find people who are difficult to recruit in their home labour market.
4 Line management and the HR department are responsible for recruitment and selection issues, the line managers being supportive of the HR department. Line managers rarely hold the sole responsibility for recruitment and selection issues.

Policies

The determination of recruitment and selection policies is carried out most of the time at the site/establishment level and not at the national level.

Group 4 (Spain, Portugal, Turkey)

The leading features which are to be found are as follows:

Practices

1 What mainly characterises the organisations in this group is their difficulty in hiring technicians, IT professionals and people speaking foreign languages.
2 In order to facilitate the recruitment of scarce skills, they have introduced measures related to flexible working practices – flexi-time, part-time – less than in any of the other countries, but have introduced all the other possible measures, i.e. relaxed qualifications requirements, relaxed age requirements, training for new employees, retraining for existing employees, increased pay and benefits, relocation of the organisation.
3 The staffing requirements are planned for the next year or even for a shorter length of time.
4 The southern countries are among those that use the least internal advertising to fill vacancies of all kinds.
5 Line management and the HR department are responsible for recruitment and selection issues, the line managers being supportive of the HR department.

Policies

The determination of recruitment and selection policies is more than anywhere else located at the national level and less than anywhere else located at the subsidiary level.

Turning to the area of training and development, again broad distinctions can be drawn between directive and voluntarist systems. As we have already pointed out, in Germany and Japan there are strong institutional and cultural pressures to give training a high priority. In France since the 1970s legislation has been passed which compels employers to invest in training. The instrument of taxation has been used to ensure that organisations employing nine people or more allocate at least 1.2 per cent of total wages and salaries to staff training.[22] Holden[23] finds that the effects of this and other similar legislation have been quite dramatic. Not only have a number of training consultancies come into existence to meet the increased demand, but also, after seeing the advantage of investing in training, many companies have decided to exceed the minimum threshold.

In the US and the UK primary responsibility for training and development rests with employers, who may also decide how much priority is attached to it. There is little statutory or other interference in these matters from outside the enterprise.

Nevertheless there is recognition on the part of employers of the importance of training and development where the volatile nature of international competition places versatility and skill at a premium. In the US, according to Springer and Springer,[24] training and development are big business, with annual expenditure reaching billions of dollars. The 'voluntary' approach to training in the US is reflected in the fact that around 400 companies have their own training centres.

In the US emphasis is placed on training which has direct relevance for workplace experiences and problems. Moreover, attempts have been made to identify and develop key 'competencies', comprising knowledge, skills and attitudes which will enable individuals to make the maximum contribution towards the achievement of business success.

At management level, and in keeping with some central facets of the HRM concept as elaborated by Beer *et al.,* US employers are increasingly seeing the need to match the individual development and career progression of managers to the future needs of the organisation, with the use of assessment centres and performance appraisal being instrumental in the process.

In the UK a number of these practices have been emulated, particularly the competency movement. Nevertheless, in comparing the UK with its European counterparts, it would seem that the absence of statutory incentives in a time of recession has led to training being relegated in the list of business priorities. Furthermore the 'voluntarist' approach may lead to a reluctance on the part of employers to provide transferable skills, preferring to invest in company-specific skills.[25] The comparative paucity of training in the UK was highlighted by a number of authoritative surveys in the 1980s,[26] and, despite indications that British employers, like others in Europe, recognise the significance of training and development to provide skilled and knowledgeable workforces in the 1990s,[27] statistics on the actual level of training provision would indicate that such statements are quite rhetorical (see Fig. 8.2).

Vocational educational systems and styles

The inception of the Single European Market has presented HR practitioners across Europe with an important new set of challenges in the area of training and development. In particular, there is an increasing need for language and cross-cultural training, as well as for preparing individuals for expatriation. There is little evidence to cast light on progress in this direction, although it would seem that those companies which have been active across Europe for some time are continuing to make the most serious training provision in these areas.[28]

Moreover, the integration of former communist Eastern European countries into capitalist structures is likely to produce significant training and development requirements, both in respect of workers and of management. It is doubtful whether autonomous efforts will be sufficient to bring about suitable levels of development, yet there are some significant cultural and practical barriers which are likely to impede East/West collaboration in education, training and development.

The following information is reproduced from Beardwell I and Holden L (eds) (1994) *Human Resource Management: A Contemporary Perspective*, Pitman Publishing.

Britain
Vocational and Educational Training (VET) institutions:
- Youth Training for adult unemployed (Action Programme).
- Training and Enterprise Councils.
- Local Enterprise Companies – to encourage companies to train their employees.

Table 8.3 Organisations: training and development objectives/spending

% organisations with training and development as main objective			% organisations spending more than 2% on training	
%	Country ranking		Country ranking	%
34	D		F	80
31	N		S	60
31	DK		T	47
30	S		D	43
26	NL		NL	40
25	F		IRL	40
25	T		P	39
24	P		FIN	36
22	UK		N	36
22	IRL		UK	26
19	E		DK	25
12	FIN		E	23

Source: Larsen H H (1994) 'Key issues in training and development' in Brewster C and Hegewisch A (eds) *Policy and Practice in European Human Resource Management*, The Price Waterhouse/Cranfield Survey, Routledge, p.109

- Apprenticeships – declining, about 13 000 places.
- Colleges of higher and further education.
- Universities (including the 'old polytechnics').
- Business schools, usually part of universities.

Training culture – voluntarist: finance rather than industry oriented; class based; public/private education.

Germany
VET institutions:
- Dual system: in-company training (practical).
- Vocational school (theoretical).
- Apprenticeships – 319 000 places, although demand is decreasing.
- Technical colleges.
- Universities.

Training culture – directed: functionalist; industry oriented, particularly engineering.

France
VET institutions:
- Much VET in school system.
- Apprenticeship places 300 000.
- University institutes of technology.
- Universities.
- *Grandes écoles*.
- Law requiring employers to spend 1.2 per cent of total gross salaries on training employees.

A little knowledge is a dangerous thing

UK vocational education is under fire in a new report, write **John Authers** and **Lisa Wood**

Vocational education: UK at bottom of class
% of upper secondary students in vocational education including apprenticeship (1991)

Germany, Austria, Switz., Sweden, Italy, Neths., Denmark, Norway, Belgium, Finland, France, Turkey, Spain, Australia, Japan, Ireland, UK, Portugal, N. Zealand, Canada

Source: OECD

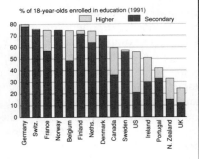

% of 18-year-olds enrolled in education (1991)
Higher Secondary

Germany, Switz., France, Norway, Belgium, Finland, Neths., Denmark, Canada, Sweden, US, Ireland, Portugal, N. Zealand, UK

An employment consultant listening to Mr Kenneth Clarke's announcement in the Budget that the UK government would introduce a "modern" apprenticeship scheme suggested to his wife that their son might like to pursue such a route.

"My son...an apprentice?" she screamed. "He is bright and will go to university."

This kind of traditional academic snobbery is one of the biggest problems facing British manufacturing today. Deep-seated skills problems threaten to stifle recovery and leave the UK vulnerable to competition from both European and increasingly high-tech Asian economies.

A report* published today pinpoints the crisis. It says the system of vocational qualifications phased in by the government over the past three years is a "disaster of epic proportions".

Professor Alan Smithers and his team from Manchester University's Centre for Education and Employment concentrate their attack on two reforms: national vocational qualifications (NVQs), which are work-based and measure an individual's ability to do a task, and the general national vocational qualification (GNVQ), intended as an alternative to A-levels mainly for students in full-time education. Both qualifications – introduced in workplaces and schools – are based on what a student can do, rather than the knowledge or theory acquired about a particular subject.

In comments which will intensify the debate between adherents of the new system and its critics, Prof Smithers claims both NVQs and GNVQs are inferior to previous training schemes and to comparable European courses.

Response to the report has been swift. Mr Tony Webb, director of training at the Confederation of British Industry, one of the driving forces behind the new qualifications, said: "There is a great deal of misunderstanding about what NVQs are. To an employer it is what somebody can do that matters."

In marked contrast, Professor Sig Prais, of the independent think tank, the National Institute for Economics and Social Research, a noted critic of NVQs, said: "The government may now be sufficiently embarrassed in order that it reconsider the whole system."

Such a move is highly unlikely despite the fact that training for 16-to-19-year-olds in the UK is unco-ordinated and controlled by different government departments, GNVQs, for example, are an education department responsibility, while NVQs come under the employment department.

Both departments are trying to give more status to the new qualifications. For instance, the apprenticeship scheme announced in the Budget, under the employment department, will be based on NVQs. Meanwhile, the current review of the National Curriculum for 14-to-18-year-olds, by Sir Ron Dearing for the education department, is expected to recommend a stronger emphasis on GNVQ.

So what has the government been trying to do with its vocational education standards and provision? Mr Tim Boswell, further education minister said: "We believe the broad structure is right and that we can build on it to have a really powerful range of qualifications."

Nevertheless the problem is plain.

Britain's workforce is under-educated and under-qualified. Only 18 per cent of the UK workforce, for example, is qualified to craft level – skilled carpenters for example – whereas in Germany the figure is 56 per cent, France 33 per cent and the Netherlands 38 per cent.

Other international comparisons are revealing although direct contrasts along the lines attempted by the Organisation for Economic Co-operation and Development (see accompanying graph) are difficult because countries use different training schemes.

Prof Prais points out that the German figure for 16-to-18-year-olds in full-time vocational educational is swollen by the numbers of apprentices on the country's "dual scheme", who spend most of the week with their employer, spending only one or two days at a college.

However, his own figures also rank the UK's vocational provision low compared with its main economic competitors. He says that 64 per cent of the British workforce has no vocational qualifications, compared with 26 per cent in Germany, and 23 per cent in Switzerland.

An awareness that there is a shortage of skilled workers has forced the government to rethink vocational education. It has sought to establish three routes into the world of work for young people: a work-based route built on NVQs; the GNVQ (now renamed "vocational A-levels" by the education department); and the "A" level.

An effective, competence-based qualifications system is critical to reform, the government believes. But here is the rub – deciding what amounts to competence pits academics such as Prof Smithers against business bodies such as the CBI.

According to Prof Smithers, the educational theory of NVQs "is loosely derived from behavioural psychology, and argues it is what people do that counts, their competence (to perform a task)". Examiners assume that what pupils know or understand can be inferred from what they do.

By contrast, Prof Smithers and other conservative academics believe that both practical ability and trainees' theoretical grasp of their tasks must be tested. In most European countries, trainees take practical and written examinations, both of which must be judged acceptable by external examiners, before they can gain a qualification.

The added theory can be vital, critics of the current system claim. One college lecturer suggests that a young NVQ-qualified craftsman could build a brick wall, but "because he had never been taught about the effects of freezing weather on water, he would not know what to do when it was cold, and neither would he know what to do in hot weather. So your wall would probably fall down within a couple of years."

Testing on the continent is also more rigorously linked to the needs of the workplace. In Switzerland, for instance, trainees lose marks for taking more than a fixed time to complete work, and must produce consistent quality. Prof Prais says that in the UK, examiners are more concerned to ensure candidates can reach a certain standard – not necessarily that they do so consistently – and do not set a time limit for the work.

According to Prof Prais: "It's vital for the economics of production for someone to be trained to do something reliably and punctually. We have given up testing for that kind of thing."

A National Institute study of workplace practices in Europe found serious UK inadequacies which could be attributed to training.
• Machinery maintenance was found to be routine on the continent, but in Britain was left to smaller "firefighting" teams of qualified craftsmen. Normal machine operators did not understand how to practise good maintenance.
• In the clothing industry, qualified German workers could reach an efficient working speed on a new garment within three days, while an English worker would typically take three weeks.

On this evidence, British employers seem sorely let down by the education and training system. Even though they may recruit workers who are competent in their immediate tasks, they will not in the long run have a workforce with a broad range of flexible and competitive skills.

Changing the system to satisfy their needs along the lines identified in Switzerland and Germany requires both clarity of government objectives and a recognition by employers that their best interests lie in a deeper commitment to high-level training. Prof Smithers' report shows that consensus on the way forward is as far away as ever.

*All Our Futures – Britain's Educational Revolution: Prof Alan Smithers, Channel Four, PO Box 4000, London W3 6XJ; free with sae

Fig 8.2 Source: *Financial Times*, 15 December 1993

Training culture – directed: mathematical/engineering orientations; centralised; elitist, e.g. grandes écoles; educational establishment attended often decides career prospects.

Sweden
VET institutions:
• Upper secondary school – large vocational content.
• Technical and specialist universities.
• Universities.
• VET in most organisations is strong. HRD considerably emphasised.
• Retraining for unemployed.
• Labour market training board (AMU) is very influential.
• Considerable free adult education.
• Emphasis on 'self-development' and open learning systems.

Training culture – directed: state will use training to affect labour market policy. Companies are strongly encouraged to train.

Japan
VET institutions:
• High schools take up to 90% of pupils up to 18 years.
• Two-year college – vocationally specific training.
• Four year university courses.
• Five year college of technology courses.
• Considerable continuous in-company training.

Training culture – directed/voluntarist: central and local government set and enforce training standards; meritocratic – top companies will take from top universities etc.; lifetime employment and training in large companies; self-development emphasised.

United States

VET institutions:

- Junior or community college two-year associate degree course.
- Technical institutes.
- Vocational, trade and business schools.
- 'GI Bill' federal loans/grants for four years higher education after completion of four years military service.
- Private schools and colleges.
- University courses.
- Apprenticeships are increasingly less common and of low status.
- Excellent training by leading companies but this is not universal.

Training culture – voluntarist: anti-federalist in nature with wide variation; uncoordinated with emphasis on individual effort and individual payment.

There is a close association between the processes of pay determination and approaches towards collective bargaining, which we have discussed in a previous chapter.

In broad terms, a distinction may be drawn between centralised structures which involve the collective involvement of trade union and employer institutions at an industrial (or national) level, and where agreed terms and conditions have a pervasive influence across industrial sectors; and more decentralised approaches where remuneration and reward packages will be decided predominantly at the level of the corporation or the plant. In practice, centralised bargaining does not necessarily preclude more localised bargaining. According to Filella and Hegewisch,[29] in Finland, France and Sweden negotiations at company level complement national or industry-level negotiations, although in Portugal, Spain, Turkey and UK company-level bargaining has tended to displace bargaining at a higher level.

Where pay determination is mainly decentralised, although there may still be involvement of trade union representatives at a local level, individual employees will be able to formulate pay policies which take into account the local labour market and other circumstances surrounding the concern, and also, importantly, they will be able to devise pay policies which can be instrumental in the achievement of broader corporate goals.

Approaches to reward may therefore be viewed as a useful 'lever' for management to achieve more performance-orientated or flexibly deployed workforces.

It is also the case that the extent of state intervention into processes of pay determination may vary. Filella and Hegewisch note that 'There is in Europe, compared to other geographical areas, greater regulation and institutionalisation of pay bargaining.'[30] They find that in most European countries provision exists to protect low paid workers. Taking a historical perspective, in the 1970s, high levels of inflation prompted governments and Members of European countries to enter the arena of pay determination through somewhat controversial application of income policies.[31]

In Europe such interventions were consistent with, and feasible owing to, an emphasis having been placed on collective determination of pay and a concern for equity and standardisation within grading structures.[32] Indeed, those principles may be viewed as being in keeping with the 'Fordist' paradigm which we have described earlier, which placed an emphasis on continuity and stability of production for mass markets and which implied standardisation of terms and conditions of employment.

Nevertheless, considerable variation exists in patterns of reward, and in the assumptions underlying them. Undoubtedly many of the features of the wage/work bargain are rooted in, and may be seen to reflect, more profound cultural and ideological tendencies of the society in question. Thus, in those countries where there are strong individualistic tendencies and a deregulated approach is taken to national economic management (notably the US and the UK), a relatively high priority is attached to the rewarding of individual performance (particularly in more recent years). In Japan, however, the rewarding of individual performance has not generally been viewed as being consistent with the 'groupist' ethos and, as we have noted previously, seniority remains an important factor in approaches to pay.

Deeper ideological considerations may also be manifested in the extend to which egalitarian principles are evident within reward systems. Rowthorn[33] finds that differentials are relatively compressed in Scandinavian countries, while pay discrimination on grounds of sex, although widespread, varies considerably from country to country in terms of the size of the gap between male and female earnings.[34]

Although explanations for this are complex, Filella and Hegewisch[35] assert that 'as a general finding, countries with highly centralised bargaining structure generally display greater wage equality than those where bargaining is fragmented.' This may lead to a tentative

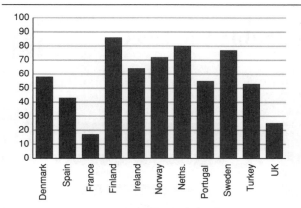

Fig 8.3 National/industry level negotiations for manual workers in the private sector (% of organisations)

Source: Fillela J and Hegewisch A (1994) 'European experiments with pay and benefits' in Brewster C and Hegewisch A (eds) *Policy and Practice in European Human Resource Management,* The Price Waterhouse/Cranfield Survey, Routledge, p.93

conclusion that egalitarian principles are most likely to be found in pay structures within the relatively regulated, neo-corporatist economies in continental Europe. A corollary of this is that any move towards deregulation may be accompanied by increased discrimination in the field of pay, and also a spreading of differentials.

Despite the diversity of approaches towards the formulation of reward, recent survey findings would suggest that some important trends are occurring. Overall, these would serve to support a view that the rigidities associated with centralised and collective determination of pay are giving way to systems in which employers are able to formulate flexible packages which are contained within cost constraints, but which also link closely with employee performance and versatility, and which meet the developing aspirations of staff at a time when effective recruitment and selection of skilled workers is necessary.

In particular, Filella and Hegewisch,[36] in analysing the results of the Price Waterhouse/Cranfield Survey, find a clear trend towards the determination of pay at lower levels (see Fig. 8.3). This is particularly pronounced in the UK and France, although multi-employer bargaining shows considerable persistence in the Nordic countries, Ireland and the Netherlands. It seems, however, that in general industry-wide bargaining is more common in the public sector than in the private sector.

A move is also identified towards increased variability in pay, although traditions and statutory pressures in different countries have meant that this has taken a variety of forms (see Figs 8.4 and 8.5). In Germany and France a preference seems to exist for profit sharing, while merit and performance pay are more prevalent in France, Italy, Switzerland and the UK, particularly at managerial and professional levels.

The move towards pay for performance is not, however, restricted to these categories. In France, IDS[37] finds that 'individualisation', or linking part or all of a pay rise to individual merit, is showing a marked increase, and that Rhône Poulenc, for example, is budgeting 1.5 per cent of the pay bill for individual awards, which may be granted to shopfloor workers as well as staff.

However, it seems that performance-related pay is not always used as a motivational tool, and that there

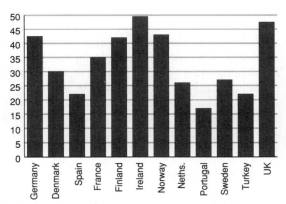

Fig 8.4 Decentralisation of pay policies to subsidiary or site/establishment level within the private sector (% of organisations)

Source: Fillela J and Hegewisch A (1994) 'European experiments with pay and benefits' in Brewster C and Hegewisch A (eds) *Policy and Practice in European Human Resource Management,* The Price Waterhouse/Cranfield Survey, Routledge, p.96

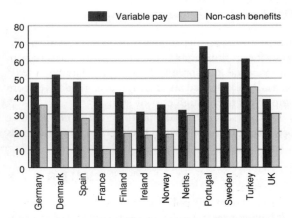

Fig 8.5 Increases in variable pay and non-cash benefits during the last three years (% of organisations)

Source: Fillela J and Hegewisch A (1994) 'European experiments with pay and benefits' in Brewster C and Hegewisch A (eds) *Policy and Practice in European Human Resource Management,* The Price Waterhouse/Cranfield Survey, Routledge, p.98

German labour costs almost double UK level

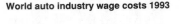

Germany has the highest total motor industry labour costs in the developed world while the UK has the lowest according to a study by the German auto industry, **writes Kevin Done.**

German costs at DM49.6 (£19) per hour in 1993 were almost double the UK's level of DM25.6 according to figures from the German automobile federation (VDA), which exclude South Korea.

The gulf in labour costs between Germany and the UK underlines a key part of the strategy behind BMW's £800m takeover of Rover, the leading UK volume carmaker, announced on Monday.

The acquisition gives the German executive and luxury carmaker access, for the first time, to a low-cost production base in Europe.

As a result of the takeover BMW has abandoned its earlier plan to develop a small car for sale under the BMW badge. It has decided to make Rover the European centre for the production of small medium-sized front wheel drive cars. They will be under the Rover, rather than the BMW, badge.

The UK position at the bottom of the labour costs league is the result of the very low level of social costs, such as payroll tax or national insurance. UK social costs accounted for only 27 per cent of total wage costs, compared with 43 per cent in Germany.

The appreciation of the D-Mark and the yen against many other European currencies and the dollar have had a substantial impact on the competitiveness of leading vehicle producing countries.

Japanese carmakers now have the highest gross wage levels in the world's auto industry at DM34.3 per hour, compared with DM28.5 in Germany, DM18.7 in the UK and only DM12.9 in Italy.

Total Japanese wage costs are still 16 per cent lower than the German level, however, thanks to much lower social costs.

Japanese carmakers have rapidly built up a large production presence in North America and Europe. Three of the leading Japanese producers, Nissan, Toyota and Honda, have chosen the UK as the location for their first European car plants.

UK car production rose by 6.5 per cent last year in contrast to sharp falls in most continental European countries and is forecast to show the strongest increase during the whole of the 1990s chiefly as a result of rising Japanese output.

The biggest improvement in competitiveness in total labour costs last year came in the UK, Spain, Italy and Sweden largely as a result of the devaluation of these countries' currencies against the D-Mark and the yen.

Italy now has the second lowest total labour costs after the UK, but it is still 6 per cent above the UK level, because of much higher social costs, which are more than double the UK level.

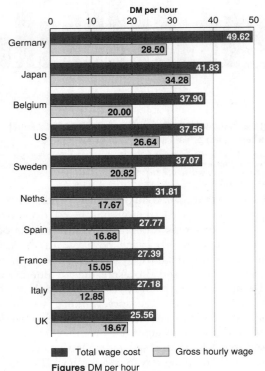

World auto industry wage costs 1993

Germany — 49.62 (total wage cost), 28.50 (gross hourly wage)
Japan — 41.83 (total wage cost), 34.28 (gross hourly wage)
Belgium — 37.90 (total wage cost), 20.00 (gross hourly wage)
US — 37.56 (total wage cost), 26.64 (gross hourly wage)
Sweden — 37.07 (total wage cost), 20.82 (gross hourly wage)
Neths. — 31.81 (total wage cost), 17.67 (gross hourly wage)
Spain — 27.77 (total wage cost), 16.88 (gross hourly wage)
France — 27.39 (total wage cost), 15.05 (gross hourly wage)
Italy — 27.18 (total wage cost), 12.85 (gross hourly wage)
UK — 25.56 (total wage cost), 18.67 (gross hourly wage)

■ Total wage cost   □ Gross hourly wage

Figures DM per hour

Source: Verband der Automobilindustrie (VDA)

Fig 8.6 Source: *Financial Times*, 2 February 1994

are circumstances in which it may be used as an aid to staff recruitment and retention. In the Paris region, for example, the spread of merit pay may be at least partially explained as a pragmatic response from employers to the high cost of living.[38]

It is perhaps in the US that the greatest efforts have been made to tailor reward packages to meet the needs of individual employees or workforces. Increasingly, flexible or 'cafeteria' benefits are being designed which enable employees to select from a menu of benefits including healthcare and childcare or pension provision. This represents a cost effective but nevertheless sophisticated method for attracting and retaining valuable staff, particularly women.

SUMMARY AND CONCLUSION

This review of HR policy areas has only been partial. We have concentrated on the key policy areas of recruitment, training and development and remuneration.

Nevertheless, this discussion has indicated that it is not realistic to view HR policies in isolation. The shortage of skills in certain job categories means that increased attention may need to be given to the effectiveness of recruitment mechanisms, but there will need to be corresponding manipulations in the reward and training 'levers' to ensure that valuable staff are recruited and retained; or, if not, that necessary compensations can be made from within the corporation.

We have also suggested that there is no single 'best practice' in human resource management and that policy decisions in this area are conditioned by underlying cultural, ideological or institutional factors. In broad terms, we have drawn a distinction between 'directive' and 'voluntary' approaches. Directive approaches are found in those more regulated systems in which the state possesses an active role in the conduct of the employment relationship, thus fitting closely with the notion of 'corporatism'. In 'directive' systems we would expect to see greater state and trade union involvement in matters affecting the mobility and procurement of labour, which is likely to impede employer discretion to advertise and select employees with a completely free hand. In such systems, too, the state is likely to play a more directive role with respect to training and development, so that laws may be passed to compel training, or more intangible, 'cultural' pressure may be exerted on employers to undertake training. Perhaps inevitably, the 'reward' lever will also be influenced by prevailing value systems. The greater visibility of statutory forces is likely to make itself felt in more centralised arrangements for pay determination, with an emphasis being placed on 'tripartitism', and with at least minimum rates of pay and other conditions of employment applying across industries. We have already pointed out that such approaches may be associated with greater egalitarianism in pay determination.

There are obvious difficulties in attempting to categorise complex and sometimes inherently contradictory national systems, although previous analysis in this text would suggest that we would see Germany, the Nordic countries and possibly some countries in Southern Europe displaying a number of the features we have outlined.

In contrast 'voluntary' approaches imply a non-interventionist role for the state, and are consistent with more deregulated, liberal individualist traditions. In effect, this translates into greater autonomy for employers in hiring and firing staff, implying discretion in formulating and operating recruitment procedures in relatively open labour markets. Moreover, it is likely that employers will have direct access to the 'reward' lever, as it is in these economies that decentralisation of bargaining arrangements is likely to have occurred (although trade

union organisation at local level may still be an important factor). Furthermore, it is in the deregulated countries that responsibility for training tends to be vested primarily in employers. It is in these countries (and we would see the UK and US as approximating most closely to this stereotype), where companies have been exposed most acutely to the realities of the marketplace, that we would expect to see an increasing sophistication of recruitment procedures to include, for example, psychometric testing for attitudinal commitment to organisation cultures, a direct linking of pay to performance, and training provision where it can be applied to develop those competencies which will contribute towards organisational adaptability and survival.

In addition to suggesting that there is no single best practice, we have indicated that HR policies, and the broader approaches on which they are based, are subject to change over time. Drawing on the work of Pieper[39] and the evidence of the Price Waterhouse/Cranfield Survey, it would seem to be the case that there are overriding trends towards flexibility in the organisation of employment practices, and a 'decollectivisation' in terms and conditions of employment, particularly in the area of pay, which are impinging on even the most 'directed' of systems.

These trends are borne out in a rather anecdotal way in the case studies in Section 2 which relate to a number of our sample countries. Key developments include:

● greater line management responsibility for recruitment decisions and using selection tools to establish the link between personal attributes and the requirements of the organisation;

● shifts towards relating pay specifically to individual contribution (and performance appraisal outcomes) and to skills/competencies required by the organisation, as opposed to collectively determined and standard 'rates for the job';

● the provision of training to develop individual skills/competencies which relate specifically to organisational requirements, and to match individual career progression with the dynamics of organisational change and development.

The authors are grateful to Chris Brewster and Ariane Hegewisch and to Routledge for the use of material from *Policy and Practice in European Human Resource Management*, The Price Waterhouse-Cranfield Survey, first published in 1994.

DISCUSSION QUESTIONS

1 How can employers be encouraged to invest in training and development?

2 Is high pay consistent or inconsistent with economic performance at corporate and national levels?

3 Is performance related pay likely to be effective in all cultures? Why? Why not?

4 What are the benefits/drawbacks of decentralising pay determination from the point of view of (a) employers (b) trades unions?

NOTES AND REFERENCES

1. Pieper R (ed) (1990) *Human Resource Management: An International Comparison*, de Gruyter, New York, p.11

2. Brewster C and Bournois F (1991) 'Human Resource Management: A European Perspective,' *Personnel Review*, volume 20, no 6, 1991, pp.8–9

3. Guest D E, June 1988, First annual Seear lecture at the London School of Economics, 'Human Resource Management – is it worth taking seriously?'

4. Beer M *et al.* (1984) *Managing Human Assets*, The Free Press, New York, p.26

5. Guest D E, op. cit., p.6

6. Brewster C and Hegewisch A (ed) (1994) *Policy and Practice in European Human Resource Management*, 'The Price Waterhouse/Cranfield Survey,' Routledge, London and New York p.28

7. Lawrence P (1993) 'Human Resource Management in Germany', in Tyson S *et al.*, *Human Resource Management in Europe, Strategic Issues and Cases*, Kogan Page, London, p.35

8. Dany F and Torchy V, (1994) 'Recruitment and Selection in Europe: Policies, Practices and Methods', in Brewster C and Hegewisch A, *Policy and Practice in European Human Resource Management*, The Price Waterhouse/Cranfield Survey, Routledge, London and New York, p.81

9. Filella J and Hegewisch A (1994) 'European Experiments with Pay and Benefits Policies', in Brewster C and Hegewisch A (eds), *Policy and Practice in European Human Resource Management*, The Price Waterhouse/Cranfield Survey, Routledge, London and New York, p.102

120. Holden L (1994) 'Training', in Beardwell I and Holden L (eds) *Human Resource Management: A Contemporary Perspective*, Pitman Publishing, London, p.358

11. Ibid.

12. Ibid.

13. Thorn J (1988) 'Making of a Meister', *Industrial Society Magazine*, June

14. Dany F, and Torchy V (1994) 'Recruitment and Selection in Europe', in Brewster C and Hegewisch A *Policy and Practice in European Human Resource Management*, The Price Waterhouse/Cranfield Survey, Routledge, London and New York, p.84

15. Langtry R (1994) 'Selection', in Beardwell I and Holden L, *Human Resource Management: A Contemporary Perspective*, Pitman Publishing, London, p.249

16. Springer B and Springer S (1990) 'Human Resource Management in the US – Celebration of its Centenary,' in Pieper R, *Human Resource Management: An International Comparison*, de Gruyter, New York

17. Wright M and Storey J (1994) 'Recruitment', in Beardwell I and Holden L, *Human Resource Management: A Contemporary Perspective*, Pitman Publishing, London, pp.213–14

18. Danny F and Torchy V, op. cit.

19. Incomes Data Services, 1990, European Management Guides, Recruitment, IPM, London, p.163

20. Wood S and Peccei R (1990) 'Preparing for 1992: Business versus Strategic Human Resource Management', *Human Resource Management Journal* 1 (1), pp.63–9

21. Dany F and Torchy V, op. cit., p.83

22. Maurice M *et al.*, (1982) *Politique d'Education et Organisation*, Industrielle en France et en Allemagne, Paris

23. Holden L (1994) op. cit.

24. Springer B and Springer S (1990) op. cit., p.51

25. Holden L, op. cit., p.360

26. Coopers and Lybrand Associates, (1985) *A Challenge to Complacency: Changing Attitudes to Training*, MSC/NEDO, London

27. Larsen H H (1994) in Brewster C and Hegewisch A (eds), *Policy and Practice in European Human Resource Management*, The Price Waterhouse/Cranfield Survey, Routledge, London and New York, pp.109–10

28. Wood S and Peccei R op. cit.

29. Filella J and Hegewisch A, 'European Benefits with Pay and Benefits Policies,' in Brewster C and Hegewisch A, *Policy and Practice in European Human Resource Management*, The Price Waterhouse/Cranfield Survey, Routledge, London and New York, pp.94–5

30. Ibid.

31. Ibid.

32. Ibid.

33. Rowthorn R E (1992) 'The Centralisation, Employment and Wage Dispersion,' *Economic Journal* 102, May, p.502

34. Incomes Data Services, (IDS), 1992, 'Equal Pay – A Distant Goal?', *IDS European Report* 371, November I–VIII

35. Filella J and Hegewisch A, op. cit., p.90

36. Ibid.

37. Incomes Data Services Focus, 1989, The European View 53, December

38. Ibid.

39. Pieper R, (ed) (1990) *Human Resource Management: An International Comparison*, de Gruyter, New York, p.11

FURTHER READING

Pieper R (ed) (1990) *Human Resource Management*, De Gruyter, New York

Sparrow P and Hilltrop J (1994) *European Human Resource Management*, Prentice Hall International, New York

Section 2

AN OVERVIEW OF NATIONAL SYSTEMS, THE EU AND THE ILO

In this section we shall present a holistic and integrated view of national systems of HRM. A common format has been adopted for this analysis in respect of each country, as described in Figure S2.1.

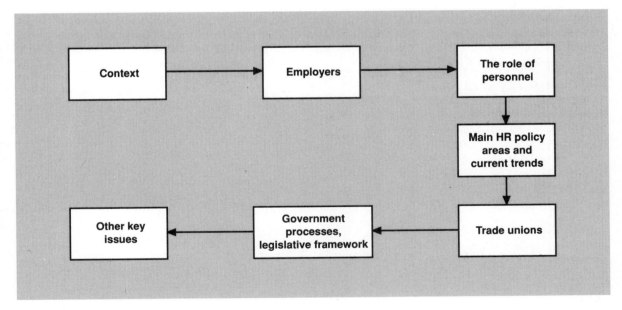

Fig S2.1 Format of analysis

The authors are indebted to Brewster C, Hegewisch A, Lockhart T and Holden L, editors of *The European Human Resource Management Guide*, published in 1992, and to Harcourt Brace and Company Ltd, for allowing use of the Price Waterhouse/Cranfield data in the European country sections on labour markets, recruitment, remuneration, training and development, and current issues.

9 · GERMANY

BACKGROUND

It has been recognised for some time that Germany's competitive strength rests on its 'only natural resource'[1] – the people – and on their ability to utilise technology. Since reconstruction after the second world war, considerable emphasis has been placed on training and developing staff, to ensure that they possess the technical skills and the versatility to cope with technological change. This formula was integral to the phenomenal success of the German economy (the economic miracle, in German *Wirtschaftswunder*) until the early 1990s.

The value placed on the human resource has been reflected in comparatively high rates of pay, and suggests that people have traditionally been viewed as an asset rather than a cost. German companies themselves have tended to concentrate on the types of production and service that demand skilled workers and high technology. Intensification of competition is demanding even more effective ways of deploying human resources.

The German model is characterised by the 'social market' approach, a central feature of which has been co-determination, in which workers control up to one-third of places on supervisory boards of large companies. At company level, works councils have been established which possess rights of information, consultation and co-determination. For example, in organisations with more than 20 employees, the employer must obtain agreement of the works council for each new appointment, grading, regrading or transfer.

In recent years economic recession, declining confidence and rising social problems across Germany have led to serious questioning of the continued viability of the social market model. *Business Week*[2] pointed to the high cost of German labour as impeding international economic competitiveness, and saw the emergence of a new German model comprising:

- Heavier reliance on cheaper manufacturing bases, more goods to be made outside Germany.
- Greater flexibility with labour costs, work rules and social requirements.

- Concentration on delivering what consumers want and not making expensive, over-engineered products.
- Moving into newer, higher-value-added technologies.
- Depending on a much more deregulated and privatised economy.

These developments are occurring in conjunction with the ramifications and repercussions of one of the most fundamental world events of the second half of the twentieth century, the dismantling of the Berlin Wall on 3 October 1990.

EMPLOYERS

Since the immediate post-war period German employers have, individually, played relatively little part in the determination of terms and conditions of employment. The need for unity and consensus after the second world war, which was considered essential to the effective reconstruction of Germany, facilitated the fairly rapid emergence of a system which reflected common interests, a desire to avoid competition on wages and wage costs, and adherence to the principle of bargaining autonomy. The national emphasis on democracy and its reinstatement encouraged the creation of formal structures for co-determination within the enterprise. Employers relatively readily accepted the legitimacy of employee participation via the co-determination mechanisms created, which are described in the following sections of this chapter. Only relatively recently have employers begun in any numbers seriously to question the continuing appropriateness of these systems in the face of the enhanced need to reorganise work and production processes, introduce new technology and obtain productivity and labour-cost improvements. The extent to which employer autonomy has actually been constrained by co-determination, is, however, arguable, since on issues of this kind co-determination often only requires employers to inform or consult. Particularly in the car industry, German employers have begun to experiment with 'lean production' techniques, teamwork and group working and more flexible working time schemes. Some 100 000 jobs have been lost in the car industry since 1991 and many more are to go over the next few years. Estimates are that costs must be reduced by between 20 and 30 per cent in the period 1993–95 in order to facilitate competition with Japanese standards of lean production. Volkswagen's realisation in 1993 that it could only make profits on 104 per cent capacity utilisation has encouraged massive cost-cutting pressures on jobs and suppliers and new emphases on teamworking, quality and satisfying the customer. Major manufacturers such as BMW and Mercedes Benz have also announced significant new investments abroad in line with their decisions to globalise their manufacturing capacity.

Early in 1994, employers in engineering and the public sector were in dispute with employees over the need to limit pay increases, reduce jobs and achieve greater labour force flexibility without additional expenditure. In some instances, employers were seeking longer hours of work at no extra cost, while in others they were seeking a shorter working week and reductions in weekly pay. The Volkswagen agreement towards the end of 1993 provided for a four-day working week and a 10 per cent cut in gross annual salaries, equal to a 20 per cent reduction in the overall wage bill through reductions in employer's contributions to social insurance.

The majority of employers belong to associations which represent them in collective bargaining. These associations have been organised so that they are relevant to the structure of collective bargaining and they therefore also tend to mirror the structure of trade union organisation. There are both vertical and horizontal dimensions to the structure, with employers being organised industrially but also across industrial boundaries at land or district level. It is not uncommon for employers to be represented in negotiations within the enterprise by representatives from the appropriate Land or district employers' associations.

In joining collective associations employers give up considerable autonomy; they are obliged to accept and apply the agreements arrived at on their behalf, non-compliance presenting possibilities of fines or expulsion.

Some large employers, Volkswagen being the most frequently cited example, have remained outside employers' associations, and in the last couple of years there have been instances of large organisations withdrawing (IBM) and increasing discontent among smaller employers confronted with recession and working hours and wage agreements which they felt to be too generous. Figure 9.1 suggests that increasing numbers of employers are leaving these associations and doing their own deals with works councils. The scale of the discontent must, however, be viewed against the rejection by employers of the opportunity to introduce different, more individual bargaining systems in the East after reunification. By and large the employers' associations have ensured that very similar arrangements pertain. However, there is little doubt that in 1994 the employers' associations, prompted in large measure by the problems of the smaller members, are ready to pursue a more determined effort to 'stand up' to the unions and take the steps they consider essential to enhance flexibility, productivity and competitiveness, even if these comprise pay cuts and job losses.

The peak association to which industrial and regional associations are affiliated is the Bundesvereinigung der Deutschen Arbeitgeberverbande (BDA), which before the recent departures represented some 70 per cent of eligible employers, employing up to 80 per cent of employees. Public sector organisations remain separate as does that representing iron and steel producers.

The BDA represents its members centrally to government and internationally, co-ordinates, but does not engage in, collective bargaining in the various sectors and regions, and seeks to ensure that individual employers do not take advantage of others in a situation where selective industrial action is occurring. It is a source of information and advice to its members and can provide financial assistance to members, subject to industrial action.

THE ROLE OF PERSONNEL

Lawrence[3] describes the personnel function in Germany as being relatively reactive and legalistic in the area of pay; the main concern of the function is with implementation rather than determination, as rates of pay are normally established at regional level through collective agreements. Nevertheless, the job of implementation is often complex, involving the evaluation of jobs to determine whether individuals fit into the payment structure.[4]

It will be necessary for personnel managers to have effective working relationships with works councils members, as many important personnel issues are arrived at through a consultative process involving these bodies.

According to Arkin[5] much of the personnel practitioner's time will be spent interpreting the considerable volume of employment legislation and also comprehensive corporate regulation, as well as undertaking succession planning within structures geared towards internal promotion, and identification of training needs and administration of training programmes.

The personnel function itself tends to be the preserve of lawyers, economists and social scientists, and a growing number of institutions now offer courses in personnel management. The professional association for personnel management (DGFP) organises approximately 1300 corporate members. It has recently extended its sphere into the former East Germany where its concerns are to reduce overstaffing. A tendency has been noted for personnel practitioners in the East, who were often alleged (although this remains unproven) to have close links with the secret police, to have been replaced with personnel managers from the West.

LABOUR MARKET

- In the 1960s virtually no unemployment existed in West Germany so additional workers had to be procured from abroad. At first refugees from East Germany filled gaps, but subsequently foreign workers, particularly Turks, were recruited. In 1990 8 per cent of the West German workforce was foreign.
- The number of women entering the labour force has grown considerably over the past decade.

Recruitment

- Recruitment is a highly significant area as wage costs are high and constraints exist on staff severance.
- Decisions regarding recruitment and selection require the agreement of works councils in larger plants. In organisations with more than 20 employees the employer must obtain the agreement of the works council for each new appointment, and the latter can also see all relevant documents (application forms, job descriptions, etc.) during the recruitment process.

Selection

- The state has a monopoly on the placement of labour through the Federal Department of Employment and an independent placement service by public job centres operates free of charge in larger firms. Companies can publicise job vacancies in newspapers and journals.
- Common methods include application forms, CVs and references, which are of great importance in the preliminary screening of candidates.
- Shortlisted candidates attend interviews which normally involve a personnel specialist and a member of the relevant department. Following the interview candidates may be required to undertake medical, aptitude and psychological tests, and to attend an assessment centre. Successful candidates are frequently required to serve a satisfactory period of probation before employment is confirmed.

Remuneration

- Collective agreements at industry level determine the general framework for pay, benefits and working conditions, and restrict the scope for corporate regulation of pay. At plant level, works councils have important rights in respect of the application of pay policy. The processes of job evaluation and grading are also frequently specified in collective agreements.
- Discretion is available to individual employers with regard to the setting of salaries for managers and the determination of incentive payments for all staff. This is in addition to collectively agreed levels, although works councils have rights in the structuring of incentive payments. Many large employers have introduced performance related pay (PRP) for technical/professional staff in the early 1990s. While profit sharing is common among managerial staff, other employees can benefit from share ownership and from rewards for an adopted suggestion where there are suggestion schemes.
- Different collective agreements exist to account for different labour market conditions. Currently there is a hiatus between east and west German levels. The aim is to achieve harmonisation by 1996. Employees in former West Germany are used to generous fringe benefits, including subsidised meals, provision of works canteens, recreational facilities and subsidised visits to health spas. Although legislation exists to avoid discrimination in the area of pay, women's remuneration is still, on average, inferior to that enjoyed by men. Parents are allowed to return to work up to three years after the birth of a child, and many companies allow unpaid breaks of up to seven years. Although some companies in former West Germany provide kindergarten facilities or subsidise childcare, reunification has in fact led to a reduction of crèche provision in the East, which was designed to promote female employment.

Training and development

- Training is usually provided by co-operative arrangements between companies, state schools and universities.
- The apprenticeship system controlled by the state provides standard curricula for nearly 400 vocational qualifications, but also general courses ranging from language to sport.

- Chambers of commerce and companies offer additional training leading to a foreman's qualification.

TRADE UNIONS

After the second world war, as part of the reconstruction process, trade unionism was reaffirmed as a legitimate mechanism for the representation of employees' inter-

---

Flagging spirits test new union supremo

Germany's trade union federation badly needs a confidence boost, writes **David Goodhart**

Mr Dieter Schulte, the steel industry union boss who has just been elected to lead the German Trade Union Federation (DGB), inherits an organisation badly in need of a boost to its confidence.

On the face of it this seems odd. At its congress this week in Berlin the entire political establishment, including Chancellor Helmut Kohl, came to pay homage to the principle of social partnership and the important role of organised labour in national political life.

Just how integrated it is into that political life was evident on Wednesday night. In one hall Mr Rudolf Sharping, leader of the Social Democrats, gave an address to the majority of delegates, while elsewhere a group of Christian Democratic trade unionists was addressed by several ministers from Bonn. Even the Greens threw a little party.

But the DGB is not only a political force. Its 16 industry-based unions still have more than 10m members, representing a higher proportion of the workforce than in almost any other large industrial country. And only a few months ago the unions were being widely praised for their restraint in this year's pay round.

So why does the 54-year-old Mr Schulte inherit such an anxious organisation? German unions *are* still central to the political and industrial life of the country – as this year's wage round underlined – but they fear they are beginning to lose their critical mass.

Membership, although still high, has fallen by 1.5m over the past two years. That is mainly because of job losses, especially in east Germany, but the unions are not recruiting many new members in the growing service sector and remain unattractive to women and young people.

The trends have contributed to the rapid decline of unions elsewhere in Europe and Mr Schulte and his colleagues know that unless they take action it could be them next. In his address to the congress he talked of the dangers of becoming "dinosaurs" and of the need to "abandon dreams of a lost utopia".

Mr Ulf Fink, a Christian Democrat DGB official, even warned congress of the French example, where union membership has fallen to 8 per cent of the workforce.

After his speech Mr Schulte said the "French option" would be avoided in Germany and added that there were some special factors behind the recent decline in union standing, "including the disappointment that many of our new members in east Germany felt when we could not prevent their jobs being lost".

The other key challenge to the unions is the growing interest of the government in labour market deregulation as an aid to creating more jobs, and the emergence of a two-tier labour market with an increasingly large group of workers not covered by centralised collective bargaining.

The unions are happy to accept some aspects of the new flexibility. They are keen to reduce non-wage labour costs and are not opposed to an expansion in part-time work, although they do want to improve the social protection of part-timers.

Mr Schulte stressed the unions' favoured means of job-creation: reducing working time, with some corresponding reduction in pay without undermining existing hourly pay rates. "Ten years ago it would have been unthinkable to talk in this way", he said. That may be true, but so far only a handful of companies have followed the lead of Volkswagen, the car group, in cutting hours and pay to create or retain jobs.

The more insidious threat to the unions' centralised collective agreements comes from the growing number of companies leaving the industry associations which enforce them, or are drawing up special deals with their own company works councils to undermine the national unions.

Mrs Ursula Engelen-Kefer, Mr Schulte's deputy, says the flight from collective agreements seems to have been stopped by the moderate wage deal earlier this year. But Mr Charly Schübel, an official of the engineering union IG Metall in Schweinfurt, says an increasing number of small metal industry companies in his area are paying skilled workers only DM8 or DM9 (£3.60) an hour – about half the national rate.

Given the continuing solidity of most German labour market regulations it is tempting to ask whether the decline of the unions will make much difference.

"It would make a big difference," says Mrs Engelen-Kefer, "We are part of the political and social structure but our arguments are only listened to because of our strength on the ground".

Fig 9.1 Source: *Financial Times*, 17 June 1994

est. The Federal Constitution of 1949 grants employees the right to organise and associate freely and the Collective Agreement Act of 1949 (TVG)[6] guarantees free collective bargaining, as noted earlier.

When trade unionism was reconstructed it was determined that the basis for organisation and membership would be industrial, the principle of one union for one plant being integral to the structure. The DGB[7] (the German Trade Union Federation) was formed in 1949 as the peak association with 16 individual industrial affiliates. This simple and coherent structure has remained very largely unchanged since then, and has been hailed worldwide as a model example of how trade unions should be organised, particularly in those countries which have lived with multi-unionism, fragmentation and competition.

Reunification, however, has pointed up the tensions within the DGB, with unions arguing over demarcation issues and which of them should represent sectors in the East. For example, OTV[8], the public sector union, was in dispute in 1990 with the energy workers union, IG Bergbau, and with the banking and insurance workers union on the issue of rights to organise workers in the East. It was clear before reunification that the changing structure of industry and the development of new industries were likely to make the reorganisation and restructuring of the union movement an issue; reunification brought it to a head. DGB has begun to examine structural reform and, not surprisingly, there are numerous views on the subject. It is unlikely that the principle of industrial unionism will be forsaken, but it does seem quite likely that reorganisation will eventually result in fewer unions. Already existing affiliates are in some cases discussing merger, for example IG Chemie (chemical) and IG Bau (construction).

Trade union membership density in West Germany was remarkably stable in the decades between the war and reunification, and between 1970 and 1990 density varied only within a narrow range of 33 and 37 per cent[9]. In the East completely different systems operated with union density being estimated at more than 90 per cent. Reunification and transfer of membership resulted in significant DGB membership increases, for example in the first year IG Metall, the largest trade union in the world, recorded an increase in membership from the East of just under 950 000, increasing its total membership at the end of 1990 to 3.6 million. However, by the end of 1992 the figure had fallen to 3.39 million and total membership was slightly above 11 million, compared with 11.8 million at the end of 1991.[10] The massive increase in unemployment since

1991 has resulted in considerable reductions in trade union membership in both East and West, and this is referred to in Figure 9.1 where a total in excess of 10 million is quoted and reference is made to a decrease in membership of 1.5 million between 1992 and 1994. The much higher female participation rates in the labour force and in union membership in the East contributed to a significant DGB female membership percentage increase from 24.4 per cent in 1990 to 33 per cent in 1991.[11]

In addition to DGB unions, there are three independents and federations of significance: DAG[12] – the German Salaried Employers Union – a white collar union that recruits and organises across industrial boundaries; DBB[13] – the German civil servants federation; and CGB[14] – the Christian Federation of Trades Unions. Respectively, these organisations represent approximately 600 000 (1992), 800 000 and 250 000–300 000 (1989–90) members.[15] The DGB has in affiliation the vast majority of trade union members in Germany, in excess of 80 per cent. There have been problems between DGB unions and the independents, particularly the DAG.

The majority of DGB unions have informal political ties with the Social Democrats and many members and officials are also members of the Social Democratic Party (SPD). However, the Christian Democratic Union (CDU) also has union members and in most of the DGB unions a proportion of executive committee seats are reserved for CDU members. In recent years it may well be that this maintenance of CDU links and influence within the DGB has worked to the unions' advantage, making it more difficult for a CDU government to pursue an openly hostile policy towards trade unionism, collective bargaining or co-determination.

Unions in Germany are representative democracies often with oligarchic tendencies, centralised, with bureaucratic power vested in the hands of small groups of officials. Members do not participate directly except in elections for local representatives or if balloted on industrial action.

Traditionally, German trade unions have objectives extending beyond the workplace encompassing full employment, a more equitable distribution of income and wealth and a role in economic planning, in addition to co-determination according to the model in the coal and steel-producing industries. As Jacobi et al.[16] summarise it, this is a programme of objectives which combines socialist rhetoric with pragmatic accommodation to capitalism.

In the 1980s trade unions in West Germany were particularly concerned with humanisation of work and quality of work life issues; reducing the working week to 35 hours if possible, health, safety and the working environment, protection against rationalisation. Outside the workplace peace, ecology and nuclear issues were prominent. The 1990s, post-reunification and its costs and in recession, have seen the unions return to pay and job protection issues, as well as seeking to resist the decentralisation of collective bargaining and extend its scope to incorporate new management strategies and techniques associated with Japanisation, new technology, lean production, quality circles and team and group working.

By and large, the unions have adopted a welcoming stance to these latter changes, seeing them as opportunities for improving the work experience and enhancing involvement, participation, autonomy, job satisfaction and development opportunities for employees. However, they seek to resist such innovations where they see them as a device through which management is simply seeking to rationalise. IG Metall developed a proposal for qualified teamwork which sought to ensure that the productivity benefits were accompanied by enhanced employee development and satisfaction.[17] Currently, managements are able to process such changes at the level of the workplace through discussions with works councils, which as discussed below are not formally part of the union structure.

Job protection and associated policies facilitating greater flexibility of working hours, without pay cuts where possible, are the unions' priority in 1994. The unions are also having to face the problems associated with employers leaving employers' associations and increasingly making use of plant-level agreements with works councils, themselves in a weak position given the recession and high unit-labour costs.

GOVERNMENT

As indicated in Chapter 3, government in the former West Germany has been dominated by the Christian Democrat/Christian Social Union (CDU/CSU), the latter being the Bavarian sister party of the former, but in coalition with others. The state has intervened considerably in providing a legislative framework which specifies and regulates many employee rights and protections, for example on issues such as pensions, maternity pay, hours of work, holiday entitlements and termination, and which establishes the co-determination mechanisms described below. Additionally, it has

created a structure of labour courts to resolve disputes and grievances concerning the application or interpretation of existing agreements or statutes. These operate at local, Land and federal level. The process and content of collective bargaining is not regulated, the parties being free to agree rates of pay and other working conditions. The government does often seek to influence bargaining outcomes, particularly in the context of seeking to achieve particular economic, social and welfare objectives, such as lower levels of unemployment or inflation and parity or equity between men and women, or East and West.

Government seeks to influence labour market activity and supply quality through various active training and job-creation mechanisms. The Federal Institute for Labour finances many of these interventions in the labour market and the Institute's administration is tripartite, being comprised of employer, union and government representatives. In the last two years, government has been anxious to reduce expenditure in some of these areas because of the massive costs of unemployment in the East. The positive and active labour market role dates from the Work Promotion Act of 1969 which proposed an active and preventative labour market policy.

Another example of tripartite administration is the national vocational training scheme which seeks to ensure vocational training for all up to the age of 18. Tripartite co-operation at a national level was much more common in the late 1960s and 1970s when forms of bargained corporatism were adopted, the bargain usually comprising some form of wage and price restraint in return for macro-economic policies in pursuit of stable economic growth and employment.

The 1980s and early 1990s have seen some relaxation of protections for employees, often in response to employer pressures for greater flexibility which it is argued is necessary to assist and enhance work reorganisation, international competitiveness, the introduction of new technology and indeed employment. It is in this context that the Employment Promotion Act 1985 allowed new recruits to be offered fixed-term contracts for 18 months where the previous limit had been 6, and the government has put forward a 30-point action programme at the beginning of 1994 which has as its main objective reducing public expenditure and encouraging job creation through further deregulation of the labour market and employment relationship. In addition to the 1993 reductions in the rate of unemployment benefit for the childless and long-term unemployed, government put forward proposals to limit unemployment benefit to two years' duration and had given the go-ahead for a publicity campaign encouraging part-time work. Germany has a low proportion of part-time workers compared with some other European countries.[18]

The government does not provide conciliation facilities or indeed require conciliation or mediation in the event of failures to agree. In the case of matters of right arbitration is, in a sense, provided by the labour courts, but in matters of interest it is eventually up to the parties to fight it out.

In addition to the provision of a legislative framework protecting employees, prescribing co-determination mechanisms within organisations, the funding and implementation of various policies and programmes geared towards improving the quality of the labour force, and employment and co-operation with unions and employers in the achievement of these and other objectives, the government at local, Land and federal level is also a significant employer and is able through this role to promote certain models or systems of human resource management.

The public sector, comprising government, government agencies, the post office and the railways, employs in all in excess of 4.5 million people. Public employees generally have the same rights as the other employees, but civil servants (Beamten) are not allowed to take strike action and do not have the usual collective bargaining rights and freedoms. Civil servants, as opposed to public sector salaried staff or wage earners, have a special employment status by law.

In the past the public sector provided employee benefits, particularly in terms of security of employment, which were a model for the private sector, but in recent years public sector employers have moved closer to the private sector in terms of an emphasis on flexibility and productivity and the increasing use of part-time staff and fixed-term contracts. Indeed there are indications from government that a widespread programme of privatisation may be embarked on with Lufthansa, the telecom and the postal services, savings bank, gas and electricity monopolies in the firing line.

As in other countries, governments sometimes seek to influence wage rounds by forcing restraint on their own employees. This often requires public sector employees to take the lead in the wage round. In spring 1992 more than 2 million public sector employees took strike action for 11 days in pursuit of a pay claim, an indication of public sector employees' dissatisfaction at the rise offered and the government's tactics. Ironically, the employees secured an increase, by virtue of their action, in excess of what government had claimed 'affordable', and this did act as an example for the private sector. A similar situation developed early in 1994 as government sought to impose a pay freeze on civil servants and local council employees, though this time the outcomes were more moderate.

PROCESSES

As has been indicated earlier, within the German system there are two distinct sets of processes for achieving consensus (or resolving conflict) between employers and employees. One of these is collective bargaining between trade unions and employers' associations, usually at Land or industry level. It is through this bargaining process that the main terms and conditions of employment, other than those which are determined or protected via legislation, are agreed. The other system is legislatively prescribed and referred to as co-determination, has a number of dimensions including two-tier boards and works councils, and varies according to the size of the organisation and the industry concerned. It is convenient to deal with these processes separately.

Collective bargaining

It has been unusual for the main terms and conditions of employment to be determined through bargaining at enterprise level. They have usually been the product of agreement at Land or industry level between appropriate employers' association representatives and trade unions. Approximately 90 per cent of employees have been covered by collective agreements. These agreements, once made, have the force of law, incorporate a peace clause for the duration of the contract and can be extended via a declaration of general applicability by the Land or Federal Minister of Labour. Most agreements also provide for the parties to seek mediation or conciliation assistance in the event of a failure to agree a renewal at the appropriate time. Industrial action cannot lawfully be taken in pursuit of a claim on a substantive issue unless the contract has expired. Industrial action can only lawfully be organised by a trade union or employers' association, and in the case of strike action must have been supported in a ballot by at least 75 per cent of those voting.

The tendency in the former West Germany has been for a form of pattern bargaining, whereby IG Metall as the largest trade union would seek a new agreement first in the Land where they considered it likely that they would get the best deal. Once agreed, the unions would then seek to extend the same or very similar terms across the industry and even into other sectors, the first agreement in a sense determining the 'going rate'. These selective tactics also made it easier for the unions to finance industrial action, since it need only be partial. Prior to the Work Promotion Act of 1986, employees affected by a strike in their industry but in another Land or district were entitled to short-time or unemployment benefits from the state. This facilitated a union's taking selective strike action which it knew would affect its members across the whole economy, but which it knew also would not involve it in country-wide expenditure.

There are three different categories of collective agreement: pay agreements, framework agreements, e.g. those setting out payment systems and principles, and general or umbrella agreements dealing with issues such as hours of work, holiday entitlements, and dismissal and redundancy provisions.

In recent years there have been pressures, initially from the smaller employers and some interests in government, for a decentralisation and opening up of the bargaining system, primarily motivated by dissatisfactions with agreements on pay and reductions in the working week, and desires for greater flexibility and the tailoring of agreements to individual employers' circumstances. Early in 1994, each party was accusing the other of threatening the system of industry-level collective bargaining. Employers criticised the unions for not being prepared to accept greater flexibility, and unions were critical of employers taking advantage of the recession to push through plant-level agreements and, in some instances, unilateral action.

Co-determination

The essence of co-determination within the enterprise is a combination of employee involvement at board of directors level with representative participation of employees via a works council which, depending on the subject matter, has legislatively determined rights of co-decision, information or consultation.

One of the characteristics of German companies is a two-tier board structure comprising a supervisory board and a management board. The former appoints the latter. The supervisory board oversees the management board; it does not initiate policy but its approval should be obtained for substantial changes in the scope and purpose of the company's business. The management board is the executive board. It is on the super-

visory board that co-determination provides for employee representative involvement. These employee representatives do not have to be employees of the organisation in question. Simultaneous membership of the supervisory and management boards is not allowed.

In the coal and steel industries, the special Co-determination Act 1951 prescribes the 'Montan' model of co-determination which provides for parity of employee influence at supervisory board level, allied to a proviso that the labour director on the management board must be appointed with majority approval of the employee representatives on the supervisory board. This renders the labour director a representative of employee interests at management board level, and indeed is one of the main reasons why companies in these, albeit declining, industries are not allowed into membership of the BDA. This is the model most favoured by the union movement.

Outside the coal and steel-producing industries, different legislation and systems apply. In companies with more than 2000 employees the Co-determination Act of 1976 specifies a requirement for employee representatives to comprise 50 per cent of the supervisory board, but with shareholders' representatives having an effective majority in the event of disagreement. Non-employee representatives on supervisory boards often represent the company's main bankers, suppliers and customers. Additionally, employee representatives on supervisory boards in this category do not have the effective right of veto over the appointment of the labour director.

In companies with more than 500 employees, the Works Constitution Act 1952 provides for employee representatives on the supervisory board to be one-third of the total.

The other legally prescribed workplace mechanism are works councils. These should be established in all enterprises employing five or more people. The legislation – the Works Constitution Act of 1972 – gives employees the right to elect a council, and once elected it has certain statutory rights and roles. The size of the council varies with the size of the enterprise or workplace. In multi-site companies there may be workplace and group-wide councils. In the public sector there is legislative provision for staff councils but with fewer rights and powers.

Works councils are councils of employees elected by all employees. The councils are not trade union bodies, although in practice there are usually very close relationships between local union representatives and their organisation and the works councillors. There is considerable mutual dependence. Many councillors are union members, and the unions often suggest a list of approved candidates. The union will often take part in the training of councillors and the council members often act as recruiting agents for the trade union. Trade union dominance of the councils often outweighs union density. The legislation imposes an obligation on the councils to work with management in a spirit of mutual trust for the good of both employees and the enterprise.

The councils have various rights of participation or involvement in management decision making. On many personnel issues, such as promotions, dismissals, transfers and regradings, on matters concerning working conditions and health and safety and on pay-related matters such as performance-related pay, bonuses, daily and weekly work schedules and overtime working, the council has the right either of co-decision or to give its consent to management proposals. This latter effectively constitutes a power of veto. Employers can refer a veto to a Labour Court, and co-decision disagreements are referred to a joint conciliation mechanism. The parties are required when entering into such discussions to do so with a serious desire to reach agreement on matters such as changes in work processes and organisation, the introduction of new technology and the working environment. Councils also have rights to information and consultation; on matters such as financial performance and prospects the councils have information rights only. Of course, the initiative for giving information remains with management and *de facto* this probably preserves managerial prerogative to a greater extent than was initially intended. There are no *status quo* clauses, so management, having informed and consulted, can implement even if the works council is opposed to a proposal.

Works councils are not allowed to initiate industrial action and legally they are not supposed to negotiate on any matter that is the subject of collective bargaining or determination at a higher level. In practice this distinction is sometimes blurred. Collective agreements at higher levels can, via 'opening clauses', enable negotiations on particular issues at works council level, for example on flexible working times and patterns. It seems that recession and unemployment have provided a background for an increase in the extent of such works council agreements.

THE IMPACT OF REUNIFICATION ON WORK AND EMPLOYMENT IN THE FORMER EAST GERMANY

The euphoria which accompanied the dismantling of the Berlin Wall on 3 October 1990 extended into all walks of life, including management and employment.

Hopes ran high that the former East Germany would be delivered swiftly from a state of affairs characterised by old-fashioned technology, chronic overstaffing, productivity levels one-third those of the West, protected markets, a seeping loss of technicians and specialists, and rampant pollution.

The entire West German state and constitutional system was extended into the East including, in the employment sphere:

- Freedom of association and right to organise.
- Protection of individual employees in respect of job security, equal opportunities, health and safety, hours of work and sick pay. A comprehensive social security system also exists.
- Collective negotiations are regulated by statutory law, agreements being legally enforceable in respect of union members.

In addition, the jurisdiction of trade unions and employers' associations has been widened to include the East. Their structures are now established in the East.

Co-determination is also formally applied throughout the unified state. At company level, works councils have been established which possess rights of information, consultation and co-determination.

The main features of the East German economic and employment picture before reunification were:

- A continuing reliance on the heavy industrial sector.
- Protected markets in Eastern Europe. Comecon, the socialist trade bloc, accounted for more than 75 per cent of exports.
- A high level of monopolisation. In some sectors only one company existed. Companies with more than 1000 employees made up almost 70 per cent of industrial workplaces.
- Production and employment structures highly influenced by the political decisions for the Party, the *Sozialistiche Einheitspartei Deutschlands* (SED).
- Terms and conditions of employment were fixed universally, with no collective bargaining. An independent labour code was ideologically linked to the socialist system.
- A trade union structure, the East German Confederation of Trade Unions (FDGB), which was primarily a political institution to ensure socialistic attitudes.
- Full employment.

Personnel management concentrated on two main topics:

- *Kaderarbeit* – the selection and induction of the managerial elite, which was influenced more by political attitudes and affiliations than by professional knowledge. Senior and junior managers were also party officials.
- *Sozialpolitik* – social welfare was an important function of organisations in the absence of effective social security. This involved provision for occupational health and welfare, training and education, social integration of the disadvantaged, company housing, subsidised meals, childcare, kindergarten and holiday camps. Some 85 per cent of women had a job outside the home and provision to support this was more generous than in the West.[19]

At workplace level, full employment influenced power relations. Without sackings, disciplinary sanctions could be fatuous. Poor logistics and shortages of materials meant periods of very low work activity followed by intensive production. Production workers found themselves in a powerful strategic position, as first-line managers would be blamed by the Party for not meeting deadlines, and through overtime production earnings could exceed that of supervisors. The intrinsic motivation of workers was assumed, and a strong emphasis placed on the humanisation of work.[20]

The West and East German governments decided that mass privatisation was the way to transform the East German economy from a centrally planned to a social market system. To bring this about the Treuhandanstalt (trust agency) was set up in Spring 1990 and, until the end of 1994 when it will be wound up, it is charged with renewing the East German economy by selling off those companies that could be restructured and made viable, and shutting down those considered unsalvageable. 90 per cent of newly privatised concerns in former East Germany have been purchased by western German concerns, with France, the US, Canada and Britain being the main acquirers of the remaining 10 per cent. Manufacturing bases in the East have been established by Volkswagen, Siemens, Daimler-Benz, General Motors/Opel, Bosch, AEG, GKN and Toshiba. An Anglo-American consortium headed by Britain's PowerGen and NRG of the US has bought the lignite mines, which provide industrial and domestic energy, but which contribute to the highest per capita level of sulphur dioxide emission anywhere in the world.

The Treuhandt principles apply to companies locating in the East:

- Commitment to certain levels of funding over set periods.

- Businesses cannot be acquired, then closed, to prevent competition.
- A regional office to be established in East Germany.
- Guarantees of a fixed number of jobs over specified periods.

Yet some major sticking points remain, which would work to the disadvantage of the German economy, including the harmonisation of wage levels.

In March 1991 IG Metall, the engineering trade union, together with former East German managers and West German employers, agreed that harmonisation should occur by 1994. In May 1993 industrial action in former East Germany, the first for more than 60 years, was taken by 14 000 workers to reinstate this contract which had been cancelled by employers. Under a compromise solution, the new target for harmonisation is 1996.[21]

Adjustment is also necessary to curb the migration of young skilled workers from the East to the West. This means, however, that firms in the East will have to carry the high cost burden of West German concerns while productivity levels remain inferior.

Much of the unemployment in the East (and West) has been mitigated by implementation of employment schemes (*Beschäftigungsgesellschaften*) which allow workers up to 90 per cent of normal income. Although these schemes are having a positive effect on social stabilisation, an argument is emerging that they are draining resources and artificially supporting the position of poorly motivated and qualified workers.

At the time of writing the broader structural problems which have contributed to this malaise show little signs of abating. The free convertibility of German currencies and the removal of state subsidies have meant that former East German products have been uncompetitive in the West. This has been aggravated by the collapse of the Eastern European markets on which the economy was dependent. A shaft of light is the overall growth of the former East Germany economy, and the increased buoyancy in the construction industry accompanying obvious improvements in roads, the water network and telecommunications.[22]

In retrospect, it seems that the top-down and highly deterministic approach towards transforming former East German employment structures and cultures neglected the real complexities, particularly at grassroots level. Perhaps this explains why the change process has been more protracted and costly than originally anticipated. At the level of the enterprise the following disorientating shifts can be noted:

- Wholesale changes in staff, particularly at upper levels, where party members have been replaced, and the consequent ruptures in managerial approaches.
- Increasing, and possibly retaliatory, authoritarianism exerted by first-line managers accompanying the move towards Western methods of managerial control. This could well impede the effective operation

of modern production technology which depends on self-motivated and co-operative workers.[23]

Throughout a period of crisis, there is evidence that works councils and collective bargaining mechanisms in the former East Germany have tended towards working with management to ensure corporate survival.

CASE STUDIES

GM/Opel: Low labour cost
The plant at Eisenach was one of the world's oldest car factories.

Following the collapse in demand for the pollutive Wartburg vehicles produced there, the Treuhandt wanted Opel to take over Automobilwerk Eisenach. This was refused as it involved paying 'western level wages'.

A compromise was reached in which Opel bought the concern for DM 30 million and set up a new plant outside the town. It also spent DM 100 000 on cleaning up the environmental mess that came with the old plant.

US/Japanese working practices have now been introduced involving production facilities which will run round the clock uninterrupted for five days a week. Before poaching the plant manager responsible for negotiating the introduction of these practices, Volkswagen denounced Opel for an 'attack on the economic structure of Germany'.

Bittefield: Rationalisation and new technology
In the 1970s this 1500-acre site for chemical production in Saxony produced such contamination that breathing around it was difficult.

The Treuhandt divided the site, and some of western Germany's high technology chemical and pharmaceutical manufacturers have moved in, including Bayer and Heraeus Quartzglas, which has set up the first plant in Europe producing synthetic quartz glass for semi-conductors and the optical fibre industry.

DM 11 billion has been spent on cleaning up the site, installing new waste water treatment plants, and a solid toxic waste disposal recycling centre. The site now includes digital telephone and satellite networks.

The Finns in Eilenburg: market opportunities
Enso Gutzeit, Finland's and Europe's largest paper manufacturer, has built its new recycling plant in Saxony. It received investment grants of between 15 and 20 per cent for a greenfield site. After tax relief and depreciation allowances, investment outlay is likely to be only 53 per cent of the total.

Attractions, according to the company, included the minimum of red tape, and the strategic market position of

Saxony which, states the MD, 'was one of the great European crossroads. Today it is two hours drive from Berlin, slightly longer to Prague .... and four hours to Munich .... we cannot ignore the growing demand in the countries of Eastern Europe, by being here we will be in a position to capture these markets.'

Source: *Financial Times Survey*, Germany, 26 October 1993

Mercedes Benz: Merger plan for blue-collar and white-collar personnel sections.
The personnel and social services department in the Bremen plant of car manufacturer Mercedes Benz has 288 members of staff. They are responsible for catering and social welfare, as well as personnel services, which are handled by separate sections for blue-collar and white-collar workers. However, with harmonisation of employees' conditions now on the agenda, there are plans to merge these two sections in the next five to ten years.

With the holding company, Daimler Benz retaining overall responsibility for personnel policies, much of the work of the personnel department in the Bremen plant involved dealing with the works council. This council is directly elected by the plant's 16 000 employees and has 35 members, of whom a third are full-time officers and the rest ordinary employees who receive time off work to attend council meetings. Although council members do not have to be union appointees, in the Bremen plant they are all members of IG Metall.

Mercedes Benz uses the federal employment institute, BFA, to recruit blue-collar workers to low-level jobs but operates an internal promotion scheme for most other vacancies. Professional and other white-collar workers, including those in the personnel department, are usually recruited straight from high school or university and, again, internal promotion is used to fill more senior jobs. The selection process used by the company is less structured than in many UK companies, possibly because within the highly standardised German conventional training system employers can safely assume that a person with a given qualification has a certain range and level of skills. Neither assessment centres nor psychometric tests are used in staff

▶ selection, and interviewers generally rely on situation questions of the 'what if' variety, rather than schematic plans. Personnel and line managers tend to interview the same candidate separately.

The company's approach to appraisal is more structured. All employees take part in annual appraisal interviews, which are carried out by departmental managers using criteria agreed with personnel managers to identify training needs and set both production and individual targets.

Training needs identified through appraisal are met by the company's internal training centre, which offers 180 different courses as part of an advanced vocational training and adult education programme. An average of 4 000 employees a year take advantage of this programme, in addition to the 600 young people receiving training in a range of technical and commercial occupations. There is also a modular management development package.

The Bremen plant is highly automated, but manual and robot production lines are used interchangeably. According to one supervisor, the company is prepared to leave some of its robot lines idle in order to retain the services of a well-qualified and loyal workforce.

Source: *Personnel Management*, February 1992, p.33

SUMMARY

The outstanding features of the German system have been the degree of central regulation of main terms and conditions, allied to co-determination in the enterprise, the coherence and centrality of trade unions and employers' associations, the principle of bargaining autonomy, the traditional search for consensus and emphasis on unity and social democracy.

These traditions are confronted by enormous challenges: reunification and its consequences and opportunities, the technological revolution, maintaining international competitiveness, new work processes and organisational methods, the costs of a welfare-oriented state, increasing feminisation of the labour force, post-Fordism, the decline of communism and socialist values, and increasing violence from far-right interests as recession and unemployment bite.

Many of these changes can be seen as presenting a challenge to the centralist tradition in particular. While, at the time of writing, the main institutional actors appear resistant to any significant decentralisation of the structures through which consensus has been achieved, there is evidence that government is beginning to accept arguments in favour of deregulation and reduction of social costs as a precursor to regaining competitiveness in international markets and facilitating enhanced employment. There is also evidence that employers are increasingly leaving employers' associations and conducting their own negotiations at enterprise level with their works councils, so that the trade union movement is confronted by two main challenges, declining membership and an increase in decision making at the level of the enterprise or workplace, involving not the local union organisation but the works councils.

NOTES AND REFERENCES

1. Conrad P and Pieper R (1990) 'Human Resource Management in the Federal Republic of Germany', in Pieper R (ed) *Human Resource Management: An International Comparison*, p.123

2. *Business Week,* cover story, Germany, 31 May 1993

3. Lawrence P (1993) 'Human Resource Management in Germany', in Tyson S *et al.* (eds) *Human Resource Management in Europe: Strategic Issues and Cases*, Kogan Page, London, p.35

4. Ibid.

5. Arkin A, 'At Work in the Powerhouse of Europe, Personnel Management in Germany,' *Personnel Management*, February 1992, pp.32–5

6. TVG – Tarifverkragsgesetz – Collective Agreement Act

7. DGB – Deutscher Gewerkschaftsbund – German Trade Union Federation

8. OTV – Gewerkschaft Offentliche Dienste Transport und Verkehr – Union for Public Services, Transport and Communication

9. See appendix 14

10. EIRR (European Industrial Relations Review) – Sept 1993

11. EIRR – Aug 1992

12. DAG – Deutsche Angestelltengewerkschaft – German Salaried Employees Union

13. DBB – Deutscher Beamtenbund – German Civil Servants Federation

14. CGB – Christlicher Gewerkschaftsbund – Christian Federation of Trade unions

15. Adapted from Lawrence P (1992) 'Human Resource Management in Germany' in Tyson *et al. HRM in Europe*, Pitman Publishing pp.28–9 and EIRR Apr 1992 'Debate on Union Reform'

16. Jacobi O, Keller B and Muller-Jentsch W (1992) 'Germany: Codetermining the future' in Ferner A and Hyman R *Industrial Relations in the New Europe*, p.235

17. EIRR Aug 1992 – Response to Lean Production

18. See appendix 10

19. Wachter H and Stengelhofen T (1992) 'Human Resource Management in Unified Germany', *Employee Relations*, volume 14, no 4, MCB, University Press, pp.21–37

20. Ibid.

21. Dempsey J, 'Mission Unpopular', *Financial Times*, 25 May 1993

22. Jacobi O, Keller B and Muller-Jentsch W (1992) 'Germany – Codetermining the Future?', in Ferner A and Hyman R (eds), *Industrial Relations in the New Europe*, Blackwell, Oxford, p.225

23. Wachter H and Stengelhofen T, op. cit.

FURTHER READING

Arkin A (1992) 'Personnel management in Germany', *Personnel Management*, February

Berghahn V R, Karsten D (1987) *Industrial Relations in West Germany*, Oxford: Berg

Buchtemann C and Schupp J (1992) 'Repercussions of reunification: Patterns and trends in the socio-economic transformation of East Germany', *Industrial Relations Journal*, 23 (2) pp.90–106

Jacobi O and Muller-Jentsch W (1991) 'West Germany: Continuity and structural change' in Baglioni G and Crouch C (eds), *European Industrial Relations: The Challenge of Flexibility*, Sage, pp.127–53

'Industrial relations in the public sector' (1993) *European Industrial Relations Review*, 233, June, p.25–27

Lane C (1989) *Management and Labour in Europe: The industrial enterprise in Germany, Britain and France*, Edward Elgar.

Mueller F (1992) 'Designing flexible teamwork: Comparing German and Japanese approaches', *Employee Relations*, 14 (1), pp.5–16

Markovits A S (1986) *The Politics of West German Trade Unions*, Cambridge University Press.

'Public sector position on DGB reform' (1993), *European Industrial Relations Review*, 235, August, p.8

Schnable C (1991) 'Trade unions and productivity: the German evidence', *BJIR*, 29 (1), pp.15–24

Schregle J (1987) 'Workers participation in the Federal Republic of Germany in an international perspective' *International Labour Review,* 126, May–June, pp.317–27

'Trade unions in Germany' (1993) *Labour Research,* 82, p.22

'Union membership figures' (1993) *European Industrial Relations Review*, 236, September, p.8–9

Wächter H and Stengelhofen T (1992) 'Human resource management in a unified Germany', *Employee Relations*, 14 (4), pp.21–37

Williams K (1988) *Industrial Relations and the German Model,* Gower

10 · FRANCE

BACKGROUND

The French economy has the reputation of being highly dynamic. This seems paradoxical in the light of highly legalistic and bureaucratic traditions in employment relations. According to Crozier[1] French organisations are highly stratified, with absolute power being concentrated with a ruling elite of administrators and top managers who have been groomed by passing through the highly selective system of *grandes écoles*. Within this milieu, where the emphasis is on the observation of rules, attempts to introduce management by objectives and more flexible and participative management systems have foundered. The shackles have loosened somewhat in the 1990s in a climate of globalised competition, differentiation within product markets, increasing importance of product quality, availability of new technology and a growing service sector. Flexibility is being injected into contractual arrangements between individual employees and organisations regarding working time and methods of remuneration. Many of the features which emphasise social welfare and democracy at workplace level remain intact. In particular, it is necessary for management to take account of the views of works councils, which discuss the broader aspects of the company's economic and social affairs.

EMPLOYERS

French companies have traditionally been relatively small and predominantly owned and managed by families, and there are still a large number of family-controlled operations employing less than 50 employees. Nevertheless, perhaps inevitably, technological change, international competition and economies of scale have encouraged increasing concentration of employment in France, as in most other developed economies, particularly in the industrial sector. This has the consequence that, as Goetschy and Rozenblatt[2] point out, in 1987 some 36 per cent of the employed workforce were in companies employing in excess of 500 people, a statistic that compared reasonably with those for Germany, Britain and the Netherlands.

The traditions of management style and attitude in France are of autocracy, paternalism, rigidity and bureaucracy. Management has been elitist and it would also seem very militaristic in structure. Poirson[3] comments on and illustrates the relationship between levels in the pyramid hierarchy of the French company and educational background. Senior managers are likely to have had an engineering or technical education and Poirson argues that this does not seem to equip them with the interpersonal skills necessary for managing people effectively. Mobility between the layers in the hierarchy, from which considerable status may be derived, is also apparently difficult.

In the context of these traditions of ownership, attitudes of antagonism towards sharing decision making and the implications of the educational backgrounds of managers, it is perhaps not surprising that French companies have tended to resist trade unionism, particularly within the workplace. French employers have tended to rely on multi-employer bargaining at industry level and state regulation. They seem to have taken the view that industry-level bargaining between unions and employers' organisations would facilitate the retention of employer/managerial prerogative at local, workplace level.

The main employers' confederation at national level is the Conseil National du Patronat Français (CNPF), to which approximately 75 per cent of French companies are affiliated. The CNPF has traditionally pursued policies consistent with 'enlightened capitalism', accepting the need for a limited dialogue with trade unions. There are industry and regional associations as well, but these tend to be affiliated to the CNPF. The CNPF, with the trade union confederations, has participated in bargaining at national level, represents employers to government, participates in various consultative organisations, e.g. the Economic and Social Council, and assists in the administration of various national welfare benefit and training programmes. CNPF has been subject to criticism from among its membership as well as from non-affiliated employers for being too acquiescent in its attitude towards both government and trade unions.

Since the late 1980s there has certainly been increasing evidence that French employers are beginning to develop more effective mechanisms for managing employee relations at workplace level. This is, no doubt, prompted at least in part by their desire to achieve enhanced flexibility of contract and work organisation, viewed as prerequisites to achieving the productivity gains necessary to remain competitive and make full use of the new technologies. Allied to this has been an increasing interest in linking pay, performance and quality, and enhanced individualisation of the employment contract. The creation and use of quality circles has increased considerably, but primarily as a mechanism for achieving quality standards and making better use of employees' capabilities.

THE ROLE OF PERSONNEL

The origins of the personnel function lie in industrial relations and salary administration. HR specialists are not represented by an exclusive professional association, and there is no need for them to obtain a diploma or certificate to practise. A postgraduate programme in HRM offered by universities is, however, regarded favourably by potential employers. Meetings between HR specialists and training officers occur on a regional basis for sharing of information. The trend is towards lawyers, business school graduates, engineers and division heads passing through the function as part of their career development, and emphasis is being placed on managerial competence. This is, according to Besse[4], instead of, or in addition to, psychologists in charge of recruitment or former military personnel specialising in discipline.

The orientation of the function has tended to change from independent professional to active manager. In a study of 16 large enterprises and groups carried out in 1986, it was noted that the personnel function was being well integrated into enterprises, gaining a strategic role, and that its scope was being ceaselessly enlarged. Around 74 per cent of personnel directors interviewed sat on management committees. There is also a trend towards HR responsibilities being shared with line management.

LABOUR MARKET

- Since 1985, the rate of growth of the working population, which stood at 21 million, has slowed for two main reasons:

A slowing down in the feminisation of the workforce, following a boom in the entrance of women to the labour market which lasted until the mid-1980s.

The extension of studies for younger workers. In addition, there has been an increase in early retirements, therefore the span of working life is, on average, decreasing. More generally, the level of unemployment has remained at approximately 2.8 million since 1986.

Recruitment

- French industry suffered badly at the time of the oil crisis in 1915. However, a continuous revival has promoted some recruitment difficulties, particularly in respect of managerial and professional staff. At manual level there are some shortages of qualified skilled workers. A number of bodies, public and private, assist in matching people to jobs for managerial and manual staff. Some companies have sought to establish a longer-term approach towards managing recruitment and have developed links with schools, training centres and universities.
- Recruitment departments have been under increasing pressure in recent years and have tended to resort to speedier and cheaper methods than used previously. Along with more conventional selection tools, asytrology and graphology are in wide use. The government is considering regulating recruitment procedures. Search and selection consultancies are being used with increasing frequency, particularly in order to hire managerial talent.

Selection

- It is unlawful to take up references by phone or in writing. When an employee leaves the employer must provide a work certificate, the contents of which are legally prescribed, but which must not make any reference to the employee's performance.

Remuneration

- Minimum terms and conditions of employment are defined by law. Negotiations, which are undertaken nationally, regionally and locally, enhance statutory minima.
- Remuneration can also include bonuses and fringe benefits. In effect there is a three-tier process of pay determination. Legislation is supplemented by regional collective bargaining, which is in turn aug-

mented at company level. An extensive welfare system exists, covering matters such as health insurance, old age benefits and unemployment, and run jointly by representatives of employers and unions. Recently a trend towards wage individualisation has occurred.

- A survey carried out by Hayfrance in 1987 revealed that, out of 220 companies, 37 per cent granted only individualised wage increases.[5] Participation in the country's main profit-related pay scheme is compulsory for firms with over 50 employees, and voluntary schemes also exist. For manual workers there is a 15 per cent disparity between female and male earnings, which widens to 50 per cent for senior managers.

Training and development

- Technical education is integrated into the school and university system, most notably at secondary level, through the CAP and BGP. At higher level a technical Baccalauréat can be obtained.
- Although many universities are open to all aspiring undergraduates, a closed, elitist system operates in respect of the *grandes écoles*. These operate a very competitive entrance system, and their graduates often gain exclusive access to senior and protected positions across industry and commerce. It may be argued that such restrictive elitism is prejudicial to the overall prospects of business.
- Since 1919 there has been statutory support for an apprenticeship system balanced between classroom and practical in-company work. In addition, employees are entitled to maximum leave of up to one year for vocational training.
- Companies with over ten employees must contribute financially towards employees' training to the extent of a minimum of 1.2 per cent of total gross salaries paid through the year. Nearly 15 per cent of continuing training is conducted in house by companies themselves. Around 25 per cent of the working population undertake professional/vocational training.

Current issues

The economic recession has promoted concern over long-term and youth unemployed. A number of strategies have been adopted to try to remedy these problems.

- Job creation has occurred, involving part-time and socially valuable forms of employment.

- A scheme exists whereby firms can recruit unqualified young people without having to pay full social security charges.
- There has been an ongoing commitment, spearheaded by government, towards practical training.
- A number of large firms are successfully operating international and global strategies. Familiarity with a highly regulated HR system is thought to dispose French management favourably towards European integration and the Social Chapter.

According to Rojot, France's new approach towards HRM can be characterised by a new legitimacy for managerial authority and a move towards flexibility. New practices include formulating types of contract to fit particular business demands, including short-term employment, call contracts and subcontracting.

In 1988 18 per cent of the workforce was on atypical contracts, which included 12 per cent part time. Systems of production have also been modified to embrace fast-operating machinery and minimum stock.

TRADE UNIONS

French trade unionism has been, and still is, dominated by five main confederations. These confederations differ primarily not on grounds such as industry or occupation but in terms of ideology and political/welfare objectives. The five are usually separated into two groups, the revolutionary and reformist.

The revolutionary union confederations and their member unions have traditionally sought a fundamental transformation of society and they have considered political and direct action as the most useful mechanisms for achieving their objectives. Collective bargaining and other participatory mechanisms have not been seen as particularly attractive or useful alternatives, the danger being primarily that involvement in such power-sharing mechanisms might make it more difficult for the union to retain its ability to contest employers. This lack of interest in collective bargaining is consistent with the strand of radical Marxist thought that sees it as a process which assists the preservation of the *status quo* in a capitalist system serving only to diminish revolutionary zeal. Nevertheless, collective bargaining does provide evidence of the balance of power between the parties at any one time and as such is useful. These confederations support workers' control of production.

The reformist confederations tend to accept some legitimacy in managerial prerogative in economic decision making within organisations. These unions have tended to adopt a contractual approach to industrial relations and are, in the main, supporters of certain mechanisms for co-determination. There is evidence of increasing militancy from some of these unions in recent years and they are prepared to take direct action. Evidence of this continuing willingness to take militant action was provided by the employees of Air France in autumn 1993 when a strike against proposals for significant job losses turned into a bloody confrontation with riot police.

Perhaps not surprisingly, given the nature of the objectives of the main confederations, there has been a tradition of affiliation and association between unions and political parties. Additionally, there is a tradition of centrality in terms of both organisation and activity. The various confederations have competed with one another for influence and membership and the confederations often all have a presence in any particular workplace, employees joining or supporting the union that most suits their own objectives or ideology.

Generally, the unions have not pursued recruitment policies aimed at mass membership, preferring to recruit a core of activists and militants.

The confederations are as follows:

1. CGT – *Confédération Générale du Travail* – traditionally the largest confederation with a communist/socialist ideological orientation, strong in traditional industries and public services. Leaders associated with the Communist party. Membership around 1 million, declining in recent years.
2. CFDT – *Confédération Française et Démocratique du Travail* – revolutionary and left wing but not communist, anti-Catholic, supports workers control, strength in metal industries, health service and banking. Membership around 600 000, declining in recent years.
3. FO – *Force Ouvrière* – supports contractual policies, strongly anti-communist, unions should act as a counterweight not as a counter power, accepts management prerogative in economic decisions. Strong in public sector and among white-collar workers. Politically mixed membership. Membership 1.1 million and rising.
4. CFTC – *Confédération Française des Travailleurs Chrétiens* – strong doctrinal links with the Catholic church. Essentially contractual but is prepared to be militant. Supports co-determination and collective bargaining. Rejects the class struggle and politi-

cisation. Membership approximately 250 000 and fairly stable.
5. CGC – *Confédération Générale des Cadres* – recruits among professional and managerial staff, with particular strength in areas such as engineering and sales. Contractual orientation and particularly concerned with protecting the position of middle and production management and maintaining their pay differentials. Membership approximately 240 000.

Source: The figures above for membership of the various confederations are derived from the study by Bibes G and Mauriaux R (1990) *Les Syndicats Européens à l'Epreuve*, Paris.

Membership figures for the French unions are to some extent 'guesstimates', since the unions have not traditionally sought mass membership or strong financial reserves to support organisation or direct action. Consequently, there is no tradition of consistent paying of dues or of efficient and comprehensive membership recording. The membership figures above are for about 1988 and are the unions' own; they may well be inflated and the unions do not necessarily use consistent bases for calculation. There is no tradition of the closed shop in France and additionally the longstanding mechanism of extension by government of collective agreements to companies and even sectors not party to the agreement has meant that the benefits of trade union activity could be gained without the need to become a member.

A very different picture of trade union membership is presented by the figure quoted in Goetschy and Rozenblatt's note No. 2[6], where they quote the CFDT's estimate of all the representative confederations' membership in 1990 based on regular contribution-paying members. These figures are, with the previously given figure in brackets:

- CGT   682 000   (1 million)
- CFDT   539 000   (600 000)
- FO   416 000   (1 100 000)
- CFTC   106 000   (250 000)
- CGC   115 000   (240 000)

Arguably, therefore, trade union membership figures in France should not be accepted as a realistic or reliable measure of worker support for trade unionism. However, low trade union membership density is a feature of industrial relations in France, and it seems that around the end of the 1980s membership in the private sector might have been as low as 9 per cent.[7] Certainly, membership was in decline throughout the 1980s and is unlikely currently to be in excess of 12 per cent overall.[8] The Price Waterhouse/Cranfield project data[9] confirm that in 75 per cent of the organisations surveyed union membership density was 25 per cent or less, and the data estimating influence showed hardly any organisations saying that trade union influence had been increasing.

Goetschy and Rozenblatt[10] discuss the undeniable decline in union membership since the mid-1970s and arguably also in union influence and militancy, pointing out the decline in CGT and CFDT membership and the increase in membership of the reformist FO. They also point out the same trends in industrial tribunal, employee delegate and works council elections, combined with an increase in the vote for non-union candidates. For much of this period France has been governed by socialists seeking to enhance the role of trade unions, particularly in the workplace, and the rights of employees.

The five main confederations discussed above are all 'representative'. This is a legal status conferring on each of the so-called Club of 5 various privileges and rights. Whether or not a union is to be afforded this privileged status is determined using a number of criteria such as whether the union was patriotic during the second world war, its membership, its experience and most importantly its independence from employers. Once conferred, representativeness entitles the union to participate in collective bargaining, nominate candidates for works councils and other representative institutions, participate in consultative arrangements at national level with employers and government, and take part in the administration and implementation of various employment, unemployment and social security benefit schemes.

Only since 1968 have trade unions had the legal right to form a branch in workplaces with more than 50 employees.

There are many variables influencing levels of trade union membership and in France the decline in membership that has occurred since the late 1970s can be attributed to a number of these as follows:

- Changes in the structure of industry and the decline of traditional manufacturing and extractive industries.
- Increasing disenchantment with the politics of revolution and a shift in social attitudes and values in the direction of individualism and instrumentalism.
- The principle of extension which gives employees the benefits of collective bargaining without their needing to be members of the participatory unions.

Allied to this is the tradition of legal regulation of many terms and conditions of employment.
- The lack of unity within the movement and between the confederations.
- A disenchantment with the cosy relationship between union leaders and socialist government. Certainly there has in recent years been an increase in industrial action not organised by the unions, but by unofficial co-ordination groups, particularly in the public sector.
- Employer opposition and resistance, particularly in smaller companies.
- The increasing trend towards part-time, temporary and home working.
- The anti-inflationary economic policies pursued by government since 1982, which have arguably contributed to increased unemployment.
- The government's granting of more rights to employees as individuals may have assisted the anti-collectivist trend mentioned above.
- The advancing age of the traditional revolutionary and militant core membership.
- Improved employee relations management practices.

GOVERNMENT

French governments have tended to perform the traditional 'industrial relations' roles as employer, economic manager and regulator, legislator and conciliator, although with somewhat different emphasis depending on ideological approach and affiliation. It is often difficult for government to achieve its industrial relations objectives given economic and other circumstances, and France over the last decade provides an illustration of these difficulties.

The socialist government after 1982 undoubtedly sought to enhance the role of trade unions in the workplace; it also sought to give greater protection to employees at work and to further employee participation. It legislated in a number of instances to achieve these objectives, yet economic circumstances in the latter years have been such as to encourage the government to take austerity measures, imposing pay freezes and restrictions on public and in particular welfare expenditure. It is also possible that the measures to enhance employee protection and participation have actually undermined the role of the unions and contributed to the decline in membership referred to previously. These measures are outlined below.

As employer

The size of the public sector was significantly increased in the early to mid-1980s through nationalisation. As employer, governments of the left have tried to lead the way for the private sector, setting a good example. To this end, or at least as examples, we have the legislation in 1983 concerned with democratising the public sector by providing worker representatives with rights to up to one-third of the seats on the board, and later, in the 1980s, state enterprises such as Thomson and Rhône-Poulenc who were seen to be in the forefront of the creation of European-level employee-consultative mechanisms. On the other hand, of course, government can seek to influence pay levels throughout the economy via the policies it pursues towards its own employees, and during much of the last decade government has pursued a policy of cash-limiting civil service pay. In 1990 it further promoted revision and restructuring of public sector pay and grading systems, the first significant revision for decades, and encouraged hierarchical, bureaucratic and rigid private sector organisations to do the same, thereby facilitating improvements in labour flexibility and productivity. As noted earlier, the right-wing coalition elected in 1993 is engaged in a widespread programme of privatisation and inevitably this will herald a substantial decrease in the size of the public sector.

As legislator/regulator

Governments in France have tended to regulate both procedural and substantive dimensions of employee relations, providing a framework, creating rights and obligations, encouraging particular processes and mechanisms, and embodying minimum and maximum substantive outcomes of collective bargaining in statutory rights. There have been various important legislative interventions, e.g. the Collective Bargaining Acts of 1936, 1950, 1971 and 1982; legislation in 1968 giving unions the right to create branches in organisations with more than 50 employees and to have union delegates; the Constitutions of 1946 and 1958 in which certain basic rights are guaranteed; the legislation in 1945 creating works councils in organisations of an appropriate size; and the 1982 legislation granting employees the right of direct expression. Many of these are expanded on below.

Government legislatively regulates many terms and conditions of employment: minimum wage rates, maximum hours, hours linked to age, redundancy rights and pay, sickness leave and pay, maternity leave and pay, and paid holiday entitlements. As noted earlier, the government elected in 1993 is proposing to vary some of these regulations so as to facilitate flexibility in the labour market.

Legislative intervention, regulation and extension have been central to the French system. There is insufficient space here to detail comprehensively the content of all the various enactments, some of which are in any event probably more appropriate to subsequent discussions of processes and workplace organisation. Nevertheless, it is important to emphasise the constitutional rights to a job, to belong to a trade union and defend your interests through it, to take strike action, and to have representatives with rights to information, consultation and participation. These rights are embodied in the constitutions of 1946 and 1958.

Government can seek to influence pay levels through its operation and administration of the SMIC – *salaire minimum interprofessional de croissance* – or minimum wage. This may be adjusted to keep it in line with inflation, usually at 2 per cent intervals, but government can otherwise increase this minimum wage and thereby influence rates of pay throughout the various sectors, and/or it can encourage both unions and employers to negotiate rates in excess of the SMIC. The most recent increase in the SMIC was 2.1 per cent with effect from 1 July 1994; at that time the SMIC rate was for 169 hours' work per month and it was estimated that it was received by 1.48 million employees. Government can also influence living standards through its control of the social security, unemployment and welfare benefits systems as, for example, was done with the introduction in 1988 of the RMI – a minimum income level for the unemployed, initially set at approximately £200 per month and limited to those participating in some training or work experience scheme aimed at improving the recipient's employment prospects.

Socialist governments over the last 15 years have sought to address the unemployment 'problem' via various training and retraining schemes for the young and long-term unemployed. They have also provided incentives to employers to recruit by granting exemptions to social security contributions, and in the mid-1980s they encouraged employers and unions to agree to shorter working hours and early retirement plans as other mechanisms to encourage recruitment from among the ranks of the unemployed. The right-wing Chirac government concentrated on relaxing regulation on redundancy and working time and on various forms of atypical contracts, essentially relaxing official restrictions on employers. As noted already, the 1993 government seems to be availing itself of a mix of these initiatives pursuing greater flexibility in the use of labour and providing additional recruitment incentives, pursuing the objective of enabling a more efficient use of labour at the same time as seeking to reduce unemployment.

As conciliator

Collective agreements are usually for a fixed period, they are legally enforceable and they often prohibit industrial action during the term. The government does not usually intervene directly to resolve conflicts between employee and employer, but does encourage participants to collective agreements to provide for conciliation or mediation in the event of disputes or failure to agree. In the absence of such provision, the government can impose conciliation on the parties and appoint a conciliation board or commission which may result in mediation. Bipartite conciliation committees are often established to deal with individual grievances that cannot be resolved via the employee delegates.

PROCESSES

Collective bargaining

The structures, incidence, content and outcomes of collective bargaining have been significantly influenced over the years by government. The tradition has been for multi-employer/union bargaining at industry level, according to the framework established in the 1936 Collective Bargaining Act. Both parties preferred to locate their bargaining at this level. For the unions, it was consistent with their ambitions to influence the centre and did not force them to confront the issue of workplace organisation or activity, something they would have found very difficult given their lack of organisation and resources. It was also consistent with their egalitarian orientation. Employers preferred to bargain at industry level because it discouraged inter-company competition on wages and working conditions; wage rates not, therefore, being in any sense linked to a particular company's ability to pay. At the same time, employers were able to retain autonomy within their own organisation, they could improve on the industry minima if they wished, and importantly there was no need for them to recognise or deal with unions in their own company.

The 1936 Act also established the principle of extension, whereby the Ministry of Labour can extend terms and conditions agreed at sector level to all companies and employees within the sector whether signatory to the agreement or not. Sector-level agreements could be extended even if only one representative union was signatory.

The bargaining structure established by this early legislation is, in many ways, still dominant, although bargaining does now occur at different levels, at company and at multi-sector level. These are, however, relatively late developments. In the 1960s and 1970s there was some bargaining activity at multi-sector and plant level, but it was not until the Auroux report[11] and the subsequent Collective Bargaining Act of 1982 that significant changes occurred, and there has been an increase in the incidence of bargaining at all levels since.

The 1982 Act imposed on the parties in organisations with union workplace branches an obligation to negotiate at least annually at company level on pay and hours of work. There was no obligation to reach agreement and no obligation even to bargain in good faith. Nevertheless, there was a subsequent expansion of bargaining at this level, approximately a five-fold increase in company agreements between 1982 and 1991, 6750 agreements being reached in 1991.[12] It, to some extent, fitted with employers' desires to decentralise decision making and improve flexibility of contract and work organisation. However, there was also considerable resistance from employers, who argued that dual bargaining at industry and company level would encourage inequity and wages based on an employer's ability to pay. This Act also strengthened the Ministry of Labour's powers of extension.

Supporting the requirement to bargain, employees were given additional rights to elect delegates and workplace committees to negotiate with employers within the organisation. These delegates were also granted rights to the receipt of certain information relevant to the negotiations, and time off and other facilities to enhance their capability to negotiate effectively.

Additional rights were also given to non-signatory unions at plant level, giving them a power of veto over agreements at plant level which contradicted agreements reached at a higher level or which were in contravention of terms and conditions enshrined in the law.

As indicated earlier, the legislation appears to have had some success in encouraging bargaining and other industrial relations activity and organisation in the workplace, but it was certainly not universally complied with. After about 1988 there was a drift back to sector-level bargaining and even to multi-sector bargaining, and it was estimated that by the end of the 1980s only about 20 per cent of employees[13], predominantly in larger firms, were covered by plant bargaining. However, the results of the Price Waterhouse/Cranfield project in 1991[14] indicated a much greater degree of company-level bargaining over basic pay than previous studies might have suggested: 46 per cent of organisations were bargaining over basic pay for manual workers at company level.

The government seems to have stimulated a resurgence of multi-sector bargaining in the late 1980s by encouraging the parties to enter into framework agreements at that level dealing with issues particularly relevant to the modernisation and restructuring of French industry. Over the two years 1988–90, agreements at this level were negotiated dealing with issues relating to:

- the introduction of new technology, in particular job grading and training issues and their implications;
- the reorganisation of working time, flexibility and rules relating to the hiring of temporary and fixed-term employees;
- working conditions, health and safety training, and equal pay between the sexes for work of equal value.

The increasing unemployment of 1992–94 has encouraged the parties in some companies to engage in a form of concession bargaining at company or plant level, whereby the employees agreed to accept wage cuts in some instances as an alternative to redundancies.

In November 1993 the government put forward legislative proposals to vary the system so that changes could be made to agreements with the backing of only one signatory union. Where such changes removed or reduced one of employees' material advantages, the new proposals give any one signatory union the right to oppose the change.

Rights of expression

Additional legislation in 1982 sought to encourage direct communication and consultation between employees and employers outside the framework of collective bargaining, trade unions or works councils. The legislation provides that, in companies with more than 200 employees, the employees should have the right to meet with management on at least three occasions per year to air any grievances or views they may have on working conditions or the content and organisation of work. Usually employees exert this right as members of 'expression groups' of 15–20 employees.

It would not be surprising if this right of direct expression, bypassing representative mechanisms and despite the limited scope of its subject matter, had contributed to the decline in trade union membership evident in the last decade. Certainly one can imagine it being argued that with this right trade union membership and representation in the workplace were not necessary.

The intention of the legislators was that these expression groups would be created in practice through agreement between unions and employers; however, the legislation facilitated unilateral establishment by employers.

Employee delegates

The institution of the non-union employee delegate, taking up and processing employee grievances with management at plant level, was initially the product of the 1936 Act. The law applies to organisations employing more than 10 people. Employees have the right to elect delegates annually, these should meet management at least monthly and they are given time off to perform their duties as delegates. The grievances pursued this way may be about wages or working conditions. In organisations where there is company bargaining, a works council and expression groups, the role of the employee delegate is sometimes diluted and confused. Again, this right to non-union representation and pursuit of grievances, allied to the newer rights of expression above, has not always assisted the 'cause' of the union movement at plant level. It must be remembered in both instances, however, that the unions had in the main not actively pursued a workplace role.

Works councils

Works councils or committees ought to exist in all organisations employing in excess of 50 employees. Their role is essentially consultative, they have rights to certain categories of company information regarding the progress of orders, production and finances, and they ought to meet at least monthly. In addition, they may discuss health and safety issues, the introduction of new technology, company plans with regard to expansion, production problems and working conditions.

The council is made up of between three and eleven employee representatives, elected by the workforce, and is chaired by a senior member of management.

The council may send up to four members as observers to company board meetings. Representatives are elected initially from lists put forward by the unions; however, if less than 50 per cent of the employees entitled to vote actually do vote then there is a second stage to the election procedures in which non-union candidates may stand. It is obviously possible for these councils to be made up of non-union members, and representative unions do have attendance rights in an observer capacity. It has already been pointed out that the non-union vote in these elections has been increasing.

These councils do not have co-determination rights; the obligation on the employer is to inform and consult, not to agree. In companies operating several plants, plant and company councils are likely.

The 1982 legislation required large, multi-plant companies whose registered office is in France to form a group or combined committee. The role of the committee is to receive at least annual information on the financial and employment situation. The investigative powers of the councils were widened in 1982, particularly those of the council accountant.

French companies in both public and private sectors have been at the forefront of multi-national company development of corporate-wide information and consultative mechanisms for their employees. As noted earlier, public sector corporations such as Thomson-Grand Public and Rhône-Poulenc led the way, followed by others such as Bull and Elf-Aquitaine. In 1986 BSN-Gervais Danone and the International Union of Food set up a permanent mechanism for consultation with employee representatives from seven European countries, and most recently in June 1994 have reached agreement guaranteeing the company's employees in Europe, the Americas and Asia (56 000) rights to trade union representation.

CASE STUDIES

Peugeot

In spite of the complexities of French employment law a new shift system has been successfully introduced at Peugeot's Poissy plant.

The complicated system of employment law and representative machinery for employees does not mean that French companies are strangled by red tape or unable to achieve adventurous new ways of working.

Peugeot's huge production site at Poissy, west of Paris, has been experimenting for the past 18 months with a four-day week for two-thirds of its 9000 strong workforce.

The idea arose because of the company's desire to increase production from 1200 cars a day to 1500 after the launch of the Citroën ZX family car, to cater for an improvement in market share.

Peugeot decided to achieve the 25 per cent increase in car production by increasing the amount of time machinery was in use rather than adding to the size of the factory. But it did not want to increase individuals' working time by the same amount.

The management's approach was influenced by a workforce poll which showed huge opposition to weekend working. There was also strong union resistance to a night shift. So a new two-shift system was devised within a framework of a four-day week and a further 2000 employees taken on. The two shifts are from 6.15 am to 4.29 pm and from 4.29 pm to 2.42 am. They include a 36-minute meal break and a further 30-minute break.

Employees still work a 38.5 hour week, changing shifts every 15 days. But each works these hours within four days. Time off now includes two three-day weekends in every five, with an additional weekday off in each of the three other weeks.

Because one employee in five is off work every weekday, the new system means that five people rotate around four jobs, demanding greater flexibility among the workforce. A major training programme has been mounted to back this up.

The new shift system was the result of a nine-month consultation between Peugeot's management and unions using the normal plant negotiating machinery. (It is not the type of issue that the factory council would be involved in.)

Talks culminated in a plant-level agreement signed in October 1990 with three of the six unions, which together represent about two-thirds of the Poissy workforce.

Three of the unions present during negotiations – the CGT, CFDT and CFTC – failed to agree, one objection being the hours of the late shift. However, the company was able to implement the agreement since their members were in a minority among the workforce.

The company believes that the new shift system secures the future of the Poissy site, which some years ago had looked bleak.

Source: *Personnel Management*, August 1992, p.43

Moulinex

Since the mid-1980s two Moulinex factories assembling electrical appliances in Falaise and nearby Caen have pioneered an equal opportunities programme under France's 1983 Equality at Work law.

Yvette Roudy, the Député (Member of Parliament) for Calvados in Normandy, whose constituency includes the Moulinex factory at Falaise, was France's Minister for Women's Rights in the mid-1980s, and the Equality at Work law has become widely known as 'Roudy's Law'.

From 1981 to 1986 she introduced five major laws on equality. 'I took the principle of positive discrimination in remedial measures that the EC endorses,' she says, 'and I introduced them into law. That law enables firms to establish equality programmes.'

Mme Roudy visits the Moulinex factories regularly to see how things are progressing. As she puts it, 'it is important both to create structure models and then to stimulate policies.'

The Moulinex factories ran a pilot training programme for women in which they gave 100 women on the production line up-skilling training. Those women are now in better paid, semi-skilled jobs. Five years ago, when she first joined the company, Martine Doléans was working on the all-female assembly line, a monotonous job which involved assembling Moulinex appliances. 'Yes, since our training we have been paid a higher wage and we've progressed within the company,' she confirms.

Martine Doléans now works as a service engineer for special electrical machinery, a job that has traditionally been done by men. She says, 'I find it very interesting. It's a job where, unlike the production line, I never repeat the same thing.'

Like the other women employees on Moulinex's up-skilling course, when the offer of training came along Doléans seized the chance to escape the low-paid repetitive work on the assembly line. She recalls, 'I went to college one day a week for a year and a half, and then for one year full-time. At college I studied industrial drawing, panelling, riveting, a lot of mechanical engineering work as well as general subjects. After that year I gained a CAP professional certificate in mechanical maintenance.'

Spurred on by her success on the up-skilling course, she now has dreams of further advancement. 'I may eventually go on to do automation programming. But let's just say I try not to dream too much because I've already achieved a great deal by taking this training.'

Moulinex's pilot equality training scheme has proved so successful that the company is extending it to 1000 other employees.

The company's innovative programme shows just how wrong Britain's Duke of Edinburgh was when he visited an all-female British assembly line and remarked how much better women did monotonous, repetitive jobs than men, implying that women had a natural tendency to stay at the bottom.

Moulinex's work makes a monkey out of such misguided remarks.

Source: *Personnel Management*, August 1992, p.41

SUMMARY

The French system is one characterised by the legal regulation of employee relations processes and basic terms and conditions of employment. The dominant process has been collective bargaining at industry level; however, in the last decade there has been a tendency towards decentralisation, promoted both by government as legislator and by employers seeking flexibility, enhanced productivity, individualisation of the employment relationship and a clear link between pay and merit or performance. National or industry-level bargaining seems now to be largely concentrated in the public sector.

Employers have retained considerable autonomy over both economic and production issues and there is a tradition of autocracy, rigidity and poor employee relations management at plant level.

In addition to collective bargaining, other mechanisms exist at plant level for processing of grievances and consultation. Some of these mechanisms are non-union.

The union movement is fragmented along ideological lines and competitive. It is also small and declining in size and arguably influence, although employees at Air France showed in autumn 1993 that they are still capable of militant action and also that such action can still be successfully used to influence employers and government.

NOTES AND REFERENCES

1. Crozier M, *Le Phenomene Bureaucratique,* Paris

2. Goetschy J and Rozenblatt P (1992) 'France – the Industrial Relations system at a Turning Point?' in Ferner A and Hyman R (eds), *Industrial Relations in the New Europe*, Blackwell, p.419

3. Poirson P (1993) 'Human Resource Management in France' in Tyson S *et al.* (eds) *Human Resource Management in Europe*, Kogan Page, pp.53–8

4. Besse D (1992) 'Finding a New Raison d'Etre', *Personnel Management*, August, pp.40–3

5. Unpublished HAYFRANCE survey in Rojot J (1990) 'Human Resource Management' in Pieper R, *Human Resource Management: An International Comparison*, de Gruyter, Berlin and New York

6. Goetschy and Rosenblatt op. cit., p.441

7. Ibid.

8. See appendix 14

9. Gunnigle P, Brewster C and Morley M (1994) 'European Industrial Relations: Change and Continuity', in Brewster C and Hegewisch A, *Policy and Practice in European HRM*, Routledge, p.17

10. Goetschy J and Rozenblatt P op. cit., pp.413–9

11. Auroux J – Report on Workers Rights 1982. Auroux was the minister of labour in the French government

12. European Industrial Relations Review No. 225 October 1992.

13. Goetschy J and Rozenblatt P op. cit., p.433

14. Brewster C, Hegewisch A, and Mayne L (1994) 'Trends in European HRM, Signs of Convergence?' in Kirkbride P S (ed), *Human Resource Management in Europe, Perspectives for the 1990s*, Routledge, p.116.

FURTHER READING

'A decade of the "Auroux" laws' (1993) *European Industrial Relations Review*, 233, June, pp.31–2

Barsoux J L and Lawrence P (1990) *Management in France*, Cassell

Besse D (1992) 'Finding a new raison d'être', *Personnel Management*, 24 (8), August, pp.40–43

Blanc-Jouvain X (1988) 'Trade union democracy and industrial relations: France', *Bulletin of Comparative Labour Relations*, 17, pp.7–26

Bridgford J (1990) 'French trade unions: crisis in the 1980s', *Industrial Relations*, 21 (2), Summer, pp.126–37

Brunstein I (1992) 'Human resource management in France', *Employee Relations*, 14 (4), pp.53–70

Delamotte Y (1988) 'Workers' participation and personnel policies in France' *International Labour Review*, 127 (2), pp.221–41

'Radical five-year employment law proposals' (1993) *European Industrial Relations Review*, 237, October, pp.20–23

Goetschy J and Jobert A (1993) 'Industrial relations in France' in Bamber G and Lansbury R (eds), *International and Comparative Industrial Relations: A study of industrialised market economies*, Routledge, pp.149–74

Lane C (1989) *Management and Labour in Europe: The industrial enterprise in Germany, Britain and France*, Edward Elgar

Lash S (1984) *The Militant Workers: Class and radicalism in France and America*, Heinemann

Moss B H (1988) 'Industrial law reform in an era of retreat: The Auroux Laws in France', *Work, Employment and Society*, 2(3), September, pp.317–34

Rojot J (1986) 'The development of French employers' policy towards trade unions', *Labour and Society*, January pp.1–16

Rojot J (1988) 'The myth of French exceptionalism', in Barbash J and Barbash K (eds), *Theories and Concepts in Comparative Industrial Relations*, South Carolina Press pp.76–88

Segrestin D (1990) 'Recent changes in France' in Baglioni G and Crouch C (eds), *European Industrial Relations: The challenge of flexibility*, Sage, pp.97–126

Sellier F and Sylvestre J J (1986) 'Unions' policies in the economic crisis in France' in Edwards R, Garonna P and Tödtling F (eds), *Unions in Crisis and Beyond*, Auburn House, pp.173–277

Smith R (1987) *Crisis in the French Labour Movement*, Macmillan

11 · ITALY

BACKGROUND

The Italian state may be caricatured, not unrealistically, as two nations within one. The northern triangle of Milan, Turin and Genoa encompasses one of the wealthiest regions in Europe, while the *mezzagiorno* south of Rome is an area hampered by economic backwardness and troubled by organised crime and corruption. The level of subsidy from the North has been resented in some quarters by tax payers in these more affluent areas, where there have even been calls to declare independent regions (e.g. Lombardy). A further aspect of this is the level of migration from the South to the North, significant proportions of the large northern industrial cities comprised of southerners. The North also encompasses some of the most successful regions in Europe, e.g. in Emilia Romagna and the Po Valley areas, where small firms have also been viewed as models of industrial democracy.[1] Some of the major Italian organisations e.g. Fiat, are surrounded by satellites of small concerns which supply them. The family company provides a focus for commitment and loyalty in a country where there is considerable disenchantment with a highly volatile national political paraphernalia and with formal structures of authority. It is therefore somewhat paradoxical that employment relations are subject to a high degree of statutory regulation.

EMPLOYERS

Italy is a nation of relatively small employing organisations. It is estimated[2] that some 40 per cent of employees work in organisations employing less than 10 people. There are large organisations, but often the employer has chosen to expand the operation by means which do not significantly expand the numbers of employees, e.g. through means of franchising, licensing or joint ownership arrangements. Benetton[3] is an example of expansion of this kind: 50 000 people are involved in the Benetton empire but only 6000 are on the payroll. There are various reasons for Italian employers' choosing to operate in this way. It may facilitate the continued domination of the organisa-

tion and its enterprise by relevant family interests; and the legal regulation and determination of employment terms and conditions can be avoided in this way, thereby maintaining the autonomy and prerogative of the employer. Family interests still dominate a large number of enterprises, large as well as small. An example of this, as well as of many of the pressures and responses referred to below, is given in Figure 11.1.

Similar to those in many other countries, Italian employers have been encouraged in recent years by the competitive pressures of the world economy and the availability of new technology to seek changes in the work organisation, structures and employment relationships. The search for flexibility seems to have occurred within the confines of existing employee relations structures and systems, although there has been increasing emphasis on workplace mechanisms and some argue that relationships have become more realistic, co-operative and less conflictual as both parties search for solutions to the problems posed. Nevertheless, it is doubtful that employers have, in practice, given much in terms of autonomy over economic and production decision making. As we see later, the bargaining tends to be about outcomes and implications rather than strategic or policy issues, and much of the increased joint activity at the workplace is of the consultative type, certainly not co-determination.

There has been an increased desire by employers to link pay and performance, company performance rather than individual, and employers have also been more willing both to utilise and extend the discretionary scope in pay and benefits packages left them by legislation and sectoral agreements.

Employers, like others in Italy, have joined together to further and protect their interests. Employers' organisations tend to have trade and business roles as well as an industrial relations role, although there are organisations in one or two industries and the public enterprises manufacturing sector that have only industrial relations roles.

The main employers' organisation is Confindustria (the General Confederation of Italian Industry)[4] which has particular strength in manufacturing and con-

The retuning of Fiat's engine

The Italian group's big losses have overshadowed far-reaching changes in its culture, writes **Andrew Hill**

During its 95-year history, Fiat has often behaved as though it were an arm of the Italian government – a strict hierarchy with diplomatic, commercial and industrial functions parallel to those of the state, headed by a patriarchal chairman, Gianni Agnelli.

Over the last few years, however, Fiat, in common with Italy, has been struggling to change deep-rooted management and working habits. "Fiat today is a different Fiat compared with the company of five years ago," says Giorgio Garuzzo, chairman of Fiat's three core divisions – cars, commercial vehicles and agricultural and construction equipment. "We're not talking about revolution, because we have never sought to break with the past, but undoubtedly an evolution of far-reaching importance."

But as the group starts to recover from last year's record loss, the same questions are being asked about the "new Fiat" as about the new Italy: how deep do these changes go, and will they last?

The first indication that Fiat would attempt to change its culture came in 1989, when the group's blunt-talking chief executive, Cesare Romiti, presented 200 Fiat managers with a highly critical analysis of problems facing the group, which he described as "sad, laggardly and bureaucratised".

Fiat Auto was the most obvious culprit. In spite of earlier efforts to reform the Fiat car business, the group's principal operation was heading for a new decade with an outdated product line – it was six years since the launch of the acclaimed Uno in the popular small-car range – and a reputation for poor quality.

That reputation was not helped by an unspoken assumption within the company that customers were prepared to compromise on quality if the price was low enough – a fallacy which was about to be exploded by more efficient Japanese car manufacturers. Protected from Japanese competition at home, and coddled by a comparatively buoyant Italian market, Fiat Auto had been able to defer important decisions.

This was dangerous, not only for the division itself, but for the whole group. Fiat operates in more than 60 countries and has 15 distinct activities, including aviation, railway rolling stock, chemicals, publishing and financial services. But Fiat Auto still accounts for more than half of group industrial turnover and nearly 70 per cent of group revenues are drawn from the three principal divisions (cars, trucks, farm and building equipment). The group's top managers are almost invariably drawn from these businesses.

Analysts now criticise Fiat Auto for moving too slowly and not anticipating the inevitable cyclical downturn in the car industry after the years of plenty. But Garuzzo points out that the company was working gradually on a change of management strategy from the end of the 1980s.

For example, Fiat started to introduce the "total quality" concept from 1989 across the group, attempting to change attitudes, reform relationships with suppliers and involve workers more closely in devising solutions to production problems. Garuzzo concedes this is "not a strategy that gives results overnight", but five years later it has spawned Fiat

Auto's first "integrated factory" at Melfi, in southern Italy, which is producing the new Punto small car.

Melfi, which came on-stream this year, is one of the main reasons why Fiat believes the changes introduced over the last five years will stick.

There, Fiat is trying to delegate more responsibility to units of workers and managers. There is no separate building for central staff and the old blue-collar/white-collar distinction is abolished: everybody wears the same overalls, distinguished only by small coloured labels, and decisions are made by work teams on the factory floor.

"At Melfi, the worker doesn't exist any more" read a recent headline on an admiring article in Il Sole 24 Ore, Italy's business daily.

Practically, it is easier to establish an integrated factory from scratch – on a site such as Melfi, where production lines can be mapped out for ease of access and component suppliers located next door, for example – than impose it on to a well-established plant such as Turin's Mirafiori, originally built for a different production strategy.

Garuzzo admits as much: "Undoubtedly Melfi is a workshop for [the management strategy], because starting with a greenfield site is always more simple. There aren't any old concepts and no psychological resistance to overcome."

Fiat executives believe the enthusiasm of the Melfi workers, who are mostly in their mid-20s, compared with an average age of 46 at other Fiat factories, will infuse the whole group. However, Fiat unions claim that although Melfi's employees – drawn from a region with high unemployment – were keen on the project at the outset, disillusionment is beginning to set in as some of their high expectations are confounded.

Melfi is not the only element of the Fiat Auto strategy, however. Parallel changes in the company's approach to product development are also beginning to bear fruit. Fiat Auto has long since abandoned the accepted wisdom that you can introduce new basic models as rarely as once a decade and keep the range fresh with occasional restyling. At eight to 10 years, Fiat's product cycle in the mid-1980s was short compared with the industry average, but by the early 1990s, the changeover period looked sluggish, particularly when compared with Japanese competitors.

From 1991, the company began working on reducing this renewal cycle to five to six years. The full impact of this change will be obvious in 1996, by which time 18 new models should have been launched and the Punto will be one of the oldest Fiat models still produced.

Alas for Fiat, this heavy investment of time and money coincided with a reduction in the competitiveness of Italian industry, due partly to high labour costs. The competitiveness problem was eased in 1992, when the Italian currency was devalued and the link between wage increases and inflation cut. But it was at that point that the European car market, and Italy in particular, slipped further than anyone had predicted.

"We suddenly found ourselves with an extraordinary mix of problems to manage, issues to face up to and programmes to take forward," explains Garuzzo. "Our basic decision was not to stop any of the programmes which were going on, because that would have further damaged our competitiveness."

As a result, as Fiat has been eager to point out, although the group recorded its largest loss in 1993 – L1,780bn (£736m) after tax, extraordinary charges and minority interests – it also devoted a record L8,900bn to research and development and capital expenditure, much of it to improving Fiat Auto's sales network in preparation for the launch of new models.

Meanwhile, the number of employees in the whole group has fallen from more than 300,000 in 1990 to just over 260,000 in 1993, and in Fiat Auto from 133,000 to 120,000. Cuts in Italy have been eased by government-sponsored redundancy agreements, while the number of Fiat Auto employees abroad has increased.

But in spite of the confidence of top Fiat management, Susanna Camusso, national secretary responsible for Fiat at Fiom, the main Italian engineering union, believes the cultural changes have not yet permeated through all levels of the group. "There are people within Fiat who have chosen this new culture, but others who still think that the old system was fine," she says.

"Companies develop characters like people," agrees one analyst. "Sometimes after the age of 15, or even five years, or six months, there's nothing more you can do about changing that character."

As Fiat finally tries to reap the benefits of its painfully implemented management strategy, it must try to dispel three main concerns.

One is the danger that complacency will again set in as the recession begins to lift. Garuzzo and his colleagues say the risk of "decadenza" [decline, or decay] still exists, "but this new system of management which increases everybody's participation should create motivation internally to resist this trend". Whether this is true may not become obvious until the next downturn in the market, by which time it could be too late to amend the strategy.

A second risk is that Fiat's foreign plants – for example in Poland, Turkey and Brazil – begin to generate the sort of industrial relations problems which have largely been banished from the main Italian operations. Last week, for example, Fiat Auto's Polish workers voted to strike to try to force a 40 per cent pay increase.

Finally, there is the open question of the Fiat succession. Gianni Agnelli is 73 and Romiti is 71. Last year both of them decided to stay on rather than handing on the chairmanship to Umberto, Gianni's brother, this summer as originally planned.

Agnelli argued at the time that the market turmoil, the poor group results and the fact that Fiat had just launched a complex L5,000bn package of measures to raise cash meant investors did not want a new hand on the tiller. Some now believe the real reason was that neither Agnelli nor Romiti wanted a new chairman and chief executive to claim the credit for Fiat's recovery.

Certainly there was no hint of impending change at last month's shareholder assembly, where Agnelli forecast a return to profit for the group this year. But in a company attempting to eliminate unnecessarily hierarchical management and to create, in the words of one executive, "a flat and wide [management] unit", the dynastic structure of Fiat's top management is beginning to look increasingly out of date.

Fig 11.1 Source: *Financial Times*, 11 July 1994

struction. Confindustria is the peak association to which are affiliated industrial organisations at a national level and, often at regional or provincial levels, multi-industrial organisations. Confindustria tends to co-ordinate national-level bargaining in the various major industrial groupings and act on behalf of members on multi-industry, national-level issues. This sometimes involves entering into a bargaining relationship with both unions and government. Politically, Confindustria has had links with DC (Democrazia Christiana – the Christian Democrats), although many smaller employers appear to have supported the right-wing alliance in the 1994 election.

Despite being the only peak association, Confindustria has sometimes found it impossible to unite different interests among its members, and has found it difficult to adopt and present a single coherent policy. In recent times, the balance of power and influence seems to have changed within Confindustria and some of the industrial associations, the smaller employers perhaps flexing their muscles in favour of flexibility.

There is a separate association of independent small and medium-sized firms called CONFAPI[5], and other small associations in particular specialised industries. The public enterprise sector also has employers' organisations linked to each of the state holding companies. INTERSIND is for public enterprise, ASAP[6] is for public sector oil and petrochemical enterprises.

THE ROLE OF PERSONNEL

The origins of the personnel function were in the regulated areas of labour relations and payroll. It gained strategic significance, and board-level representation, in the 1960s and 1970s when labour relations were highly volatile. The personnel managers' association AIDP, which has only 2200 members, is not very influential. Many personnel practitioners have legal backgrounds and much time is spent dealing with works councils and interpreting legislation and national constraints. Companies employing more than 15 people must have employee-only works councils which bargain at company level on local collective issues and represent individuals on disciplinary and grievance matters.[7]

LABOUR MARKET

- Italy suffers from a declining birth rate and ageing population. This problem is more acute in the wealthy North.

- There is a total labour force of just over 24 million, with approximately 2.7 million unemployed. Women represent 51 per cent of the population and 37 per cent of the total workforce.

Recruitment

- There have been restrictions on employers in recruiting directly from the labour market. Under the system of *collocamento,* run by the Ministry of Labour, all prospective employees are obliged to register at a district employment bureau. According to the state placement system, requests by an employer to a local placement office may be *numerica,* for a specified number of employees, or *nominative,* for a specifically named individual. In recent years there has been a decline in hiring by numbers, which has been the tradition with manual staff, fostered by legislation in 1991 giving the employer greater discretion.
- In response to labour market shortages there has been a growth in recruitment consultants and executive search firms, which are able to advise companies on suitable managerial talent.
- Close links have been established between companies and universities, and greater flexibility has been applied in respect of new contracts of employment to encourage part-time and women workers.

Selection

- For managerial staff in larger concerns CVs or application forms are normally required and interviews are common, with psychometric tests gaining in popularity. Small businesses are likely to use less formal methods such as personal recommendation and word of mouth.
- Several categories of worker are subject to compulsory hiring practices. Any employer with more than 35 employees must retain a minimum of 15 per cent of staff from one or more of the following categories: disabled, blind, deaf and mute, orphans and widows of those killed at work or in war.
- The Sex Rights Equalisation Law (1977) prohibits all forms of sex discrimination in recruitment, with certain exceptions.

Remuneration

- Collective agreements are negotiated by employers' associations and trade unions at national level and establish minimum wages, taking into account job category, seniority and cost of living, as well as maximum working hours (48 per week), holidays, sickness and maternity benefits. These apply nationally to all employees, including managers, directors, non-union members and non-signatory employers. There are further agreements at company level, as well as individual contracts between employer and each employee, which contain specific terms and conditions. National agreements deal also with training, disclosure of strategic information, and the *scala mobile* (wage indexation agreement) under which automatic increases related to the cost of living are paid every six months.

- Job evaluation has been largely rejected on the grounds that it is divisive; although some large concerns, e.g. Olivetti, do have such schemes.
- Performance-related pay is most widespread in the commercial sector and is predominantly negotiated at individual level. Fringe benefits tend to be available at senior management and director level only.
- The laws on equality in the workplace (1977) and affirmative action on sex discrimination (1991) guarantee women equal salaries and benefits at the workplace. There is a state-run service of daycare facilities for working mothers, looking after children from the age of one.
- Social security and pension provisions are generous and Italian employees have significant job protection rights as well as protection indemnities.

Training and development

- Three types of school exist, including technical schools. Leavers of such schools are normally qualified to find employment without having to go to university.
- At university level, there are only a few institutions specialising in technical and management studies, including *politderic* of Milan and Turin which specialise in engineering and architecture, and Bocconi (Milan), LUISS (Roma) and the European Business School (Parma), which specialise in business and management and have been highly influenced by north American schools.
- At company level there has been an emphasis on continuous training. Traditional apprenticeships have given way considerably to *contratti di formazione,* job training contracts available to 15–29 year olds which last for two years. If employers enter into these, employment contributions are reduced.
- The education and training system is under review, with the government undertaking to increase investment in this area.

Current issues

The dynamism of the Italian economy has largely been maintained by the growth of small, family-owned businesses, which have spearheaded the use of flexible employment contracts despite the complicated and restrictive nature of labour legislation. Small businesses often obtain economies of scale by forming co-operatives. In 1986, legislation was passed to encourage young people to start their own co-operatives. By the end of 1989 4000 such projects had been approved. This has been parallelled by a trend towards decentralisation of production in larger enterprises.

A number of large organisations are also introducing flexibility into reward packages. Credito Italiano is introducing new salary schemes which pay greater attention to merit. Fiat is to some extent cutting across Italian cultural and structural arrangements by introducing HRM-type practices. It now runs an integrated programme covering job evaluation of training needs and assessment potential. This contributes to a company's internationalism by establishing a common culture linking operating units round the world, and facilitating international job mobility.[8] More generally, it would appear that restructuring is likely to occur in employment, geared towards job security and benefiting from automatic pay increases, as well as a hefty social security provision, especially in the area of pensions. The need for management development would appear to be pressing, as few employees are university educated. Furthermore, women only occupy around 5 per cent of managerial positions.

TRADE UNIONS

Employees' rights to organise collectively and indeed to strike are embodied within the Constitution of 1948, and further legislative support for workers' rights to join, establish and undertake trade union activities was contained within the 1970 Workers' Statute[9], discussed in more detail below.

Trade unions in Italy have traditionally pursued objectives of a social and political nature and have always claimed to represent interest groups broader than those of their membership. The movement has tended to concentrate on activity at industrial, multi-industrial and national level. Company and workplace organisation has become an issue for the trade unions in recent decades, prompted in part by the 1970 statute.

The traditions of trade union organisation are industrial and multi-industrial at provincial, regional and national levels. In recent years occupational unionism has become a more common feature amongst professional and managerial employees, particularly in the public sector. However, the absence of a craft or job base for trade union membership may explain why the trade unions' response to pressures for labour flexibility and the introduction of such schemes as job enlargement, enrichment, multi-skilling and autonomous work groups has been more positive than in some other countries. Nevertheless, this does not mean that the unions simply accept job losses and restructuring plans, as disputes within Alitalia and Fiat in 1994 show. In the Alitalia case, proposed job losses were cut from 4000 to around 1600 plus 800 early retirements, and proposals to rewrite contracts unilaterally were modified. However, and no doubt a sign of the impact of recession and market environment, the Alitalia agreement reached in July did require union concessions on pay – a freeze until 1996 – and on many restrictive working practices, longer hours and greater labour use flexibility.

The main manual worker trade unions are affiliated to one of three national confederations.

Union confederations, orientations and membership
CGIL – *Confederazione Generale Italiana del Lavoro* – Italian General Confederation of Labour.

- Communist/socialist political affinity.
- Largest membership at approximately 5.15 million, of which 2.725 million were employed. Wide, class-based, revolutionary traditions and objectives.
- Coming to terms with new political and industrial realities and has modified objectives, the 1991 Conference effectively giving up class struggle, favouring collective bargaining and industrial democracy.

CISL – *Confederazione Italiana dei Sindacati Lavoratori* – Italian Confederation of Workers Unions.

- Catholic, Christian democrat affinity in early postwar period, but the Catholic dimension has been eroded and replaced by socialism and currently a concern for social solidarity.
- Membership approximately 3.5 million, of which 2 million are employed.

UIL – *Unione Italiana del Lavoro* – Italian Union of Labour.

- Centre/socialist.
- Class-based traditions but currently emphasises the representation of workers as citizens.

- Membership approximately 1.5 million, of which 1.1 million are employed.

The membership figures are derived from Ferner and Hyman[10] and apply to 1990. The estimates given in Figure 11.2 are close to these figures and certainly do not indicate substantial overall decline.

These confederations have strong political affiliations. Initially, the largest of the confederations, the CGIL was formed by the opponents of Mussolini. After the war, political differences and schisms at national level resulted in splits within the CGIL, eventually resulting in the late 1940s in the formation of the two other main confederations, the CISL and the UIL.

Each of these confederations has national 'representative union status' and this entitles them to participation in a number of consultative and administrative tripartite organisations and mechanisms, for example the CIG, the earnings maintenance fund which pays laid-off employees up to 80 per cent of wages during the period of lay-off.

Relationships between these three main confederations have in recent years become more co-operative and, since the decline of communism and subsequent political upheavals and developments, increasing pressures exist for the confederations to unite. Indeed, it has become increasingly difficult to identify significant policy differences. They did unite once before, in 1972/3, after agreement was reached between them that union officials would not also hold political party or parliamentary positions. However, they eventually separated again in 1984 after several years of difficulties and differences between them. The final separation in 1984 was the direct result of disagreements over the *scala mobile* (see Chapter 3, p.48).

Another distinguishing feature of trade unionism in Italy is the high level of union membership among managers. Managers have their own national confederation, the CIDA – *Confederazione Italiana Dirigenti di Azienda* – and it is by no means unusual in large organisations for a majority of managers to be members of a union. One of the reasons for the relatively high level of union membership among managers may be the high proportion of their pay and benefits packages determined by agreement at levels outside the organisation. Usually managers' terms and conditions are covered by a separate agreement at sectoral or national level. Even in the 1990s it is uncommon for more than 20 per cent of the total pay for managers to be determined within the organisation, and it is argued that the scope for conflict between managers

Italian unions – facing up to crisis

Unions have a central and legally protected place in the Italian system of industrial relations. The constitution specifically guarantees "the free right of trade unionism" and the main law on employees' rights, the Workers Statute, prohibits an employer from: "Impeding or limiting union freedoms, including the right to strike". In addition the Workers Statute also allows unions to draw up legally enforceable collective agreements binding on the categories covered in the agreement, regardless of whether or not they are members of the union.

The majority of Italian trade unionists are in three separate trade union confederations. The largest, CGIL (Confederazione Generale Italiana del Lavoro), has 5.2 million members. The second largest union is CISL (Confederazione Italiana dei Sindicati Lavoratori) with 3.5m members. The third confederation, UIL (Unione Italiana del Lavoro), is much smaller than the other two with a membership of 1.6m. In total about 40% of the Italian workforce is organised in the three confederations.

All three confederations have a similar internal structure in that they are made up of industrial federations and geographical organisations. Unlike the situation in the UK or Germany these lower level organisations broadly reflect the positions of the confederations rather than having an independent role.

The three major Italian confederations are divided by differing trade union strategies and on political lines, although they are all formally separate from political parties.

CGIL has traditionally been linked with what was the Italian Communist Party (PCI), now the Party of the Democratic Left, and its general secretary has consistently been a member of the party.

However, the confederation has always had within its membership a strong grouping of socialist supporters and at its October 1991 congress in a major shift, the party-based factions within CGIL were dissolved and the confederation committed itself to "modernisation and moderation".

CISL, in comparison, although officially non-denominational, has traditionally had a large base of catholic workers among its members and much of its leadership has been Christian Democrat. It has therefore, more or less, supported the dominant grouping in Italian politics since the war. However, since the 1970s it has sought to reduce its links with the party to adopt a more trade union role.

UIL, the smallest confederation, was founded in 1950 in opposition to the international policy pursued by CGIL. Politically it supports the social democratic and republican parties, but also has a socialist current.

Despite these differences the three Italian confederations have been able to co-operate with one another in the past – they are all affiliated to the European TUC for example – and in the last few years there have been some moves towards greater unity. In 1991 a pact between them was signed to establish new workplace representative organisations, to identify the essential points of agreement and to establish a framework for discussion of more contentious issues.

In part the pressure to reach agreement between the confederations is accounted for by a decline in employed membership. The overall membership figures for all three confederations rose over the 1980s. But this increase is explained by an enormous growth in the number of retired members in the unions. Figures from the CGIL research body, Ires, indicate that, while in 1981 20% of members

in the three confederations were pensioners, by 1990 39% of the membership consisted of those who had retired. The employed membership of the unions fell by 15% between 1981 and 1990, with CGIL worse affected with a 20% drop.

The three confederations also face a challenge from the activities of the Cobas (comitati di base). These are unofficial workplace organisations which developed in the 1980s with particular strength in parts of the public sector, such as teaching and the railways, and in large scale manufacturing. Although they do not formally have trade union status they have organised effective industrial action on several occasions and have concluded some agreements with employers. Their aim is winning equal status to the established unions.

Italy's current economic and political crisis has affected the trade union movement. The government's 1992 austerity programme and trade union reaction to it has produced divisions both between the confederations and within the largest of them, CGIL. The general secretary of CGIL, Bruno Trentin, resigned following severe criticism by his own executive of an agreement he had signed with the government. However he later agreed to withdraw his resignation. There have also been a number of instances of senior trade union figures being involved in the broader bribery and corruption scandal currently affecting Italy and to forestall further criticism the unions have withdrawn their nominees from a number of public bodies.

The lasting impact of these events is unclear. National strikes organised by the unions last year were strongly supported. But the confederations have also been criticised for failing to respond more vigorously to the government's plans.

Fig 11.2 Source: *Labour Research*, June 1993

and their employing organisation is correspondingly limited. Managers are, therefore, relatively unlikely to experience conflict between their role as manager and that as union member.

As in many other countries, the 1980s and 1990s have been difficult for the traditional trade unions in Italy: recessions, unemployment, structural change to industry and the labour force, enhanced activity in the workplace often prompted by management initiatives concerning work organisation and the introduction of new technology, political scandal and upheaval, and in some instances rank-and-file discontent, both with the policies being pursued at the centre and with deals done locally. Against this background union membership has declined, the CGIL and CISL being the main losers while the UIL has retained relative stability. In sectoral terms, there has been a decline in both membership and density in manufacturing, agriculture and services, with perhaps the most worrying being the trend in services where employment increased but membership decreased. Trade union membership in the public sector increased through the 1980s and much of this was in autonomous unions, often occupationally based and in certain sectors, e.g. education; the degree of support has justified the unions' inclusion in collective bargaining. Nationally the scale of the decline in density among employed members of the three main confederations was from 49 per cent in 1980 to 39 per cent in 1990[11]. This was after a decade of growth in the 1970s.

Union membership in Italy includes both retired and unemployed members, which explains the difference between total membership and employed membership. In both the CGIL and the CSIL these categories constitute an increasing proportion of aggregate membership. In Figure 11.2 there is an estimate of 39 per cent of total retired membership of the three confederations. This reflects trends in the population at large, and it was estimated in June 1994 that the more than 20 million pensioners outnumbered the working population despite the increase in compulsory retirement ages in 1993.[12]

Although there has been a decline in union membership the traditional confederations are still able to mobilise their support, as was apparent on a number of occasions in 1992 and 1993 when all three confederations organised strike action in protest at government policies or lack of policies to deal with economic crises.

The position of the three main confederations has, if anything, worsened since 1993; politically only the CGIL has retained traditional links and direction, the others have been rendered almost 'lost' by the considerable political upheavals. Currently they retain their representative status but they are under attack from CISNAL[13] (a neo-fascist confederation which currently claims a membership in excess of 2 million[14], which would put it above UIL in size) and also from some of the militant shop-steward committees known as Cobas.[15] CISNAL has the potential advantage of

its affinity with the MSI, one of the governing coalition parties.

Workplace organisation

The trade unions were not present in the workplace in any active sense before the 1970s. The rank-and-file activity associated with the autumn of 1969 and the Workers' Statute of 1970 are significant milestones in the development and formalisation of workplace-based trade union organisation and activity.

The 1970 Statute gave employees in organisations with more than 15 employees (not trade unions) the right to organise, carry out trade union activities and form a new workplace union representative structure called the RSA (*rappresentanza sindicate aziendale*). These have to be formed within the context of the main confederations or trade unions signatory to the appropriate agreement, and members were given various legal rights and protections from discriminatory and disciplinary action by employers. The legislation did not prescribe any particular organisational format or representative structure; that was left to the participants and has been a continuing source of difficulty, with the federations often unable to agree on which should have how many seats and how to deal with the representation of non-union members.

Before the 1970 Statute, spontaneous development had led in many organisations to the election of non-confederation delegates to represent workers' grievances and demands to management, and also to the organisation of non-confederation-based rank-and-file committees within companies to negotiate and if necessary organise industrial action. These committees were often consolidated into factory works councils (CdF – *consiglio di fabbrica*). These factory councils represented all employers whether union members or not and contained non-union delegates.

After the 1970 statute, and particularly after the reunification of the three main confederations in 1972/3, the Statute's provisions were often used by the unions to confirm the *de facto* CdF mechanism as the unitary vehicle of shopfloor and workplace-based organisation. In many organisations the RSA and CdF became one and the same and the CdF, with no statutory basis of its own, was given rights to bargain by collective agreement. However, inter-union rivalries and tensions have bedevilled the establishment of successful and lasting mechanisms at this level, and the tensions between the unions at national level in the late 1970s and early 1980s posed particular and significant difficulties. The fact that such organisations have survived is tribute more to the activities of shopfloor delegates and activists rather than to any activity at national level. Often CdFs have shown their opposition to policies being pursued at confederation level, particularly when the confederations have co-operated with government and employers in corporatist-style arrangements incorporating wage restraint, as for example in the late 1970s.

The three main confederations and affiliates have sought throughout the last decade to enhance their influence and control of workplace representation, threatened as they have been by declining membership, the emergence of autonomous unions, declining significance of national bargaining and increasing initiatives by employers to restructure work and employment. They have sought on a number of occasions to agree an alternative and satisfactory workplace representative structure, one of the most recent being a preliminary agreement in 1991 to create at workplace level unitary union representative bodies – RSUs, *rapprasentanza sindicate unitaria*. This structure provides for workforce election of representatives, nominated by the appropriate trade unions, but with each confederation being guaranteed a proportion of the seats on the council. It therefore did not address the continuing problem of representation of non-union members and/or the workplace role of non-representative unions and the rank-and-file movement. The intention was that these bodies would act as channels of communication between workplace and union, between management and workforce, and that they would negotiate where appropriate with management, at the same time preserving agreement between the unions. A further agreement on the issue of 'fair' and appropriate workplace representation was reached towards the end of December 1993, seeking to build on the RSU concept and the Accord of July 1993 (see Chapter 3, pp.48–9).

The July 1993 tripartite agreement provided for the possibility of legislation on workplace/company-level representation since the RSUs were given an important role in the new agreed two-tier bargaining structure. This possibility of legislation, allied to the establishment in the Accord of a number of agreed principles relating to company-level representation, seems to have provided the impetus needed to persuade the employers and representative confederations to reach the December 1993 agreement.

This latter bipartite agreement was divided into two chapters, one dealing with the establishment and operation of RSUs and the other with election procedures. As a result of this agreement, the three main confederations are guaranteed at least one-third of the seats on every RSU established. RSU members are to be elected by the whole workforce by secret ballot and there was agreement on mechanisms for trying to ensure that the membership of the RSU reflects the structure of the workforce, including middle managers. The number of seats is related to size by a simple numerical formula. Rights granted to RSA representatives under the Workers' Statute are transferred to RSU representatives and the role of the RSA is also transferred – the RSU replaces the RSA and is empowered to bargain and agree within the constraints established by the appropriate national collective agreement.

It must be remembered that this is an agreement between the three main representative union confederations, INTERSIND and Confindustria; it is not legislation and not surprisingly has been subject to criticism by other union confederations, autonomous unions and rank-and-file committees. The tendency towards workplace activity has also forced the confederations to strengthen their provincial arrangements and organisation, and has placed greater emphasis on the activities of individual affiliate unions rather than the confederations.

GOVERNMENT

We have already noted that elements of the system, in particular employee rights and substantive outcomes in terms of minimum standards, are highly regulated. Additionally, there is substantial state intervention in ownership of enterprises and a sizeable public services sector. The government has also involved both union and employer confederations at a national level, sometimes via fairly direct bargaining, sometimes via tripartite consultative mechanisms, and sometimes in the administration of employment and social welfare schemes, all indications of corporatist traditions.

Some employee rights are contained within the constitution, others were granted via the Workers' Statute 1970, and many others are the product of the legislative enforcement of terms of collective agreements made at industry and multi-industry levels. The latter process was first used in 1959 when legal force was given to existing collective agreements as effective minimum entitlements for employees. Collective agreements are normally universally applicable to organisations within the relevant sector(s) irrespective of whether the employer is a member of the relevant organisation and whether the employees are unionised. Examples of legislative intervention in and regulation of the employment relationship include areas of subject matter such as:

- minimum pay;
- maximum hours of work;
- night working;
- recruitment processes;
- disciplinary and dismissal processes and compensation;
- rights to issue fixed-term or part-time contracts;
- rights to introduce change unilaterally;
- employees' rights to information and consultation on certain issues and in certain circumstances;
- rights to undertake trade union activities and not to be discriminated against;
- right to strike (recently regulated in public sector);
- earnings maintenance during lay-off.

The process of interaction in the private sector is by and large unregulated and has been left to the parties to devise and operate; the December 1993 agreement on RSUs is an example. The incentive for the employer to recognise trade unions and to bargain with them is to some extent provided by the fact that a weakening of the minimum standards created by statute and in favour of the employer is only allowed as a product of collective agreement.

The state is a major employer with approximately 16 per cent of all employment being in the public services sector and a considerable number employed indirectly via the state holding companies which control the public enterprise sector.

Public services sector

The public services sector includes national and local government public services such as education, social security and health. Public service employees were traditionally privileged in terms of working conditions, security of employment and retirement benefits, and levels of union membership have been high. However, over the last two decades this privileged position has been eroded and this erosion has, no doubt, contributed to increasing public sector employee militancy, as evidenced in the late 1980s and early 1990s. Government in Italy, faced with economic crises and the perceived need to exert control over wage increases and public expenditure, has in common with other countries sought to use the public sector as an example.

In recent years efforts to limit wage increases in the public sector have often failed, with final agreements breaching the guidelines established and often also exceeding increases won in the private sector. Efforts by government to introduce wage freezes in the public sector in late 1992 and early 1993 prompted resistance and widespread strike action. Strike action in the public sector has often been unofficial and organised by the rank-and-file committees called *cobas* and autonomous union 'groupings' representing white-collar, professional and other occupational groups not affiliated to the major confederations and not content with the essentially socialist and egalitarian policies and objectives pursued by them. Often these groups of employees have been unhappy with the policies pursued nationally, the *scala mobile* and other flat-rate agreements which have resulted in an erosion of differentials.

These problems prompted government in 1990 to enact legislation for the first time regulating public service sector employees' right to strike. Employees contemplating such action are required to give 10 days' notice and in essential services to maintain a minimum service.

In 1983 government and the main confederations had agreed a framework for the rationalisation and institutionalisation of collective bargaining in the public sector. This agreement proposed eight sectors, each of which would conclude its own agreement on pay, subject to cabinet approval, with cross-sectoral negotiations on issues such as training provision and equal opportunities. There was also some provision for decentralised bargaining, but not on pay. The law enacting this framework specifies also the areas of prerogative retained by the state as employer – framework law for Public Employment (Law 93) 1983.

Public enterprise sector

There is a strong tradition of government intervention via complete or partial ownership of enterprises. Government directly controls some large operations, for example the railways, but in most cases these enterprises are controlled via one of three state holding companies. The two main holding companies are IRI[16], the Institute for Industrial Reconstruction, which controls hundreds of subsidiaries organised into industrial groupings; and ENI[17], the National Petrochemical Agency. IRI had been used for many years as a mechanism for ensuring the continued existence of companies that were in difficulties, but in the 1980s rationalisation was pursued, with some of the companies being effectively privatised.

Companies in the public enterprise sector are operated through the holding companies as if they were privately owned, but government obviously can influence the employment relationship and terms and conditions of employment through indirect mechanisms and pressures. Each holding company has its own employers' association, the largest and most influential of which is INTERSIND which represents companies within the IRI complex.

As noted earlier, there are in 1994 plans to privatise large sections of this sector, which comprised close to 500 companies towards the end of 1993, employing 400 000 people. The Berlusconi government has announced its intention to proceed with the privatisation previously devised and including telecommunications, electricity, oil and gas, and insurance. This programme obviously has significant implications for the various holding companies.

The public enterprise sector has been used in the past to set an example to the private sector with respect to employment and employee relations policies, procedures and practices. The most notable instance of this was in 1984 and is referred to as the IRI protocol. This is, in essence, a procedural agreement which seeks to establish procedural mechanisms for dealing with minor disputes, and for ensuring fairly comprehensive consultation. It proposed a structure of group, sector enterprise and plant-level joint consultative committees, and specified rights to information and consultation on a specified range of subject matter including investment decisions, introduction of new technology, acquisitions, employment levels and prospects, and corporate strategy. Some individual sector agreements have gone further. It must be remembered that the protocol proposed consultation only; employers did not give up as part of this agreement their right to decide these issues. The protocol, as was intended, has had an influence on private sector institutions and systems.

PROCESSES

The main process for resolving differences between employers and employees and for determining terms and conditions of employment and parties' employment rights is collective bargaining. This occurs at a number of levels, national, industrial, regional and provincial and within companies, although as noted

earlier the July 1993 Accord envisages a simplified two-tier bargaining system. In recent years, bargaining at plant or company level has become more common, partly in response to employer initiatives with respect to enhancing flexibility of work organisation and employment contract, linking pay and performance, and introducing new technology; and partly due to employees who, disaffected with the outcomes of national and sectoral agreements, have been seeking more influence over work organisation and their terms and conditions of employment. There is evidence that employees have become more instrumental in their attitude towards work and less concerned with ideological objectives such as solidarity and egalitarianism. At the same time, white-collar, professional and similar occupational groupings, particularly in the public service sector, have been keen to pursue their own interests. Since these groups have not traditionally been catered for by the main confederations and have not as yet been widely included in the bargaining machinery or processes at national and industrial levels, they have sought to secure their objectives through activity and pressure at the level of the organisation or enterprise. It is arguable whether the new RSU procedures will do much to help resolve these problems of the effective representation of interests not affiliated to the three main confederations.

Plant- or company-level bargaining was encouraged by the 1970 Workers' Statute and, as was noted above, the main union confederations have been seeking ways since then of encompassing bargaining within the company, at the same time as maintaining some sort of acceptable pro rata influence between themselves in the national framework.

It is important also to reiterate that the outcomes of bargaining are frequently given legal effect and are effectively extended to cover companies and other employing organisations within the appropriate sector. The bargaining process has not been significantly regulated, there is no legal compulsion on employers to recognise or to bargain, but employees do have rights to organise and take part in such activities. Agreements, certainly at higher levels, are usually for a fixed period but industrial action can be taken at any time, there being no legal regulation and no legal distinction drawn between rights and interest.

Different subject matter tends to be dealt with at each level and, despite the increase in bargaining at plant level in recent years, it still seems to be the case that more than 80 per cent of pay and benefits packages are the product of bargaining and legislation outside the firm. Many large organisations are seeking to enhance their discretion in order to link pay and benefits to organisational performance and in order to enhance individualisation of the employment contract.

At national level, the subject matter of bargaining includes minimum wage rates, holiday entitlements, pension provisions, maximum hours of work, and for many years, until 1992, included the *scala mobile* system of automatic wage indexation. At this level relationships have been highly politicised, with conflict between the union confederations being as likely as conflict between them and employers' associations. Bargaining at this level has been favoured by the main union confederations, given their political and social objectives.

At industry level there are many agreements, and the proliferation of bargaining within industrial sectors and within companies has tended to result in a shift of emphasis away from the confederations to the industrial organisations of employers and unions. Bargaining at this level has tended to occur at approximately three-year intervals, and usually excludes topics dealt with at a multi-sector national level. The subject matter might well include job descriptions and classifications, vacation arrangements, disciplinary procedures, disclosure of information to employees, introduction of new technology, regrading procedures, and training provision and entitlements. Often, and increasingly in recent years, agreements at this level have taken the form of seeking to provide appropriate procedural and other frameworks within which issues could be dealt with at lower levels, provincial or in-company. The 1994 sectoral agreement covering engineering workers provides for wages to rise only in line with the official inflation index until 1996. The agreement is for a 39-hour week and makes provision for increases above this figure to be agreed locally but linked to improvements in productivity or profitability.

Plant or company bargaining has been expanding as indicated above, and it is at this level increasingly that agreements made at higher levels are 'tailored' to suit the situational requirements. It is at this level that discretionary pay and benefits will be determined, technology is actually introduced and implications discussed, health and safety issues are dealt with, jobs are located within agreed grading and classification schemes, and hours of work are agreed and distributed. It has been common at this level for claims to be formulated within the workplace committee or factory council but for the negotiations to be dealt with by provincial or industrial representatives of the appropriate unions and employers' organisations, although the size of the company is likely to be a consideration and in larger organisations management is more likely to bargain itself and to do so at company as opposed to plant level.

It seems possible that relationships at company level have become more collaborative. The unions in Italy have, in recent years, been ready to collaborate in the introduction and management of change. No doubt this has been facilitated by the existence of schemes such as the CIG, providing for the maintenance of earnings in periods of lay-off, which cushion the financial implications for employees of employment and work reorganisation. However, it may also be a product, as noted earlier, of the industrial/ideological base of union organisation and membership, which has not encouraged a 'job control' approach and arguably has contributed to a less suspicious and insecure response to proposals involving multi-skilling and flexibility.

CASE STUDIES

Benetton

Benetton, the leading manufacturer and retailer of casual clothes and accessories for adults and children, is an owner-managed company whose unique way of working is a prime example of Italian flexibility.

The company employs 1700 people in a core unit, which produces the resources needed to drive and control the outside. A further 50 000 work within the Benetton empire but are not on the payroll. Most of Benetton's production and distribution operations are subcontracted, or in some countries carried out under licence or through joint ventures. The 6000 Benetton shops in 100 countries are managed by private enterprises in partnership with Benetton. The network is connected by 'agents', entrepreneurs who are responsible for developing and controlling areas and regions. Many of them own or part-own shops.

The personnel function selects, trains and socialises these agents into the Benetton way. It also keeps the network connected, which is not just a matter of information technology, but also of influencing attitudes. This is no mean task considering how dramatically the company has grown in a short time.

Agents and factory heads are trained within the system to work outside it, as subcontractors or shop owners. Most of the training is on-the-job, but conventional training is used to impart the firm's values and philosophies.

While respecting the national contracts, Franco Furno, Benetton's personnel director, regards them as obsolete. 'They don't cater for rapid change and rapid staff development as we have here.' With a larger number of creative staff who often have a high individual worth, he does not find traditional salary surveys particularly relevant either because they look at relativities and differentials. Performance appraisal is carried out every year, but does not use sophisticated techniques. Benetton's approach to management is back to basics.

The Benetton family takes a strategic view of the business, but they also made a choice to stay involved in day-to-day issues. This may seem an inefficient use of senior resources, but it enables them to keep in touch with the business and still switch quickly to the big decisions.

Because of the family control, two systems of reporting have grown up. Everyone has two bosses – their manager and one of the Benetton chiefs. This can cause crises because, as Furno puts it: 'You talk to your immediate boss in a language of costs and control and talk to the padrone in another, of quality and vision.'

Source: *Personnel Management*, April 1992, p.32

Alitalia

The Italian airline Alitalia is part of the IRI state holding company. In the late 1980s the company was divided into strategic business units, each with its own personnel function. However, a central personnel department retains responsibility for company-wide strategy and works with personnel and line managers from the business units to ensure consistent standards in selection and training.

Alitalia runs several large, professional training centres to train air crew, ground staff and management in technical as well as management skills. In 1989 the company launched a total quality management programme which is just entering the second of four phases of operation. This represents a major culture change for the whole group.

Alitalia has a highly sophisticated 'integrated personnel plan' which links all areas of organisation and management development. It includes a Hay-designed 'management by objectives' performance appraisal programme and assessment centres.

National contract negotiations are handled for Alitalia by INTERSIND, the employers' association for the whole IRI group. Because of its size, however, the airline is well represented in this association and its industrial relations staff are able to influence negotiations with the unions.

Although the national contracts prescribe a significant part of the remuneration package, personnel staff in the strategic business units review salary trends in the market to ensure that Alitalia remains competitive. Under a recently introduced scheme for sales staff, bonus payments can make up 25 per cent of their salaries.

Alitalia's personnel manager for the UK and Ireland, Lucio Rigo, finds British trade unions easier to deal with than their Italian counterparts. 'Here you have room to manoeuvre,' he says. 'Relations are oriented towards involving staff in the problems of the business and the trade unions are more inclined to understand the realities of business life. But things are also moving in that direction in Italy.'

Certainly labour relations in Italy are improving. While Alitalia was plagued with strikes in the 1970s, in 1990 it was judged by the Association of European Airlines as the most punctual and reliable airline in Europe.

Source: *Personnel Management*, April 1992, p.33

SUMMARY

The Italian system is still relatively centralised and regulated, and the July 1993 Accord tended to reinforce this despite the references within it to decentralisation and deregulation.

The political scandals and upheavals allied to economic crises of the early 1990s have resulted in relatively weak government, and this has mitigated any desire there might have been at government level to limit union and employee influence and involvement through collective bargaining. Employers are keen to pursue objectives of labour flexibility, individualisation and productivity, but so far largely within the existing institutions and framework. Structural decline and change are significant issues and government is still seeking to address them through corporatist arrangements, although we must expect the new coalition to rely more on market forces in the long run.

The union confederations have been tainted by their involvement with government. The demise of communism and diminution of differences between them raise the issue of whether there is now any real justification for their remaining separate. They have been forced to confront their objectives, and to some extent the movement can be characterised as lacking direction and grappling with the choice between class solidarity and social transformation, on the one hand, and social partnership on the other. One of the main threats facing the confederations is how to cope with shopfloor movements and autonomous unions of an occupational or professional nature. Should they be brought into the existing, formalised bargaining structures and, if so, how, given the different interests and objectives that they represent? Neither of the 1993 agreements really comprehensively and satisfactorily addresses this issue.

So far there has been relatively little progress in developing participatory mechanisms other than collective bargaining. Employers have not been keen to do this, and the unions have found it difficult to agree on the detailed arrangements for any such representation, although the December 1993 agreement does hold out the possibility that an effective workplace representative and participatory mechanism has been devised. Nevertheless, collective bargaining is to remain the dominant process.

NOTES AND REFERENCES

1. Piore and Sabel (1994) *The Second Industrial Divide,* Basic Books, New York

2. Ferner A and Hyman R (1992) 'Italy between political exchange and micro corporation' in Ferner A and Hyman R (eds), *Industrial Relations in the New Europe,* Blackwell, p.555

3. Caplan J (1992) 'It's the Climate that Counts – Personnel Management in Italy', *Personnel Management*, April, pp.32–5. See case study at end of this chapter.

4. Confindustria – Confederazione Generale del Industria Italiana

5. CONFAPI – Confederazione della Piccola & Media Industria.

6. ASAP – Associanione Sindicate per le Aziende Petrochemicale e Collegate a Partecipazione Statate

7. Caplan J, op. cit.

8. Ibid.

9. Workers statute – Statute dei Lavoratori – 1970

10. Ferner A and Hyman R op. cit. p.545

11. Ibid. and appendix 14

12. *Financial Times* 16 June 1994

13. Confederazione Italiana Sindicati Nazionali Lavoratori

14. *Guardian* 4 May 1994 – 'Italian Unions ready to do business with Berlusconi', John Glover

15. COBAS – Comitat di base

16. IRI – Instituto per la Ricostruzione Industriale

17. ENI – Ente Nazionale Idrocarburi

FURTHER READING

Baglioni G (1991) 'An Italian mosaic: Collective bargaining patterns in the 1980s', *International Labour Review*, 130 (1) pp.81–93

Giugni G (1987) 'Social concertation and the political system in Italy', *Labour and Society,* 12, 379–83

Hegewisch A (1991) 'The decentralisation of pay bargaining: European comparisons', *Personnel Review* 20 (6), pp.28–35.

'Italy: Central agreement on company level representation' (1994) *European Industrial Relations Review*, no. 241, February

'Italy: Central agreement on incomes policy and bargaining reforms' (1993) *European Industrial Relations Review*, no. 236, September

Negrelli S and Santi E (1990) 'Industrial relations in Italy' in Baglioni G and Crouch C (eds), *European Industrial Relations*, Sage, pp.154–98

Pellegrini C (1993) 'Industrial relations in Italy' in Bamber G and Lansbury R (eds), *International and Comparative Industrial Relations,* 2nd edition, pp.126–48

Sirianni C A (1992) 'Human resource management in Italy', *Employee Relations*, 14 (5), pp.23–8

Treu T (1988) 'Trade union democracy and industrial relations', *Bulletin of Comparative Labour Relations,* 18, pp.51–4

Treu T (1989) 'Industrial relations, tripartism and concerted action: where do we stand?', *International Journal of Comparative Law and Industrial Relations*, 5, pp.43–55

12 · THE NETHERLANDS

BACKGROUND

A number of the world's leading companies have originated in the Netherlands, including Shell, Philips and Unilever. This has promoted a secure, internal economy with solid international linkages.

An emphasis on democracy. has fostered participative leadership styles and has been built on the effective working of collaborative arrangements at the workplace. Companies with 35 or more employees must establish a works council which is selected directly by employees. This council is consulted on mergers, closures and significant reorganisations, and has to consent to decisions on pensions, working time, merit systems, safety, training and appraisal. However, a number of articles of faith are now being questioned in the more volatile economic climate of the 1990s.

EMPLOYERS

Dutch employers are well organised and fragmented along the fault lines of the various religious and ideological pillars referred to in earlier chapters. They have been willing to participate with the unions and government in centralised mechanisms for determining terms and conditions of employment and social and economic policy and, while they have been in the forefront of company-level bargaining developments in recent years, they show little interest in totally disbanding industry-level arrangements for greater activity within the company. The Price Waterhouse/Cranfield project[1] data indicate that in 1991 in the Netherlands, 78 per cent of organisations still bargained at national or industry level over the basic pay of manual workers. It is open to the parties to improve on the terms of such industry-level agreements and to do so at company level, and while there has been a tendency towards increased use of the company-level flexibility, many employers are reluctant to engage in bargaining over the same subject matter at two different levels. Visser[2] estimates that company-level agreements now affect approximately one-third of employees.

In recent circumstances of relatively high unemployment, employers have been able to dictate more the direction, nature and scope of collective bargaining, and the pressures imposed by the need to compete both within and outside the Single European Market have facilitated employers' achieving greater flexibility in the use of labour working laws and temporary contracts. The Price Waterhouse/Cranfield data again confirm this[3] and indicate that, when asked whether they had increased the use of certain working arrangements in the preceding three years, 58 per cent said that they had increased the use of part-time work and 66 per cent reported more use of temporary/casual contracts. Of the 10 countries referred to in the project, the Netherlands ranked second and first respectively in the increased use of these more flexible arrangements. Employers would like more deregulation of the labour market and lower taxes and social costs, but show no great inclination to derecognise trade unions or deal more with the works councils rather than union representatives/officials. They prefer stability and predictability. It must be noted (see below) that employers' autonomy over a range of issues and practices is potentially constrained significantly by the rights of works councils.

The role of the employers' associations is changing also, with somewhat less importance attached to strategies of defence against the unions and more emphasis placed on providing members with advisory, diagnostic and consultancy services regarding the implications to the work organisation of changes in demand, the implementation of technology and increasing legislative intervention and regulation.

There are a mixture of employers' organisations; some perform both business and employment roles, some are specifically concerned with furthering the interests of small and medium-size employers. The major industries tend to have their own associations and there are peak associations that reflect to some extent the traditional segmentation of society, so that, for example, the Federation of Dutch Enterprises (VNO) encompasses both business and employment roles, whereas the Christian Employers Federation (NCW) is only an employers' organisation and is a product of the merger in 1970 of previously separate Catholic and Protestant federations. Political influence is also exerted by these associations, the VNO through the Christian and Liberal parties, and the NCW through the Christian Democrats. Some organisations, perhaps particularly some of the large multinationals, are members of both these peak associations. The VNO is by far the larger of the two, representing as it does most of the large employers and close to three-quarters of the total.

The interests and policies of the various employers' federations are co-ordinated through the Council of Central Employers Organisations (RCO), and nowadays there are relatively few differences between them. They all tend to want deregulation of the labour market, reduced taxes and social costs, and a reduction in the size of the public sector.

Many of the larger enterprises conduct their own bargaining with trade unions, even though they are members of appropriate employers' associations.

We have already noted that Dutch employers have encouraged decentralisation of collective bargaining to company level and that they are making increasing use of flexible, particularly part-time and temporary work contracts. There has also been a tendency for the substantial devolution of personnel responsibilities to line management. The Price Waterhouse/ Cranfield project[4] also provides evidence to suggest that Dutch employers have been making greater efforts to communicate with their employees via a number of different mechanisms, incorporating both direct communication and indirect communication via works councils and trade unions. Employers have also been placing greater emphasis on productivity, quality, employee involvement, flattening organisational structures and linking pay to some criterion of performance, whether it be qualitative or quantitative. The combined effects of the need to be internationally competitive and the new notions of human resource management can be detected in the Netherlands as in many of the European countries.

THE ROLE OF PERSONNEL

The Dutch Association for Personnel Management (NUP), which organises conferences and seminars, and publishes magazines, has 4000 members, representing only about 15 per cent of human resource managers. Entrance into the profession is typically through the 'Social Academy', education in personnel management and labour relations.

Around 20 institutions provide this kind of education, and the programme takes three or four years. The supply of graduates wishing to join the profession far exceeds demand. According to the Price Waterhouse/Cranfield project, 23 per cent of the most senior Dutch personnel and HR managers were recruited from outside the personnel discipline. The survey also suggests that strategic considerations are becoming more important within HRM, taking on board longer-term planning. However, only 48 per cent who say that they have an HR strategy translate this into work programmes and deadlines. Some recent surveys in the Netherlands have revealed that most importance is being attached to the HR activities of training and education, management development, and manpower planning and recruitment in the context of more competitive corporate environments.[5]

LABOUR MARKET

- In the early 1990s the rate of unemployment was a cause for concern, reaching nearly 5 per cent.
- The Dutch population and labour force progressively comprise a greater proportion of older people.

Recruitment

- In the early 1990s, according to the Price Waterhouse/ Cranfield Survey, 18 per cent of larger employers said that they were not experiencing recruitment difficulties.
- Problems were most generally experienced in respect of management functions, professional staff, and people with intermediate technical qualifications.
- In order to prevent shortages of necessary skills employers have adopted two broad strategies. First, underused groups, particularly women, have been targeted. In addition, some recruitment requirements, e.g. age ranges, have been revised and many organisations have improved pay and benefits packages for those categories of staff which are in great demand. Thirdly, a greater emphasis has been placed on training and retraining of staff.
- District labour offices (GAB), which are operated by the Ministry of Social Affairs and Employment, maintain databanks of vacancies and job seekers.
- Private employment bureaux are widely available, through which employers can obtain temporary staff. Most employers advertise jobs externally, and executive search agencies are in demand for the recruitment of managerial staff.

Selection

- A variety of selection methods are in common usage, including interviews, psychological tests, and assessment centres. For management staff, selection is often contracted out to professional agencies.
- There is legislation to prevent discrimination on grounds of race or ethnic origin in the selection procedure. In addition, a company is obliged to employ 3 to 10 per cent of its workforce who are disabled.
- Probationary periods are common and must not last for more than two months.

Remuneration

- In most industries rates of pay are established by collective labour agreements between federations of trade unions and employers' organisations. However, in the case of large companies, independent agreements are arrived at. There are about 200 sectoral agreements and 649 company agreements. The government may curtail agreed wage increases if the economic situation necessitates it. Such agreements are normally valid for one year. Exceptionally, individual negotiations can be used to top up the total package for manual or clerical workers.
- A minimum wage applies to all employees who work more than one-third of normal working hours.
- Job evaluation is widespread, applying to over 70 per cent of all jobs. Less than one third of employers use merit/performance-related pay in determining annual remuneration, although there is a move towards linking pay to appraisal ratings. Profit sharing is used by around a third of employers.

Training and development

- The government provides financial backing for vocational training and retraining. Employers can obtain grants towards the wage costs of employees' training and the costs of training itself. It is possible for scholars to transfer to vocational training at various ages.
- Current priority is being given to developing management skills, particularly in HRM, among management grades, which typically possess a strong technical orientation. In the 1980s there was a rapid growth in provision of managerial studies at undergraduate level.

Trends within HRM

Two further forms of evolution within HRM itself are affecting the position of the HR specialist. First, personnel tasks are increasingly being contracted out to management consultancies and training, recruitment, outplacement and data processing firms. Secondly, personnel tasks are being increasingly devolved to line management. Over half of Dutch organisations transferred personnel responsibilities to line managers between 1985 and 1990. Personnel still normally takes the lead role in areas such as wages/salaries.[6]

TRADE UNIONS

Trade unions in the Netherlands are fragmented along religious and ideological lines in accordance with the traditional pillarisation, and multi-unionism is therefore a feature of Dutch employee relations. The unions and confederations were initially mobilised by political or religious movements. There is no craft tradition and unions have not emphasised workplace organisation, believing that their most effective means of influencing and furthering members' rights and interests was via political and legislative mechanisms. After the second world war, the unions were willing to participate in centralised determination of wages and other terms and conditions of employment, to bargain at this central and national level, and where necessary make use of the legal mechanisms for extension of collective agreements to employers and employees not actually party to the agreement (the Collective Agreement Extension Act 1937). They were also keen to participate in the formation and enhancement of the welfare state, since this also was consistent with their 'inclusive' approach which accepts a responsibility to society as a whole and to employees generally, whether a member of the union or not. The unions have also been willing participants in the many tripartite consultative, advisory and administrative fora and institutions that are integral to the corporatist search for consensus determination and implementation of social and economic policy. All the main confederations tend to be represented in union membership of the main tripartite and bipartite institutions such as the Social and Economic Council (SER) and the Foundation of Labour (SvdA).

Employee consultation and representation within the workplace are more commonly achieved via the statutorily enforced system of works councils which are non-union bodies, although there are some examples of union plant committees. One of the issues confronting trade unions today is how to deal with trends towards decentralised decision making and determination of terms and conditions of employment, and how to encompass within their organisation and activities, demands from employees for greater participation and democracy. The unions, given their traditional orientation and structure, are not generally equipped to cope with demands for internal democracy and workplace representation.

Formally the union confederations and political parties are not affiliated, but 'pillarisation' has inevitably meant that there are relatively close ties between some of them.

The activities of the unions are generally not legally regulated – they are free to determine their own internal procedures and objectives. Legal status is necessary if they are to make legally binding collective agreements, and these agreements can and often do provide them with various rights and facilities. Legislation at European Union level has provided the unions with some rights; for example, in areas such as collective dismissals and rights to consultation, and the SER has made recommendations that certain facilities should be afforded union representatives in the workplace.

The main source of trade union membership has, as in many other countries, been male, blue-collar workers in the industrialised sector and manual workers in the public sector. As the industrialised sector has declined in significance, union membership has also declined. Union membership density reached a high point of around 40 per cent in the 1950s but has been in gradual decline ever since. The 1980s saw relatively sharp decreases down to a figure of around 25 per cent by the end of the decade.[7]

The unions have not effectively recruited among white-collar workers, workers in the service sector or those working part time, and they have also been ineffective in recruiting women and young workers. In the latter case, this has become a particular problem as the traditional industrial sector and the role of the blue-collar worker has declined, and as far as the unions are concerned this represents the demise of a union member role model for the young. These structural changes have consequences for trade union membership and tradition and are mirrored in many other countries. There is, however, some evidence to indicate that the Dutch union movement, fragmented and divided as it is, has had some success recently in recruiting new members in the service sector and among female and part-time workers, as well as making further inroads in the public sector.

It is important to note that the influence of trade unions in the Netherlands has been greater than might be indicated by union membership density; the centralised system, extension of collectively determined terms and conditions, and the unions' role in economic, social and welfare policy determination and administration have all served to assure the unions of greater influence. Visser[8] estimated that twice as many employees were covered by collective bargaining as were union members, and the Price Waterhouse/Cranfield Survey[9] evidence suggests that over the three years up to and including 1992 union influence had increased in more organisations than it had decreased in.

It is important also to appreciate that this 'corporatist' role can only be performed with the acquiescence of both other participants, government and employers. Even as membership density has declined, the other parties have exerted very little pressure to disband corporatist arrangements, and employers also have tended so far to resist pressures allied to decentralisation to give the non-union works councils a greater bargaining role within the workplace. Employers, even with their recently enhanced bargaining power, have shown little inclination to derecognise trade unions or to disband or leave the established joint arrangements.

The union movement used to be more fragmented or segmented than it is now. In the late 1970s, culminating in 1981, the socialist movement (the largest in terms of total membership) and the Catholic movement (second largest) merged to form the Dutch Federation of Trade Unions (FNV). In addition to the FNV, there is the Christian Union Federation (CNV) which is the Protestant movement, plus a few smaller and non-FNV-affiliated Catholic unions. In addition to these two federations, there is a relatively new Federation of White Collar Organisations (MHP). Affiliates of FNV and CNV tend to be organised on a sectoral or occupational basis. There are some other non-affiliated associations and in 1990 the ACV was formed as a federation of predominantly public sector unions representing mainly civil servants. This federation has subsequently claimed that it should also be represented in and on the SER and other major corporatist institutions. The FNV represents almost 60 per cent of the total of trade union members and the CNV nearly 20 per cent.

GOVERNMENT

As noted in Chapter 3, government since the end of the second world war has been the product of coalition, alternating between centre-left and centre-right but dominated generally by Christian democracy. There has been a strong corporatist search for consensus and conflict resolution through the integration of diverse interest groups into the decision-making and implementing processes. However, there are signs that this tripartite co-operation and search for consensus has been in decline in recent years, and certainly moves in the direction of decentralisation and greater democracy and autonomy at a lower level pose significant threats to the combined strength of the national corporatism. Nevertheless, the two main institutions through which governments have sought to achieve these objectives remain intact – the SER and SvdA, the former being more influential and tripartite as opposed to bipartite in terms of its membership. These corporatist institutions and processes have often been used by government to achieve wage moderation in order to promote other socio-economic objectives such as reindustrialisation, economic growth, stability of exchange rates and welfare protection.

In recent years, government has found it more difficult to maintain consensually determined and driven socio-economic policies. The burgeoning welfare state and consequent social costs and tax burden have led to pressures for a considerable reduction in public expenditure via a scaling down of benefits and entitlements; the conversion of a comprehensive system into one of minimal provision and protection, with individuals expected to provide for themselves via private sector insurance and similar schemes. Employers have been keen to promote these changes, since they argue that their competitiveness is severely hampered by the high level of social costs necessary to finance such a comprehensive and 'generous' system. Government is also anxious to control/reduce the public sector deficit in order to satisfy requirements linked to the introduction of a single currency within the European Union.

Dutch governments have not tended to intervene in order to promote full employment and active labour market policies have not been a tradition; as noted earlier, the emphasis has been on income maintenance while people are unemployed rather than on creating jobs or easing mobility via retraining or relocation allowances, or the provision of effective job-seeking services to the unemployed. In many instances, the government has contrived to reduce the official unemployment statistics by facilitating early retirement and by easing the transfer from work to disability status.

There is a relatively large public sector and government therefore has a significant role both directly and indirectly as an employer. Only in relatively recent times have public sector workers begun to enjoy the freedoms to bargain collectively and influence management decisions that have been the norm in the private sector for many years. Public sector unionism is more widespread than in the private sector, and in 1990 union density in this sector was estimated at about 50 per cent, twice the national figure. Public sector workers have often been subject to pay freezes in periods of austerity and as an example to the private sector. When not subject to a freeze, public sector wages and terms and conditions of employment have for long periods been formally linked to those in the private sector.

The Social and Economic Council

The SER is a tripartite body with equal numbers of members representing trade unions, employers and the national interest via government-appointed experts. In recent years, the role of the SER has in practice become predominantly advisory rather than consultative. However, the relationship between government and the SER still lies at the heart of socio-economic policy and decision making, and government is obliged to seek its advice on proposals for social and economic legislation.

To some extent, the SER has tended to act as a buffer between government and the other main actors, since it is the SER that they have pressured and lobbied rather than government itself. SER recommendations have normally been accepted and ratified by the government, but not always. Decentralisation of decision making and greater autonomy to the parties are obvious threats to the role and importance of the SER. The SER rarely makes recommendations on issues of pay – these are more likely to be the province of the bipartite SvdA.

PROCESSES

In the years immediately following the second world war, the main parties co-operated centrally to control wages and determine socio-economic policy. To the extent that collective bargaining occurred, it was undertaken at a central level via the SvdA, the Board of Mediators and government officials. Below this level, the vast majority of employers and unions did not bargain and they had very little input into the process or the outcomes. It was not until the early 1960s that this centralised determination of main terms and conditions of employment came under significant pressure from below. This centralised approach helped to extend bargaining coverage, as did use of the Collective Agreement Extension Act (1937), so that by the end of the 1950s the industry-level, multi-employer agreement had become the main source of the terms of the employment contract for blue-collar workers in the private sector. The 1937 Act gave the Minister of Social Affairs and Employment the power to extend collectively agreed terms and conditions to employers in the industry, irrespective of whether they were signatory to the agreement via membership of a participating employers' association.

By the early 1960s many employers were confronted by labour shortages, full order books and expansion opportunities, and they began to exert pressure for a relaxation of the centralised determination of rates in order to obtain labour and encourage productivity. The 1960s saw a wage explosion as the centralised approach was abandoned and many of the larger employers began to negotiate their own agreements.

Attempts were made subsequently to reimpose centralised control of wages, but with little long-term success. Increasingly, employers and their unions sought a greater role in determining their own contractual terms. A central agreement was reached in 1982 and provided for a reduction in working time as a means of combating the rise in unemployment and in return for agreement to cease the price indexation of wages. Since then, as noted earlier, income and wage differentials between firms and between skilled and unskilled, employed and unemployed have widened, and the policies pursued at national level have been less egalitarian in nature. Increasing unemployment has also made it easier for employers to achieve wage moderation via industry- and company-level bargaining, and national multi-industry regulation has become less necessary to ensure the maintenance of labour-cost competitiveness in the international marketplace.

In recent years attention has been directed towards the Collective Agreement Extension Act as the mechanism that protects employees and employers from the full force of wage- and cost-cutting competition. Indeed, those arguing that it is necessary to deregulate and reduce wages further in order to compete more effectively internationally see the legislation as something to be dispensed with.

Today collective bargaining is more decentralised, to the level of the company, than has been the case since the end of the war and, while multi-employer bargaining still occurs at the level of the industry, these agreements are increasingly viewed as establishing minima and the scope of the content is narrowing. Visser[10] estimates that company-level bargaining now covers approximately one-third of all employees.

Works councils

All enterprises in the Netherlands employing 35 or more employees are statutorily required to establish an employee-only works council. Different rules apply to enterprises employing more than 100 people; the scope of the council's activities are different, as are its rights. Initially in 1950 the councils were established as joint employer–employee bodies. In 1971 the legislation was amended to limit the employer's role to that of chairman and in 1979 further amendment confirmed the council as employee-only bodies. Trade unions can put forward candidates for election to the councils, but they are quite firmly employee as opposed to trade union councils.

The councils are not supposed to engage in collective bargaining with the employer and collectively negotiated agreements between employers and unions both take precedence over and constrain the activities of the council, since councils should not make decisions which are inconsistent with or contravene the terms of a collective agreement. Collective agreements can give the councils powers and a role that is more extensive than those granted by legislation. The discretion and role of the council are often related to the degree of detail contained within collective agreements; the more detail, the more constrained the council's role. Some arguments have been forwarded that the councils should generally be allowed to engage in collective bargaining, and indeed that they should be the main employee representatives in company-level negotiations over pay as well as other terms and conditions. As noted earlier, employers and unions are both generally against these suggestions.

Council members are particularly protected from dismissal and disciplinary action and are legally entitled to time off for training and other council-related activities. The councils themselves have legislative rights to information from the employer that is reasonable and required to enable it to function effectively. The council is required or has the right to meet the employer at least six times a year and is entitled twice a year to a report from the employer that deals with the conduct and performance of the business and, in particular, the financial performance, employment trends and social policy. These reports should look both backwards and forwards for a twelve-month period.

The councils have two distinct sets of rights – the right to information and consultation, and the right to agree or approve. Both parties have legal recourse if these rights are infringed or exercised unreasonably.

The rights to consultation specify not only a particular range of subject matter, e.g. transfers of control, closures, relocation, recruitment and the use of temporary staff, but also that the consultation must be at a time allowing the council's views to have significant impact.

The councils have the right to approve changes or initiatives in areas such as works rules, arrangements regarding hours of work or holidays, pay or job evaluation schemes, grievance procedures, health and safety regulations, and the procedures or rules regarding recruitment, dismissal, promotion, training and employee appraisal. If the council refuses consent unreasonably, the employer can appeal to the courts. If the employer ignores the council's refusal to approve or acts without seeking approval, then the council can apply to the court and the employer's decision is null and void.

As noted above, councils in enterprises employing 35–100 people have very much more limited rights to information and consultation. For example, consultation applies only if the proposal will lead to job losses.

Conciliation and arbitration

In the private sector and on a voluntary basis, disputes can be referred to a body of experts nominated by the SvdA and they may recommend a solution. Alternatively, collective agreements can stipulate arbitration procedures and a list of arbitrators. There are no publicly provided conciliation and arbitration services and no legislative requirements.

CASE STUDY

Outsourcing at DSM

The number of personnel jobs at Dutch chemical and plastics company DSM is being cut by nearly a half as part of a massive, company-wide shake-up.

Of an original 600 in personnel and organisation, 245 are moving to external contractors as their function is outsourced, or being made redundant. A few may move to non-personnel jobs in the company.

Only 355 people will remain, of whom 85 are being deployed among business units in line with a partial decentralisation of head office and other corporate functions. Others will move to an internal consultancy being set up to sell in-house personnel services to business units.

Etha van de Wiel, director of corporate industrial relations, said that, in outsourcing activities, the aim was to move the jobs together with the people involved. The activities included anything which could be done as well outside the company, from shopfloor training to testing for recruitment and career development. But works such as labour market co-ordination – selling DSM to potential recruits – was something better done in-house.

The move was first planned in 1990 and is expected to be complete by 1995. It is part of a wider change programme, Strategy 2000, developed by the company to carry through its decentralisation into business units.

DSM, which began as the chemical arm of the Dutch state-owned mining company, has been expanding, restructuring and decentralising since the early 1970s. So the current reorganisation is seen as the latest phase in a continuous process.

Van de Wiel commented: 'A few years ago we created our business units and we now want to give them all the tools to enable them to be fully responsible for every aspect of their operation.'

She said the personnel department had got the agreement of the works council to its blueprint for change. It also had trade union approval for the 'social plan': the conditions for redundancy or transfer to a contractor. Both approvals were legal requirements.

The practice of offering people jobs with external consultants when their function was being outsourced was also part of the agreement. If they declined the offer, they knew there was a strong possibility they would be made redundant. Other redundancies were caused by the need to become more efficient.

Source: *Personnel Management*, December 1992, p.45

SUMMARY

After the second world war the Netherlands exhibited the characteristics of a strongly corporatist system. As old religious and ideological ties and divides have weakened and the socio-economic objectives of prosperity, stable exchange rates and welfare for all were achieved, pressures grew for more democracy and participation at lower levels, more diversity and more flexibility. Increasing unemployment has provided employers with the power and confidence to rely increasingly on the market, at the same time as international competitive pressures and new technology and production systems have also emphasised flexibility, decentralisation and devolution. These trends have coincided and are consistent with the adoption of 'new' human resource management approaches and techniques.

Government and the other main actors have failed to address positively the issue of rising structural unemployment; although they are beginning to grapple with the scale and cost of the welfare state, without much success so far.

It seems as if the trade unions may have halted the decline in membership and support, but have not as yet begun to consider seriously their future role at company level, if indeed they are to have one. This will involve organisational and structural changes, since the unions are still very much orientated towards the centre and the traditional corporatist and tripartite institutions and mechanisms.

Multi-employer bargaining at industry level is still important and sets minimum standards, but increasingly bargaining is being decentralised to company level and the absence of effective union structures at this level is facilitating an enhanced bargaining role for works councils. Other influences for decentralisation, participation and involvement within the organisation may well exert pressure for an enhanced role for the works council at the expense of trade unions and collective bargaining.

NOTES AND REFERENCES

1. Brewster C, Hegewisch A and Mayne L (1994) 'Trends in European HRM, Signs of Convergence?' in Kirkbride P (ed), *Human Resource Management in Europe*, Routledge, p.116

2. Visser J (1992) 'The Netherlands, The End of an Era and the End of a System', in Ferner A and Hyman R (eds), *Industrial Relations in the New Europe,* Blackwell, p.354

3. op. cit. p.120

4. Brewster C (1994) 'European HRM, Reflection of, or Challenge to, the American Concept?' in Kirkbride P (ed) *Human Resource Management in Europe*, Routledge, p.66

5. Hoogendoorn J 'New Priorities for Dutch Human Resource Management, Personnel Management in Holland', *Personnel Management*, December 1992, pp.42–5

6. Ibid.

7. See appendix 14

8. Visser J op. cit. p.332

9. Brewster C and Hegewisch A (eds) (1994) *Policy and Practice in European HRM*, Routledge, p.143

10. Visser op. cit. p.351

FURTHER READING

Albeda W (1987) 'Recent trends in collective bargaining in the Netherlands', in Windmuller J P (ed), *Collective Bargaining in Industrialised Market Economies: A re-appraisal*, ILO, pp.253–64

Hoogendoorn J (1992) 'New priorities for Dutch HRM – personnel management in Holland', *Personnel Management*, 24 (12), December, pp.42–4

Hoogendoorn J and Brewster C (1992) 'Human resource aspects of decentralisation and devolution', *Personnel Review*, 21 (1) pp.4–11

Looise J (1989) 'The recent growth in employee representation in the Netherlands: Defying the times?' in Lammers C J and Szell G (eds), *International Handbook of Participation in Organisations Vol. 1*, Oxford University Press, pp.268–84

Sorge A (1992) 'Human resource management in the Netherlands', *Employee Relations*, 14 (4), pp.77–84

Van Voorden W (1984) 'Employers Associations in the Netherlands' in Windmuller J P and Gladstone A (eds), *Employers Associations and Industrial Relations: A comparative study,* Clarendon, pp.202–231

Visser J (1990) 'Continuity and change in Dutch industrial relations' in Baglioni G and Crouch C (eds), *European Industrial Relations: The challenge of flexibility,* Sage, pp.199–242

13 · SWEDEN

BACKGROUND

Much HRM activity in Sweden takes place in the main urban conurbations around Stockholm, Gothenburg and Malmö, where 35 per cent of the population live.

Since the 1940s the Swedish model has rested on co-operation between central employers and union institutions at national level, and provides a national framework for the determination of terms and conditions of employment. Joint commitment to economic growth and welfare has been underpinned by a generous social security system, one aspect of which is provision whereby 90 per cent of the cost of childcare is split between central and local government, allowing 80 per cent of women with pre-school children to be employed. Collaborative approaches have also been emphasised at corporate level, where there is legal provision for co-determination, requiring employers to negotiate before taking important decisions and to provide information.

In recent years the continued viability of this model has been questioned, with growing emphasis being placed on decentralisation and market orientation. SAS, the famous airline, set the example by stressing customer relations, training, corporate culture and reorganisation of work. Mass unemployment has put considerable strain on the welfare state, and current costly pension arrangements, as the population grows older, are going to be difficult to sustain.

EMPLOYERS

Swedish employers in the private sector organised and centralised relatively early, SAF (the Swedish Employers Confederation) was formed only a few years after LO (the Swedish Federation of Trades Unions) in 1902. There is little doubt that centralisation of the employers' organisation was a response to the activities of the trade unions. To some extent the employers organised in a form that was consistent with the organisational characteristics and structures adopted by the LO in the early years of the twentieth century, even though the LO was not fully centralised until the early 1940s and

centralised bargaining between LO and SAF did not materialise until the 1950s. Very early on, the SAF was allowed by its members considerable authority over them in areas such as the authorisation of lock-outs and use of lock-out funds, and it was the employers who finally took the initiative to create the centralised bargaining processes and institutions that became the cornerstone of the Swedish model for the next 30 years. In the favourable economic climate of the 1950s with low unemployment and rapid economic growth, and with the LO influenced by the Rehn-Meidner[1] proposals, and prepared to restrain wages in return for government pursuit of particular economic policies and strategies, SAF took the opportunity to create centralised pay bargaining, thereby rendering employers safer from union activity against them as individuals and from competitive wage bargaining.

SAF is the peak confederation, but its membership is primarily from the private sector. Other arrangements are made in the public sector, where employers bargain with the various union cartels referred to below; although the SAF was influential in the 1960s and 1970s in encouraging this centralisation of bargaining in the expanding sectors of employment, white-collar and public sector. SAF has in membership the vast majority of private sector employers, in the region of 40 000 individual employers organised into 36 sectoral organisations.

In the early 1970s there were a series of essentially pro-union legislative interventions and these, coupled with the election of a conservative government in 1976, encouraged employers to begin moving in the direction of seeking to decentralise industrial relations and withdraw from corporatist arrangements. They sought to maintain their prerogative over production issues, regain control of pay determination locally and link it to performance or productivity, enhance labour flexibility and reward skill. To some extent, they have been assisted in the achievement of these objectives by the less friendly economic climate and the increased need to reorganise production and control costs in order to remain internationally competitive. Further assistance has been given by the conflicts within the union movement, encouraged by the changing balance of power and changing attitudes and objectives, with less emphasis on solidarity and a keener interest on the part of some union groups in the enhancement of pay linked to improved skills and productivity.

That is not to say that comprehensive decentralisation has been achieved. Indeed, in 1989 a two-year central agreement was struck between LO and SAF, but the deteriorating economy, rising prices and the likelihood of LO taking up its option to renegotiate linked to price rises forced the government to intervene with an austerity package. The failure of the package resulted in the Rehnburg mediation proposal but, as described earlier, it was short lived.

The 1980s in particular is a story of very mixed feelings among employers with respect to the relative merits of decentralisation, with many still seeing the advantages of centralisation in preventing competitive and inflationary wage bargaining, despite their desire to link production and wage issues. However, in the current economic and political climate, with low growth and rising unemployment and with a conservative-led coalition government pursuing policies consistent with the wishes of employers – reducing the public sector, a greater reliance on market forces, anti-union legislative proposals and the reduction of taxation and welfare benefits – employers seem to feel relatively safe from the risks of decentralisation.

The 1993 bargaining round saw agreements establishing overall wage increases at sector level, but providing for ever more discretion for the parties at company level to determine actual distribution of the sectorally agreed 'global' figure. Some agreements, such as that in engineering, specifically acknowledged the employers' concerns with linking pay and individual performance and job responsibility. These agreements were often viewed by employers as a transitional stage in achieving the ultimate goal of enterprise-based wage determination.

THE ROLE OF PERSONNEL

The origins of personnel management can be traced to 1921 when the organisation of Social Workers within Industry and Business (SAIA) was founded. Subsequently the profession has changed its profile considerably to reflect political social developments in the country. There were approximately 30 000 personnel managers and specialists in 1990, with 10 000 being members of the SPF.

Personnel departments are now well accepted across Swedish industry, particularly in large companies, and in the public sector, with a trend towards business administration and law graduates entering the profession. A government commission has proposed a new 3½-year study programme in human resource management.[2]

Currently there is a trend away from administration towards a more strategic role for personnel, as is borne out by a survey carried out in 1990 by the Uppsala Institute of HRM,[3] in which about 60 leading personnel directors in service industries and the public sector stated how they spent their time and discussed their expectations for 1992.

There is also an anticipation that the role will increasingly involve providing non-standardised internal consultancy to managers in decentralised organisations. In the 1980s an economic perspective on HRM has gained ground, with an emphasis on the 'economics of personnel' and the 'economics of people'.

A number of Swedish companies have included personnel factors in their final accounts and balance sheets, and a government commission is enquiring into modifying accounting law to facilitate this practice on a broader scale.

LABOUR MARKET

- The total workforce is approximately 415 million and rates of unemployment are relatively low.
- Growth has occurred in white-collar employment. From 1980 to 1990, employment in the service sector grew by over 1 per cent to reach around 7.3 per cent of the total workforce, although in the early 1990s the recession has had a negative impact in jobs, chiefly in the public and financial sectors.

Recruitment

- Most jobs (8 out of 10) are in the service or public sectors. The Swedish Labour Market has established local job centres in all towns and cities. Regional Labour Market Boards also exist to co-ordinate recruitment, and to inform interested parties of the current labour market situation.
- Since the 1930s, with a few exceptions, private recruitment agencies have not been allowed. Advertising is therefore predominantly public, through job centres and internal procedures.

Selection

- The interview is a common method, with some resurgence in interest in psychometric testing in large concerns.

Remuneration

- Salary differentials are narrow, with high salary levels being decreased further by progressive taxation. Since 1951 there has been a cohesive wage policy, whereby all wages and salaries have been determined through annual negotiations, normally at national level.
- In the late 1980s negotiations became more decentralised. This was reversed by the Rehnberg Commission, which undertook to supervise all negotiations for 1991 and successfully moderated wage and salary increases.
- Incentives, both individual and group, vary much in use. The introduction of such schemes must be agreed at annual wage negotiations.
- The social welfare system provides free and cheap services in the areas of healthcare, childcare, social services, education, public transport, pensions and sometimes housing allowances. An allowance makes it possible for either parent, under certain conditions, to stay at home with each child up to 15 months in age.

Training and development

- The basis of adult education in Sweden is the principle of continuous education, voluntary study assistance, and a well-developed system for labour market training widely available at a low cost.
- Vocational training has increased considerably since the 1970s.
- A government commission has suggested a 'national strategy for competence and development'. University colleges are becoming more market orientated, providing a variety of training and development programmes to companies.

Current issues

- A decline in productivity has contributed towards an economic crisis in which previously secure groups of workers have been made redundant, including managers and technical specialists.
- Companies such as Asea Brown-Boveri, Saab, SKF and Atlas Copco,have carried through programmes of rationalisation. Trade unions have co-operated in the introduction of new production methods, multi-skilled teams and time-based manufacturing systems.
- At national level, the emphasis has been placed on attempting to retrain redundant workers.

- Most of Sweden's large organisations, including Volvo, already have significant interests abroad, and according to the Price Waterhouse/Cranfield study, most personnel managers expect the EU to have positive effects, although there is little evidence of serious preparation for further economic integration.

TRADE UNIONS

Between the 1930s and the 1990s, trade unions in Sweden operated in a relatively friendly environment with their political allies, the Social Democrats, in government for all but nine years since 1932. The right to organise freely was agreed in the Saltsjobaden Agreement in 1938, and employers have generally been willing to negotiate with the unions and to some extent share decision making, although not on production issues. Additionally, the trade unions have participated in the administration of unemployment and other benefit schemes. There is, however, evidence of a considerably more hostile union environment in recent years, with government and employers keen to regain the initiative and control over wage determination locally. There has additionally been a significant increase in unemployment levels.

The friendly climate undoubtedly contributed to the very high levels of trade union density that are characteristic of the Swedish system, with a peak of 86 per cent being reached in the mid-1980s. There was a dip in membership after that but Figure 13.1 suggests that membership density has been rising again since the early 1990s. The Price Waterhouse/Cranfield Project data[4] confirm that union influence remained strong in 1992 with 61 per cent of organisations saying that their influence had remained the same; however, 29 per cent said union influence had decreased – an increase from 21 per cent in 1991.

The union movement in Sweden, like most European movements, began as a socialist-oriented movement among manual workers. The very early unions were craft based, but by the 1890s they were increasingly organised on a company or site basis with the same union representing all manual employees. The trend towards company and industry-based unionism was assisted in many cases by geographic isolation of employment locations and, as the relatively late industrialisation and mass-production techniques resulted in relatively large semi-skilled labour forces, general and industrial unionism was encouraged.

Membership still growing

Robert Taylor

The forced resignation of Mr Stig Malm as head of Sweden's LO blue-collar union federation earlier this month – for his sanctioning of "golden parachute" pay-off deals for failed executives in union-dominated companies – has thrown a harsh light on the inner machinations of what remains one of the strongest trade union movements in the world.

The scandal was only the last of many involving Mr Malm during his 11 years as LO leader and his departure was met with barely concealed sighs of relief from Sweden's labour establishment who believed he had grown into a serious liability.

Previously, Mr Malm had been able to ride out the storms by mobilising support behind himself but this time he found no sympathisers among the rank and file. LO's headquarters was inundated with letters, fax messages and phone calls calling for his dismissal.

Mr Malm, already a figure of fun, lost all credibility with the exposure of the enormous gap that exists between the harsh shopfloor realities and the lavish, cushioned world of the nomenklatura.

Now the LO executive is looking for his successor and the choice will be put to a special meeting of the LO on February 2 for approval.

The Malm affair is unique in Swedish labour history. His predecessors at the LO were sober, modest men of power, vision and responsibility who combined idealism with administrative competence. They built the movement into one of the most respected and influential in the industrialised world.

Union leaders wonder whether they can restore the LO to its former pivotal role and they are taking the opportunity presented by Mr Malm's abrupt departure to re-examine the role of organised labour in Sweden and plan its reform.

At first sight, the Swedish unions look in reasonable shape, despite the return of mass unemployment, deindustrialisation, and the waning of the old centralised corporatism that made the LO almost an arm of government. Union membership is actually going up at the moment. It rose from 82 per cent to 86 per cent of the employed workforce in the past six years. Compare this with today's official figures of less than 33 per cent in the UK; 34 per cent in Germany; 15 per cent in the US and a mere 8 per cent in France.

The huge size of Sweden's organised workforce suggests no social stigma is attached to belonging to a union. Nor is there any hostility to trade unionism among the country's white-collar salariat, with 83 per cent of them organised. Indeed, the overwhelming majority of Swedes regard union membership as a necessary protection at a time of labour market crisis.

The reason for this is understandable. The Swedish unions do not only try to provide strong job security for their members in work but they continue to administer the unemployment insurance benefit system as they have done since 1935.

Commentators believe that if the unions were ever to lose their key role in the welfare state, their membership would tumble to 50-60 per cent of the employed labour force; the norm in other Scandinavian countries.

But other factors in Sweden are perhaps just as important. First and foremost the country's employers remain strong supporters of workplace trade unionism. While some dislike the political role the unions like to play in national life, they see the value of having unions in their own plants. During the current deep and long recession in Sweden, companies such as Asea Brown-Boveri, Saab, SKF and Atlas Copco have carried through sweeping programmes of workplace rationalisation. Job losses have been heavy but workers and unions have co-operated in the introduction of lean production methods, multi-skilled teams and time-based manufacturing systems aimed at improving cost competitiveness.

After a prolonged period of stagnation, the growth in Swedish manufacturing productivity is now the highest in the industrialised world. Employers recognise these radical changes would have been much harder to achieve if they had not enjoyed the wholehearted support of the unions.

In fact, Sweden's unions have a long tradition of accepting technological change. Innovative, not reactive, they have developed internal structures flexible enough to enable them to turn the demands made on them by capital to their own advantage.

Such adaptability has made it easier for the Swedish unions to reassess parts of the old model that have grown obsolete. Support for centralised, solidaristic wage bargaining where workers were paid the same level of wages for the same kind of work has waned. There is also much less enthusiasm among the rank and file for retaining close links between the unions and the Social Democratic party.

The most significant change in collective bargaining this year has been the joint two-year agreement for the first time in the engineering industry that has united the white-collar unions SIF and CF with the metalworkers' union.

Such single-table bargaining is likely to spread to other sectors and it may lead to an eventual merger between the LO and the TCO white-collar union federation, particularly as the LO has all but abandoned its role as central wage bargainer or even pay co-ordinator.

There are clear signs of a new consensus emerging in the workplace between capital and labour. Mr Heinrich Blauert, head of VF the engineering employers body, points out: "In the new agreement, the role of co-operative groups is even more important. This is a step in the right direction." By enhancing the position of company-based union negotiators in the bargaining process, the employers believe they can establish a more effective basis for keeping down costs.

Four joint employer-union working parties are examining the future of Swedish engineering. "Our approach is low-key," says Mr Blauert. "In a peaceful way we are moving to a position where our member companies have the room for manoeuvre in reaching the kind of wage settlements which they want." There is a more conciliatory tone nowadays among Sweden's employers. The neo-liberal rhetoric of SAF, their main national organisation, is less in evidence. Only limited moves have been made to deregulate the Swedish labour market and rolling back union power remains little more than an aspiration on the far right.

A new generation of young union leaders and employers is starting to emerge. They are keen to find a new way of working together. This will not mean any cosy return to the certainties of the old Swedish model. But nor is the country about to see a marginalising of organised labour.

In fact, Sweden may turn out to be an example of how organised labour can still have a positive role to play in an open market economy. By accepting the global realities of Sweden's manufacturing companies and embracing new forms of work organisation, the Swedish trade unions may escape the steep decline suffered by trade unions elsewhere.

Fig 13.1 Source: *Financial Times*, 21 December 1993

The LO, which is the confederation that represents nationally the vast majority of manual workers, was originally formed in 1898 and has dominated the union movement in Sweden ever since. We have already mentioned the affiliation with the Social Democrats and its role in the Saltsjobaden Agreement in 1938. The LO was not fully centralised until the early 1940s, but since then has pursued a fairly authoritarian role with respect to affiliated organisations, these organisations relinquishing much autonomy in return for the influence LO could wield centrally. As the public sector expanded LO successfully recruited and represented manual workers in both central and local government sectors; SF[5] was the state sector union affiliated to LO and Kommunal[6] the municipal sector affiliate. LO is still the largest union confederation, representing close to 2 million members in private and public sectors.

However, LO does not represent white-collar workers in private or public sectors; these are represented by cartels of unions, formed mainly in the late 1960s and 1970s. In the private sector co-ordinated bargaining involving LO and PTG[7] (the white-collar cartel) was not established until 1977, and not until 1980 was there a successful attempt at co-ordinated action between LO unions and those affiliated to TCO (the central organisation of salaried employees) in the public sector. There is another important confederation in the public sector, SACO (the Swedish Confederation of Professional Associations), which represents primarily professional employees.

The union movement has become a considerably less coherent entity over the last 25 years and there has been increasing inter-union conflict. Increasingly, white-collar and public sector employees and their organisations have assumed prominence as the structure of industry and employment has changed. These organisations have often not shared the same values, allegiance and objectives as LO; indeed, the public sector affiliates to LO have seen their power within LO increase with their membership. Union co-operation with government and support for solidaristic wage policies, narrow differentials and wage restraint have become more problematic and bargaining at national level has been more complex.

LO has recently adopted a strategy of seeking to respond to employer strategies of decentralisation and linking pay and production by developing the notion of solidaristic work, which comprises and emphasises the enhancement of work and job satisfaction and the use of pay differentials to encourage individuals to take on new skills and work.

The Swedish union movement is still not fragmented along religious or political lines, but there have been clear divisions on grounds of interest, objectives and approach.

Despite these divisions and other potentially negative influences on trade union membership and density, such as employer policies of decentralisation and individualism, changing societal values in the direction of less egalitarianism and a greater concern with self, the recession, unemployment and a considerably less friendly government between 1991 and 1994, trade union membership appears to have held up remarkably well and the unions seem to have retained a central role both nationally and at local level within the workplace (see Fig. 13.1).

Union confederation, orientation and membership
LO – Swedish Federation of Trades Unions.

- Manual workers.
- Public and private sectors.
- Public sector affiliates Kommunal and SF.
- Membership approx 2.3 million (1991).
- Industrial basis of organisation.
- Established 1898.

TCO – Central Organisation of Salaried Employees.

- Salaried, white collar workers.
- Public and private sector cartels.
- Majority of membership is female.
- Primarily industrial basis of organisation.
- Membership approximately 1.3 million (1991).
- Established 1944.

SACO – Swedish Confederation of Professional Associations.

- Public and private sector cartels with TCO.
- Associations with members having similar academic qualifications, doctors, dentists, teachers, etc.
- Membership approximately 300 000 (1991).
- Established 1947.

Local organisation

Swedish unions are renowned for being a centralised and coherent movement, and there is a tendency sometimes to ignore the fact that they also traditionally have effective and active local organisation. The Saltsjobaden Agreement of 1938, in effectively granting employees the right to organise freely, facilitated union organisation and activity at local level, although even before this union activity at the workplace and its integration into the wider union organisation were commonplace.

These local-level organisations are often referred to as workplace clubs. They will be part of a local union branch, and this will be affiliated to a national union which is, in its turn, affiliated to a national confederation. The national unions rely on the workplace organisations to recruit and represent members on their behalf.

National/industry-level agreements have always been renegotiated at workplace level to tailor them to local circumstances, and it may well be that this visible local activity has contributed to high membership density. Local activity and the importance of the role of the union at local level have been expanded as a result of legislative interventions in the 1970s and no doubt also by the increasing decentralisation of bargaining and decision making favoured by many employers in more recent times. It is important to note also that Swedish unions have traditionally facilitated the introduction of new technology and restructuring of work organisation. While the employers have tended to retain managerial prerogative over such production decisions, the unions at local level have been in a position to negotiate on the outcomes of this process.

Local union stewards, particularly perhaps safety stewards who have the power to order a stoppage of work where they consider it hazardous to continue, have considerable influence. It is estimated that between 10 and 20 per cent of union members have some designated union role or activity to perform or engage in union-run training activities each year.[8]

Unions at local level represent individuals with a grievance and have the final say when it comes to certain disputes of 'right' concerning the interpretation or application of an existing agreement, this being incorporated in the legislation on co-determination.

GOVERNMENT

As has been described earlier, government in Sweden has been dominated since 1932 by the Social Democrats. Not surprisingly the government has predominantly been pro-trade union and pro-centralised self-regulatory arrangements. Nevertheless, despite these ideological and historical links, by the end of the 1980s the Social Democrat government was being more and more influenced by economic circumstances to pursue policies at odds with the traditions of self-regulation. These economic circumstances included the need to remain internationally competitive, the

necessity to reintroduce incentive, the requirement for a stable currency given its wish to join the European Union, the size and drain of the public sector and welfare provision, increasing unemployment and relatively low growth combined with rising inflation.

The 1980s can be seen as another decade during which government was increasingly drawn into intervention in and regulation of bargaining processes and outcomes, and it must be remembered that this followed hard on the heels of a decade during which government had intervened via legislation more than before. The culmination of this increased interventionism can be seen in the attempt by the Social Democrat government in 1989 to force the parties to return to centralised pay bargaining. When by early 1990 it was clear that inflation was going to trigger renegotiation of the agreement, the government, initially with LO agreement, proposed a two-year wage freeze, a ban on strikes, heavier penalties on wildcat strikes and ceilings on prices and dividends – a fairly thoroughgoing, statutorily backed prices and income policy. Rank-and-file opposition quickly forced LO to withdraw from any involvement with the policy, reflecting again the changing interests, allegiances and distribution of power within the movement.

The government, faced with the failure of these proposals to gain union support, proposed the Rehnberg Commission, referred to earlier, arguably the most centralised and corporatist arrangement of all. One of the main objectives was to prevent wage drift in the private sector and it was proposed that this would be done by prohibiting local negotiations in 1991, any drift in 1991 being subtracted from wage increases determined centrally by the Commission in 1992. The unions were pressured by government and employers to join the attempt at regaining control of wages nationally and centrally. Employers favoured the Rehnberg proposals, partly because they thought that, in the absence of local collective negotiations, they would actually have more autonomy locally to introduce and expand individual and performance-related payment arrangements linked to greater flexibility and restructuring of work organisation. The return of a conservative coalition government later in 1991 signalled a change of policy and direction, with government very much more keen to control the power of the unions.

Government presides over a large public sector. While it does not negotiate as employer directly with the unions, which is done through appropriate employers' organisations in the various sectors, nevertheless the government is obviously in a position to have a significant influence on the outcomes of these negoti-ations. As in other countries, the public sector tended to lead the way on non-wage issues, setting standards for others to follow. However, towards the end of the 1980s public sector groups began to set the pace on pay as well and this undoubtedly prompted employ-ers in the private sector to exert pressure on govern-ment to intervene more directly in pay determination. The 1980s was also a decade of increasing industrial action, particularly in the public sector, and again this can be seen as a product of numerous influences, includ-ing the increased conflict within the union movement consequent on changing power relationships, and the emergence of different interests, approaches and ide-ology among those groups of employees in expanding sectors of employment.

Legislative framework

While the traditions have been of self-regulation, there is a body of legal rights and obligations and in the 1970s there was considerable legislative intervention aimed at encouraging employee participation, securi-ty and safety in the workplace.

Collective agreements are generally for a fixed peri-od and legally binding. Industrial action during the period of an agreement is unlawful. However, most agreements contain a provision for termination on notice and so it is possible for disputes of interest to be pursued through cancellation of the existing agree-ment. Disputes of right can be pursued during the peri-od of an agreement, but these are settled via mediation or arbitration, not industrial action.

There are generally no other limitations on the right to strike. Public sector workers are not, for example, prohibited, although the government can effectively halt strike action in certain sensitive occupations, police, nurses, etc., by intervening legislatively and declaring the action dangerous, inhumane or damag-ing to the country.

As indicated above, there were a number of statu-tory interventions in the 1970s which are outlined below.

Worker Director Act 1972 (revised 1976)

This legislation provides for employee organisations to appoint two employee representatives to the board of directors of companies in the private sector with more than 25 employees. Generally the representa-tives will be one LO and one TCO appointee. The value of this role is primarily informational, since there are not enough employee directors to determine com-pany policy. Employee directors do have the same rights and obligations as other directors.

Security of Employment Act 1972

This act protects the rights of employees on dismissal and employers are required to consult the unions before any dismissal.

Shop Stewards Act 1974

The legislation provides for shop stewards to have time off for trade union activities.

Work Environment Act 1977

This act gives enhanced rights to union safety repre-sentatives, including ordering a stoppage of work, and to safety committees on which there is usually a major-ity of employee representatives.

Co-Determination At Work Act 1977 (MBL)

This was an attempt to establish a framework in which capital and labour representatives would jointly agree to extend collective bargaining and joint decision mak-ing to include some of the production issues, e.g. work organisation and/or technical change, that employers had reserved as their prerogative. It was additionally proposed that employers should have an obligation to negotiate (although not to agree) before making changes affecting any employee, and that employers should have an obligation to disclose information on matters such as production plans and manpower policies. Additional rights to information disclosure on demand by unions during negotiations were also envisaged. Finally, the Act gave unions priority rights of interpretation in disputes concerning existing rights and agreements, subject to subsequent nation-al negotiations or decision of the appropriate legal authority.

The parties at national level in the private sector did not conclude the necessary development agreement (UVA) giving effect to the legislation until 1982 and when they did so, it was primarily concluded on employers' terms, as the agreement acknowledged the need for enhanced flexibility and decentralisation stressing common endeavour to improve efficiency, competitiveness and profitability. There is evidence of an increase in bipartite decision making within organ-isations on production issues in recent years, and it is possible that this is a product of this legislation.

CASE STUDIES

How a new strategy took a bank back into profitability

Svenska Handelsbanken (SHB) is the second biggest and most successful bank in Sweden. SHB was the first big company in the service sector to introduce and carried out a totally new management strategy – 10 years before Jan Carlzon's work with the SAS airline became well known.

The SHB model was characterised by systematic decentralisation, an obvious market orientation and a strong vision. This strategy meant changing from highly traditional personnel management to strategic human resource management concentrating on corporate issues of importance for business success.

SHB was originally established in 1871 and got its present name, as well as country-wide organisation, in 1919. SHB played a crucial role in the industrialisation of Sweden and later on became an important bank for small business as well.

The bank has about 500 local branches all over the country as well as international operations in the UK, USA, Luxembourg, Singapore and Hong Kong among others.

The bank's employees totalled 7700 in 1991, and it has around 80 000 shareholders, a widespread ownership for Sweden.

During recent years Svenska Handelsbanken has taken over the RKA, a large life assurance company, a provincial bank in the south, and a mortgage bank.

In the early 1970s, SHB suffered a real crisis, and Jan Wallander became chief executive with a mission to reorganise the bank and make it profitable again.

The bank had 26 geographical districts reporting to three regional managers at head office, which had a number of hierarchical levels and all kinds of staff departments.

The main principles behind Wallander's new strategy were:

- to organise the bank to match customers' needs more closely: the customer should only have one banker to talk to and get support from
- to create a high degree of cost awareness in all operations, which meant decentralising responsibility for profitability
- to maintain a restrictive control system, which was assumed to become still more important in a decentralised organisation.

The bank was then changed from a central hierarchy to eight regional, almost independent banks where all the main decisions in practice had to be made. Local branches of the bank received full responsibility for all their operations and customer relations.

The new strategy was a great success and has since been an inspiring example to many other service companies as well as some public bodies.

SHB has shown strong growth since the 1970s, has been able to create new services and, at the same time, avoid most of the financial problems which have afflicted some of the other Swedish banks in recent years.

While the biggest bank in the country, together with three other leading banks, has been forced to ask for governmental support because of enormous losses, Svenska Handelsbanken is still successful, although it has experienced some decline.

Ninnie Aldergren, director of training in SHB in the 1970s, says the new strategies meant 'a lot of change and upside-down thinking to all of us on the human resource management side.

'The local branch managers became the real personnel managers. Our mission became more strategic – we developed a first-class system for management education to support the new organisation. We worked a lot with corporate culture and all other kinds of training.'

The main task for human resource management was to develop high professionalism, adds Aldergren – 'and I think we have succeeded in this.'

Source: *Personnel Management*, June 1993, p.30

How the recession hit a Swedish City Council

Uppsala, 70 km north of Stockholm, has a population of 170 000. There are two universities, many knowledge-intensive firms, research-based public authorities and a lot of private service businesses.

In 1850 Uppsala was still a small town in the shadow of the old university and cathedral. There was a local magistrate and few public employees. The industrial revolution brought about the introduction of manufacturing, business and handicrafts. Bicycles, mechanical equipment, chemicals, food and drugs were produced. Then the first manufacturing crisis in the 1960s changed it again and all was closed down.

Since the 1950s the city council had a small personnel department for negotiations, training, recruitment and administration of salaries and pensions. The main decisions on personnel matters were made by a political board, the Personalnamnden.

Local politicians decided in 1987 to decentralise and split up most of the organisation into 14 local councils, Kommundelsnamnder, for schools, childcare and social care. The aim was to improve local influence and support responsibility and cost-effectiveness. This has achieved more integration and flexibility in public services but has also been criticised for increasing costs. Some other public services, for example secondary schools, estate and technical services, fire-brigade and public health services, were still kept in separate divisions.

▶

Most operational HRM issues were moved to local management. In 1988 a new training department was organised as a profit centre to provide training services to all other bodies. The political Personalnamnden continued with a coordinating role and was, according to law, still the formal employer for all staff.

A third step has now been taken. The economic decline in Sweden has dramatically changed the financial basis for cities like Uppsala by cutting tax income and government support. The city council had to reduce its total staff of about 13 000 by more than 1000 employees in 1992. More cuts are expected this year.

The HRM function, however, had to handle a situation which was new to most Swedish local government, as people had never been fired before.

First, the decentralised structure had obvious difficulties in managing the problem. The remaining central personnel department, on behalf of the Personalnamnden, had to co-ordinate all redundancies and resignations. Secondly, the situation demanded much professional knowledge in employment law as well as manpower planning and crisis psychology.

HRM people were able to respond to the demands and they have been appreciated, not the least by the local union, for their professionalism and fair play.

However, the next step in the development of Uppsala City Council seems to involve a decreased emphasis on HRM. A new 'market concept' is being introduced where most responsibility for HRM has been integrated with general management and the Personalnamnden has been abolished. The training department, however, has been given a more strategic role.

Source: *Personnel Management*, June 1993, p.30

SUMMARY

The Swedish system has traditionally provided employee participation through negotiation and other mechanisms of co-operation at various levels, and the parties have been organised effectively to deal with this three-tier national, sectoral, workplace system. As has been detailed above, the traditional emphasis on centralisation and coherence has been subject to many competing influences in recent years, and there is little doubt that negotiation and co-operation between the parties are increasingly occurring at local levels. The Price Waterhouse/Cranfield Project[9] evidence supports the contention that industry level multi-employer bargaining on basic pay for manual workers was still dominant in 1991, with 68 per cent of employers represented in these negotiations. However, these agreements do now leave greater scope for local, company-level variation and implementation, as was evident in many of the sector agreements reached in 1993. There are still pressures for co-operation at national level, but the thrust is downwards. The expansion of company and local workplace-based activity and range of subject matter may necessitate organisational adjustments.

The early 1990s have seen recession, unemployment and considerable change. The move to the right, signalled by the election of a conservative coalition in 1991 may have been halted and the election of a new social democrat government in 1994 and entry into the European Union in 1995 both signify a period of further changes and adjustments. The labour movement appears to have survived the 'crises' of the late 1980s and early 1990s remarkably well.

NOTES AND REFERENCES

1. Named after LO economists G Rehn and R Meicher

2. Söderstrom M, 'An HRM role struggling for survival, Personnel Management in Sweden', *Personnel Management*, June 1988, pp.28–33

3. IPF (the Uppsala Institute of Human Resource Management) study, 1990, in Söderstrom M, op. cit.

4. Brewster C and Hegewisch A (eds) (1994) *Policy and Practice in HRM*, Routledge, p.146

5. SF: Swedish State Employees Union

6. Kommunal: Swedish Municipal Workers Union (SKAF)

7. PTG: Federation of Salaried Employees in Industry & Services

8. Kjellberg A (1992) 'Sweden – Can the Model Survive?' in Ferner A and Hyman R (eds), *Industrial Relations in the New Europe*, Blackwell, pp.88–142

9. Brewster C, Hegewisch A and Mayne L (1994) 'Trends in European HRM – Signs of Convergence?' in Kirkbride P S (ed), *Human Resource Management in Europe*, Routledge, pp.114–32

FURTHER READING

Ahlen K (1989) 'Swedish collective bargaining under pressure' *British Journal of Industrial Relations*, 27 (3), pp.330–46.

Delsen L and Van Veer T (1992) 'The Swedish model: Relevant for other European countries?', *British Journal of Industrial Relations*, 30 (1), pp.83–105

Fulcher J (1991) *Labour Movements, Employers and the State: Conflict and co-operation in Britain and Sweden*, Clarendon Press.

Hammarstrom O (1993) 'Industrial relations in Sweden' in Bamber G S and Lansbury R D (eds), *International and Comparative Industrial Relations*, Routledge.

Lansbury R (1991) 'Industrial relations in Australia and Sweden: Strategies for Change in the 1990s', *Economic and Industrial Democracy*, 12 (4), pp.527–34

Olsson A S (1990) *Swedish Wage Negotiation System*, Dartmouth, Aldershot

Rehn G and Kiklind B (1990) 'Changes in the Swedish model', in Baglioni G and Crouch C (eds), *European Industrial Relations: The challenge of flexibility*, Sage pp.300–25

14 · UNITED KINGDOM

BACKGROUND

The UK, despite its physical proximity to the European mainland, possesses many political, cultural and geographical features which distinguish it from its European partners. Indeed, since the late 1970s the economic philosophy which has influenced events and processes in the areas of employment relations and HRM would suggest a greater affinity with the US than with European counterparts. The onset of Thatcherism in the 1980s signalled a move away from previous tripartite modes of industrial and economic management, and implied a reliance on free interaction of supply and demand in all sections of the economy, including the labour market. Consequently, the objective of reducing the level of unemployment has been overtaken by the need to establish realistic wage rates in a market environment. The strong belief in the working of the market, particularly at government level, helps explain why the Social Charter and Social Chapter of the Maastricht treaty were both rejected. Significant cuts have been made in public expenditure and this has been accompanied by the extensive privatisation of nationalised industries. In the course of this, large concerns such as British Telecommunications, British Gas and British Airways have been transferred from state to private ownership.

EMPLOYERS

We have already noted that the tradition of employers in the private sector combining together for protection and advantage has been weakened during the 1980s. These combined associations tend to be trade or industrial in terms of membership base. Changes in the structure of industry have an impact on association membership and influence as they do on trade unions, so that in industries most affected by the competitive and technological pressures of the last decade, one should expect substantial change in membership numbers. The annual reports of the Certification Officer[1] are the most reliable source of information on employers' association numbers and a comparison of reports for 1980 and 1990 shows substantial proportionate membership decreases in the following industries: engineering 36 per cent, chemicals 53 per cent, road haulage 24 per cent, civil engineering 31 per cent. In addition to the competitive and technological pressures mentioned above, there are other explanations for the decline including:

- a desire to regain control within organisations over terms and conditions, combined with the declining threat posed by trade unionism;
- the introduction of new working practices rendering traditional payment structures irrelevant;
- decentralisation of operational decision making and with it decentralisation of employment and human resource management, and new fragmented organisational structures.

It may well be that the representative, diagnostic, consultancy and advisory services offered to members become the attraction of membership rather than the traditional protection offered against the activities of trade unions via multi-employer bargaining. This implies a change of emphasis and role, from collective bargaining to advisory and lobbying.

Consistent with processes of decentralisation, fragmentation and localisation, it may be that local inter-industrial and commercial associations become more relevant, so that we may see further expansion of the activities and influence of associations at this level, e.g. the Chambers of Commerce.

Employers and employers' associations in the UK have tended to support the Conservative Party, seeing it as the natural ally of business and employers. Political parties in the UK are financed by membership and donations, and many industrial and commercial organisations contribute financially to the Conservative party.

While employers' association activities and developments in the UK are still important, more interest in recent years has been focused on individual organisations and their management of human resources and the employment relationship.

Since the election of a Conservative government in 1979, the combined and cumulative effects of the economic, political and legal environments have undoubtedly strengthened the employing and bargaining power of management. In the early 1980s, it was suggested that management had taken advantage of their new-found strengths to pursue policies and strategies consistent with the term 'macho-management'. This term signifies:

- a willingness to stand firm against the demands of employees through their trade unions and less inclination to compromise;
- management placing more emphasis on opening up and utilising direct communication links with employees, bypassing what had become the accustomed channels of communication via the employees' trade unions;
- and an increased willingness to use the new rights and freedoms granted to management through the early legislative interventions of the then recently elected Conservative government.

In brief, it represented an attempt to regain control and managerial prerogative, if necessary through confrontation.

The two most famous instances of management adopting the new macho-management approach are probably the dispute between the print unions and News International, proprietors of the *Times* newspaper (1986), and the dispute between the National Union of Mineworkers (NUM) and the National Coal Board (NCB), one of the nationalised public corporations (1984–85). In both instances, some of the main issues were projected job losses and the introduction and utilisation of new technology. Both disputes resulted in violent and bloody confrontations between employees and the police in their role of trying to maintain order.

However, it would be inaccurate to suggest that many managements took advantage of the new situation to this extent. Purcell and Sisson[2] suggested that most managements in the UK fell into their standard modern category, being essentially reactive and pragmatic; if so, one can only conclude that the pragmatic approach they adopted did not often fit with the notion of macho-management.

The Confederation of British Industry (CBI) also refuted any suggestion that companies are pursuing a widespread offensive against trade unions. In their evidence to the House of Commons Employment committee's enquiry into the future of the trade unions[3], they argued that the sharp decline in collective bargaining and trade union membership since the mid-1980s reflected a shared wish in the workplace for

dealings on a different basis. They further suggested in this evidence that they saw a continuing role for trade unions so long as the latter adapt to change rather than seeking to obstruct it. Individual relationships and dealing directly with the workplace can be complementary to collective bargaining.

Undoubtedly, managements in many organisations have sought over the last 15 years to introduce:

- new technology, new production methods and more flexible working practices;
- new mechanisms for communicating with their workforce;
- new mechanisms for involving employees in decisions about their work, its organisation and quality inspection;
- new performance appraisal and related payment schemes emphasising either the workgroup or the individual;
- new consultative arrangements regarding issues above the level of the job or task;
- new initiatives regarding the recruitment, selection, training and development of employees and a more flexible approach to resourcing activities, encompassing a shrinking of their permanently employed labour force;
- an expanded use of temporary, part-time and fixed-term contracts and also of subcontracting where possible. There has also been increased use of individual contracts as opposed to the tradition of collective terms and conditions of employment.

Additionally, we have seen the acceptance and introduction of 'Japanese' terms, techniques and mechanisms, such as 'just-in-time management', quality circles and lean production.

However, while nearly all these initiatives are consistent with one or more of the varieties of human resource management identified in the literature, there is little evidence that many organisations have adopted strategies in this direction which could be viewed as coherent and integrated. As Guest[4] suggests, it is easier to adopt such a strategic, integrated approach on greenfield sites and probably also in non-trade-union situations, but the bottom line appears to be that the vast majority of managements have introduced such changes on a piecemeal, pragmatic and even in some cases opportunistic basis. This impression also seems to fit fairly comfortably with Purcell and Sissons'[5] earlier assertion that most managements seem to fit into their standard modern category.

The 1990 Workplace Industrial Relations Survey (WIRS) results confirm many of the above assertions. Managements are reported to be using a wider variety of communication channels and they were also substantially more likely to have taken new initiatives for securing employee involvement (up from 35 per cent to 45 per cent 1984–90). Part-time working had increased, as also had the use of subcontracted services. Additionally, managers in a third of workplaces reported changes to working practices geared towards achieving more flexible working between 1987–90. In the third report in the 1990 WIRS series[6] (and see Fig. 14.1), Millward argues that there is evidence of increasing autocracy on the part of management, a tendency towards treating labour as merely another factor of production, and little evidence that the substantial growth in non-unionism was accompanied either by more 'progressive' management practices or enhanced use of HRM. Nevertheless, using the same research data Fernie and Metcalf[7] have concluded that in those workplaces where HRM techniques were introduced they do seem to produce more productive workforces. HRM did not appear to have improved employee relations, but it had led to enhanced productivity.

THE ROLE OF PERSONNEL

The Institute of Personnel Development (IPD) is the association for personnel staff and has 45 000 members. Most of these members have taken its professional development scheme, offered in universities, colleges of further education and by distance learning programmes. The IPD also offers a range of benefits to members, including regular publications, courses and conferences, and a library and information service. Moves towards HRM would appear to be gaining ground, and this involves a devolution of personnel responsibilities to line management and a more strategic role for personnel specialists, which could also involve acting in the capacity of an internal 'consultancy'. The profession is aiming to justify its contribution by demonstrating how it is 'adding value' to the organisation and its activities.

LABOUR MARKET

- There has been a continued decline in primary and manufacturing sectors of industry, but with a continuing growth in the services sector. Related to this has been an expansion of manual occupations and a rise in female employment.
- There is a marked reduction in the number of under 25s entering the labour market. The demographic dip is now having a particular effect in engineering, IT, health services and education.
- There has been a persistently high level of unemployment, with significant regional variations.

Recruitment

- A combination of private and public methods are used to match potential employees with job vacancies. Frequently, employers advertise in newspapers, and management consultants provide executive selection and search services. Job centres, which provide local services and act mainly in respect of manual workers, are organised by the state.
- Employers may try to establish links with schools, and the 'milk round' is frequently used by larger employers, involving visits to universities to attract graduate applicants. Certain groups are being targeted to compensate for skills shortages, particularly women and school leavers.
- The interview continues to be the popular selection method, with CVs normally being used. There is an increasing interest in the use of psychometric tests and assessment centres.

Remuneration

- There is little statutory involvement in pay determination processes. The principle of state absenteeism has ostensibly become even more entrenched with the winding up of wages councils which stipulated minimum rates of pay in poorly paid sectors.
- Terms and conditions of employment are normally established through collective bargaining processes. In recent years there has been a trend towards devolving this process to the level of the enterprise, and to setting up semi-autonomous profit centres within larger concerns. In the public sector, which is declining in terms of numbers employed, national-level bargaining is still important.
- Job evaluation is established in most larger concerns.
- The importance of establishing internal relativities is to some extent giving way to a notion of rewarding individual contributions and performances. Performance-related pay is now being used by around 66 per cent of British companies for managerial staff, and is well established for clerical and

Workers losing 'access to decisions'

By Robert Taylor,
Labour Correspondent

The increasingly unregulated labour market is returning to the way it was in the 19th century before trade unionism, according to a government-commissioned survey of workplace industrial relations published today.

Its author – Dr Neil Millward of the Policy Studies Institute – argues the country is approaching the position where most workers lack any means of influence in the way their workplace is run beyond their own job.

The report was commissioned by the Employment Department as part of a long running inquiry into Britain's changing industrial relations.

The third report in the series says: "The recent growth in inequality in wages and earnings which has been widely observed to be greater in Britain than in almost all other developed economies is being matched by a widening in the inequali-

ties of influence and access to key decisions about work and employment."

The study suggests the sharp decline in workplace trade unionism since 1980 (with a fall from 58 per cent to 40 per cent in membership) has not led to any spontaneous move by employers to introduce alternative forms of worker representation or joint consultation.

Instead, the author argues British industry and commerce "appear to be moving towards the situation in which non-managerial employees are treated as a 'factor of production'".

Increasingly management is growing more autocratic in its wielding of unilateral power.

At the same time Dr Millward points out no laws have been passed in Britain unlike in "almost all other developed economies" to "provide a basic floor of employment rights and minimum labour standards" for workers.

The comprehensive survey covers 1,500 establishments with more than 25

employees in industry and commerce in 1990.

Dr Millward found few companies are following human resource methods of management. Only 10 establishments had "new style agreements" that included "management control over work organisation" combined with a functioning consultative system; single status in benefits for blue and white collar workers; and "final offer" arbitration. The survey found few companies have introduced profit sharing or share ownership schemes to strengthen the commitment of their employees.

It also found human resource management techniques are more common in unionised than non-unionised enterprises. "We could find little evidence the very substantial growth in non-unionism was accompanied by a growth in human resource management or more 'progressive' management practices," says Millward.

Fig 14.1   Source: *Financial Times*, 15 February 1994

manual workers. Profit sharing has also become increasingly popular following modification in the tax system to favour it.

- Certain basic benefits are regulated by law, including maternity pay, sickness pay, redundancy pay, equal pay and pensions. Many companies enhance these basic provisions, and the government has encouraged private pension arrangements.

Training and development

- The current government limits its role to providing guidance and research in the area of training, and being directly involved in training the unemployed. The onus is therefore on employers to provide training and development.
- In the mid-1980s National Vocational Qualifications (NVQs) were introduced as a departure from standard craft apprenticeships, to relate training directly to the needs of commerce and industry. The Training Agency was established by government to co-ordinate schemes, a number of these involving

employers in partnership arrangements.

- Management development is seen as a priority area, yet surveys indicate that adequate investment is not yet made in this.
- In higher education the binary divide between universities and polytechnics was abolished in the early 1990s, and both sets of institutions are entering into closer partnerships with commercial and industrial bodies.

Current issues

- There have been moves towards flexible working practices in relation to the hours worked and the tasks performed. A number of organisations have broken down demarcation between jobs. The introduction of new technology into offices and factories over the last 10 years has continued the removal of division of labour.
- There has been a significant increase in part-time working, in casual employment (which accounts for 7 per cent of total employment), subcontracting and

self-employment. These developments have coincided with the challenge posed by the demographic time bomb. Employers have had to consider changing familiar work patterns and retaining female and retired employees. The ageing population is likely to promote reconsideration of pension provision.

- Although some companies in the UK are already European in their outlook, the inception of the Single European Market in 1992, which formalised the principle of free movement of labour, may cause problems for many companies who have not reacted positively to European integration. Graduates, managers, and those with special skills could be attracted by the more generous remuneration packages offered in continental Europe. European legislation is making British companies review their approaches to, for example, health and safety. The areas which have caused most controversy in deregulated Britain have been the establishment of works councils and consultation arrangements with employee representatives, but these have been rejected at national level.

GOVERNMENT

For many years it was argued that government in the UK played little part in the human resource system other than in its role as employer in the public sector. Certainly it has been commonly suggested that, both before and after the second world war, the UK system was one that was stable and bound together by a common ideology – the parties to the system sharing the belief that the two main participants to the employment relationship and their respective representative institutions should be allowed jointly and voluntarily to regulate the relationships between them and to resolve the conflicts that inevitably arose. This ideology was given the name voluntarism. The implications of such a voluntarist approach are that government should remain on the sidelines, intervening only when absolutely necessary to protect minority groups who might otherwise be exploited and to protect the national and public interest. Before the 1960s, government acted in a manner consistent with this principle of voluntarism. There was very little legislative intervention: some to protect women and children; some to establish minimum standards with respect to health and safety (a series of Factories Acts); and some to protect employees in industries where it was difficult, often

for logistical reasons, for trade unions to recruit and represent, and where employees might otherwise be exploited. In some of these sectors National Joint Councils, created as a result of Whitley (see Chapter 5) and resurrected in the second world war, were in many cases converted into Wages Councils. These latter bodies, tripartite in nature, set minimum main terms and conditions of employment which were legally enforceable. The intention was that Wages Council activity would encourage the formation of voluntary collective bargaining.

The voluntary nature of the system applied both to collective relationships and to individual employment matters, and it is still the case in the UK that collective agreements are not legally enforceable, although their terms may well be implied in individual contracts of employment. The notion of voluntarism is consistent with liberal collectivist perspectives and can be seen to have lasted as the dominant perspective into the mid-1960s.

However, in the 1960s there were numerous pressures working on government to adopt a more interventionist role and, even before the election of a Labour government in 1964, (perhaps by inclination more interventionist and potentially corporatist in orientation), government had begun to intervene to protect the interests of employees and this continued throughout the decade. The Contracts of Employment Act 1963, the Industrial Training Act 1964, the Redundancy Payments Act 1965 and the Trades Disputes Act 1965, the Race Relations Act 1968 and Equal Pay Act 1970 collectively constituted a significant departure from the voluntarist tradition.

Among the pressures for greater intervention, employers were becoming concerned at the increasing evidence of unofficial strikes. Trade unions were concerned at some judicial decisions affecting their traditional rights and immunities, and the government was becoming increasingly concerned with issues concerning the performance of the economy and the need to control inflation.

This raises another peculiarity of the system in the UK: its emphasis on legislative immunities and negative as opposed to positive rights. The absence of a written constitution and code of positive rights is reflected in the legislative arrangements concerning employment; primacy has often been given to contract and common law and trade unions in particular have had to rely on immunity from legal action rather than positive rights. Even much of the protective legislation of the last 30 years has been negative in character and emphasis, e.g. rights not to be unfairly dismissed, not to be discriminated against and not to be disciplined by your trade union.

In 1965 the government established the Royal Commission on Trades Unions and Employers' Associations (Donovan) to investigate the problem posed by increasing unofficial action and, at or about the same time, it felt obliged to establish, initially voluntarily but subsequently compulsorily, limits on increases of both rates of pay and prices. The recommendations of the Donovan Commission were essentially procedural and structural and did not recommend further statutory intervention. It was the Labour government's only partial acceptance of the Commission's recommendations and its subsequent proposals for further legislative reform and sanctions which signalled the end of both its period in office and the dominance of voluntarism and liberal collectivism.

The Conservative government elected in 1970 rejected Donovan and the liberal collectivist proposals for change, and proceeded in the belief that trade unions had become too powerful, so statutory intervention was necessary to curb them. The Industrial Relations Act of 1971, in addition to creating specific rights and protections for employees for the first time in certain 'unfair' dismissal situations, also banned pre-entry closed shops and created a Trades Union Registrar with powers to vet trade unions' rules, to assess their independence and suitability for collective bargaining, and with whom trade unions were required to register if they were to retain certain legal protections, rights and immunities. The Act effectively nullified post-entry closed shops by giving employees the right to belong or not to belong to a trade union. It also sought to make collective agreements legally binding, created new provisions to assist trade unions gain recognition from relevant employers, and gave the Secretary of State for Employment powers to apply to the newly created National Industrial Relations Court to delay strike action for 60 days and order a compulsory ballot of members to assess support for the action. The Act was complex, to some extent contradictory and was widely avoided, employers and trade unions often colluding together to nullify some of its provisions, in particular the provision that collective agreements were to be legally binding unless both parties specified in writing at the end of the agreement that this was indeed not their intention – most did so.

In 1974, a new Labour government was elected with a very much more macro-corporatist intent. The government and the trade unions agreed that unions would

exercise voluntary wage restraint in return for pro-trade-union legislation and a return to free collective bargaining. The 1971 Act was repealed and there was another tranche of legislative intervention. The Trades Union and Labour Relations Acts of 1974 and 1976, the Employment Protection Act of 1975 and the Employment Protection Consolidation Act of 1978 all served to restore trade union rights, freedoms and immunities to approximately the pre-1971 position, and created new rights for employees in such areas as maternity leave, lay-off pay and paid leave in redundancy situations. The Advisory, Conciliation and Arbitration Service (ACAS) was created to provide the services included in its name and to promote good industrial relations through collective bargaining. Shop stewards were given rights to paid time off for training and other legitimate activities, a procedure was created for assisting trade union recognition, employers were legally required to give unions information for bargaining purposes, and compulsory consultation before collective redundancies was introduced as a legal obligation on employers. The legislative support for collective bargaining was consistent with earlier liberal collectivist traditions, but not so much with voluntarism.

In addition, in 1974 the Health and Safety at Work Act was enacted, giving employees and trade unions new rights, and further individual rights were created in the Sex Discrimination Act of 1975. The administration and enforcement of many of these new rights was given to new tripartite institutions created for the purpose. In addition to ACAS, the period between 1974 and 1979 witnessed the creation of the Equal Opportunities Commission, the Commission for Racial Equality and both the Health and Safety Commission and the Health and Safety Executive. Industrial tribunals, initially created by the Industrial Training Act of 1974, were used to hear applications from individuals that one or more of these rights had been infringed, particularly those relating to dismissal and sexual or racial discrimination.

The corporatist nature of this period of government is most clearly shown by its efforts to secure wage and price restraint through voluntary macro-level bargaining with both the TUC and employers. The government succeeded in reaching a number of agreements with the trade unions until pressures built up from the unions, in the face of declining real living standards and rising unemployment, for increases in excess of the limits required by the government. This culminated in the infamous 1978–79 'winter of discontent' and the Labour government's subsequent defeat in the 1979 election.

In many respects the period 1974–78 represents the high point of trade union influence in the UK, yet the unions failed to obtain legislation extending industrial democracy. The government, at the behest of the trade unions and prompted also by proposals and discussions within the European Community, had set up the Bullock Commission in 1975 (the Royal Commission on Industrial Democracy) with a view to its proposing mechanisms for the achievement of trade union involvement at board level in company decision making. The proposals of the Commission were so strongly resisted by employers that the government was forced to reconsider.

The collapse of these corporatist experiments, the militancy of the trade unions and the anguish experienced by the general public through the winter of 1978–79 provided fertile ammunition for the Conservatives in the 1979 general election. They campaigned on the grounds that the unions were too powerful and they clearly paraded before the electorate their liberal individualist, neo-classical, *laisser-faire* beliefs and policy proposals. Consequently, when elected they proceeded with a series of legislative interventions which, piece by piece, served effectively to limit the power and influence of the unions, dissolved many of the tripartite institutions, diminished the rights and protections of employees at work and from the arbitrary actions of their employers, and increased the rights of trade union members in their relationships with the union in the name of enhancing trade union democracy. At the same time, the government's neo-classical, monetarist and supply-side leanings resulted in economic policies which concentrated on reducing price inflation in pursuit of international competitiveness and economic growth in the longer term, if necessary at the expense of short-term unemployment. Industries and companies that could not compete were to be allowed to founder. Over a relatively short period, 1979–81, unemployment doubled from 1.14 million (4.7 per cent) to 2.3 million (9.4 per cent), and by 1986 it had reached over 3 million (11.4 per cent), most of this in manufacturing industry.[8] Employment in manufacturing industries declined by over 2 million between 1979 and 1987.

The new government's belief in the efficiency and effectiveness of free markets and market forces inevitably posed significant threats to the public sector, particularly that part of the public sector engaged in 'business' activities, the public corporations, nationalised industries and government institutions and agencies providing services to the general public. Over the period since 1979 many of these operations have either been privatised or forced to confront market forces in various other ways, in order to achieve the improvements in efficiency, in particular cost-effectiveness, which would thereby result.

Unlike that of 1971, the Conservative government elected in 1979 approached the task of tackling trade union and employee power gradually. The rights, protections and immunities afforded to these groups were sources of imperfection in labour markets and were therefore ripe to be reformed. Within organisations, these rights and protections enabled employees to insist on restrictive practices which significantly hampered management's abilities to introduce the new technology, production and working methods and flexibility essential to restoring competitiveness.

In 1980 the first Employment Act began the process of legislative reform by repealing the procedure whereby unions could obtain recognition; making it more difficult for unions to maintain closed shops; repealing procedures whereby the Central Arbitration Committee could extend collective agreements within industries; giving employers legal remedies against secondary action and picketing; and making public funds available to unions to encourage them to hold postal ballots for electing officers and before important policy decisions. Employees' unfair dismissal and maternity-leave rights were significantly affected by increasing the relevant qualifying period from six months to two years. This was followed in 1982 by another Employment Act which continued the fight against the closed shop by requiring periodic ballots on the issue, and in tightening the definition of a trade dispute reduced the scope of issues on which trade unions could lawfully take industrial action and thereby retain their immunities from being sued in respect of loss suffered by others as a result. Excluded from the scope of lawful action were secondary and political actions.

The Trades Union Act followed in 1984 and was outwardly geared towards encouraging and enhancing democracy within the trade unions by requiring that union executives should submit themselves to periodic re-election; that unions wishing to have a political fund should have this approved by the membership in a secret ballot at least every 10 years; and that pre-strike ballots should be a legal prerequisite for strike action to be lawful.

In 1986 the Wages Act removed young persons (arguably those in greatest need) from the protection of the Wages Councils and also reduced the scope of the

Councils' activities. The government made it clear that the role of Wages Councils in setting minimum rates of pay was not consistent with its belief in the efficiency of free markets and that they would like to abolish them.

The Employment Act of 1988 further strengthened the rights of trade union members, giving them the right not to be disciplined for not taking part in lawful industrial action and the right to take legal action against the union if that industrial action was taken without the appropriate secret ballot. The Act further stipulated that all senior union officials were to be chosen by secret ballot, and a new role of Commissioner for the Rights of Trade Union members was established.

The 1989 Employment Act repealed laws regulating the hours and working conditions of young people, limited trade union øfficers' rights to time off for trade union activities, and exempted small firms from the requirement that they should have written disciplinary procedures.

In 1990 another Employment Act effectively made the closed shop inoperative. Action in support cannot now be lawful and refusal of employment on grounds related to union membership is also not lawful. Employers were given greater freedom to dismiss employees taking unofficial industrial action, and the Act also rendered unlawful industrial action taken in support of employees dismissed for taking unofficial action. The balloting provisions were tightened up and almost all secondary action now falls into the unlawful category.

In 1993 the Trades Union Reform and Employment Rights (TURER) Act was enacted. The legislation incorporated European Community requirements with respect to both details to be given to employees on employment and to maternity pay and leave. Wages Councils were finally abolished. Employees were given a right to belong to any union of their choice, thereby undermining longstanding jurisdictional and no-poaching agreements within the TUC-affiliated union movement, and employers were given the responsibility of ensuring that individuals authorise deduction of union dues from their pay (check-off) at least once every three years, thereby posing a threat to union finances. The Act also diminished the role of ACAS by removing from it the responsibility to encourage the extension of collective bargaining. The Transfer of Undertakings regulations (1981), which protect employees' job rights and terms and conditions in such circumstances, were amended (in accordance again with EC requirements) to include public sector transfers. Employees were given further protections from

being penalised for undertaking legitimate health and safety activities, and unions and employees were given further rights in the event of redundancy, each of these also being the result of EC directives.

Subject to the receipt of qualified legal advice, employees have also been given the right to conclude compromise agreements with their employers by which they opt out of their statutory rights regarding termination of employment and sexual and racial discrimination. Very importantly, the Act makes it lawful for employers to offer inducements to employees to switch to individual contracts, including inducements to opt out of collective bargaining and/or leave a trade union. The traditional tripartite nature of Industrial Tribunals has been potentially weakened by allowing certain cases to be heard by the chairperson alone with just one lay member. Finally, the Act further affects trade unions and the taking of industrial action by requiring the union to give the employer at least seven days' notice of its intention to hold the necessary ballot and/or take industrial action. Citizens are given the right to take legal action in cases of unlawful industrial action affecting the supply of goods and services, and there are other provisions concerning trade union amalgamation ballots, political funds and other financial matters.

Whichever way you look at the period of Conservative government since 1979, it has contained an unprecedented willingness to legislate in areas affecting the rights and protections of employees, employers and their representative institutions. The actions of government over the period are not consistent with liberal collectivist traditions; they exemplify a conviction that trade unions and employees were too powerful within the employment relationship. The government has returned to management and employers greater freedom to employ on their own terms, and its actions are by and large consistent with a belief in the efficiency of free markets and deregulation (exceptions to this most commonly being the product of EC directives). Lawful industrial action has been made more difficult and narrowed in scope, and it must be remembered that this is in a context whereby employees in the UK do not have a constitutional or statutorily backed right to strike and such action has always effectively rendered the employee in breach of his or her contract of employment. Consistent with their beliefs governments since 1979 have not been keen to pursue active labour market policies, there have been initiatives to encourage training provision and take-up via the private sector, to encourage the provision of vocational courses within the state education sector, to extend the numbers going on to higher education, to improve job-seeking services for the unemployed and to encourage small business start-ups. However, job creation via direct intervention has not been on the agenda.

At the end of 1994, after another recession which saw unemployment rise again close to the three million mark and another substantial erosion of employment in manufacturing, the government showed no real signs of deviating from its predominant concerns with inflation and international competitiveness or from its belief in the efficiency of market deregulation, supply-side reforms, and its desire to limit public expenditure. The UK labour market is now one of the least regulated among industrialised nations, and some interesting and different perspectives on the impact of deregulation, enhanced flexibility and employment levels are expressed in Figure 14.2. At the end of 1994 unemployment had fallen to just below 9%.

In, out, share the work about

FT

David Goodhart tests how far labour flexibiity has reduced UK unemployment

The UK labour market is behaving with all the unpredictability of the weather at Wimbledon. As the economy came out of recession, unemployment began falling earlier than most experts had expected. It stopped falling last summer, continued falling in the autumn, and then stopped again in January.

At the core of most explanations for this erratic behaviour is the notion that the labour market has experienced a significant change in flexibility. The government says that its policies of promoting flexibility – by, for instance, reducing the power of trade unions – responsible for the earlier than expected fall in the jobless total. That is the success story Mr Kenneth Clarke, the chancellor, was parading at the two-day Detroit job summit yesterday.

Similarly, businessmen (see below) agree that increased flexibility explains the unexpected fall in unemployment, though they claim the credit for themselves. But critics say that far from being a straight-forward positive development, flexibility has merely allowed full-time jobs to be repackaged as part-time ones, creating an illusion of more work in the economy. Some go further, adding that whatever the advantages of flexibility to individual employers, it has the big disadvantage of increasing employee insecurity, damaging consumer confidence in a fragile economy.

Amid the conflicting explanations, there is one certainty: unemployment has been falling. Even using International

Employment: part-time Britain?

Part-time employees in Great Britain

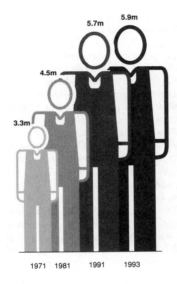

Sources: Employment Department, Datastream

Full-time employment in GB manufacturing sector

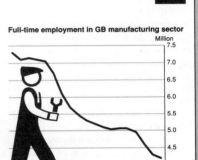

UK growth in male part-time employees*

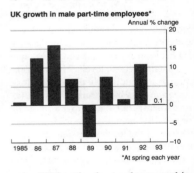

*At spring each year

Labour Organisation figures (which are based on survey evidence and are judged a better indicator than the government's unemployment benefit claimant statistics), the jobless total fell by nearly 100,000 between winter 1992 and winter 1993. Most City analysts expect that trend to continue when the government tomorrow publishes its seasonally-adjusted total for February.

The main reason for falling unemployment has been a reduction in the flow of people coming on to the jobs market. Companies have been sacking fewer people and the number of young people coming on to the market is lower than in the early 1980s, thanks to demographic changes and more pupils staying on at school after reaching 16.

More debatable is whether many jobs are being created. This does not seem to be the case in manufacturing, where employment has been sliding since 1968, with only a slight upward blip in the late 1980s. In the economy as a whole, there was a small increase of 67,000 in the number of employees in work between January and September 1993, from 21.183m to 21.250m, according to the Labour Force Survey, published by the Department of Employment.

But over the same period the number

Fig 14.2 Source: *Financial Times*, 15 March 1994

of full-time jobs fell by 40,000 and part-time jobs increased by more than 100,000. Thus, when the figures are calculated in terms of "full-time equivalent" jobs, the increase is negligible. Further supporting the conclusion that work is being spread around rather than growing, are figures for working hours, which fell from 936m per week in 1992 to 927m in 1993 (the 1990 peak was just over 1bn).

The idea that work is being spread may seem beneficial, but many people are being excluded: employment market experts say job losses are concentrated among lower-skilled male workers whose partners do not work (voluntarily or because the welfare system provides a disincentive to enter employment) while new part-time jobs are in general being taken by women whose partners are in work.

There is some evidence that the male share of part-time work is starting to rise, as manufacturing follows the service sector in increasing its use of part-time labour, but men still constitute only 15 per cent of the 5.9m part-time workforce.

The government says, nevertheless, that growth in part-time employment is a welcome development, shortening the time lag between changes in economic output and unemployment levels. This has some truth to it – but is only part of the story. According to a recent analysis by the US investment bank Goldman Sachs, the main reason why unemployment fell faster after the end of the latest recession than after the 1981–83 downturn was because the working population was growing faster in the early 1980s.

Another important part of the improvement, was the result of "bounce-back"; over pessimistic employers shed labour too rapidly at the time of the autumn 1992 European Exchange Rate Mechanism crisis and had to increase employment when the impact on the economy turned out to be less detrimental than feared. But it was also, says Goldman Sachs, due to an improvement in labour market flexibility which led to employers taking on more part-time workers instead of increasing overtime. As a result, the average hours worked by full-time employees fell between summer 1992 and summer 1993

from 36.6 hours a week to 36.3.

So is Mr Kenneth Clarke right to claim that the current government is responsible for creating that more flexible market? If he is claiming credit for the growth of part-time work, the answer is no. The weakening of union power in the 1980s may have removed an obstacle to the increasing use of part-timers and outside contractors. But many of the legislative and financial incentives for employers to take on part timers – such as exemption from many work-related benefits – have been largely unchanged for 25 years.

Moreover, contrary to the view that part-time work has only recently started to accelerate, it increased at a slightly faster rate in the more regulated and union-dominated labour market of the 1970s than in the 1980s. In 1971 the number of part-time employees was 3.3m or 15.3 per cent of all employees, by 1981 the figure had jumped to 4.5m and 21.2 per cent of all employees. By the end of 1991 the total had increased to 5.7m or 26.4 per cent of all employees.

This suggests that the rise in part-time work is driven as much by broader business and social trends – such as the growing demand of married women for part-time employment – as by deregulation. For that reason this month's House of Lords ruling, based on European Union law, that part-time workers should have the same rights over redundancy pay and unfair dismissal as full timers, may prove to have relatively little impact on demand for part-timers.

However, the government can claim some credit for other factors which may be contributing to job creating flexibility. The growing divergence between the pay of skilled and less skilled workers, encouraged by measures such as the abolition of wages councils, may have prevented demand for low skill labour falling further.

The reduction in benefit payments relative to income from employment may also have encouraged some people to accept jobs which they would not have done in the 1970s.

The government is on firmer ground in claiming credit for creating more flexibility among those with jobs. Over the

past decade, government-inspired curbs on union power, as well as the shadow of high unemployment, has certainly reduced resistance to moves by employers to take more control over pay and working practices.

The corollary of this new flexibility within companies, according to some analysts, is a pervasive insecurity in the British workplace. Mr Eric Salama, joint managing director of the Henley Centre, says that the combination of employment insecurity and the feeling that the state will no longer provide for people is having a strong impact on consumer confidence and savings. Nearly one-fifth of respondents to a recent Henley survey said that concerns about job security had prevented them from making major purchases in the last 12 months.

However, worries about greater insecurity in the workforce may be exaggerated. Employment department figures on the number of people in "atypical work" – casual, temporary, contract or seasonal – show a slight fall over the past 10 years. The total fell from 1.08m in 1984 to 1.05m in 1993, although within that total, contract work has doubled to 600,000.

It may be that such statistics are not picking up other aspects of a more flexible and less secure labour market: the increase in the proportion of the working population who fear losing their jobs and the increase in job-hopping.

But it may also be that consumer spending, now back at pre-recession levels, can adjust to the new labour market flexibility thanks to the creativity of the consumer finance industry, for example by adapting hire purchase schemes to be more like leasing deals.

In any case, recent improvements in labour market flexibility are unlikely to be reversed: as markets and technology change rapidly, the relationship between employers and employees is becoming more fluid. The British experience is that not everyone benefits; the picture is still of some people moving into employment – but others moving out. That suggests flexibility alone is insufficient to make a large dent in the unemployment mountain.

Fig 14.2 Cont.

The public sector

Despite the reductions in the size of the public sector that have occurred as a result of government initiatives since 1979, the sector still employed approximately 5.9 million in 1991, and still encompasses a substantial civil and local government service which implements and administers government policy, purchasing and providing public services including education, healthcare, emergency services and the police service. There are still significant business activities such as the postal services and the railways – all of which are due for privatisation in the future. Public sector employment decreased from approximately 7.5 million, 29 per cent of total employment, to 5.87 million (21 per cent) between 1979 and 1991, the latter figure including nearly 600 000 civil servants. The decline over this period has been mostly in the public corporation sector, where employment decreased from in excess of 2 million in 1979 to under 750 000 in 1991.

As indicated in Chapter 6, it used to be the case that the public sector set an example to the private sector with respect to the employment and management of human resources, public sector organisations being heralded as model, liberal collectivist employers. The Conservative government has encouraged public sector managements to stand firm against employee and trade union demands and has often refused to allow disputes to go to arbitration. It has used its ultimate control over funding to encourage public sector managements to introduce changes to work practices and payment schemes, the most common example in recent years probably being some element of individual performance-related pay. Government has also used its control of funding indirectly to influence and contain rates of wage increase, making use of the cash limits mechanism to encourage the directly involved parties to confront a trade-off between employment, efficiency and wage rates.

By and large, public sector employees have the same or equivalent employment rights and protections as those in the private sector, although some groups (most noticeably nurses in membership of the Royal College of Nursing) have voluntarily relinquished the use of strike action as a weapon or action of last resort, and some have had their freedom to join a trade union and rights to be represented arbitrarily removed. The latter happened in 1984 to employees at GCHQ, a highly sensitive national security establishment. Teachers had their collective bargaining rights removed from them by the Remuneration of Teachers Act 1987.

In the public sector, one of the other traditions that has been eroded over recent years is that of pay and many other substantive conditions of employment being determined through some form of comparability activity or mechanism. Certain groups of essential service workers, such as the police, fire service, the armed forces and senior civil servants, still have access to arrangements of this kind, but government is always in the position of deciding whether to implement the awards recommended or not.

Interestingly, there is little evidence to suggest that as yet the creation of internal markets in the health service, which remains part of the public sector, has achieved the employee relations results that were hoped for. The government intended that the new freedoms would encourage managements of the new employing trusts to determine their own terms and conditions of employment, and to move away from the traditional nationally negotiated system towards human resource management policies and practices more readily associated with the private sector and a liberal individualist perspective, and more closely linked to local labour market conditions. In most cases it seems that these managements have recognised their lack of expertise and rely on the nationally negotiated framework and recognise the same trade unions as before. As time passes and experience is gained, the outcome may of course move closer to the government's target.

The public sector has seen *pro rata* more overt industrial conflict over the last decade than has been the case in the private sector. Managements in public sector organisations have been put under considerable pressure by government to introduce and implement organisational and cultural reforms emphasising performance, efficiency, cost-effectiveness and individualism, to stand firm against employees and trade unions and to operate a *de facto* incomes policy perceived by government to be consistent with its economic and fiscal policies. They have been encouraged to decentralise and localise collective bargaining arrangements and terms and conditions of employment where possible, in contrast to the national liberal collectivist public sector tradition, and indeed in some instances have been encouraged to withdraw from mechanisms of joint regulation. The protracted series of stoppages in 1994 involving railway signalmen was symptomatic of many of these influences and pressures.

Again, government shows little sign of deviating as proposals emerge to reduce further the number of civil servants to less than 0.5 million, privatise further non-core civil service activities, put senior civil servants on to individual contracts, with their pay more closely linked to their success in achieving cost reductions, and give individual departments responsibility for pay bargaining, thereby eroding the centralised tradition.

TRADE UNIONS

The trade union movement in the UK has a long history. Associations among skilled workers, craftsmen etc. can be traced to the earlier parts of the nineteenth century, and the Trades Union Congress (TUC) was formed in 1868. This is the peak association for the majority of the movement comprising more than 80 per cent of trade union membership in the early 1990s.[9] The associations among craftsmen led on in the latter part of the nineteenth century to the emergence and development of trade unions among less skilled workers, this development being linked to the development of large-scale employment locations, stronger markets and relatively full employment. These latter groups were not possessed of a skill which they could seek to control monopolistically and they tended to form general or industrially based movements. This meant that even before 1900 in the UK there was a structurally fragmented labour movement comprising craft, industrial and general unions. It was among the general and industrial groupings that the desire for political and social transformation emerged and it was this which motivated the formation of a political wing to the labour movement, the Labour Party (initially formed as the Independent Labour Party in 1883, becoming the Labour Party in 1906). Ever since the trade union movement, as represented by TUC affiliation, has played a significant role within the Labour party providing the vast majority of its finance (mainly through a political levy on individual members' subscriptions) and playing a significant role in the determination of party policy and leadership elections. The issue of the appropriate mechanisms through which this role should be exerted is currently being discussed, with the leadership of the Labour party seeking to 'democratise' the party by introducing internal policy-determining mechanisms based on the principle of one member one vote, while sections of the TUC-affiliated movement wish to preserve the system of the block vote whereby trade unions arguably have had a disproportionate influence. Behind the particulars of this debate is the conviction that from an 'electability' perspective, the Labour party needs to loosen its ties with the trade unions, thereby convincing the electorate that it is not dominated by the unions. The dilemma is that the Labour party relies overwhelmingly on the unions for its income and, in the absence of the state funding of political parties, is likely to do so for the foreseeable future. It was noted above that in the Trades Union Act 1984 the Conservative government imposed additional periodic balloting requirements on unions wishing to have a political fund. However, early in 1994 there were signs that the TUC-affiliated movement was embarking on a policy of seeking fresh relationships with the other political parties.

The fragmented, multi-union structure of the movement was established early on, as was the development of organisations that were national in their membership coverage. Union activity at an industrial or sector level was encouraged significantly by the recommendations of the Whitley Committee for the creation of national-level joint industrial councils, the employee side of such arrangements often requiring multi-union co-ordination.

The multi-union nature of the movement has often been criticised as inefficient since it complicates collective bargaining and provides scope for inter-union disputes over such issues as jurisdiction and representation, job demarcation and membership poaching. Since 1939 the TUC has had agreed procedures and mechanisms for preventing and resolving such disputes between affiliates, these procedures being referred to as the Bridlington Principles. It is these procedures that have been weakened and in some cases made unlawful by the 1993 TURER Act which gives individuals a right to belong to a union of their choice, rather than necessarily the one currently recognised by the employers, or the one that unions have agreed among themselves should represent employees of a particular type, doing a particular kind of work or working in a particular location or for a particular employer.

The number of trade unions has significantly diminished as the years have passed.[10] Many have found the basis of their membership, whether it be possession of a particular skill or working in a particular industry, no longer relevant in the face of international competition and/or technological development. These unions have either ceased to exist or ceased to be a separate entity, combining instead with other(s) by way of merger or amalgamation. The two big general unions, the Transport and General Workers and the General Municipal and Boilermakers Unions (TGWU and GMB) have absorbed many of these groups, and mergers themselves can create general unions out of industrial or occupational ones. The trend is certainly towards fewer, larger unions. Whether the process has simplified and rationalised the structure of the movement is arguable – certainly some mergers fall into the rationalising category, but others have occurred for reasons other than membership proximity. Two of the more recent and important mergers are those between the engineering and electricians unions to form the Amalgamated Engineering and Electricians Union (AEEU), and between three unions in the public sector, the Confederation of Health Service Employees (COHSE), the National Union of Public Employees (NUPE) and the National Association of Local Government Officers (NALGO), to create the largest union in the UK with 1.5 million members, UNISON.

An additional dimension to the first of these mergers was that the electricians had been expelled from the TUC in 1988 for being in breach of agreed policy with respect to the signing of single-union agreements involving no-strike clauses, and in competition with other affiliates. At the TUC Conference of 1993 the electricians were readmitted.

Despite the multi-union nature of the movement, it has long been the case that unions in certain industries, each representing particular sectors of the labour force, have co-operated with one another, at least to the extent that they have formed confederations of a loose nature to facilitate industry-, enterprise- or plant-level bargaining on common issues, as for example within Whitley-type arrangements. There is a long tradition of multi-union and multi-employer bargaining. More recently, such arrangements have been encouraged and the term 'single-table bargaining' has been coined. At workplace level, these loose associations are often of lay representatives, the shop stewards.

The Donovan Commission examined workplace bargaining and the role of the shop stewards and determined that such, often informal, arrangements should be formalised. Subsequent to that report, and as mentioned above, various legal rights were given to workplace representatives in areas such as time off with pay for various activities, rights to information and consultation on issues such as redundancies and health and safety, and rights to information for collective bargaining purposes. Trade unions have also devoted considerable resources over recent years, although one could argue not enough, to training and equipping their lay representatives so that they can perform their role more effectively. The shop steward role initially developed as a recruiter of members and collector of dues, the latter role having been largely replaced by the widespread use of automatic deduction or check-off arrangements. As time went by, the role of the shop steward developed into one much more concerned with the presentation and taking up of grievances, the representation of employees subject to disciplinary proceedings, and negotiation on substantive issues in the workplace. The TURER Act of 1993 may re-emphasise the dues collecting role if the widespread acceptance of check-off is adversely affected. The impact of this legislative change is potentially significant in other ways; unions may well find their finances adversely affected if they do not succeed in persuading their members to agree again to automatic payment of dues, perhaps particularly those unions representing members employed in fragmented locations and in mobile occupations such as in construction. On the other hand, some may use the requirement to gain a periodic approval of automatic deduction by employers as motivation for a recruitment drive. In mid-1994 the GMB claimed a 4 per cent membership increase attributable to such renewed activity.

We have already noted that the union movement has found itself on the receiving end of a considerable amount of unwelcome legislative intervention since 1979, particularly in the areas of making it more difficult to take industrial action lawfully, narrowing the scope of lawful action and seeking to encourage internal democracy. In the latter regard, the unions have been encouraged or required to make much more use of postal and secret ballots in connection with elections of officers and main policy decisions and before taking strike action. Additionally, members have been given statutory rights not to be disciplined in certain circumstances, not to take part in lawful strike action, not to be discriminated against, not to be prevented from working by virtue of non-membership, and the right to seek injunctions or compensation in respect of such rights being violated. Much of this legislative intervention was based on an assumption on the part of the government that the unions were not internally democratic and that members were not being encouraged to participate in internal decision making processes; also that in some cases they were being intimidated and that the unions were being run by militant minorities and/or popular bosses. Whether the legislation has tackled issues of democracy, and indeed whether this was really the reason for intervention, are matters of subjective judgement, democracy being a multi-dimensional concept.

Trade unions in the UK have tended to see collective bargaining as the main means of achieving employee participation and reducing the scope of managerial pre-rogative and, as noted earlier, the traditions have been conflictual and distributive. However, there are signs that, as with many employers, more co-operative and integrative approaches are emerging and there is a great deal more talk of partnership and joint problem solving. Many trade union leaders, however, are also sceptical of such developments, suspicious that initiatives encouraging employee participation through non-union mechanisms, and which are concerned with issues of quality, the job and working methods, are devices for achieving improved productivity and output, rather than representative of an enhanced and genuine desire for consensus and partnership. They feel also that such developments could pose a threat to trade unionism by making it easier for managements to bypass them.

The 1970s and 1980s were markedly different decades as far as the fortunes of the union movement were concerned. The 1970s saw significant membership growth, particularly among white-collar workers who were actively recruited by a number of relatively new and specialist white-collar unions, the most active probably being the Association of Scientific, Technical and Managerial Staffs (ASTMS), now part of the Manufacturing, Science and Finance Union (MSF). The highpoint of trade union membership in the UK was in 1979, with 13.29 million members, a density of 57.2 per cent[11], and at this point white-collar union membership constituted approximately 40 per cent of the total. Waddington[12] suggests that throughout the 1980s white-collar membership as a proportion of the total continued to increase and by 1987 accounted for almost half, 48 per cent. Certain white-collar unions, often outside the TUC, had continued to expand during this period, an example being the Royal College of Nursing (RCN), and banking, insurance and finance had also been growth areas. The trend towards an increasing proportion of white-collar and professional trade unionists was further confirmed in 1994 in a MORI poll[13] which indicated a substantial increase since 1979, broadly in line with the changes that had occurred in the structure and composition of the labour force. This same poll also indicated a substantial increase in the proportion of female trade unionists and a decline in the proportions employed in manufacturing, again broadly reflective of labour force changes. See also Figure 14.3 for a diagrammatic representation of the make-up of trade union membership in 1993.

The 1980s and early 1990s have seen considerable membership decline from 13.29 million in 1979 to 9.48

Union membership

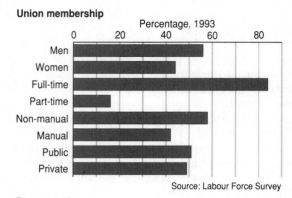

Source: Labour Force Survey

By occupation

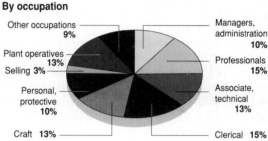

Fig 14.3 Source: *Guardian,* 5 September 1994 – 'Unions must widen appeal' by Keith Harper. Reproduced with permission. © *Guardian* 1994.

million at the end of 1991,[14] and, as noted earlier[15], the proportion of the total movement affiliated to the TUC also declined during the 1980s, although the readmittance of the electricians in 1993 will affect this percentage. Therefore the TUC is arguably less representative of the movement as a whole than it was at the beginning of the Conservative government's period of office in 1979.

The substantial decline in membership has promoted a number of different responses and is attributable to a number of interrelated factors, the most significant including:

- massive unemployment in the union strongholds of manufacturing and extractive industries;
- declining employment in the other main stronghold – the public sector;
- the public relations and legislative campaign mounted by the government and its supporters;
- a greater willingness by management to stand firm;
- the development by management of alternative non-union mechanisms for communicating and seeking involvement;
- some derecognition and failure on the part of the unions at first to appreciate the magnitude of what was happening;
- relative failure on the part of the unions to organise and recruit in those sectors of the labour force

which were expanding and in which they had poor organisation and membership traditions, e.g. female workers, the service sector and younger employees.

The response of the movement so far has perhaps been barely adequate; membership services have been expanded, some attempts have been made to organise and recruit in the traditionally difficult sectors of the labour force, and some unions have begun to confront the financial and organisational implications of declining membership and new check-off legislation. Perhaps most interestingly, the decline or crisis has prompted a debate about purpose and objectives, with two main groupings emerging which have been labelled the new realists and the new traditionalists. The new realists argue that what members and potential members are concerned about are essentially instrumental issues, main terms and conditions of employment and individual protection and representation, and that this is what unions should realistically seek to achieve. They should not concentrate on wider social, economic and political issues, debates and objectives, since these are largely an irrelevance to the membership. (The electricians and engineers are both associated with this view.) The new traditionalists, however (exemplified by the general unions), emphasise a wider community and political approach and objectives. To some extent, as Towers[16] points out, these differences are prompted by the disparate labour market stature of the organisations, respective memberships and the direction of their recruitment activity. The new realists are more fortunate in that they represent members whose skills are likely to ensure their membership of core workforces, whereas the general unions are much more likely to represent and seek to recruit employees without such skills, people much more likely to be on the periphery of labour forces – 'the new servant class'.

The role and purpose of the TUC have also been thrown into the melting pot of trade unionism in the UK in the 1980s and 1990s, primarily as a result of the refusal of government to consult or listen or to continue with corporatist arrangements. Mergers leading to the formation of super-unions also raise the issue of what these organisations have to gain from TUC membership. Again, the attack on the traditional Bridlington arrangements contained within TURER 1993 also potentially diminishes the value of membership. The TUC is beginning to respond to some of these issues and dangers. It is approaching wholeheartedly the opportunity of a European Union role via the ETUC and social dialogue, and at the 1993 TUC Conference the new General Secretary announced that in 1994 the TUC was to relaunch itself and change its ineffectual and bureaucratic image. It would also concentrate on a tightly defined set of priorities: full employment, Europe, employment rights, services to affiliates and a new voluntary code of practice to replace Bridlington. The TUC seems to have a new mission: job insecurity was to be put further up the political agenda, and there are signs in 1994 that the TUC is trying to resurrect a dialogue with government.

The 1990 WIRS[17] again confirms many of the developments discussed above relating to the 1980s. Union density had fallen from 58 per cent to 40 per cent between 1980 and 1990 in both public and private sectors. These first findings indicated that recognition of trade unions for jointly determining rates of pay had declined from two-thirds of workplaces with at least one recognised union to just over a half, and Millward, in the third report in the series,[18] states that the number of employees in workplaces with recognised unions fell from 58 per cent in 1984 to 43 per cent in 1990. He argues that the decline in recognition was the result primarily of lower rates of recognition in new workplaces allied to derecognition in others. Unions were recognised in 40 per cent of all workplaces, but only 30 per cent of new ones. Union recognition had been withdrawn in 9 per cent of all workplaces between 1984 and 1990 and nearly a fifth of workplaces operating union recognition at the beginning of that period were not doing so at the end. The closed shop, which as already pointed out had come under significant attack via legislation (and which is also counter to the direction of EU developments), had covered some 5 million employees in 1980 and this figure was only half a million in 1990. Another finding was that workplace committees of lay representatives from the same and different unions were more common in 1990 than before.

It is easy to present the experience of the unions over the last 15 years as one almost invariably negative and depressed; certainly they have been confronted by strongly negative economic and political environments. However, Hancke[19] comments that in the face of such a hostile environment it is remarkable that membership density has held up so well, and this he attributes to the strong shopfloor role. This role was identified in the 1960s by Donovan and subsequently somewhat protected by various legislative interventions in the 1970s. If Hancke's analysis is well founded, it poses many issues for the movement, its emphasis, organisation and structure.

PROCESSES

As indicated earlier, other than unilateral managerial determination, the main process, through which the employment relationship has been regulated, terms and conditions determined, and grievances and conflicts resolved, has been collective bargaining freely entered into and primarily of the distributive variety. The scope of this bargaining has been limited and it has made relatively few inroads into issues of an economic or business nature. Few managements have or would accept employee participation (whether via collective bargaining or other mechanisms) in decisions on issues such as where to invest and locate, what objectives to pursue, what strategies should be used to achieve the objectives, what kind of technology and production processes should be used, or marketing and pricing policy. Collective bargaining on procedural issues, for example discipline and grievance handling, was encouraged by legislative intervention in the 1960s and 1970s and collective bargaining was generally encouraged and supported by governments that were of a liberal collectivist persuasion prior to 1979. As noted earlier, it was only in 1993 through the TURER Act that ACAS' responsibility to encourage collective bargaining was removed.

Structurally collective bargaining occurs at a number of levels. Multi-employer bargaining at the level of the industry, trade or locality has been dominant in the UK. Workplace bargaining involving shop stewards and local management became more common in the early 1960s in the industrial sector, often facilitated, if not necessitated, by particular forms of technology and payment schemes linked to that technology. Donovan recommended the formalisation of workplace bargaining into enterprise-level bargaining, and developments in the 1980s seem to have further encouraged the decentralisation of collective bargaining, both from multi-employer to single employer and within enterprises. These developments include:

- The desire to link payment to performance.
- The need to introduce new technology and change working practices.
- The decentralisation of operational decision making, partly in response to market pressures.
- Information technology developments facilitating communication between the centre and establishment, plant or workgroup management.
- The government's belief that national bargaining results in wages and other terms and conditions which are insufficiently reflective of local labour market conditions.

- The need for increasing flexibility among the labour force at the level of the plant or workgroup.

The 1990 WIRS[20], however, indicates that where collective bargaining occurs, multi-employer bargaining still affects more workplaces than either single-employer, multi-site or plant-level bargaining, although fewer employees have their pay at least partially determined this way. Other relevant findings were that non-personnel specialist managers' involvement in personnel and industrial relations decision making at an operational level had increased, and managers in a third of workplaces had changed working practices between 1987 and 1990 in order to achieve greater flexibility. According to the initial survey report: 'It is not unreasonable to conclude that the traditional distinctive "system"... based on collective bargaining is no longer characteristic of the economy as a whole.'[21] The authors also concluded that no new system could be said to have emerged to replace the old. Millward[22] in a sense goes further and argues that most workers in the early 1990s lack any means of influence in the way that the workplace is run beyond their own job. The gap left by the rapid shrinkage in trade union representation has not been filled by any significant growth in other methods of representing employees' views and interests.

For many decades the government has provided facilities for disputes to be resolved through conciliation or arbitration. Since 1974 these facilities have been available through ACAS, and that still is the case. The 1990 WIRS[23] found no decline in the frequency with which recourse to such third-party intervention was provided for within pay dispute procedures. However, in the public sector, we know that government seems to have set its face against such involvement in practice. The ACAS Annual Report for 1992[24] noted that after three years of increases in collective conciliation requests, requests for such assistance in 1992 fell 13 per cent to 1200. Individual applications that one or more individual employment rights had been infringed continued to increase in number, and ACAS attributed this in part to higher levels of redundancy in the recession and an increasing individual awareness of rights. The report for 1993[25] noted almost exactly the same number of requests for collective conciliation and a continued increase in individual applications.

The position and role of joint consultation as a mechanism through which management and employees discussed and resolved issues of a collective nature have traditionally been less certain. Managements have often seen joint consultation as a preferable alternative to trade unionism and collective bargaining, a mechanism through which they could communicate and consult but which did not impinge substantially on their managerial prerogative. Trade unions, although sceptical, have been heavily involved in such arrangements and they have been common, although again the 1990 WIRS[26] reports them to be in decline with 21 per cent of workplaces having them in place, compared with 34 per cent in 1984. The problems of differentiating between negotiable and consultative issues in practice continues in situations where both mechanisms exist or where one mechanism is used for both consultation and bargaining.

It has been noted earlier that managements have expressed greater concern in recent years to involve employees more, particularly in issues concerned with quality, the implementation of new working methods and practices, and the job itself. Initiatives have taken numerous different forms including quality circles, suggestion schemes, self-managing work groups, new mechanisms for communicating with and/or consulting employees, and specific projects or problem-solving groups. However, as Guest[27] among others has noted, there is little evidence of organisations approaching the issue with, or as part of, a coherent strategy linked to the achievement of specific objectives or outcomes. The initiatives have often been *ad hoc* and, as Marchington *et al.*[28] have identified, founded in assumptions of positive relationships between employee involvement, commitment and performance.

SUMMARY

The human resource system in the UK in 1994 is substantially different to that which dominated the period from the 1940s to the end of the 1970s. The main authors of change have been the Conservative governments since 1979 which, with their belief in the advantages of free markets, liberal individualist ideology and neo-classical economic policies, have transformed the legislative framework and, in the process, have transformed a system based on individual and collective freedoms into one of individual rights (often specifically against collective institutions) and collective prohibitions. The role of collective bargaining and trade unions has been considerably diminished, the size of the public sector has been significantly reduced, the structure of industry transformed, the government has resisted liberal collectivist initiatives from within the European Union and, wittingly or not, has contributed to the climate of uncertainty and insecurity which pervades employment in 1994.

The other main actors have been relatively passive observers of these changes. Managements have taken a primarily reactive, pragmatic or opportunitistic stance, with little evidence of coherent strategic interventions geared towards the achievement of specific human resource or organisational outcomes. The trade unions have been physically and psychologically traumatised by the onslaught and are still uncertain of how to respond, what the objectives of the movement should be, or quite how to reorganise their relationship to the Labour party; and they are seemingly looking to the EU for salvation. Employees have been on the receiving end of unemployment, impermanence and insecurity, with many being marginalised from employment and experiencing considerably greater emphasis on their performance as individuals.

No new system appears to be emerging – there are piecemeal initiatives but little coherence, and one wonders about the extent to which the old traditions are in permanent decline or opportunistically awaiting resurrection by a change of government and/or EU intervention.

NOTES AND REFERENCES

1. Certification Office. Annual Report of the Certification Officer for Trades Unions and Employers' Associations (annually)

2. Purcell J and Sisson K (1983) 'Strategies and Practice in the Management of Industrial Relations' in Bain G S (ed), *Industrial Relations in Great Britain*, Blackwell, pp.95–120

3. Quoted in *Financial Times*, 26 January 1994

4. Guest D (1992) 'Human Resource Management in the UK' in Towers B (ed), *The Handbook of Human Resource Management*, Blackwell, pp.3–26 and Guest D (1989) 'Human Resource Management, Its Implications for Industrial Relations and Trades Unions' in Storey J (ed), *New Perspectives in Human Resource Management*, Routledge, pp.44–55

5. Purcell and Sisson op. cit.

6. Millward N (1994) *The New Industrial Relations*, Policy Studies Institute

7. Fernie S and Metcalf D (1994) 'What has HRM achieved in the Workplace?' *Employment Policy Institute*, London

8. Employment Gazette Historical Supplement

9. Towers estimated a TUC membership in 1991 of 7.8 million of a total 9.48 million, comprising 82.3% compared with 91.6% in 1979. Towers B. British Industrial Relations and Trade Unions in Towers B. (ed) (1992) *A Handbook of Industrial Relations Practice*, Kogan Page 3rd edition p.32.

10. The total number of unions decreased from 453 at the end of the 1970's to 287 in 1990 of which 74 were TUC affiliates. 28 of these unions had membership in excess of 100,000 in 1991 and they accounted for more than 80% of total trade union membership. Various Annual Reports of the TUC and Certification Officer

11. Density in this instance being as a percentage of civilian employees in employment

12. Waddington J (1992) 'Trade Union Membership in Britain 1980–87', *BJIR*, 30.2, pp.287–335

13. MORI poll reported in *Financial Times* 20 June 1994

14. Towers B, op. cit. p.32

15. Ibid.

16. Fernie and Metcalf op. cit. p.42

17. Millward N, Stevens M, Smart D and Hawes W R (1992) *The 1990 Industrial Relations Survey – First Findings*

18. Millward N, op. cit.

19. Hancke B (1993) 'Trade Union Membership in Europe, 1960–90, Rediscovering the Local Unions,' *BJIR* Vol 31 No. 4, pp.593–610

20. Millward *et al.* op. cit.

21. Ibid.

22. Millward N, op. cit.

23. Millward *et al.* op cit.

24. ACAS Annual Report for 1992, 1993

25. ACAS Annual Report for 1993, 1994

26. Millward *et al.* op. cit.

27. Guest D op. cit.

28. Marchington M *et al.* (1992) 'New Developments in Employee Involvement', *Employment Department Research Series No. 2*

FURTHER READING

Beaumont P (1992) *Public Sector Industrial Relations*, Routledge

Bird D and Corcoran L (1994) 'Trade Union Membership and Density 1992–93,' *Employment Gazette*, June 1994, 189–98

Blyton P and Turnbull P (1994) *The Dynamics of Employee Relations*, Macmillan

Brown W (1994) 'Bargaining for Full Employment,' *Employment Policy Institute Economic Report*, Vol. 8 No. 7

Brown W and Walsh J (1991) 'Pay determinants in Britain in the 1980s: The anatomy of decentralisation' *Oxford Review of Economic Policy*, 7 (1), pp.44–59

Cave A (1994) *Managing Change in the Workplace – New Approaches to Employee Relations*, Coopers and Lybrand

CBI (1990) *Employee Involvement in Shaping the Future*, Confederation of British Industry

Clegg H A (1979) *The Changing System of Industrial Relations in Great Britain*, Blackwell

Coates D (1989) *The Crisis of Labour*, Philip Allan

Coates K and Topham T (1986) *Trades Unions and Politics*, Blackwell

Disney R (1990) 'Explanations of the decline of trade union density in Britain, an appraisal', *British Journal of Industrial Relations*, 28 (2), pp.165–78

Edwards P, Hall M, Hyman R, Marginson P, Sisson K, Waddington J and Winchester D (1992) 'Great Britain, still muddling through' in Ferner A and Hyman R (eds) *Industrial Relations in the New Europe*, Blackwell, pp.1–68

Farnham D and Horton S (eds) (1993) *Managing the New Public Services*, Macmillan

Flanders A (1974) 'The tradition of voluntarism', *British Journal of Industrial Relations*, 12 (3), pp.352–70

Freeman R and Pelletier J (1990) 'The impact of industrial relations legislation on British union density', *British Journal of Industrial Relations*, 28 (2), pp.141–64

Gallie D (ed) (1988) *Employment in Britain*, Blackwell

Gospel H F (1992) *Markets, Firms and the Management of Labour in Modern Britain*, Cambridge University Press

Marginson P, Edwards P, Martin R, Sisson K and Purcell J (1988) *Beyond the Workplace, Managing industrial relations in multi-establishment enterprises*, Blackwell

Marsden D and Thompson M (1990) 'Flexibility agreements and their significance in the increase in productivity in British manufacturing since 1980', *Work, Employment and Society*, 4 (1), pp.83–104

McCarthy W. E. J. (ed) (1992) *Legal Intervention in Industrial Relations*, Blackwell

McLoughlin I P and Gourlay S N (1992) 'Enterprises without unions: The management of employee relations in non-union firms', *Journal of Management Studies*, 29 (4), pp.669–91

Pollert A (1988) 'The flexible firm: Fixation or fact?', *Work, Employment and Society*, 2 (3), pp.281–316

Ramsay H, Pollert A and Rainbird H (1992) 'A decade of transformation? Labour market flexibility and work organisation in the United Kingdom' in Rojot J and Tergeist P (eds), *New Directions in Work Organisation: The Industrial Relations Response,* OECD

Rubery J (ed) (1988) *Women and Recession,* Routledge

Storey J and Sisson K (1989) 'Limits to transformation: Human resource management in the British context', *Industrial Relations Journal* 20 (1), pp.60–65

TUC (1988) *Meeting the Challenge,* Trades Union Congress

TUC (1992) *The Quality Challenge,* Trades Union Congress

Sisson K (ed) (1989) *Personnel Management in Britain,* Blackwell

15 · JAPAN

BACKGROUND

The rise of the Japanese economy to the status of world leader in the years since the second world war has been spectacular. A number of explanations have been given for this, ranging from eulogies about culture to more pragmatic explanations of corporate practices and strategies. At the centre of the success story has been the priority given by Japanese manufacturers to 'quality' production; in this sense, quality is taken to mean ability to satisfy the customer rather than the production of highly prestigious items. More than this, Japanese manufacturers have been second to none in their ability to respond rapidly to market changes and to attack new niches.

At the centre of this success story has been the workforce and the way it has been deployed. Most notably, responsibility for quality remains in its 'natural' place, at the point of production with the producers, who are themselves responsible for quality control and improvement. Lean and adaptable production systems are serviced by multi-skilled teams. Underlying such features are some of the structural properties of the Japanese economic system. These include long-term and high-trust relationships between buyers and suppliers, and between companies and subcontractors, which facilitate longer-term planning. Many subcontractors have in fact been integrated into larger concerns, which is thought to explain the prominence of teamworking. Moreover, the economic revival has been guided by strong central institutions at national level, and has been inspired by semi-religious, as opposed to *laisser-faire* ideology. All the same, in recent years it seems that the economic bubble has burst, and a number of the corporate principles on which the Japanese system is based have been tinged with measures of deregulation.

EMPLOYERS

The Japanese business enterprise is different in nature from those in other developed economies; it is often described as being a family, paternalist, an example of welfare corporatism. It can be characterised as demo-cratic, with decision-making processes which are consensual in nature. They are social organisations in which people are nurtured and developed and given the opportunity to build social relations. Whitehill[1], for example, argues that any accurate model of Japanese management must give priority to human resource development. To the extent that these descriptions are accurate, they are likely to apply only to the larger organisations and mainly to their regular employees, those benefiting from lifetime employment.

Such a model of the enterprise is consistent with a culture influenced by Confucius, except that democracy is apparently inconsistent with the duties of serving and obeying. In fact, it is the part of the model description that is most contested; the decision-making processes can alternatively be described not so much as democratic in nature, but as giving a semblance of participation and involvement which in practice does not impinge on managerial prerogative and control.

If these Japanese enterprises are social organisations nurturing and developing employees ('peoplism' is a term sometimes used to contrast them with capitalism), they are considerably aided in this intent by the legal system surrounding enterprises which, unlike those in the West, does not give priority and control to the interests of shareholders. Shareholders are treated as bondholders; the company owes them money but this does not give them primacy as an interest group. This situation has been further aided by the government, which over the years has provided funds for research and development and assisted investment. Companies have not been primarily motivated to make profit to distribute to shareholders and have been able to take a much longer-term view, concentrating on growth and security. The directors of companies are mostly employees who have themselves benefited from the practices of lifetime employment, internal training and development, and seniority-based pay and promotion. Shareholders, mostly financial institutions and banks, have been content to receive relatively small payments by way of dividends in return for the capital appreciation of their holdings consequent on expansion.

As indicated earlier, enterprises have tended to develop both horizontal and vertical affiliations, so that the main companies tend to form into conglomerates comprising contractors, suppliers and customers. The vertical links are particularly useful from a human resource perspective, since they can be used as a 'safety valve' for near retirement age or otherwise redundant, regular employees without prejudicing the lifetime employment guarantee.

These groups tend not to have holding companies or dominant shareholdings, but they deal with and complement each other. The groups are commonly referred to as *Keiretsu* and the big six of these groups – Mitsubishi, Matsui, Sumitome, Fuji, Daiichi Kangyo and Sanwa (the last three being banks) – are said to control 25 per cent of total Japanese assets. Each group is likely to have between 20 and 30 large commercial or industrial firms as members, with maybe ten times this number also part of the group, and the groups possess considerable influence.

The main enterprises are members of the Federation of Economic Organisations (*Keidanren*), an association which is claimed to be the most important in Japan, significantly influencing (if not controlling) government policy in the areas of economics and business. It is an organisation which speaks for business and management, presenting the image of management as economic statesmen choosing the best course for Japan.

The Federation of Employers' Associations (*Nikkeiren*) is the main employers' association dealing with labour issues. It performs a primarily representative and promotional role externally and a co-ordinating and advisory role internally. It does not engage directly in collective bargaining or dispute resolution; these matters are usually kept within the enterprise family.

As indicated earlier, management preserves control, it encourages the involvement of employees at all levels within the organisation, quality control circles being probably the best-known mechanism securing this involvement, but suggestions or decisions made at one level always have to be approved at a higher level before implementation. It is this aspect of the 'consensual' decision-making process that takes time, but it is argued that any extra time taken in making a decision is more than made up for by the fact that the decision is accepted by employees because they have been involved in making it. Not all suggestions are approved.

Management within the enterprise is multi-layered, each layer being associated with a particular rank and status to which subordinates owe the duty of service and obedience. All regular employees can aspire to the lower management levels in accordance with the seniority principles. Promotion to *bucho* or departmental manager level and above that to director is more difficult and inevitably involves an assessment of merit in addition to having sufficient seniority, although there is a lack of clarity as to what might constitute merit and an absence of criteria against which individual performance can be measured. The assessment of individuals is difficult in a cultural context which emphasises the group and subjugates the individual. Promotion to *bucho* would normally occur at around the age of 45 and to director in the early 50s.

LABOUR MARKET

Since 1965 the Japanese labour market has gradually evolved from an over-supply of the young labour force to an over-demand because of declining birth rates and an increase in university admissions. Until the beginning of the first world war, there was a fluid labour market. It was recognised that excessive labour mobility could be at the expense of national competitiveness, and so a dual structure was set up. Core employees were assumed to have lifetime employment and were surrounded by more malleable and dispensable, peripheral employment. In general, female workers have found themselves peripheral. The labour mobility is now within a company. Since before the second world war the Japanese employment system has been characterised by three principal elements:

1. *Lifetime employment* – those in the core labour force are assumed to stay with the same company for their working lives, a strong emphasis being placed on internal labour markets.
2. *Seniority-based wage system* – incremental pay according to time served.
3. *Enterprise unionism* – collaborative relations without external interference between management and union representatives.

The inception of these practices accompanied the integration of subcontractors, which had previously been prominent, into large enterprises. These three elements are themselves founded on strong binding cultures within enterprises, and personal commitment to corporate values. The team is the linchpin of Japanese concerns. Separate HR practices should be viewed within this broader context.

Recruitment

- Selection is vital, as the expectation is that core employees will remain until retirement. Major companies recruit directly from educational establishments.
- Careful screening ensures that candidates will endorse company values. Entrance ceremonies may involve extensive induction programmes, including team activities.

Remuneration

- Many Japanese companies have a seniority-based wage system. This encourages employees to stay with companies, and contributes towards predictability in wage costs. Job evaluation and performance-related pay systems have therefore not been used with any frequency.
- A range of other benefits are frequently available to core employees which may include subsidised housing, holiday homes, company schools and shops, assistance in cases of sickness, accident and death. At Toyota, 4000 workers have purchased houses with the assistance of company loans.[2]

Training and development

- The assumption of lifetime employment is a positive one as far as training is concerned. A view of employees as assets, rather than costs, means that employers are willing to train and develop human resources at their own expense. There is collaboration between schools/universities and companies, and the education system incorporates a strong vocational orientation. General disciplines may include the philosophy of the 'company man'.
- A main aim of training and development under the internal labour market is to provide employees who are readily transferable between jobs. Multi-skilling is therefore a fundamental ingredient of 'off-the-job' and 'on-the-job' programmes, in which job rotation is a prerequisite for promotion. According to a survey conducted in 629 companies by the Ministry of Labour,[3] 86.6 per cent of all surveyed companies mentioned 'the enrichment of education and training systems' as being the most important aim of personnel and labour management in the future.

Other important features of Japanese HRM

- Just-in-time production is a group of related practices aimed at ensuring that the exact quantity and quality of raw materials, parts and subassemblies are delivered 'just in time' for the next stage of the production process.
- The concept of 'internal customers' is applied to those at progressive stages within the production process.
- Flexible and responsive forms of work organisation are based on group technology and cellular work groups. This can be viewed as an adjunct of 'just in time'.
- There is a high incidence of face-to-face communication and an absence of visible hierarchy. In theory communications are on an equal basis. Managers spend considerable time on the shopfloor, and there is an emphasis on open planning in offices and on the shopfloor.
- Quality circles are common, in which small groups of workers meet voluntarily to make suggestions for improving quality and productivity in their work areas. Such suggestions may then be taken up by management.
- *Kaizen*, or continuous improvement, is emphasised in which all staff constantly consider methods of improving quality and efficiency.

Current issues in HRM

- The boom period would seem to have abated, with contraction of the economy being predicted in the short term. Consequently, some of the basic tenets are now being questioned. The ageing population is becoming increasingly burdensome on two main counts. First, under seniority-based wage systems there is a costly accumulation at the upper end of scales. Secondly, the generous state pension scheme, which allows for 70 per cent of average salaries to be paid after the age of 60, means that, if it remains unchanged, by 2020 some 2.2 million workers will be supporting one pensioner with more than 30 per cent of gross salary.[4] (See Fig. 3.4).
- A survey carried out by the Ministry of Labour[5] found that nearly 28 per cent of 629 companies revealed that ability factors would be used in making promotion decisions. 84 per cent indicated that they would decide wage increases and promotion of employees on the basis of ability and job performance.
- An increasing practice is for certain employees to be lent or transferred to related companies at a lower rate of pay. Also, there is a growing use of part-time working and of micro-electronic technology.

- Personnel or HRM is viewed as an integral part of management both in academic circles and in business, where recognition of the importance of HRM has been fundamental in economic recovery. Further, since the second world war there has been no demarcation between line and staff management functions. Nevertheless, broad personnel policies are more commonly being established beyond individual companies, across enterprise groups. Such policies include co-ordinated approaches of education and training, performance evaluation and pay determination.

GOVERNMENT

Government in Japan has not been actively involved in the conduct and operation of human resource systems. It has pursued a relatively non-interventionist role for most of the post-war decades, although there is some more recent evidence of a developing interest in issues such as the quality of work life and equal opportunities. By and large government has satisfied itself with the provision of a legislative framework and facilities and mechanisms for the resolution of certain kinds of disputes, allied probably to a belief that economic growth would result in greater prosperity for all. Certainly government has been more concerned with assisting and restructuring industry than with the protection of employees' interests. There is a public sector comprising civil service at both national and local levels and some public enterprises, and government has certainly sought to influence the nature of the human resource systems operating within these organisations.

Legislative framework

The allied occupation administrations in the late 1940s set the basic legislative framework with a series of enactments:

- The Trade Union Law of 1945 gave workers the rights to organise, bargain and take collective action including strike action. It also introduced into Japan the notion of an unfair labour practice, borrowed directly from the legislative system operating in the US. Some amendments to the unfair labour practice legislation were made in another Trade Union Law in 1949 and these employee rights were embodied in the Constitution in 1947.
- The Labour Standards Act 1947 specified that employers should create minimum standards usu-

ally known as works rules, in areas such as wages, hours of work, rest periods and holidays. The law did not specify what the minimum standards should be, just that there should be works rules in which employees' rights and entitlements were specified. This Act was revised in 1987 to incorporate an ultimate goal of a 40-hour week with additional hours paid at overtime rates.
- The Labour Relations Adjustment Act 1949 created machinery for conciliation, mediation and arbitration.

Further significant legislation includes the Minimum Wages Act of 1959, followed in 1968 by the creation of Minimum Wages Councils. These councils are tripartite and operate within each prefecture or region and at national level. They advise on appropriate rates, they do not set them; this is done by the government, sometimes through Labour Relations Commissions. New minimum wage rates for each region or industry are established yearly and according to Whitehill[6] tend towards 50 per cent of the average wage in the industry or region concerned.

The law on unfair labour practice is enforced either through the civil courts or by reference to one of the local or central Labour Relations Commissions, each of which is tripartite in its membership. It is possible to pursue an allegation that an unfair labour practice has been committed with both the courts and the Commission, one taking a legal perspective and the other a more administrative approach. There are three kinds of unfair labour practice: discriminatory treatment of workers because of union membership or activities, refusal to bargain (in good faith) and control of union administration. Only employers can commit an unfair labour practice.

In addition to being a Commission of first instance, the central Commission also reviews local Commission decisions and Commission orders can be judicially reviewed by the courts if one party is dissatisfied. One of the criticisms of the system for dealing with alleged unfair labour practices is the long time that can be taken before the various processes are exhausted.

Some of the most intractable of unfair labour practice cases concern multi-unionism. The employer often runs the risk of one or other union alleging unfairness. If the employer bargains with one and then extends the agreed terms to the other, this second union might allege that the employer is being unfair and not bargaining with them in good faith; whereas if the employer comes to separate deals through bargaining with each union in good faith, one party may allege discrimination in that their terms and conditions are not as good as those achieved by another union. There is no notion of an exclusive bargaining agent in Japanese law.

The Labour Relations Commissions also conciliate, mediate and arbitrate in labour disputes and have the power of extending collective agreements in an industry or region.

The above legislation and machinery applies in the private sector. The public sector is covered by a separate legislative framework, which is arguably far less advantageous to employee interests.

The public sector

The public sector includes four subsectors: central government and local government each of which employ civil servants; national public corporations and enterprises, and local public enterprises. National-level corporations and enterprises include postal services, the mint and national forests, and local enterprises include local railways, tramways and public utilities. Several public corporations and monopolies have been privatised in the last decade, and government is currently proposing to privatise others, and it is likely that this process will continue.

Each of the four subsectors within the public sector is covered by different legislation, which itself varies from that applying in the private sector. Government employees, civil servants at both national and local level, are free to organise, but are not free to bargain collectively with their employer, nor can they lawfully take strike action. Registered unions can negotiate with management on working conditions, although not on matters of management or administration, but they cannot conclude agreements.

In the public corporation and enterprise sectors, employees are free to organise and their unions can negotiate and conclude agreements on working conditions (again, matters of management and administration are excluded), but national-level agreements are subject to Diet (parliament) approval if they would occasion above-budget expenditure. Employees in this sector cannot lawfully take industrial action. The prison, fire and police services are not even allowed to organise.

In practice, as is shown by Hanami,[7] the prohibition on industrial action and reaching collective agreements has not stopped the unions in the public sector from being among the most political and militant, and the incidence of strike action in the public sector has often been far greater than that in the private sector.

It is argued that despite the legislation, public sector employees have been prepared to be more militant because they have considerably enhanced job security and are not exposed to market forces, when compared with private sector employees.

It is also common for negotiation and consultative discussions to take place on issues which are not strictly allowed. Managements, however, are in a very strong position when it comes to deciding what they will discuss with the unions, partly because management and administrative matters are difficult to define and it is relatively easy for management to argue that subject matter falls into these prohibited categories if it wants to.

TRADE UNIONS

Japanese workers, as we have just seen, have constitutional rights with respect to being free to organise and act collectively. However, in practice this right means little in the large organisations unless you have permanent or regular employee status. This is because the dominant organisational type of trade unionism in Japan since the late 1940s has been enterprise unionism, and most enterprise unions limit membership to regular or permanent employees. There are other kinds of union – some craft, general, industrial and occupational unions do exist, for example in the public sector, and some do try to cater for non-regular employees – but the overwhelming majority of trade unions are centred on and exist within a particular enterprise. It is often argued that the union is part of the enterprise family and, certainly in this context at least, the union exists because the company exists. Enterprise unions account for more than 90 per cent of Japanese trade unions and it is estimated that they number in excess of 70 000.

Overall, trade union density is approximately 25 per cent.[8] There are quite wide industrial variations in density levels and the public sector has tended to exhibit the highest density figures.

Enterprise unionism was included as one of the four distinctive traditions or 'sacred treasures' of the Japanese system. There are obvious links between various cultural dimensions and this particular organisational type. The importance of loyalty, family, obedience and group status all tend to encourage employees to see the enterprise union as the most logical form. Joining an external organisation would create strains and conflicts of loyalty, exacerbated by an acceptance that self-interest should be subordinated to group interests.

The enterprise union is open to all regular employees (thereby excluding women who rarely have this status), blue collar and white collar. The leaders of the union are employees of the enterprise and elected by the employees. It is by no means unusual for junior management ranks to provide the union leadership and such experience is generally considered as evidence of leadership qualities that render the employee suitable for further promotion. Union dues are collected by check-off and the majority of employees are usually members. The enterprise often provides office and other administrative facilities, although they are not supposed to finance or control the union.

The enterprise union system has been widely criticised, particularly by external observers, as being too cosy and not really providing a mechanism through which employee interests and grievances are likely to be satisfied in conflict with the interests of the enterprise. As Kawanish[9] argues, the union really acts as an auxiliary to management rather than as a bona fide representative of the employees. Certainly, it is relatively easy for management to dominate the union. Some authors have argued that there will have to be change, that indeed employees will increasingly seek different forms of representation as recession, change and insecurity occur.[10] Certainly any expansion on the political left is likely to generate increased disaffection with enterprise unionism.

Most enterprise unions are affiliated to industrial federations and to the national peak association Rengo. Before 1987 there were three main and politically differentiated peak associations,[11] but they merged into the one association in 1989. Rengo represents unions and federations with approximately 8 million members (about two-thirds of the total trade union membership). These industrial and national federations tend to perform certain co-ordinating and political lobbying activities on behalf of the enterprise unions, but do not usually engage in collective bargaining themselves; this tends to be the province of the enterprise union and is discussed below. Rengo has until very recently supported the Social Democrat party, but there is now some evidence of this 'block' support weakening, with unions representing nearly 2 million workers announcing in March 1994 that they intend to cut their links with the Social Democrats.

PROCESSES

The fourth of the sacred treasures of the Japanese system was identified earlier as consensus decision making. The implications of this are that Japanese employees participate to a great extent in the decision-making process and that they are, therefore, sharing power with management who give up unilateral control. This seems to be far from the truth. Certainly consensus decision making and the employee involvement generated are consistent with a culture which emphasises harmony and views the enterprise as an enlarged family, the status of an individual being derived from the status of the group. However, it is not consistent with the findings of Hofstede[12], who discovered that Japanese work systems exhibited high power distance and strong uncertainty avoidance; employees were accustomed to taking orders (this is, of course, consistent with the Confucian duty to serve and obey) and work tasks were tightly structured so that employees were left with little doubt as to both the 'what' and the 'how', with very little leeway or freedom to control their own activities at work. It must also be borne in mind that much of the tight structuring of work tasks is technologically driven. Conti and Warner[13] confirm that the principles of scientific management are still a significant influence on manufacturing processes and job design.

There are two main processes through which, it is often argued, employees participate in decision making: the quality control circle and joint consultative committees. The former is an example of direct participation, while the latter is representative in nature.

Quality control circles are small groups of people who voluntarily meet regularly to examine and resolve problems with product quality and operations, potentially including also employee development and job enrichment. These circles are consistent with the 'ringisei' or consensus decision-making model, which encourages changes in procedures and routines to be originated by those involved, and with the philosophy that quality is the responsibility of everyone. These groups make suggestions or recommendations but crucially are not in a position to decide and implement. All suggestions are referred upwards for approval; often the approval process will go through various stages and layers of management and is inevitably time consuming. However, as pointed out earlier, the system is defended on the grounds that, while it takes time, it does result in changes being implemented which already have the commitment of those to be affected, since they have participated in the origination of the proposal.

Quality circles are, therefore, an example of 'bottom-up' management, but importantly they seem to have very little to do with democracy or power sharing and are motivated mostly by management concerns with quality and production. The voluntary nature of these circles is debatable, since many commentators would argue that there is much pressure on individuals to participate.[14]

Similarly, critical comments have been made about the joint consultative committee system. Ostensibly this is another mechanism enabling employees indirectly to influence corporate decision making and receive information about the state of the company, but, as Morishima[15] argues, they can also be viewed as mechanisms used by management to obtain labour's consent and co-operation in potentially conflictual situations. This study also showed that labour-intensive continuous processes, which give employees greater disruptive capacity, seem to encourage greater willingness on the part of management to share information and engage in consultation. Increasingly, it seems that enterprise management is using joint consultative fora before collective bargaining as a mechanism for informing employee representatives of the financial position of the enterprise, and perhaps particularly setting the scene for arguing that certain levels of wages and benefits cannot be afforded. Joint consultative committees do exist in the majority of larger enterprises.

Collective bargaining

Collective bargaining is the preferred method for determining wages and working conditions, at least in the larger enterprises. The majority of the bargaining takes place at enterprise level, but only after a pattern or 'rate' has been established at industry level via the annual *shunto* spring wage offensive. Usually what happens is that the national and industrial union federations co-ordinate wage bargaining, select an industry and seek to reach agreement in that industry on the rate of increase to be applied to wage rates. Once established, the rate is taken as a rate around which enterprise bargaining is concentrated.

The *shunto* system has its critics. Some of the problems or disadvantages associated with the system apparently include a concentration on wages to the detriment of other issues, and wage rate bargaining becoming divorced from the workshop.

Bargaining within the enterprise is also likely to cover issues such as the twice-yearly bonus payment characteristic of the larger organisations, other supplementary payments and allowances, retirement allowances, hours of work and rest periods. The twice-yearly bonus payment is loosely linked to organisational performance and commonly equates to four or five months' pay.

This enterprise bargaining, it must be remembered, takes place within a context encompassing the alleged disadvantages of enterprise unionism referred to earlier and the cultural influence encouraging consensus and the avoidance of conflict. Nevertheless, disputes do occur and industrial action is sometimes taken, although this is usually demonstrative in nature and of short duration.

Collective agreements are legally enforceable and there is legislative regulation of certain terms and conditions of employment.

SUMMARY

Japan's is a distinctive system, with cultural value and traditions that have undoubtedly contributed to a remarkable economic and technological success and which also have served to set the Japanese system apart.

However, recession, declining profits, political corruption and scandal, increasing international competition, structural change, increasing consumerism and interest in leisure, the ageing population and inadequate social security system, increasing concerns about the quality of life and working hours and conditions, and the dilemma surrounding the future role of women in industry and society, all cast doubt on the future of the system and the ability of the old order to survive.

NOTES AND REFERENCES

1. Whitehill A M (1991) *Japanese Management: Tradition and Transition*, Routledge, p.149

2. Oliver N and Wilkinson B (1988) *The Japanisation of British Industry,* Oxford

3. Ministry of Labour (1987)(a) *The Change and Propsect of Japanese Employment Practice* (in Japanese), Onkwashoa Press, Tokyo

Ministry of Labour (1987)(b) *The Research of Employment*, Onkwashoa Press, Tokyo

4. 'Japanese face up to getting old,' *Financial Times* 10 December 1993

5. Ministry of Labour, op. cit.

6. Whitehill A M op cit p.182

7. Hanami T (1991) 'Co-operation & Conflict in Public Sector Labour Relations in Japan', in Gladstone A, Lansbury R, Steiber J, Keu T and Weiss M (eds) *Current Issues in Labour Relations, An International Perspective*, Berlin DeGruyter

8. See appendix 14

9. Kawanish H (1986) *The reality of Enterprise Unionism. Democracy in Contemporary Japan*

10. Tokunaga S (1983) 'A Marxist Interpretation of Japanese industrial relations with special reference to large private enterprises', in Shirai T, *Contemporary Industrial Relations in Japan*, pp.313–30

11. Sohyo – General Council of Trade Unions of Japan.

Domei – Japanese Confederation of Labour.

Churitsuroren – Federation of Independent Unions of Japan.

12. Hofstede G (1984) 'The Cultural Relativity of the Quality of Life Concept', *Academy of Management Review*, July 389–98

13. Conti R F and Warner M (1993)'Taylorism, new technology and Just-in-Time systems in Japanese manufacturing', *New Technology, Work & Employment* Vol. 8-1

14. Woronoff J (1991) *Japan is Anything but Number One*, Macmillan

15. Morishima M 'Use of Joint Consultation Committee by large Japanese firms', *BJIR* Sept. 1992, 405–23

FURTHER READING

Blanpain R (1985) *Comparative Labour Law and Industrial Relations*, 2nd edition, Kluwer

Chalmers N (1989) *Industrial Relations in Japan: The peripheral workforce*, 2nd edition, Routledge

Jain H C (1990) 'HRM in selected Japanese firms', *International Labour Review*, 129 (1), pp.73–90

Koike K (1988) *Understanding Industrial Relations in Modern Japan*, Macmillan

Kuwahara Y (1993) 'Industrial relations in Japan' in Bamber G and Lansbury R D *International and Comparative Industrial Relations* 2nd edition, Routledge, pp.220–44

Ohta T (1988) 'Works rules in Japan', *International Labour Review*, 127 (5), pp.627–40

Ozaki M (1987) 'Labour relations in the public service: Labour disputes and their settlement' *International Labour Review*, 126, pp.405–22

Schrofe J (1993) 'Dismissal protection in Japan', *International Labour Review*, 132 (4), pp.507–20

Shirai T (1983) *Contemporary Industrial Relations in Japan*, University of Wisconsin Press

Pascale R T and Athos, A. G. (1986) *The Art of Japanese Management*, Penguin Business

Takahashi Y (1990) 'Human Resource Management in Japan' in Pieper R (ed) *Human Resource Management: An International Comparison*, De Gruyter

Trevor M, Schendel J and Wilpert B (1986) *The Japanese Management Development System*, Frances Pinter

16 · AUSTRALIA

BACKGROUND

Australia is a large country with a relatively small population. A distinct feature is its degree of federalism, with federal governments able to pass laws, including the sphere of employment relations. The Australian economy is dominated by multinational concerns, many of which are run from overseas. As a result of this, a diversity of HR practices will be apparent, any of these having been influenced by cultures and structures within the multinational country of origin. Despite this, much consideration has been given to HR issues over recent years. These have been linked with economic success and there is evidence of a shift away from a highly centralised and legalised system of employment regulation towards one that is more devolved and performance orientated.

EMPLOYERS

Employers in Australia have traditionally adopted a unitarist, individualist and enterprise-level approach towards human resource management and the nature of the employment relationship. At a relatively early stage in the development of the system in Australia, managements were confronted by trade unions representing the collective interests of employees, and employers responded by forming a number of organisations representing their interests. However, coherence and unity within the employers' organisation movement proved difficult. Numerous co-ordinating efforts, committees and other mechanisms were tried out over the years, but it was not until 1977 that the Confederation of Australian Industry (CAI) was established as a single peak association to represent and lobby at federal level on behalf of employers.

Even this arrangement proved relatively short lived, with many large employers experiencing sufficient dissatisfaction with the objectives, role and services of the CAI to de-affiliate and establish the Business Council of Australia (BCA) in 1983, and it is this organisation which seems to have been carrying the flag for Australian employers in the last decade. In 1992, the CAI merged with the Australian Chamber of Commerce to form the Australian Chamber of Commerce and Industry (ACCI).

The early establishment of compulsory conciliation and arbitration as mechanisms for preventing and resolving disputes between employer and employee also contributed to the pressures encouraging the formation of organisations representing the collective interests of employers. The widespread utilisation of arbitration tribunals has resulted in many instances in managements losing substantial control over the determination of main terms and conditions of employment and thereby control over wage costs. The scope of the arbitration awards, and arguably the influence of trade unions within organisations, has been fairly narrow, with managerial prerogative and issues related to organisation and production substantially protected and preserved by the arbitration boards and tribunals. However, control over wage costs has also been influenced over the last 15 years by the substantial use of incomes policies and wage indexation as mechanisms for exerting pressure on inflation with a view to improving the competitiveness of Australian industry in both domestic and international markets.

Over the last decade, employers have been confronted by numerous interrelated pressures encouraging change, some of the more influential being:

- A Labour government committed to trade unionism, employee participation and the interests of employees and their families, but also seeking to restructure and regenerate Australian industry in the face of a primarily negative international economic environment, and looking to do so through corporatist and tripartite mechanisms. This government has become increasingly committed to collective bargaining at enterprise level as a preferred alternative to centralised and compulsory arbitration.
- Increasing technological innovation and the need to utilise it in order to remain competitive.
- Increased exposure to alternative methods of work organisation and human resource management, particularly as practised by Japanese and 'excellent' American employers.

In response, employers and employers' organisations have adopted various approaches and responses, among which they have sought to do the following:

- influence arbitration awards and seek tax concessions;
- cut costs through mechanisms such as lay-offs and redundancies, just-in-time management and total quality production;
- enhance employee involvement in job issues through team and workgroup-based mechanisms such as quality circles, taking advantage where appropriate of employees' insecurity;
- introduce new technology and production methods, encouraging flexibility, multi-skilling and broadening task ranges where possible;
- place greater emphasis on employee development and skill-related career paths;
- increase use of communication schemes emphasising direct communication with employees rather than through trade unions;
- extend joint consultative arrangements with trade unions at enterprise level to discuss and possibly resolve problems related to the issues above, sometimes extending into a form of enterprise-based productivity bargaining.

It would be inaccurate to suggest that Australia has witnessed employers discovering and implementing *en masse* coherent, strategic, developmental human resource management, but there is evidence of managements moving, often in a reactive and piecemeal fashion, in these directions, utilising one or more of the approaches detailed.[1]

The adverse economic climate has helped, in that unions and their members have been left in no doubt of the seriousness of the threats facing the Australian economy and the necessity to accept some change to their traditionally restrictive and conflictual approach towards work organisation, working practices and task flexibility. The close relationship between Labour governments and the trade union movement has probably assisted employers in this respect. Certainly the Labour government has accepted the need to change and indeed has introduced a number of initiatives aimed at assisting the regenerative process, including encouraging the restructuring of arbitration awards and the system of wage determination to facilitate and encourage joint enterprise-level productivity bargaining.[2]

LABOUR MARKET

- More than 60 per cent of the population lives in Sydney, Melbourne, Brisbane, Perth and Adelaide. The bulk of the working population is concentrated with a few large employers. Large workplaces with 400 or more employees account for approximately 1 per cent of workplaces, but employ 24 per cent of the workforce.
- There has been a substantial increase in women employees. In 1961 women made up approximately 25 per cent of the workforce. By 1990 the figure had reached 41.5 per cent.[3] Women tend to be concentrated in the service sector, and in part-time, low-status work which carries poor pay and conditions.

HR practice

Traditions of adversarial collective bargaining and centralised arbitration have affected the nature and content of HR practice. Basic rates of pay and related matters have been legally determined at a central level. Personnel policies in the early 1980s were established at central level to apply across industries concentrating on precedent, rather than performance.

Since the mid-1980s change has been apparent, with the Labour government and the national trade union association, the Australian Council of Trade Unions (ACTU), entering into Accords to reconstruct the Australian economy for greater competitiveness. In particular, these have been highly influenced by the Swedish neo-corporatist tripartite model of employment regulations, which had combined economic progress with low unemployment, social cohesion and more balanced national growth.[4] Interestingly, UK policies were rejected by the unions as they 'had been pursued in a socially disruptive and inefficient way and had resulted in disastrous levels of unemployment and high social and regional inequality'.[5]

The Accords have produced the following:

- Legislation for equal employment opportunity and for health and safety.
- More flexible education abolishing the distinction between universities and polytechnics.
- A training guarantee scheme to encourage employers to spend at least 1.5 per cent of their payroll on structured training.
- Structural efficiency programmes, which aim to promote multi-skilling, flexible working patterns and consultative arrangements.

More and more pressure is being exerted, mainly by employers, to move away from the industrial relations mindset, and instead to promote individualism and flexibility in employee relations. This could be promoted by decentralising bargaining arrangements to enterprise level.[6]

There is some evidence that HRM is gaining ground in Australia. A survey reported in 1990[7] found in medium- to high-performing enterprises:

- a decentralisation of the HR function to business units, away from centralist HRM departments;
- a more strategic orientation for HRM, with most senior HRM executives reporting directly to the chief executive;
- an increasing prominence for HR issues in the formulation of business plans.

GOVERNMENT

As indicated earlier, government occurs at federal, state and local level with considerable devolution of powers, and there is a substantial public sector comprising public administration and services at each level and a number of public sector business activities.

Here we examine first the regulatory and legislative roles of federal government as they impinge particularly on the private sector, and then we look at the government's role as employer in the public sector.

Regulatory and legislative roles

Governments of all political persuasions have sought at various times to regulate, or at least influence, the rate of wage increases. There are two main ways in which they have sought to achieve this in the private sector:

1 By seeking to persuade the parties to moderate their aspirations and demands in the interests of the economy, controlling inflation and enhancing competitiveness and employment. Often they have encouraged automatic indexation schemes.
2 By trying to manipulate the rate of wage increases through putting pressure on the various arbitration tribunals and commissions and influencing the awards made for strategic groups, thereby setting a pattern which it is hoped the rest will follow.

In addition to the rate of increase in wages, government within the last decade has started to encourage the parties, including the arbitration commissions, to link wage increases to restructuring and greater productivity.

On some occasions, efforts on behalf of government to influence the arbitration commissions brought the two parties into conflict, since the commissions, as noted earlier, are autonomous and independent of government, with roles prescribed by legislation and the constitution. Resistance to government intervention of this kind has also come from employers and unions with each, depending on the precise circumstances, alleging that the arbitration commissions were in breach of their legally prescribed duty if they yielded to government pressure.

Over the last decade, government at federal level has sought to achieve corporatist consensus, involving employers and unions in decisions relating to economic objectives and strategies and the restructuring and regeneration of Australian industry. Employers' organisations have been reluctant and unable to participate fully with the federal Labour administration and trade unions in these 'corporatist' endeavours, and there have been a number of primarily bipartite as opposed to tripartite 'Accords' in consequence. Employers, with their unitarist, individual and free market ideological roots, and with the absence of a strong and coherent federal-level organisation, have found participation in such national and industry-level planning activities difficult. Additional problems were initially posed by the closeness of the relationship between the Labour party and the unions, and the fact that the original Accord of 1983 was the basis on which the Labour party fought the 1983 election and was the product of an agreement between the Labour party and the ACTU.

The main aims of the original Accord were:

- price and income restraint;
- better industrial relations;
- enhanced tripartite involvement in economic and industrial planning via a system of advisory councils, e.g. the Economic Planning Advisory Council;
- the introduction of Medicare;
- creation of employees' rights to be notified and consulted through their unions about proposals for technological change.

This latter objective was achieved in 1984 as a result of the Federal Conciliation and Arbitration Commission Decision on Termination, Change and Redundancy, which required employers to consult before introducing significant changes to production methods or company structure. The decision also dealt with notice periods and severance pay provisions in the event of redundancy. This federal decision was quickly incorporated into industry awards throughout the country.

Despite employers' objections to some provisions of the original Accord, primarily on grounds that proposals such as that detailed above would inevitably increase costs and diminish competitiveness, some employers' organisations did subsequently approve it. Employers can perhaps best be described as reluctant and junior partners. Since the original Accord, a number of subsequent Accords have been agreed[8], many of them involving agreement on the part of the trade unions to restrain their wage demands in return for changes of a fiscal and/or social nature benefiting at least some of their members.

The scope of Accords has tended to narrow as the years have gone by, and the dangers of centralisation inevitably linked to corporatist arrangements of this kind have been noted by all parties. Government and employers have both frequently emphasised and encouraged enterprise-level bargaining geared towards gaining improvements in productivity and efficiency. The trade unions have generally been less keen on this trend since they feel it may reinforce the position and prerogatives of management. They do not have a tradition of competent workplace organisation, and the economic environment of recession and high unemployment may well favour the employer in any such bargaining. Nevertheless, the most recent Accord (1993) goes further in encouraging enterprise bargaining to determine wage increases and assigns top priority to reducing unemployment.

This Accord goes a long way towards creating a new model of wage determination, at least as favoured by the federal Labour government and the ACTU. The Accord states that collective agreements freely entered into should become the preferred method of delivering increases and that these should be certified by the tribunals. Where parties are unable to reach agreement, the Australian Industrial Relations Commission (AIRC) may require the parties to bargain in good faith and may help through conciliation and arbitration. There was to be a system of arbitrated safety-net awards protecting those on low incomes and not covered by workplace/enterprise-level agreements. Negotiated agreements should seek to enhance productivity and competitiveness. Arbitrated safety-net awards adjustments were to be consistent with the twin objectives of promoting sustainable employment growth and reducing unemployment. National-level wage policy was to be determined between government and the ACTU. In

sum, it represents a shift towards collective bargaining at enterprise level, with conciliation and arbitration available as support and protection for those unable to agree or not covered by such arrangements. The emphasis will also be on productivity and efficiency as the justification for wage increases.

In June 1994 the government announced agreement with the ACTU on increases in the national minimum wage applicable to low income earners not covered by enterprise agreements. These increases were to cover the two years of 1994 and 1995 and amounted to $16 over the two-year period, building on the $8 increase granted in October 1993 as part of a safety-net national wage decision. These agreements and increases were determined within the terms of the 1993 Accord but did not link pay to improvements in efficiency or productivity, and have subsequently been criticised by employers' organisations on these grounds and because they will discourage employment.

It is difficult at this early stage to assess the impact of the 1993 Accord. The intent certainly is to transform the system of wage determination, to decentralise it and to significantly enhance the role of collective bargaining. Many trade union leaders are concerned by the developments, given the absence in many plants/enterprises of trade union organisation and the inadequacy of the skills and experience of those who may be called on to participate. There are questions relating to the adequacy of the existing legal framework and the legitimacy of industrial action and the rates to be applied; also about what is going to happen in non-unionised companies and how the new emphasis for decentralisation bargaining will fit with the structural changes happening in the trade union movement.

In addition to the 1988 Industrial Relations Act which established the AIRC, governments at federal and state level have in recent years legislated in the areas of equality of opportunity, e.g. the Federal Affirmative Action (Equal Employment Opportunity for Women) Act 1986, and health and safety. In both these areas, the legislation has required the development of consultative arrangements, and in the case of health and safety these have taken the form of relatively permanent health and safety committees.

Federal governments have sought to encourage private sector investment in training and skills development, but there are signs in 1994 that government is about to pursue more active policies to deal with structural, long-term and youth unemployment. In May, it published a set of proposals in a white paper on employment and growth which involve a $6.5 billion programme over a four-year period, the objective being to reduce unemployment by 5 per cent by the end of the 1990s. The package comprises subsidies to employers for employing long-term unemployed, training and work-experience initiatives, direct job-creation schemes in some of the more remote areas, and changes to the social security system to provide more of an incentive to work.

It is also important to note that federal and state governments do not always see eye to eye, the potential implications of which are exemplified by the Conservative Victoria state government wishing to abolish many employees' rights and benefits in conflict with the direction taken by federal government.

The public sector

The public sector in Australia encompasses various business activities including utilities as well as the common public services, their administration and health and education.

As a whole, the sector has employed between 25 and 30 per cent of total civilian employment. Trade union membership and density have traditionally been higher in the public sector compared with the private sector, and this has been attributed primarily[9] to a combination of size of establishment, check-off facilities being common, more favourable employer disposition towards trade unions and greater employment security.

As indicated earlier, government and therefore public sector employment (excluding business activities) occurs at three main levels – federal, state and local. At the local level, where services such as refuse collection, welfare services, road construction and maintenance, and parks and gardens are provided, the employer is the local council. At other levels there is less consistency, but in each state and at federal level there is a Public Service Board which is the employer for the majority of employees. At local level, employers have often formed loose associations at state level in order to facilitate consistency of outcome in discussions and bargaining with the trade unions.

Conciliation and arbitration provisions and tribunals have operated in the public sector in a similar fashion to those in the private sector. Tribunals have been more likely to have employee representation and there are numerous distinct and different sets of arrangements. Grievance procedures have been more common in the public sector, although as has been noted earlier the private sector is catching up in this area. Employee participation in consultative arrangements has also

been more common in the public than private sector. At federal level, the Public Sector Reform Act 1984 extended federal employees' rights to information and consultation, Joint Councils have been established to advise the Public Service Board, and federal government has encouraged each department to devise plans and proposals for enhancing industrial democracy; although democracy in this context is perhaps a misnomer and 'employee participation through consultation' would be a more appropriate description of what is envisaged. In this context, as in others, government has perceived its role as one of leading by example.

The craft and occupational origins and traditions of trade unions in Australia extend into the public sector and, like the private sector, it is characterised by a multiplicity of unions in most departments, services and establishments. Union multiplicity provides plentiful opportunities for inter-union demarcation and jurisdictional disputes, but the unions have devised mechanisms both for preventing such disputes and for acting together in loose associations for bargaining purposes.

Strikes also occur in public sector departments and services. Some essential services are legally prohibited from taking strike action and the law varies from one state to another, but the laws prohibiting industrial action have rarely been used and certainly such industrial action has been taken.

While there are no hard and fast rules, developments in the federal sector, whether through voluntary bargaining and agreement or as a result of an arbitration award, do tend to set patterns and trends for other groups at different levels.

TRADE UNIONS

As has been mentioned earlier, the trade union movement in Australia shares common origins with other 'Anglo' countries which have significantly influenced its structure. There are still many trade unions, several of them relatively small and with craft or occupational origins. However, the number of unions has fallen quite rapidly in recent years, there have been many mergers and amalgamations, and unions have been encouraged in many instances to open up their membership base and thereby move towards the industrial or general type. The amended registration requirements of the 1988 Act and its 1990 amendment have undoubtedly contributed to this rationalisation, and both government and the ACTU foresee a movement comprising 20 or so large unions probably organised on industrial/occupational lines.

There is a single peak association, the ACTU, to which the more significant unions representing the vast majority of union members belong and which represents the movement at national level with employers and government and in any corporatist or tripartite mechanisms.

The union movement has tended to be economistic in its objectives, traditionally concentrating on wages and other terms and conditions of employment, although in recent years there is evidence of an increasing concern with the social wage and with employee participation as well as with the reconstruction and regeneration of Australian industry.

There have been close ties with the Australian Labour party for many decades and the Labour party is often described as the political wing of the labour movement. The closeness and significance of this relationship has been particularly important since the early 1980s, and the Prime Minister between 1983 and 1991 was an ex-president of the ACTU. Indeed, as noted earlier, the ACTU and the Labour party collectively formulated the policies on which the 1983 election was fought and which formed the basis of the Accords since then. The original Accord, which Frenkel[10] ascribes in large measure to initiatives by the Australian Metal Workers Union (AMWU), sought to provide for the unions a system whereby real wages could be maintained through indexation; improvements in the social wage could be gained through spending on education, health and welfare benefits; and greater union participation could be achieved in planning as well as implementing change. In return, the unions were to support government measures to restructure and regenerate industry which required that they adopt a more flexible approach to traditional working practices, production methods, wage and salary structures and differentials, redeployment, retraining and their approach towards employers. Further evidence of a changing approach by the unions can be detected from the recommendations of the ACTU mission to Europe in 1986, which included achieving a tripartite, consensual, positive and innovative approach to the management of change.

Undoubtedly the Accords have facilitated some progress in these latter areas. However, employers have been resistant to employee participation through their trade unions in decision making prior to change. Employers have tended to view these sorts of strategic and policy issues as within their prerogative, although they may be more amenable to consultation or participation in decisions concerning implications

and consequences. Similarly, trade unions have been sceptical of new working practices and participative mechanisms which emphasise team or group working and employee consultation at the possible expense of trade union involvement and joint decision making.

Government, the AIRC and employers have emphasised the need to develop workplace, enterprise-based co-operation and productivity bargaining, and this has been given additional impetus in the 1993 Accord. However, as noted earlier, this poses problems for the unions since they have not traditionally given much emphasis or resources to this level of trade union activity. Their net gains in terms of wages and other terms and conditions have been won via the compulsory conciliation and arbitration process, which has encouraged a centralised rather than decentralised perspective and structure. The 1988 and 1990 registration requirements referred to above have also tended to emphasise size and centrality rather than enterprise-level organisation and activity.

For many years it appeared that trade union membership figures and density held up throughout the 1980s at a density level in excess of 50 per cent.[11] However, Deery and DeCieri[12] have cast doubt on this with their suggestion that trade union density fell from 51 per cent in 1976 to 42 per cent in 1988 and Australian Bureau of Statistics (ABS) figures for 1990 at 41 per cent density, and less than 40 per cent at the end of 1992, support this contention. Certainly, the public sector traditionally exhibits density figures in excess of those in the private sector.[13] The causes of the reduction include the decline of traditional manufacturing membership bases, allied to a failure to organise, recruit and represent the expanding service sectors, female and part-time employment.

Geographically based branches have formed the base level of formal organisation within the movement with, as implied above, workplace organisation being informal. In the larger workplaces shop steward networks and committees may be active, but it is the full-time officials of individual unions and the ACTU that have played active roles in bargaining and conciliation and arbitration processes. At state level, there are trade and labour councils which assist in the co-ordination of activity and communication of information.

EMPLOYEE PARTICIPATION

The return of a Labour government in 1983 heralded a much more prominent position for employee participation. The government, through legislation and example, through its Accords with the ACTU and through exerting pressure on the AIRC, has sought to encourage and persuade employers to adopt more participative approaches, arguing that efficiency, productivity, quality and employee relations may all be improved. The unions have generally welcomed initiatives in this area, although there has been scepticism about employer motives. Employers' organisations have also expressed their support, although they have tended to have a somewhat narrower perception of participation than the other parties, seeing it primarily as a communication improvement activity.

Lansbury and Davis[14] have documented developments in a number of large organisations such as the postal service and Ford, and the Australian Workplace Industrial Relations Survey(AWIRS) 1990[15] incorporated questions on the extent and nature of participatory activity. It is clear from the (AWIRS) data that on almost every dimension participation is more common in public sector workplaces than in workplaces in the private sector. However, it is also clear that formal health and safety committees are the only arrangements present in more than 20 per cent of the private sector companies surveyed employing 20 or more. Other arrangements such as quality circles, employee representatives on boards of directors, *ad hoc* task forces and formal joint consultative committees each occur in less than 20 per cent of such workplaces. It would seem from this evidence that many managements still need to be convinced of the advantages of employee participation.

SUMMARY

The Australian system is in the process of change. Economic and technological pressures seem to have been the catalysts for a gradual and eventually substantial reorientation of decision-making mechanisms. The centralised and compulsory system of wage determination and conflict resolution that has dominated the twentieth century is being curtailed, and encouragement is being given to enterprise-level activity and decision making with an overwhelming emphasis on improving efficiency and productivity, eliminating restrictive practices and modernising traditional methods of working, so that Australian industry can regain competitiveness and stimulate economic growth and employment.

Government has been in the forefront of encouraging these changes and has recently shown itself willing to play an even more active labour market role. The unions have been confronted by membership decline and a need to rationalise and restructure, but the extent to which they are currently fit to represent their members adequately and participate in decision making at enterprise level is arguable. Employers generally favour the recent developments: they welcome the diminished role of compulsion; they want to retain decision making within the enterprise; they want to improve efficiency, productivity and competitiveness; and decentralisation of decision making and wage determination are likely to facilitate their control of wage costs as well as their prerogative over other issues of business policy and strategy, particularly in a period of high unemployment.

It is impossible at this stage to assess the impact of the changes encouraged by the 1993 Accord, but there are many unanswered questions and further legislative interventions may be necessary.

NOTES AND REFERENCES

1. Callus R, Moorehead A, Cully M and Buchanan J (1991) 'Industrial Relations at Work', *The Australian Workplace Industrial Relations Survey*, Australia Government Publishing Service

2. The agreement between ACTU and the Federal Government in February 1990 and known as "Accord" Mark VI

3. Bamber G J and Davis E M (1993) 'Australia' in Rothman M, Briscoe D R and Nacamulli R C D (eds), *Industrial Relations Around the World. Labor Relations for Multinational Companies*, De Gruyter, New York

4. Bamber GJ (1992) 'Industrial Relations and Organizational Change: Is Human Resource Management Strategic in Australia?' (p.87) in Towers B (ed) *The Handbook of Human Resource Management*, Blackwell, Oxford

5. 'Australia, Commonwealth of 1987: Australia Reconstructed: ACTU: TDC. Mission to Western Europe' – A report by the Mission Members to the Australian Council of Trade Unions and the Trade Development Council, Canberra, Australian Government Publishing Service

6. Bamber G J op. cit., p.90

7. Dunphy D and Stace D (1990) *Under New Management: Australian organisations in transition*, McGraw Hill, Sydney

8. Accords have been agreed between ACTU and Federal Government covering the periods: 1985–6, 1987–8, 1988–9, 1989–90, 1990–92 and 1993–96

9. Isaac J (1989) 'Co-operation and Conflict in Public Sector Labour Relations' in Australia' in Gladstone A, Lansbury R et al., *Current Issues in Labour Relations*, De Gruyter, pp.335–48

10. Frenkel S (1988) 'The Australian Metalworkers Union and Industrial Change: A Labour Movement Offensive', in Hyman R and Streeck W, *New Technology and Industrial Relations*, Blackwell, pp.233–46

11. Gospel H and Palmer G (1993) *British Industrial Relations*, Routledge, p.145

12. Deery S and DeCieri H 'Determinants of Trade Union Membership in Australia', *British Journal of Industrial Relations* 29:1, March 1991 pp.59–73

13. Isaac J op. cit.

14. Lansbury R D and Davis E M (1992) 'Employee Participation in Some Australian Cases', *International Labour Review,* Vol.131, No. 2, pp.231–48

15. Callus R *et al.*, op. cit.

FURTHER READING

Davis E M and Lansbury R (1993) 'Industrial relations in Australia' in Bamber G and Lansbury R (eds), *International Comparative and Industrial Relations*, 2nd edition, Routledge pp.100–25

Deery S and Plowman D (1991) *Australian Industrial Relations,* 3rd edition, McGraw Hill

Frenkel S (1988) 'Australian employers in the shadow of the labour accords', *Industrial Relations*, 27 (2), pp.166–79

Hancock K and Isaac J (1992) 'Australian experiments in wage policy', *British Journal of Industrial Relations,* 30 (2), pp.213–36

Hancock K and Rawson D (1993) 'The metamorphosis of Australian industrial relations', *British Journal of Industrial Relations,* 31(4), pp.489–513

Kyloh R H (1989) 'Flexibility and structural adjustment through consensus: Some lessons from Australia', *International Labour Review*, 128 (1), pp.103–23

Lansbury R (1991) 'Industrial relations in Australia and Sweden: Strategies for change in the 1990s', *Economic and Industrial Democracy*, 12 (4), pp.527–34

Lansbury R and Bamber G (1993) 'Australian industrial relations in transition', *International Labour Review,* 132 (4), pp.451–2

Lansbury R and Davis R M (1992) 'Employee participation: Some Australian cases', *International Labour Review,* 131 (2), pp.231–48

Niland J R (1976) *Collective Bargaining in the Context of Compulsory Arbitration,* New South Wales University Press

Omaji P O (1993) 'The state and industrial relations: Background to the adoption of compulsory arbitration law in Australia', *British Journal of Industrial Relations*, 31 (1), pp.37–55

Plowman D H (1988) 'Employer associations and bargaining structures: An Australian perspective', *British Journal of Industrial Relations*, 26, pp. 371–96

Plowman D H (1989) *Holding the Line: Compulsory arbitration and national employer coordination in Australia,* Cambridge University Press

Schuler R S, Dowling P J, Smart J R and Huber V L (1992) *Human Resource Management in Australia,* Harper Collins

17 · UNITED STATES OF AMERICA

BACKGROUND

Change is endemic in the US, and the pace of change has quickened in recent years, which has reverberated across the world. Several bestselling authors have influenced thinking far beyond America by investigating the ramifications of market change and challenging complacency at all levels. Commercial reorganisation has occurred relentlessly, often taking the form of mergers and amalgamations, and inevitably staff have been shed, with 'downsizing' being feared at all levels. Within corporations, it has been predicted that the nature of management itself will soon be almost unrecognisable. Delayering, blurred job categories and more complicated forms of communication will be commonplace by the end of the twentieth century.[1] Relations between management and employees are also in transition, not only being remoulded through the necessity to achieve greater cost-effectiveness and performance, but also because the nature of the agenda, especially in HR, is changing as the negative aspects of an increasingly competitive and stress-promoting society filter into the workplace.

The origins of HRM can be found in the US. Although hailed as a new marvel, its roots can be located in a strong tradition of 'personnel welfarism', which has existed since the early twentieth century.

A rich vein of theory emanating from the US has influenced the way in which jobs have been designed. Frederick Taylor[2] advocated standardisation and specialisation of tasks, which was clearly manifested in Fordist organisational principles. Behavioural science writers, such as Frederick Herzberg[3], exhorted management to pay attention to the internal motivation of workers and to consider the enrichment of jobs.

EMPLOYERS

There is a strong tradition in the US of employer independence and hostility towards trade unionism and any incursion into the realms of managerial prerogative. The employment-at-will doctrine was upheld by the courts in the 1908 case of Adair v United States,

and employers have sought as far as possible to maintain the doctrine and their rights as enunciated by it. It was partly due to fierce employer opposition to trade unionism and negotiating with their employees as a collective interest group that government in the mid-1930s legislated to facilitate union negotiation and collective bargaining.

Despite the legislation employers continued to try to thwart trade unions and maintain their unilateral right to manage. Subsequent legislation after the second world war did, as we detail below, to some extent redress what employers perceived as an imbalance in the power relationship between themselves and their employees. However, many employers have successfully resisted trade unionism and in recent years not only has the incidence of unfair labour practice allegations against employers increased, but many employers have successfully used union avoidance tactics, going so far in some cases as to close down plants which were unionised and relocate them elsewhere, usually in a site where unionism can be resisted or avoided. The relocation may be to one of the so-called 'right to work' states, where it is illegal for unions to insist on union membership as a condition of employment. Through the formation of the National Right to Work Committee, and successful lobbying, employers were largely responsible for the Labour–Management Relations Act (Taft-Hartley) of 1947 in which states are given the opportunity to enact the appropriate right-to-work legislation.

This instance of collective employer action is not typical of employers in the US, who have generally preferred to remain independent and have shown no great inclination to combine together against the trade unions at either industry, regional or national levels. There are some employers' organisations in specific trades or industries that do bargain with trade unions on behalf of members, but there is no coherent structure to the employers' association 'movement'. Multi-employer bargaining has tended to occur in those trades where there were a relatively large number of employers, most of them relatively small and in competition. In such circumstances a single strong trade union was able to target employers in a position to pay, secure a favourable agreement and then utilise pattern bargaining to extend it to the whole trade or industry. It was usually this danger which prompted employers to combine for bargaining purposes. Consequently there is multi-employer bargaining in industries such as construction, transport, hotels and restaurants, but it does not tend to be found in manufacturing, where large-scale employment occurred relatively early.

Where employers have and do combine for bargaining purposes they tend also to create institutions which provide the members with other services such as wage and salary surveys, lobbying, advice and research.

In industries where single-employer bargaining is the norm and one would expect employers to be acting independently, it is not uncommon for 'patterns' to be established with one or two leading employers which then and at the least act as guidelines for the rest of the industry, even though there are no formal employer organisations or multi-employer arrangements.

In the non-union sector employers have formed organisations which include among their roles that of combating the threat of unionism; examples include the National Association of Manufacturers (NAM) and the United States Chamber of Commerce. These will assist and advise members confronted with the threat of unionism on how to avoid recognition and bargaining. They will also support anti-union litigation, for example unfair labour practices by trade unions, and conduct publicity and lobbying campaigns.

In recent years, many employers have been confronted with difficult trading and competitive circumstances which have encouraged them to reappraise their production and work methods and organisation. Japanese and other international competition and investment in the US, the new automated technology available, an enhanced awareness of the importance of quality and customer satisfaction, and increasing pressures on costs have all combined to encourage employers to seek greater labour force flexibility. These include some instances of multi-skilling and a decreasing reliance on seniority as a basis for work allocation. More co-operative and participative approaches and mechanisms for the management of human resources are being investigated which emphasise communication, commitment, collaborative problem solving and employee development. In some instances, for example in the motor industry, this has been tackled in a unionised environment with the involvement of the union concerned. Examples of the latter might be

General Motors' new Software Division and its joint venture with Toyota–NUMMI. Strauss[4] suggests that different techniques or mechanisms might be appropriate in non-union as opposed to unionised plants, and quotes job enrichment, quality circles and autonomous work groups as more common in the former, with joint committees more common in the latter. Examples of developments of this nature are illustrated in Figure 17.1.

To the extent that employers are adopting a more collaborative approach and style, it is very doubtful whether many see this extending beyond production issues, beyond employee participation in the design and operation of production arrangements to produce a more efficient and effective process, a higher quality product and at a lower cost. There is no evidence to suggest that employers are willing to relinquish any of their prerogative in business and economic areas of decision making.

LABOUR MARKET

- By the end of the twentieth century the average age of the workforce will be 36, six years older than at any time in US history. Women, minorities and immigrants will supply five-sixths of the net additions to the workforce between 1990 and 2000. Senior citizens too will be in demand. There is a growing discrepancy between the supply of labour and employer requirements.

- 20 per cent of the adults are considered to be functionally illiterate.[5] It is estimated that women are the only group with adequate education levels to match projected needs of employers.

- 2.3 per cent of the workforce are engaged in the service sector in which new technology, through office and home work automation, is altering the nature of work. Currently, about three million people work through computers in their home, connected to the company's mainframe.[6]

- Part-time and temporary work are becoming more common.[7]

Recruitment

- Rigorous legislation on recruitment requires employers to act on a fair and objective basis. Personnel decisions must be made on the basis of economic and scientific criteria. Discrimination is unlawful on grounds of sex, race, colour, age, national ori-

Blue-collar team, white-collar wise

FT

Victoria Griffith on how a better-educated workforce is helping the US car
industry to raise productivity

When a handful of Chrysler assembly
workers gathered late last year with suggestions on cost-cutting, they came up with
an innovative solution to replace the expensive sealer used in car boots. The idea
amounted to an annual saving of $250,000
(£171,000).

The car company says this is just one
example of the boost in productivity
derived from a better-educated, more participative workforce.

"The days of the cattle-call are over,"
says Dennis Pauley, executive vice-pres-
ident of manufacturing at Chrysler. "We
used to put out the word on Fridays that
we needed X number of workers Monday
morning. If you could walk and breathe
you were in. That's not how it is anymore."

US car manufacturers hope tougher hiring standards will ensure they get the
skilled workers they need to stay competitive. Blue-collar employees in the industry are looking more like white-collar
workers in terms of educational background.

At Chrysler's Windsor plant in Ontario,
for instance, some 20 per cent of new
assembly plant workers are college graduates, while nearly 5 per cent of new blue-
collar employees for Ford Motor Company
are university graduates, up from almost
none 10 years ago.

Even more striking is the surge in the
number of workers who have completed
high school. About 97 per cent of the blue-
collar employees Ford has taken on since
1991 possess a high school diploma or
higher degree. More significantly, since
nearly half the blue-collar workers at US
car manufacturers will become eligible for
retirement over the next five years, "this
offers us a major opportunity to reshape
our workforce", says Pauley.

The American car sector is taking its
cue from Japan, where groups such as
Toyota and Honda have built up a highly-
skilled employee base. "The Japanese
assembly-line workers graduated in the

top 20 per cent of their technical school,"
says David Jones, president of the consulting group HR Enterprises, which advis-
es US car companies on assembly line
hiring. "They put the same energy into
blue-collar recruiting that the companies
here put into management recruiting at the
top universities."

US car manufacturers now realise that
to compete with the Japanese, they need a
workforce with similar accomplishments.
"In the past, we put our energy into making sure we had a well-educated management force," says Pauley. "Now, we know
that assembly-line workers are just as
important. My workforce needs to be at
least as good as that of the Japanese, or
I'm out of the game."

Recruitment of the highly-educated is
made easier because university graduates
are finding assembly-line jobs appealing.
The work is less physically strenuous, and
more intellectually challenging, than it was
just a decade ago. High salaries are also
enticing. Hourly wages usually range from
between $15 and $18 an hour, generous
even by university graduate standards.

To select the best workers, car makers
have adopted strict new screening methods. Potential employees are required to
take examinations which measure reading, writing and mathematics ability, manual dexterity and inter-personal skills. No
specific degree is required, but the tests
automatically favour the well-educated.

"It is more likely that people with high
school diplomas will do better on the
exams, and individuals who score higher
clearly are more productive on their jobs,"
says Jones.

Changes in the industry over the last
decade have made educated workers more
of a necessity. Companies have been
eliminating middle management to slice
costs; as a result, more workers are being
left to their own devices.

At Chrysler there are now 50 workers
to every manager. Ten years ago that number was 20; soon, says the company, it will
be 100.

"Once you back out the supervisor, you
need more self-directed workers," says

Pauley. "By having fewer managers, you
redefine the job of the assembly plant
worker."

Manufacturing jobs are also more technical than they once were. "Many jobs have
changed beyond recognition," says Arthur
Johnson, supervisor in charge of employment and training planning at Ford. "For
instance, a welding line used to consist of
a man holding a piece of metal on to the
car, and someone welding it with a hand-
held machine. Today, robots do all that."

These changes require new skills. The
ability to read an instruction manual is now
more important than brute strength, and
with new technology being adopted all the
time, workers must be capable of learning
new tasks quickly.

Workers must have the flexibility to perform more than one job. To keep the plant
running smoothly, and cut down on overtime pay, assembly-line employees are
often expected to fill in for absentee workers, or ease the work load in another section of the plant.

Employees are also asked to participate
in the daily running of the company. At
the Dodge City Complex, a Chrysler operation which opened last July, each worker has the right to halt the assembly line at
any time. The company says it helped them
iron out the wrinkles and address ineffi-
ciencies which under the old system would
never have come to light.

"One guy suggested we put in a computer program which would tell him what
materials he'd need for a particular vehicle in advance. Now, he prepares the stuff
ahead of time," explains Norman Hunt, a
supervisor assistant who will soon receive
an engineering degree.

Even General Motors, which because it
is not hiring has less flexibility in shaping
its workforce, is attempting to improve
blue-collar educational levels. The company, in conjunction with the Auto Workers
Union, has launched a programme which
subsidises employees' tuition at university and technical schools. The company
says that 17 per cent of assembly-line
workers involved in the initiative are working towards a college degree.

Fig 17.1   Source: *Financial Times*, 11 May 1994

gin or religion. This applies in hiring, firing, promotion and training.

- It is important, therefore, that selection methods have been properly validated, and so more controversial methods, including personality tests, are avoided by many companies. Structured interviews with set questions on a rating scale are frequently used.[8]
- Job description, job specification and job evaluation methods are increasingly used to define jobs. Promotion from within is emerging as the preferred way.

Remuneration

- Pay, hours and terms and conditions of employment are normally established through collective bargaining between trade unions and employers. Most collective bargaining contracts are negotiated between a single union and single employer.
- There is a move towards flexible reward packages which enable individual employees to choose from a set of alternative benefits the ones which best suit his or her needs. Not only does this appeal to dual career families, who may, for example, require only health insurance, but it also promotes cost-effectiveness on the part of the employer.[9]
- Approximately 38 per cent of compensation is in the form of non-wage benefits, about a third of which is required by government for social security, unemployment and workers' compensation.[10]
- Many employers provide health insurance, although the escalating costs of healthcare are giving rise to concern. Employees are now being asked to cover part of the cost, and HR managers are designing new packages.[11]
- About half the American workforce is covered by a pension plan, with any abuse of voluntary schemes regulated by law. The HR role includes design of pension plans, which provide a significant source of capital. Many US employees forfeit pension entitlement due to a high propensity to change jobs.[12]
- In the non-union sector, pay and conditions are typically determined by a combination of job evaluation (i.e. systematically assessing the relative worth of the job to the firm) and individual performance evaluation techniques.

Training and development

- Training and development is viewed as a priority area, with many companies providing their own training centres. The emphasis, at all levels, is placed on job-related training and on developing competencies which will contribute towards effective job performance.[13]
- At managerial level, there is a strong psychological underpinning in much developmental activity, and an objective underlying much recent HR development has been to enable managers to cope with high levels of change and feelings of insecurity. Consequently, popular programmes include stress management, effective negotiating techniques and cross-cultural communication.[14]
- Assessment centres are in common usage, involving interactive and simulated work activity, which can be evaluated by trained observers. Results may be used to identify employees with potential for promotion, or to help individuals in planning their own careers.[15]

Current trends

The publication of the greatly influential *In Search of Excellence* by Peters and Waterman and the books which followed connect the success of America's top-performing companies to an ability to draw on the talent of their human resources. Many companies have introduced employee involvement programmes and are seeking to enhance the quality of working life. The aim of such programmes is to reduce product cost, improve product quality, ease communications, raise morale and reduce conflict.

HR managers are now finding themselves confronted with decisions which pull them into the arena of ethics and public controversy. Negative behaviour by employees in the form of alcoholism, drug abuse and employee theft constitutes a significant cost for companies. Drug abuse was estimated to have cost firms $50 billion in absenteeism in 1987. Employee theft is estimated to cost about $10 billion a year.[16] Balanced against this is the right to privacy, which restricts the ability of employers to use tests. Despite legal restrictions on polygraph tests, whose validity is questionable, they have been used quite frequently for screening potential employees and for investigating thefts. Similarly, about 34 per cent of 1000 firms surveyed by the American Management Association (AMA) have a drug-testing policy.[17] So HR practitioners are responsible for establishing fair and workable company policies in the vital areas of controlling negative behaviour at work and managing changes in reward systems.

GOVERNMENT

Here we concentrate on government's intervention in providing a legislative framework within which the relationship between employers and employees and their respective representative institutions is conducted, government regulation of substantive issues and protection of employee/employer rights, and government as an employer in the public sector.

It is important to bear in mind that while this is mainly concerned with events and interventions at federal level, the states can and do legislate in employment matters and the majority of public sector employees are employed at state or lower levels.

Legislative framework

Government at federal level first intervened significantly in the 1930s. The National Recovery Act 1933 provided legal protection for employees' rights to bargain collectively and to be represented by a union and in a unit of their own choosing. However, employers continued to oppose unionism and in 1935 the National Labour Relations or Wagner Act was passed. This piece of legislation, subsequently amended, has formed the bedrock of the system ever since and was significant in enshrining employees' rights to 'self-organisation, to form, join or assist labour organisations, to bargain collectively through representatives of their own choosing and to engage in concerted activities for the purpose of collective bargaining' (Section 7), concerted activities in this context including the taking of industrial action.

The Act further created the notion of an unfair labour practice (initially only able to be committed by employers) and specified that it was to be an unfair labour practice for an employer to 'interfere with, restrain or coerce employees' in the exercising of the rights conferred. It therefore became an unfair labour practice for employers to seek to encourage or discourage employees from joining or taking part in a trade union and its activities.

The above rights would count for relatively little if employers could easily avoid or refuse to engage in collective bargaining, and so the act created a mechanism whereby employees and their trade unions could effectively force employers to recognise and bargain if there was sufficient support. Employee organisations, armed with authorisation cards from 30 per cent of the appropriate labour force, were given the right to petition an institution newly created by the Act, the National Labour Relations Board (NLRB), to conduct a representation election for the purposes of assessing employee support for the union. If a majority of those voting voted in favour, then the NLRB was given the right to make a legally enforceable order that the employer should both recognise and bargain with the trade union in respect of employees within the specified bargaining unit.

There are two types of representation election conducted by the NLRB: a consent election, as described above, when there is only the one union petitioning; or a stipulation election in the event of there being more than one union in competition, or where there is opposition from the employer. Employees must have the option of voting for no union.

The NLRB determines the bargaining unit, which should be appropriate and not, for example, contain a mix of antagonistic interests, and which usually operates on the basis of exclusive jurisdiction; once the unit is determined a single trade union is given the right to bargain, this being the one supported in the election. The NLRB can also be petitioned to decertify a trade union and again would conduct an appropriate election.

After the Wagner Act was passed union membership and recognition did increase and in subsequent years employers frequently argued that the legislation was far too one-sided, some evidence of this bias being that while employers could be found guilty of committing an unfair labour practice, trade unions could not. In 1947 an additional piece of legislation was enacted called the Taft-Hartley (Labour–Management Relations) Act. This legislation amended the Wagner Act, creating the notion of an unfair labour practice by trade unions, for example refusing to bargain collectively with an employer or attempting to force recognition from an employer when another union is already the certified representative. Additionally the 1947 Act imposed other obligations on trade unions, for example:

- the requirement to give 60 days' notice of strike action;
- the requirement to prepare and provide annual financial statements;
- the pre-entry closed shop was declared illegal although the post-entry union shop remained lawful;
- the President was given emergency powers to intervene in and stop strike action which endangered national health or safety;

- unions were also required to express their opposition to communism and state that they did not believe in violent revolution.

Additional amendments to the Wagner Act were made in the Landrum-Griffin Act 1959 (Labour–Management Reporting and Disclosure Act). This legislation was enacted in a climate of scandal following the exposure of racketeering and corruption in a number of trade unions, perhaps most notably the Teamsters Union.

This legislation incorporated a Bill of Rights of Union Members giving them legal rights to inspect union accounts and records, and rights with respect to nominating candidates, voting in elections and participating in union meetings. It was an act which sought to enhance democratic practices within the union as well as opening them up to greater financial scrutiny. National union officials were given greater power to supervise local union officials and their activities, particularly where it was alleged that members' rights were being violated.

These three major pieces of legislation, Wagner, Taft-Hartley and Landrum-Griffin together have provided the framework of legal regulation within which collective relationships must be conducted.

The NLRB was created by Wagner and, in addition to its role in representation issues and elections, it has the overall responsibility for dealing with allegations of unfair labour practices, whether they be committed by employer or union. Both parties are legally required to bargain in good faith which, in this context, requires them to:

- meet at a reasonable time and place;
- confer to reach an agreement;
- draw up a written, legally binding contract;
- give 60 days' notice of the intention to terminate or modify the agreement;
- make proposals and counter proposals which should be realistic;
- where an employer argues financial inability to pay, it must provide the union with substantiating financial information.

Failure on the part of either party to bargain in good faith constitutes an unfair labour practice and the other party can petition the NLRB to investigate and, where appropriate, make a suitable order. Orders by the NLRB have the force of law, and in the case of established unfair labour practices usually take the form of a 'cease and desist' order or provide for financial compensation to the injured party, for example an employee dismissed for taking part in a union-organising

campaign. Failure to reach an agreement is not an unfair labour practice.

The NLRB defines the duty to bargain as applicable to all matters concerning pay, wages, hours of employment, or other conditions of employment. These are referred to as the mandatory topics, refusal to bargain on them constituting an unfair labour practice. Other permitted issues or permissive topics, can be bargained over, but it must be lawful to do so and the parties cannot be compelled to. They are therefore free to bargain on certain issues other than those which are mandatory but failure to do so does not constitute an unfair labour practice. Certain topics, however, are not considered appropriate to bargaining and are prohibited. Examples of prohibited bargaining topics would be a pre-entry closed shop, a post-entry or union shop in states which have enacted right-to-work legislation effectively prohibiting such agreements, and perhaps also discrimination. The distinction between mandatory and permissive issues is difficult to determine and the NLRB is often required to decide this issue between parties.

In addition to strikes at the end of the contract period on mandatory issues, employees can also lawfully take industrial action in protest at an unfair labour practice by the employer. In the event of the NLRB eventually ruling in favour of the employees, they would be entitled to re-employment, but it is risky for employees to take such action since the NLRB decision is likely to take some time and if they lose then there is absolutely no obligation on the employer to re-employ. A legislative proposal to effectively outlaw the permanent replacement of strikers was rejected in July 1994. Strikes and lock-outs can themselves constitute an unfair labour practice; generally strikes during the period of an agreement are unlawful, most agreements contain no-strike clauses and the law upholds the distinction between matters of interest and right. Only in the event of the employers having committed an unfair labour practice are strikes over matters of right likely to be lawful. When the collective agreement specifies no strikes during the agreement term and employees nevertheless take strike action rather than pursue the grievance to conciliation or arbitration, the strike will be referred to as a 'wildcat'. It is necessary to point out that during the Reagan and Bush presidencies the appointments made to the NLRB resulted in pro-labour legislation being enforced in a much less rigorous manner than before. Many employers pursued anti-union activities during representation campaigns and elections with little risk of the activities being found illegal.

The other main federal agency created by the government is the Federal Mediation and Conciliation Service (FMCS). This was established by Taft-Hartley in response to the increasing incidence of strikes in the years following the second world war. The FMCS has no enforcement powers and generally relies on being invited to assist with a dispute.

Government regulation of employee rights and terms and conditions of employment

There has been increasing federal and state government intervention in the area of protecting and enhancing employee rights and benefits at work. The main areas of concern have been compensation and related non-wage benefits, equal opportunities and payment for jobs of comparable worth, rights with respect to discrimination, unfair disciplinary action and job security encompassing the notion of property in a job.

Compensation, equal opportunity and other benefits

The majority of states have minimum wage laws or wage boards that fix minimum wage rates industry by industry. Most of them also regulate hours of work and overtime premia.

There are three principal federal laws regulating these issues:

1 The Davis-Bacon Act 1931, which is also known as the Prevailing Wage Law. Its aim was to ensure that people employed on federal public works projects were paid at least the prevailing rate and that overtime hours should be paid at at least 1.5 times the normal hourly rate. The prevailing rate for this purpose is linked to the rates paid to only 30 per cent of the workers in the area.
2 The Walsh-Healy Act of 1936, which is officially known as the Public Contracts Act, covers workers employed on government contract work for supplies, equipment and materials exceeding $10 000 in value. Again, workers on such contracts must be paid the prevailing rate for the area, in the case as determined by the Secretary of Labour for the area, and overtime hours must be paid at the 1.5 premia rate, overtime hours being those in excess of 8 per day and/or 40 per week.
3 Fair Labour Standards Act 1938 (FLSA), commonly known as the Wage and Hours Act. This legislation applies to most employees in the US, in particular those employed in interstate commerce or the production of goods for interstate commerce, enterprises with volume of sales or business exceeding

$500 000 p.a., most educational and health establishments and agriculture. The Act provides for the specification of a federal minimum wage, payment for hours worked in excess of 40 at 1.5 times the normal rate, a training wage minimum of 85 per cent of the appropriate minimum (the result of an amendment in 1990), and it also imposes limitations on child labour.

The above legislation, in particular the FLSA, has been much amended over the years, but it must be remembered that the initial legislation was enacted in the 1930s, as were the National Recovery Act and Wagner, and it should be acknowledged that enactment was motivated more by government desire to boost aggregate demand and employment than the pursuit of social welfarism.

One of the more significant amendments to the FLSA was the Equal Pay Act of 1963 which requires employers not to discriminate by gender in the payment for equal work. This was followed in 1964 by the Civil Rights Act which prohibits discrimination in employment on the basis of sex, race, colour, religion or national origin, and in 1967 the Age Discrimination in Employment Act extended this legislation to include discrimination against people of 40 or older on the grounds of age. As amended, this legislation prohibits mandatory retirement before age 70 except on grounds of safety. The latter act provides for exemption on the base of age being a bona fide occupational qualification (BFOQ). The Pregnancy Discrimination Act of 1978 extends the provisions of the Civil Rights Act to include pregnancy as an unlawful basis for discrimination, pregnancy in this context being regarded as a disability. The Equal Employment Opportunity Act of 1972 extends the Equal Employment Opportunity Commission's (EEOC) powers of enforcement and the coverage of the Civil Rights Act to include government employees, academic staff in higher education and others previously excluded. The Americans with Disabilities Act 1990 prohibits discrimination in employment against people with physical or mental disabilities and the chronically ill, legislation in 1993 seeks to require employers to give employees sick leave in the event of pregnancy/maternity and in order to care for children and other dependents.

Much of the above federal equal rights legislation has been further extended at state and local level and these are referred to as Fair Employment Practice Laws.

Despite legislative intervention, the median earnings level of female workers in the US in 1989 was 72 per cent of the median for all working men, and while this was an improvement of 10 per cent over 1979, it indicates that there is probably institutionalised discrimination which will be difficult to eliminate unless the equal pay issue becomes one which concentrates more on equal pay for work of comparable worth. This is an issue which interested parties are likely to pursue in the 1990s, difficult though it is likely to be to define and measure worth in such a context.

Government intervention with respect to the provision by employers of benefits other than wages now includes the legal requirement for employers to contribute towards social security insurance, unemployment insurance and workers' compensation insurance in respect of work-related accidents and illness, which is compulsory in most states.

Employee rights

The tradition in the US has been that the employer could employ (and terminate) at will. This right or doctrine has been curtailed by the development and increasing acceptance by the courts of the job-as-property doctrine allied to Amendments 5 and 14 of the Constitution, which provide that an individual should not be deprived of property without the protection of due process. Additionally, specific legislative interventions have made it unlawful for employees to be dismissed for various reasons or in specific sets of circumstances, for example it is unlawful to dismiss for taking part in the activities of a trade union, and it is unlawful to dismiss on grounds of sex, race or colour.

Other areas in which employees have been granted rights at work, either by specific legislation or as the result of court decisions, include:

● Rights to privacy and access to employment records.
● Rights not to be sexually harassed, EEOC guidelines in 1980 making it clear that sexual harassment constitutes discrimination.
● Rights to plant/office closure notification; the Plant Closing Act of 1988 requires employers to give employees and their communities 60 days' written notice of closure or lay-off affecting 50 or more employees.

Public sector

The public sector in the US is relatively small by international standards and comprises employment at federal, state and local levels. In 1990 this totalled in excess of 16 million employees, the vast majority of these being employees of sub-state-level authorities, approximately 60 per cent, compared with 23 per cent at state level and the remaining 17 per cent federal. Union membership among public sector employees is high compared with the private sector, and it is arguable that this is in part a response on the part of employees to the somewhat 'worse' entitlements that employees in the public sector have with respect to participation in the determination of their terms and conditions of employment. There are still substantial restrictions on public sector bargaining, the scope of bargaining tends to be narrower and many public sector employees do not have a legal right to take strike action, though in many cases this has not stopped them. Trade unionism and collective bargaining, where allowed, are relatively recent developments in the public sector.

It was not really until 1962 and President Kennedy's Executive Order No. 10988 that federal employees were given the right 'freely and without fear of penalty or reprisal to form, join or assist any labour organisation or to refrain from such activity.' There were also provisions for the establishment of bargaining units and for bargaining collectively with government.

Another Executive Order in 1971 defined the bargaining rights of federal employees more closely and created the Federal Labour Relations Council to hear appeals relating to unfair labour practices and bargaining issues, and also created the Federal Services Impasses Panel to deal with collective bargaining disputes and failures to agree.

The Civil Service Reform Act of 1978 created the Federal Labour Relations Authority (FLRA), which is similar in role to the NLRB.

Federal employees have no rights to bargain over pay, pensions or other economic benefits; these are determined by management. Bargaining in the federal sector tends to be at department level.

At state level, there is considerable diversity of legislative provision, with some states having no legal provision of collective bargaining rights whereas others do. Some states have administrative and enforcing mechanisms and bodies analogous to the NLRB and FLRA. Commonly, state employees are not given the right to negotiate an agreement, they may only be granted the right to meet and confer with a view to developing a memorandum of understanding.

Given that many public sector employees do not have the right to strike, it is quite common for compulsory and binding arbitration to be provided as a means of resolving apparently intractable disputes.

This is commonly the case for groups such as the police and firefighters who are employed at local level, along with educational staff.

The Clinton administration has already reversed three major anti-union/employee orders of the Reagan–Bush years. The air traffic controllers sacked by Reagan and banned from future federal employment (1981) have had the latter restriction removed; and the requirement for federal agencies to employ union members or pay union rates on construction projects has been reinstated, along with a rescinding of the 1992 requirement for federal contractors to post notices advising employees that they did not have to join a union.

TRADE UNIONS

Trade union membership density has been in decline for some years. In 1992, overall density was no more than 16 per cent. In the private sector it was estimated to be 12 per cent and in the public sector 37 per cent[18], the only sector in which there has been significant membership growth in recent decades.

The strategies and objectives of trade unions in the US have been traditionally consistent with strong individualistic and masculine cultural dimensions and traditions; they have tended to concentrate on economic goals and satisfying the direct interests of their members. Certainly there is no tradition of a movement with a desire to transform society or with strong political affiliations. As Bean[19] says, this phenomenon of business unionism is characterised by job consciousness and job control, placing emphasis on economic struggle, collective bargaining and the pragmatic satisfying of the job-related economic and social conditions of members. However, there is some evidence that objectives and orientations are changing. Certainly some unions and their leaders are adopting more co-operative approaches and abandoning the conflictual and distributive traditions; and unions in the last two decades have shown themselves more adept at pursuing broader social, economic and legislative programmes. To some extent this latter widening of the scope of their activities and interests is a response to and product of the structure of trade union membership and potential changes in membership. In the past, the stereotypical union member was white and a blue-collar worker in the manufacturing, construction or transport industry. Now the movement must organise and recruit in the public and service sector, and among white-collar and minority groups. Some com-mentators argue that membership decline will continue unless the movement does find a new social purpose and convince the American population that it stands for more than maximising the interests of its members. We comment on this issue of change and challenges confronting the trade unions in Chapter 5.

The movement is comprised of a single peak association, the American Federation of Labour-Congress of Industrial Organisations (AFL-CIO), to which are affiliated the majority of national unions (approximately 80 at the beginning of the 1990s) and their 70 000 or more local union affiliates. It is estimated that the AFL-CIO represents somewhere around 75 per cent of total union membership and is primarily involved in public relations, representational and political programmes. These dimensions of the role and the relationship with the Democrats are illustrated in Figure 17.2. The AFL-CIO does not engage in collective bargaining, although it does seek to limit disputes between affiliates, particularly those of a jurisdictional nature.

Trade unionism in the US has been concentrated both industrially and regionally. The strongholds of union membership have been industries such as those referred to above plus mining, automobiles and metal manufacturing, and regionally membership has been concentrated in California and the central Northern Atlantic states. As has been noted earlier, 21 states have passed right-to-work laws and in these predominantly southern and mid-western states union membership tends to be very low. The low success rate of unionism in the southern states is owing to a mixture of reasons, including:

- high levels of employer antipathy and resistance;
- relatively few large-scale manufacturing enterprises;
- strong cultural traditions of employment at will in the dominant agricultural and textile industries.

As the traditional industrial centres of unionism have declined, membership has declined and unions are faced with the challenge of attracting members in different kinds of industry, with different backgrounds, interests and aspirations.

The union member will have most contact with the local level of union organisation. At this level, he or she will have a shop steward, a fellow employee, representing him or her and keeping an eye on the administration of the contract and handling employee grievances. The steward does not negotiate the contract; this will probably be undertaken by an employee of the union at local or district level, often the 'business representa-

Lane Kirkland, internationalist

Before he left office, Lyndon Johnson presented a framed array of 100 presidential signing pens to the trade-union federation, the AFL-CIO. Each pen signified a piece of legislation enacted thanks to union support. Yet relations between Johnson and the unions were not always so cosy. Earlier in his presidency, Johnson had summoned the AFL-CIO's boss, George Meany, to an angry meeting at the White House, to complain about union defiance of his wages policy.

Present at that meeting was Lane Kirkland, Meany's long-time assistant and, since 1979, his successor as union chief. Nowadays Mr Kirkland likes to recall the tiff with Johnson – and similar incidents with every Democratic president from Harry Truman to Jimmy Carter – as a way of explaining that the unions' current contretemps with Bill Clinton over NAFTA is really nothing out of the ordinary. In time and on other matters, relations can improve.

They could hardly get worse. Organised labour has waited a long time to have a "friend" in the White House, after being frozen out by a former strike-leader named Ronald Reagan. During the Reagan-Bush years, the share of the workforce belonging to unions continued to slip, from 22% in 1980 (already low compared with other rich western countries) to some 16%. Mr Clinton's election brought hopes of influence regained.

Only last month, at the AFL-CIO's convention in San Francisco, Mr Kirkland was extolling Mr Clinton's early achievements in office, from laws on family and medical leave to easier voter-registration. "By and large," Mr Kirkland told the delegates, "his agenda is our agenda." With one exception.

The NAFTA argument flared up with shocking intensity. Mr Clinton complained on television about the unions' "rough-shod, muscle-bound tactics", including private threats to end campaign contributions to Democratic congressmen who voted for the free-trade agreement (labour unions are the biggest single contributor to Democratic campaigns). Mr Kirkland responded by solemnly declaring that the president had "clearly abdicated his role as the leader of the Democratic Party" by promising to defend Republicans attacked for supporting NAFTA.

This was strong stuff, stronger than can easily be explained even by the heat of a hard-fought political battle. Behind the angry words lay something verging on a mutual sense of betrayal. Mr Kirkland seemed genuinely taken aback by the lengths to which Mr Clinton was prepared to go to push "this lousy agreement" through Congress. Mr Clinton, ready to work with Mr Kirkland in many other areas, was stunned by the ferocity of labour's formidable anti-NAFTA campaign.

Had he taken a short walk from the White House to the AFL-CIO's headquarters, Mr Clinton might have spotted some clues to the intensity of Mr Kirkland's feelings. In a large frame on the wall of his meeting room is the distinctive red logo of Solidarity, the trade union that brought freedom to Poland. Nearby is a poster of Mr Kirkland with Lech Walesa. Over the years Mr Kirkland, married to a Czech survivor of the concentration camps, took a great interest in communist Europe and was always on the right side, shunning the official trade unions and backing the likes of Solidarity. He waxes eloquent on the theme of repression, whether in Eastern Europe or in China. In other words, Mr Kirkland is no isolationist. He is in many ways conspicuously internationalist. He cares deeply about freedom of association, in America and beyond.

It may seem odd to draw a link between the struggles of recent weeks in Washington and Solidarity's struggles in Gdansk in 1980. But in Mr Kirkland's eyes the link – defence of basic freedoms – certainly seems to be there. NAFTA, he said this week, would "give corporate America a virtual veto over every piece of social and economic legislation designed to establish minimum conditions of life and labour in this country." His warnings about a "back door" escape from America's labour standards were oddly reminiscent of Margaret Thatcher's warnings about socialism returning to Britain by way of Europe.

However, the evident strength of Mr Kirkland's feeling on NAFTA is not the only reason for the vehemence of his campaign against the agreement. You do not become head of the labour federation by letting your feelings run away with you. Mr Kirkland is only the fourth in a line that stretches back – through Meany, William Green and Samuel Gompers – to the foundation of the modern American trade-union movement in 1881. Such men can afford to think long.

What was the long-term thinking behind the strategy of bitterly opposing NAFTA? It carried risks. Defeating the trade agreement might ruin a presidency which otherwise had much to offer the unions. Failure to defeat the agreement might leave the unions looking weaker than ever and encourage Democrats to break free from unions' influence for good. Either way, bitterness between the government and the unions would linger.

But Mr Kirkland presumably calculated that the benefits outweighed the risks. Whatever the result of the vote, Democrats would have had a sharp reminder of union clout, and the government would want to reingratiate itself with labour in setting its legislative agenda. Top of that agenda is an item – universal health care – for which Mr Kirkland has been campaigning virtually since Mr Clinton was a toddler. The unions may have lost their NAFTA battle; but they can still dream about where to hang the framed array of presidential pens that, they hope, should one day arrive from the Clinton White House.

Fig 17.2 Source: *Economist*, 20 November 1993. Reproduced with permission. © The Economist November 1993.

tive', who will both negotiate and administer the agreement, dealing with grievances and issues that the stewards are unable to deal with satisfactorily.

The national union is arguably the centre of power within the movement, as it is at this level that broad policy and collective bargaining goals are determined. The national union determines the rules and conditions governing local membership. They provide professional, legal and other advisory services for the locals in membership. The national may provide financial assistance to a local, for example to help run an organising campaign or finance a strike, and the national will also, where required, provide guidance and sometimes direct assistance in negotiating an agreement. Additional services are likely to include education, training and, if necessary, disciplining union members.

We have noted earlier the procedures through which unions can gain certification and the requirements to bargain in good faith and act fairly. Since Taft-Hartley, unions can and do commit unfair labour practices; 10 800 were alleged in 1989.[20] They do lose certification elections: during the 1980s they were winning only a minority, compared with the 1950s and 1960s when unions tended to win 60 per cent plus.

One of the distinguishing features of the legal framework within which American unions have to operate is the requirement imposed on them by the courts to represent fairly all members. This is particularly relevant in respect of contract administration and the union pursuit of employee grievances. Undoubtedly union officials do at times pursue grievances raised, not necessarily because they think the grievance justified but because they are afraid that the union will be sued by the employee/member if they do not. The union has an obligation to its members to provide them with fair and adequate representation and to process and investigate grievances brought by its members speedily.

As indicated earlier, the union movement in the US is confronted by change, some would argue crisis. Some of these changes include the following:

- Foreign competition has encouraged employers to introduce new technology and new working methods to survive. This has often implied the redundancy of traditional skills and it is arguable whether we are seeing a process of deskilling and degradation or whether flexible specialisation is a more apt description of the outcome.
- Competition and technological innovation have caused changes in the structure of industry; old industries are declining and in some cases withering away, and others emerging. Unemployment of a structural nature has increased.
- Increasing legislative intervention protecting employees and creating new legal rights has, in some instances, removed part of the traditional role and *raison d'être* of trade unions.
- The decline in union membership is a problem since it reduces income and influence and may require structural adjustments. In addition to the reasons already given, this decline can be attributed to:
  (a) hostility from employers, increasing decertification and employer strategies of union avoidance;
  (b) the introduction by management of more participative processes, seemingly giving employees more involvement in job control without the need for trade unions;
  (c) the image and credibility of the union leadership, corruption, scandal, political activity and lack of responsiveness to members.

These changes confronting the movement have, to some extent, also brought to the fore a difference of opinion within the movement between those Katz[21] refers to as the co-operatists and the militants. The co-operatists are willing to participate in concession bargaining, the militants do not want to; the co-operatists view new 'team'-based working methods and job enlargement, rotation and quality circle developments as enhancing employee control over their work and its environment, while the militants view such techniques as means by which management obtains greater productivity and weakens the union movement.

PROCESSES

It must be pointed out that the overwhelming, most frequent and common mechanism for resolving matters between employees and an employer, and for determining rates of pay and other terms and conditions of employment, is in fact unilateral managerial determination allied to statutory intervention to establish and protect minimum standards and employee rights.

Approximately three-quarters of all employees in the US are not working in situations where their terms and conditions are determined through collective bargaining, and therefore are arguably working in situations where they have no real opportunity to participate collectively in decision making about their work or working environment and lives.

In the last decade or so, employers have introduced other mechanisms facilitating employee participation and involvement, but they are predominantly restricted opportunities, limited to particular, production-related areas of subject matter. The most popular are:

- Problem-solving teams comprised of 5–12 people, often not distinguishable from quality circles, which meet regularly to examine issues such as quality, efficiency, productivity and the work environment. Rarely do such groups have the power to implement decisions.
- Special purpose teams which are joint employee –management groups set up to design, plan and introduce particular changes, usually of a technological nature. Some examples of this kind of arrangement can be found in unionised environments.
- Self-managing teams, where the workgroup manages itself in terms of issues such as work/job allocation and rotation, scheduling work, ordering materials and vacation planning. This particular arrangement can have long-term consequences for organisational structures.

Ford, Kodak, Corning, Westinghouse Electric and Warner Gear are internationally known organisations that have introduced one or more of these participatory mechanisms, usually in response to international competition, the need to introduce new technology and an enhanced concern with issues such as quality and efficiency. Negrelli[22] has suggested that either unilateral or participative structures are necessary for problem solving and the successful introduction of change such as new technology; both distributive and integrative approaches are inadequate since they ultimately emphasise and are primarily concerned with the division of the spoils generated via the labour process. Wood[23] describes similar developments in the automobile industry and suggests that one of the attractions to management of these participative schemes is that they preserve managerial prerogative intact since they are focused on production, operational and quality issues, giving employees only some measure of autonomy or control over job issues. He comments that any increase in industrial democracy is likely to require unions to form new sets of objectives and initiatives, and it is unlikely such initiatives will come from management. These schemes also have the potential to undermine the union within the workplace, and it may be that in some instances these schemes have been introduced as part of a union-avoidance strategy.

Despite the limited coverage of collective bargaining, it has been the main mechanism through which employees have sought, via their trade union, to limit management's prerogative and challenge its unilateral control of the employment relationship. As has been discussed earlier, the employment-at-will doctrine has dominated and only relatively recently has this been challenged through legislation and judicial interpretation. Collective bargaining in the US has been adversarial in nature and predominantly an economic trial of strength.

Collective bargaining has been promoted and underpinned by legislation; interested parties are required to bargain and to do so in good faith, failure constituting an unfair labour practice. The NLRB has distinguished mandatory and permissive subject matter, a distinction which supports the notion of managerial prerogative and control; the unions are allowed to challenge management, the two are not partners.

Consistent with the above, most collective agreements contain a management's rights clause, often referred to as defined rights. These clauses reinforce and clarify (or at least that is the intention) which rights are exclusively management's. Another alternative is for the agreement to contain a reserved rights clause, in which case the clause is likely to state that, except where otherwise specified in the agreement or legislatively restricted, management's authority is supreme.

Most collective bargaining has been relatively decentralised, single employer and single union at local level. There are industries in which multi-employer bargaining is more common, and there are also some instances of coalition or co-ordinated bargaining in which an employer bargains with a number of unions together, which has been increasingly common in the public sector. In the absence of industry-wide bargaining, pattern bargaining has also been quite common, agreement with one employer setting the pattern for the rest of the industry. Another feature of the system in the US is that principles of seniority are often reinforced by collective agreements which may contain provisions that seniority should be the basis for lay-offs, redundancies, transfers, promotion and work transfers.

A bargaining development in the 1980s has been concession bargaining. Employers, confronted by harsh economic realities, have persuaded unions to make concessions, e.g. with respect to pay, both pay rates and performance-related pay, working practices, productivity and output, in return for which the unions have sought guarantees about the security of employment, retraining and redeployment. Employers in this position can sometimes realistically threaten to deunionise, either via a decertification election, or outsourcing, or subcontracting, or closing and relocating. In 1993, three of the main American airlines, Transworld, Northwest United traded equity strikes via employee share-ownership schemes in return for various packages of labour concessions. As an example in the last case, employees via their trade unions agreed wages cuts, reductions in other benefits and changes in working practices which are projected to yield savings over a six-year period of $5 billion. It is projected that the employees in return for these concessions will eventually control between 53 and 63 per cent of United's equity.[24]

Collective agreements are legally binding, effectively constituting an enforceable contract, many providing a peace no-strike clause for the duration of the agreement, usually between one and three years. Disputes of interest at the end of the agreement can result in lawful industrial action, but, as indicated earlier, disputes of right within the term of the agreement, about applicability, interpretation or application, are usually dealt with via conciliation, mediation or arbitration if the parties cannot agree. The vast majority of agreements in fact provide for recourse to arbitration on such issues of right. In the public sector it is quite common for compulsory arbitration on matters of interest to be conceded as a *quid pro quo* for not having the legal right to strike.

Many disputes of right will be raised as individual grievances, a grievance technically being a complaint that management has violated part of the contract, or federal or state law, or unfairly applied parts of the contract. More and more companies now have formal grievance procedures. Unions have persuaded many employers to introduce such procedures, partly because of their duty to represent fairly all employees covered by the agreement, but many employers in non-union situations have also introduced them. In some cases this has been encouraged by the increasing acceptance by the courts of the job-as-property doctrine and the employers have to show that due process has been followed. Increasing legislation in areas such as equality and discrimination has placed a premium on being able to show that fair and adequate procedures exist to deal with employees' complaints within the organisation, particularly if they are alleging that their legal rights have been infringed.

Also managements have introduced individual grievance procedures, ostensibly protecting the employee against arbitrary management action, as part of a strategy to avoid unionism. The majority of procedures do provide recourse to arbitration in the event of the complaint not being resolved internally.

SUMMARY

The system in the US has a number of distinctive features:

- A regulatory framework which ostensibly supports trade unionism and the right for employees to be represented and to challenge management, but has not given them a right to participate in management. Management prerogative and control over non-distributive subject matter have been protected.
- A declining trade union movement, which has traditionally pursued objectives of an economic nature, has adopted a conflictual and distributive approach and currently faces many challenges, not the least of which is the issue of its objectives and role.

- Management has been traditionally anti-trade union, and has jealously guarded its right to manage. In recent years, confronted by global competition, the need to introduce new technology and new management ideologies and methods, some managements have begun to adopt a more co-operative, collaborative and participative approach towards their employees. There has been much discussion of the creation of new, high-commitment cultures in companies. There is also evidence that managements have continued to develop union-avoidance strategies, the more co-operative approach and union avoidance often being related.

NOTES AND REFERENCES

1. Drucker P (1988) 'The Coming of the New Organization', *Harvard Business Review*, Jan/Feb

2. Taylor F W (1911) *Scientific Management*, Harper and Rowe, New York

3. Hertzberg (1988) 'One more time: how do you motivate employees?' *Harvard Business Review*, vol. 46, pp.357–62

4. Strauss G (1992) 'Human Resource Management in the USA' in Towers B (ed) *The Handbook of Human Resource Management*, Blackwell p.33

5. *Training America: Learning to work in the 21st Century*, American Society for Training and Development

6. Rothman M, Briscoe D R and Nacamulli R C D (eds) (1984) 'Introduction' in *Industrial Relations Around the World: Labour Relations for Multinational Companies*, DeGruyter, New York

7. Data from the Hudson Institute (1987) *Workforce 2000*, a report prepared for the US Department of Labour. Reported in Springer B and Springer R (1990) 'HRM in the US: A celebration of its centenary' in Pieper R, *Human Resource Management: An International Comparison*, DeGruyter, New York

8. Springer G and Springer R, op. cit.

9. Ibid.

10. Ibid.

11. Ibid.

12. Beth S (1988) 'Complementing the Welfare State: The Development of Private Pensions, Health Insurance and other employee benefits in the US', *Labour Management Relations Series*, International Labour Office, Geneva

13. Springer B and Springer R, op. cit.

14. Ibid.

15. Ibid.

16. *Business Week*, 28 March 1988

17. Ibid.

18. Strauss G op. cit., p.30.

19. Bean R (1994) *Comparative Industrial Relations*, Croom Helm, 2nd edition, p.21

20. Fifty Fourth Annual Report of the National Labor Relations Boards –1989, US Government Printing Office 1991

21. Katz H (1988) 'Policy Debates over Work Reorganisation in North American Unions', in Hyman R and Streeck W, *New Technology and Industrial Relations*, Blackwell, pp.220–232

22. Negrelli S (1988) 'Management Strategy: Towards New Forms of Regulation?' in Hyman R and Streeck W op. cit., pp.89–100

23. Wood S (1988) 'Between Fordism and Flexibility? The US Car Industry' in Hyman R and Streeck W, op. cit. pp.101–27

24. *Financial Times*, 17 December 1993

FURTHER READING

Adams R J (1989) 'North American industrial relations: Divergent trends in Canada and the United States', *International Labour Review*, 128 (1), pp.46–64

Blanchflower D G and Freeman P B (1992) 'Unionism in the United States and other advanced OECD countries', *Industrial Relations*, 31, pp.56–79

Clark G L (1989) *Unions and Communities Under Siege: American communities and the crisis of organised labour*, Cambridge University Press

Donn C V and Lipsky D G (Eds) (1987) *Collective Bargaining in American Industry*, Lexington

Forbath W E (1991) *Law and the Shaping of the American Labor Movement*, Harvard University Press

Goldfield M (1989) *The Decline of Organised Labor in the United States*, University of Chicago Press

Hecksher C (1988) *The New Unionism: Employee involvement in the changing corporation*, Basic

Katz H C and Kochan T A (1992) *Collective Bargaining and Industrial Relations*, McGraw Hill

Piore M J and Sabel C (1984) *The Second Industrial Divide: Possibilities for prosperity*, Harper-Row

Schuler R S (1992) *Managing Human Resources*, 4th edition, West

Sherman H W and Bohlander G W (1992) *Managing Human Resources*, 9th edition, South Western

Strauss G Gallagher D G and Fiorito J (eds) (1991) *The State of the Unions*, IRRA

Troy L (1990) 'Is the US unique in the decline of private sector unionism?', *Journal of Labour Research*, 11, pp.111–43

Troy L (1992) 'Convergence in international unionism: The case of Canada and the USA', *British Journal of Industrial Relations*, 30 (1), March, pp.1–43

18 · INTERNATIONAL LABOUR ORGANISATION

INTRODUCTION

The International Labour Organisation (ILO) celebrated its 75th anniversary in 1994. It is a United Nations agency that was created alongside the League of Nations in 1919 as part of the first world war peace settlement. Underlying its creation was an acceptance by the relevant parties that international peace was linked to the creation and maintenance of social justice both within individual member states and internationally, and that social unrest caused by unfair and exploitative treatment of workers and other vulnerable and disadvantaged groups might well pose a threat to peace, possibly through violent and bloody revolution.

There were further economic motivations, since it was also realised that social reform and the pursuit of social justice would impact on production costs and international competitiveness. Consequently it was important that these objectives were pursued as universally as possible, otherwise those not doing so might gain competitive advantage. The preamble of the ILO constitution expresses this: 'The failure of any nation to adopt humane conditions of labour is an obstacle in the way of others which desire to improve the conditions in their own countries.'

These motives are of current interest and are reflected in the debate within the European Union and more widely at the Group of Seven major industrialised nations (G7) conference in 1994 about the impact of labour market and social regulation on international competitiveness, in the context particularly of seeking solutions to the widespread unemployment in Western Europe and, to a lesser extent, the United States of America.

In 1944 the basic mission of the ILO was restated in the Declaration of Philadelphia and it is this document which, annexed to the constitution of the ILO, constitutes the charter of the organisation's aims and objectives. It embodies a number of fundamental principles:

- labour is not a commodity;
- freedom of expression and association are fundamental to sustained progress;
- poverty anywhere poses a threat to prosperity everywhere;
- all human beings, irrespective of race, creed or sex, have the right to pursue both their material well-being and their spiritual development in conditions of freedom and dignity, of economic security and equal opportunity;
- member states commit themselves to these principles.

The organisation has sought to pursue its objectives of social justice, peace and the promotion of productive employment via a number of different mechanisms, probably the most well known of these being the gradual development of what now constitutes an international labour code. This code consists of instruments which specify minimum standards to be achieved by member states on a wide range of work-related issues and areas of subject matter.

Two different types of instrument may be adopted. One is called a 'convention' and these are legally binding on member states, and the other is called a 'recommendation' with which compliance is voluntary. So far 174 conventions have been adopted. Collectively, these instruments are referred to as 'international labour standards'.

The ILO also seeks to pursue its objectives via the provision of technical advice and assistance; it undertakes development projects, runs and provides training courses and collects and disseminates a wealth of statistics and other information.

Currently 169 countries are members of the ILO. Confronted by the accelerating development of a global economy and new technology (and consequent structural change and adjustment), and by the collapse of communism in Eastern Europe, the organisation has identified a number of specific current and interrelated problems and priorities. The problems are:

- growing economic polarisation both between and within countries;
- increasing poverty, unemployment and economic migration;
- continuing widespread use of child labour;
- in many countries, growing social tension and political instability.

The priorities encompass the support and encouragement of democratic development, the fight against poverty, and the continuing fight to protect the more vulnerable groups of working people: children, women and migrants.

ORGANISATION

A dominant feature of the ILO is that it is tripartite; it seeks to bring together representatives of employers, employees and governments and each group has a voice in the formulation of policies and indeed in other areas of decision making and administration. This tripartism and the search for consensus and co-operation were inspired in the very early days of the organisation's existence by the recommendations of the UK's Whitley Commission in 1916.

The International Labour Conference is the senior body within the ILO. The conference is held annually and debates and adopts conventions and recommendations and oversees compliance by member states. The conference also elects the governing body and adopts the organisation's budget. Delegations from each member state may attend the conference and each delegation contains two government representatives, one employer and one employee representative. The employee and employer delegates participate independently and equally.

The governing body is the executive of the organisation and has the normal responsibilities of ensuring that policies are pursued and that appropriate programmes of work are undertaken. It comprises 28 government members and 14 each representing employers and employees. Ten of the major industrial nations have permanent representation among the government members, and the other members, government, employer and worker representatives are elected every three years by the annual conference. The governing body inevitably becomes involved in the pursuit and investigation of complaints of non-compliance with conventions by or in individual member states. It may establish an *ad hoc* commission of inquiry to pursue a particular complaint and indeed has established a

standing committee to examine complaints against two of the rights central to the objectives and mission of the ILO – the right to organise and the right of freedom of association. This standing committee has examined over 1700 cases since its creation in 1951.

The secretariat of the organisation is provided by the International Labour Office and it also acts as the centre of the advisory, research and information-gathering and dissemination services, as well as co-ordinating the technical assistance activities.

INTERNATIONAL LABOUR STANDARDS

It has already been noted that the ILO creates international standards in one of two forms – conventions and recommendations – and so far standards have been created in the following areas:

- the abolition of forced labour;
- freedom of association;
- equality of treatment and opportunity;
- the promotion of productive employment and vocational training;
- social security;
- conditions of work including hours;
- minimum age of entry into the labour market;
- maternity protection;
- prevention of work-related accidents;
- protection of various minority groups including migrant workers, seafarers and fishermen.

Conventions have the same legal status as international treaties and must be ratified at national level. In other words, the convention only becomes legally binding on the member state once it has been ratified by that state's legislature or by some other appropriate mechanism.

Member states are required periodically to report to the ILO on the measures taken to enforce the conventions which they have ratified. These reports are examined by a committee of experts and they in turn report to the conference. If member states do not comply with conventions that they have ratified, then employers' and workers' organisations, or indeed another member state that has ratified the same convention, can lodge a complaint with the ILO and this is then investigated. If the governing body establishes a committee of enquiry which effectively finds that compliance is not effective, it is likely to formulate recommendations to the member state's government as to how compliance can or should be achieved. The member state government then has a period of three months in which to accept the measures proposed. If it does not, the disagreement may be referred to the International Court of Justice.

Recommendations do not have the same legal status and are not subject to ratification by individual member states. Often recommendations are issued as guidance accompanying the adoption of a new or revised convention.

As noted earlier, there were 174 adopted conventions at the beginning of 1994. However, ratification by member states varies considerably as indeed does compliance, and member state governments cannot at the end of the day be forced to ratify particular conventions nor indeed can they be compelled to comply with those that they have ratified.

It is not practical to give details here of all these adopted conventions, but it is perhaps illuminating to elaborate briefly on some of the more central ones.

- Convention No. 83 on Freedom of Association and Protection of the Right to Organise establishes the right of all workers and employers to form and join organisations of their own choosing without prior authorisation. It also specifies a series of guarantees for the free functioning of organisations, free, that is, from interference from public authorities.
- Convention No. 98 on the Right to Organise and Collective Bargaining. This provides protection from anti-union discrimination, protects both workers' and employers' organisations from interference by each other, and provides also for certain measures to promote collective bargaining.
- Convention No. 111 on Discrimination calls for national policies eliminating discrimination in access to employment, training and working conditions on grounds of race, colour, sex, religion, political opinion, national extraction or social origin. It also calls for policies to promote equality of opportunity and treatment for all.
- Convention No. 100 calls for equal pay for men and women for work of equal value.
- Convention No. 138 on Minimum Age for Entry into Employment aims to achieve abolition of child labour and stipulates that the minimum age should not be less than the age of completion of compulsory schooling.

Of the countries that we are studying in this text, the US has not ratified any of the above conventions. With this exception, Conventions 83, 98 and 100 have been ratified by all other countries with the exception of the Netherlands who have not ratified Convention 98. Convention 111 is not ratified by either Japan or the UK, and Convention 138 is not ratified by Australia, Japan or the UK.

TECHNICAL ASSISTANCE AND CO-OPERATION

By its own estimates, at least 60 per cent of the ILO's member states may be classified as less developed countries and a number of the others are in the process of making the transition from centrally planned to democratic market economies. The ILO plays a considerable role in assisting development through its programme of providing technical advice and assistance, and in the early part of 1994 approximately 500 technical co-operation programmes were active in more than 100 countries.

This help covers a broad range of activities and initiatives encompassing:

- vocational training and rehabilitation;
- employment promotion and development;
- occupational health and safety;
- working conditions;
- industrial relations;
- small enterprise and co-operative development.

The ILO has instituted what it refers to as its active partnership policy. As part of this policy, officials seek to agree with developing country governments and social partners a set of objectives which the ILO then helps to pursue through one of the 14 multidisciplinary teams of experts that have been established on a regional/geographical basis. The hope is that these teams will facilitate a quicker and more meaningful response to the needs of countries in a particular region, which are also often at similar stages of development and confronted by similar problems and issues.

An example of such a multi-disciplinary team is the Central and Eastern European Team (CEET) which has been established in Bucharest. One of the most urgent priorities for the team is the problem of unemployment associated with the demise of central planning and exposure to market forces. In most of these formerly communist countries with command economies, adjustment strategies are required to cope with the inevitable and massive industrial restructuring. Therefore, the team is engaged in devising means to promote productive employment, improve the social security systems and in particular unemployment benefits, develop effective trade union and employer organisations and mechanisms for the efficient resolution of grievances and conflict, and in some instances the development of national institutions to facilitate dialogue and co-operation between the government and the social partners. Much of the team's work is inevitably educational and developmental.

EMPLOYMENT CREATION AND DEVELOPMENT

The promotion of productive employment is central to the activities of the ILO, part of which is the promotion of entrepreneurship and competent management, considered essential to economic and social development. Many member states obtain assistance to enhance productivity and improve the competence of management. This assistance can take many forms and often encompasses the design, development and delivery of training policies and programmes, frequently geared particularly to the needs of the entrepreneur and small employer, the development of more effective production and quality improvement, promotion of self-help organisations of small producers and help for managers to cope with changing business and social environments. In Eastern and Central Europe, much of the activity is undertaken now in the context of privatisation and the development of democratic market economies.

The organisation has always recognised the importance of co-operatives and has supported their development, particularly as participatory institutions contributing to alleviating poverty as well as the promotion of productive employment. Much of the support given is again by way of the design and implementation of specific co-operative training and development programmes.

Whenever the ILO assists member states and social partners to improve employment opportunities, it does so bearing firmly in mind its concerns with the achievement of social justice and labour protection. Achieving an appropriate and equitable balance between labour protection and employment promotion is often hazardous.

The ILO is often active in encouraging and facilitating the creation of free, comprehensive and effective employment services, encompassing guidance and counselling as well as putting job seekers in touch with potential employers. Again, economies in transition have been particularly in need of such a service since traditional employment sources have closed as industry and the economy are restructured in the face of exposure to market forces and international competition.

As is evident from the above, the ILO expends a great deal of its effort and energy on designing and encouraging training and development activities orientated to the promotion and development of productive and effective employment. In 1975, Convention No. 142 was adopted and member states ratifying the convention are required to 'adopt and develop comprehensive and co-ordinated policies and programmes of vocational training in co-operation with workers and employers organisations.'

Much of this assistance is provided directly at the organisation's International Training Centre in Turin. Courses and subjects taught in the centre include management training and development, workers' education, industrial relations, health and safety, and programmes aimed at promoting women and their employment.

INDUSTRIAL AND LABOUR RELATIONS

As noted earlier, the ILO is firmly tripartite in its constitution and structure. It is inevitable therefore that much of its activity over the years has been concerned to promote and preserve the institutions and organisations of employers and workers necessary to the effective operation of such tripartism. The organisation has granted consultative status to four main international federations of trade unions (the International Confederation of Free Trades Unions, the World Confederation of Labour, the World Federation of Trades Unions and the Organisation of African Trades Union Unity) and, on the employers' side, the International Organisation of Employers acts as the umbrella organisation for the 107 national employers' organisations that have members active within the organisation.

In addition to the formal representative and consultative roles performed at the conference and within the governing body, representatives of both social partners participate actively in a multitude of standing and *ad hoc* committees and in various project teams.

The activities of the trade union and employers' organisation representatives and their interests are co-ordinated centrally and respectively by the Bureaux of Workers Activities and Employers Activities.

As indicated above, much of the work undertaken by the ILO in promoting effective organisation within member states is educational. The enactment of labour laws, their effective enforcement, collective bargaining and other co-operative mechanisms are all encouraged by the ILO as a means of promoting both social justice and economic efficiency. The organisation is similarly concerned to promote equitable individual employment relationships and fair and efficient payment policies and procedures. The standards set by the ILO conventions and recommendations often form the basis for legal enactment within member states, and in recent years considerable assistance has been provided to the transitional economies of Central and Eastern Europe concerned to develop mechanisms and standards consistent with emerging democracy.

Relationships between workers' and employers' representatives at industry level have also been encouraged by the ILO. There are established sectoral committees which facilitate joint discussion of issues and problems within particular industrial sectors and across national and regional boundaries.

HEALTH AND SAFETY

The organisation has been consistently concerned with health and safety at work issues and in excess of 20 conventions have been adopted on such issues. One of the earliest was concerned with regulating night work. In recent years there has been a particular concern with alcohol and drug abuse and the ILO is emphasising preventative training and informational campaigns.

The long-term belief that limits on working hours were essential for workers' health and safety, as well as for productivity and efficiency, has come under increasing pressure in recent years as employers have sought greater flexibility of working hours and labour usage as part of their response to new technologies and increasing competitive pressure within the developing global economy. The ILO has not been shifted from its position with respect to the need for employees to be protected, but it is also aware that existing

conventions are perhaps not as relevant as they once were. Consequently new initiatives are in process: a draft convention on part-time work was put to the 1994 conference and other measures include the production of an educational manual highlighting and emphasising the productive possibilities of work organisation and ergonomics.

EQUALITY ISSUES

Equality is another area of longstanding ILO interest and activity, particularly with respect to seeking to improve conditions for people with family responsibilities, and achieving gender equality both in terms of opportunity and treatment and pay for work of equal value.

There is a convention (156) and a recommendation (165) which address the particular problems and potential solutions of those workers with family responsibilities. Convention 156 requires member states to formulate a national policy to enable such people to be employed without discrimination and without conflict between their responsibilities and their employment. A number of mechanisms and practices are suggested which may facilitate the achievement of these latter objectives, ranging from the provision of adequate childcare facilities to greater flexibility in the organisation and allocation of work and work schedules.

Sexual harassment is another area with which the organisation has been particularly concerned in recent years, and after much research, analysis and discussion a Code of Practice is planned for 1994–95.

The organisation is also concerned with devising structural adjustment packages that achieve the twin objectives of productive employment and social equity, mitigating the effects of unemployment, insecurity, greater income and wealth polarisation, and inequity. The organisation again emphasises the importance of seeking tripartite consensus in the search for practical solutions to these common current problems.

SUMMARY

The ILO remains a significant international organisation creating labour standards and seeking to protect the vulnerable, promoting productive employment but not losing sight of social equity, and doing so within the context of promoting democracy in both national, political and industrial senses. The organisation has

consistently pursued consensus and co-operation between the main actors, government and the social partners, the trade unions and employers' organisations. The integration and mediation of these various interest groups in the decision-making processes within the organisation has provided an example to member states, and some of the corporatist developments in Europe after the second world war were no doubt influenced by this example.

However, the ILO and its objectives and mechanisms have often posed problems for states in which a more liberal and *laisser-faire* philosophy dominates, such as the US, and any significant move in the direction of liberalism and individualism in Europe represents a threat to the continuing influence of the ILO within these developed economies. The organisation is obviously well aware of this danger, hence its current concern to find solutions to the problems of industrial restructuring which are consistent with the achievement and maintenance of social equity, and the prevention of social unrest and the threat such unrest poses to international peace.

FURTHER READING

Annual World Labour Reports, ILO

Annual Yearbook of Labour Statistics, ILO

'Combating Sexual Harassment at Work' (1992) *Conditions of Work Digest,* 1, ILO

Hastings S and Coleman M (1992) *Women Workers and Unions in Europe: An analysis by industrial sector,* IDP Women's Working Paper No. 12, ILO

ILO (1994) *Defending Values, Promoting Change: Social justice in a global economy: An ILO agenda,* ILO

International Labour Conventions and Recommendations, ILO

International Labour Review, ILO

International Standards and Guiding Principles on Labour Law and Labour Relations (1989) ILO

Kassalow E (1993) *White Collar Unionism in Selected European Countries,* Sectoral Activities Programme, Working Paper No. 60, ILO

Khan A R (1993) *Structural Adjustment and Income Distribution: Issues and experience,* ILO

Report of the Committee of Experts on the Application of Conventions and Recommendations (1994) Report III, 81st Session, International Labour Conference, ILO

Standing G (1993) *Labour Market Developments in Eastern and Central Europe,* Working Paper, CEET, ILO

Standing G (1993) *Restructuring for Distributive Justice in Eastern Europe,* Policy Paper No. 2, CEET, ILO

Standing G and Tokman V (1991) *Towards Social Adjustment: Labour market issues in structural adjustment,* ILO

The Role of the ILO in Technical Co-operation (1993) Report VI, 80th Session, International Labour Conference, ILO

19 · THE EUROPEAN UNION

Most of the countries that we are focusing on in this text are full members of the European Union (EU). The Netherlands, France, Germany, Italy, the UK and Sweden are already full members, Sweden acquiring full membership in January 1995. The size of the expanded single market created via the 1995 enlargement of the European Economic Area agreement (EEA)[1] now numbers some 380 million people, more than equal to the combined markets of Japan and the US. While these latter countries cannot be members of the EU, their companies can gain many of the benefits of membership by locating one or more of their facilities in a member state. Consequently we have seen many Japanese and American companies investing in the European Union, bringing with them many of their own cultural traditions, attitudes towards work, working practices and ways of managing human resources, but at the same time having to adapt in order to operate successfully within the cultural traditions, legislative and human resource systems of the member state in which they locate. These systems have been increasingly influenced by those countries' membership of the EU.

The European Union and its predecessors[2] has always envisaged that labour (as well as capital, goods and services) should be free to move between the member states with little or no inhibition and that the member states should constitute an effective single market. However, deliberations surrounding the decision to achieve this single market revealed that eliminating barriers to mobility might, through the process known as social dumping (which we elaborate on later), result in social and employment dislocation within and between the member states. There had always been a social dimension to the Communities/Union, but this realisation gave impetus to its enunciation and achievement.

Pappandreou[3], representing the European Commission, pointed out the need for a social dimension, arguing that to be more productive and competitive European labour forces have to be flexible, multi-skilled and capable of utilising the new technologies to produce quality products. She further expressed the Commission's opinion that good working conditions are essential to improving productivity, quality and therefore competitiveness, and that the Commission would therefore seek to establish throughout the Union a general framework of minimum basic requirements with respect to the working environment, employee rights, and terms and conditions of employment.

There were therefore two main incentives to the achievement of this 'social dimension': on the one hand the agreement to create a single European market required a levelling of the social and wage cost 'playing field' if serious dislocation was to be prevented; and, on the other hand, to be competitive internationally companies had to emphasise quality, and to achieve a quality product it is necessary to have a quality labour force and quality working conditions.

There has been considerable disagreement within the Union on these issues, with the UK government seemingly leading the argument against Union-level regulation and interference, reasoning in essence that regulation and harmonisation are likely to lead to less flexibility and increased social and labour costs, which diminishes competitiveness and will in the long run cost the Union and its member states both economic growth and jobs. As we discuss elsewhere, government in the UK since 1979 has been of a liberal individualist and neo-classical persuasion, while within the Union the other influential governments have tended towards collectivism, intervention and the achievement of tripartite consensus. This ideological divide has both contributed to and been compounded by divisions over the role and legitimate use of the institutions and decision-making processes of the Union.

We briefly explain below the way the Union works, before returning to look in more detail at the social dimension and the measures that have been taken so far and the dilemmas and challenges that confront the Union now and in the foreseeable future.

HISTORY AND MEMBERSHIP

In the 1950s six European countries – Belgium, France, Italy, Luxembourg, the Netherlands and West Germany – joined together in formulating the Treaty of Rome 1957 which created the European Economic Community (EEC), the forerunner of the current European Union. The broad aims of the original members were to create a Europe that was economically more interdependent, thereby rendering war between European countries less likely, and to create a large economic block capable of trading more effectively and successfully on the world stage. A common market was to be created between the members by eliminating barriers to the free movement of goods, labour, capital and services.

In 1967 the EEC merged with the Coal and Steel and Atomic Energy Communities, also formed in the 1950s to create the European Community (EC). Subsequently the number of nations in membership of the European Community increased to 12, with Ireland, Denmark and the UK joining in 1973, Greece in 1981 and Spain and Portugal in 1986. The Treaty on European Union agreed at Maastricht in December 1991 paved the way for the Community to become the European Union with effect from November 1993 and Austria, Sweden and Finland became full members in January 1995. Many others, including Turkey and a number of the countries formerly contained within the Communist Eastern European bloc, have applied or indicated their desire to join. At a Council of Ministers meeting in Copenhagen in 1993 it was agreed that certain countries in Eastern and Central Europe could join when they satisfied economic and political conditions. The countries concerned are sometimes known as the 'Visegrad Four' and are the Czech Republic, Poland, Hungary and Slovakia. It is unlikely that they will become full members before the twenty-first century. Nevertheless, the 1994 Corfu Summit meeting welcomed the formal applications in the Spring of 1994 from Poland and Hungary and indicated that the association agreements with them, the Czech and Slovak Republics and Slovenia should be used to propel them towards entry. Cyprus and Malta were also given recognition as probable future members. The December 1994 meeting of heads of government in Essen also gave positive consideration to these further enlargements.

Despite the initial enthusiasm among the members for the creation of a single market, relatively little success had been achieved before the mid-1980s.

Consequently in 1985 the member states agreed, this agreement being embodied in the Single European Act of 1987, that additional measures were necessary if the single market was to become a reality, and they set a deadline for the achievement of this of the end of December 1992. As indicated in the introduction to this chapter, many of the measures proposed as necessary before the achievement of a single market concern social and employment issues and practices, and we examine these later.

THE INSTITUTIONS AND THE LEGISLATIVE PROCESS

Proposals for EU legislation must be based on one or more articles of the original Treaty of Rome as amended. At the heart of the Union are four main institutions with a role in the initiation, enactment, interpretation and application of Union law:

- The European Commission (Commission of the European Communities);
- The European Parliament;
- The European Council;
- The European Court of Justice.

The main legislative roles of the first three of these are summarised in Figure 19.1.

The Commission

Probably the two most important roles of the Commission are to initiate proposals for policy and legislation, and to ensure that member states comply with Union legislation once enacted. The Commission does not, however, legislate. It is divided into divisions on the basis of subject area – e.g. agriculture, transport or social policy – and there are 23 such divisions, each of which is called a Directorate-General (DG). Each DG has a Commissioner in charge of it. Commissioners are appointed by individual member states, with Germany, France, Spain, Italy and the UK having the right to appoint two commissioners each, and the others one each. Some of the Commissioners look after more than one DG.

There is a President of the Commission and he or she is appointed by agreement among the member heads of state; and the President and Commission are now appointed subject to the approval of the European Parliament. Commissioners are required to act in the interests of the Union as a whole. Proposals for legislation initiated by the Commission will usually have

The Commission
Makes proposals

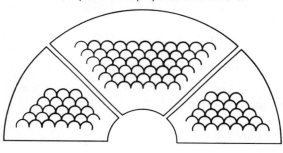

The European Parliament
Gives opinions and proposes amendments

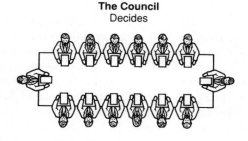

The Council
Decides

Fig 19.1 The process summarised

Source: DTI – The Single Market, 'Brussels, Can You Hear Me?', p.13. Crown copyright is reproduced with the permission of the Controller of HMSO.

originated within a particular Directorate. Once formulated, they are discussed and agreed by a simple majority of the Commission as a whole before being put to either the Parliament or the Council.

The Commission and its staff are generally answerable to the Parliament, which determines its budget, not to the Council.

European Parliament

The Parliament has the power to veto enlargement of the Union and to determine the Commission's budget. However, before the implementation of the Treaty on European Union (Maastricht) it only had a consultative and advisory role with respect to the determination and adoption of Union policy and legislation (see Fig. 19.2(a)). In recent years this limited role has become a matter of some debate, with many interest groups arguing that the Parliament should be allowed a stronger role in the legislative process. The Single European Act had given the Parliament enhanced opportunities to influence legislation adoptable via qualified majority voting (see below). The Act introduced what is termed the Co-operation Procedure (see Fig. 19.2(b)) which gave Parliament two opportunities to comment on and amend legislative proposals, and between July 1987 and September 1991 the Parliament made 2734 amendments of which 1410 were accepted by the Council and which therefore became law.

Nevertheless, it was the Treaty on European Union which arguably has given real impetus to the role and influence of the Parliament. Now the Parliament has co-decision powers with the Council of Ministers on most matters that are subject to qualified majority voting, including consumer protection, health and safety at work, vocational training, and research and devel-

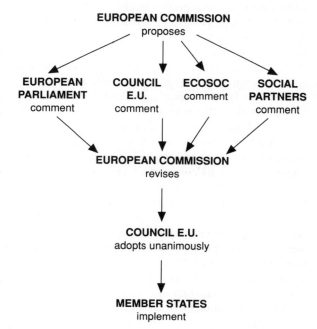

Fig 19.2(a) Consultation procedure

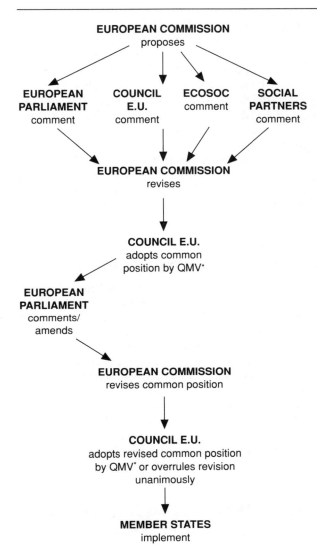

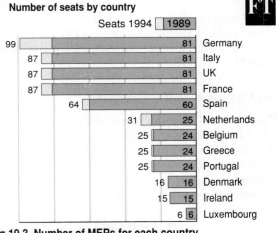

subsequent elections, the Parliament was to be expanded from a total of 518 directly elected members to a total of 567. The motivation for this expansion primarily came from the consequences of German reunification and Germany gained 18 extra seats. Eight other countries also gained representation, and the total numbers of Members of Parliament (MEPs) for each country are shown in Figure 19.3. Those countries that joined in January 1995 are initially to be represented by nominated members and the numbers for each of the three new states are 21 for Austria, 22 for Sweden and 16 for Finland, bringing the total Parliament size to 626.

Political allegiances and alliances within the Parliament are of a cross-national nature.

Fig 19.3 Number of MEPs for each country

Source: *Financial Times*, 14 June 1994

The Council and Council of Ministers

The European Council and Council of Ministers are the legislating bodies within the European Union, although as noted above, in some areas of subject matter it now shares this responsibility with Parliament. Twice a year, heads of government meet as the European Council to decide main issues of policy, amend existing treaties and/or adopt specific legislative proposals. In between these heads of government meetings, the Council of Ministers meets on a subject matter basis, so that if there are social or employment proposals to be adopted or rejected, the appropriate subject area ministers from the government of each member state meet under the aegis of the Council of Ministers.

The Council receives legislative proposals from the Commission and is required also to receive consulta-

*QMV: see description in section on *Voting and the legislative process*

Fig 19.2(b) Co-operation procedure

opment projects and expenditure. This right of co-decision has been somewhat unclear, but it does seem that it constitutes the ability to veto or reject a Council of Ministers' position. The Parliament took this step for the first time in mid-July 1994 when it rejected a Council decision liberalising aspects of the telecommunications market.

The Edinburgh Summit meeting in December 1992 of the 12 heads of state agreed that for the 1994 and

tive opinions from Parliament and a number of other interested and relevant groups and committees. For example, in the area of Economic and Social Policy, there is a Union committee called EcoSoc[4] which the Council has to consult before adopting legislative proposals. However, as with the Parliament, there is no obligation on the Council to take note of or incorporate the opinions expressed.

Within the Council structures, other important committees and working groups, staffed usually by civil servants from the various member states, do much of the detailed work on Commission proposals and much of the negotiating of acceptable compromise. For example, the Social Question Working Group (SQWG)[5] would do much of the detailed work on social and employment proposals and aim to present the Ministers with a position sufficiently acceptable for it to be adopted as Union policy or law; and there is a Committee of Permanent Representations (CoREPER)[6] which is made up of 'permanent representatives' from each member state.

The European Court of Justice

The Court's roles are to interpret and apply Union law, including the founding treaties. The Court is made up of 13 judges, at least one from each member state, and 6 advocates-general all of whom, despite coming from member states, are required to act independently of national interests. Decisions of the Court on the interpretation or application of Union law are binding on all within the Union and have primacy over national law.

Often cases or issues are referred to the Court of Justice by a national court seeking an interpretation. However, individuals can succeed in progressing to the Court a complaint in which national law is inconsistent with Union law[7], or one in which Union law is not being implemented within a particular member state. The Commission is responsible, as noted earlier, for ensuring compliance with Union law, and it is therefore to the Commission that complaints must initially be made. The Commission may seek to resolve the issue itself by effectively making an order that a member state must rectify the particular apparent infringement or lack of compliance. Only if this instruction itself is not complied with will the Court become involved. The Maastricht Treaty introduces provisions for the Court to fine member states for non-compliance.

An example of a case pursued by an individual is *Marshall v Southampton and South West Area Health Authority 1986*. In this case, the Court of Justice ruled

that retirement ages should be equalised between men and women in accordance with the Union's Equal Treatment Directive of 1975. The UK's Sex Discrimination Act 1975 did not require retirement ages to be equalised between the sexes, but the judgement was to the effect that the Union Directive did and it was this that should prevail. Subsequently many employers have sought to equalise at the higher of the previously unequal ages, and it is arguable whether this is consistent with the spirit of the original Directive or indeed with the Court of Justice ruling. The UK government has also now proposed to equalise entitlement to state retirement pensions at age 65 for both men and women, the current position being 65 and 60 respectively.

Trade union and employers' associations

In addition to these main Union institutions, there are institutions at Union level representing trade unions and employers and their associations. The European Trade Union Confederation (ETUC), the Union of Industrial and Employers Confederations of Europe (UNICE), and the European Centre of Public Enterprise (CEEP) are the main umbrella organisations concerned and it is these bodies which are often referred to as the 'social partners' at Union level and through which employer and employee representatives are appointed to various consultative groups and working parties. It is also through these groups that the Social Dialogue occurs, and we return to this later.

VOTING AND THE LEGISLATIVE PROCESS

As has already been explained, Union policy and legislation are proposed by the Commission, considered by Parliament and a number of other consultative fora and working groups, and decided by the Council or Council of Ministers.

Depending on the nature of the subject matter of any proposals, the Council either has to agree unanimously or can create policy or legislation given a sufficient majority in favour. Associated with these different voting requirements are different consultation processes and, in particular, different requirements concerning the number of opportunities Parliament has to consider the proposals and give an opinion and/or propose amendments. If a proposal, because of the nature of the subject matter, can only be adopted or enacted by the Council given unanimity, then the Consultation Procedure (Fig. 19.2(a)) will be used giving the Parliament only one reading or opportunity to comment on and seek to amend the proposal. If, however, the proposals concern subjects which could be adopted by the necessary majority, but not unanimity, of Council, then the Co-operation Procedure is used and the Parliament has a second reading or opportunity to comment (see Fig. 19.2(b)).

Prior to the enlargement in January 1995, the majority required in this second instance above is 54 of 76 votes. When the Co-operation Procedure is appropriate, each of France, UK, Italy and Germany have 10 votes, Spain 8 and the others variously fewer (see below). This meant that at least three countries were needed to block a proposal. This method is known as the Qualified Majority Voting (QMV) or blocking minority procedure. In 1994 the UK and other member states were in dispute over changes to the blocking minority required on enlargement of the Union. The outcome of this dispute was that, at least until the 1996 review, the blocking minority required should remain the same percentage of the total votes available. The three new member states have been allotted votes taking the total from 76 to 87. Austria and Sweden have four votes each and Finland has three.

Co-operation Procedure – the distribution of votes

UK	
France	
Germany	10 votes each
Italy	
Spain	8 votes
Greece	
Netherlands	
Belgium	5 votes each
Portugal	
Denmark	
Ireland	3 votes each
Luxembourg	2 votes

1995 new members

Austria	
Sweden	4 votes
Finland	3 votes

Over recent years, the Commission in particular has been keen to extend the range of subject matter to which the QMV system can be applied. The Single European Act made various amendments to the original EEC Treaty, one of which was to add to the Social Chapter of that Treaty Article 118(a) which provides a specific legal basis for the adoption of Directives on health and safety matters to be by QMV. Legislation on other areas of subject matter such as employee rights and freedom of movement of labour require unanimity and are covered by Article 100.

The UK government, in particular, has been critical of the way in which the extensions of QMV contained within the Single European Act have been used by the Commission and other member states to seek to introduce legislatively backed rights for employees, under the guise of being matters concerned with the health and safety of workers. If treated as employee rights, unanimity within the Council would be required. This dissatisfaction with the activities of the Commission no doubt fuelled the UK government's unwillingness to accept the proposals for the further extension of QMV on social and employment matters that were contained within the proposed European Union Treaty eventually agreed at Maastricht in December 1991.[8] The UK government's refusal to accept these proposals encouraged the other 11 member states to conclude an agreement among themselves. It is important to note that the UK government's reluctance to accept an extension of QMV in the social field should also be seen in the context of its fundamental disagreements with other member states and the Commission on both the nature and extent of Union intervention in and regulation of social and employment matters. These are matters to which we return below.

Types of legislation

There are three forms in which Union legislation may be passed.

Regulation
A Regulation is binding in its entirety on all member states and effectively becomes absorbed, more or less immediately, into the national law within each member state. Regulations, however, are relatively few and far between.

Directive
A Directive is the more common form that legislation takes. Usually Directives specify an objective, outcome or result to be achieved and the time period within which it should be achieved, but they do not normally specify the method to be used. Directives apply to all member states but do not necessarily require each member state to legislate if the outcome specified with-

in the Directive can be achieved in other ways, e.g. through the negotiation and implementation of collective agreements. Directives only have legal force if not implemented and are only directly enforceable in domestic courts in relation to the public sector.

Decisions

A decision is binding on the parties to whom it is addressed and these may include the government of a member state as well as organisations, companies and individuals. Decisions are often made by the Commission where other legislative requirements have not been complied with, e.g. non-achievement of the requirements of a Directive, or where Union law has been infringed. As was stated earlier, the Commission has the general duty of trying to ensure member states' compliance with and implementation of Union law and Decisions, and accompanying fines may be the way in which the Commission seeks to achieve such compliance.

SUBSIDIARITY

The principle of subsidiarity has long been central to the issue of determining whether EU legislative intervention is necessary, but for many years it was undefined. As indicated earlier, some governments (particularly that of the UK) have become concerned that too many legislative initiatives were being taken at Union level when it might have been possible and more appropriate to have achieved the same objectives through action at the level of member states, particularly in the context of very different regulatory frameworks and traditions from one state to another. Briefly, 'subsidiarity' means that the EU should only act when common objectives can be better achieved by action at that level than by member states acting individually. Article 3 of the Maastricht Treaty on European Union sought to reaffirm commitment to the principle and to define it:

> The Community shall take action . . . only if and in so far as the objectives of the proposed action cannot be sufficiently achieved by the member states and can therefore, by reason of the scale or effects of the proposed action, be better achieved by the Community.

Problems also tend to occur as a result of different judgements on the applicability of the words 'sufficiently' and 'better' in particular instances, and linked to this issue are debates concerning flexibility and centralisation. Concerns about overcentralisation prompted a heads of state meeting in Edinburgh in December

1992 to reaffirm their commitment to the principle of subsidiarity and to ensure that it is respected in future initiatives.

THE SOCIAL DIMENSION

One could be forgiven for concluding that the European Union only discovered or became concerned about the social dimension relatively recently. The agreements embodied within the Single European Act certainly gave fresh impetus to consideration of the social and employment implications of creating a single market, but many of these concerns can be traced back to the Treaty of Rome in 1957. Rights to free movement within the Union (Articles 48–51) and to equal pay between the sexes (Article 119), and co-operation between member states in areas such as employment, working conditions, health and safety at work, vocational training, social security benefits and entitlements, rights to free association, collective bargaining and the social dialogue (Articles 118, 118(a) and 118(b)), were all referred to in articles of the 1957 Treaty. However before 1974 little was achieved; certainly no Union-wide legislative measures were taken in these areas and this early period has been characterised as one of 'benign neglect'.[9]

In 1974 the Council adopted the first Social Action Programme which did lead to legislative intervention on a Union-wide basis on a number of dimensions of the employment relationship. Employees were given protective rights in situations of collective redundancies, transfers of undertaking and employer insolvency. Directives were adopted on equal pay and equality of access to work, working conditions, training and promotion, and a few particular health and safety concerns were dealt with, such as noise and lead and asbestos levels. Proposals concerning parental leave, employee participation and equal state retirement ages were, however, not adopted. We would not be the first to suggest that despite much thought and consideration, not a great deal was actually achieved in terms of Union-wide employment, social protection or integration before the Single European Act of 1987 and subsequent developments.

The setting of a deadline of the end of 1992 for the creation of a single market served to concentrate the minds of many within the Union on the need for action in the areas of employment and social policy, in order to prevent the single market resulting in exploitation of the weak and social dumping. This latter concern is, in essence, a concern that unless the social and employment costs of production are roughly harmonised, market forces would encourage the diversion of investment within the Union to those areas or countries in which social and labour costs were lowest and the potential for profit arguably the greatest. Alternatively, there might be mass relocation of labour from low-wage economies or regions to high. Notwithstanding that other factors, for example proximity to markets, infrastructure, availability of other resources, skill levels of the labour force, and wider economic circumstances, such as rates of inflation and interest rates, are all relevant to investment decisions, any diversion of investment would inevitably pose considerable problems for employment levels and standards of living in those areas of the Union that 'lost' as a result of the investment decision.

The counter-argument is that, while there might be some short-term reallocation in the medium to longer term, the market mechanism would tend towards an equalisation of wage costs in a single market. In an interesting report of enquiries conducted by McWilliams[10] the latter view is rejected, and the judgement is made that barriers created by various institutional, cultural and social factors would tend to limit any natural tendencies towards such convergence. He further asserts in the report that the UK should continue to attract inward investment owing to its relatively low labour costs, in particular its low non-wage labour costs; thereby in a sense confirming the fears of those who argue the need for intervention to create a level playing field. These fears have been further confirmed by the Hoover relocation from France to Scotland in January 1993, when it was acknowledged by Hoover spokespeople that the lower non-wage labour costs in Scotland had been a factor in the decision.

These concerns, among others, eventually resulted in 1989 in the production by the Commission of a statement of intent with respect to the creation of a common 'baseline' of minimum employment and social rights and protections across the Union. In December of 1989, 11 of the 12 member states agreed with this 'Social Charter', otherwise known as the Community Charter of the Fundamental Social Rights of Workers. The UK government did not accept its contents and vetoed its adoption by the Council.

The Social Charter

The Charter sets out three overall aims: increased growth and competitiveness for EU industry, job creation, and improvement and greater harmonisation of living and working conditions. It then states that in order to achieve these objectives, it is important that:

- measures to facilitate free movement of labour should be expanded;
- training, health and safety and equality of opportunity should be improved;
- workers throughout the Union are guaranteed fair wages and decent living standards, and that other terms and conditions of employment are improved;
- employers and workers be guaranteed the right to join or not join a trade union of their choice, to negotiate and conclude collective agreements and to resort to collective action, including the right to strike, under the conditions laid down by national legislation and practice;
- employees be given additional encouragement and opportunity to participate in certain areas of decision making;
- and finally that particularly vulnerable groups, such as the young, atypical part-time or temporary workers and the disabled, are given additional protections.

Subsequent to the failure to achieve Union-wide agreement to the Charter, it was adopted as a solemn declaration by the 11 and required the Commission to set out an action programme to achieve at least some of its objectives. To this end the Commission produced a second Social Action Programme containing 47 separate proposals, about 20 of which were envisaged as proposals requiring legislation by the Council.

Social Action Programme

The Social Action Programme reflected a pragmatic rather than a coherent approach by the Commission. Many of the legislative proposals have been adopted, but some seem unlikely to succeed. Particularly, the programme contained proposals concerned with:

- written statements of main contractual terms;
- protection of pregnant women's rights and benefits at work and enhanced rights to both maternity leave and pay;
- mutual recognition of qualifications to assist freedom of movement;
- rights, benefits and protections in the case of some atypical employment contracts, particularly part-time and temporary contracts;
- maxima and minima concerning hours of work and rest periods respectively;
- the creation of organisation-wide works councils in large pan-European companies;

- dealing with certain issues of collective redundancies in pan-European companies, particularly employee representatives' rights to information and consultation in such circumstances.

As indicated earlier in this chapter, the issue of whether particular proposals require unanimous or only qualified majority approval has been relevant in a number of specific instances in determining the degree of progress made towards adoption, and the Commission and a number of the member states have sought to progress as many proposals as possible via qualified majority voting, arguably taking a very broad view of the limits to QMV agreed and contained within the Treaty as amended by the Single European Act.

The UK government has been the most public opponent of many of the proposals referred to above. However, at the time of writing, agreement has been reached on Directives concerned with written proof of contract, equivalence and recognition of professional and vocational qualifications and experience, and Directives have been adopted on rights to maternity leave and pay and on maximum working hours and minimum rest periods, the latter two having been subject to QMV as health and safety measures. Some of these Directives are very much watered-down versions of the original proposals, and others, particularly those concerning atypical contracts and pan-European works councils, have not been adopted by the Union as a whole.

The UK government's opposition to many of the proposals referred to above is grounded in both ideological and practical considerations. From an ideological viewpoint, increased regulation is perceived as the introduction of further sources of imperfection into labour markets, with the consequent distortions to the efficient operation of the market mechanism leading to artificially high wage rates and labour costs and resulting in unemployment.

From a practical viewpoint, the UK government has said that it supports a social dimension of the single market focused on creating and sustaining employment, but any and all proposals for action at Union level should and must be measured against criteria concerned with job creation, intervention at the lowest possible level and in accordance with national traditions. If these criteria are not satisfied, then the proposals should not be adopted. In effect, it seems that the UK government has opposed, and will continue to oppose, proposals for intervention in the employment field which it can be argued are likely to raise employers' costs, make them less competitive and/or have a damaging effect on jobs.

Against the background of this approach, it was predictable that the UK government would oppose the original Social Action Programme proposals concerning pregnant women, part-time and temporary contracts, works councils in pan-European companies and limits on working time and rest periods. Nevertheless, the UK is one of the more readily compliant member states, as can be seen in the passage in 1993 of the TURER[11] in which legislative effect is given to a number of Directives and Decisions regarding pregnant workers[12] and the implications of the Dekker[13] case, a form of proof of contract[14], and enhanced employee representatives' rights to information and consultation in the event of redundancies.[15]

MAASTRICHT – THE EUROPEAN UNION TREATY

The heads of state met in December 1991 to agree the Treaty on Political Union. Like the 1957 Treaty, this contained a chapter concerned with the social dimension of the Union and creation of the single market, consisted largely of proposed amendments to Articles 117–122 of the 1957 Treaty. The purpose of the chapter was again to state the Union's intent to give effect to the Social Charter of 1989, and more specifically to incorporate into the Treaty provisions giving the member states considerably greater capacity to proceed with the legislative harmonisation of employment rights, obligations and law. It proposed that the Union should be able to act in this regard on a unanimous basis in a further five main areas:

- social security and protection of employees;
- protection of employees whose contracts are terminated;
- representation and protection of collective interests of both employers and employees, including co-determination;
- financial contributions for the promotion of employment;
- conditions of employment for third-country nationals resident in a member state.

Further extension of the capacity to act via QMV was also proposed, to include:

- health and safety – specifically improving the working environment to protect workers' health and safety;
- working conditions;
- information to and consultation of workers;

- equality between the sexes both in terms of access to and treatment in employment;
- some training issues.

These proposals are consistent also with the desire to speed up progress.

However, the chapter also specifically excluded Union-wide legislative action in the areas of pay, rights of association and the right to strike or lock-out. The majority of these changes were proposed as amendments and additions to Article 118 of the 1957 Treaty.

The UK government was not prepared to agree to the Treaty containing the revised Social Chapter and eventually won agreement that it should stay out of an agreement among the other 11 to adopt the proposed amendments. It did not opt out of the original Social Chapter and to all intents and purposes the situation remains in a pre-Maastricht state as far as the UK is concerned. As noted, the 11 came to a separate agreement between themselves to adopt the changes proposed to the original Social Chapter, and this is annexed to but does not form part of the 'new' Treaty. The agreement by the 12 that the UK could stay out of the agreement to adopt the Social Chapter, that the 11 could adopt it on their own, is contained within the social protocol which does form part of the Treaty. This protocol became effective when the Treaty was ratified, which in practice was November 1993.

The issue of quite how the new arrangements will work has not been fully resolved at the time of writing, although it is clear that the Commission and other member states will use the pre-Maastricht rules and procedures wherever possible, the protocol agreement being used only in those circumstances where the UK's position renders progress unlikely or at a pace unacceptably slow. The protocol also authorised the 11 to use the mechanisms and institutions of the Union for the purpose of taking decisions among themselves and applying them as far as they are concerned. Quite how any new laws agreed by the 11 through the protocol processes will be interpreted by the European Court of Justice and whether they will become part of the Union's body of laws, regulations and practices, are also unclear. One thing that does seem clear, however, is that when the 11 are considering issues on their own, QMV will require 44 out of 66 to be in favour of proposals, the 10 votes of the UK being discounted on both sides.

Certainly the possibility now exists for the members, excluding the UK, to press ahead with a range of legislative proposals giving effect to more of the aims of the Social Chapter. The extent to which such an approach is consistent with progress towards full monetary union is debatable, as indeed is the achievement of that objective. At the time of writing, the 11 have recently reached a common position on legislative proposals concerning information and consultation to and of employees in community-scale undertakings and we deal with this below. The three new 1995 members will join the eleven others in utilising protocol arrangements.

There is evidence that some other member states are themselves concerned at the implications of giving effect to all the aims of the Social Chapter, particularly as it effects employment costs and, in the context of continuing concern about social dumping, it seems quite likely that they may decide individually or collectively that progress should be slowed if not halted completely. Additionally there is concern that the UK will gain competitive advantages in terms of production costs and as a potential home for non-European company investment within the Union. Non-European Union members seeking access to the single market often invest within the Union, and if labour and social costs and the degree of regulation are lower in one member state, this may just be sufficient to tip the balance in favour of investing in that member state rather than another. The UK government is well aware of this potential advantage and is willing to exploit it.

A policy paper for the rest of the decade agreed by the Commission in July 1994 is indicative of a slowing down in pursuit of the aims of the Social Chapter. It was proposed in the paper that currently stalled Social Action Programme directives concerned with extending rights to part-time workers (on a *pro rata* basis with full-time workers) and widening rights to parental leave should be pursued via the protocol procedures if necessary (this will be necessary since the UK has on many occasions indicated that it will not agree to these proposals). The commission was also concerned that the necessary action be taken to ensure that non-EU nationals cannot be used by contractors to undercut EU minimum standards. However, the emphasis of the rest of the paper is on consolidation and enforcement of existing Directives rather than on an active pursuit of further Social Chapter aims.

SOCIAL DIALOGUE

In addition to the above, the Union Treaty Social Chapter proposals included a considerably enhanced role for the social partners, described in the document only as 'management and labour at community level', in initiating and implementing Union legislation through the process of social dialogue. These proposals were adopted by the 11 and form part of the agreement between them that is annexed to the Treaty.

The promotion of dialogue between management and labour is incorporated as an objective in Article 117 and the detail of the new provisions is contained in the proposed revisions to Articles 118(a) and 118(b). These two revised articles now give the partners to the social dialogue:

- the right to be consulted before the Commission puts proposals to the Council;
- the right, on agreement between them, to request the Commission to formulate proposals in accordance with that agreement;
- the right to be consulted on Commission proposals;
- the right to formulate agreements of a contractual nature at EU level which could be given the force of law by a Council decision or which could be implemented at national level by the parties to the agreement subject to the approval of the member state.

Figure 19.4 illustrates the possible decision-making processes when matters are dealt with by the protocol arrangements.

Again, it is too early yet to assess the impact of these provisions. Clearly they might encourage collective bargaining at a Union level. They also afford a potential status and role to the social partners which is not currently available to them in all member states, and reflect a liberal collectivist approach consistent with the achievement of consensus and macro-corporatism, but not consistent with liberal individualism. The last item above indicates at least two types of agreement that could be the output of the social dialogue, one which is given legislative effect at Union level by a Council decision (a practice common in many member states where national governments/parliaments give legal effect to collective bargaining outcomes), and another which envisages agreement at Union level being voluntarily implemented by the partners at a national level.

The lack of specificity about who the participants to the social dialogue may be certainly enables the possibility that the social policy agreement annexed to the Treaty encompasses bargaining at both inter-sectoral and sectoral level. Certainly it raises the likelihood that the central representative groups/organisations – ETUC, UNICE and CEEP – may engage in bargaining and produce either kind of outcome referred to above. However, it is also possible that the representative organisations in a particular industry could do

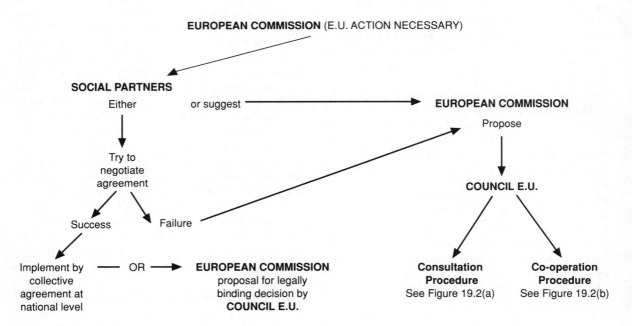

Which procedure and whether by Q.M.V. or unanimity is determined by subject matter

Fig 19.4 Protocol decision-making procedures

the same: either produce an agreement given legal effect by a Council decision, or one which is voluntarily implemented by the partners/participants and their affiliates in each member state.

It is debatable whether collective bargaining at a Union level will be encouraged by these arrangements. Where the central organisations are invited to reach agreement on a particular issue, for example on the Social Action Programme Directives that have been stalled by the UK veto, then collective bargaining is being encouraged. However, if UK employers' representatives within UNICE use the opportunity to prevent or sabotage any such agreement (as arguably was the case early in 1994 on the first occasion that this mechanism was used[16]) then the potential for any meaningful enhancement of collective bargaining at this central, inter-sectoral level does seem limited. These first discussions and attempts to use the newly agreed arrangements were concerned with the proposed Directive on the information and consultation rights of employees in community scale undertakings.

As was the case above, where such bargaining does occur it seems that it is likely to be most appropriate where it is framework, umbrella or procedural agreements that are the desired outcome. In the near future, the scope for inter-sectoral substantive agreements seems very much more limited given the arguable representiveness of the central associations, their lack of mandate and the considerable variations within the Union of substantive terms and conditions of employment. At a sectoral level such agreements may be more feasible, but there is a shortage of effective and representative employers' associations at this level in many sectors; indeed, over the last two years there has been a noticeable trend for employers to leave employers' associations in several member states.

The apparent decision of the Commission and some member states that over the next few years further prescriptive legislative interventions should be avoided where possible may also imply an increased emphasis on the voluntary route rather than on bargaining resulting in a Council decision giving the agreement legislative effect, although the partners at an inter-sectoral level may be given further opportunities to produce agreement on the relatively few stalled Social Action Programme proposals.

FREEDOM OF MOVEMENT

As noted earlier, freedom of movement has always been an objective of the Union but little was achieved before the agreement on creating a single market that is embodied within the Single European Act. Subsequent to this, a number of initiatives have been taken and a number of Directives adopted. It was soon realised that practical restrictions on mobility concerned with rights to work and reside could relatively simply be eased, but that there were other barriers that would prove far more intractable. Examples of these include:

- access to vacancy and opportunity information;
- differential social security and superannuation provisions;
- cultural differences and attachments;
- language;
- housing availability and affordability;
- racial prejudice;
- sexual stereotyping;
- absence of mutual recognition of qualifications and experience.

So far, the majority of Union effort has been concentrated on mutual recognition and the provision of funding for relevant activities and training programmes, e.g. language training and the establishment of Union-wide information and vacancy networks.

Initially the problems of mutual recognition were approached on an individual profession basis, but this proved far too time consuming and eventually the approach was changed to a general one. There are a number of individual Directives concerning medical professions and architecture, but in 1989 a General Directive was adopted (89/48/EEC) that required all member states to recognise as equivalent regulated professional qualifications obtained in any member states. In some instances periods of supervised practice or aptitude tests may be required, but by and large equivalent qualifications in terms of duration of training and level are now mutually recognised and in that sense transferable. A similar approach was subsequently adopted to other vocational qualifications and experience.

UNEMPLOYMENT

Since 1992 there has been a much greater awareness and concern within the Union that unemployment, particularly that of a structural nature, was increasing. The Social Affairs Council of Ministers at its meeting in December 1992 considered the problems of the Union's 17 million unemployed and concluded a resolution that had four key elements, including reference to vocational training and removing barriers to mobility, but also floating the idea of an 'individual portfolio' for every adult in the Union. This could contain a summary of their academic and vocational qualifications and experience which they could carry with them and for which they could be given credit anywhere in the EU.

In April 1994 European Union unemployment reached a record of 11 per cent – 18 million people, though by August 1994 this had decreased to 10.7 per cent. Both heads of government summits in 1993 were preoccupied with debates about cause and remedy. There was a measure of agreement within the Union that the unemployment was both cyclical and structural and that it might well increase throughout the rest of the decade unless appropriate action was taken. However, there was no such common position on either the distribution between cyclical and structural causes or on the remedies to be adopted, or indeed on whether action could or should be taken at Union level. Similarly, it is important to record that unemployment experience varies considerably within the Union and between countries (see Fig. 19.5) and dimensions, e.g. youth unemployment in Germany in 1993 was 4.9 per cent compared with 24.6 per cent in France; female unemployment was 8.1 per cent in the UK but 28.9 per cent in Spain. These differences were further acknowledged in a Franco-German report issued by the respective governments at the end of May 1994, and preceding the year-long co-ordinated German and then French Presidency of the Union. The report identifies German weaknesses as high wage costs, short working hours and overcomplex products; the French weaknesses are too high a social security burden on companies that invest too little in research. Both countries were reported to suffer from far-reaching labour regulation, insufficient training and retraining, and lack of wage differentiation. Among other suggestions, the report recommends relaxing rules governing dismissals, more flexibility in working hours and basing wage policy on performance and productivity.

The Commission declared its position on the various issues in its white paper on competitiveness, growth and unemployment presented to the December 1993 heads of government summit. In this it argues for lifelong training and retraining, reducing non-wage labour costs on unskilled labour, investment in infrastructure networks, improvement of employment services for job seekers, job sharing and more part-time work, but crucially not at the expense of living standards. The alternative and more deregulatory viewpoint was expressed in UNICE's report *Making Europe More Competitive* in which the remedies necessary are seen to be reducing the high non-wage labour costs that have contributed to Europe's increasing lack of competitiveness in comparison with the US, Japan and Pacific-rim states, keeping real wage increases below the rate of increase in productivity, and an encouragement of incentive through a widening of wage differentials at least partly facilitated by cutting minimum wage rates. The employers also required relaxation of rules on working hours, easier laws with respect to employment and termination, lower unemployment benefits and a more limited access to social security benefits.

These viewpoints can be seen to represent the difference between those who see the role of government and the Union as minimalist, intervening where necessary to facilitate the operation of the market, and those who see the role of government and the Union as interventionist, facilitating business competitiveness and economic growth but not at the expense of social justice and equity.

The December 1993 summit endorsed the Commission white paper, which can be summarised as calling for greater flexibility in labour costs and a better balance between protection for the employed and access to work for the unemployed. The white paper and its endorsement have also been seen as evidence of the beginnings of a move away from a detailed EU-wide legislative agenda protecting those in work.

Subsequent work by the Commission in advance of the June 1994 Corfu summit meeting, the outcome of that meeting and the July 1994 Commission social policy paper, all tend to confirm movements in the direction of less detailed and prescriptive legislation, greater sympathy for the principle of subsidiarity, achieving greater flexibility in the use of labour, and putting more effort into reducing non-wage labour costs, but not at the expense of the social dimension of the Union. The Corfu summit reaffirmed the social dimension as an indispensable corollary to the single market, and the progress report on the December 1993 white paper that was prepared for the Corfu meeting stressed that labour market efficiency should not be sought through the dilution of the traditional European model of social protection. The burden should not be borne by the weakest in society. What was needed was action to adapt, rationalise and simplify regulations in order to establish a better balance between social protection, competitiveness and employment creation.

Critics might well argue that these 'official positions' seek the best of both worlds and run the risk of

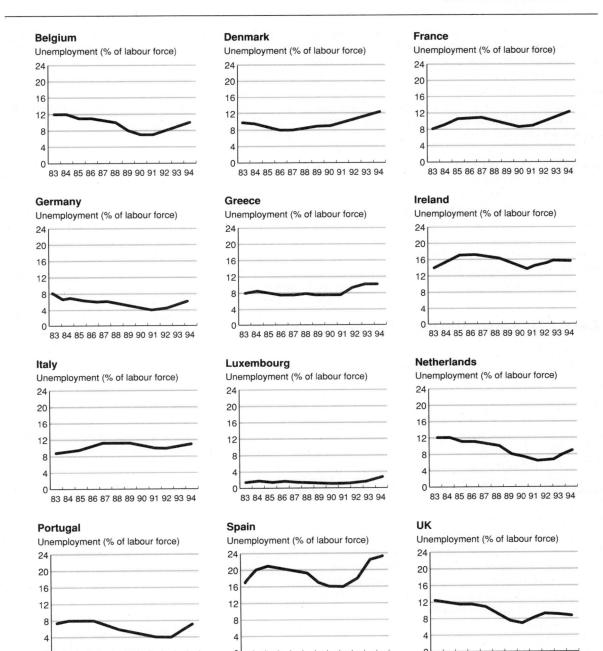

Belgium
Unemployment (% of labour force)

Denmark
Unemployment (% of labour force)

France
Unemployment (% of labour force)

Germany
Unemployment (% of labour force)

Greece
Unemployment (% of labour force)

Ireland
Unemployment (% of labour force)

Italy
Unemployment (% of labour force)

Luxembourg
Unemployment (% of labour force)

Netherlands
Unemployment (% of labour force)

Portugal
Unemployment (% of labour force)

Spain
Unemployment (% of labour force)

UK
Unemployment (% of labour force)

Source: Datastream, OECD

1994 figures are latest values

Fig 19.5 Where Europe isn't working

Source: *Financial Times*, 17 May 1994

achieving neither; that unless the EU allows the costs of employing low-skilled labour to fall and at the same time creates a greater incentive for that labour to accept employment, very little positive impact is likely to be made on overall and long-term levels of unemployment; indeed that the European social welfare model is incompatible with job creation and employment levels as high as those in the US and Japan.

The December 1994 summit meeting of heads of government endorsed a set of non-legislative proposals aimed at shifting the emphasis away from protecting or expanding the rights of those with jobs towards giving the unemployed greater opportunities for employment. Specifically the proposals concern better training, greater working time flexibility, lower non-wage labour costs, changes to social security arrangements encouraging re-employment and greater help for unqualified youth.

EMPLOYEE PARTICIPATION/DEMOCRACY

The issue of employee participation has been on the agenda of the EU for many years now and there have been a number of initiatives and proposals, none of which has amounted to much in terms of outcome. Rights to information and consultation have been agreed in certain limited areas of subject matter, e.g. health and safety matters, transfers of undertakings and collective redundancies, but by and large each member state has different traditions, laws and practice. This issue is examined more thoroughly in Chapter 7. The initiatives that have been taken include:

- European Company Statute: in return for incorporation as a European company, which would yield certain legal and potentially financial benefits, certain information and consultation rights would be granted to employees. A number of participatory models have been proposed including worker directors, works councils and other equivalents achieving the criteria established.
- The Vth Directive: applies to companies employing in excess of 1000 people, very similar to the first initiative above.
- The Vredeling Directive: again applying to companies with more than 1000 employees, but interestingly this proposal incorporated a requirement that agreement be the aim of consultations with employee representatives on matters affecting employee interests.

None of the above has proceeded beyond relatively early stages.

The most recent proposal, based on Article 100 of the Treaty of Rome and requiring unanimity, was the draft Directive requiring community scale undertakings to establish a company level or European works council. These undertakings are sometimes also referred to as pan-European or trans-European companies. The original proposal envisaged that the works council would have to be informed and consulted on issues affecting employees in more than one member state, and visualised the Commission specifying a model constitution and appropriate subject matter, but it was also intended that any Directive would seek to facilitate flexibility and individual models that suited the requirements of both the management and labour in a particular organisation. Pappandreou[17] considered that the standard model decided on would in fact only be used in circumstances where management and labour are unable to agree on alternatives.

The opposition of the UK government eventually resulted in these proposals being the first dealt with by the 11 under the social protocol provisions. The social partners sought to negotiate an agreement, but opposition from UK employers seems to have been influential in ensuring that agreement was not achieved.

Proposals were presented in a number of different forms and drafts, and eventually the 11 adopted a Directive in September 1994.[18] The requirements apply to community scale undertakings employing more than 1000 people, with at least 150 employed in each of two member states excluding the UK. However, UK companies that satisfy these criteria excluding their UK operations will be subject to the legislation. Estimates vary as to how many companies are likely to be covered by the Directive: – a German study[19] estimated that 450 German, 250 US and 220 French corporations would be eligible, and that nearly 300 UK companies would have been had UK-based operations been calculable. Even without their UK operations, between 50 and 100 UK companies seem likely to qualify in respect of their mainland European operations.

The scheme adopted was more flexible than some of the earlier drafts and provides that, if the requisite number of employees or other representatives request it, companies must enter into negotiations with a view to agreeing and establishing information and consultation procedures at corporate or European level. If employers refuse to negotiate or if agreement is not achieved within three years, then a specific form of works council arrangement contained in an annex to the Directive can be imposed within the organisation.

This annexe specifies a range of subject matter that must be covered by the information and consultation process to include: the economic and financial situation; business developments and trends; investment plans; substantial organisational change; the introduction of new working methods or production processes; transfers of production; mergers, cutbacks, closures and collective redundancies.

It is important to note that these proposals will have no impact on companies where the workforce does not ask for negotiations or relevant procedures.

Employers' organisations have criticised the proposals on the grounds of cost and time delay to decision making. It must be remembered that these are proposals for informing and consulting employee representatives and, by some criteria, this does not constitute participation in decision making.

THE IMPACT OF THE EU ON HRM

As will have been evident from the foregoing analysis, governmental commitment to the principle of European integration has been varied and this seems to have impinged upon the extent to which indigenous companies have prepared for European integration.

It is within the European context that the creeds of 'social partnership' and deregulation are most poignantly juxtaposed. At HR policy level a preference for a deregulated, free market approach, most evident in the UK, translates into HR policies which are to enhance competitiveness through actions such as lowering wage costs and increasing working hours.

This has led Hendry to argue:

> although the Social Chapter was conceived with polarisation between northern and southern Europe more particularly in mind, by consistently opposing it the Conservative government in Britain seems to have wanted to retain "social dumping" as a policy option.[20]

Indeed a survey carried out in the UK of industry responses to the Single European Market in the late 1980s, which concentrated particularly on the insurance and furniture industry[21] found little action had been taken in anticipation of the Social Charter or perceived

---

SINGLE MARKET CONFLICTS: TWO IDEAL TYPES

Deregulation

Ideology
- emphasis on free movement of labour, capital and goods

View of State:
- non-interventionist

HR Policy Formulation:
- flexibility
- individualisation in
  - pay
  - reward
  - recruitment
- 'empowerment'

IR Orientation:
- tendency to marginalise trade unions

Hopes:
- competitiveness with other trade blocs through cost-effective production

Fears:
- 'red tape'
- unnecessary restrictions on employers

Harmonisation

Ideology
- establishment of a democratic, liberal and peaceful political order

View of State:
- more active involvement

HR Policy Formulation:
- harmonisation
- standardisation
- collectivism in pay etc.
- statutory involvement in recruitment
- training

IR Orientation:
- 'social partnership'

Hopes:
- competitiveness through high skill base

Fears:
- 'sweat shops'
- deskilling
- 'social dumping'

language problems, and that HRM issues were taking second place to marketing and business decisions. Also there had been little or no anticipation of any significant increase in cross-national mobility and training of management within Europe. However, some concern was expressed about 'poaching' by European firms.

Yet, as Thurley argued:

> It can be argued that the free market 'laissez-faire' approach is unlikely to be acceptable to most Europeans in its extreme form, as the development of a revitalised 'common market' economy must depend on the existence of a democratic, liberal and peaceful political order – it is also true that what appears to be idealistic to pragmatic Anglo Saxons, such as the emphasis on dialogue, actually takes place with a considerable degree of success in, for example, Dutch, Danish and German Works Councils.[22]

Moreover, it may be argued that those countries which adhere most to the 'social partnership' model are likely to view deregulation with a degree of scepticism, or even resentment and the existence of relatively 'favourable' economic conditions elsewhere, particularly in the form of low labour costs, may act as an incentive for businesses to locate in these areas where codes of employment are more rigorous.

Nevertheless European integration does throw up an important set of challenges to HR practitioners across Europe, albeit on a differential basis, according to factors such as sector, or degree of current involvement of concerns within Europe.

These have been described quite clearly by the British IPD in *IPD Executive Brief*, an extract of which is reproduced below.

GENERAL IMPACT OF THE EU ON HR MANAGEMENT

PERSONNEL POLICY

The general effects of the increased competition and opportunities offered by the liberalisation of movement of goods, services, capital and labour are impacting on all aspects of personnel management, as more UK and Irish companies expand their activities into other Member States, and more companies in other Member States start operating over here.

The extension of the Single Market to five of the EFTA countries from January 1994 has widened this impact still further.

Issues for particular companies regarding the implications of the Single European Market depend on the size and nature of their business and their current or potential involvement in the European Market – i.e. whether they are expanding into new markets and/or facing new competition in their home market.

However, most organisations will be affected in some way, even if indirectly, and particularly in the areas of organisation, recruitment, training, and retention. Organisations expanding beyond national frontiers will face additional challenges. The major effects are outlined below.

Organisation

New competition and opportunities for expansion may result in a complete overhaul of structure for some companies, bringing change management and personnel planning and resourcing issues to the fore.

Reorganisation and rationalisation: Many companies have relocated their manufacturing or distribution sites to low-cost countries, or have established a central site or headquarters in Europe to serve the whole of the European market in place of several national sites. Choice of location varies enormously and depends on many factors. Quality, flexibility and cost of labour tend to be important factors on the personnel side particularly where production is concerned. However, inward investors, such as US and Japanese companies, are keen to locate in what they see as the heart of Europe, so communications and politics are also important.

There has been substantial rationalisation in many industries – particularly the steel, car, banking, tool and transport industries as organisations adapt to greater competition, compounded by the current global recession. The European Commission has predicted a growth rate for the EU of only 1.3% for 1994, and the average EU unemployment rate is expected to reach nearly 20 million, or about 12% by the end of the year.

Mergers and takeovers: The development of the Single European Market has led to a surge in mergers and takeovers as companies seek alliances or reinforcement to face competition or take new opportunities for expansion.

This has resulted in some radical culture changes for many companies having to adapt to a new national as well as a new corporate management culture.

Recruitment

Free movement of labour is enshrined in the EEC Treaty; employers may recruit throughout the EU and employees may work in any Member State without a work permit – a right which was extended to five EFTA countries in January 1994.

Opportunities and competition: Many employers and employees now see Europe as a single labour market. More employers are looking now beyond their national borders to find the best candidates for their vacancies and are keen to develop a 'European' workforce. This means increased competition in home labour markets as employers in other Member States reduce the pool of national labour available.

Mobility and skills shortages: Mass movements of labour are not expected as a result of the gradual consolidation of the Single European Market. In fact only 2 million EU citizens work permanently in another EU country, fewer than the number ten years ago. In the UK the number of EU nationals working or seeking work is 1.5% of the workforce. Of these, 61% are from Ireland.

All Member States are affected to a varying degree by the demographic trends leading to a shortage of younger workers and a gradually ageing workforce across the EU, and it is expected that certain categories of staff, especially senior managers, graduates and technical/specialist staff will become more mobile as the supply of such personnel as a whole decreases and competition for them intensifies. The 'Euro-executive' is likely to become a rare and highly sought-after commodity.

Recruiting from other Member States: Employers wishing to recruit from other Member States need to acquire new skills and knowledge, for example:

- locating supplies of labour in other Member States;
- where and how to advertise;
- how to assess qualifications and experience gained in other Member States;
- how to deal with induction and training to overcome language and cultural differences between the new recruits and existing staff.

Pay and conditions

Remuneration: The more mobile employees and those in generally short supply – particularly senior managers, graduates and specialists/technicians – are increasingly aware of more advanced practices in Europe and compare remuneration packages on a European rather than a national basis, so employers will need to ensure that they are offering competitive packages to attract and retain these key personnel at European level. Remuneration is likely to become more uniform for such people, although national differences will remain in the remuneration of most employees for a long time to come, and disparities in cost of living, tax, social security and pension systems still cause big differences.

Collective bargaining: Cross-border comparison of pay levels, working hours, training, investment and productivity are likely to increase as unions develop cross-border links – particularly once the Directive on European Committees is implemented. There is also the likelihood of the development of pan-European collective bargaining in the larger pan-European companies.

Industrial relations: Trade unions in the UK are actively developing a more European approach to industrial relations, based on consensus or 'Social Partnership' rather than conflict.

Training

Skills: Greater and higher quality training is essential if organisations are to compete successfully with other European firms in an increasingly competitive home market or if they are to expand their operations successfully into other Member States.

Languages/culture: Companies working on a European rather than a national basis need to ensure that certain employees are adequately trained in other languages and in cultural awareness – particularly senior managers, and sales and support staff, such as receptionists and secretaries. The UK Languages Lead Body has developed a set of language standards for the use of foreign languages at work and NVQ qualifications based on these standards are now available. Skills such as selling skills also need adaptation to different markets.

New rules/knowledge: changes made to free up the movement of goods, services, capital and labour mean new knowledge requirements for many employees working in those areas. They must learn and adapt to new technical standards, and be up to date in their knowledge of new rules, e.g. on exporting.

Impact of Single Market: For some organisations it will be essential to ensure that someone in the company is provided with the training and resources to assess the effects of the Single European Market on the business.

According to the Industrial Society's report, *Training Trends* (November 1993), 50% of UK companies have not carried out any single market training, and those that have concentrated mostly on languages.

Additional issues for European companies

Companies expanding into other Member States will have additional considerations. These will already be familiar to international companies, and include:

- deciding whether to employ local or send out national staff;
- learning about local laws, customs, employment conditions, tax and social security differences;
- training national staff dealing with other countries in the linguistic/cultural differences;
- creating competitive but compatible pay and benefit systems for staff working in different Member States;
- structuring the organisation's reporting and communication systems;
- managing multi-cultural teams;
- succession planning.

European-wide policies need to be flexible, compatible between the different Member States and well-coordinated from the centre.

Source: *IPD Executive Brief: Personnel Management and Europe*, July 1994. Reproduced with kind permission of Cherry Mill, IPD advisor on EC affairs.

SUMMARY

The Union comprises 15 countries and is facing future enlargement. Initially, its processes and institutions were relatively conservative and emphasised unanimity. The long-awaited agreement to make the single market a reality prompted concerns about its processes and institutions, specifically the need to speed up decision making, the practical application of the principle of subsidiarity and the role of the Parliament. Interwoven with these concerns are the issues of national sovereignty and the 'need' for Union-wide/level action. In many instances, the UK has stood apart from the others in its opposition to the extension of qualified majority voting and its determination to retain its power of veto whenever possible. It is arguably responsible for much of the attention recently given to the issues of subsidiarity and sovereignty and the critical evaluation of the need for and nature of Union-wide intervention and regulation. Other interests have pointed up the so-called 'democratic deficit' whereby the parliament of directly elected representatives was constrained to an advisory and consultative role.

The agreement to create the single market also significantly increased concerns about social dumping and whether the market mechanism should be allowed to operate freely in respect of investment and employment decisions. The collective decision that regulation and mediation of the process was necessary, allied to the majority belief that employees will be exploited by the market and that they therefore need the protection afforded by collectives and legislative regulation, served to raise both the profile of social issues and the temperature of the debates.

Events in recent years – the initiatives taken to create a level playing field on the social front and to improve working environments and terms and conditions within those environments – have highlighted the ideological divide that was brought into the open at Maastricht. Proposals to extend the scope of qualified majority voting and the influence and role of the social partners in formulating and implementing social policy proved too much for the UK government to accept.

However, since Maastricht, the liberal collectivist and corporatist direction of the Union (or at least the 11 excluding the UK) has been thrown into doubt by the election of right-wing governments in a number of member states and by the recession. By late 1994 it seemed very much more likely that the pace of social regulation over the next few years was about to slow down as its costs and impact on international competitiveness were reassessed. The Union is confronted with declining competitiveness and increasing unemployment and these issues are likely to be afforded considerably greater attention in the future. In the meantime, it does seem that investment and production decisions are being taken within the Union which will benefit those economies with lower social and other production costs. Continuation of the process of social dumping in the context of relatively high levels of unemployment may well lead to a considerably greater degree of tension within the Union, both between advantaged and disadvantaged social and ethnic groupings, and at the level of the member state between those seen to be gaining and those perceived to be losing.

The Treaty agreed at Maastricht has enhanced the influence of the Parliament. This experience, the 1995 enlargement and proposals for further enlargement to the East in a few years time will put considerable pressures on the 1996 review of the treaty on political union to appraise critically the adequacy and appropriateness of existing institutions and procedures.

NOTES AND REFERENCES

1. European Free Trade Association (EFTA) members, with the exception of Switzerland have since January 1994 been members with EU countries of a grouping called the European Economic Area agreement (EEA). By way of this agreement, the single market is extended to include these other countries: Iceland, Norway, and Liechtenstein, who in return, accept much (about 60%) of the Union legislation, including social legislation, and accept the principles of the Social Charter (see later). They are also able to participate in some of the Union's consultative but not decision making processes. They will not be required to implement any further EU legislation unless and until they become full members. The agreement facilitates transition to full member status for those that wish it and that satisfy the criteria. These minimum criteria being that a country is in Europe, is democratic and economically developed.

2. Particularly the European Economic Community (EEC) and the European Community (EC)

3. Pappandreou V (1991) 'Flexible Approaches to Involvement', *Personnel Management*, May

4. EcoSoc – The Economic and Social Committee, this committee is made up of representatives of various interest groups across the Union. For example, employees, employers and consumers. The employee and employer members of this committee are usually proposed by trades unions and employers' associations respectively. The committee is quite large with almost 200 members.

5. Working groups are usually comprised of both permanent representatives and civil servants from relevant government departments or ministries.

6. Each member state keeps a form of embassy to the EU in Brussels, and it is representatives from these embassy staffs that make up CoREPER and, in conjunction often with specialised working groups, deal with much of the detailed preparatory work.

7. Member states exhibit varied rates of compliance. In the IPM's European Community Update of Nov. 1993, p.16, it is reported that only half of the single market directives had been implemented by all member states. In the social and employment field, the UK, Denmark and Ireland had taken implementing measures for over 90% of the directives, whereas in the cases of Germany, Italy and Luxemborg, the figure was below 70%

8. It was proposed that the Social Chapter of the EEC Treaty be amended to facilitate the pursuit and implementation of the social action programme accompanying the social charter, some aspects of which to be via QMV. Specifically articles 117–122 were to be amended.

9. Mosley H (1990) 'The Social Dimension of European Integration', *International Labour Review*, Vol 129.2, pp.147–164

10. McWilliams D (1992) *Will the Single European Market Cause European Wage Levels to Converge?* London Economics (MES) Ltd.

11. Trades Union Reform and Employment Rights Act 1993

12. EC Directive 85/92/EEC on Safety and Health at Work of Pregnant Workers or Workers who have recently given birth

13. Dekker; European Court of Justice 1991 ruled that discrimination on grounds of pregnancy or maternity leave constitutes direct sex discrimination since only women can become pregnant.

14. EC Directive EEC/91/533 on Form of Proof of Employment Relationship

15. EC Directive(s) 75/192/EEC and 92/56/EEC on Collective Redundancies

16. Comments of P. Flynn – the Commissioner for Social Affairs, reported in *Financial Times*, 20 May 1994

17. Pappandreou V, op. cit.

18. Council Directive 94/95 on the establishment of a european works council or a procedure in community scale undertakings and community scale groups of undertakings for the purpose of informing and consulting employees

19. *Financial Times* 23 June 1994

20. Hendry C (1994) 'The Single European Market and the HRM response' in Kirkbride P S (ed) *Human Resource Management in Europe: Perspectives for the 1990s*, Routledge, London

21. Wood S and Peccei R (1990) 'Preparing for 1992: Business versus Strategic HRM', *Human Resource Management Journal* 1 (1) pp.63–9

22. Thurley K (1990) 'Towards a European Approach to Personnel Management', *Personnel Management*, Vol. 22, No. 9, September pp.54–7

FURTHER READING

A Proposal for a European Constitution – 1993 European Policy Forum

Blanpain R (1992) *Labour Laws and Industrial Relations of the European Union*, Deventer, Netherlands Kluwer

Brewster C and Hegewisch A (1993) 'A Continent of Diversity', *Personnel Management,* January, 36–40

Bridgeford J and Sterling S (1994) *Employee Relations in Europe,* Blackwell

Burgess S (1993) 'The Ins and Outs of Unemployment', *Economic Review*, Vol II No 1, September

'Can Europe Compete?' *Financial Times*

Coldrick P (1990) 'Collective Bargaining in the New Europe', *Personnel Management*, October

European Commission Annual Employment Reports

'European Works Councils – The Action Begins', *EIRR* 250, November 1994, pp.14–17

'Farewell European Works Councils?' *EIRR,* 242, March 1994

Gold M (ed) (1993) *The Social Dimension Employment Policy in the European Community*, Macmillan

Gold M and Hall M (1992) 'Report on European level Information and Consultation in Multinational Companies: an evaluation of practice,' *European Foundation for the Improvement of Living and Working Conditions*

Guery G (1992) 'European Collective Bargaining and the Maastricht Treaty', *International Labour Review*, Vol 131, No 6

Hall M (1992) 'Behind the European Works Council Debate: The European Commissions' Legislative Strategy', *BJIR* 30 (4), pp.547–66

IDE- Industrial Democracy in Europe Revisited OUP 1993

IPD – European Update(s)

Information and Consultation in European Multi Nationals, Parts 1 and 2, *European Industrial Relations Review*, Nos 228/9, Jan/Feb 1993, 31–21 and 14–20

Lasok D (1994) *Law and Institutions of the European Union*, 6th edition, Butterworths

Lintner V and Mazey S (1991) *The European Community: Economic and Political Aspects*, McGraw Hill

Lockhart T and Myers A (1993) 'The Social Charter: Implications for Managers', *Personnel Review*, Vol 22, Issue 4, pp.3–16

Messmer M (1994) 'Temporary Employees are Permanent Part of New Europe', *Personnel Journal*, Vol 73, Issue 1, p.100–1

Michie J and Smith J. Grieve (1994) 'Unemployment in Europe', *Academic Press*

Northrup HR, Campbell DC and Slavinski BJ (1990) 'Multi National Union-Management Consultation in Europe, Resurgence in the 1980s', *International Labour Review*, Vol 127, No 5, pp.525–43

Ojeda-Aviles A (1993) 'European Collective Bargaining: A triumph of the will?', *International Journal of Comparative Labour Law & Industrial Relations,* Winter

Tixier M (1994) 'Management and Communication Styles in Europe: Can they be compared and matched?', *Employee Relations Journal* 16.1, pp.8–26

'The Hoover Affair and Social Dumping', *European Industrial Relations Review*, No 230, March 1993, pp.14–20

Wise M and Gibb R (1993) *A Single Market to a Social Europe*, Longman.

20 · CONCLUSION

In concluding our review of international human resource management, it would seem opportune to address a few of the key themes and questions which emerge from our analysis. Unfortunately, much of the research done on the evolution of human resource management is at a formative stage, and as we have indicated, the conceptual framework underlying such research needs to be defined with greater rigour.

Our comments at this stage highlight the areas where we believe further research is necessary to raise the level of the debate on international human resource management.

Firstly, an important question is whether there is a positive correlation between human resource management and economic performance, either at corporate or national level. In Chapter 3 we suggested that this was a central tenet of the Harvard human resource management model, and a number of other prominent authors (for example, Porter)[1] have made similar connections.

In fact, there is little or no hard evidence to support the proposition that putting human resource management policies into place will contribute directly to economic success. At corporate level, we have argued that human resource management-type approaches tend to be most evident in the service sector, among white-collar employees, and where trade unions have a low or non-existent profile. It may also be the case that human resource management initiatives are most likely to be found among those companies which have traditionally demonstrated 'sophistication' (as described in Chapter 4) in their approaches to employee relations management. Moreover, it has been argued that the appropriateness of human resource management is dependent on the competitive strategies adopted by organisations,[2] and that human resource management policies need to evolve over time to correspond with the stages of business development.[3] It is also new 'greenfield' sites, where previous traditions in employee relations cannot constrain the initiation of new management styles, which may provide the most fertile ground for human resource management.[4]

What seems to emerge is that human resource management is likely to be appropriate in a particular set of business and employee relations circumstances. Although there are difficulties in establishing cause and effect, and comparisons of business performance are rendered difficult by the self-selecting nature of the sample, it would seem that the reason for the perpetration of human resource management policies in companies such as Hewlett Packard, Marks and Spencer and Toshiba is the perceived connection between the policies and competitive advantage. Conversely, it may be proposed that where the preconditions for human resource management do not exist, where strategic choice, for example necessitates the maintenance of a low-skilled workforce, or where trade unions are strongly organised, human resource management type initiatives will not represent a recipe for improved economic performance, and that managerial choices in this area will need to be conditioned by precise organisational circumstances.

At national level, if the proposition we have previously put forward is accepted – that human resource management has been most influential in the relatively deregulated economies of the UK, the US, and perhaps also Australasia – the economic indicators represented in Fig. 20.1 are likely to be a disappointment for advocates of human resource management.

It may therefore be significant for public policy makers, as well as for corporate managements, to note that a relatively high degree of state or trade union intervention into corporate affairs does not seem *prima facie* to be inconsistent with high economic performance.

According to Brewster:

Those nations who allow least autonomy to their managements (with most legal regulation and trade union influence) tend to have been most successful in recent years. Those successful nations in Europe, include some where organisations tend to have a human resource function close-

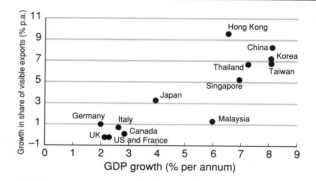

Fig 20.1 Rate of real growth of GDP compared with rate of growth of share in visible exports for selected countries (1979–1990)

ly integrated with business strategy and some where it is only represented at board level. Many successful European states have moved in the direction of external labour markets. National differences in human resource management and in practices linked frequently with views of 'good human resource management practice' have no correlation with national economic differences in economic performance.[5]

Indeed, as our discussion of human resource policies suggested, statutory or trade union influences may encourage employers to take initiatives that may not, without such influences, have assumed great priority, but which, once taken, contribute to corporate success. An example of this is the statutory requirement for employers to invest in training in France. Statutory pressure may also be important in the implementation of equal opportunities, which gains particular economic significance at a time of skill shortages, or in fostering approaches to reward which ensure that adequate skill bases are maintained.

In Japan, the guiding hand of the state has been important in that country's economic regeneration since world war two.

It may be that difficulties in demonstrating the validity of the human resource management/economic success equation may be traced to deficiencies in the human resource management concept itself. Although the Harvard model takes account of the need to 'fit' human resource management to important 'situational factors', nevertheless much of the inspiration underlying the concept is gained from examining the practices of a select number of 'excellent' companies. Hewlett Packard is frequently cited, for example, throughout *Managing Human Assets*.[6]

The difficulty here may be that, even within the domestic arena, human resource management may

have particular and limited applicability to specific organisational forms, structures and cultures. The prescriptions accompanying human resource management may therefore not be useful in highly unionised, predominantly blue-collar contexts, or where the form of technology necessitates repetitive and unskilled activity. It would follow therefore that for the human resource management concept to have greater utility within national systems, let alone across them, a greater element of contingency and adaptability would need to be built into it. This being the case, the tendency to prescribe stereotypical good practice which is evident in much human resource management literature, for example advocating the use of psychometrics 'empowering' line managers, competency based training and performance related pay systems, would need to give way to greater sensitivity in recognising the complexity of organisational forms, cultures and requirements.

In the chapter on government, we considered some of the pressures for convergence on human resource management and employee relations systems. To conclude this text, we would identify those features which are promoting a similarity of approach to the management of human resource across national systems, and those which are perpetuating diversity.

A central theme within the text has been the growing recognition on the part of the stakeholders in the employment relationship that organisational flexibility is required if corporations are to respond successfully to increasingly competitive environments.

In an interesting piece of work based on the findings of an extensive research project covering nine European automobile manufacturing engine plants, belonging to four different corporations, and located in four different countries, Mueller[7] finds that moves towards functional flexibility in terms of broadening the jobs of operatives had occurred to a greater or lesser extent in all companies.

Important explanations for this include the international system of production technology, product development and manufacturing operations to meet competitive pressures, as well as a common set of responses which take on board the 'positive' example of Japanese principles of production and organisation, which we referred to earlier. Also, Mueller suggests that the action programme by the European Commission and European Social Legislation may exert some common legalistic and collectively agreed terms across European countries.

Mueller (p.202) suggests the following causes of increasing convergence:

- internationalisation of product market;
- technological restraints;
- increasingly competitive industry environment;
- example set by Japanese transplant operations in the US and UK;
- European action programme and European legislation.

The study, which is confined to a particular industry, places the design of work, in terms of team working and job enlargement, at the centre of its analysis. However, it would seem reasonable to assume that enlarging the scope of jobs will have implications for training and development, recruitment and remuneration as well as other areas of human resource policy. Indeed, the connection between functional flexibility and change in the human resource practices is a potential area for further research. Undoubtedly, too, the increasing scale of multinational operations has a homogenising effect on human resource management in countries of operation, and we have already mentioned the particular significance of the 'Japanese' effect, as well as the influence of US operations overseas. Nevertheless, it is important to bear in mind that such corporations invariably adjust their approach in host countries to accommodate the particular features of national cultures and structures. Moreover, at the initial stages of multinational development, the focus of operations is likely to be domestic, and therefore little attempt will be made to 'export' policies and practices.[8]

Even though powerful forces towards convergence exist, our study has shown that much diversity remains across national systems, and that important national distinctions still prevail. Quite often these are perpetuated by pervasive cultural and ideological facets which may condition the selection of human resource policy choices, for example, in the area of reward, where tendencies towards 'individualism' mould policy choices. Also, interaction between 'stakeholders' occurs within a particular political or ideological milieu in which shared values exert a potent conditioning effect. As we have described, the manifestations of organisational flexibility may take quite different forms in 'corporatist' structures compared with 'liberal individualist' contexts, in which market considerations are most likely to determine approaches to change. In the former, responses will probably tend towards nurturing existing employees, while in the latter, greater use may be made of external labour markets.

In an intriguing piece of work, which may be viewed as a global parallel to the principle that at a local level, greenfield sites are most amenable to new managerial and technological initiatives, Gerschenkron[9] superimposes a historical perspective on the debate about convergence. His model consists of the following four propositions.

1 The later the industrialisation is, the faster its speed. This is because the late developer can introduce the newest production technology from the starting point of its industrialisation and the late developer can also occasionally borrow capital from early developers.
2 The industrialisation of the late developed nations must be promoted on a large scale from the starting point.
3 The industrialisation of the late developed country must be guided by a strong institution at a national level, for example, an enterprise or national bank.
4 *'Laissez-faire'*, 'individualism' and 'nationalism' cannot be applied to the late developer. Instead the latter require 'nationalism' or a 'semi-religious' orientation.

Despite receiving substantial criticism,[10] the model is useful to point out the durability of economic and organisational traditions in the early industrialised countries, and the consequent difficulties they would confront in rapidly incorporating advanced new forms of technological and work design. Returning to the 'Fordist' and 'Post-Fordist' typologies, it seems to be the case that the newer developers have had greater success in establishing flexible production systems to meet the needs of increasingly volatile global markets, as the process of transformation to arrive at this position has been less cumbersome and painful than has been the case in the older established economies, with firmly entrenched systems, procedures, ideologies and cultures.

In conclusion, our study has indicated that there are important international shifts towards flexibility in the organisation of work, and in the resourcing, reward and development of employees. Yet distinctive ideologies and cultures continue to contribute to diverse and heterogeneous scenes in the field of international human resource management.

A number of these arguments are encapsulated in a quote from Pieper, with which we shall conclude:

> Since human resource management is seen as a strategic factor strongly influencing the economic success of a single company, we can argue that it is also the strategic figure for the success of an entire nation. Since most technologies are available worldwide, technology itself no

longer forms the most important determining factor, but the way technologies are applied, ie whether people are educated or trained well enough to use them effectively, has become decisive. Neither technologies nor technical knowledge nor money for investment is confined to national borders. People, however, to a large degree are. Whether a plant is built in India or the Federal Republic of Germany makes a considerable difference to its efficiency, even if exactly the same technologies are being used, because the workforce in the two countries is different in regard to, for example, its standard of education and its culture.[11]

REFERENCES

1. Porter M (1980, 1985) *Competitive Strategies*, New York, Free Press

2. Miles R and Snow C (1984) *Designing Strategic Human Resource Systems, Organisational Dynamics,* 12(2) pp.36–52

3. Tichy NM, Fombrun CJ and Devanna MA (1982) 'Strategic Human Resource Management', *Sloan Management Review*, 23(2) pp.47–61

4. Guest DE (June 1988) 'Human Resource Management – Is it worth taking seriously?', First Annual Seear Fellowship lecture at the London School of Economics, p.15

5. Brewster C (1994) 'European HRM in the American Concept', in Kirkbride PS (ed), *Human Resource Management in Europe, Perspectives for the 1990s,* Routledge, London, p.77

6. Beer M et al (1984) *Managing Human Assets,* Free Press, New York

7. Mueller F (1992) 'Flexible Working Practices in Engine Plants: Evidence from the European Automobile Industry', *Industrial Relations Journal,* vol 23, no 3

8. Adler NJ and Ghadar F (1990) 'Strategic Human Resource Management: A Global Perspective', in Pieper R, *Human Resource Management: An International Comparison,* DeGruyter, New York, p.240

9. Gerschenkron A (1951) 'Economic Backwardness in Historical Perspective', in Hoschitz BF (ed), *The Progress of Underdeveloped Areas,* The University of Chicago Press, pp.3–29

10. Takahashi Y (1990) 'Human Resource Management in Japan', in Pieper R, *Human Resource Management: an International Comparison,* New York, DeGruyter, p.213

11. Pieper R (1990) 'Introduction', in Pieper R (ed) *Human Resource Management: An International Comparison,* DeGruyter, New York, p.4

APPENDICES

1. Population, Economically Active and Employed (Thousands)

	A	B	C	D	
	Total Population	Economically Active	Employed	%B Male	Female
USA	255 082[1]	128 548[1]	117 598[1]	54.9	45.1
Japan	124 310[1]	65 780[1]	64 360[1]	59.3	40.7
France	56 893[2]	25 330[2]	22 332[1]	56.7	43.3
Germany[3]	63 889[2]	31 360[2]	29 115[1]	58.9	41.1
Italy	57 114[2]	24 245[2]	21 595[2]	62.9	37.1
Netherlands	10 371[2,5]	7 010[2]	6 521[2]	60.3	39.7
Sweden	8 587[4]	4 491[4]	4 250[1]	52.0	48.0
United Kingdom	57 649[2]	28 769[2]	25 463[1]	57.0	43.0
Australia	13 689[1,5]	8 626[1]	7 693[1]	58.2	41.8

[1] 1992
[2] 1991
[3] Territories of West Germany prior to October 1990
[4] 1990
[5] 15+ only

Source: Adapted from ILO *Yearbook of Labour Statistics*, 1993.

2. Civilian Employment by Sector (%)

	Agriculture						Industry						Services					
	1970	1980	1990	1991	1992[1]	1993[1]	1970	1980	1990	1991	1992[1]	1993[1]	1970	1980	1990	1991	1992[1]	1993[1]
United States	4.5	3.6	2.8	2.9	−0.2	−3.6	34.4	30.5	26.2	25.3	−2.1	−0.9	61.1	65.9	70.9	71.8	1.6	2.4
Japan	17.4	10.4	7.2	6.7	−3.7	−4.4	35.7	35.3	34.1	34.4	1.6	−0.7	46.9	54.2	58.7	58.9	1.4	1.3
Australia	8.0	6.5	5.6	5.5	−2.2	1.0	37.0	31.0	25.4	24.2	0.7	0.4	55.0	62.4	69.0	70.4	0.1	0.4
France	13.5	8.7	6.0	5.8	−4.5	−4.2	39.2	35.9	29.9	29.5	−3.0	−4.0	47.2	55.4	64.1	64.8	0.7	0.2
Germany	8.6	5.3	3.5	3.4	−5.1	−6.0	49.3	43.7	39.8	39.2	−1.6	−2.9	42.0	51.0	56.7	57.4	2.5	−0.5
Italy	20.2	14.3	8.8	8.5	−4.1	n/a	39.5	37.9	32.7	32.3	−0.9	n/a	40.3	47.8	58.5	59.2	0.0	n/a
Netherlands	6.2	4.9	4.6	4.5	−10.9	n/a	38.9	31.4	26.3	25.5	−1.7	n/a	54.9	63.6	69.1	69.9	4.3	n/a
Sweden	8.1	5.6	3.3	3.2	−4.8	−0.4	38.4	32.2	29.1	28.2	−9.7	−10.8	53.5	62.2	67.5	68.5	−1.8	−5.5
United Kingdom	3.2	2.6	2.1	2.2	−1.6	0.0	44.7	37.7	28.8	27.8	−5.6	−5.0	52.0	59.7	69.0	70.0	−1.0	−1.0
OECD total	13.8	9.6	7.4	7.2	−3.9	n/a	37.0	33.8	29.6	29.1	−2.5	n/a	49.2	56.6	63.0	63.7	1.0	n/a

[1] Average annual growth rate percentage

Source: Adapted from OECD *Labour Force Statistics* 1993 and *Employment Outlook*, June 1994.

3. Real GDP (annual percent change)

	Average[1] 1967–76	Average 1976–85	1986	1987	1988	1989	1990	1991	1992	1993
United States	2.6	2.9	2.9	3.1	3.9	2.5	1.2	–0.6	2.3	3.1
Japan	6.8	4.2	2.6	4.1	6.2	4.7	4.8	4.3	1.1	0.1
Germany[2]	3.8	2.2	2.3	1.5	3.7	3.6	5.7	2.9	2.2	–1.1
W. Germany only								5.0	1.8	–1.7
France	4.3	2.3	2.5	2.3	4.4	4.3	2.5	0.8	1.2	–1.0
Italy	4.3	3.1	2.9	3.1	4.1	2.9	2.1	1.2	0.7	–0.7
United Kingdom[3]	2.4	1.9	4.3	4.8	5.0	2.2	0.4	–2.0	–0.5	2.0
Netherlands	4.4	1.9	2.7	1.2	2.6	4.7	4.1	2.1	1.4	0.3
Sweden	3.2	1.6	2.3	3.1	2.3	2.4	1.4	–1.1	–1.9	–2.1
Australia	4.6	3.1	1.9	4.4	4.6	4.6	1.4	–1.0	2.1	4.1
All industrial countries		2.8	2.9	3.2	4.4	3.3	2.4	0.8	1.5	1.3
European Union/E.C.	4.0	2.3	2.9	2.9	4.3	3.5	3.0	1.2	1.1	–0.3

[1] Source: OECD *Economic Outlook*, June 1994
[2] Data through to 1990 inc. applied to W. Germany only
[3] Average of expenditure, income, and output estimates of GDP at market prices

Source: International Monetary Fund. Adapted from *World Economic Outlook* October 1994.

4. Consumer prices[a] (Percentage changes from previous period)

	Average 1970–74	1975	1976	1977	1978	1979	1980	1981	1982	1983	1984	1985	1986	1987	1988	1989	1990	1991	1992	1993
United States	6.2	9.1	5.7	6.5	7.6	11.3	13.5	10.3	6.1	3.2	4.3	3.5	1.9	3.7	4.1	4.8	5.4	4.2	3.0	3.0
Japan	11.3	11.8	9.4	8.2	4.2	3.7	7.8	4.9	2.7	1.9	2.2	2.0	0.6	0.1	0.7	2.3	3.1	3.3	1.7	1.3
Germany[b]	6.2	5.9	4.6	3.7	2.7	4.1	5.5	6.3	5.3	3.3	2.4	2.2	–0.1	0.2	1.3	2.8	2.7	3.5	4.0	4.1
France	8.1	11.8	9.6	9.4	9.1	10.8	13.6	13.4	11.8	9.6	7.4	5.8	2.7	3.1	2.7	3.6	3.4	3.2	2.4	2.1
Italy[c]	10.0	17.2	16.5	18.1	12.4	15.7	21.1	18.7	16.3	15.0	10.6	8.6	6.1	4.6	5.0	6.6	6.1	6.5	5.3	4.2
United Kingdom	10.4	24.2	16.5	15.8	8.3	13.4	18.0	11.9	8.6	4.6	5.0	6.1	3.4	4.1	4.9	7.8	9.5	5.9	3.7	1.6
Netherlands	8.2	10.2	8.8	6.4	4.1	4.2	6.5	6.7	5.9	2.7	3.3	2.3	0.1	–0.7	0.7	1.1	2.5	3.7	3.2	2.6
Sweden	7.5	9.8	10.2	11.4	10.0	7.2	13.7	12.1	8.6	8.9	8.0	7.4	4.2	4.2	5.8	6.4	10.5	9.3	2.3	4.6
Australia	9.1	15.1	13.5	12.3	7.9	9.1	9.8	10.1	11.2	10.1	3.9	6.7	9.1	8.5	7.3	7.5	7.3	3.2	1.0	1.8
Total OECD	8.0	11.7	8.9	9.3	8.1	10.4	13.5	10.8	8.0	5.6	5.6	4.9	3.0	3.6	4.3	5.4	5.8	5.2	4.0	3.6
EC	8.9	14.4	12.0	12.5	9.1	10.9	13.7	12.4	10.9	8.6	7.2	6.1	3.7	3.3	3.6	5.3	5.7	5.1	4.3	3.3

[a] Aggregates were computed using the previous year's consumer expenditure expressed in private consumption purchasing power parities
[b] Western Germany
[c] Index for households of wage and salary earners

Source: Adapted from OECD *Economic Outlook*, June 1994.

5. Labour force participation rates[a]

	Average 1968–77	1978	1979	1980	1981	1982	1983	1984	1985	1986	1987	1988	1989	1990	1991	1992	1993	1992 Labour force (000s)
United States	66.3	70.0	70.7	71.0	71.2	71.5	71.6	72.2	72.7	73.5	74.1	74.7	75.6	75.8	75.6	75.9	75.9	128 548
Japan	71.4	71.5	71.8	71.8	72.1	72.3	73.0	72.7	72.5	72.4	72.5	72.7	73.3	74.2	75.2	75.9	75.9	65 780
Germany	68.7	67.9	68.1	68.3	68.1	67.8	67.3	67.0	67.4	68.0	68.4	68.7	68.6	69.0	71.5	70.5	69.6	30 949
France	67.8	68.4	68.4	68.1	67.6	67.3	66.4	66.2	66.4	66.5	66.5	66.4	66.2	66.3	66.5	66.5	66.4	25 108
Italy	57.8	58.3	58.7	59.3	59.6	59.0	58.9	58.3	58.1	59.0	59.4	59.5	59.8	61.3	61.5	61.4	57.7	24 612
United Kingdom	73.0	74.0	74.2	74.2	73.5	72.9	72.9	73.9	74.7	74.8	75.2	75.8	76.0	76.0	75.5	75.5	74.4	28 143
Netherlands	67.8	64.4	64.5	64.8	64.8	64.5	64.5	64.1	63.4	63.9	64.1	65.2	66.5	66.7	67.6	68.4	69.9	7 133
Sweden	75.8	79.3	80.1	80.8	80.6	80.7	80.9	81.0	81.6	80.9	81.7	82.3	82.9	84.6	83.8	82.0	79.9	4 429
Australia	69.6	70.0	69.7	70.5	70.4	70.1	69.8	69.9	70.6	71.7	71.9	72.4	73.7	74.4	74.3	74.2	73.2	8 679
Total OECD	67.5	68.6	68.9	69.0	69.0	68.8	68.8	68.8	69.0	69.4	69.8	70.1	70.5	70.9	71.1	70.9	70.6	404 533
EC	65.7	65.6	65.7	65.7	65.6	65.2	65.0	64.9	65.0	65.4	65.7	66.0	66.2	66.6	67.3	67.0	66.2	

[a] For sources and definitions, see "Sources and Methods".

Source: Adapted from OECD *Economic Outlook,* June 1994 and *Employment Outlook,* June 1994.

6. Labour force participation rates by sex (Percentages)

	Men						Women					
	1973	1979	1983	1991	1992	1993[a]	1973	1979	1983	1991	1992	1993[a]
Australia	91.1	87.6	85.9	85.6	85.8	85.0	47.7	50.3	52.1	62.2	62.5	62.5
France	85.2	82.6	78.4	75.2	74.7	–	50.1	54.2	54.4	58.2	58.7	–
Germany	89.6	84.9	82.6	79.8	78.9	–	50.3	52.2	52.5	58.2	58.6	–
Italy	85.1	82.6	80.7	79.7	79.1	75.1	33.7	38.7	40.3	46.2	46.5	43.2
Japan	90.1	89.2	89.1	88.9	89.7	90.1	54.0	54.7	57.2	61.5	62.0	61.7
Netherlands	85.6	79.0	77.3	80.3	80.8	–	29.2	33.4	40.3	54.5	55.5	–
Sweden	88.1	87.9	85.9	85.3	83.2	80.3	62.6	72.8	76.6	80.9	79.1	76.5
United Kingdom	93.0	90.5	87.5	85.2	84.5	83.3	53.2	58.0	57.2	65.0	64.8	64.3
United States	86.2	85.7	84.6	84.7	84.8	84.5	51.1	58.9	61.8	68.4	68.9	69.1

[a] Secretariat estimates

Source: Adapted from OECD *Employment Outlook,* June 1994.

7. Standardised unemployment rates (Per cent of total labour force)

	1974	1975	1976	1977	1978	1979	1980	1981	1982	1983	1984	1985	1986	1987	1988	1989	1990	1991	1992	1993
United States	5.5	8.3	7.6	6.9	6.0	5.8	7.0	7.5	9.5	9.5	7.4	7.1	6.9	6.1	5.4	5.2	5.4	6.6	7.3	6.7
Japan	1.4	1.9	2.0	2.0	2.2	2.1	2.0	2.2	2.4	2.6	2.7	2.6	2.8	2.8	2.5	2.3	2.1	2.1	2.2	2.5
Germany[a]	1.6	3.6	3.7	3.6	3.5	3.2	2.9	4.2	5.9	7.7	7.1	7.1	6.4	6.2	6.2	5.6	4.8	4.2[b]	4.6[b]	5.8[b]
France[a]	2.8	4.0	4.4	4.9	5.2	5.8	6.2	7.4	8.1	8.3	9.7	10.2	10.4	10.5	10.0	9.4	8.9	9.4	10.4	11.6
Italy	5.3	5.8	6.6	7.0	7.1	7.6	7.5	7.8	8.4	8.8	9.4	9.6	10.5	10.9	11.0	10.9	10.3	9.9	10.5	10.2
United Kingdom[a]	2.9	4.3	5.6	6.0	5.9	5.0	6.4	9.8	11.3	12.4	11.7	11.2	11.2	10.3	8.6	7.2	7.0	8.8	10.0	10.3
Netherlands[a]	2.7	5.2	5.5	5.3	5.3	5.4	6.0	8.5	11.4	12.0	11.8	10.6	9.9	9.6	9.1	8.3	7.5	7.0	6.7	8.3
Sweden	2.0	1.6	1.6	1.8	2.2	2.1	2.0	2.5	3.2	3.5	3.1	2.8	2.7	1.9	1.6	1.4	1.5	2.7	4.8	8.2
Australia	2.6	4.8	4.7	5.6	6.2	6.2	6.0	5.7	7.1	9.9	8.9	8.2	8.0	8.0	7.2	6.1	6.9	9.5	10.7	10.8
Memorandum item:																				
EC[c]	3.0	4.3	5.0	5.4	5.6	5.7	6.4	8.1	9.4	10.3	10.7	10.9	10.8	10.6	9.9	9.0	8.4	8.7	9.5	10.6

[a] Series based on EC Labour Force Surveys: see corresponding notes in *Quarterly Labour Force Statistics*

[b] Western Germany

[c] EC: only Germany, France, Italy, United Kingdom, Belgium, Ireland, Netherlands, Portugal and Spain – are included in the area total.

Note: These unemployment rates are based on the ILO/OECD Guidelines. The unemployed are defined as persons of working age who are without work, available for work and actively seeking employment: unemployment is expressed as a percentage of total labour force including all members of the armed forces. The data above are averages of quarterly or monthly figures. For a detailed description of the sources and methods used, see *Standardized Unemployment Rates, Sources and Methods* (OECD, 1985)

Source: Adapted from OECD *Economic Outlook,* June 1994.

8. Unemployment rates by sex (%)

		1983	1984	1985	1986	1987	1988	1989	1990	1991	1992
United States[1]	Total	9.5	7.4	7.1	6.9	6.1	5.4	5.2	5.4	6.6	7.3
	Male	9.7	7.3	6.9	6.8	6.1	5.3	5.1	5.4	6.9	7.6
	Female	9.2	7.6	7.4	7.1	6.2	5.5	5.3	5.4	6.3	6.9
Japan[2]	Total	2.6	2.7	2.6	2.8	2.8	2.5	2.3	2.1	2.1	2.2
	Male	2.7	2.7	2.6	2.7	2.8	2.5	2.2	2.0	2.0	2.1
	Female	2.6	2.8	2.7	2.8	2.8	2.6	2.3	2.2	2.2	2.2
France	Total	8.4	9.8	10.2	10.4	10.5	10.0	9.4	8.9	9.4	10.2
	Male	6.5	7.9	8.4	8.5	8.4	7.8	7.1	6.7	7.3	8.1
	Female	11.2	12.4	12.7	12.9	13.3	12.9	12.4	11.7	12.1	12.8
Germany[3,4]	Total	9.1	9.1	9.3	9.0	8.9	8.7	7.9	7.2	6.3	6.6
	Male	8.4	8.5	8.6	8.0	8.0	7.8	6.9	6.3	5.8	6.2
	Female	10.1	10.2	10.4	10.5	10.2	10.0	9.4	8.4	7.0	7.2
Germany[5]	Total									10.3	14.8
	Male									8.5	10.5
	Female									12.3	19.6
Italy	Total	9.9	10.0	10.3	11.1	11.9	12.0	12.0	11.0	10.9	11.5
	Male	6.6	6.6	6.8	7.4	8.1	8.1	8.1	7.3	7.5	n/a
	Female	16.2	16.5	16.7	17.8	18.5	18.6	18.7	17.1	16.8	n/a
Netherlands[3]	Total	13.9	14.1	12.9	12.0	11.5	6.5[6]	5.8	5.0	4.5	n/a
	Male	14.5	14.6	13.0	11.8	11.1	6.8	5.8	5.0	4.4	n/a
	Female	12.7	13.3	12.8	12.3	12.1	6.1	5.8	5.1	4.7	n/a
Sweden[7]	Total	3.5	3.1	2.8	2.2[8]	1.9	1.6	1.4	1.5	2.7	4.8
	Male	3.4	3.0	2.8	2.2	1.9	1.6	1.3	1.5	3.0	5.7
	Female	3.6	3.3	2.9	2.2	1.9	1.6	1.4	1.5	2.3	3.8
United Kingdom[9]	Total		11.8	11.2	11.2	10.7	8.8	7.2	6.8	8.3	9.6
	Male		12.0	11.6	11.6	11.1	9.0	7.4	7.0	9.2	11.5
	Female		11.5	10.7	10.6	10.2	8.4	7.0	6.5	7.2	7.2
Australia[2]	Total	10.0	9.0	8.3	8.1	8.1	7.2	6.2	6.9	9.6	10.8
	Male	9.7	8.7	7.9	7.7	7.8	6.8	5.7	6.7	9.9	11.4
	Female	10.4	9.5	8.8	8.7	8.6	7.9	6.9	7.2	9.2	10.0

[1] 16 yrs and over
[2] 15 yrs and over
[3] Persons aged 15–64 inc.
[4] Territory of Federal Republic of Germany before October 1990
[5] The 5 new Länder
[6] Methodology changed
[7] Persons 16–64 inc.
[8] Prior to 1986 persons aged 16–74 included

Source: Derived from ILO *Yearbook of Labour Statistics* 1993, Explanatory notes and sources, p.633.

9. Employed females as percentage of total employed

	1984	1986	1988	1990	1992
United States	43.7	44.4	45.0	45.4	45.7
Japan	35.6	36.2	36.8	38.0	38.6
France	41.0	41.8	42.3	42.5	43.2
Germany[1,2]	38.6	38.8	39.3	40.0	41.4
Italy	32.4	33.2	33.8	34.6	34.7[3]
Netherlands[1]	33.0[4]	33.6[5]	36.9	37.8	38.6[3]
Sweden[1]	46.8	47.9	48.0	48.0	48.5
United Kingdom[1]	41.4	42.3	43.1	43.9	45.2
Australia	37.8	39.3	40.2	41.3	42.1

[1] Includes armed forces
[2] Relates to territories of Federal Republic of Germany prior to October 1990
[3] 1991 data
[4] 1983 data
[5] 1985 data

Source: Derived from ILO *Yearbook of Labour Statistics* 1993.

10. Part-time work (%)

| | As % of total employment | | | | | As % of total employment | | | | | | | | | | Womens' share of the total of part-time employment | | | | |
| | | | | | | | | Men | | | | | Women | | | | | | | | | |
	1979	1983	1991	1992	1993	1979	1983	1991	1992	1993	1979	1983	1991	1992	1993	1979	1983	1991	1992	1993
Australia	15.9	17.5	22.6	24.5	23.9	5.2	6.2	9.2	10.6	10.3	35.2	36.4	40.8	43.3	42.3	78.7	78.0	76.4	75.0	75.3
Germany	11.4	12.6	15.5	14.1	n/a	1.5	1.7	2.7	2.2	n/a	27.6	30.0	34.3	30.7	n/a	91.6	91.9	89.6	91.0	n/a
Italy	5.3	4.6	5.5	5.9	n/a	3.0	2.4	2.9	2.9	n/a	10.6	9.4	10.4	11.5	n/a	61.4	64.8	65.4	68.5	n/a
Japan	15.4	16.2	20.0	20.5	21.1	7.5	7.3	10.1	10.6	11.4	27.8	29.8	34.3	34.8	35.2	70.1	72.9	69.9	69.3	69.7
Netherlands	16.6	21.4	34.3	32.8	n/a	5.5	7.2	16.7	13.4	n/a	44.0	50.1	62.2	62.9	n/a	76.4	77.3	70.1	75.0	n/a
Sweden	23.6	24.8	23.7	24.3	24.9	5.4	6.3	7.6	8.4	9.1	46.0	45.9	41.0	41.3	41.4	87.5	86.6	83.4	82.3	81.3
United Kingdom	16.4	19.4	22.2	23.5	n/a	1.9	3.3	5.5	6.3	n/a	39.0	42.4	43.7	45.0	n/a	92.8	89.8	86.1	85.2	n/a
United States	16.4	18.4	17.4	17.5	17.5	9.0	10.8	10.5	10.8	10.9	26.7	28.1	25.6	25.4	25.3	68.0	66.8	67.2	66.4	66.2
France	8.2	9.7	12.0	12.7	n/a	2.4	2.6	3.4	3.6	n/a	16.9	20.0	23.5	24.5	n/a	82.2	84.4	83.7	83.7	n/a

The definition of part-time work varies considerably across national boundaries. Details of the sources and methods used in these calculations are given in the source below, p.199.

Source: Adapted from OECD *Employment Outlook*, June 1994.

11. Hours of work per week in manufacturing

	1983	1984	1985	1986	1987	1988	1989	1990	1991	1992	1992 M	1992 F
United States[1]	40.1	40.7	40.5	40.7	41.0	41.1	41.0	40.8	40.7	41.0	n/a	
Japan[2,3]	46.2	46.0	46.2	46.0	46.3	46.8	46.3	45.7	45.0	43.8	47.6	37.9
France[2,4]	38.9	38.7	38.6	38.6	38.7	38.7	38.7	38.7	38.7	38.7	n/a	
Germany[1,5]	40.5	41.0	40.7	40.4	40.1	40.0	39.9	39.5	39.2	38.9	38.9	37.6
Germany[1,6]									40.4	40.7	40.8	40.0
Netherlands[1,7]	40.5	40.3	40.3	40.1	39.9	39.8	39.8	39.9	39.9	n/a	40.0[8]	39.3[8]
Sweden[2,9]	37.7	38.1	38.3	38.3	38.4	38.5	38.5	38.5	38.4	38.5	39.9	34.3
United Kingdom[10,2]	42.9	43.5	43.7	43.7	43.8	44.3	44.5	44.3	42.9	43.2	44.0	40.2
Australia[2]	35.5	36.2	36.9	37.0	37.3	37.9	37.7	38.1	37.6	37.9	39.6	33.2

1 Hours paid for, including hours paid for but not worked such as paid annual leave, paid public holidays, paid sick leave, paid meal breaks etc
2 Hours actually worked including overtime, short periods of waiting time and tea and coffee breaks
3 Civilian labour force employed
4 Employees
5 Territory of Federal Republic of Germany before October 1990
6 5 new Länder and Berlin East
7 Employees including juveniles
8 Figures for 1991 adults only
9 Employees. Labour force sample survey
10 Full-time workers on adult rates of pay
11 The figures represent the average per wage earner

Source: Adapted from ILO *Yearbook of Labour Statistics* 1993.

12. Average hours actually worked per person per year[a]

	1979	1983	1991	1992	1993
Total employment					
France	1 813	1 711	1 667	1 666	–
Germany	1 764	1 733	1 603	1 618	1 588
Italy	1 788	1 764	–	–	–
Japan	2 126	2 095	1 998	1 965	–
Sweden	1 451	1 453	1 468	1 485	1 507
United States	1 808	1 787	1 770	1 768	1 776
Dependent employment					
France	1 667	1 558	1 540	1 542	–
Germany	1 699	1 668	1 551	1 563	1 534
Netherlands	1 591	1 530	1 423	1 415	1 409
United States	1 767	1 754	1 736	1 736	1 743

a Includes part-time work
Sources:
France: Data supplied by INSEE on a National Accounts basis.
Germany: Data supplied by the *Institut für Arbeitsmarki-und Berufsforschung*
Italy: Data supplied by the Italian authorities (ISTAT)
Japan: Secretariat estimates based on data from the Monthly Labour Survey of Establishments and the Labour Force Survey
Netherlands: Data are annual contractual hours on the basis of Labour Accounts data and were supplied by the national authorities (CBS)
Sweden: Data estimated from National Accounts data
United States: Data provided by the *Bureau of Labour Statistics*

Source: Adapted from OECD *Employment Outlook*, June 1994.

13. Competitive positions: relative unit labour costs[a] (Indices, 1991 = 100)

	1976	1977	1978	1979	1980	1981	1982	1983	1984	1985	1986	1987	1988	1989	1990	1991	1992	1993	Projections 1994	1995
United States	122	122	114	119	124	131	142	146	156	160	132	112	105	106	103	100	94	92	90	89
Japan	92	100	115	97	86	90	78	86	86	85	117	120	123	108	95	100	113	141	151	151
Germany	80	84	87	89	90	83	86	87	85	83	92	102	102	99	103	100	106	111	107	107
France	111	104	105	107	111	110	106	105	106	108	110	109	104	99	102	100	100	104	105	104
Italy	96	95	91	91	89	88	89	95	93	90	91	91	90	94	99	100	96	80	80	82
United Kingdom	73	72	80	94	115	119	113	103	99	101	93	93	98	100	97	100	96	86	87	87
Netherlands	133	134	132	129	121	109	112	111	100	97	105	110	107	99	101	100	104	106	103	101
Sweden	123	120	111	104	103	104	90	81	83	87	86	87	91	95	97	100	95	75	75	76
Australia	130	116	107	100	100	113	121	115	121	100	85	84	94	103	103	100	90	81	85	86

[a] In manufacturing, expressed in a common currency

Source: Adapted from OECD *Economic Outlook*, June 1994.

14. Evolution of trade union density rates 1970–90
(Trade union membership as a per cent of wage- and salary-earners)

	Type of data*	1970	1980	1990
Australia	E	50.2[a]	48.0[b]	40.4
France	E	22.3	17.5	9.8
Germany	E	33.0	35.6	32.9
Italy	E	36.3	49.3	38.8
Japan	E	35.1	31.1	25.4
Netherlands	E	38.0	35.3	25.5
Sweden	E	67.7	79.7	82.5
United Kingdom	E	44.8	50.4	39.1
United States	E	23.2[c]	22.3	15.6

* E = Based on employed members only
[a] 1976
[b] 1982
[c] 1977

Data supplied by Jelle Visser, University of Amsterdam. See also Table 4.1 and Annex 4.A in OECD, *Employment Outlook*, 1991.

Source: OECD *Employment Outlook*, June 1994.

INDEX